Image *and* Word

in the Theology of John Calvin

Image *and* Word

in the Theology of John Calvin

RANDALL C. ZACHMAN

University of Notre Dame Press

Notre Dame, Indiana

Manufactured in the United States of America

Library of Congress Cataloging-in-Publication Data

Zachman, Randall C., 1953–
Image and word in the theology of John Calvin / Randall C. Zachman.
p.   cm.
Includes bibliographical references and index.
ISBN-13: 978-0-268-04500-5 (cloth : alk. paper)
ISBN-10: 0-268-04500-3 (cloth : alk. paper)
1. Calvin, Jean, 1509–1564. 2. Image (Theology)—History of doctrines—
16th century. 3. Word of God (Theology)—History of doctrines—16th century.
4. Reformed Church—Doctrines—History—16th century. I. Title.
BX9418.Z32   2007
230'.42092—dc22
2006039828

Contents

CHAPTER 2

Symbols of God's Goodness in the Present Life   55

CHAPTER 3

The Manifestation of the Providential Care of God   73

Part II. The Living Images of God the Redeemer

Preface

The insights into Calvin's theology that have come to fruition in this book first arose through the generous invitation of David Foxgrover to have a session at the Sixteenth Century Studies Conference in 1993 on the ramifications of my previous work comparing the theology of Martin Luther and John Calvin. The paper I prepared for that session, "Word and Image in the Theology of John Calvin," set me on the path that eventually led to this book. The initial research for this book was made possible by a Summer Research Stipend from the Institute for Scholarship in the Liberal Arts at the University of Notre Dame in 1994. Final production was made possible by the Henry Luce III Fellowship from the Association of Theological Schools, which funded my leave from teaching and administrative work from August 2003 to May 2004.

This book is dedicated to my wife, Carolyne Call. I will always be grateful to Carrie for her encouragement, love, and support throughout the long and difficult process of research and writing and for reading and critiquing every chapter as it emerged from the printer. Carrie saw from very early on the importance for theology and the Church of Calvin's insights into the self-manifestation of God in the beauty of creation, and her passion for this theme in Calvin's theology has helped me to see its importance more clearly. Her love is to me a vivid mirror and image of the love and care that God shows for all that God has created.

Introduction

The Essential Interdependence of Image and Word
in Calvin's Theology

If God is essentially invisible, can God nonetheless be seen? If God is essentially above the heavens, and the heaven of heavens, can God nonetheless be present on earth? If the Kingdom of God is yet to be manifested in the future, can it nonetheless be seen in the present? If only God can see the human heart, can the thoughts and affections of the heart nonetheless become manifest to others in what we say and do?

If these questions were to be addressed to John Calvin, one would expect that his answer to all of them would be negative. After all, Calvin used the essential invisibility of God to deny that God could be represented in any kind of visible image, and this claim formed one of his foundational arguments against the use of human-made images in worship. Calvin used the transcendence of God, as of greater "altitude" than the highest heavens, to reject the human attempt to create signs and symbols of God's presence on earth, especially in the reserved host of the Roman mass. Calvin often claimed that all of the promises of God are contradicted by our experience, so that we must close our eyes and cling only to the Word of God, which alone cannot lie. Finally, Calvin thought that humans used the gestures and ceremonies of worship to conceal their hearts via hypocrisy and was continually suspicious of their use, urging instead the worship of God "in spirit and in truth."

I will argue, however, that Calvin insisted throughout his theological career that the invisible God does become somewhat visible, in what he called "living icons or images of God," while nonetheless remaining invisible. God manifests Godself in "signs of God's presence" while nonetheless remaining on high above the highest heavens. The reality that is awaited in the future is in fact manifested here and now in symbols and images of that reality, both in the history of Israel and in the Church, in which the power of that reality can be experienced in the present. Finally, Calvin argued that human thoughts and affections, while ultimately known to God alone, can and should be manifested to others in what we say and do, including the rites and ceremonies of worship, so that others might be influenced by our example. Calvin insisted that none of this can happen without the simultaneous presence of the Word of God, which he describes as the "soul" of such living images, along with the internal illumination of the Holy Spirit, which alone gives us the eyes to see these living icons. However, he also insisted that the Word of God never comes to us alone but is always accompanied by the visible self-manifestation of God and the corresponding self-manifestation of the human heart. We must always hear the Word in order to be able to see the living images of God; but concomitantly we must always open our eyes to see the living images of God even as we hear the Word of God.

To frame the question from a slightly different angle: what is the role of the three "transcendentals"—truth, goodness, and beauty—in the theology of John Calvin? One would expect, from the received picture of Calvin, that only one of these categories, truth, fits his theological approach. Calvin is thought to approach all theological issues on the basis of the truth of the Word of God in Scripture, which he is thought to combine not with goodness and beauty but with power. God declares what is true in God's Word, and we must submit to this truth with docile obedience. God decides what is to be on the basis of God's power, both in providence and in eternal election and reprobation, and we must submit ourselves to this decision. The truth and power of God are all that ultimately matter to Calvin, not God's goodness and beauty.

I argue, on the contrary, that goodness is central to Calvin's understanding of God. God for Calvin is ultimately and essentially "the fountain and author of every good thing," and although he certainly considered power to be one of those good things, it is always seen in the context of other good things such as wisdom, righteousness, life, mercy, and goodness. Moreover, the fountain of every good thing manifests itself to us in two essentially related ways: in the beauty of God's works and in the truth of God's Word. The goodness of God not only proclaims and attests itself in truth, but it also manifests and exhibits itself in beauty. We need the truth of God to be able to discern the beauty of God in God's works; but we also need the beauty of God to be sweetly allured and gently invited to God, so that we might be ravished with admiration for the beauty of God's goodness, and seek God from the inmost affection of our hearts.

I. MANIFESTATION AND PROCLAMATION IN CALVIN SCHOLARSHIP

There is no question that the thesis of this book appears to contradict not only commonly received impressions of Calvin but also a good deal of scholarly analysis of Calvin's thought. There does in fact appear to be abundant evidence in Calvin's writings that he denied that the invisible God can be seen, and in which he exhorts us to hear the Word of God alone in order to come to the knowledge of God. Not only does Calvin insist on the binding nature of the second commandment forbidding the use of images in worship, but he undergirds that commandment with Deuteronomy's description of the giving of the Law from Sinai: "Then the Lord spoke to you out of the fire; you heard the sound of his words, but you saw no form; there was only a voice" (Deut. 4:12). Commenting on this verse, Calvin said, "It is a confirmation of the Second Commandment, that God manifested himself to the Israelites by a voice, and not in a bodily form; whence it follows that those who are not contended with his voice, but seek his visible form, substitute imaginations and phantoms in his place."[1] In response to Rome's claim, following Gregory the Great, that "images are the books of the uneducated," Calvin stated that God "has set forth the preaching of his Word as a common doctrine for all."[2] The primacy of hearing over against seeing appears to be reinforced not only by the removal of images, statues, stained glass, paintings, and altars from places of worship but also by the substitution of the Sermon for the daily offering of the Mass, embodying Calvin's vision of the Church as the "school of Christ" in which the faithful would hear daily expositions of the Scriptures and be exhorted to read the Scriptures for themselves.

Calvin's focus on the exposition and application of Scripture to the life of the Church has led several scholars to conclude that Calvin emphasized hearing the Word to the exclusion of seeing any "living icons" of God. Edward Dowey states that Calvin's theology "is overwhelmingly a 'theology of the word,'" for according to Calvin "the only successful medium of intercourse between God and the fallen world is the word."[3] David Willis echoes this impression: "Calvin emphasizes the priority of hearing over seeing as a means of receiving revelation."[4] Thomas F. Torrance concurs, insisting that even when Calvin speaks of "living images of God," he primarily means the Word. "Where the thought is of the mirroring of God, properly speaking the mirror is always the Word."[5] The image of God in humanity is similarly said to depend entirely on the Word of God. "Therefore man's true life consists in the light of his understanding in so far as that is reflexive of the glory of God revealed through His Word. It is thus that men resemble God."[6]

Roman Catholic scholars tend to agree with this description of Calvin's theology. Lucien Richard links the seat of the knowledge of God in the inmost affection of the heart with an emphasis on hearing the Word to the exclusion of seeing. "We know God through the direct impact and causality of his divine being in and through his Word. God manifests himself and acts towards man and is present to him through his word. Thus knowledge of God is attained primarily by hearing rather than by seeing."[7] Alexandre Ganoczy notes the same dynamic at work in Calvin's rejection of the use of images in worship. "These severe criticisms, except for what is legitimate, seem to reveal Calvin's invincible distrust of a largely sacramental and 'incarnational' understanding of the Christian religion. . . . Since God is by nature spiritual and invisible, it is not only forbidden but absurd to express or represent him by material images."[8] Carlos M. N. Eire credits Calvin with making a transition from a form of religion based primarily on visible symbols to a form of religion based primarily on the Word as expounded by learned clergy. "It was a cerebral, learned sort of religion, one that only allowed for the Word to stand as an image of the invisible reality of the spiritual dimension. In practical terms, this meant a very concrete shift from a world brimming over with physical, visible symbols that were open to a wider range of interpretations—some intentionally ambiguous—to one charged principally with verbal symbols that were subject to the interpretation of a carefully trained and ostensibly learned ministry."[9] Eire claims that Calvin combined this "shift from pictures and concrete symbols to words" with a rejection of the possibility of miracles after the time of the apostles: "there is no intrusion of the divine, spiritual sphere into the material. The world operates on its own divinely appointed principles."[10] According to Eire, the move from symbols to words, and the rejection of miracles, is based in Calvin's metaphysic, which highlighted the transcendence and omnipotence of God, making impossible the representation of God in visible images. "Calvin's primary concern in his struggle against Catholic piety was to defend the glory of the God who is 'entirely other,' who transcends all materiality, who is 'as different from flesh as fire is from water,' and whose reality is inaccessible. . . . Calvin forcefully asserted God's transcendence through the principle *finitum non est capax infiniti* and His omnipotence through *soli Deo gloria*."[11]

Even scholars who wish to highlight the centrality of the sacraments in Calvin's theology emphasize the verbal nature of the sacraments for Calvin. According to Brian Gerrish, "The key to a Calvinistic interpretation of the sacraments is, in short, to construe them as essentially word, promise, or proclamation. It is the efficacy of the word that is brought to light in a sacrament, for a sacrament is a proclamation of the gospel—different in form, but not in function, from the preaching of the word."[12] Dawn de Vries concurs with this description, stating that the Word itself is sacramental—that is, the means of grace—for Calvin, making the Word "the primary means of grace."[13]

Two of the most recent biographers of Calvin agree with this description of the primacy of preaching and hearing in his theology. According to William Bouwsma, "Calvin suggests, at times, a bias against visual experience. He thought it impossible to give visual representation to the spiritual; neither God nor the human spirit can be painted, he observed. . . . We must rise above 'what is revealed to our eyes.' The Christian depends on 'God's mouth': because 'mute visions are cold,' he always speaks to us, and faith begins when we listen to his voice."[14] Bernard Cottret seems to sum up this whole line of Calvin interpretation with the following statement: "'It is God who speaks.' This is undoubtedly the most perfect summary of Calvin's theology: God speaks, God chooses, God summons."[15]

In spite of the apparent consensus that Calvin privileges hearing over seeing, recent scholarship has begun to notice the importance of visual manifestation for Calvin. Mary Potter Engel notes the many different "living images of God" that Calvin exhorts believers to contemplate, over against Torrance's focus on the Word of God alone. "Calvin does speak of men and women contemplating God in the mirrors of the world, their bodies, the scriptures, exemplary Christians, and Christ."[16] Susan Schreiner notes that the dialectic of the visible and invisible God is central to Calvin's interpretation of Job, for the "issues of revelation and hiddenness determine his exegesis of the text."[17] Philip Butin has observed the pervasiveness of visual imagery in Calvin's theology, noting "Calvin's typically dramatic visual imagery for the knowledge of God."[18] Most recently, Barbara Pitkin has emphasized Calvin's understanding of faith as a kind of vision: "faith is a kind of perception that looks beyond or even away from the objects presented to the physical senses and apprehends in a preliminary and proleptic fashion the full vision of God that the elect will someday enjoy."[19] Even Bouwsma notes that Calvin "often seemed much impressed by the special value of sight," though he seems to limit this to Calvin's discussions of astronomy.[20] And in one revealing sentence, Eire notes that for Calvin "God is quite visible, making himself manifest in the church: 'When God represents himself according to his good wishes, and gives us marks and signs so that he can be known by us, then it is as if he took a face.'"[21]

Calvin scholars have also noted the essential interdependence of manifestation and proclamation in Calvin's theology, though usually only in isolated instances of his thought and not as an essential element of his theological thinking. T. H. L. Parker has argued that "Calvin's theology is, . . . throughout his life, a theology of the Sacraments. God will not encounter man directly but by means of that which is already a human term of reference, the human means of communication and visible symbols."[22] In particular, Parker has noted the interrelationship of the Word and works of God in Calvin's description of the knowledge of God. "Revelation is indirect, as we have said; knowledge is always by way of the sacramental form of revelation. We know God in His Word and in His works, because they are the image of God, mirroring His *effigies,* His portrait."[23] The Word of God confirms the work of God, even as the work of God confirms the Word of God. "The *oracula Dei* both confirm the *opera Dei* and in turn are confirmed by them."[24] Edward Dowey has noted the same interrelationship between divine oracles on the one hand and visions and miracles on the other. "The oracle preserves the vision from indefiniteness, the vision prepares the mind for and confirms the oracular message."[25] The Word of God and the contemplation of the universe manifest the same interdependence of proclamation and manifestation. "With Scripture as our 'guide and teacher,' we actually see God at work in creation."[26] The same relationship between Word and symbol has been observed in Calvin's understanding of the sacraments. According to Gerrish, "Word and sacrament, correctly understood, fit naturally together. On the one hand, the sacraments make the promises of God clearer to us; on the other hand, they stand in constant need of the word to make us understand their meaning."[27] Thomas Davis agrees: there is an essential interdependence of symbol and word, manifestation and proclamation. "The sign and the words are interdependent: the sign reinforces the words, paints a picture of them for the senses. The words explain the sign. Together, they present to the believer the fullest expression of Christ as spiritual food."[28]

As I show in the following chapters, the interdependence of the Word and work of God, or proclamation and manifestation, is not present in a few isolated topics of Calvin's theology but is central to the way he thinks theologically. Calvin did not think that we could come to the knowledge of God by seeing the self-manifestation of God alone, or by hearing the proclamation of the Word of God alone. Instead, we must use our eyes and our ears in order to behold the living images that God presents to our view, in order to be led from the visible to the invisible, from the earthly to the heavenly, from the present to the future, from the carnal to the spiritual. Our faith is never firm or certain for Calvin unless we can see with our eyes evidence of the goodness of God that we hear with our ears. Even if that goodness is for a time hidden under an appearance that seems to contradict it, the goodness of God will once again manifest itself, and confirm our faith by experience, even as we held to the truth of the Word when it was hidden from view. Indeed, far from making hearing the primary way of knowing, Calvin associated words themselves with visible symbols and images in which unseen reality manifests itself to us. As Lucien Richard notes, "'Words are nothing else but signs.' But when God gives a sign, he comes himself to be present. Signs form a veil behind which God conceals his presence in human affairs. They are at the same time focal points for the meeting between God and man. Calvin understood a sign to point to another reality. 'As he was not tied to any place, so he meant nothing less than to tie his people to the earthly symbols, but he descends to them that he might take them to himself.'"[29]

2. Removing "Dead Images" for the Sake of "Living Images"

If manifestation is as essential to Calvin as proclamation, how then can he repeatedly insist that God is invisible, and cannot be represented in visual images and pictures? The answer to that question will occupy us throughout the book, but for now I want to note first that Calvin distinguished between the "dead images" that human beings create and the "living images" that God alone can create. Since for Calvin the Word of God is the life and soul of images and symbols, human images that lack the Word therefore lack life, and so are "dead." But what in particular makes them dead, beyond the lack of the Word? First, Calvin thought that living images live in the field of tension created by the essentially invisible, infinite, and spiritual God becoming somewhat visible in finite reality. This field of tension—that the God who cannot dwell in temples made by human hands nonetheless dwells in a Temple made by human hands—keeps the living image from creating the illusion that it can somehow enclose or contain God in itself, as is the case with dead images. Whereas Calvin thought that dead images were forged in an attempt to drag God down from heaven, living images represent God's descent to us so that we might use them as "ladders" or "vehicles" whereby we might ascend to God.

Second, Calvin thought that living images transform the person contemplating them into the image of God, from one degree of glory to another, so that we might become more and more like God in order to be united to God. Dead images, on the other hand, attempt to transform God into our own image, in order to make the spiritual and infinite God carnal and finite, a prisoner of the image that we create to represent God. Third, living images have both an analogical and anagogical relationship to the reality they represent. They refer the mind and heart of the one contemplating them to the reality being represented, by means of the similarity amid dissimilarity they have with that reality, and raise the mind up anagogically to that reality. Dead images lack this analogical and anagogical relationship to God but instead contradict the reality they claim to represent and keep our minds and hearts firmly planted on earth. Fourth, living images not only represent and portray reality but also offer and present the reality being represented. To take but one well-known example, the bread and wine not only represent the body and blood of Christ; they also offer and present that body and blood to us for the nourishment of our souls unto eternal life. Dead images, on the other hand, simply represent a reality that is and remains absent from the representation. Human beings are incapable of making images that offer the reality that they represent—only God can do this.

Calvin did not seek to remove "dead images" from places of worship so that there might be no images of God at all but only the preaching of the Word. Instead, Calvin sought to remove the dead images so that the faithful might apply their eyes and ears to the "living icons" that God uses to represent Godself to us. "When I ponder the intended use of churches, somehow or other it seems to me unworthy of their holiness for them to take on images other than those living and symbolical ones which the Lord has consecrated by his Word. I mean Baptism and the Lord's Supper, together with other ceremonies by which our eyes must be too intensely gripped and too sharply affected to seek other images forged by human ingenuity."[30] The same can be said of the making of images out of creatures, for such images keep our eyes from contemplating the living image of God in the whole of creation, as well as the image and likeness of God in other human beings. Calvin carried on a "war against the idols" to direct the attention of the faithful to the living images and icons of God all around them, from creation itself, to the living images of God and Christ in the history of Israel, culminating in the living portraits of Christ in the preaching, sacraments, and ceremonies of the Church.

3. Beholding the Image in the Mirror: Calvin's Seneca Commentary, 1532

Calvin's thoughts about self-manifestation continued to develop throughout his career, but it is important to note that he demonstrated an interest in this issue from the beginning of his writing career in 1532. Of particular note is Calvin's interest in the phenomenon of "beholding an image in a mirror" in his earliest written work, the Commentary on Seneca's *De Clementia*. In the first paragraph of his comments, Calvin says of Seneca's treatise, "Skillfully therefore does Seneca propose to write about clemency in such a way that Nero may recognize the reflection (*imaginem*) of his own clemency in the description of that virtue. . . . He says therefore he does not so much intend to instruct and educate Nero by precepts, as to show him a mirror with the image of virtue (*illi exhibere speculum in imagine virtutis*), in which he can recognize himself and contemplate his own gifts. For as a mirror displays (*repraesentat*) a man's face to himself, so in the description of strength does a strong man recognize something of himself; in that of prudence a prudent man; in that of justice a just man."[31] By 1536 Calvin will describe the Law as the mirror that reveals to us our sin; and by 1546 he will describe the Gospel as the mirror in which we behold the image of Christ, who is himself the living image of God.

Calvin also makes use of Cicero's statement, "History is life's school-mistress," to discuss the role of historical examples and exemplars, which will be central to his understanding of exemplary figures such as Abraham, David, Paul, and Christ. "In [history], as in a mirror (*speculo*), we see our own life. We discern with our eyes what we are to avoid, what to follow."[32] Calvin notes the power that language has when it can portray something so vividly that it places it before our eyes, which became his ideal as a teacher and formed the category by which he would analyze prophetic speech in particular. "Now what in this context is called 'description,' is so called by Cicero in his *Rhetoric* and in Greek is called *energeia*, that is *perspicuitas* and *evidentia*, which conceives images of things (*rerum imagines*) as here as if before our eyes Seneca represents (*quasi oculis repraesentat*) a populous city."[33]

Calvin describes the exemplary instruction that others should receive when the punishment of some is manifested to all, which will become central to his description of the way the godly are to profit from the open punishment of the reprobate, such as the destruction of Sodom and Gomorrah. "The Greeks call this sort of punishment *paradeigma*, the Latins, *exemplum*, when the punishment of one is the fear of many, as Gratian and Valens say, for which reason punishments are sometimes made more severe than usual. Plutarch, *On the Slowness of Divine Vengeance*: 'The punishments of criminals are openly displayed (*ostenduntur*) to all, inasmuch as the function of vengeance inflicted with reason is to deter and restrain some by the chastisements of others.'"[34] Calvin also cites Plutarch's description of kings as "the image of God," something that will carry into his theological understanding of kings, given their greater participation in the governance of human affairs by God. "And in the same Plutarch, one finds a similar saying by Artabanus: 'Kings, likenesses (*simulacra*) of God who sustains all.'"[35]

Calvin notes the importance of distinguishing realities, such as virtues and vices, that can be easily confused by impressing them with "certain marks," which will become central to his theological dialectics, such as distinguishing the children of God from the reprobate, the true God from false gods, the true Church from the false church. "Thus Seneca: ' . . . there is great danger if one goes astray in these matters. So stamp them with special labels (*certas notas imprime*).' The opposite is 'to confuse the marks (*signa*),' as used by Cicero."[36] The necessity of "certain marks" is made more urgent given the way evil people can represent themselves before others as virtuous, a theme that Calvin tirelessly addresses throughout his career as teacher and pastor. "What? Are there not also in our own age 'monsters of men, dripping with inner vices,' yet putting forth the outward appearance and mask (*speciem et larvam*) of uprightness?"[37] Calvin traces the use of such descriptions of hypocrisy to the theater, in which actors appear to be other than they are by the wearing of masks. "What Seneca previously called a 'goodness assumed for a time' he now calls, wearing a mask (*personam*), a metaphor drawn from comedy and tragedy, in which masked persons act in the theater. Hence, 'to wear a mask' means to lay aside one's natural form. And we speak of a counterfeit and hypocritical man as 'masked.'"[38] On the other hand, upright people will eventually give evidence of their character, which others can infer from their behavior, which Calvin will later use in his attempt to give signs of adoption that others should be able to discern. "Seneca means that Roman affairs had been in great jeopardy before Nero had established a sure way of life; in other words, when he had not yet displayed any proof (*specimen exhibuisset*) of natural disposition, from which one might infer an upright character."[39]

4. HISTORICAL INFLUENCES ON CALVIN'S THEOLOGY OF MANIFESTATION

How is one to account for Calvin's interest in the issue of visible manifestation and concealment? The obvious reason is that it is suggested to him by the classical authors, usually compiled by Budé, whom Calvin cites to interpret Seneca's treatise. This appears to be the case with Calvin's discussion of "certain marks" from Seneca, which one also finds in Plato, as well as his understanding of hypocrisy, and the rhetorical figure of description from Cicero, as well as the use of historical examples and exemplars. However, Budé himself does not evidence anywhere near the interest in visible manifestation that Calvin does.[40] Moreover, most of the references to seeing images in mirrors come from Calvin's own comments on Seneca and not from the classical sources he is citing.

The most likely source for Calvin's interest in contemplating images in mirrors comes from the world of French literature in the first half of the sixteenth century, in particular the circle around Marguerite of Navarre, to which Calvin belonged while he was in Paris and with whom he corresponded even after he went into exile. Of particular note is Marguerite's *Le Miroir de l'âme pécheresse* (*The Mirror of the Sinful Soul*), first published in 1521. Marguerite appears to have been influenced rather decisively by Augustine of Hippo, an influence no doubt reinforced by her correspondence with

Briçonnet. According to Robert Cottrell, Marguerite developed two related but distinct uses of the mirror in her poem. First, the mirror reflects back the image of the person looking into the mirror, which would correspond with the way Calvin speaks of the image in the mirror in his Seneca commentary. However, the text then moves into another sense of the mirror, one in which Christ is the image in the mirror, and what is reflected in the mirror is not the sinful soul that she perceives herself to be but the way Christ sees his image in her. The move between the first and the second meaning of the mirror takes place by means of what Cottrell calls "allegorical or anagogic interpretation."[41] "At the beginning of the *Miroir*, reality is resolutely anthropomorphic. Marguerite herself is the source. The text reflects the image of the sinner that she is. . . . Soon, however, it begins to acquire symbolic resonance. As it becomes increasingly anagogic, one level of reality gives way to another. Christ is now identified as the source. Man, to the extent that he participates in the Incarnation, is seen as Christ's image."[42] These two uses of the image in the mirror can be seen in earlier medieval literature, tracing the influence of Augustine. "As Sister Ritamary Bradley observed in her seminal article on the use of the word *speculum* in medieval literature, the mirror image, at least from Augustine on, has had two basic connotations: a mirror may reflect a faithful image of what is, or it may serve as a paragon of what should be."[43] It should be noted that in the Seneca commentary, Calvin's use of the mirror follows the first meaning: Nero should recognize himself in the description of clemency. By 1534, however, Calvin will incorporate the second meaning as well: the image in the mirror is Christ, who reveals the invisible God to us. The mirror as the faithful image of what is, in turn, will no longer be the virtue in which we can recognize ourselves but the mirror of the Law revealing to us our sinfulness before God.

The awareness that a text itself can function as a mirror already begins to suggest the essential conjunction of hearing and seeing that I will argue is essential to Calvin's theological thinking. The relationship between seeing and hearing would receive even more of an impetus from two other sources: Cicero and Augustine. According to Cicero, sight is the keenest of the senses; and we therefore know things with greater constancy if we can see them as well as hear about them. "[T]he keenest of all our senses is the sense of sight, and . . . consequently perceptions received by the ears or by reflexion can be most easily retained in the mind if they are also conveyed to our minds by the mediation of the eyes, with the result that things not seen and not lying in the field of visual discernment are earmarked by a sort of outline and image and shape (*imago et figura*) so that we keep hold of as it were by an act of sight things which we can scarcely embrace by an act of thought."[44] Cicero therefore preferred metaphors drawn from visible reality, as they penetrate more fully into the mind: "the metaphors drawn from the sense of sight are much more vivid, virtually placing within the range of our mental vision objects not actually visible to our sight."[45] Moreover, this explains why Cicero prefers oratory that has lucid brevity, for it appeals the most clearly and directly to the eyes, even though it is speech. "For it is this department of oratory which almost sets the fact before the eyes—for it is the sense of sight that is most appealed to. . . . For brilliance is worth considerably more than the clearness above mentioned. The one helps us to understand what is said, but the other makes us feel that we actually see it before our eyes."[46] For Cicero, the most effective words are those that place the reality being described before the eyes of the listener. We can see this ideal already reflected in Calvin's interpretation of Seneca, and it will emerge decisively in his understanding of the Gospel as the portrayal of Christ from life, following Galatians 3:1.

The Ciceronian combination of hearing and seeing would be further reinforced in Calvin's thought by Augustine of Hippo, with particular reference to Augustine's description of sacraments as "visible words," which first makes it appearance in the *Institutes* of 1536. Calvin clearly relates Augustine's description of the sacraments with the theme of beholding an image in a mirror, which we have seen as early as the Seneca commentary. "Augustine calls a sacrament 'a visible word' for the reason that it represents God's promises as painted in a picture (*velut in tabula depictas repraesentet*) and sets them before our sight, portrayed graphically and in the manner of images (*graphice atque eikotos*)."[47] Unlike the use of rhetoric, in which words are used to portray the reality before the eyes of those who hear them, in the sacraments things are used to portray in a graphic and iconic way the words that God proclaims to us in the promise. The words are not only portrayed as in a painting in the sacramental symbols; they are also essential to setting forth the analogical and anagogical relationship between the symbol and the reality it represents. "[Augustine] says, 'Visible sacraments were instituted for the sake of carnal men, that by the steps of the sacraments they may be transported from things discernable by the eyes to those understood.' . . . In another place, he says: 'A sacrament is indeed so called because in it one thing is seen, another understood. What is seen has bodily form; what is understood has spiritual fruit.'"[48] It is quite likely that the development of

Calvin's understanding of living icons and symbols takes place as he extends Augustine's understanding of sacraments as "visible words" to all forms of divine self-manifestation, from the universe itself to the symbols and visions given to the fathers under the Law to the symbols and visions of the Gospel. He never ceases to point out the essential conjunction between the symbol and the word, or between manifestation and proclamation, and to draw the proper analogy between the sign and the thing signified.

Calvin was also influenced by Desiderius Erasmus, whose writings he surely knew by the time of his Seneca commentary, and whom he continued to read as he worked on his expositions of the New Testament. Erasmus, like Calvin, speaks of texts that mirror the image of the person to herself, as in the discussion of the knowledge of self in his *Enchiridion*. "I shall set before you a kind of likeness of yourself, as in a painting, so that you may have a clear knowledge of what you are on the inside and what you are skin-deep."[49] Erasmus also refers to Jesus Christ as "the reflection of the glory of the Father," echoing the other sense of mirror as reflecting unseen divine reality to us.[50] Erasmus encouraged his readers to contemplate the image of Christ in the Gospels rather than seek after relics of Christ to venerate. "You give homage to an image of Christ's countenance represented in stone or wood or depicted in colour. With how much more religious feeling should you render homage to the image of his mind, which has been reproduced in the Gospels through the artistry of the Holy Spirit? . . . And you do not gaze with wonder upon this image, do not worship it, scan it with reverent eyes, treasure it in your mind?"[51] Indeed, Erasmus insists in his *Paraclesis* that we see Christ more vividly in his image in the Gospel than his contemporaries ever did: "these writings bring you the living image of His holy mind and the speaking, healing, dying, rising Christ Himself, and thus they render Him so fully present that you would see less if you gazed upon Him with your very eyes."[52] That Erasmus uses the term "living image," which will become a favorite of Calvin's, suggests that he may have had a decisive influence on Calvin's thinking about images.

Erasmus was also highly critical of the use of ceremonies for their own sake, as though they alone constituted the true worship of God. "With what spite they exact these same ceremonies of others, with what a sense of security they trust in them, with what temerity they judge others, with what jealous rivalry they defend them. They think heaven is owed to them because of these actions of theirs."[53] For Erasmus, it is far more important to represent Christ in one's way of life than to perform ceremonies. "Where is the image of Christ in your morals?"[54] Erasmus holds up Christ as the exemplar to whom we should always seek to conform our lives and norms all other examples by whether they conform to Christ. "Painters hold up the best paintings to themselves as models. Our example is Christ, in whom alone are all the patterns of the holy life. You may imitate Him without exception. From men of tried virtue you may take single qualities as a model according as they correspond to the archetype of Christ."[55] Erasmus reminds his readers, as Calvin will later, that God does not see externals but the heart. "The eyes of the Lord do not see what is manifested externally, but what is in secret."[56] Since God is Spirit, he must be worshiped by spiritual sacrifices, as even the pagans knew. "It is shameful that Christians do not know what a certain pagan poet did not fail to recognize: 'If God is spirit, as poets say / With purest mind must he be worshipped.'"[57] Calvin will later cite the same poet in support of his claim that God must be worshiped in spirit and truth.

Finally, Calvin shared with Erasmus the sense that human life is properly lived if we ascend as by steps from the temporal to the eternal, from the visible to the invisible, from the carnal to the spiritual: "raise yourself as on the steps of Jacob's ladder from the body to the spirit, from the visible to the invisible, from the letter to the mystery, from sensible things to intelligible things, from composite things to simple things."[58] This anagogical ascent as on steps of a ladder would be reinforced by the influence of Marguerite of Navarre, whose own poems are built on the theme of the ascent to God by steps, and by the theological vision of Briçonnet, who influenced Marguerite.[59] Calvin cites Augustine's statement that the sacraments are like "steps," and he will increasingly call the visible symbols of God's goodness "steps," "ladders," or "vehicles" by which we ascend from the temporal and visible world to the eternal and invisible God.

Such language of anagogical ascent reflects not only the influence of Briçonnet, Marguerite, Augustine, and Erasmus but also the thought of Plato.[60] It is clear from the increasing number of citations from Plato's works that Calvin read Plato throughout his career. However, the influence of Plato on Calvin's theology does not emerge explicitly until the 1539 edition of the *Institutes*. Calvin describes Plato as the most religious of all philosophers and the most circumspect (I.v.11), and cites in approval Plato's statement that the highest good of the soul is likeness to God (I.iii.3) as well as his discussion of the five senses or organs of the human being (I.xv.6). Most strikingly for our purposes, Calvin paraphrases Plato's description of the effect in the soul once beauty has been beheld, and applies it to the taste of divine love brought about by faith. "But how can the mind be aroused to taste the divine good-ness without at the same time being wholly kindled to love God in return? For truly, that abundant sweetness which God has stored up for those who fear him cannot be known without at the same time powerfully moving us. And once anyone has been moved by it, it utterly ravishes him and draws him to itself."[61] This is a clear paraphrase of Plato's description of the way beauty awakens love in the *Phaedrus,* as is clear from a later citation of Plato by Calvin. "Granted that Plato was groping in the darkness; but he denied that the beautiful which he imagined could be known without ravishing a man with the admiration of itself—this in *Phaedrus* and elsewhere."[62]

For Plato, the beautiful itself is perceived in images of beauty perceived by human sight. "For sight is the keenest mode of perception vouchsafed us through the body; wisdom, indeed, we cannot see thereby—how passionate had been our desire for her, if she had granted us so clear an image of herself to gaze upon—nor yet any other of those beloved objects, save only beauty; for beauty alone this has been ordained, to be the most manifest to sense and most lovely of them all" (*Phaedrus* 250.d). For those whose souls are rightly prepared, the vision of beauty "ravishes" the person with awe and reverence as by the visible image of deity on earth. "But when one who is fresh from the mystery, and saw much of the vision, beholds a godlike face or bodily form that truly expresses beauty, first there come upon him a shuddering and a measure of awe which the vision inspired, and then reverence as at the sight of a god, and but for fear of being deemed a madman he would offer sacrifice to his beloved as to a holy image of deity" (251.a).

The vision of beauty in the image of beauty draws the person up as on wings, by the power of love, or *eros,* that the vision of beauty awakens. "Such a one, as soon as he beholds the beauty of this world, is reminded of true beauty, and his wings begin to grow; then is he fain to lift his wings and fly upward: yet he has not the power, but inasmuch as he gazes upward like a bird, and cares nothing for the world beneath, men charge it upon him that he is demented" (249.d). Such madness and dementia are caused by the ex-perience of being rapt or ravished out of oneself by the vision of beauty in its earthly image. "Few indeed are left that can still remember much, but when these discern some likeness of the things yonder, they are amazed, and no longer masters of themselves, and know not what is come upon them by rea-son of their perception being dim" (250.a). As we shall see in the chapters that follow, Calvin draws on Plato's understanding of the vision of beauty in its earthly images to describe the effect in the soul of the person who rightly beholds the living images and icons of God's goodness manifested in this life. "Now, it must be the case that the grace of God draws us all to Himself and inflames us with love of Him by whom we obtain a real perception of it. If Plato affirms this of his Beautiful, of which he saw only a shadowy idea from afar off, this is much more true with regard to God."[63] The influence of Plato further underscores the claim that the author and fountain of every good thing proclaims itself by the truth of the Word of God even as it manifests itself by the beauty of the living images of God portrayed in the world.

5. CALVIN ON THE HISTORICAL DEVELOPMENT OF LIVING IMAGES

My analysis of Calvin's understanding of the living icons of God attends in every instance to the historical development of his thought, addressed in the context of each topic. However, my analysis also attends to Calvin's own understanding of the way the living images of God develop throughout history, beginning with creation itself and then progressing through the symbols of the Law to the symbols of the Gospel, both of which manifest Christ, the living image of God. Calvin had a Pauline and Irenaean understanding of God's relationship with humanity, in which God adapts God's proclamation and manifestation of Christ to the capacities of human beings at various stages in history. Following Paul and Irenaeus, Calvin claims that humanity develops over history from infancy to adulthood, though he often suggests that we have only reached the level of adolescence even after the appearance of the Gospel. According to Calvin, this economy of divine self-manifestation means that we must be careful to locate the symbols that God institutes in the period to which they were specifically adapted. His primary criticism of Rome is that it does not attend to this economy, and thus imposes symbols on the Church *after* Christ that were only adapted to the capacities of the people *before* Christ. To ignore this distinction would be like using a primary school textbook to teach college students. Calvin discerns different symbol systems being employed by God in at least six distinct epochs: Adam and Eve before the fall; the period after the fall from Adam to Babel; the time of the patriarchs from Abraham up until the Exodus; the period of Moses and Aaron beginning with Sinai and the creation of the tabernacle; the establishment of the Davidic kingdom and the building of the Temple in Jerusalem up until the Babylonian captivity, including the prophetic critique of Israel and Judah; the restoration of the Kingdom of David, which extends from the return from Babylon to the ascension of Christ; the time of the Gospel, which begins on Pentecost and extends to Calvin's day; and the day of the revelation of Jesus Christ, culminating in the face-to-face vision of God. The time of the Gospel is itself divided into periods by Calvin, beginning with the purer form of the Church under the apostles; the addition of misleading symbols by the fathers; the rise of the papacy and the subsequent ruin of the Church; and the restoration of the Church in Calvin's day. Since Calvin's observations about the latter periods take place in his discussion of the former, I take the former as foundational for this study.

One of the central methodological problems for this study involves the relationship of the historical development of Calvin's thinking about manifestation and proclamation and Calvin's description of the historical development of manifestation and proclamation in creation, Israel, and the Christian Church. On the one hand, to arrive at an adequate picture of the development of Calvin's thought, one must study his works in the order in which he wrote them. On the other hand, to arrive at an adequate picture of Calvin's understanding of the development of symbols through history, one must follow the canonical order of the books on which he commented, beginning with Genesis, published in 1554 (at the same time as the commentary on Acts 14–28), and ending with the Pauline epistles, which were the first commentaries published by Calvin.

Calvin's thinking about the relationship of manifestation to proclamation, of living icon to the Word of God, was present from the beginning of his writing career and continued to develop throughout his life. Since that development is different for each of the topics considered here, it seems best to trace the history of each development under each topic rather than attempt an overall picture of such development, which would need a study in its own right. For example, Calvin taught from 1534 onward that the powers of God are vividly portrayed in creation: the Lord "has, in all parts of the world, in heaven and on earth, written and as it were engraved the glory of his power, goodness, wisdom, and eternity."[64] However, Calvin does not use the widely cited metaphor of theater to describe the self-manifestation of God in creation until his commentary on 1 Corinthians in 1546: "For it is true that this world is like a theater in which the Lord shows to us a striking spectacle of His glory."[65] To take another example, Calvin denied that the laying on of hands was a sacrament in the 1536 *Institutes,* but by the 1543 edition he argues that it is a sacrament and should be restored to the practice of ordination, something he confirms in his comments on 1 Timothy 4:14 in 1548.[66] I thus trace the development of each theme of manifestation as it arises, so that a complete picture of the development of Calvin's understanding of self-manifestation will only emerge by the end of the book. For the sake of the clarity of the presentation, I have taken as my major organizational theme Calvin's description of the development of the living icons of God from creation to the vision of God in eternal life, and discuss the historical development of Calvin's understanding of the living images of God in the context of each chapter. The major sources used in this study are the Latin treatises written by Calvin, with a focus on the biblical commentaries, as these offer the clearest picture of the historical development of living images.

6. Objectives of This Study

The goal of this study is fourfold. First, this exploration hopes to reawaken interest in the self-manifestation of God in creation in Protestant theology, which is especially timely in light of our current ecological crisis, to counter the one-sided emphasis on the proclamation of Christ introduced by twentieth-century theologians such as Karl Barth and Rudolph Bultmann. Calvin insisted that one of the reasons that God instituted the Sabbath was that we should take at least one day out of the week to contemplate the wisdom, power, goodness, and mercy of God revealed in the works of God in creation, which he consistently described as "the most beautiful image of God," even after the fall into sin and wrath. He was as passionately interested in the contemplation of the heavens, both by the unlearned and by trained astronomers, as he was in the study of the intricacies of the human body, including the anatomical work of Galen and the medical work of contemporaries such as Benedictus Textor.[67] For Calvin, the various sciences, which he regarded as a form of philosophy, were rightly understood as providing us with a more vivid sense of the powers of God at work in all aspects of creation, and were perfectly compatible with genuine piety—indeed, they fostered genuine piety. The feelings of awe and reverence that the image of God in creation awakened in Calvin are a far cry from the heartless manipulation of the natural world for our own profit that one sees in modern industrialized societies. Calvin's countless exhortations that we should spend the whole of our lives contemplating this most beautiful image of God would be a serious check on the participation of Christians in the denigration of the environment.

Second, by showing the centrality of seeing as well as hearing in Calvin's theology, this study hopes to create avenues of further research by those interested in theological aesthetics, and to encourage a greater appreciation of visual contemplation in Protestant theology, including efforts of liturgical renewal in the Reformed and Presbyterian traditions. Given Calvin's awareness that the fountain of every good thing manifests itself in beauty as well as in truth, and can only rightly be sought when we hold beauty and truth together, it is not surprising to see one of the heirs of Calvin, Jonathan Edwards, making beauty central to his understanding of God. Contrary to the suspicions of Luther and Kierkegaard, Calvin shows that it is in fact possible to combine a radical theology of the cross with an equally radical emphasis on visible manifestation. We cannot rightly behold any of the living images of God until we have been humbled by the cross of Christ and submit ourselves to its wisdom. However, once we have been transformed by the cross of Christ, we are given the eyes of faith to behold the glory of God's goodness not only in all of creation but also, especially, in Christ crucified, who, when we behold him in the mirror of the Gospel, transforms us into his image from one degree of glory to another.

Moreover, Calvin thought of visible manifestation not only in terms of the sacraments but also in terms of the rites and ceremonies of Christian worship. All of these should manifest and represent Christ to the congregation, and should be set forth in such a way as to hold the attention of the worshiping community, so that they might be more deeply stirred to worship, call upon, praise, and thank God. It often seems to be the case that Calvin was not able in fact to set forth his theory of worship in the actual worship life of the Geneva Church. He describes preaching as painting Christ to the life so that the congregation can vividly see him set before them, while in practice his sermons were mostly line-by-line expositions and applications of the text of Scripture. He taught that all rites and ceremonies should represent Christ and manifest his grace and power in the community, but his own liturgical rites were often heavily penitential. His failure to realize his vision of worship in the practice of worship he helped to create should not undermine his concern to have worship that is both true to the Word of God and visually moving and stimulating, appealing as much to the eyes and the affections as to the ears and the intellect.

Third, the essential conjunction of manifestation and proclamation with regard to the knowledge of God is mirrored by Calvin's attention to the words, gestures, and actions of others as they communicate with us. For Calvin, language is the image of the mind, and represents our otherwise hidden thoughts and affections to others. However, our thoughts and affections are also externally represented by the gestures we use, as well as by our actions. Calvin is always sensitive to the ways a person's gestures or actions either correspond to or contradict what the person is saying. He strove for a harmony among heart, word, and gesture, so that our communication with others might have integrity. Moreover, Calvin became increasingly convinced that the external representation of pious affections not only awakens greater fervor of piety in the individual but also stirs up others by its forcefulness. This communication and stimulation of piety forms one of the central purposes of public worship for Calvin, and leads him to an increasing appreciation of the role of rites and ceremonies in worship. One can see a line of development on this issue extending from Calvin through the pietists to the theory of religious communication in Friedrich Schleiermacher. Calvin's attention to gestures and actions would be a salutary corrective to an overemphasis on words, and his attention to the communication and strengthening of the pious affections would be a healthy corrective to the neglect of affectivity in modern Protestant theology, which has been deeply influenced by the suspicion of pietism in Ritschl and Herrmann, as well as Bultmann and Barth. Calvin's increasingly positive assessment of gestures, rites, and ceremonies also opens avenues of access to Roman Catholic, Greek Orthodox, and Anglican understandings of worship.

Fourth, and most important, by showing the importance of manifestation in both creation and redemption, this study hopes to demonstrate the ecumenical promise of Calvin's theology in light of the strong emphasis on manifestation in the Roman Catholic and Greek Orthodox traditions, without losing sight of the essential role for Calvin of proclamation in clarifying the living icons of God. Roman Catholic theologians, such as David Tracy and Hans Urs von Balthasar, have contrasted Catholic and Protestant forms of thought by saying that the former emphasizes manifestation and a sacramental way of thinking, whereas the latter emphasizes proclamation and a verbally oriented way of thinking. This study shows that Calvin thinks in terms of the essential interrelationship of manifestation and proclamation, which may provide interesting bridges between the Protestant and Catholic Churches, without ignoring the major differences between them. Calvin may not agree with Roman Catholic or Greek Orthodox theologians about how many "living images of God" there may be, but it is nonetheless significant that he urges his readers to contemplate the living images of God as an essential part of their piety. Calvin always claimed that his theology was both evangelical and orthodox, and it is my hope that by highlighting the sacramental character of the entirety of Calvin's theology, Calvin may be able to claim his place as a member of the broader catholic tradition.

PART I

The Living Images of God the Creator

CHAPTER I

The Universe as the Living Image of God

The self-manifestation of God in the works of creation emerges in the first writing Calvin published as an evangelical, and remained an essential element of his theology throughout his theological career. Our objective in this chapter will be first to set forth the development of Calvin's understanding of the universe as the living icon of God, in which the invisible God makes Godself somewhat visible, beginning with his French preface to Olivetan's Bible in 1535, and culminating in the final edition of the *Institutes* in 1559. We will then turn to the exposition of his teaching on this topic, which is most fully expressed in his commentaries on the Psalms and the Prophets, from 1557 to 1564. In contrast to the approach to this topic that many have taken since the argument between Barth and Brunner regarding the knowledge of God the Creator, which has tended to focus on the way the self-manifestation of God in the universe renders sinful humanity without excuse, we will be especially interested in the ways the contemplation of the universe operates in the lives of the pious, according to Calvin. In this way, we hope to show that the contemplation of the living image of God in the universe is as essential for Calvin as is the contemplation of the living image of Christ in the mirror of the Gospel.

A. The Development of Calvin's Theology of God's Self-Manifestation in the Universe

1. The Powers of God Engraved in the World: Preface to Olivetan, 1535

The theme of the self-manifestation of God in the universe emerges in the first writing Calvin published as an evangelical, his preface to Olivetan's New Testament, titled the *Epistle to the Faithful Showing that Christ Is the End of the Law*. Calvin discusses the self-revelation of God in the universe in light of Paul's sermons in Acts 14 and 17, where it serves the purpose of showing the Gentiles that God did not leave them without witness throughout the time of his self-revelation to Israel through the Law.[1] Central to the self-manifestation of God to the Gentiles are the "powers of God" set forth in all parts of the universe, especially "his power, goodness, wisdom, and eternity."[2] The powers of God mentioned here will remain central to Calvin's understanding of the self-manifestation of God.

According to Calvin, the powers of God "engraved" in every creature both bear witness to God and invite all people to seek after God, "and, after having found him, to meditate upon him and to render him the homage befitting his dignity as so good, so mighty, so wise a Lord who is eternal; yea, they are even capable to aiding every man wherever he is in this quest."[3] The powers of God set forth in the works of God reveal to us the nature of God, in this instance God's goodness, power, wisdom, and eternity. Since these powers are revealed everywhere in the universe, all of the creatures we behold seek to lead us on the right path in our search for God.[4] However, there is no need to go outside ourselves, as Paul indicates in Acts 17, for we find evidence of the powers of God within ourselves.[5]

For Calvin, the display of God's powers both outside and within us reveals to us the goodness of God, from which all of these powers flow.[6] In spite of their perception of God's goodness, the Gentiles did not glorify God for God's goodness but rather created for themselves gods to their own liking, so that each region had its own god. However, the Law did not fare any better with the Jews, for they, like the Gentiles, refused to be taught by God.[7] The failure of creation and the Law to teach Gentiles and Jews the true knowledge of God led God to send forth Christ the Mediator, to reconcile both Gentiles and Jews to God. At this period of Calvin's life, the self-manifestation of God in the universe is not prior to the clarifying testimony of the Law, but rather both creation and the Law are parallel revelations that are powerless to overcome sin, and therefore need to be replaced by the Mediator, Jesus Christ.

The *Institutes* of 1536 adds little to the discussion of the self-manifestation of God in the universe, but it does reinforce the centrality of the powers of God for the self-disclosure of God. In the opening section, Calvin mentions the powers of God in his discussion of what we need to know of God, namely, that he "is infinite wisdom, righteousness, goodness, mercy, truth, power, and life [Bar. 3:12–14; 16:4]. And all of these things, wherever seen, come from him."[8] Calvin associates the powers of God with the Name of God, an association that will remain to the end of his life. "By God's name is indicated his power, which comprises all his powers: as, his might, wisdom, righteousness, mercy, truth."[9] Moreover, Calvin identifies three of the powers of God with the three subsistences of the Trinity. "Indeed Scripture so distinguishes these as to attribute to the Father the beginning of acting and the fountain and source of all things; to assign to the Son the wisdom and plan of acting; to refer to the Spirit the power and effective working of action."[10] This association of powers with persons continues to inform his discussion of God the Creator in the Apostles' Creed.[11] Although Calvin will often list many powers in his discussion of the self-revelation of God, his association of goodness with the Father, wisdom with the Son, and power with the Holy Spirit will make these three powers central to his thinking about God, with the priority being given to the goodness of God the Father.

2. The World as the Visible Representation of Invisible Things: *Catechism*, 1537

The first major development in Calvin's thinking about the self-disclosure of God in creation occurs in his *Catechism*, which he published in French in 1537 and in Latin in 1538, during his first period of ministry in Geneva. Calvin makes several moves in this catechism that will remain foundational for all subsequent discussions of this issue. First, he distinguishes between seeking knowledge of God's essence and seeking knowledge of God through God's works, an issue already indirectly alluded to in 1536 in his definition of the Name of God.[12] Second, he turns to his unique (some would say eccentric) translation of Hebrews 11:3 to describe the self-exhibition of God in the universe. "Accordingly, we are to search out and trace God in his works, which are called in the Scriptures 'the reflection of things invisible,' because they represent to us what otherwise we could not see of the Lord."[13] The New Revised Standard Version translates the same phrase, "so that what is seen was made from things that are not visible" or "was not made out of visible things." Calvin will later link Hebrews 11:3 with other texts of the same nature, such as Romans 1, Acts 14, Acts 17, and Psalm 19, but Hebrews 11:3 will always have pride of place as the foundational text on this topic, even in the introduction to his commentary on Genesis in 1554.

Third, Calvin clearly links the "representation of invisible things" in the world with the development of piety in the soul.[14] By linking the self-manifestation of God in the universe with the creation and nurturing of piety, Calvin clearly indicates the positive role that the contemplation of the reflection of the invisible God will have in the lives of the pious, over and above its role in rendering the impious without excuse. Fourth, Calvin describes in greater detail the way the powers of God are set forth in the works of God in the world, which is what makes the world the reflection of invisible things, focusing on the immortality, power, wisdom, goodness, righteousness, and mercy of God, which the godly are to contemplate. These powers should teach us "what God is like," as the powers of God disclose the nature of God. However, human blindness and perversity keep us from seeing and judging the works of God aright.

Fifth, Calvin turns to the self-attestation of God in God's Word to clarify our consideration of the powers of God set forth in God's works, unlike the 1535 preface, in which the Word was parallel to the powers of God engraved in creation. "Therefore, we must come to God's Word, where God is duly described to us from his works, while the works themselves are reckoned not from the depravity of our judgment but the eternal rule of truth."[15] The addition of the Word of God (Truth) to the representation of God in God's works (Beauty) leads to the acknowledgment of God as the fountain of every good thing (Goodness), for God alone is the source of all the powers we behold. "From this, therefore, we learn that God is for us the sole and eternal source of all life, righteousness, wisdom, power, goodness, and mercy. As all good flows, without any exception, from him, so ought all praise deservedly to return to him."[16]

Finally, Calvin reinforces the move, seen in the 1535 preface, from the contemplation of the powers in the universe to the consideration of the powers within us, though he expands the list of these powers. "And even if all these things appear most clearly in each part of heaven and earth, yet we at last comprehend their real goal, value, and true meaning for us only when we descend into ourselves and ponder in what ways the Lord reveals his life, wisdom, and power in us, and exercises toward us his righteousness, goodness, and mercy."[17] This descending order of contemplation, from heaven to earth to ourselves, is reflected in the order of my discussion of this theme below, as it is a consistent theme in Calvin's discussion of the pious contemplation of the works of God in the universe.

3. The Lord Manifests Himself by His Powers: *Institutes*, 1539

The remarkable and foundational expansion of Calvin's understanding of the universe as the reflection of the invisible God between the 1536 *Institutes* and the 1537/8 *Catechism* is further developed in the 1539 edition of the *Institutes*. Calvin continues to use Hebrews 11:3 as his leading text to describe the universe as the representation of the invisible God. "The reason why the author of the letter to the Hebrews elegantly calls the universe the appearance of things invisible is that this skillful ordering of the universe is for us a sort of mirror in which we can contemplate God, who is otherwise invisible."[18] Calvin's association of reflection or appearance with a mirror is reinforced by his commentary on Romans of 1540: "God is invisible in himself, but since his majesty shines forth in all his works and in all his creatures, men ought to have acknowledged him in those, as they clearly demonstrate their Creator. For this reason the Apostle, in his Epistle to the Hebrews, calls the world a mirror or representation of invisible things (Heb. 11:3)."[19] In the *Institutes*, Calvin reinforces the citation from Hebrews 11:3 with Psalm 19:1 and Romans 1:19–20, along with Acts 14:16–17 and 17:27–28, to further his claim that God has "revealed himself and daily discloses himself in the whole workmanship of the universe."[20]

Calvin also makes explicit the relationship between the powers of God and the self-manifestation of God, setting forth the following definitional statement: "For the Lord manifests himself by his powers, the force of which we feel within ourselves and the benefits of which we enjoy."[21] The right way to come to know God, therefore, is to behold and contemplate God's powers until one both feels their force within oneself and enjoys the benefits that they offer, leading to the acknowledgment that God is the author and source of these powers, that is, of every good thing. Moreover, God acts like an artist painting a self-portrait in the way he sets forth his powers in his works. "We must therefore admit in God's individual works—but especially in them as a whole—that God's powers are actually represented as in a painting."[22] The works of God portray the powers of God as in a painting, so that the powers of God might become for us the representation or mirror in which we can behold and contemplate the invisible God.

As noted in the introduction, in the 1539 *Institutes* Calvin begins to cite Plato quite extensively, describing him as "the most religious and the most sober" of the philosophers. [23] Perhaps in light of the growing influence of Plato, Calvin also begins to associate the category of beauty with the appearance or mirror of God in the universe. "You cannot in one glance survey this most vast and beautiful system of the universe, in its wide expanse, without being completely overwhelmed by the boundless force of its brightness."[24] The emergence of Plato indicates that Calvin begins to redeploy the classical sources he studied so extensively for his commentary on Seneca, using them now in support of his teaching of the truths of the Catholic Church. In particular, Calvin expands on his discussion of the way the powers of God are set forth in the works of God by explicitly referring to the classical arts and sciences, leading him to distinguish between the ways the learned and the unlearned would contemplate the universe.[25] Though both the learned and the unlearned can see enough in the universe to be aware "of the excellence of divine art," the liberal arts allow the learned to "penetrate with their aid far more deeply into the secrets of the divine wisdom."[26] In particular, astronomy allows one to behold and admire the wisdom of God set forth in the movement of the stars, planets, sun, and moon.[27] On the other hand, following the movement from the heavens to ourselves, anatomy helps us to admire the wonderful wisdom of God in the composition of our bodies.[28] Similarly, in his discussion of the power of God revealed in God's works, Calvin makes an implicit reference to the science of meteorology, which will become increasingly prominent in his commentary on the Psalms in 1557.[29] It is not at all surprising then to see Calvin adding a spirited defense of the liberal arts in the same edition of the *Institutes*. "Shall we say that the philosophers were blind in their fine observation and artful description of nature? . . . No, we cannot read the writings of the ancients on these subjects without great admiration."[30]

Finally, Calvin expands on the idea first presented in the *Catechism* of 1538 that the truth of the Word of God is needed for us rightly to behold the representation or mirror of the invisible God in the universe. "We must come,

I say, to the Word, where God is truly and vividly described to us from his works, while these very works are appraised not by our depraved judgment but by the rule of eternal truth."[31] Calvin returns to Hebrews 11:3 to clarify that it is only by faith in the Word of God that we can rightly behold the appearance of the invisible God in the universe. "For this reason, the apostle, in that very passage where he calls the worlds the images of things invisible, adds that through faith we understand that they have been fashioned by God's word [Heb. 11:3]. He means by this that the invisible deity is made manifest in such spectacles, but that we have not the eyes to see this unless they be illumined by the inner revelation of God through faith."[32]

Moreover, to clarify his expectation that the godly will seriously aspire to contemplate God in God's works under the guidance of the Word and faith, Calvin asks "whether the Lord represents himself to us in Scripture as we previously saw him delineate himself in his works."[33] To answer this question, Calvin turns to the Name of God that was proclaimed to Moses in the theophany on Mount Sinai (Exod. 34:6–7). "Indeed, in certain passages clearer descriptions are set forth for us, wherein his true appearance is exhibited, to be seen as in an image (*eikonikos*)."[34] Calvin summarizes the description of God's face given by Moses in a way that focuses on the powers of God revealed to Moses, which we are not only to behold but also to feel.[35] Since the same powers described by Moses are also seen in creation—that is, kindness, goodness, mercy, justice, judgment, and truth—we find that "nothing is set down there that cannot be beheld in his creatures. Indeed, with experience as our teacher we find God just as he declares himself in his Word."[36] The Word of God does not replace the self-representation of God in the universe but rather makes it possible for us rightly to behold it, so that we are led to feel and enjoy the powers of God represented therein.

4. CONTEMPLATING THE WORKS OF GOD ON THE SABBATH: *INSTITUTES*, 1543–1545

Calvin accentuates this order of seeing, feeling, and enjoying the powers of God depicted in the works of God in a sizable addition he made to the discussion of the first article of the Creed in the *Institutes* of 1543. After a lengthy discussion of the creation of angels, Calvin turns to consider the visible creation, with the remark, "although it is not the chief evidence for faith, yet it is the first evidence in the order of nature, to be mindful that wherever we cast our eyes, all things they meet are works of God, and at the same time to ponder with pious meditation to what end God created them."[37] To guide their pious meditations of God's works, Calvin advises the godly to read Moses's brief account of creation in Genesis along with the more copious illustration of this account given by Basil and Ambrose, among others. He then turns to a brief consideration of the direction our contemplation should follow, namely, that "we contemplate in all creatures, as in mirrors, those immense riches of his wisdom, justice, goodness, and power."[38] Calvin then sets forth what he calls a "universal rule" to guide such contemplation. The first part of the rule is to reflect on the order and beauty of the heavens, including the power of God in upholding and governing the universe.[39] This would relate to the theme of beholding the powers of God that Calvin describes in 1539. The second part of the rule is "to contemplate his power and grace in ourselves and in the great benefits he has conferred upon us, and so bestir ourselves to trust, invoke, praise, and love him."[40] Such contemplation would lead to our feeling and enjoying in ourselves the powers of God we initially contemplate in the heavens, so that piety might be nurtured.

In 1545 Calvin reinforces his understanding that the pious are to contemplate God in the beautiful machine of the universe by expanding the purpose of the Sabbath to include the contemplation of God's works and by noting that this aspect of the commandment is still in force for Christians. In the 1545 edition of the *Institutes*, Calvin says, "each one of us privately, whenever he has leisure, is to exercise himself diligently in pious meditation upon God's works."[41] He makes the same point more extensively in his Latin *Catechism* of 1545. "When he finished the creation of the world in six days, he dedicated the seventh to the contemplation of his works. To incite us more strongly to this, he sets before us his own example."[42] The more we contemplate the works of God in creation, the more we obey the spirit of the Sabbath, and the more we image God in our lives.

5. The World as Theater, School, and Image: Corinthians and Hebrews, 1546–1549

After 1545 the primary line of development regarding the self-manifestation of God in the universe lies in the various metaphors Calvin develops to describe God's self-representation. Beginning in 1537, Calvin took his lead from his translation of Hebrews 11:3, in which the universe is the "representation of invisible things," which he expands by 1539 to include the universe as a "mirror" or even an "image." However, it is only in 1546, in his comments on 1 Corinthians 1:21, that Calvin begins to use his best-known metaphor for creation, that it is like a theater of God's glory. "For it is true that the world is like a theater in which the Lord shows to us a striking spectacle of his glory."[43] Calvin also calls the universe a "school" in which we were originally to be taught the true knowledge of God but which now functions to render all without excuse.[44] Finally, building on his use of Hebrews 11:3, that it is only by the illumination of faith that we can rightly behold God in the mirror of the universe, Calvin coins the phrase "the eye of faith," which will play a prominent role in his subsequent writings.[45]

In 1549 Calvin published his interpretation of the text that had been foundational to his understanding of the self-manifestation of God in creation, Hebrews 11:3. In his exposition of this text, Calvin reinforces his description of the world as a mirror in which we can see the invisible God, due to the evidence of God's powers in God's works.[46] Calvin also reinforces his description of the world as the theater of God's glory, making it clear in the process that the godly in particular are the spectators in this theater.[47] Finally, Calvin introduces a term that will become central to his description of the universe, that it is the living image of God: "in this world we have a clear image of God, and in this passage our apostle is saying the same thing as Paul in Romans 1:20, where he says that the invisible things of God are made known to us in the world, since they are seen in his works."[48] In light of this passage, it is not at all surprising that Calvin introduces the theme of the image of God when he returns in 1556 to do the final edition of his commentary on Romans 1:19. "By saying 'God manifested it' he means that man was formed to be a spectator of the created world, and that he was endowed with eyes for the purpose of being led to God himself, the Author of the world, by contemplating so beautiful an image."[49]

6. The Beautiful Fabric of the Universe: Genesis and Acts, 1554

In his commentary on Genesis, published in 1554, Calvin confirms the foundational status that he gives to Hebrews 11:3 in terms of understanding the world as the visible self-manifestation of the invisible God.[50] However, in his expansion of this theme, Calvin introduces a new metaphor for the visible manifestation of the invisible God, the idea of fabric or clothing. "This is the reason why the Lord, that he may invite us to the knowledge of himself, places the fabric of heaven and earth before our eyes, rendering himself, in a certain manner, manifest in them."[51] Calvin links this idea with his other favorite texts, Romans 1:19–20 and Psalm 19:1, as well as Acts 14:17,[52] and in one passage combines it with an earlier metaphor for the universe, that of school.[53] He also combines the idea of clothing with another favorite metaphor, that of the image of God.[54] One reason that Calvin turns to the metaphor of clothing may be that it combines the hiddenness and revealedness of God: the clothing manifests the invisible God even as it hides God from being viewed directly. He will develop this metaphor much more fully in his commentary on Psalm 104, published in 1557.

In his Genesis commentary, Calvin continues to develop his understanding of the world as the theater of God's glory.[55] However, he makes it clear that the only ones who know that they are spectators in the theater of God's glory are those who not only see the universe with their eyes but also hear the proclamation of Moses with their ears. "For if the mute instruction of the heaven and the earth were sufficient, the teaching of Moses would have been superfluous. This herald therefore approaches, who excites our attention, in order that we may perceive ourselves to be placed in this theater, for the purpose of beholding the glory of God."[56] Calvin also emphasizes that we are not merely created to be spectators in this theater but are also to enjoy the good things we behold: the godly are "not indeed to observe them as mere witnesses, but to enjoy all the riches which are here exhibited, as the Lord has ordained and subjected them to our use."[57] He makes the same point in his commentary on Acts 14:17, published later the same year.[58] Such statements reinforce the dynamic of seeing, feeling, and enjoying that Calvin sets forth in the 1539 *Institutes*.

Calvin continues to reflect on the powers of God not only as they are manifested in the universe but also as they are exhibited in each person. He develops this thought by borrowing from Aristotle the metaphor of humanity as a microcosm: "if you rightly weigh all circumstances, man is, among other creatures, a certain preeminent specimen of Divine wisdom, justice, and goodness, so that he is deservedly called by the ancients *mikrikosmos*, 'a world in miniature.'"[59] Calvin uses the same idea to explain why Paul says we do not have to search for God outside ourselves, for we can feel him within ourselves (Acts 17:27).[60]

Calvin also clarifies the relationship of the teaching and preaching of Moses to the contemplation of the image of God in the universe, to make it clear that the Word of God clarifies, but does not replace, the self-manifestation of God in the works of creation. He does this first by using a new metaphor to describe the Word of God, claiming that it acts as "spectacles" to clarify poor vision.[61] Faith in the Word leads us directly towards the proper contemplation of God in God's works. "For faith properly proceeds from this, that we being taught by the ministry of Moses, do not now wander in foolish and trifling speculations, but contemplate the true and only God in his genuine image."[62] Calvin reinforces this aspect of the godly life by repeating that the Sabbath is meant to lead us to the contemplation of the powers of God in the works of God, even though such contemplation should occupy us every day.[63] Calvin adds in this commentary the new thought that God divided the work of creation into six days so that it would not be too burdensome to meditate upon it.[64]

Calvin also seeks to clarify the relationship between the self-manifestation of God in the beautiful image of the universe and the self-representation of God in Christ crucified. On the one hand, he points out that the universe as described by Moses has been transformed by sin and wrath so that it no longer reveals only God's goodness, but it also reveals the curse of God against our sin.[65] The favor of God is now portrayed alongside signs of God's wrath.[66] On the other hand, Calvin for the first time conjoins his use of Hebrews 11:3—that it is by faith that we can contemplate God in God's representation or mirror in the universe—with the teaching of Paul in 1 Corinthians 1:21: "After that, in the wisdom of God, the world through wisdom knew not God, it seemed right to God, through the foolishness of preaching, to save those who believe." According to Calvin, Paul means that we are not able to behold God in the beautiful image of the universe until we are first humbled by the preaching of Christ crucified.[67] According to this statement (which is unique in Calvin's writings on this topic), one would not only need the spectacles of the teaching of Moses, and the eyes of faith through the inner illumination of God, but also faith in Christ crucified by the preaching of the Gospel before one could rightly contemplate the image of God in the universe.

The difficulty with this way of presenting the right order of teaching is that it seems to contradict the order set forth by Calvin later that same year, in his comments on Acts 14:15. "We know that in teaching the right order requires a beginning to be made from things that are better known. Since Paul and Barnabas were preaching to Gentiles, it would have been useless for them to attempt to bring them to Christ at once. Therefore, they had to begin at some other point, not so remote from common understanding, so that, when assent was given to that, they could then pass over to Christ."[68] It is significant that Calvin follows this order of teaching in his final edition of the *Institutes* in 1559, and uses 1 Corinthians 1:21 to make the transition from the knowledge of God the Creator to the knowledge of God the Redeemer, supported by the signs of God's wrath against sin in the universe.[69] However, in his commentary on Genesis, Calvin seems to be especially concerned that one not use Paul's statements in 1 Corinthians 1:21 to explain away the need for the faithful to contemplate the living icon of God in the universe, as though Paul meant that "we must not therefore commence with the elements of this world, but with the Gospel, which sets Christ alone before us with his cross, and *holds us to this one point*."[70] Even if one must begin with the Gospel of Christ crucified, one must nonetheless move on to the contemplation of the works of God in the universe in distinction from Christ crucified, for these works are included in Christ himself.[71] Such an interpretation would be supported by the fact that Calvin had given a spirited defense of the liberal sciences in his comments on 1 Corinthians 1:20 eight years earlier.[72] Indeed, far from taking the gifts of the liberal sciences away from the godly, Calvin insists that only in the hands of the godly are such gifts rightly used.[73] Calvin thinks that Christ himself confirms this claim by the order in which various stations of people were called.[74]

7. The Proclamation of the Heavens: Psalms, 1557

The final developments of Calvin's understanding of the universe as the living icon of God come in his commentary on the Psalms in 1557. When Calvin turns to his exegesis of Psalm 19:1—a text that he frequently associates with Hebrews 11:3, Romans 1:19–20, and Acts 14 and 17—he develops yet one more metaphor for the self-disclosure of God in the universe, that of proclamation. "It is indeed a great thing, that in the splendor of the heavens there is presented to our view a lively image of God; but, as the living voice has a greater effect in exciting our attention, or at least teaches us more surely and with greater profit than simple beholding, to which no oral instruction is added, we ought to mark the force of the figure which the Psalmist uses when he says, that the heavens by their preaching declare the glory of God."[75] This metaphor recalls Calvin's fondness for Augustine's dictum that the sacraments are "visible words" of God, and indicates his willingness to extend this sacramental way of speaking to the self-disclosure of God in the universe. Calvin reinforces the theme of visible words in his interpretation of the fourth verse, in which he uses the metaphor of the orations of a teacher.[76] He then combines the similitude of teaching and preaching with the metaphor of a written volume set forth for us to read.[77] Even without the addition of the "spectacles" of the Word or the eyes of faith, Calvin sees the living image of God in creation to be so compelling that on its own it combines both manifestation and proclamation.[78] The metaphor of the open volume will be used in the 1559 edition of the *Institutes* in conjunction with the metaphor of the spectacles of Scripture developed in the Genesis commentary.[79]

Calvin also directly addresses the difficulty presented to the faithful by their use of the liberal sciences, especially Aristotle, to understand the world. One sees this issue emerge in the commentary on John in 1553, and appear again in the commentary on Genesis a year later, but it is addressed directly and extensively in the commentary on the Psalms.[80] According to Calvin, the liberal sciences rightly attend to what he calls the "mediate causes" that give rise to natural phenomena. There is nothing wrong with studying such mediate causes so long as one ascends by their means to the ultimate cause. For example, bread is nourishing to human beings (mediate cause), but the real cause of all nourishment is the blessing of God freely given with the bread (ultimate cause). Calvin began to suspect that philosophers such as Aristotle sought to confine our attention to mediate causes, making them obstacles to the ascent to the ultimate cause.[81]

So long as one rises from mediate causes to the ultimate cause, God, there is nothing wrong with the scientific study of nature, even when it leads to descriptions of the way the world works that appear to contradict the descriptions of the universe given in Scripture. According to Calvin, the liberal sciences are for the learned, whereas Scripture is written for the unlearned: hence there can be no real conflict between their descriptions of the universe. "He who would learn astronomy, and other recondite arts, let him go elsewhere. Here the Spirit of God would teach all men without exception."[82] The danger with Aristotle and other philosophers is not that they study mediate causes in a way that contradicts the descriptions of Scripture but rather the way they weave mediate causes into an obstacle preventing the ascent to God, the ultimate cause and source of all that we see.[83] Rightly understood, the scientific investigation of the universe should lead to a deeper awareness of the powers of God exhibited therein, and should thus foster the piety of the learned in a way that is distinct from the contemplation of the unlearned.

8. The Knowledge of God the Creator: *Institutes*, 1559

The final edition of the *Institutes* in 1559 consolidates most of the developments I have charted between 1535 and 1557. In this text Calvin uses all of the metaphors he developed from 1535 onward to describe the self-representation of God in the universe, from representation and mirror to theater, school, image, clothing, and written volume. He uses the metaphor of spectacles to describe the clarifying effect of Scripture on our vision so that we might rightly contemplate God in God's works.[84] He claims that God broke down the work of creation into six days "that we might not find it irksome to occupy our whole life in contemplating it."[85] He confirms the central role of the powers of God for the development of piety. "For this sense of the powers of God is for us a fit teacher of piety, from which religion is born."[86] He accentuates the need for humans to contemplate the heavens by citing a saying from Ovid, which also emerges in the commentary on Isaiah, published the same year. "'While other animals look downwards toward the earth, he gave man a lofty face, and bade him look at heaven, and lift up his countenance erect towards the stars.'"[87] He describes humanity as a "microcosm" because of the powers of God revealed in human beings.[88] He even edited passages from previous editions of the *Institutes* to accentuate the association of the self-manifestation of God in the universe with beauty.[89]

Most significantly, Calvin reorganized the whole structure of the *Institutes*, and introduced in Book I the distinction between knowledge of God the Creator and knowledge of God the Redeemer, following the order of teaching he discerned in Paul's sermon in Acts 14:15 in 1554. "First, as much in the fashioning of the universe as in the general teaching of Scripture the Lord shows himself to be simply the Creator. Then in the face of Christ he shows himself the Redeemer."[90] Moreover, the reason for adopting the order of teaching from Acts 14 seems to be the same. In his commentary Calvin noted, "The minds of the men of Lystra were possessed by the error that there were many gods. Paul and Barnabas show, on the other hand, that there is one Creator of the world. With the removal of that fictitious crowd of deities the way was open for the second step, to teach them what that God, the Creator of heaven and earth, was like."[91] In the *Institutes,* Calvin makes a similar point, using in this instance Seneca's "distinguishing marks" to make the point.[92] Calvin uses 1 Corinthians 1:21 to make the transition from the knowledge of God the Creator to the knowledge of God the Redeemer, showing that he decided to follow the order of teaching in the Acts commentary instead of the introduction to Genesis.[93] By distinguishing between the knowledge of God the Creator and the knowledge of God the Redeemer, he further underscores his lifelong concern that the self-disclosure of God in the universe not be eclipsed by the self-revelation of God in Jesus Christ. Both are necessary for the creation and strengthening of faith and piety. Our knowledge of God the Creator must lead us to the knowledge of God in Jesus Christ; but our knowledge of God in Christ will also lead us back to the knowledge of God the Creator.

B. The Universe as the Self-Manifestation of God

1. Contemplating the Powers of God in the Works of God

Calvin has developed an increasingly rich set of visual metaphors by which to describe the ways in which the invisible God makes Godself somewhat visible in the universe. The universe may be described as a "mirror or representation of invisible things" (Heb. 11:3).[94] The world may also be described as the theater of God's glory, which, when we behold it, should lead us to the knowledge of the God who created it.[95] The universe is the living image of God, in which God represents Godself to us.[96] The world is the clothing that the invisible God wears so that we might behold God therein.[97] Because the invisible God appears to us in the fabric of God's works, the world is also the school in which we should be taught to know the God who created us.[98] Finally, the universe is the speechless proclamation or the mute teaching that would instruct us in the true knowledge of God, who is the Author of all things.[99]

By making Godself somewhat visible in God's works, God accommodates Godself to the capacities of human beings.[100] We would be overwhelmed by the majesty of the invisible God were we to behold it directly—hence the folly of those who seek to know the essence of God in disregard for the works of God—but in God's works the invisible God becomes somewhat visible so that we might see God in a way that suits our capacities.[101] According to Calvin, human beings were created with reason and understanding so that we might contemplate the living icon of God in the universe and thereby come to the true knowledge of God.[102] However, one does not have to have acute intelligence or be especially learned to discern the visible representation of God in the world, for "God manifests himself even to the simple, and even to mere women and children."[103] The same may be said of the human sense of sight, through which our reason and understanding would contemplate the image of God in the universe.[104] However, even those who lack the sense of sight can still come to know God, by feeling the force of the powers of God within them. "For each one undoubtedly feels within the heavenly grace that quickens him."[105]

In particular, the works of God set forth and portray to us the powers of God, which are essential to the self-manifestation of God, according to Calvin. "Wherever they turn their eyes, upwards or downwards, they are bound to fall on living, and indeed countless, images of God's power, wisdom, and goodness."[106] The powers of God make the universe the living image of God, for they portray the nature of God in God's works.[107] Calvin would not have us contemplate one of these powers to the exclusion of any of the others, as some scholars suggest by focusing almost exclusively on God's power. Rather, all the powers together constitute the self-disclosure of the eternal nature of God. "In the whole architecture of the world God has given us clear evidence of his eternal wisdom, goodness, and power, and though he is invisible in himself he shows himself in some measure in his work."[108] All these powers are caught up in the meaning of the Name of God for Calvin, which he defines directly in light of the powers and works of God.[109]

Calvin accentuates the powers of God's goodness, wisdom, and power, with particular attention to God's wisdom and goodness. Following Paul, Calvin will describe the whole self-delineation of God in creation as "the wisdom of God," the proper contemplation of which would make human beings wise.[110] He makes the same point via Psalm 19, which does not directly mention the wisdom of God, stating that "this most beautiful order of nature silently proclaims his admirable wisdom (Ps. 19:1)."[111] Since all the powers are ultimately "good things of God," the ultimate power that is both revealed in the universe and nourishes piety is the goodness of God. "To whatever subjects men apply their minds, there is none from which they will derive greater advantage than from continual meditation on his wisdom, goodness, righteousness, and mercy; and especially the knowledge of his goodness is fitted to build up our faith, and to illustrate his praises."[112]

2. The Spectacles of Scripture and the Eyes of Faith

Even though the self-representation of God in the living image of the universe is accommodated to the capacities of the most unlearned, and even the blind, Calvin insists that we lack the ability to see this image properly on our own but need the assistance of God to do so. "But as, although surrounded by so clear a light, we are nevertheless blind, this splendid representation of the glory of God, without the aid of the word, would profit us nothing, although it should be to us as a loud and distinct proclamation sounding in our ears."[113] The assistance of the Word does not replace the image of God in the universe but rather clarifies our weakened vision so that we can see more clearly the powers of God set forth in the works of God.[114] In this way Scripture acts as spectacles for bleary-eyed people, for "Scripture, gathering up the otherwise confused knowledge of God in our minds, having dispersed our dullness, clearly shows us the true God."[115] Scripture therefore directs our attention to the living image of God that is set before us, so that we rightly contemplate the God who is represented therein.[116]

However, Calvin describes the Word not only as spectacles but also as itself being a living image in which God represents Godself to us. According to this model, the faithful would contemplate God in two mirrors simultaneously, the mirror of the Word and the mirror of God's works: "although the works of God are sufficiently plain, yet by his mouth, that is, by the word, he makes them plainer to us, that we may see them more clearly. And this is the true contemplation of the works of God, when we keep our eye fixed on the mirror of the word."[117] The knowledge of God the Creator would therefore come from both the Word and the works of God, with each being seen as a living image of God. "We ought carefully to observe the word 'know'; for 'to know the name of the Lord' is to lay aside every false opinion, and to know him from his word, which is his true image, and next from his works."[118] The Word and the works of God would thus together form the self-manifestation of the Creator. "Hence the majesty of God is in itself incomprehensible to us, but he makes himself known by his works and by his word."[119]

Calvin insists that even with the spectacles or mirror of the Word, human beings still lack the capacity to see the self-representation of God in the universe without God illuminating their vision. "For notwithstanding that God shows himself openly, yet it is only with the eye of faith that we can look at him."[120] God gives us the eyes to see God's works by inwardly illuminating our eyes with faith, on the basis of Hebrews 11:3: "the invisible divinity is made manifest in such spectacles, but that we have not the eyes to see this unless they be illumined by the inner revelation of God through faith."[121] God not only heals our vision by the spectacles of the Word, but also by inward illumination, which allows us to see the universe in a way we could not before.[122]

3. Guiding the Contemplations of the Pious: From the Heavens to Ourselves

Calvin consistently and increasing exhorted the godly—those whose vision had been clarified by the Word and faith—to contemplate the powers of God set forth in the works of God in creation.[123] Because God knows that we distract ourselves with other concerns that take our attention away from such contemplation, God commands us to take at least one day a week to rest from such occupations, so that we might contemplate the beauty of creation, in imitation of God, who also rested on the seventh day of creation.[124] God also assists us in our weakness by dividing the work of creation itself into six days, to guide our meditation of it as by steps.[125]

The creation account itself begins with the creation of light, and then with the creation of the heavens. The proper way to begin our contemplation of the universe would be to begin with the heavens and descend from there to the sky, then to the earth, and finally to within ourselves. Calvin sets forth this pattern of contemplation as early as 1537/8, and reinforces it in his rule for contemplation in the 1543 *Institutes*. But he also saw this method being repeatedly taught throughout Scripture, as in Zechariah 12:1: "The word of the Lord concerning Israel: Thus says the Lord, who stretched out the heavens and founded the earth and formed the human spirit within." Commenting on this verse, Calvin says, "God, then, . . . bids us to raise up our eyes to the heavens and carefully to consider his wonderful workmanship, and also to turn our eyes down to the earth, where also his ineffable power is apparent; and, in the third place, he calls our attention to the consideration of his own nature."[126] Calvin sees the same pattern in Psalm 19.[127] Below I follow this descending order of contemplation, from the heavens above to the powers of God within us.

The Powers of God in the Heavens

God would have us begin our contemplation of the universe with the heavens because the powers of God are more clearly portrayed in the heavens than on the earth.[128] The contemplation of the heavens builds on the healing of our sight that begins with the spectacles of the Word and the illumination of the Spirit, for it leads us from the clearest image of the powers of God so that we might see the same powers on earth, down to the smallest creatures. "When a man, from beholding and contemplating the heavens, has been brought to acknowledge God, he will also learn to reflect upon and admire his wisdom and power as displayed on the face of the earth, not only in general, but even in the minutest plants."[129]

According to Calvin, the heavens provide the clearest image of the powers of God because they are also the closest to God of all creation, since "the nearer we approach to God, the more conspicuous becomes his image. For truly God there exercises his own power and wisdom much more clearly than on earth."[130] Our contemplation of the heavens, therefore, should not only train us to see the same powers on earth that we behold in the heavens but also elevate our minds to God, who is the Author and governor of the heavens.[131] The elevating effect of the contemplation of heaven is one of the best ways to come to an awareness of the transcendence of God, which frees us from confining the powers and nature of God to our carnal conceptions of them, "for the mere sight of heaven ought to carry us higher, and transport us into admiration."[132] Thus the contemplation of heaven not only leads to the descent to the contemplation of the world and ourselves, but it is also the last step of our ascent to God.[133] For this reason, from 1539 onwards Calvin always had the highest praises for the study of the heavens, even when practiced by the ungodly, and made it a close companion to the study of theology proper. "And, indeed, astrology may justly be called the alphabet of theology;

for no one can with a right mind come to the contemplation of the celestial framework, without being enraptured with admiration at the display of God's wisdom, as well as power and goodness."[134] Hence it is not surprising that Calvin claims that Moses himself was educated in this art by the Egyptians, as was Daniel by the Babylonians.[135] Calvin thinks that Jeremiah appeals to astronomy as providing the best method to free the Jews from carnal conceptions about God, as though God could be contained in anything on earth.[136] For Calvin, the proper acknowledgment of the transcendence of God takes place not with the right conception of divine incomprehensibility but rather with the experience of being ravished with admiration by the contemplation of the infinite powers of God revealed in the heavens.[137]

Of all the powers of God, Calvin thought that the wisdom of God more clearly appeared in the heavens than on earth, echoing Plato in the *Timaeus*.[138] "The wisdom of God is visible throughout the whole world, but especially in the heavens."[139] Calvin was especially impressed by the harmonious order manifested in heaven in spite of the rapid motion of so many immense bodies. "To each of them he assigns its fixed and distinct office and in all the multitude there is no confusion."[140] Calvin directs our attention to the fact that all of the stars hold to their appointed courses in spite of their vast number and varying movements "so that they do not deviate a hairbreadth from the path which God has marked out for them."[141] Such harmony and constancy of motion is even more impressive when one adds the movement of the planets and the sun and moon.[142] The movement of the sun alone is a wonderful display of the wisdom of God, "for when the sun, in its daily course, completes so great and so immense a distance, they who are not amazed at such a miracle must be more than stupid."[143] The same orderly motion of heavenly bodies, as well as their age, also discloses to us the incomprehensible power of God, since "this fair and beautiful order has been uninterruptedly maintained for ages."[144] It is noteworthy that Calvin associates the power of God with the beauty of the heavens, revealing that power for him must always be seen in the context of the manifestation of all the powers of God.[145]

The heavens also disclose God's benevolence to humanity, especially when the skies are clear and the sun and stars shine brightly. "Accordingly, when the sun and moon and stars shine in heaven, God may be said to cheer us by his bright and gracious countenance."[146] For this reason, Calvin thinks that God truly made the stars, planets, sun, and moon for signs, that God might manifest both God's favor and God's displeasure towards us.[147] Among these signs would be the appearance of comets.[148] The sun and the moon in particular manifest to us the goodness of God, in that they not only provide us with light but also make possible our cultivation of the earth, as well as our ability to tell time by the seasons of the year, which makes civic life possible.[149] Again, what manifests the goodness of God, as well as the power and wisdom of God, is the harmony of the arrangement of the heavens, so that it not only proceeds in a beautiful and orderly way but also provides useful advantages for humanity. "In the meantime, let us admire this wonderful Artificer, who has so beautifully arranged all things above and beneath, that they may correspond to each other in the sweetest harmony."[150]

The Powers of God in the Atmosphere

From the contemplation of the heavens, Calvin turns to the consideration of the atmosphere, including clouds, wind, thunder, lightning, and rain. For Calvin, the powers of God that are so clearly manifested in the constancy and harmony of the heavens are more perceptibly set forth in the sudden changes and mutations that take place in earth's atmosphere.[151] He thought that the dramatic changes produced by the weather were especially useful in compelling the ungodly to consider the power of God, which they otherwise ignored.[152] The changes in the atmosphere reveal to us the presence of God, as God approaches us either with favor or with wrath.[153] Calvin was aware that philosophers had set forth what they considered the causes of such meteorological phenomena as wind, clouds, thunder, and rain, "namely, that when the cold and humid vapors obstruct the dry and hot exhalations in their course upwards, a collision takes place, and by this, together with the noise of the clouds rushing against each other, is produced the rumbling thunder-peal."[154] He does not doubt the legitimacy of such accounts, as far as the mediate causes of such phenomena are concerned; but he does not want such accounts to blind his readers to the wonderful power and wisdom of God manifested in thunder and lightning.[155]

The same may be said about the origin of the wind. Attention to the mediate causes producing wind should not blind us to the ultimate cause, which lies in the powers of God. "Winds arise from the earth, even because exhalations proceed from it; but exhalations, by whom are they created? Not by themselves: hence it follows, that God is their sole author."[156] For Calvin, it is not the investigation of secondary causes per se that leads philosophers to divert our attention from the ultimate cause.[157] Were it not for our ungrateful and corrupt hearts, we would see countless miracles not only in those phenomena that defy explanations by mediate causes but also in those that can also be explained by mediate causality, such as the appearance of clouds over our heads. "For we see that vapors arise at a distance and immediately spread over our heads. Is it not wonderful? And were we not accustomed to such a thing, it could not but fill us with admiration."[158] Far from emptying the world of miracles, as Eire suggests, Calvin wants us to be overwhelmed by the countless miracles that present themselves so vividly to our eyes, especially in those phenomena that are the most familiar to us: "for the more carefully we attend to the consideration of God's works, we ourselves vanish into nothing; the miracles which present themselves on every side, before our eyes, overwhelm us."[159]

The Powers of God on the Face of the Earth

From the atmosphere, Calvin descends to consider the face of the earth, beginning with the wisdom of God that is revealed in the stability of the arrangement between the mighty waters of rivers, lakes, and oceans and the emergence of dry land, and including the wonderful variety that one sees on the dry land itself. "Indeed, man's industry contributes to this variety; but we see how God has fitted the earth for different purposes. Here then shines forth the wonderful wisdom of God."[160] The preservation of dry land is all the more miraculous given that for Calvin the waves and floods of water are one of the clearest evidences for the power of God.[161] The stability of the dry land in the midst of the waters thus manifests the truth of God, which is also seen in the stability of the heavens.[162]

The variety of life on the face of the earth, and the care of God for all creatures, manifests to us the power, and especially the goodness, of God. This is true even in places where no human beings dwell, and thus where the good things set forth are not for human use or enjoyment. "Rivers run through great and desolate wildernesses, where the wild beasts enjoy some blessing of God; and no country is so barren as not to have trees growing here and there, on which birds make the air to resound with the melody of their singing."[163] Once we see the goodness of God manifested in the wilderness, we should be even more aware of the amazing variety of good things that God supplies in less remote and rugged places.[164] Such variety and abundance alone would be enough to overwhelm us with astonishment, even without consideration of the good things that God freely provides to human beings.[165]

The acknowledgment of the goodness of God towards all creatures on earth is necessary so that we might rightly be amazed by the care that the Creator of the universe has for human beings. Such is the approach taken by Psalm 8: "When I look at your heavens, the work of your fingers, the moon and the stars that you have established; what are human beings that you are mindful of them, mortals that you care for them?" Calvin uses this text to highlight the dramatic condescension of God, to lower Godself from the care of the heavens and the earth to care for human beings.[166] If the wisdom and power of God are most clearly manifested in the heavens and the earth, the goodness of God is especially revealed in the care that God manifests for human beings, "for this, of all the subjects which come under our contemplation, is the brightest mirror in which we can behold his glory."[167]

The goodness of God is not only disclosed to our eyes by the abundance of good things that God presents to our view on earth; it is most particularly revealed to our hearts by our enjoyment of the good things that we behold.[168] The good things that we see and enjoy in our temporal life on earth encourage us "to praise him for the manifestation he has made of himself as a father to us in this frail and perishable life."[169] Calvin wants his readers to be especially impressed by the free gratuity of all of the good things that God so lavishly bestows upon us, which God was in no need to do, and which we in no way deserve.[170] The account of creation in Genesis only reinforces the gratuity of the care of God for humanity, for "before he fashioned man, he prepared everything he foresaw would be useful and salutary for him."[171] The only thing that God wishes from us in return is the praise we render to his goodness by our heartfelt gratitude for every good thing we are given.[172] Though Calvin directs the attention of the godly to all of the powers of God, he especially highlights the goodness of God, for it alone confirms in our hearts the self-manifestation of the fountain of every good thing to us.[173] We should still praise God for all of God's powers, for all of them together reveal to us the nature of the one God who created us, "but nothing affects us more than his goodness which descends to us, and exhibits himself as Father."[174] Our experience of the goodness of God in particular overwhelms us with astonishment, leaving us unable to express the infinite goodness of God in words.[175]

The Powers of God within Us

Our enjoyment of the good things that God so lavishly bestows upon us leads Calvin to direct us to descend within ourselves, so that we might feel the power of God's life within us. We may certainly behold the power of God's life in all forms of life that surround us, in the infinite variety of creatures with whom we live, and especially in the cycle of life and death in which we all participate.[176] Given our awareness of the fragility of all life, we ought to be all the more impressed by the manifestation of God's life that we see in the preservation of all forms of life.[177] However, we ought in particular to feel the power of God's life within us, especially in light of our awareness that our life does not come from ourselves. "Since then men live not of themselves, but obtain life as a favor from another, it follows that God dwells in them."[178] For this reason, even the blind, who cannot contemplate the works of God with their eyes, can nonetheless feel God living within them, and thus "they could by feeling find out God."[179] The power of God's life within us was known by the ungodly, as Paul's quotation of Aratus shows and as the writings of Plato also demonstrate.[180] Our awareness of the life of God within us is also the supreme proof that there is but one God.[181] Our awareness of the life of God within us is also the clearest way to come to know the distinction between God and all other creatures, which will become central to Calvin's critique of human idolatry.[182]

Our awareness of the power of God's life within us should lead us to the simultaneous awareness that many of God's powers are portrayed both within us and towards us in the universe. The goal of our contemplation of the powers of God in creation is achieved when we descend into ourselves to see and feel the powers of God within us.[183] The presence of the powers of God within us leads Calvin to endorse Aristotle's statement that humanity is a microcosm, as the same powers are seen in us as are portrayed in the works of God in the cosmos.[184] Once again, this means that there is ultimately no need to survey the vast expanses of heaven and earth to discover the self-manifestation of God in God's powers, for the powers of God can be felt within us even by the blind. "For he so influences every single one of us by his power within, that our stupidity is like a monster, because while feeling him we do not feel him."[185]

Once we descend within ourselves to feel the powers of God within us, our awareness of the powers of God ought to be such that it inevitably leads to the experience that they completely transcend our ability to comprehend them. The same powers of God that reveal God to us in a way suited to our finite capacities simultaneously reveal the infinite nature of God, due to the incomprehensibility of the powers themselves. Hence when the psalmist wishes to prove the greatness of God, "He does not speak of the hidden and mysterious essence which fills heaven and earth, but of the manifestations of his power, wisdom, goodness, and righteousness, which are clearly exhibited, although they are too vast for our limited intelligence to understand."[186] Thus the living image of God that is clear enough for infants and children to contemplate reveals that the powers of God set forth in that image vastly transcend all human understanding, and leave us with the experience of being ravished with astonishment, unable to speak. "The true and proper view to take of the works of God, as I have observed elsewhere, is that which ends in wonder."[187] Such admiration leads both to praise and to thanksgiving, which Calvin contrasts with the kind of knowledge "which philosophers presumptuously pretend to, as if they could solve every mystery of God."[188] However, the experience of the incomprehensibility of the powers of God should not take away from the very real knowledge of the powers of God that the faithful acquire from the works of God.[189] The powers of God are simultaneously revealed and hidden in God's works in creation, and the goal of all contemplation of God's works ends with this recognition.[190]

4. Human Images and the Nature of the Creator

The powers of God that shine forth in the universe and in humanity reveal to us the nature of God. Beginning with the *Institutes* of 1536, Calvin associated the proper conception of God with the powers that are manifested in the works of God.[191] He makes the same point in his commentary on Romans of 1540. "No conception of God can be formed without including his eternity, power, wisdom, goodness, truth, righteousness, and mercy."[192] Calvin contrasts the proper conception of God with the conceptions of God formed from the human mind and imagination, which are noteworthy precisely because they do not attend to the powers of God manifested in God's works.[193] The key, then, to all idolatrous conceptions of God is that they are imaginary constructions of the human mind that do not attend to the powers of God by which God manifests Godself to us. Since those powers, as we have repeatedly seen, surpass all human ability to comprehend them, any deity imagined by human beings would form a god according to human comprehension.[194] For Calvin, central to such an understanding of God is the thought that God can be represented in a form or image.[195]

Human Images Contradict the Living Images of God

Calvin's earliest critique of idolatry emphasizes the way all idols are phantoms forged by the human imagination, which contradicts the self-manifestation of God as the author of every good thing by the powers of God engraved in God's works.[196] According to this line of reasoning, the manufacturing of images by human beings is both unnecessary, because God already manifests Godself to our eyes in the works of creation, and false, because such images are forged by the human mind and do not correspond to the powers of God engraved in the works of God. Calvin continued to follow this line of thought throughout his writings, as in the citations from his 1540 Romans commentary above. Thus when the prophet speaks of the forging of the golden calves in the wilderness, Calvin says, "The prophet again repeats that the people had sinned not simply through ignorance, but willfully, inasmuch as God had already given them a very palpable manifestation of his power and glory. And as he makes himself known in the creation of the heavens and the earth, the blindness of men is totally inexcusable."[197] Because the living image of God shines forth throughout the universe, it is both foolish and futile to seek to make images of God ourselves, as these divert our attention from the self-representation of God in God's works.[198]

Calvin makes this argument about the falsehood of human images not by appealing to the secret essence of God but, following Paul in Athens, by appealing to the self-representation of God in God's works. In this instance, Paul proves that the source and Creator of the world cannot dwell in temples made by human hands because the powers of God that manifest God to us are, as we have repeatedly seen, infinitely beyond human comprehension, and thus cannot be confined to any location in the universe.[199] Indeed, in this line of thinking, a direct appeal to God's essence would leave us with an empty abstraction instead of the nature of the true God.[200] Since the powers of God ravish us with astonishment and since the life of God in particular reveals the clear distinction between God and all creatures, the true knowledge of God should correspond to the self-portrait of God given in God's powers by clearly distinguishing the source of the good things of the universe from the universe itself.[201]

The argument from the self-manifestation of God in God's powers not only shows the futility of making images when the whole of the universe is a living image already but also shows how easy it is for human beings to make the mistake of taking part of this living image for the whole.[202] Since everything we see is the self-revelation of God, there are as many ways to mistake part of the image for the whole as there are things in the universe.[203] For instance, Moses warns the Israelites not to worship the stars because the stars themselves form one of the clearest images of the wisdom and power of God, and might be mistaken for the one who created them.[204] The same thing may happen with trees, in which God's "power is illustriously displayed," as well as God's goodness, "for the wood cannot be applied to various uses without bringing before our eyes the bounty of God" that makes it possible for us to bake bread, cook meat, and warm ourselves. Even a heathen such as Horace knew it was folly to take half of the log and bake bread while making a god out of the other half. "But they did not actually know the fountain of impiety, because they did not apply their minds to consider the goodness and the power of the one God, which is displayed in all creatures."[205]

Human Images Contradict the Invisible Essence of God

By 1536, however, Calvin develops another argument against images, not based on the contrast between the living image of God in God's works and the false images created by human hands, but based instead on a direct appeal to the secret essence of God. In his interpretation of the second commandment in the 1536 *Institutes*, Calvin says, "[God] is incomprehensible, incorporeal, invisible, and so contains all things that he can be enclosed in no place. Let us then fervently pray against our imagining he can be expressed in any figure, or represented in any idol whatsoever, as if it were God's likeness. Rather, we are to adore God, who is Spirit, in spirit and truth."[206] Calvin makes the same point in his *Catechism* of 1538, appealing to the dialectical opposition of spirit and body.[207] Unlike the previous argument, which contrasts the way God makes Godself somewhat visible in living images with the way human beings ignore this image by making images of their own devising, the argument from God's essence is based on the essential invisibility of God, making it impossible for God to be represented in anything visible. Calvin intensifies the opposition between the visible and the invisible in his expanded discussion of the second commandment in the 1539 *Institutes*.[208] Calvin interprets Isaiah's question, "To whom then will you liken God, or what likeness compare with him?" as a direct warrant for appealing to the invisible, infinite, eternal, immeasurable, and incorporeal essence of God, claiming that there is no likeness or similarity at all between that essence and anything in the universe. Any attempt to give a visual representation of God is false, because God is essentially invisible and cannot be visibly portrayed. "Careful attention must be given to the reason: 'an idol is nothing because there is no God but one,' for he is invisible and cannot be represented by a visible sign."[209]

By 1546 Calvin begins to appeal to the statement of Habakkuk, that a cast image is "a teacher of lies" (Hab. 2:18), to underscore the lack of similarity between the invisible God and the visible world.[210] He bolsters his appeal to this text by adding to it passages such as Isaiah 40:18 and Jeremiah 10:8. "Every statue, every image, by which foolish men seek to represent God, is a teacher of falsehood. So our prophet says,—that the teaching of vanities is found in all statues, because God is thus misrepresented; for what can be in a wood or stone that is like the infinite power of God, or his incomprehensible essence and majesty?"[211] Calvin contrasts the true knowledge that one should have of God's infinite essence with the false knowledge of God taught by manufactured images.[212] According to Calvin, there is no likeness between anything in creation and the invisible and infinite God. This is especially true of "dead material" such as silver, gold, and stone.[213] He claims that "it is impossible to frame out of dead matter an image which shall have any resemblance to the glory of God."[214] However, he extends his understanding of "dead materials" to include things such as trees, which in his previous argument were to be contemplated as living images of the goodness and liberality of God.[215] The same may also be said of other living creatures, including both animals and human beings: neither have any affinity or likeness to God.[216]

According to this argument, the essence of God is invisible, and is unlike anything else in all creation. It is therefore impossible for God to be represented in any visible way whatsoever. "It is wrong for men to seek the presence of God in any visible image, because he cannot be represented to our eyes."[217] Far from seeing countless images of God wherever our eyes may turn, we now seem to find ourselves in a universe in which there neither are nor can be any images of God whatsoever.[218] If this second argument from the essence of God is taken to its logical conclusion, then it would be impossible for the invisible God to become somewhat visible before our eyes in any way whatsoever, not only in images made by human artistry, but also in the works that God does in the universe. The prevalence of this second argument may explain why the theme of manifestation has been neglected for so long in Calvin's theology, as it seems to be directly undercut by his appeal to the invisible essence of God.

Calvin apparently never sought to reconcile the two arguments against images, one based on the manifestation of God's powers in the universe and the other based on God's invisible essence. However, the apparent contradiction created between them might be resolved if we turn not to the question of God's invisibility but rather to the question of who has the right and ability to represent the invisible God so that the invisible God becomes somewhat visible to human beings. After all, Calvin repeatedly insists that God is invisible even when he is describing the way God represents Godself to us in the works of God in the universe. "We know God, who is himself invisible, only through his works."[219] According to Calvin, God always remains invisible even when God renders Godself somewhat visible, which explains why Calvin always says "somewhat visible" and not simply "visible." His own translation of Hebrews 11:3—that in the world we have a representation of unseen things—makes this point more clearly than any other text he cites, such as Romans 1:20, Psalm 19:1, or Acts 14 and 17, which may explain why he prefers it to all others. God always remains invisible, even when God is representing Godself to us in God's works as in a mirror, theater, or image.

Since God is invisible, only God has the ability to render Godself somewhat visible in the beautiful fabric of the universe, which, as noted above, unveils God precisely by veiling God. Since God is invisible, only God has the ability to make living images of God that do not contradict, but maintain, the essential invisibility of God, even as God renders Godself somewhat visible before our eyes. Moreover, since God manifests Godself by God's powers, and God is the source of all such powers, only God has the ability to manifest God's powers in God's works in a way that creates a likeness and similarity between the visible work and the invisible God. We cannot on our own establish the similarity between God and the created world, any more than we can by an act of our imagination render the invisible God visible. When we think we can do so, we inevitably transform the truth into a lie, change God into something that God is not, and drag God down from heaven to be confined in an image we both created and can comprehend.

Our inability to represent God lies in the nature of human artistic creation. According to Calvin, we can only rightly represent those things that we can see with our eyes. Since we cannot see God in this way, we cannot represent the invisible God in the images we create.[220] Moreover, since "in God's individual works—but especially in them as a whole— . . . God's powers are actually represented as in a painting," there is no need for us to try to represent God, for "the Lord represents himself . . . in the mirror of his works with very great clarity."[221] Instead of spending our time and energy attempting the impossible—rendering the invisible God visible in images of our creation—we should rather devote our attention to the contemplation of the self-representation of God in the universe, for we were "endowed with eyes for the purpose of being led to God himself, the Author of the world, by contemplating so beautiful an image."[222]

CHAPTER 2

Symbols of God's Goodness
in the Present Life

The beautiful image of God in the universe not only portrays the powers of God to our eyes but also offers us a multitude of good things that we can and should enjoy. "God did not place man on earth that he may idly contemplate his works as if in a theater, but that, while enjoying the riches of heaven and earth, he may exercise himself in praising the bounty of God."[1] The enjoyment of the good things of God is the ultimate goal of our contemplation of the powers of God, as set forth by Calvin in his definition of divine self-manifestation. "For the Lord manifests himself by his powers, the force of which we feel within ourselves and the benefits of which we enjoy."[2] The previous chapter focused on the way the Lord manifests himself by his powers and the way Calvin directed the godly to meditate on those powers as portrayed in God's works. I now turn to Calvin's treatment of our enjoyment of the good things of creation per se, as it forms a distinct locus of discussion in his theology. According to Calvin, the good things of this life are symbols and pledges of God's love and goodness towards us, as well as steps and ladders by which we might ascend from this life to God, the Author and source of every good thing. Our enjoyment of the good things of creation should sweetly allure us to the enjoyment of the source of all goodness in God.

1. The Manifold Blessings of God in This Life

Calvin first addressed the role of our enjoyment of the good things of cre-ation in his discussion of Christian freedom in the 1536 *Institutes*. According to Calvin, Christians are free to use those things that are "indifferent," pro-vided that they do so with thanksgiving, in recognition of the goodness of God.[3] However, it was not until the expansion of the *Institutes* in 1539 that Calvin devoted more attention to this theme, both in the context of the life of the Christian per se, and in the context of the differing economies of the Old and New Testaments.

In his description of the life of the Christian, Calvin claims that the Christian should have contempt for this life out of an ardent longing for eternal life.[4] However, Calvin does not want contempt of this life to lead us to be ungrateful to God for the many blessings bestowed upon us.[5] Even though believers hope for eternal blessings in Christ, God still manifests God's favor and goodness towards us in this life in the benefits we enjoy.[6] According to Calvin, there are three reasons that we are to be grateful for the good things of this life. First, as already noted, the benefits of this life bring us to a greater apprehension of the goodness of God we hope to enjoy in eternal life. "Since, therefore, this life serves us in understanding God's good-ness, should we despise it as if it had no grain of good in itself?"[7] Second, this life serves as a necessary preparation for the glory of the Kingdom of heaven, and should therefore not be despised even in light of the suffering we might experience. Third, the goodness we enjoy in this life ought to lure us towards the enjoyment of the eternal blessings God wishes to bestow upon us, for "we begin in the present life, through various benefits, to taste the sweetness of the divine generosity in order to whet our hope and desire to seek after the full revelation of this."[8]

The role of temporal benefits in both revealing God's love and goodness to us and inviting us upwards by their sweetness to eternal benefits is central to Calvin's argument that the Old and New Testaments are one in substance, though different in dispensation. Calvin is especially concerned to refute the Anabaptist claim that the promises of God to Israel were only temporal, having to do exclusively with blessings such as descendants and wealth in the land of Canaan. Calvin argues against this claim by first noting that the fa-thers did not enjoy happiness in their own lifetimes, but rather the hardship of the cross, and so must have placed their hope elsewhere in God.[9] He then goes on to delineate the differences between the Old and New Testaments by noting how God trained the Israelites for a better hope by alluring them with temporal benefits, whereas in the Church the future life is more plainly revealed.[10] The good things of this life were to allure the Israelites by their sweetness to seek the eternal blessings of God. Thus the land of Canaan and other temporal blessings were meant to be images of spiritual blessings and not ends in themselves.[11]

Thus, for both the Israelite and the Christian, the blessings of this life are meant to manifest to us the goodness of God in this life that we hope to enjoy more fully in eternal life, even as our enjoyment of these good things is meant to allure us by their sweetness to the source of all goodness in God. For both the Israelite and the Christian, the blessings of the present life are mixed together with suffering, so that we might realize that the true blessings of God are eternal and not place our hope in the good things of this life. The difference lies in the nature of the promises of God: God called the Israelites to eternal blessings through the image and mirror of temporal blessings, whereas God calls Christians directly to the eternal blessings of the Kingdom of God while still manifesting God's favor in temporal blessings.[12]

Calvin's concern that we be grateful for all the blessings God showers on us in this life, combined with his concern not to denigrate God's promises of temporal blessings to Israel, made him increasingly concerned to magnify the importance of the good things God gives us in the present life. This concern is intensified by Calvin's interest in showing how the enjoyment of the good things of this life renders the ungodly without excuse, as he states as early as 1535. "It is true enough that the Gentiles, astonished and convinced by so many goods and benefits which they saw with their own eyes, have been forced to recognize the hidden Benefactor from whom came so much goodness."[13] Such an acknowledgment by the ungodly makes it even more imperative for the godly to be grateful for every blessing from God. "Exceedingly base, therefore, is our ingratitude, if, when God acts kindly towards us, we pass by his benefits with closed eyes."[14] If even the ungodly can acknowledge God to be the fountain of every good thing through the blessings of this life, then the godly must acknowledge such blessings as signs and testimonies of God's love and favor towards them.[15]

2. The Goodness and Care of God
from Birth to Old Age

In his Genesis commentary of 1554, Calvin begins to note the way faith in Christ is confirmed by the experience of the goodness of God in this life, by distinguishing between the knowledge of God through the Word and the knowledge of God through experience. "The best method of seeking God is to begin at his word; after this, (if I may so speak) experimental knowledge is added."[16] Thus David appeals to the help God has given him in this life to confirm his confidence that God has forgiven him.[17] Such visible and experiential confirmation of faith is necessary, according to Calvin, for we are so created that we will not have confidence in God's favor only by hearing about it in the Word. We must also see with our eyes the goodness about which we are told in the Word, "for unless we have ocular demonstration of the divine goodness, we are not spiritual enough to rise upwards to the apprehension of it."[18]

The godly should recall to their minds the many blessings that God has freely bestowed upon them throughout the course of their lives, to confirm their faith, especially in a time of trial and tribulation when God's goodness is not so evident to them.[19] Following the example of David in the Psalms, we should begin with the blessings shown to us before we were born. According to Calvin, one of the most vivid, but frequently overlooked, symbols of God's love and care for us takes place before our birth, when we are kept alive in what appears to be a watery tomb. "Have we not equal reason to marvel that the infant, shut up within its mother's womb, can live in such a condition as would suffocate the strongest man in half an hour?"[20] The answer lies in the incomprehensible power of God, making life possible where it seems to be impossible. "What prevents the child from perishing, as it might, a hundred times in its own corruption, before the time for bringing it forth arrives, but that God, by his secret and incomprehensible power, keeps it alive in its grave?"[21]

The safe emergence of the child into this world is no less astonishing evidence of the goodness and favor of God towards us. Though the mother and midwife do all they can to deliver the child and feed it on its safe emergence from the womb, were it not for the activity of God as nursemaid, the child could not be kept alive.[22] As we have seen before, the most striking miracles are those that seem the most common. "But if ingratitude did not put on our eyes the veil of stupidity, we would be ravished with admiration at every childbirth in the world."[23] Thus when Jeremiah curses the day he was born, Calvin says that such a thought lacks both piety and humanity, and even breathes of madness, for "this life, though exposed to many sorrows, ought yet to be counted as an evidence of God's inestimable grace."[24] Calvin seems to have come a long way from the position of the Stoic philosophers he endorsed in 1539. "I confess that those showed a very sound judgment who thought it the best thing not to be born, and the next best thing to die as quickly as possible."[25]

God not only provides for us when we are born, but continues to feed and nourish us in this life, by providing us with food from the earth and sea for our use and enjoyment. Noting the way Christ gave thanks over the loaves and fish, Calvin says, "all those things that God has appointed for our use summon us to praise him as symbols of his infinite goodness and fatherly love toward us."[26] Calvin wants us to see the meat and drink we enjoy as "remarkable testimonies" of God's paternal kindness, "for we cannot eat a crumb of bread or drink a drop of water, except God's goodness, and the care he takes for our safety, shines upon us."[27]

The care God has for us is manifested by the way various animals are used by us both to help in our labors and to clothe and feed ourselves. "And the more this dominion is apparent, the more we ought to be affected with a sense of the goodness and grace of our God as often as we either eat food, or enjoy any of the other comforts of life."[28] The same may be said about the way the arrangement of the seasons allows us to cultivate the earth.[29] Calvin also sees the arts and skills human beings have developed as remarkable signs of the goodness of God, including not only "agriculture and mechanical arts" but also "the learned and exalted sciences, such as Medicine, Jurisprudence, Astronomy, Geometry, Logic, and the like."[30]

Since "God wishes his favor to be conspicuous in all his gifts," we should acknowledge God's favor in all of the gifts we receive, in those that provide for our necessities as well as those that ornament our lives. "If therefore riches are a glory and ornament, so also are bodily health, and honors, and things of this kind."[31] The goodness of God is revealed to humanity in the gifts of wealth and health, for "whatever God has given to men is testimony of his paternal favor."[32] The problem is that human beings tend to luxuriate in such gifts, and even begin to trust in them. This violates the nature and intent of such gifts, for God manifests God's favor towards us in all of these ways so that we might be more and more grateful to God.[33] When wealth and honors are brought to us, God may be testing us to see if we can control ourselves amid such abundance, primarily by means of our gratitude to God.[34] Finally, it is a manifestation of God's favor when God prolongs our life, even in spite of the hardship and misery that may be involved in our present life.[35] The main blessing of a long life primarily involves "tasting God's fatherly love which he bears towards us, by which we may be led to cherish the hope of immortality."[36]

3. The Blessings of This Life as Ladders and Vehicles to Heaven

All the blessings that God bestows on us in the present life are ultimately meant to lead us on in the hope of eternal life.[37] The very blessings that exhibit to us symbols and signs of the love and favor of God also allure us, through our enjoyment of them, to the enjoyment of the eternal blessings of God.[38] To make the upward movement from temporal to eternal blessings more clear, in his Psalm commentary of 1557 Calvin begins referring to temporal benefits as "ladders" by which we might climb step by step from this world to heaven. For example, David was given a great abundance of temporal blessings. To guard himself against being unmindful or ungrateful for all of the blessings he had received, David "not only testifies that he is mindful of God, but calling to remembrance the benefits which God had conferred upon him, makes them ladders by which he might ascend nearer to God."[39] If we use the blessings of this life as ladders, we will still be grateful to God for all of them, but we will not rest in them. Rather, we will use them to ascend to the eternal blessings of God, so that we might approach ever nearer unto God, the source of all blessings.[40] To make the same point, Calvin also speaks of temporal blessings as "vehicles, to lift up our minds on high."[41]

The very gifts that manifest to us the love and goodness of God also become the means by which we might ascend to the source of all goodness in God.[42] Such an upward ascent is made possible by the upward force of gratitude and praise, by which we lift our hearts to God, even as the heart is drawn upwards by the alluring sweetness of the goodness we enjoy in this life to the fountain of every good thing in God.[43] Finally, our upward ascent from temporal blessings to God takes place when we are ravished with admiration as we call to remembrance and seriously contemplate the overwhelming abundance of good things that God has lavished on us from our birth to the present day. "Let us learn then not to taste God's goodness slightly, and, as it were, with loathing, but to apply all our faculties to it in all its amplitude, that it may ravish us with admiration."[44]

4. ENJOYMENT MIXED WITH AFFLICTION: FINITUDE AND SIN

In order that we might more clearly distinguish between temporal and eternal blessings, God qualifies our enjoyment of the present life by mixing in the experience of affliction and misery.[45] One reason for adding misery to our enjoyment of this life is to reveal to us that we have lost our right to the good things on earth due to Adam's fall into sin, an idea Calvin first seems to develop in his Hebrews commentary of 1549. Though God blesses us by giving us animals we can domesticate and land we can cultivate, we also experience the fury of other animals against us, and the resistance of the land to all our efforts to grow food on it.[46] Calvin develops this line of thinking further in his commentary on Genesis in 1554. The fall of Adam into sin not only entailed the loss of our dominion over the rest of creation but also brought about a transformation of the appearance of the universe itself, so that it now manifests not only the blessing of God towards humanity but also the wrath of God against sinful humanity.[47] The curse of God against sin is manifested in the corruption evident in all the benefits of this life. The food we eat can very quickly rot and spoil. The riches that so splendidly ornament our lives may rust away, "in order that everywhere our eyes should light upon the punishment of sin."[48] Even when one is directly blessed by God in this life, as was Esau, this blessing lacks stability, "and the whole of his pomp departs like the passing scene of the stage."[49] The same may be said about the passing character of all the good things of this life, as when Paul states that "the fashion of this world passes away" (1 Cor. 7:31). "But he seems to have been making an allusion to the stage in the theater, for, on the instant that the curtain falls, their appearance intervenes, and what held the gaze of the audience is immediately swept from their sight."[50]

The clearest evidence for the transitory nature of all earthly blessings appears in the termination of all human life in death. Were we to think seriously about our approaching death, we would quickly lose our trust in any earthly benefit, no matter how glorious. "And as soon as they open their eyes, they see that they are dragged and carried forward to death with rapid haste, and that their excellence is every moment vanishing away."[51] Death accompanies us from the womb to the grave.[52] For this reason, Calvin commends

David's description of human life: "Surely everyone stands as a mere breath" (Ps. 39:5–6). "David speaks truly and wisely in declaring that man, even when he seems to have risen to the highest state of excellence, is only like the bubble which rises upon the water, blown up by the wind."[53] However, in spite of the evidence of our finitude that reveals itself to all people, we fail to take this evidence to heart, and act as though we were to live on earth forever, "because we do not lift our eyes above the world."[54]

5. WHEN LADDERS BECOME OBSTACLES

In spite of all God's efforts to reveal to us the distinction between temporal blessings and eternal life with God, we are all tempted to make the mistake of limiting all the blessings of God to the good things of this life. When we do so, the very gifts that were meant to lift us up to God suddenly become obstacles blocking our access to God.[55] When we seek all our good only in the good things of this life, we suddenly find that no matter how much we hoard the blessings of this life to ourselves, we always need more, and are never close to being satisfied.[56] We may even make the mistake of judging the eternal blessing of God only on the basis of our fortune in this life, without realizing that such blessings of God are an invitation to the ungodly to repent. "It is the disposition of men not to look so much on themselves as on external circumstances."[57] Calvin does not deny that God lavishes good things upon the ungodly, for "he does not cease to cherish and preserve those whom he has created, although they be unworthy."[58] However, God does so to draw them to repent by alluring them with God's goodness, not that they might think that they are loved by God the way they are.[59]

To keep the godly from turning the vehicles of God's benefits into obstacles, God will often give fewer of the benefits of this life to the godly, and will mix in more afflictions with their benefits, than is the case with the ungodly, "lest the faithful should become self-indulgent or sleep on earthly blessings, but that they may ever seek higher things."[60] Moreover, even though Christ restores to us the right to the good things of this life, God keeps reminding us of all that we lost in Adam, to keep us humble.[61] We should not, therefore, blame God if we cannot see an unmixed image of God's goodness in this life. "For were we in right order as to our obedience to God, doubtless all the elements of the world would be conformable, and we should thus observe in the world an angelic harmony."[62] However, neither the afflictions that turn the godly from earth to heaven nor the confusion that reveals to us the extent of our sin can keep God from revealing God's goodness to us in the blessings of this life. Thus "the condition of the godly is always better than that of others: for although they are not satiated with good things, yet they are continually made to experience a sense of the fatherly love of God."[63]

6. Humanity Created in the Image and Likeness of God

Central to all of the blessings that God shows to us in this life is our creation in the image and likeness of God. The image of God manifests the goodness of God to us in the present life, and also directs us to ascend from this life to the next.[64] The image of God also provides one of the reasons that longevity of life is one of the blessings of God in this life.[65] Our having been created in the image of God is directly related to the original plan of creation, which was to come to know God in the image of God in the universe, so that we might ascend to eternal life with God.[66]

Calvin was intensely interested in the image and likeness of God in humanity from the beginning of his theological career. The image of God plays a prominent role in two of his writings from 1535. The opening of the preface to Olivetan's New Testament celebrates humanity as the crowning achievement of God's creation. "Man is endowed with a singular excellence, for God formed him in his own image and likeness, in which we see a bright refulgence of God's glory."[67] Human beings are the surpassing work of God's visual self-expression in the universe, expressing in a unique way the glory of God in creation. This idea is even more clearly set forth in the *Psychopannychia*, as Calvin seeks to refute the idea that the human soul sleeps with the body after death by appealing to our having been created in the image and likeness of God. "But as a bodily image, which exhibits the external face, ought to express to the life all the traits and features, that thus the statue or picture may give us an idea of all that may be seen in the original, so this image of God must, by its likeness, implant some knowledge of God in our minds."[68] Human beings are therefore the unique self-representation of God in creation, for they vividly represent the God who created them, even as a statue or painting ought to represent faithfully the exemplar being represented.

Since human beings are created to be the "singular manifestation" of God, Calvin goes on to describe more clearly "what resemblance this image bears to the archetype." Building on Paul's descriptions of the renewal of the image in Colossians 3:10 and Ephesians 4:24, Calvin locates the similarity in the powers of God in which human beings participate. "When we would comprehend all these things, in one word we say, that man, in respect of spirit, was made partaker of the wisdom, justice, and goodness of God."[69] Human beings are the unique self-representation of God in creation because in their spirits they manifest the powers of God. The more clearly the powers of God are manifested in our souls, the more clearly we represent the archetype after which we were created. Calvin makes the same point in his Genesis commentary of 1554, describing human beings as "a living image of the Divine wisdom and justice."[70] The beginning of his discussion of the image of God in humanity in the *Institutes* of 1559 also echoes this thought, noting that humanity "is the noblest and most remarkable example of his justice, wisdom, and goodness."[71]

The *Institutes* of 1536 intensify the association of the powers of God with the image of God. Turning from the knowledge of God to the knowledge of ourselves, Calvin points us directly to the image of God. "That is, he was endowed with wisdom, righteousness, holiness, and was so clinging by these gifts to the grace of God that he could have lived forever in him, if he had stood fast in the uprightness God had given him."[72] The powers of God are rightly manifested in us when they are set forth in the integrity of our nature, by which Calvin means the right ordering of our soul, which is especially related to humility, gratitude, and obedience. The loss of such integrity by sin directly entails the loss of the powers of God in the soul, and their replacement with their opposites. "As a consequence, nothing was left to him save ignorance, iniquity, impotence, death, and judgment [Rom. 5:12–21]."[73] The loss of the powers of God in the soul leads Calvin to describe the image and likeness of God as "cancelled and effaced" in Adam and his descendants.[74]

7. Lineaments of the Image in Reason and Intelligence

In his *Catechism* of 1538, Calvin repeats his claim that the image of God was "wiped out" in Adam and his descendants. However, Calvin turns again to the image in order to warrant the commandment not to kill, echoing the appeal to the image of God in humanity in Genesis 9:6: "Whoever sheds the blood of a human, by a human shall that person's blood be shed; for in his own image God made humankind." According to Calvin, "if we recall that man was created in God's image, we ought to hold him sacrosanct, as he cannot be violated without God's image also being violated."[75] If this is the case, then the image of God cannot be entirely obliterated, for that would undermine the reason we are forbidden to kill other human beings. However, at this point Calvin gives no hint of what the remnant of the image of God might be.

In the *Institutes* of 1539, Calvin appeals to the image of God in all human beings not only to warrant the prohibition of violence against them but also to explain how it is that we can love those who do not deserve to be loved by us. "But here Scripture helps us in the best way when it teaches that we are not to consider what men merit of themselves but to look upon the image of God in all men, to which we owe all honor and love."[76] Only by looking at the image of God in others can we love them, especially when they repay our love with hatred and our blessings with reproaches. "It is that we remember not to consider men's evil intention but to look upon the image of God in them, which cancels and effaces their transgressions, and with its beauty and dignity allures us to love and embrace them."[77] If the image of God remains to such an extent that its beauty and dignity can allure us to love even our enemies, it is clear that the image of God cannot be entirely obliterated, or else love of our enemies would not be possible.

Calvin returns to this issue in 1550. Commenting on James's description of the way we use our tongues both to bless the Lord and to curse people "who are made in the likeness of God" (James 3:9), Calvin says, "If God is blessed in all his works, this should be true in men above all, in whom his image and glory cast a particular radiance."[78] Were someone to cite Calvin's own teaching that the ungodly do not deserve such blessings because the image of God has been deleted in them, Calvin gives the following response. "If it is objected, that the image of God in human nature was removed by the sin of Adam, we must admit that it was sadly deformed, yet in such a way that certain lineaments still appear."[79] Such lineaments are not enough to unite us with God in eternal life—for it is precisely these powers that have been lost—but they are enough to distinguish us from the rest of creation.[80]

In his commentary on John of 1553, Calvin adds yet another reason that we should love all people, even those who do not seem to deserve our love. "Love is, indeed, extended to those outside, for we are all of the same flesh and are all created in the image of God."[81] When we behold other human beings, we should see in them not only the image of our mutual Creator but also the image of our own human nature, which we cannot hate without hating ourselves. Commenting on Isaiah's warning "that thou hide not thyself from thine own flesh," Calvin observes, "It is therefore a proof of the greatest inhumanity, to despise those in whom we are constrained to recognize our own image."[82] He adds our recognition of one another as one flesh in his treatment of why we should love our enemies in the 1559 edition of the *Institutes*.[83] We ought, therefore, to behold the image of God, as well as the image of ourselves, when we look upon our neighbors, even those we consider the most estranged from us. However, the "lineaments of the image" remain as yet unspecified.

Calvin does not concretely describe the lineaments of the image of God until his commentary on Acts of 1554. Interpreting Paul's quotation of Aratus that human beings are "the off-spring of God," Calvin says that even in their fallen state, human beings "represent something divine in the superiority of their nature. This is what Scripture teaches, that we are created in the image and likeness of God."[84] What is it, then, that makes all people represent God by their resemblance to God? In spite of the fact that "the image of God is almost obliterated in them, so that scarcely the faint outlines of it appear," Calvin claims, "All mortal men, without distinction, are called 'sons,' because they resemble God in mind and intelligence."[85] Calvin seems to be linking the lineaments of the image of God with his observation a year earlier about the light of the Word in all human beings. "It is as if he were saying that the life given to men was not life in general but life united with the light of reason."[86] To warrant this claim, Calvin appeals to Acts 17:27, making it clear that the life of humanity is the self-revelation of God in us, especially the powers of life and wisdom.[87]

Calvin draws out the consequences of the lineaments of the image of God in his Genesis commentary of 1554, showing that it guides our behavior not only towards others but also towards ourselves. Any behavior that threatens to undermine our own reason and intelligence is a direct assault on the image of God in ourselves. Thus when Noah made himself intoxicated, Calvin says, "Drunkenness in itself deserves as its reward, that they who deface the image of their heavenly Father in themselves, should become a laughing-stock to their own children. For certainly, as far as possible, drunkards subvert their own understanding, and so far deprive themselves of reason as to degenerate into beasts."[88] He makes a similar observation nine years later, when he discusses those who pride themselves on their stubborn disobedience to God. "And assuredly it is the climax of all sins that a wretched man, who is abandoned to vice, should extinguish the light of his own reason, and destroy the image of God within him, so as to degenerate into a beast."[89]

The remnant of the image of God in all humans also explains why human beings cannot have a natural desire for death. The image of God means that we were created to pass from this temporal life to eternal life without experiencing death.[90] The life that remains to us, essentially linked to the remnants of the image of God within us, is one that is haunted throughout by the shadow of death.[91] Calvin will appeal to this idea nine years later, to explain why dead bodies horrify us: they remind us of the loss of the image of God, as well as the curse of God against sinners. "And assuredly, if we consider its origin and cause, the corruption of nature, whereby the image of God is defaced, presents itself in every dead man; for, unless we were altogether corrupt, we should not be born to perish."[92]

In his commentary on Psalms of 1557, Calvin gives a much fuller description of what remains of the image of God in our mind and intelligence. When David says that God has "crowned [human beings] with glory and honor" (Ps. 8:5), Calvin takes this to refer to "the distinguished endowments which clearly manifest that men were formed after the image of God, and created to the hope of a blessed and immortal life."[93] Calvin then describes all the wonderful gifts that remain in all human beings. "The reason with which they are endued, and by which they can distinguish between good and evil; the principle of religion which is planted in them; their intercourse with each other, which is preserved from being broken by certain sacred bonds; the regard to what is becoming, and the sense of shame which guilt awakens in them, as well as their continuing to be governed by laws; all these things are clear indications of pre-eminent and celestial wisdom."[94] Even in the ruin of fallen human nature, there is enough of a manifestation of God's wisdom, grace, and love in us that it "ought justly to strike us with amazement" and "should suffice to fill us with admiration."[95]

Calvin builds on his claim that the light of reason and intelligence is essential to the image of God in the 1559 *Institutes*, by associating the integrity of the soul with the governance of human life by reason. In light of Paul's description of the renewal of the image in knowledge, righteousness, and holiness (Col. 3:10, Eph. 4:24), Calvin says, "From this we infer that, to begin with, God's image was visible in the light of the mind, in the uprightness of the heart, and in the soundness of all the parts."[96] He links this integrity with Plato's description of reason as the governing power of the soul (*to hegemonikon*), which should guide human beings through this life to the next.[97] The principal use of reason, as noted above, is to lead us to the knowledge of God by the contemplation of the image of God in God's works. "Hence the more anyone endeavors to approach God, the more he proves himself endowed with reason."[98] It would follow that the more we come to know God, the more the image of God shines in us.[99]

If enough of the image of God remains in fallen human beings to prevent us from murdering them, to draw us to love them even when they hate us, and to urge us to respect the reason and intelligence within ourselves, could it also be the case that God cares for all human beings because God still sees God's image in them? "Men are indeed unworthy of God's care, if respect be had only to themselves; but since they bear the image of God engraven on them, . . . he looks upon his own gifts in them, and is thereby excited to love and to care for them."[100] I explore the providential care of God for all humanity in the next chapter, but for now it is important to note that Calvin begins to link such care with the image of God that God beholds in every human being. "And we know also the reason why God undertakes to protect the life of men, and that is, because they have been created in his image."[101]

If our recognition of the image of God in others draws us to care for and protect them, even if they are strangers or enemies, the same may be said of God. Because God recognizes the remnants of the image of God in all people, God cares for all, even those outside the covenant community.[102] Explaining why God commands the Israelites, "You shall have one law for the alien and for the citizen" (Lev. 24:22), Calvin observes, "because he created all men without exception after his own image, he takes them under his care and protection, so that none might injure them with impunity."[103] When people are injured or killed with impunity, as when tyrannical rulers slaughter their subjects, these acts call into question the providential care of God itself, "for they have, after all, from the least to the greatest, been created in God's image."[104] Although Calvin will describe all rulers as "the image of God" because God is reflected in their superior authority, he also uses the image of God in all people as a check to the tyrannical abuse of power by rulers. Rulers only properly image God when they care for their subjects the way God cares for all people, and for all creation.

8. The Image of God in Men and Women

Calvin first addresses the question of the quality of the image of God in men and women in his commentary on 1 Corinthians of 1546. In 1 Corinthians 11:7, Paul describes the man as "the image and reflection of God," whereas he calls the woman "the reflection of man." Calvin attempts to interpret this text without having it come into conflict with Genesis 1:27, which explicitly states that God created men and women in the image of God. "But when he is speaking about image here, he is referring to the conjugal order. Accordingly, it has to do with this present life."[105] Since both men and women were created in the image of God in the hope of eternal life, and both are reformed by the grace of God into that image by innocence and holiness, the kind of image being spoken of by Paul refers to the relationship of men and women to each other, not their relationship to God. "The glory of God is seen in the higher standing that the man has, as it is reflected in every superior authority."[106] The man is the image of God in relation to the woman even as kings are the image of God in relation to their subjects, because their superior authority is more reflective of God.

When Paul calls the woman "the glory of man," Calvin takes him to mean that the woman is both the helper and the ornament of the man's life.[107] This is true not only of wives in relation to husbands but also of the whole sex, if one looks to the ordering of God. "For that is what Paul is endorsing here, showing that the woman was created in order to be the splendid ornament of the man."[108] Since the woman is both the ornament and the helper of the man, she is subject to his authority and should therefore wear an external symbol of her subjugation, which should be some kind of veil, "either a robe, or a linen cloth, or some other kind of covering."[109] If a woman decides to forgo the symbol of subjugation by going about with a bare head, she acts "against the Law both of God and men" by appropriating the symbol of domination for herself, for her subjection to the man is rooted in "the eternal law of God."[110] Calvin took this ordinance of Paul's seriously enough to argue for an exemption to be made for pastors preaching in the winter, when they need to wear a covering on their heads.[111]

Calvin returns to the question of the image of God in men and women in his commentary on Genesis of 1554. Calvin repeats his claim that Paul's denial of the image of God to women pertains only to government and not to the shining forth of God's glory in human nature, "where the mind, the will, and all the senses, represent the Divine order."[112] However, if Calvin's comments on 1 Corinthians 11 indicate that men and women are equally created in the image of God, his interpretation of Genesis 2 suggests that women are not equal to men in this regard. He claims that the woman as well as the man was created in the image of God, since Genesis 1:27 speaks of God creating humanity (*hominem*) in the image of God; but the reason is that the woman "was nothing else than an accession to the man (*viri accessio*)."[113] Calvin first notes the role of the woman as an "accession" to the man in his commentary on 1 Timothy of 1548, where it is clearly limited to the male-female relationship.[114] However, in his Genesis commentary the priority of the male over the female extends beyond the temporal authority the man has over the woman to influence the degree to which the woman is created in the image of God. "Certainly, it cannot be denied, that the woman also, although in the second degree, was created in the image of God; whence it follows that what was said in the creation of man belongs to the female sex."[115] This passage makes it clear that for Calvin the image of God resides primarily in the man, and only by accession does it reside also in the woman.

In his Genesis commentary, Calvin repeats his claim that the woman was created to be the helper and companion of the man, but he does not describe her as an ornament but rather emphasizes her role as the man's companion.[116] Calvin also speaks of the "mutual obligation" the man and the woman have towards one another, and how they are not complete without one another. However, the basic structure of the companionship remains one of superiority and subordination: "the woman is assigned as a helper to the man, that he may fill the place of her head and leader."[117] Calvin makes the same point in his commentary on 1 Corinthians: "Let the man therefore carry out his function as the head, having supremacy over her; let the woman perform her function as the body, giving help to him."[118] According to Calvin, these offices extend beyond marriage to include all "public obligations," even for those who are not married.[119] Thus it is not surprising to hear Calvin say that "we know that males are preferred to females,"[120] and to see this preference reflected in the way men and women are educated, for young women "are not so liberally educated as the male sex, being considered as born for domestic offices."[121] The differing methods of education, combined with the essential relationship between the image of God and the light of the intellect, clearly suggest that Calvin thinks that women's intellects are not as keen as men's.

Calvin reinforces the need of the woman to be veiled as a sign of subjection, but he extends the meaning of the veil to include the husband himself. In his comments on Genesis 20:16, in which Abimelech returns Sarah to Abraham, Calvin says, "For Sarah is taught that the husband to whom she is joined was as a veil, with which she ought to be covered, lest she should be exposed to others."[122] The veil in this instance protects her modesty. However, in his commentary on Isaiah of 1559, he reiterates the need for the woman to display a sign of subjection to the man, only in this instance the sign is the taking of the husband's name as her own.[123] If a woman is single, she ought to be hidden in the veil of her family, under the headship of her father. If she marries, she is veiled by her husband, and bears the signs of subjection both by taking his name and by wearing a covering. Her subjection to the superiority of the men over her and the help that she should render to them govern all aspects of a woman's life.[124]

9. THE IMAGE OF GOD IN HUMANITY AND THE REJECTION OF HUMAN IMAGES

On the basis of the image of God in humanity, Calvin develops two distinct arguments against images of God made by human beings. The first argument, found in his commentary on Acts of 1554, is formulated on the basis of Paul's statement in Acts 17:29: "Since then we are God's offspring, we ought not to think that the deity is like gold, or silver, or stone, an image formed by the art and imagination of mortals." Calvin interprets this statement to mean that, since the living image of God is found in the human soul, and the soul cannot be painted or sculpted, it is even more absurd to try to represent God in images of our devising.[125] This is an argument from the lesser to the greater. If the soul, in which the image of God resides, cannot itself be painted or represented, how much more absurd is it to try to represent God that way, whose image is reflected in the soul? "Now we see how much harm is done to God by all those who make up a physical shape for God, seeing that the soul of man, which scarcely reproduces a tiny spark of the immense glory of God, does not permit anything of the sort."[126]

The second argument is formulated on the basis of Jeremiah's description of idols as "teachers of falsehood" (Jer. 10:8). In his lectures on Jeremiah of 1563, Calvin explains why Jeremiah says that idols are teachers of falsehood by contrasting the qualities of the soul that make it like God with the absence of these qualities in idols, making them unlike God. "For some life appears at least in men, they are endued with mind and intelligence, and so far they bear some likeness to God: but dead wood and stone, which are void of sense—gold and silver, which are metals without reason, which have no life—what affinity, he says, can these have to God?"[127] It is significant that Calvin bases his critique on the lineaments or remnants of the image found in all people, namely, life, reason, and intelligence, and not on the powers of God per se. By this argument, anything lacking in life, reason, mind, and intelligence cannot be a living and true image of God.[128] "God will not have himself compared to dead things, without mind and life."[129] Human beings are truly the image of God because they have mind and life.

Calvin combines an argument from the invisibility of God (based on the invisibility of the soul) with an argument contrasting true and false images of God. On the one hand, God cannot be represented visibly because the soul, which is the image of God, cannot be painted. On the other hand, the soul truly is the image of God because it has life, reason, mind, and intellect. Images made of stone and wood lack life and mind, and are therefore nothing like God. The latter argument can be traced back to Calvin's description of the image of God in 1535, which highlights its ability truly to represent God to us, thereby referring us to the original by its representation.[130] Calvin reiterates this claim in the *Institutes* of 1559, describing humanity in the image and likeness of God as the self-representation of God. "For, when God determined to create man in his image, which was a rather obscure expression, he for explanation repeats it in this phrase, 'According to his likeness,' as if he were saying that he was going to make man, in whom he would represent himself as in an image, by means of engraved marks of likeness."[131] The very mind and reason that make it impossible to paint God also make it unnecessary to do so, since human beings are already the living self-representation of God.

CHAPTER 3

The Manifestation of the Providential Care of God

Calvin's understanding of the manifestation of God's providential care overlaps in some ways with the topics treated in the preceding chapters. The works of God that manifest God's care for and governance of heaven and earth clearly contribute to the living image of God in the universe. Moreover, Calvin's discussion of the care of God is reflected in his understanding of the benefits of God in the present life, especially in the way God sustains our lives over against the constant threat of death. However, the providence of God also constitutes a topic in its own right in Calvin's theology, as it raises issues related to the way God governs and directs every event in the universe, especially events in human history. As I discuss below, the providence of God brings into sharp relief the relationship between the self-manifestation of God and the often-troubling hiddenness of God in God's works. Calvin's discussion of providence develops in large part in light of his concern to give guidance to the godly as they navigate the field of tension created by the simultaneous revealedness and hiddenness of God in God's governance of the world. Since the order of topics covered by Calvin is also reflected in the order of the development of his thoughts on providence, the discussion below is structured along chronological lines alone and supplements each topic as it arises in Calvin's writings with statements on the same topic from later writings.

1. Early Reflections on God's Providence, 1532–1537

Calvin expressed an awareness of providence in his first writing, the Seneca commentary of 1532. Noting the way Seneca exhorts Nero to view himself as chosen by heaven to be vicar of the gods, Calvin says, "This statement, moreover, derives from the opinion of the Stoics, who attribute the superintendence of human affairs to the gods, assert providence, and leave nothing to mere chance."[1] Calvin contrasts the opinion of the Stoics with that of the Epicureans, making it clear that the issue at stake for him is the care of the gods for mortals.[2] Calvin's identification of providence with the opinion of the Stoics explains why he will be at pains later in his career to distinguish his own teaching about providence from the opinion of the Stoics.

Calvin does not directly mention providence in his preface to Olivetan's New Testament of 1535, apart from a brief mention of the goodness of God that all the Gentiles experience.[3] In the 1536 edition of the *Institutes,* Calvin expands on this theme of God's goodness to all by combining it with the power of God in his discussion of the first article of the Creed. God not only created all things by God's wisdom (the Son) and power (the Holy Spirit) but also now "sustains, nourishes, activates, preserves, by his goodness and power, apart from which all things would immediately collapse and fall into nothingness."[4]

The emphasis on goodness and power continues in his discussion of what it means to call God "Almighty." "But when we call him almighty and creator of all things, we must ponder such omnipotence of his whereby he works all things in all, and such providence whereby he regulates all things."[5] The acknowledgment that God works all things means that we must accept whatever comes to us, whether prosperous or adverse, as coming to us from God.[6] The alternation of prosperity and adversity will be one of the central themes Calvin develops in his discussion of providence. However, in 1536 the emphasis is clearly on the goodness of God, which comes to us gratuitously, due to no merit of our own. "For this reason, we must take care to give thanks for this very great goodness of his, to ponder it with our hearts, proclaim it with our tongue, and to render such praises as we are able."[7] The need for pondering the goodness of God in providence is especially great in times of adversity, which we should believe is for our own welfare and salvation. "We should also so receive all adverse things with calm and peaceful hearts, as if from his hand, thinking that his providence so looks after us and our salvation while it is afflicting and oppressing us [Job 2:10]."[8] The godly are to know that the power of God, howsoever it is exercised towards them, is always guided by God's free and unmerited goodness, which comes to them gratuitously.[9]

Calvin first speaks of the manifestation of providence in the works of God in his *Catechism* of 1538. Discussing what it means for the works of God to be "the reflection of things invisible" (Heb. 11:3), Calvin describes the powers of God to be contemplated in God's works, especially immortality, power, wisdom, goodness, righteousness, and mercy.[10] These powers should not only be contemplated outside of ourselves; we should also descend into ourselves to consider "in what ways the Lord reveals his life, wisdom, and power in us, and exercises toward us his righteousness, goodness, and mercy."[11] The powers that are particularly associated with providence are power, which sustains all things; wisdom, which orders and governs all things; goodness, without which nothing would exist; righteousness, which defends the godly and punishes the ungodly; and mercy, which invites sinners to repentance. Calvin also notes that although these powers shine forth in all the works of God, we lack the eyes to see them without the corrective influence of the Word of God.[12]

Calvin explicitly discusses providence in the *Catechism* in his interpretation of what it means to call God the "Father Almighty" in the Creed. "Omnipotence is attributed to him, by which is signified both that he administers all things by his providence, governs by his will, and directs by his power and hand."[13] The theme of God's governance and direction is accentuated here more than in the 1536 *Institutes*, and will become central to his understanding of providence in 1539. However, to say that God is the Creator also means that "all he once created he everlastingly nourishes, sustains, and quickens."[14] The providence of God therefore means that God both governs and cares for everything God has created. The power and will of God guiding all things must be seen in conjunction with the care of God nourishing and sustaining all things.

2. The Providence of God versus Fortune: *Institutes*, 1539

Calvin did not develop a comprehensive teaching on providence until the 1539 edition of the *Institutes*. He builds on the two loci of his discussion of providence in the 1538 *Catechism*, discussing providence in the first chapter regarding the knowledge of God that could be derived from God's works and in an expanded discussion of the first article of the Creed in the fourth chapter on faith. However, over and above these loci, Calvin emphasizes the importance of providence by developing a whole chapter devoted to the predestination and providence of God. Given the comprehensive scope of the discussion in 1539, it is no wonder that, apart from small additions in 1543, it remained unchanged from 1539 until 1559, when the *Institutes* was radically reorganized and more material on providence was added. The primary theme of the treatment of providence in 1539 concerns the contrast Calvin continually makes between the providence of God and fortune. He also begins to develop his understanding of the simultaneous manifestation and concealment of God's providence. On the one hand, the providence of God is so clearly manifested in God's works that the ungodly are rendered without excuse for their failure to acknowledge it. On the other hand, even to believers all things appear to be fortuitous and contingent, and they must hold to the providence of God in spite of the confusion that confronts them in the world.

The Works of God outside the Ordinary Course of Nature

The first locus of Calvin's discussion of providence is in his description of the way God manifests Godself in God's powers, which are portrayed in God's works as in a painting. After discussing the manifestation of God's wisdom in the heavens and God's power in the dramatic changes in earth's atmosphere, Calvin turns to consider the works of God in relation to the human community. "In the second kind of works, which are outside the ordinary course of nature, proofs of his powers just as clear are set forth."[15] This distinction between those works done in the ordinary course of nature and those done outside it will run through the whole discussion of providence. Calvin is as critical of those who limit the providence of God to the motion that sustains the ordinary course of nature as he is of those who attribute the works outside the course of nature to fortune. In particular, the powers that are clearly set forth in providence are the goodness, mercy, and wrath of God.[16]

The clemency and severity of God reveal that God is righteous, protecting the godly and innocent from the attacks of the wicked.[17] We ought to hold to this righteousness of God even when it is not apparent, as when the wicked prosper and even afflict the innocent and godly.[18] On the one hand, we ought to remember that God does good to the wicked in order to induce them to repent, for "he often pursues miserable sinners with unwearied kindness, until he shatters their wickedness by imparting benefits and recalling them to him with more than fatherly kindness!"[19] On the other hand, the incomplete manifestation of God's righteousness in this life ought to lead us to conclude that "there will be another judgment to which have been deferred the sins yet to be punished."[20] There is enough evidence of God's severity against sin to reveal that God will punish all sin, and enough evidence of God's protection of the godly to disclose that God will alleviate all their afflictions in a future life.[21]

Even though the full manifestation of God's mercy towards the godly must await the future life, there is still enough evidence of God's power and wisdom in the works done to protect them to manifest the providence of God to us in this life. The power of God is revealed by the way God can quickly overturn in a moment the apparently unconquerable ferocity of the impious so that they are laid low contrary to all expectation, while "the oppressed and afflicted are rescued from their extreme tribulation; the despairing are restored to good hope; the unarmed, few, and weak, snatch victory from the armed, many, and strong."[22] The wisdom of God is manifested by the way God confounds the wisdom of the wise and "catches the crafty in their own craftiness" (1 Cor. 3:19), as well as by the way "he dispenses everything at the best opportunity."[23]

In sum, the works of God outside the ordinary course of nature exhibit the goodness of God towards all; the righteousness of God in the mercy shown towards the godly and the severity shown towards the wicked; the power and wisdom of God in confounding the powerful and wise of this world; and the future manifestation of all these powers in a future life, given their incomplete exhibition to us in this life. However, in spite of the clarity of the manifestation of providence, we misjudge the works of God so that everything outside the course of nature is ascribed to fortune and chance rather than to the providence of God.[24] No matter how much evidence we have before us in God's works, we profit no more from the powers of God in providence than we do from the powers of God in the theater of the universe.[25]

In his commentaries after 1539, Calvin continues to insist that the providence of God is so clearly manifested in God's works that it cannot be denied. The providence of God clearly appears to us from the day we are born.[26] According to Calvin, "babes and sucklings are advocates sufficiently powerful to vindicate the providence of God," not because they can speak, but because they are given breasts to nourish them and tongues skilled in sucking milk from the breast.[27] The providence of God is also demonstrated in the preservation of the order and harmony of the heavenly bodies that all may behold.[28] However, God's providence also appears in the manifold changes that we perceive in the world, which reveal to us that God presides over the whole of life, lest we make a god of nature.[29] In particular, the power and wisdom of God may be seen when God overturns one form of earthly rule and raises up another.[30] The wisdom and power of God are not only manifested in the beauty and harmony of the heavens, but also in the confusing revolutions of earthly dominion.

The providence of God is particularly manifested in the prosperity and afflictions of life, which reveal to us the mercy and severity of God. An especially vivid description of the providence of God in afflicting and delivering humans is given in Psalm 107, which according to Calvin speaks of the works of God for all people and not just for the pious. We are to observe the judgments of God in all the varying changes of the world, and are to be especially attentive to discern the signs of God's wrath and mercy.[31] The providence of God shines with special clarity when those hopelessly suffering some calamity, revealing to them the wrath of God, are suddenly and unexpectedly delivered from it, manifesting the wonderful grace of God.[32] The same may be said of those who are facing death in the midst of a storm on the sea, for "the goodness of God may appear the more conspicuous when the tempest happily ceases without any loss of life."[33]

We are therefore to pay careful attention to all the events of our lives, in order to discern in them both the judgment and the goodness of God.[34] Our meditation ought to lead us to feel and experience the power of the goodness and the judgment of God, so that the force of the powers manifested to us in providence might influence our lives. "Let us know that God would have himself to be seen in daily events, so that the signs of his love may make us to rejoice, and also that signs of his wrath may humble us, to the end that we may repent."[35] We may at times see signs of wrath and love in the same person, as in the man born blind in the Gospel of John. "For so long as he was blind, there was exhibited in him an example of the divine severity, from which others might learn to fear and humble themselves. It was followed by the benefit of his deliverance, in which the wonderful goodness of God was reflected."[36] Although both wrath and love are revealed in the providential works of God, and we should accept both from God's hand when they arrive,

Calvin insists that the power of God is most clearly revealed when God delivers those whom God had afflicted.[37]

Viewing the Providence of God with the Eyes of Faith

In spite of the clarity of the manifestation of God's providence in the works that all can behold, Calvin insists that our ingratitude and perversity prevent us from beholding the providence of God without the clarification of the Word of God and the illumination of the Holy Spirit.[38] The reason we need the Word of God and the illumination of faith is that we constantly misjudge the works of God's providence, either attributing everything to fortune or considering everything the result of the universal course of nature. Calvin continues to develop the necessity of the Word and Spirit for our contemplation of providence in his commentaries after 1539, especially in his commentary on the Psalms.[39] He insists that the works that manifest God's providence are equally evident to both the ungodly and the godly, but only the godly are given the eyes rightly to perceive them. When David concludes his psalm about the works of deliverance done for the ungodly, he says, "The righteous shall see that, and shall rejoice" (Ps. 107:42). Calvin uses this statement to distinguish between the vision of the godly and the ungodly. "The prophet now draws the conclusion, that so many evident tokens of God's [superintending and overruling] providence could not transpire before the righteous without attracting their notice, and that their vision being illumined by faith, these scenes are contemplated by them with unfeigned delight; while the wicked remain perplexed and mute."[40]

One reason for this difference is that the ungodly do not ascribe the events they see to God's governance but rather to the arbitrary wheel of fortune. When David tells us God sees all human beings from heaven, Calvin says, "There are, no doubt, evident proofs of it continually before our eyes; but the great majority of men, notwithstanding, see nothing of them, and in their blindness, imagine that all things are under the conduct of a blind fortune."[41] One reason for the blindness of the ungodly is that they rush to conclusions based only on what they perceive with their senses.[42] They see the same events as the godly but do not go further than the event itself, and thus miss "the secret hand of God" directing and governing the event.[43]

If we are rightly to behold the providence of God that exhibits itself before our eyes in every event, we must turn to God for the wisdom that we ourselves lack.[44] We must therefore be instructed by the Word of God and illumined by the Spirit if we are rightly to see the providence of God that reveals itself before us. "When, therefore, we are told here that men are unfit for contemplating the arrangements of divine providence until they obtain wisdom elsewhere than from themselves, how can we obtain to wisdom but by submissively receiving what God teaches us by his Word and by his Holy Spirit?"[45] When we contemplate the works of God, therefore, we ought to pray to God to give us the eyes of faith by which we may rightly consider what we behold.[46] Such clarified vision is especially necessary given that God wants us to be "eye-witnesses" of God's works, a theme Calvin begins to develop in his commentary on Genesis of 1554. "For although God does not declare to us what he is about to do, yet he intends us to be eye-witnesses of his works, and prudently to weigh their causes."[47] If we are rightly to see the providence of God, we need to open our eyes as well as our ears.[48] We can only contemplate the works of God if God teaches us by God's Word and opens our eyes to see what is before us.[49]

However, the difficulty of rightly discerning the providence of God in the works of God goes beyond our own perversity and blindness. Calvin speaks of God's "invisible providence" and "hidden hand" in the events we experience, indicating that one major reason we cannot discern the providence of God without the eyes of faith is that it is hidden from our view.[50] Without the eyes of faith, the events of this world appear dark and impenetrable to us, and seem to be full of confusion, not only because we are blind, but also because God's providence is hidden in such events, and can only be apprehended by faith. It is perhaps for this reason that in the final edition of the *Institutes* Calvin repeatedly refers to the wisdom of God that orders all things as the "hidden counsel" of God.[51] Only when we are given the eyes of faith to see, in conjunction with the ears to hear God's word, can we begin to see and even delight in the powers of God that shine forth in God's works of providence. "But the righteous are not only able to form a good and sound judgment of these events, they also spontaneously open their eyes to contemplate the equity, goodness, and wisdom of God, the sight and knowledge of which are refreshing to them."[52]

The godly will therefore be patient when they cannot clearly discern the judgments of God in the confusing whirl of human affairs, and will wait until the time arrives for the manifestation of the judgment of God in their lives, knowing that the full exhibition of such judgment will not come until the future life.[53] When adversity comes upon them, and they can discern no sign of the love and favor of God, they will rely on the providence of God as revealed in the Word of God, and await the time when they will experience yet again the deliverance God alone can provide.[54] The providence of God cannot be completely hidden from view in this life but will emerge from darkness so long as we wait for its manifestation with faith.

The Wisdom and Power of God

The second locus of Calvin's discussion of providence in 1539 is the first article of the Creed. Here Calvin is especially concerned to distinguish God's providence from the universal motion that sustains the machine of the universe. He acknowledges that the ungodly, when they look upon heaven and earth, are compelled to rise up to the Creator, and even to acknowledge the wisdom, power, and goodness of God in creating the universe. They also contemplate "some general preserving and governing activity, from which the force of motion derives." However, "faith has its own peculiar way of assigning the whole credit for creation to God."[55] According to Calvin, we do not know what it means to confess by faith that God is the Creator unless we pass on to God's providence, which means that God is not only the universal motion preserving the order of nature "but also . . . sustains, nourishes, and cares for, everything he has made, even to the least sparrow [cf. Matt. 10:29]."[56] Such care extends to all the creatures that God has created, as David reminds us in Psalm 104, for without the particular care of God they would all perish in a moment. Without such care, there could be neither signs of God's favor in the dew and the rain nor signs of God's vengeance in drought and blight.[57]

Unlike the 1536 edition of the *Institutes*, however, Calvin's concern for the care of God leads him to focus not on the goodness of God but on the wisdom and power of God. In his discussion of the omnipotence of God in the first article of the Creed, Calvin insists that the power of God is always joined to the will and deliberation of God.[58] Calvin renews this focus on God's deliberative power when he turns to discuss providence in the newly added chapter on predestination and providence. He states that many (most likely scholastic theologians) describe providence in terms of the bare foreknowledge of God, while others limit providence to the general motion driving the order of nature.[59] Both descriptions of providence attribute the entirety of contingent actions to the free choice of human beings, even though such actions may be foreknown by God and may even be empowered by the general motion driving the natural course of the universe.[60] According to Calvin, such teaching takes away from God "the chief thing: that he directs everything by his incomprehensible wisdom and disposes it to his own end."[61] The power of God must always be seen as working in conjunction with the wisdom of God, which directs all human actions to the end intended for them by God.

Calvin is aware that his opponents will charge him with reviving the teaching of the Stoics, something that happened to Augustine before him. Calvin denies that he is doing so, because he is basing his position on the inseparable relationship between the wisdom and power of God.[62] Calvin does not deny that human beings choose their own ends by the deliberation of free choice, but he insists that it is God who directs them to their true end by God's wisdom and power, working through their own self-deliberation. "From this we declare that not only heaven and earth and inanimate creatures, but also the plans and intentions of men, are so governed by his providence that they are borne by it straight to their appointed end."[63] The wisdom of God decreed the end to which we are all appointed, and the power of God executes that decree in our lives. Nothing takes place by chance, nothing by fortune, nothing by pure contingency. Whatever God has decreed in wisdom, God will execute by God's power.

However, Calvin makes an important concession, based on his acknowledgment that the wisdom of God in providence is hidden from our view. Even though believers penetrate to God's providence by their faith, and know that all things take place by God's wisdom and power, they nonetheless experience events in the world as though they were strictly contingent and even fortuitous.[64] Calvin does not mean that the pious will actually believe that fortune rules the world but rather that the wisdom governing the world is hidden from our view, and can only be believed in spite of what we see.[65] Unlike the wisdom of God manifested in the beauty, harmony, and order of the heavens, the wisdom of God governing human events presents an image of contingency that cannot be penetrated by believers but must rather be believed in spite of what appears to them. Thus, when thieves unexpectedly murder one of the godly, the godly will hold both positions at the same time: an event that appears to be fortuitous is nonetheless governed by God's wisdom and power.[66]

According to Calvin, there are three benefits in particular that come to believers by their meditation on the providence of God. "Gratitude of mind for the favorable outcome of things, patience in adversity, and an incredible freedom from worry about the future all necessarily follow upon this knowledge."[67] Our gratitude is related to the goodness, beneficence, and love of God that we experience in this life, which will also include thanks to the instruments God uses to bring us such benefits, including other people. Our patience is fostered by the justice of God, which reveals to us the need to bear our afflictions without succumbing to anger or impatience.[68] If we have suffered loss through our own neglect, we will acknowledge our culpability as well as God's wisdom; and if we suffer through the sin of others, we will not blame God for the evil, even as we acknowledge the righteousness of God in the event.[69] Finally, freedom from worry about the future is made possible by our knowledge that in spite of all the dangers that confront us in the future, the wisdom and power of God will direct our life to the end willed by God.[70] Since the future is unknown to us, we must use our prudence and wisdom to direct our lives, even as we acknowledge our lives are governed and directed by the power and wisdom of God.[71]

Even though the faithful experience the force and benefits of God's goodness and justice by their knowledge of providence, in 1539 Calvin's emphasis falls on the wisdom and power of God, which guide all things to the end determined for them by God. In his commentaries after 1539, Calvin continues to focus on the power of God in conjunction with the plan of God. However, he tends to focus more on the promises of God than on the wisdom of God per se. The faithful should always bear in mind the power of God whenever they hope for the fulfillment of God's promises, especially the promise of God to protect and deliver them from the power of their enemies. "When God, therefore, kindly allures us to himself, and assures us that he will take care of our safety, since we have embraced his promises, or because we believe him to be faithful, it is meet that we rightly extol his power, that it may ravish our hearts with admiration for itself."[72]

The danger is that the faithful, especially in times of affliction or captivity, tend to judge their situation by appearances, and forget about the power of God.[73] This is especially true with regard to the glorious and powerful appearance of earthly kingdoms, such as Egypt or Babylon. When the faithful are taken captive by such powers, they cannot allow themselves to judge the hope of their deliverance by looking at appearances, for then they would lose all hope. Rather, they must keep in mind the power of God, which will bring about their deliverance in spite of the most powerful kingdoms. This is why Jeremiah bids the Jews to consider the power of the Creator when he promises them deliverance from the Babylonians. "He bids the faithful to raise their thoughts above the world, and to behold with admiration the incomprehensible power of God; that they might not doubt that Babylon would at length be trodden under foot; for had they fixed their eyes on that monarchy, they could have hardly believed the words of prophecy; for the prophet spoke of things which could hardly be comprehended by the human mind."[74]

Scripture so often narrates the history of the powerful being cast from their thrones to teach us to look to the governing wisdom and power of God and not to the deceptive appearance of earthly power.[75] Scripture also narrates accounts of deliverance in which the power of God is so clearly manifested that even the ungodly are compelled to acknowledge it, so that we might hope in the same power to deliver even when it works in hidden ways.[76] Our faith in the power and wisdom of God is confirmed by the experience of the faithful in history, and Scripture reminds us of these events so that we might hope for the same actions of God in our own lives.

The Providence of God and Mediate Causes

The providential governance of God is most often executed by means of mediate causes, which God uses like instruments to carry out God's will. Events in human history are usually carried out by the contingent actions of human agents, but this does not prevent the same events from being governed by God's wisdom and power.[77] If God chooses to deliver us from peril by the use of human instruments, we must give them their proper place even as we trace our deliverance ultimately to God. Calvin enlarges upon God's use of mediate causes in the 1543 edition of the *Institutes* by highlighting the way God also uses inanimate objects such as the sun and the stars as instruments of God's providence. "These are, thus, nothing but instruments to which God continually imparts as much effectiveness as he wills, and according to his own purpose bends and turns them to either one action or another."[78] Since all things are instruments of God, God's power is not bound to them for its efficacy. To make this point, Scripture narrates the creation of light before the creation of the sun, making the sun "merely the instrument that God uses because he so wills; for with no more difficulty he might abandon it, and act through himself."[79]

Calvin demonstrated an increasing interest in the relationship between divine agency and inferior causes in his biblical commentaries, especially after 1552. He was particularly concerned with the impact of the study of philosophy on his doctrine of providence. For instance, with regard to human agency, philosophers teach that the actions of human beings are by nature contingent and lacking in necessity. Remarkably, Calvin does not deny the truth of this insight but simply insists that it is not inconsistent with the same actions being governed by the wisdom and power of God.[80] Calvin appeals to the narrative of Joseph in Genesis in order to illustrate the coincidence of contingent human choice and the wisdom and power of God, over against those who play human self-determination off against divine providence. "And yet the selling of Joseph is not here interposed as a veil to hide the divine providence; but is rather set forth as a signal instance of it to teach us that whatever men may undertake, the issues are in the hand of God."[81]

Calvin makes the same point with regard to God's use of inanimate creatures. He acknowledges the right of philosophers to discover the proximate causes of earthly phenomena, such as rain, but denies that such causes eliminate divine causality, or bind God to them as necessary instruments.[82] Calvin insists that even with the creation of mediate causes, God could still provide the same effects for us without their instrumentality. However, God chooses to use such instruments in order to manifest to us in a visible way the care God has for our welfare.[83] Calvin was especially concerned that the increased interest in Aristotle might lead the godly to lose sight of the providence of God, since Aristotle sought to find the origin of any given earthly effect in another earthly cause.[84] However, philosophers only accentuate a tendency apparent in every human mind; for we all inquire into the causes of things, without ever raising our minds to the providence of God.[85] The godly are to acknowledge the role played by mediate causes in all events, whether of blessing or adversity, but are nonetheless to raise their minds to the providence of God, which governs all such events and directs them to their appointed end.[86]

Calvin was also concerned with the impact of another ancient science on the doctrine of providence, astrology. One reason Calvin addressed the relationship between God's providence and the working of the sun in 1543 was to deny the tendency that many in his day were developing of looking to the stars to discover the power directing earthly events, including their own lives. "But when unbelievers transfer the government of the universe from God to the stars, they fancy that their bliss or their misery depends on the decrees and indications of the stars, not upon God's will; so it comes about that their fear is transferred from him, towards whom alone they ought to direct it, to stars and comets."[87] Calvin expanded on this position in his 1549 treatise, *Against Judiciary Astrology,* making the same point that all blessings and curses come from God, even if stars and comets may be used as signs thereof.

Beginning in 1552, Calvin began to focus his attention on the way miracles demonstrate God's freedom over the instruments of God's providence. Calvin briefly mentions miracles in his discussion of providence in his 1552 treatise, *Concerning the Eternal Predestination of God.* He adds two distinctions to clarify the nature of God's providence, first that providence refers to past as well as future events; second, "that, sometimes with and sometimes without and sometimes contrary to all means, the highest power is to be ascribed to him who ordains and creates all things."[88] He elaborates on the role of miracles in his commentary on John of 1553, showing that our perversity is such that we misjudge the works God does via mediate causes as well as those done without any mediate causes. "For such is our pride that we take no account of anything whose cause is hidden."[89] Human beings like to confine their attention to causes they can perceive and understand. When these causes are present, they veil our eyes to the power of God. If they are absent, we are stunned, and learn nothing from it.

In spite of our ingratitude and blindness, God chooses to work above or apart from the ordinary course of nature in order to awaken our attention to the works of God, and to excite us to gratitude.[90] Even though God's hand guides and governs all events, including those involving mediate causes, God often acts without means, so that the hand hidden in other events might be more clearly perceived. "His hand may be seen with the eyes of faith in the whole course of nature; but, since he stirs up our indifference with miracles, therein it shines forth more conspicuously."[91] The means God uses often act as veils to keep us from seeing the providential care of God in all things, including the creatures God gives us for our sustenance.[92] The miracle of the manna from heaven shows that God can nourish us without any means, so we should not bind God's aid to the instruments God uses to care for us.

The miracles done by God therefore give us a clearer view of the glory of God that should be seen in all events.[93] So, for example, the power of God should be seen in all events of deliverance from captivity and oppression. However, when God uses ordinary means to accomplish this, God's power might be concealed beneath the means used. "But when he sees that this hinders men from beholding his hand, he sometimes works alone, and by evident miracles, that nothing may hinder or obscure the manifestation of power."[94] The same would apply to all the powers of God, according to Calvin. These are clearly portrayed in the works of God as in a painting, but we do not see them as clearly as when they appear in the miracles God performs.[95] The problem is that we might become so accustomed to seeking the demonstration of God's powers in miracles that this blinds us to their manifestation in all the works of God's providence.[96] It seems clear, therefore, that Calvin would have us consider the miracles of God in order to learn that God is not bound to the use of instruments and mediate causes, so that we might behold the powers of God more clearly in the works God does by means of instruments, including the ordinary course of nature.[97]

3. The Church as the Theater of God's Providence

The first major development in Calvin's understanding of providence after 1539 begins to emerge in 1550, in the treatise *Concerning Scandals*. In his treatment of scandals that are intrinsic to the Gospel, Calvin discusses at great length the scandal created by the way the Church appears in history as a weak, small, poor, afflicted, often exiled community, which hardly seems to represent the Kingdom of God on earth. "In the first place, it never shines with that splendor, which would enable the minds of men to recognize the kingdom of God. Secondly, if ever it succeeds in rising to some modest position, soon afterwards it is either crushed by the violence of tyrants or collapses of its own accord, so that that situation lasts only for a short time."[98] Calvin notes that the same could be said of the Church in Israel. "We see the insolent way Cicero scoffs at the law of God, because circumstances were by no means favorable to the Jews."[99] His first response to this scandal is to point out that it is only reasonable that "in the form of the Church the living image of Christ should appear as in a mirror."[100] The life of the Church should mirror the cruciform life of Christ.

However, Calvin is not content to leave matters at this point but rather goes on to insist that "if we were skillful and fair interpreters of the works of God," we would see in the history of the afflicted and seemingly abandoned Church the providential care, preservation, and protection of God.[101] Calvin invites his readers to investigate this matter by examining the historical sources for themselves.[102] To guide this investigation, he summarizes the history of the Church from the time of Seth to his own day, not once, but twice, in order to highlight the manifestation of the providence of God in this history, so that the reader may learn that "the more the Church has been crushed beneath the Cross, the more clearly has the power of God shown itself in raising it up again."[103]

Were we attentive to the providence of God that preserves the Church in affliction and restores the Church when it appears to be destroyed, we would realize that the history of the Church is not a scandal but is rather the theater that most clearly manifests God's providence.[104] The providence of God more clearly appears in the preservation of the poor, small, afflicted Church than it does with regard to the governance of the glorious and powerful earthly kingdoms.[105] Calvin insists the same must be said for the history of the evangelical communities since the emergence of the teaching of Luther in 1520. "Certainly when the ungodly, with their threats and terrorizing and their furious raging, however, do not go so far that the Church of God does not stay firm and erect under the humiliation of the cross, why then do we not give great praise to the glory of God for preserving it so marvelously?"[106]

Calvin had previously linked the providence of God to the care God has for the godly, especially in their afflictions, as one sees in the *Institutes* of 1536 and 1539. "Indeed, the principal purpose of Biblical history is to teach that the Lord watches over the ways of the saints with such great diligence that they do not even stumble over a stone [see Ps. 91:12]."[107] However, the focus before 1550 was on the special care of God for the pious, not on the protection and preservation of the Church throughout history. Once this theme is introduced in *Concerning Scandals*, it becomes the focal point of Calvin's discussion of providence. Thus, in his 1552 treatise, *Concerning the Eternal Predestination of God*, Calvin begins his discussion of providence by highlighting the role of the Church as the theater of God's providence.[108] Calvin uses the Church as the theater of providence to develop a new fourfold distinction to discuss the operation of God's providence. First, God cherishes and nourishes the general government of the world. Second, God governs and cares for all the particular parts of the universe. Third, God demonstrates particular care for the human race, both individually and communally, so that all human events are under a single heavenly control. "Lastly, there is the truly paternal protection with which he guards his Church, to which the most present help of God is attached."[109]

To highlight the importance of this development, one need only look at Calvin's discussions of providence before and after 1550. In his 1545 treatise, *Against the Libertines,* he developed three distinct operations of divine providence: the universal operation sustaining the whole order of nature; the operation of God in all creatures so that they serve God's goodness, righteousness, and judgment to help the faithful and punish the wicked; and the operation of the Holy Spirit governing the lives of the faithful.[110] In contrast, in the final edition of the *Institutes* in 1559, Calvin reiterates the centrality of God's special care for the Church that he first developed in 1550, making it the goal at which God's providence especially aims. "Finally, it strives to the end that God may reveal his concern for the whole human race, but especially his vigilance in ruling the church, which he deigns to watch more closely."[111]

In his commentaries after 1552, Calvin continues to develop the theme of the Church as the theater of God's providence, in the context of God's special care for all human beings. In his Genesis commentary of 1554, Calvin establishes the relationship between God's special care for human beings and their creation in the image and likeness of God.[112] Calvin appeals to the image of God in humanity to make an argument from the lesser to the greater. If God cares for the beasts and other creatures by God's providence, how much more will God care for those created in the image of God, who are thereby closer to God?[113] Even though our sins keep the favor of God from flowing as freely towards us as it ought, the goodness of God is nonetheless shown towards all, no matter how sinful they might be. "In particular mankind as a whole is evidence that the benefits of God, in which he is seen to be our Father, never cease."[114]

The special care of God for human beings means that one cannot limit the goodness God manifests in this life to the godly, for it is shown universally to all, even to the reprobate.[115] Such divine generosity not only reveals the care of God for all created in God's image, but it also creates a pastoral problem for the godly that Calvin will try to address, namely, that it often seems that God is more generous in this life to the ungodly than to the godly.[116] The very goodness of God that reveals God's care for all created in the image of God also has the effect of hiding the judgment of God that distinguishes between the godly and the ungodly, although some signs of this judgment emerge in history. The goodness of God manifested to all people creates a pastoral crisis among the godly that Calvin will increasingly address in his writings on providence after 1550. How can God be said to care in particular for the Church, when it is more often than not in much worse shape than the ungodly world that surrounds it, and that often persecutes it?

One way in which Calvin attempts to address this question is to argue again from the lesser to the greater. If God cares for those created in God's image more than all other living things, how much more should God care for those whom God has adopted as God's children in the Church? According to Calvin, the same powers that are manifested in the works of God in the theater of the universe are especially displayed in God's providential care for the Church throughout history, revealing the special care of God for the Church. "The powers of God are to be seen more conspicuously in the Church than in the constitution of the world at large."[117] Calvin makes the same point in the final edition of the *Institutes,* when speaking of the special care of God.[118] For this reason, the godly have two reasons to praise God: "first, for the display of his power, goodness, wisdom, and other powers in the common government of the world, and in the several parts of it, the heavens and the earth, but more particularly for his special goodness in cherishing and defending the Church, which he has chosen of his free grace, in restoring it when fallen down, and gathering it when dispersed."[119]

The powers of God manifested in the care and protection of the Church therefore make the Church a very prominent part of the theater of God's glory in the universe, to which special attention should be paid. "The whole world is a theater for the display of the divine goodness, wisdom, justice, and power, but the Church is the orchestra, as it were—the most conspicuous part of it."[120] However, Calvin will go beyond this description, as we have seen above, and claim that the Church is itself the principal theater in which the powers of God are displayed before us.[121] Since the Church is the primary theater of God's glory, God's preservation and care of the Church is central to God's governance of the universe. "In fine, the prophet concludes that the whole course of nature would be subverted, unless God saved his Church."[122] This is especially true since the primary task of the Church is to praise the very powers that are revealed both in the theater of the universe and in the theater of the Church. God upholds and preserves the Church in every age "that he may never leave himself without some to testify and declare his justice, goodness, and mercy."[123] One can see in this discussion a major reason for the publication of Calvin's commentaries on the Old Testament. The godly are to contemplate the powers of God manifested in the whole history of the Church, from the time of Seth to the present day. The history of Israel constitutes a major portion of that history, and must therefore be contemplated by the godly in order that they might come to know the way God cares for and governs the Church in every age, including their own.[124]

If the Church is both the orchestra in the theater and the theater itself, then the care and protection of the Church by God cannot be something entirely concealed, but "is displayed in the existence and protection of the Church, and may there be beheld."[125] The care of God for the Church is so compellingly clear that even the ungodly are compelled to be "eye-witnesses" of the works of God in protecting the Church.[126] God's protection of the Church is especially evident in those events in which it emerges from a situation of distress in which others perish, such as the exodus from Egypt.[127] In like manner, when the people wander about in exile, with no fixed abode, and yet remain in safety, the providence of God is more conspicuous than if they were in well-defended homes.[128] The same may be said of the opposition the people of Israel faced when they attempted to enter the promised land of Canaan. "Ultimately, however, all these violent attempts had no other effect than to make the power of God more manifest, and give brighter displays of mercy and faithfulness in the defense of his chosen people."[129] So also, when ungodly historians narrate events that confirm the prophecy given to the chosen people, Calvin claims that this makes more manifest God's providential care and protection of the Church.[130]

However, Calvin is aware that the history of the Church does not always clearly manifest the care and protection of God, for there are times when the Church is severely oppressed by the ungodly, who themselves seem to luxuriate under the care and protection of God. Such a confused state of affairs forms one of the severest trials of the godly, and frames the context of Calvin's discussion of providence after 1550. "Since the faithful, so long as they pursue their earthly pilgrimage through life, see things strangely confused in this world, unless they assuaged their grief with the hope of a better life, their courage would soon fail them. The more boldly any man despises God, and runs to every excess in wickedness, so much the more happily he seems to live."[131] Such a confusing state of affairs can lead the godly to conclude that there is no providence of God governing the world but rather that all things are subject to the capricious whims of fortune.[132] Although it may appear that Calvin advises the godly to withdraw from all consideration of the present world when confronted with such a trial, he knows that such a solution will not work, because God's protection of the Church must also be manifested in history, or else the purpose of history will fail.[133] The godly who

hope in God's providence must also hope for the manifestation of that providence in the restoration of the afflicted Church.[134] The hope of the godly in
affliction lies in their confidence that the work, which is most proper to God,
is the care and protection of the Church. If that care is absent for a time, they
know it cannot but manifest itself in the future. "Moses, by way of eminence,
prefers before all other proofs of God's power, that care which he exercised
in maintaining the welfare of the people, by which it was his will that he
should be principally known."[135]

God Looks upon Us So That We Might Look to God

Since the providential care of God is especially directed towards the life of
the Church in history, the eyes of the godly are ever intent upon seeing signs
of the favor of God manifested in their lives, by which they might know that
God is with them. "For our happiness consists in this, that we are the objects
of the Divine regard, but we think he is alienated from us, if he does not give
us some substantial evidence of his care for us."[136] According to Calvin, the
godly not only desire to see signs of God's favor but also want to see the face
of God graciously inclined towards them, so that they know that the signs of
God's favor really do reveal the grace of God.[137] We can only be sure of God's
favor towards us if we hold to the promise of God in conjunction with the
signs of God's favor, and vice versa.[138]

Beginning with the Genesis commentary of 1554, Calvin develops a
dynamics of mutual beholding, in which God first looks upon us, so that
we might in turn look upon God. The text that first occasions this idea is the
account of Hagar in the wilderness, in which she is not aware of the presence of God with her, even in her situation of extremity. Thus, when Hagar
names God "the God who sees," Calvin says, "It implied, indeed, a base ingratitude on her part, to be blind to the presence of God; so that even when
she knew he was looking upon her, she did not, in turn, raise her eyes to behold him."[139] According to Calvin, God's regard for us has two levels of
meaning. On the one hand, God looks upon us even when there are no signs
of God's presence or protection. On the other hand, God manifests Godself
to us in the works God does to care for us, so that we may in turn behold
God. "The former has precedence in order; namely, that God, by his secret
providence, directs and ordains what is best for us; but on this the latter is
suspended, namely, that he stretches out his hand to us, and renders himself

visible by true experimental tokens."[140] When God makes Godself visible to us in our experience of God's help, we should in our turn look upon God, so that we may be cheered and comforted.[141]

Even though the faithful can only see God when God becomes visible in their experience of God's presence and help, Calvin wants the faithful to turn their eyes to God even when God appears to be hidden and far off. "Now, we think that he is absent, when we do not perceive his present aid, and when he does not immediately supply our wants."[142] If we do not look to God in such times of God's absence, our present experience will leave us bewildered and without hope. We must therefore turn our eyes to God on high, in the hope that though all things are changed on earth, God always remains the same.[143] Since God ever remains the same, we look to God in the hope that God will again manifest Godself by helping the Church in its adversities. Thus during the Babylonian exile God seemed to have hidden from the Jews, until God again restored the people and exhibited Godself to be their Father. "For though the Lord ever looks on us, we, on the other hand, do not see him, nay, we think that he is far from us. But he then only appears to us, when we perceive that he cares for our salvation."[144]

In his 1557 commentary on the Psalms, Calvin begins to contrast the way the godly look to God alone for help with the way the ungodly look all around them for the means to save themselves and secure their own lives.[145] The godly, on the other hand, always direct their eyes to God alone, and seek all their help from God. "As God prevents his believing people with his blessings, and meets them of his own accord, so they, on their part, immediately cast their eyes directly upon him."[146] Calvin is aware that whenever the godly experience any affliction, their first impulse is not to look to God but rather to look all about themselves for help and succor. However, in spite of their weakness, their faith should direct their gaze back to God.[147] In spite of their weakness and infirmity, whenever the godly are afflicted or oppressed, they should turn their eyes to God alone, and not to their circumstances, knowing that God's providence is sufficient to take care of them even in the absence of all earthly assistance. Thus, when Isaiah says, "I looked, and there was none to help" (Isa. 63:5), Calvin says, "He shows, therefore, that from God alone they ought to expect salvation, that they may not gaze around in every direction, but have their eyes fixed on God, who has no need of the assistance of others."[148]

Looking to the Heavenly Throne of God

Calvin wanted the faithful to look to God not only for their help and protection in this world but also for the establishment of justice on earth. One of the major effects of linking the providence of God with the care and protection of the Church throughout history was to highlight the injustice of the affliction of the Church at the hands of the ungodly. If God is the governor of the universe and the protector of the Church, why does God lavish so many gifts upon the enemies of the Church, so that they have the power repeatedly to bring the Church into captivity, and at times to appear to destroy it? Where is the justice of God in the history of the Church, if the ungodly are rewarded in this life while the godly are afflicted?

Calvin first develops his response to these questions in light of the dialogue Abraham has with God over the immanent destruction of Sodom and Gomorrah, when Abraham asks God, "Shall not the Judge of all the earth do what is just?" (Gen. 18:25). No matter how confusing the works of God in human history may appear, we, like Abraham, can never lose our firm confidence in the justice of God, even if that justice does not immediately appear to us in God's works.[149] Convinced of the justice of God, the faithful will wait for the time when the hidden justice of God will manifest itself again in history, which alone can solve the contradiction they experience between the righteousness of God and the works of God. "God, when he interposed to restore the condition of his people, would bring forth openly to light his justice which had lain concealed; by which we are not to understand that he ever deviates the least in his providence from the strictest rectitude, only that there is not always that harmony and arrangement which might make his righteousness apparent to man's view."[150]

We can clearly see why Calvin in 1552 so categorically rejects the late scholastic definition of the absolute power of God. Just as he insists in 1539 that God's power can never be separated from God's wisdom, so now in light of God's dealings with the Church he insists that God's power can never be separated from God's justice.[151] For Calvin, the thought of God's power alone is terrifying, but when seen in the service of God's justice, it is alluringly beautiful.[152] We should also remember to combine the justice of God with the wisdom of God, which directs all things to their proper end, so that we see the power, wisdom, and justice of God working together in providence. "So must we infer that, while the disturbances in the world deprive us of judgment, God out of the pure light of his justice and wisdom tempers and directs these very movements in the best-conceived order to a right end."[153]

In his commentary on Psalms of 1557, Calvin expands on his understanding of the justice of God by encouraging the faithful to look to the throne of God when they do not perceive the justice of God in God's works. According to this metaphor, God sits enthroned in heaven as the Judge and governor of the world, and so beholds from on high all that is done here below. When all seems to be confused, and the Church seems near to destruction, the godly are to turn their eyes to the throne of God in the expectation that God now sees, and will therefore one day act.[154] By turning our eyes to the heavenly throne of God, we remind ourselves of God's justice, which now remains hidden, and thereby gain patience. Since nothing is hidden from the eyes of God, God's restoration of order will come in due time.[155] In particular, the godly console themselves with the awareness that God can never be blind to their misery and affliction, nor can God allow the wicked to escape with impunity for what they are doing to the godly.[156]

When we turn our eyes to the heavenly throne of God, our awareness of God's justice becomes so great that we can already see the defeat of the enemies of the Church, even though they appear on earth to be triumphing over us; for it is impossible for God to behold their iniquity, and the misery of the Church, without acting in righteousness.[157] The expectation of the godly that God will soon act to deliver them is in stark contrast to the ungodly, who think that the hiddenness of God's judgments on behalf of the Church mean that God lacks all judgment.[158] However, Calvin is clearly aware of the pain and anguish caused in the godly by the apparent triumph of the wicked over them, and does not at all underestimate the passionate longing they feel for the time when God would in justice restore order out of the chaos they experience. Thus, when the psalmist speaks of the day when the righteous will show that the Lord is upright (Ps. 92:15), Calvin says that his goal is "to allay that disquietude of mind which we are apt to feel under the disorder which reigns apparently in the affairs of the world; and to make us cherish the expectation (under all that may seem severe and trying in our lot, and though the wicked are in wealth and power, flourish, and abound in places and distinctions) that God will bring light and order eventually out of confusion."[159]

When God does act in judgment on behalf of the Church, Scripture describes this as God seeing with God's own eyes (Zech. 9:8); not that God did not see before, but because God's vision is hidden from us until it is manifested in God's works of justice. Even the godly experience the absence of justice as an indication that God does not see, in spite of their looking to the heavenly throne of God during such times. "The Jews indeed thought that they were neglected by him; for the Scripture everywhere says, that God closes his eyes, is asleep, lies down, forgets, cares not, when he hides himself and appears not as the avenger of wrongs."[160] On the other hand, God "is rightly said to see what he begins to call to judgment."[161] In a similar manner, even though the godly look to the heavenly throne of God when God's justice is hidden on earth, Scripture also describes God as ascending his throne when God acts on behalf of the Church.[162] When God does reveal God's care for the Church, the godly can perceive the judgments of God much more clearly in contrast to the darkness that surrounded them when God's justice appeared to be absent.[163] Moreover, the judgments of God against the ungodly reveal much more clearly the glory of God, which is disclosed as much by God's acts of judgment as it is by God's works of mercy.[164]

Signs of God's Judgments in This Life

Although Calvin admits that there are times when the justice of God appears to be entirely hidden, especially when the ungodly afflict the godly with apparent impunity, he was also concerned to direct the eyes of the godly not only to the hidden heavenly throne of God but also to the signs of God's righteous judgment that always appear in this life, if we have the eyes to see them.[165] Calvin is not satisfied in saying that the justice of God is entirely hidden, any more than he is content to say that it is always clearly manifested. In spite of the hiddenness of God's judgments, which will only be clearly manifested on the Last Day, Calvin directs the pious to attend to the signs of God's judgments that they can see in history and in their own day. "And as God never ceases, even in the midst of the greatest darkness, to give some tokens of his providence, it is inexcusable not to attend to them."[166]

One reason people do not discern the signs of God's judgments is that they do not look upon themselves to attain an awareness of their sin. According to Calvin, we do not see God's justice in the world because we would rather not be held accountable to God for our actions.[167] The godly discern more clearly the signs of God's judgment because their consciences have been awakened to their sin. However, it is necessary to look not only into ourselves but also to God when the justice of God appears to us, for we must acknowledge that the hand of God lies behind the punishments that come to us. "We know that the great majority of men are blinded under the judgments of God, and imagine that they are entirely the events of chance; and hardly one in a hundred discerns in them the hand of God."[168]

Beginning in the Psalm commentary of 1557, Calvin claims that we only truly profit from the signs of God's judgment if we follow Isaiah's advice to look to the hand of God even when it is striking us (Isa. 9:13). "As every chastisement of God should remind us of God's judgment, the true wisdom of the saints, as the prophet declares, Isaiah 9:13, is, 'to look to the hand of him who smiteth.'"[169] Calvin sees an example of such wisdom in Nebuchadnezzar, who is said to have raised his eyes to heaven after he was afflicted by God for his pride (Dan. 4:34). "Meanwhile, he did not raise his eyes until God drew him to himself. God's chastisements do not profit us unless they work inwardly by his Spirit."[170] Those who are blind to the signs of God's judgment, on the other hand, lack this kind of wisdom, and so never look to the hand that smites them.[171]

Calvin thought that one way to train the eyes of faith to see the judgments of God was to meditate more seriously on the judgments of God as portrayed in Scripture, so that we might be able to see the same judgments taking place in our own lives. For instance, Scripture often describes the way the plans of the wicked against the pious recoil on their own heads, yet we do not pay any attention to this, even though it happens in our own experience.[172] Scripture also describes events in which the wicked are suddenly destroyed, which we would see in our own day if we did not forget them. "Those judgments which are so evident that none can miss to observe them without shutting his eyes, we sinfully allow to pass into oblivion; so that we need to be brought daily into that theater where we are compelled to see the divine hand."[173] The same may be said for the way Scripture describes the judgment of God on the mad ambition of rulers, whose plans and kingdoms are overthrown in an instant, as happened to Alexander the Great. "These things are plainly before our eyes, and yet we do not apply our mind to the consideration of them."[174]

In order to train the eyes of faith to see the judgments of God, Calvin points out to his readers the signs of judgment he sees in his own day that mirror judgments in Scripture, so that they might be attentive to their own experiences of the same. Thus, when commenting on the way the Lord threatens to hurl Shebna out of the land for presumptuously building a conspicuous tomb for himself, Calvin points to a similar incident in his own day.[175] Thomas More had a tomb made for himself on which he celebrated his persecution of the evangelicals, and had this epitaph sent to Basel for the approval of Erasmus. "What happened? He was accused of treason, condemned, and beheaded; and thus he had a gibbet for his tomb. Do we ask more manifest judgments of God, by which he punishes the pride, the unbounded eagerness for renown, and the blasphemous vaunting, of wicked men?"[176] On the other hand, when Isaiah speaks of the removal of the righteous and devout as a sign of the great wrath that is coming, Calvin applies this to the death of Luther, which occurred just before the defeat of the evangelical forces in the Smalkaldic War.[177] In spite of the confusion that surrounds them, the pious are given the eyes of faith by which to discern signs of the hidden judgment of God. We ought to meditate on the signs of judgment in Scripture so that we might discern the same signs in our own day and not allow the confusion of our experience to call into question the justice of God.[178]

Standing on the Watchtower

Calvin was well aware of the difficulties confronting the pious with regard to the hiddenness of God's care for the Church. Even though Calvin was convinced that the godly could see signs of God's judgment in their own lives, he was also aware that the Church of his day was sorely afflicted, and that it paled in comparison to the power and glory of the Roman Church. Calvin was therefore increasingly interested in developing strategies to help members of the afflicted Church maintain their hope in God's care and protection in spite of the fact that they appeared to be defenseless before the power of their adversaries. Beginning in his 1552 treatise on predestination, Calvin appealed to the image used by Habakkuk when he was awaiting the answer from the Lord concerning his complaint of the apparent injustice of his day. "I will stand at my watchpost, and station myself on the rampart; I will keep watch to see what he will say to me, and what he will answer concerning my complaint" (Hab. 2:1). Calvin uses this image to describe the way Scripture gives us the proper vantage point from which to view the often perplexing and even dismaying works of God. "But because of the dense darkness of the human mind by which all knowledge is rendered thin and perishable, Scripture builds for us a higher watchtower from which to observe God overruling all the works of men so as to direct them to the end appointed by him."[179] Scripture allows us to see the works of God in the proper way by elevating us above the world, so that we might get a broader view of the providence of God, and begin to see the way the works of God are directed to a specific end, including the protection and care of the Church.

The need to ascend the watchtower in times of affliction and confusion can be seen in the life of David, who at one point in his life almost stumbled out of envy for the prosperity of the wicked, in comparison to the afflictions of the godly. "David, having now gone through his conflicts, begins, if we may use the expression, to be a new man; and he speaks with a quiet and composed mind, being, as it were, elevated on a watchtower."[180] When David ascends the watchtower, he sees that although the lives of the ungodly appear for a time to be prosperous, they ultimately end very badly, as appointed by the providence of God. Calvin thinks the godly should do the same thing when confronted with the distressing contrast between the present appearance of the Church and the promises of God regarding its glorious restitution. "Although, therefore, nothing appeared to the eye of sense and reason, calculated greatly to rejoice the heart, yet the prophet would have them encouraged by the word to stand as it were on the watchtower, waiting patiently for the fulfillment of what God had promised."[181]

According to Calvin, the watchtower elevates us closer to God, so that we begin to see events in the way that God perceives them, "by the light of the Holy Spirit."[182] What this means specifically is that the prophet withdraws from the world to the "recess of the mind," which is the meaning of the watchtower. The ladder by which one ascends the watchtower is the Word of God.[183] When we ascend to the recess of the mind by the ladder of the Word, we begin to see events from the perspective of the wisdom and promises of God and not from the confusion that immediately presents itself to our view. We thereby attain both patience and hope, knowing that the truth of God cannot fail, and that God will one day perform by God's power what God has promised in God's Word. In the meantime, we are exhorted to be constant in our watching, for there is much that will continue to perplex and dismay us. "It thus happens, that all our observations become evanescent, except we continue to watch, that is, except we persevere in our attention, so that we may ever return to God, whenever the devil raises new storms, and whenever he darkens the heavens with clouds to prevent us to see God."[184]

Connecting the End with the Beginning

One of the benefits of viewing the works of God from the elevated platform of the watchtower is that it allows us to see the way the end of the work of God corresponds with the beginning, an idea Calvin first develops in his Genesis commentary. The problem with our carnal judgments of God's works is that they are precipitous, drawing conclusions in the midst of the work that thereby miss the goal towards which the wisdom of God is guiding all things. "Though, therefore, the providence of God is in itself a labyrinth; yet when we connect the issue of things with their beginning, that admirable method of operation shines clearly in our view, which is not generally acknowledged, only because it is far removed from our observation."[185] The locus classicus for this perspective on the works of God's providence occurs in the Joseph narrative in Genesis. Calvin encourages his readers to meditate on this narrative in particular, for it reveals that no matter how perplexing the providence of God may be at any given time, out of all the confusion it elegantly links the end with the beginning, and thereby displays the previously hidden wisdom of God.[186]

Other events in the history of Israel reveal the same dynamic, in which the end or issue of the work of God reveals that God was governing events all along. For instance, when Moses is handed over to Pharaoh's daughter to be raised as her son, it might appear that this would be an insurmountable obstacle to the redemption of the Israelites, "but thus the providence of God, the more circuitously it appears to flow, shines forth all the more wonderfully in the end, since it never really wanders from its direct object, or fails of its effect, when its due time is come."[187] Calvin sees another example of this dynamic in the allotment of the lands of Israel to the different clans by the casting of lots. In spite of the apparently random and contingent nature of this allotment, Jacob received the land promised to him in the book of Genesis, one rich in vines and pastures.[188]

The pious should use these examples to learn to judge events in their own lives from the end or issue of them, as Calvin notes in the final edition of the *Institutes*. "It is, indeed, true that if we had quiet and composed minds ready to learn, the final outcome (*exitu*) would show that God always has the best reason for his plan."[189] Thus when the godly are perplexed and oppressed by the apparent prosperity of the wicked, they should look to the end of such lives, which will reveal their true meaning.[190] The same must be said of the prosperity of the pious: they are to wait for the end or issue of things to see the favor of God in their success.[191] Finally, the pious must learn to see the whole life of the Church in light of the end or issue towards which God is directing it, in light of their awareness of God's wisdom and goodness.[192] By exercising patience, and by taking the longer perspective afforded by the altitude of the watchtower, the pious can see the end or issue to which God is directing their lives, the lives of the wicked, and the history of the Church, and thereby have hope.

Contemplating the Nature of God

The way the end of God's providential works corresponds with their beginning reveals the constancy and consistency of God. Even though God appears to take a confusing and almost self-defeating path, the end will always reveal that God was governing all things to their end all along. The constancy of God is in turn based in the nature and essence of God, so that the works of God's providence are an expression of God's essential nature. The godly should turn their eyes and minds to the contemplation of God's nature when they cannot see the end or issue of events, but all seems to be dark and confusing to them. Calvin begins to develop this theme in his comments on Psalm 77, which he claims was dictated by the Holy Spirit as a form of prayer for the Church in all her afflictions, not limited to one author or one age.[193] The afflictions of the Church cause the psalmist to raise radical questions about the discontinuity between the nature of God and the works of God he is experiencing. "Will the Lord cast off forever? And will he be favorable no more? Is his mercy gone forever?" (Ps. 77:7–8). According to Calvin, these are not accusations or reproaches hurled against God but rather are forms of deliberation within the psalmist, by which he directs himself to consider the nature of God in the midst of his troubles. "He does not complain or find fault with God, but rather reasoning with himself, concludes from the nature of God, that it is impossible for him not to continue his free favor towards his people, to whom he has once shown himself to be a father."[194] The nature of God is such that once God has manifested God's goodness and mercy to us, God cannot but continue showing such goodness, for it is essential to the nature of God.[195] In spite of all evidence to the contrary from his present experience, the psalmist knows that God's mercy and goodness are essential to God, and as such they must be manifested in the future works of God, or else God would cease being God.[196]

The powers of God that are portrayed in the works of God, and that are felt and enjoyed by the pious, express to us the very nature and essence of God. Once we have come to see, feel, and enjoy those powers in God's works, we should appeal to them in our trials and tribulations, when God seems to hide these powers from our view.[197] The works of God manifest a living image of God, by the powers that shine forth in God's works.[198] Since God is eternal and self-sufficient, the powers of God are also eternal and abiding, as they are essential to God. We need to turn our eyes from the trying and confusing appearance of the world to these powers, knowing that they will abide forever. "We ought to contemplate the nature of God; for as soon as we turn aside from beholding it, nothing is seen but what is fleeting, and then we immediately faint. Thus ought faith to rise above the world by continual advances; for neither the truth nor the justice, nor the goodness of God, is temporary and fading, but God always continues to be like himself."[199]

To facilitate their contemplation of the nature of God, Calvin directs his readers to the Name of God as it was revealed to Moses on Mount Sinai (Exod. 34:6–7). Calvin thought that the Name of God was itself a living image of the nature of God, rooted in the vision of God vouchsafed to Moses.[200] The Name "clearly and intimately expresses the nature of God," and is understandably given a central place in the way the Jews describe the nature of God.[201] "The passage is taken from Exodus 34, where is described that remarkable and memorable vision, in which God offered to Moses a view of himself; and there was then exhibited to the holy prophet, as it were, a living representation of God; and there is no passage in the Law which expresses God's nature more to the life."[202] The Name of God therefore sets before the godly in a vivid and intimate way the nature of God that is also expressed in the powers of God revealed in God's works.[203] The godly can therefore appeal to the Name whenever God seems to act in ways that appear to be contrary to God's nature, in the hope and confidence that God will again act in ways that correspond to God's nature.[204] Calvin sees this appeal occurring frequently in the psalms. When the godly cry out, "Will you be angry with us forever?" (Ps. 85:5), Calvin interprets this cry as an appeal to the Name of God, which reveals the nature of God.[205] He encourages the faithful to appeal to the nature of God as revealed in the Name whenever God acts in a way that seems to contradict this depiction of God's nature.[206]

When dealing with their affliction, Calvin directs the godly to the consideration and contemplation of the mercy, goodness, and love of God, more than to God's justice. When David calls upon God "out of the depths," he strengthens himself by considering the mercy that is essential to the nature of God.[207] The same may be said of the goodness of God, to which David turns when he walks in the midst of troubles and experiences the wrath of his enemies. "Having once been delivered by an act of Divine mercy, he concludes that what had been done would be perfected, as God's nature is unchangeable, and he cannot divest himself of that goodness which belongs to him."[208]

The godly should consider the powers of God not only in their own experience but also in the history of the Church; for as God has delivered the Church in the past, so God will deliver the Church in the future. "We may not doubt that God, who always continues to be like himself, and never degenerates from his nature or swerves from his purpose, will also be our deliverer; for such have believers found him to be."[209] The life of the Church reveals the harmony and correspondence between the truth and the justice of God, by the way God acts in correspondence with what God promises.[210] The same may be said of God's power and kindness. Even though these powers may at the present time be concealed from our view, we can see them in the relationship of God with the Church in the past, and therefore have hope that God will continue to manifest these powers in the Church in the future, "for God never ceases to care about his people, since he governs unceasingly every part of the world."[211]

The pious also know that it is essential to God to act with justice, which means to protect the Church from the wicked, and to punish the wicked for their insolence. "When anyone takes away these things from God, he leaves him an idol."[212] The godly therefore know that it is essential to the nature of God that God punishes them for their own sins, the knowledge of which leads them to anticipate the judgment of God by judging themselves. "It is necessary that he should punish sins or be displeased with us; but, as it has been said, he cannot be inconsistent with himself or dissimilar in his nature, since no change can take place in him."[213] However, the pious also know that the justice and punishment of God cannot obliterate God's mercy; and so if they submit to the judgment and punishment of God, they may then with confidence turn to the mercy which is also essential to God. This is why the prophet has hope that God will not reject the Church forever, even though the pious are languishing in Babylon after the destruction of Jerusalem, "for otherwise his mercy would be obliterated, yes, that mercy which is inseparable from his eternal essence and divinity."[214]

Because the mercy of God is essential to the nature of God, the pious know that God will hear their prayers as they cry out to God in their distress, including such distress as has been brought on by their own sins. Thus, when Daniel prays to God from Babylon for the redemption of Jerusalem and the restoration of the Church, he strengthens himself by appealing to the nature of God itself. "He argues thus, To God belong loving-kindness; therefore, as he can never deny himself, he will always be merciful."[215] Indeed, because of the love and mercy of God, Calvin goes so far as to claim that it is essential to the nature of God to hear prayer. The godly should therefore never cease calling upon God even when God does not appear to hear, for God cannot be deaf to our cries without ceasing to be God. "When God claims to himself this prerogative, that he answers prayers, he intimates that it is what cannot be separated from his eternal essence and divinity; that is, that he is ready to hear prayer."[216]

If it is the nature of God to hear the prayers of the afflicted, even when they are being punished for their sins, then it must be the case that although the pious know God to be powerful, just, true, and wise, the heart of their knowledge of God lies in their awareness of the goodness of God. Not even the majestic glory and transcendence of God can undermine their awareness of the goodness and mercy of God. "The amount is, that God's dwelling above the heavens, at such a distance from us, does not prevent him from showing himself to be near at hand, and plainly providing for our welfare."[217] The godly are not to ignore the majesty of God but ought to hold the goodness and majesty of God together, so that they might rightly appreciate the wonderful condescension of God's mercy.[218] Indeed, the glory of God is primarily the manifestation of the goodness of God, which constitutes the very beauty of God, for God "would have the splendor and beauty of his character manifested in dealing bountifully with us, as if his beauty is obscured when he ceases to do good."[219]

Ultimately, then, the hope of the pious that God will continue to care for, protect, and restore the Church, lies in their confidence that it is the very nature of God that comes to expression in God's care of the Church. Over and above every other work of God's providential rule, the care of the Church is the proper work of God.[220] This care may at times be hidden under a darkness that threatens to reduce the godly to despair. However, the pious console themselves with a knowledge that is more certain than their experience of affliction, namely, that God can no more cease caring for the Church, and manifesting that care in history, than God can cease to be God.

PART II

The Living Images of God the Redeemer

CHAPTER 4

The Manifestation of Christ in the Law and in the Gospel

The self-manifestation of God by the powers portrayed in the universe and in human history would have been sufficient not only to reveal God to humanity but also to lead humanity from this life to eternal life with God. The problem, as noted in chapter 2, is that human beings no longer manifest the powers of God the way they were created to manifest in Adam. Rather, due to the sin of Adam, they are now destitute of the good things that God had bestowed on them, and are now filled with every evil that opposes these good things. "For this reason, he went down in ruin and lost all the dignity and superiority of the state in which he was first created; he was despoiled and divested of all his glory and deprived of all the gifts that were his."[1] God can no longer recognize God's image and likeness in us so that we might inherit eternal life in enjoyment of the face-to-face vision of God. "Therefore, seeing that God's image and likeness was thus defaced, and man was without the graces which God in his goodness had bestowed upon him, God began to hold man in abhorrence and disavowed him as his handiwork."[2]

The defacing of the image and likeness of God in humanity means that if humanity is again to be reconciled to God, and to inherit eternal life, God must manifest Godself in another image over and above the living image of

God in the universe. According to Calvin, this reconciling and reuniting image of God is to be found in Jesus Christ alone. "In short, if we have Jesus Christ with us, we shall come upon nothing so accursed that he will not turn it into a blessing; nothing so execrable that it shall not be made holy; nothing so evil that it shall not turn into our good."[3] In Jesus Christ alone, every evil we have brought on ourselves is removed, and every good thing we need to be reunited with God is restored. "It follows that every good thing we could think or desire is to be found in this same Jesus Christ alone. . . . In short, mercy has swallowed up all misery, and goodness all misfortune."[4] This theme emerges in the very first writing from Calvin's pen as an evangelical, and remains central to his message for the rest of his life.

Christ as the living icon of God is discussed more fully in chapter 9. For now, it is important to highlight that for Calvin Jesus Christ is manifested to us both by the Law and by the Gospel. From the very beginning of his theological career, Calvin insisted that the living image of God in Christ had to be sought from both sources, for the Christ whom the apostles proclaim was the one foretold by the Law and the prophets. "Therefore, when you hear that the gospel presents you Jesus Christ in whom all the promises and gifts of God have been accomplished . . . as it was foretold in the Law and to the Prophets—it ought to be most certain and obvious to you that the treasures of Paradise have been opened to you in the gospel."[5] We only have the fountain of every good thing in Jesus Christ when we seek him in both the Law and the Gospel.

However, although Christ manifests himself to us in both the Law and the Gospel, Calvin was also at pains to distinguish between the two, lest the manifestation of Christ to Israel be mistaken for the manifestation of Christ in the Gospel, as Calvin thought had happened in the Roman Church. In the years between 1534 and 1549, Calvin developed a total of nine models by which to distinguish between the Law and the Gospel, according to the differing ways they manifest Christ to us.[6] In what follows, I discuss each model as it arises in Calvin's career and then supplement the discussion of the model with writings from later periods. All nine models trade on visual manifestation for their meaning, each in its distinctive way. We only come to a full understanding of what Calvin meant by the unity and distinction of the Law and the Gospel when we keep in mind all the different ways he related them to each other.

1. The Law Is the Figure of the Truth and the Shadow of the Body

One of the first, and most common, ways Calvin distinguishes between the Law and the Gospel is by means of the description in Colossians of the meaning of ceremonies such as the Sabbath: "These are only a shadow of what is to come, but the substance belongs to Christ" (Col. 2:17). Calvin interprets the distinction between shadow and substance by means of the distinction between figure and reality. "And, God has confirmed his people in every possible way during their long waiting for the great Messiah, by providing them with his written law, containing numerous ceremonies, purifications, and sacrifices, which were but the figures and shadows of the great blessings to come with Christ, who alone was the embodiment and truth of them."[7] The distinction in this case is not between the Law and the Gospel but between the Law and Christ himself. The law is the shadow cast by the coming body of Christ, or the figure of the coming truth in Christ. The metaphor of the shadow and substance seems to echo Plato's image of the cave, in which people first come to know reality by means of the shadows cast on the wall of the cave, only then to see the objects themselves upon their emergence from the cave. Now that the body is here, we would not want to return to the shadow. The distinction between figure and truth seems to trade on a sacramental way of speaking, in which the figure refers one to the reality or truth being figured. Now that the truth is here, we would not want to return to the figures.

Calvin reiterates this model in his interpretation of the Sabbath commandment in the 1536 edition of the *Institutes*. "Therefore at the coming of Christ, who is the light of the shadows and the truth of the figures, it was abolished, like the remaining shadows of the Mosaic Law, as Paul clearly testifies [Gal. 4:8–11; Col. 2:16–17]."[8] In this paraphrase of Colossians 2:17, the Law as shadow is contrasted with Christ as the light, emphasizing the obscurity of the manifestation of the Law, as opposed to the lack of its solidity, as is the case in the contrast between shadow and body. However, in his *Catechism* of 1538, Calvin again returns to the contrast between shadow and body, in conjunction with the parallel contrast between figure and truth, again in conjunction with the interpretation of the Sabbath. "For he is truth at whose presence all figures disappear. He is body at whose advent shadows are left behind. On this account Paul declares that the Sabbath was the shadow of the reality to come."[9] Calvin repeats this description of the Sabbath in the 1539 edition of the *Institutes*.[10] However, he does not use Colossians 2:17 to develop any of the five differences between the Old and New Testaments that he sets forth in this edition of the *Institutes,* primarily because the contrast is not between the Law and the Gospel, but the Law and Christ.

Calvin elaborates on his understanding of the contrast between shadow and body in his commentary on Colossians of 1548. In his exposition, Calvin uses the contrast to highlight the difference between the absence of Christ in the time of the Law and the presence of Christ now. "He frees Christians from the observances of them because they were shadows at a time when Christ was still in a sense absent. For he contrasts shadows with revelation, and absence with manifestation."[11] The shadows of the Law manifest Christ in a way that shows he is yet absent and hidden, as one would be able to judge the coming of a person by the appearance of his or her shadow. The shadow would give an accurate but incomplete manifestation of the person who is still absent, which would pale in comparison to seeing the person for oneself. "Those, therefore, who still adhere to the shadows act like one judging of a man's appearance from his shadow, while he has the man himself before his eyes to look at. For Christ is now manifested to us, and hence we enjoy him as being present."[12]

The shadow and figures point one to the future, when the body and truth itself will appear before our eyes.[13] To return to the shadows and figures after the appearance of Christ would be to act as though Christ were not yet present. "Hence anyone who calls back the ceremonies into use either buries the manifestation of Christ, or robs Christ of his power, and makes him as it were empty."[14] Calvin thus uses Colossians 2:17 both to explain why the Sabbath has been abrogated and to give a warrant for his critique of the redeployment of the ceremonies of the Law in the Roman Church. Calvin reiterates in later commentaries the way the Law shadows forth Christ. Speaking of the way the prophets knew Christ, Calvin says, "They therefore possessed him as one hidden, and as it were absent; I say not in power of grace, but because he was not yet manifested in the flesh."[15] The prophets thus figure Christ in such a way as to reveal that he is yet to come but is not yet present. "The word 'prophesying' is important, because the Law and the prophets did not set God before men's eyes but represented him in figures as absent."[16]

Calvin develops the relationship between the Law as figure and Christ as truth in his commentary on Hebrews of 1549, in a way that makes clear the sacramental understanding lying behind this contrast. Speaking of the way

Hebrews acknowledges that the sacrifices of the Law were in fact efficacious signs, Calvin says, "There occurs often in the writings of Moses this kind of sentence—When a sacrifice has been duly performed iniquity is taken away. This is surely the spiritual teaching of faith. It is so all the more since all sacrifices have this aim in view that they lead to Christ."[17] Since the sacrifices all figure and point to Christ, they are true testimonies of the salvation to be found in Christ. However, Hebrews seems to limit the efficacy of the sacrifices of the Law to the cleansing of the flesh. Calvin explains this as being a sacramental way of speaking.[18] Since the efficacy of the signs of the Law come from the reality they figure, it is only to be expected that once the reality appears, it will have much greater efficacy than did the signs that manifested its coming. "The argument is from the signs to the thing signified because the effect preceded by a long way the reality of the signs."[19]

Once the reality of the signs and the truth of the figures appear, the ceremonies that testified of Christ's coming, and that offered the effect of his appearing, will necessarily come to an end, according to Calvin.[20] Calvin underscores this point in his commentary on John of 1552, by interpreting the words of Jesus from the cross, "It is finished" (John 19:30), to mean that the ceremonies of the Law have come to an end with the coming of the truth of the sacrifices in his death. "To this doctrine is attached the abolition of all the rites of the Law. For it would be perverse to pursue shadows when we have the body in Christ."[21] Far from undermining the meaning and efficacy of the rites and ceremonies of the Law, Calvin claims that their abolition at the coming of Christ confirms their veracity.[22]

The cessation of the use of the ceremonies of the Law does not mean that they have no meaning for the Christian community, and can therefore be safely ignored. Since the figures represent Christ and the meaning of his presence, they should still be considered carefully by Christians in order to come to a fuller understanding of the manifestation of Christ in the flesh. Thus, when the author of 1 Peter compares the blood of Christ with that of a lamb to be sacrificed, Calvin says, "Although the rite of sacrificing is abolished, it yet greatly assists our faith to compare the reality with the types, so that we may seek in the one what the other contains."[23] Calvin makes the same point when coming across the description of Christ in 1 John that speaks of him as coming with the water and the blood. Calvin takes this to be an allusion to the rites of the Law, which we should consult not only to see how Christ is the reality that they figure but also to learn from them the riches that are to be sought in Christ.[24] The abundant variety and richness of ceremonies in the Law means that they can vastly enhance our understanding of the coming of the one who fulfills them, even as their use comes to an end by his appearing among us.

However, one must always remember that the ceremonies are figures and shadows compared to the truth and body of Christ, so that one does not bring them back into the Church after the time appropriate to their use has come to an end. "We can ascribe to this ignorance the huge mass of ceremonies with which the Church under the Papacy has been buried."[25] Calvin became convinced that this was the way the Church fathers behaved, leading to the creation of the sacrifice of the Mass. "The Jews had their sacrifices; and therefore, that Christians might also not be without a show, the rite of sacrificing Christ was invented. As if the state of the Christian Church would be any worse if all the shadows should pass away that obscure the brightness of Christ."[26]

2. PHYSICAL SYMBOLS OF THE SPIRITUAL GIFTS PLAINLY REVEALED IN THE GOSPEL

The second distinction Calvin develops between the Law and the Gospel has to do with the nature of the symbols of the Law in comparison with the reality that they represent. The symbols of the Law are earthly and temporal, whereas the blessings of Christ are spiritual and eternal. This does not mean that the Israelites only hoped in earthly blessings, whereas Christians hope for eternal blessings, for this would create an insurmountable division between Israel and Christ, and would undermine the ability of the Law to shadow forth and figure Christ. Rather, the earthly symbols of the Law represent in corporeal ways the spiritual blessings of God in Christ. Calvin makes this point in the *Psychopannychia* of 1534/36, when speaking of Ezekiel's description of the Spirit of God as a wind. "In both passages we see examples of what is ever occurring in the Prophets, who figure spiritual things too high for human sense by corporeal and visible symbols."[27] The prophets use bodily symbols to create iconic images of spiritual realities that cannot otherwise be expressed. According to Calvin, one must not take such images literally but rather attend to the similitude between the corporeal images and the spiritual realities they represent.

The relationship between corporeal symbol and spiritual reality became especially acute for Calvin in his engagement with Anabaptists in the 1539 edition of the *Institutes*. He developed an entire chapter to address the similarity and difference of the Old and New Testaments, with the focal point of his discussion being the relationship between the corporeal images of the Old Testament and the spiritual realities attested in the New Testament. According to Calvin, the Anabaptists take the symbols of the Law literally, and thereby misunderstand them, making the Israelites no better than animals, and severing them from the covenant made in Christ.[28] To counter this description of the Israelites, Calvin shows from the narratives of the Old Testament itself that the fathers under the Law did not look to the earth for their happiness, for they were more often than not miserable in this life. Rather, they looked directly to God as being the goal of their hope, according to God's promise to be their God.[29] Calvin acknowledges that God does set before the fathers earthly images of the happiness they could have only in God, but this was done not to keep the minds of the people on earth but rather to raise them up to the spiritual life. "But they painted a portrait such as to lift up the minds of the people above the earth, above the elements of this world and the perishing age, and that would of necessity arouse them to ponder the happiness of the spiritual life to come."[30] Calvin considers this the key that his readers should use to discern the proper relationship between the Old and New Testaments.

Not surprisingly, Calvin makes this distinction the first of the five differences he develops between the Old and New Testaments in the 1539 *Institutes*. "Now this is the first difference: the Lord of old willed that his people direct and elevate their minds to the heavenly heritage; yet, to nourish them better in this hope, he displayed it for them to see and, so to speak, taste, under earthly benefits. But now that the gospel has more plainly and clearly revealed the grace of the future life, the Lord leads our minds to meditate upon it directly, laying aside the lower mode of training that he used with the Israelites."[31] The relationship between the figures of the Law and the reality of Christ emphasizes the analogy between the signs and the thing signified, whereas the corporeal nature of the symbols of the Law in relation to Christ makes necessary an anagogic elevation from the corporeal and temporal to the spiritual and eternal. Calvin claims that the scriptural warrant for this interpretation is found in Galatians 4:1–2, in which Paul speaks of the law as the tutor of children. The corporeal nature of the symbols of the Law is adapted to the capacities of human beings as they had developed by the time of the fathers.[32]

Chief among the earthly promises of the Law was the land of Canaan. Calvin claims that the Israelites never confined their hopes to the land, but saw the land as a symbol of God's love and favor towards them, thereby elevating their minds and hearts from the earthly symbol to God. "Thus Abraham is not allowed to sit idly by when he receives the promise of the land, but his mind is elevated to the Lord by a greater promise."[33] The saints in their childhood beheld the love of God in the symbol and type of the land, but elevated themselves from that type and symbol to God, who was experienced as their real blessing.

Calvin reinforces the anagogic relationship between the earthly symbols and the heavenly inheritance in his commentary on Genesis of 1554, by speaking of the earthly blessings as helps and steps by which the Israelites might rise to the heavenly inheritance. "Thus he appointed the land of Canaan as a mirror and pledge to them of the celestial inheritance [so that] being aided by such helps, according to the time in which they lived, they might by degrees (*per gradus*) rise towards heaven."[34] Thus, when Jeremiah promises those about to go into exile in Babylon that God would once again give them wine, oil, and wheat, Calvin claims that "something better and more excellent than food and sufficiency is promised; and that what is spiritual is conveyed under these figures, that the people might, by degrees (*per gradus*), ascend to the spiritual kingdom of Christ, which was yet involved in shadows and obscurity."[35]

God's accommodation to the childlike capacities of humanity at the time of the Israelites also accounts for the way both the love and the wrath of God were manifested to the Israelites primarily through earthly symbols and signs.[36] Those who interpret the comparative lack of earthly blessings and punishments in the Gospel as indicating a change in God, such as the Manichaeans, do not understand the nature of God's accommodation to the capacities of human beings. The change took place not in God but in the developing capacities of the Church as it progressed from childhood to adolescence. Calvin reinforces this point in his later commentaries, again taking exception to the Manichaean view that there must have been a change in God between the Old and New Testaments. "But this error springs from gross and disgraceful ignorance; for, by not distinguishing his different modes of dealing, they do not hesitate impiously to cut God himself in two."[37] The difference lies not in God but in the different way God taught the Church before it had been fully educated with regard to the heavenly inheritance.[38] Once the fuller revelation of eternal life is made in the Gospel, God resorts less frequently to external rewards and punishments to reveal God's mercy and wrath.[39]

In spite of the different ways God manifests love and favor in the Law and in the Gospel, Calvin does acknowledge the continuity between the two forms of manifestation. There was a spiritual dimension to the pedagogy of the Law even as there is a material dimension to the pedagogy of the Gospel. The difference between the two is not qualitative but quantitative: there was more of an emphasis on the material in the Law, without neglecting the spiritual; and more of an emphasis on the spiritual in the Gospel, without neglecting the material. Thus, when the author of Hebrews tells the Church that they "have not come to something that can be touched" (Heb. 12:18), Calvin makes the following qualification. "If anyone objects that there was a spiritual meaning in all former things, and that today we have external exercises of holiness by which we are carried up to heaven, I reply that the apostle is speaking comparatively. . . . There is no doubt that when the Law and the Gospel are contrasted what is spiritual predominates in the latter while earthly symbols are more prominent in the former."[40]

The same might be said of earthly benefits. The Church after Christ enjoys the benefits of this life in a way similar to the Church under the Law, as discussed in chapter 2.[41] However, the Gospel nonetheless calls us directly to eternal life, whereas the Law led Israel to eternal life by the steps of earthly blessings and symbols: "since God has revealed to us the heavenly life in the Gospel, he now calls us directly to it, whereas he led the fathers to it as it were by steps (*per gradus*)." The continuity between the Law and the Gospel lies in the persistence of human childishness in spite of our having matured to adolescence. We still need earthly helps, as did the Israelites, only the helps we now have do not obscure the upward call of the Gospel to eternal life. "There are indeed among us today certain outward exercises of godliness which our childishness needs. But they are moderate and sober enough not to obscure the naked truth of Christ."[42]

3. Glimpsing Christ at Dawn in Distant Shadows; Beholding Christ at Noonday

Calvin wants to hold together two claims with regard to the Law. On the one hand, he insists that the fathers under the Law really did see the same Christ who is now fully exhibited to us in the Gospel. On the other hand, he insists that they saw Christ in a way that revealed to them that he was not yet present, and not yet clearly beheld, but was on his way to approaching them. The third model Calvin develops to relate the Law to the Gospel combines these two concerns by means of the image of seeing a distant figure approaching on a road at early dawn. He first uses this image in the *Psychopannychia* of 1534/36, in his attempt to describe how the fathers were "imprisoned" by their expectation of Christ, following 1 Peter 3:19. "As they saw the light at a distance, under a cloud and shade, (as those who see the remains of the day at late twilight, or who sense the coming day before dawn), and had not yet an exhibition of the divine blessing in which they rested, he gave the name of prison to their expectancy."[43] In his later use of this model, Calvin will refer to this time as before sunrise, in order to combine the dynamic of seeing an approaching figure in darkness with a gradual increase of both proximity and light. As time goes on, the figure gets nearer, and the light increases, which only serves to increase the sense of expectation.

The advantage of this model is that it can bring the progressive manifestation of Christ into correspondence with the increasing maturation of the Church in Israel. Calvin makes this correlation in the 1539 edition of the *Institutes*. "The Lord, therefore, so meted out the light of his Word to them that they still saw it afar off and darkly. Hence Paul expresses this slenderness of understanding by the word 'childhood.'"[44] The contrast between the Law and the Gospel therefore has to do with the clarity of Christ's manifestation and the proximity of his presence.[45] For this reason, even though the fathers saw the same Christ in the Law that is fully exhibited in the Gospel, Christ can say that they longed to see what his followers saw, yet did not see him (Matt. 13:16). All this took place by the deliberate plan of God, who administered the manifestation of Christ so that it would correspond with the spiritual capacities of the Church through history. "The Lord held to this orderly plan in administering the covenant of his mercy: as the day of full revelation approached with the passing of time, the more he increased each day the brightness of its manifestation."[46]

Thus when the first epistle of John claims that life was revealed in Christ (1 John 1:2), Calvin can interpret this claim by means of the expectation of the fathers of a clearer manifestation of Christ. "Life was only manifested in Christ when he put on our flesh and completed all the parts of our redemption. For although even under the Law the fathers were associates and partakers of the same life, we know that they were shut up under the hope that was to be revealed."[47] The fathers share with us the life that was manifested in Christ, but they also eagerly hoped for the manifestation of that life in him. If they share the life of Christ with us, then it must have been manifested to them as well, but not as clearly and as presently as it is in Christ.[48] The prophets therefore set forth Christ to the Israelites; but even they knew that they were serving not themselves but those to whom Christ was fully exhibited. "In descending to earth, he in a manner opened heaven to us, so that we might have a near view of those spiritual riches, which before were exhibited under types at a distance. This fruition of Christ as manifested discloses the difference between us and the prophets."[49]

Calvin appeals to the dynamic of the increasing brightness and proximity of Christ's manifestation to harmonize two apparently contradictory statements of Christ. On the one hand, Jesus says that Abraham rejoiced when he saw his day (John 8:56); on the other, he says that the fathers longed to see his day, yet did not see it (Luke 10:24). "I reply, faith has its degrees (*gradus*) of seeing Christ. The ancient prophets beheld Christ afar off, as he had been promised to them, and yet were not permitted to behold him present, as he made himself intimately and completely visible when he came down to men from heaven."[50] Calvin also notes differing degrees of seeing Christ in the time of the fathers themselves. For instance, Jacob asks to be told the Name of the Lord with whom he had wrestled, but is denied his request, for "the time of full revelation was not yet completed: for the fathers, in the beginning, were required to walk in the twilight of morning; and the Lord manifested himself to them by degrees."[51] However, the Lord did manifest his Name to Moses, revealing that there was more light and proximity at his day than at the time of Jacob: "because he occupied an intermediate place between patriarchs and apostles, he is said, by comparison with them, to have seen God face to face, the God who had been hidden from the fathers."[52] The greater light and proximity of Christ in one age makes the light of a previous age seem more dim and distant, until Christ himself comes and reveals the dimness of the Law compared to the brightness of his presence.[53]

The description of Christ as the "Sun of Righteousness" (Mal. 4:2) fits in very nicely with Calvin's description of the Law as a time when Christ was glimpsed approaching in shadows in the distance. "And for this reason Christ is also called the light of the world; not that the fathers wandered as the blind in darkness, but that they were content with the dawn only, or with the moon and the stars."[54] Calvin appeals to this model of the sunrise in the chapter on the Law and the Gospel that he added to the 1559 edition of the *Institutes,* for it allows him to illustrate quite clearly the continuity amid discontinuity between the Law and the Gospel. "By these words he teaches that while the law serves to hold the godly in expectation of Christ's coming, at his advent they should hope for far more light."[55] The same Christ is manifested in both the Law and the Gospel; but over time the manifestation becomes nearer and brighter, until it shines forth like the noonday sun. "From this we infer that, where the whole law is concerned, the gospel differs from it only in clarity of manifestation."[56] Calvin uses the faithfulness of the fathers even in the dimmer light of the Law to chastise the ingratitude of those who are not grateful for the full light of day that they presently experience.[57] If the fathers could remain faithful even in the predawn hours when Christ was still absent, what excuse do we have for our faltering faith, as Christ stands present before us at noonday?[58]

4. From Shadow Outline to Living and Graphic Image

Calvin was aware that although Christ is more clearly manifested in the Gospel than in the Law, both the Law and the Gospel are not themselves Christ but representations of Christ. As such, both use doctrine and sacraments to portray Christ to us. Calvin acknowledges this continuity between the Law and the Gospel in the 1536 edition of the *Institutes*. "Yet those ancient sacraments looked to the same purpose to which ours now tend: to direct and almost lead men by the hand to Christ, or rather, as images, to represent him and set him forth to be known."[59] The difference between the Law and the Gospel must therefore lie in the way each represents Christ to us: "the former foreshadowed Christ promised while he was yet awaited; the latter attest him as already present and revealed."[60] Calvin makes this the second difference between the Law and the Gospel in the 1539 edition of the *Institutes*.[61] The dichotomy between figure and shadow on the one hand and truth and body on the other echoes Calvin's use of Colossians 2:17. However, in this instance the comparison is between the nature of the representation in the Old and New Testaments: the former reveals an image of the substance, whereas the latter reveals the very substance as present. Calvin turns not to Colossians 2:17 but to Hebrews 10:1 to draw the comparison. "He therefore concludes that there was in the law 'the shadow of good things to come,' not 'the living likeness of things themselves' [Heb. 10:1 p.]."[62] The New Testament portrays to the life what is outlined in shadows in the Old Testament.

In his commentary on Romans of 1540, Calvin makes explicit the comparison between the two methods of representation. "For a double manifestation is to be thought of here—the first is the Old Testament, which consisted of the word and sacraments, and the other in the New, which, in addition to the ceremonies and promises, contains their fulfillment in Christ."[63] Calvin reinforces this understanding of the twofold representation of Christ in the Law and the Gospel in an addition to the discussion of the Law in the 1543 edition of the *Institutes*. "Thus it was necessary with one kind of sign to represent Christ absent and proclaim him about to come; but it is fitting that, now revealed, he be represented with another."[64] He repeats this comparison five years later in his discussion of Paul's statement that the Jews were under the Law until faith was revealed (Gal. 3:23). "For whereas the ceremonies sketched out an absent Christ, to us he is represented as present."[65] The representations of Christ in the Law make it manifest that he is yet to come, whereas the representations of Christ in the Gospel reveal that he has exhibited his presence to us, even though he is not now present before us.[66] Calvin claims that the different forms of representation can be seen in circumcision and baptism. "Baptism, therefore, is a sign of the thing exhibited, which when it was absent was figured by circumcision."[67] The language of this comparison sounds similar to that used in Colossians 2:17; but there the difference was between the figure and the truth being figured, whereas in this instance it is between an adumbration of the truth yet to be revealed and the representation of the truth having been exhibited.

To make this comparison more clear to his readers, Calvin turns to the art of painting. Both the Law and the Gospel represent Christ. However, the Law is like the shadowy outline a painter traces in charcoal before he applies the paint, whereas the Gospel is the living likeness of the person painted in full color and detail. "For as painters do not in the first draft bring out a likeness in lifelike colors and as in an image, but first sketch rude and obscure lines with charcoal, so the representation of Christ under the law was unpolished, and was, as it were, a first sketch, but in our sacraments a true likeness is seen."[68] In his commentary on Hebrews of 1549, Calvin goes into even more detail about the nature of painterly representation by means of the distinction between an adumbration and a living likeness. "Before they put on the living colors artists usually draw an outline in pencil of the representation which they intend. This less distinct picture is called in Greek *skiagraphia*, just as you say in Latin shadowy, and just as for the Greek an *eikon* is the full likeness. *Eikones* are called in Latin likenesses which represent the true appearance of men or beasts or places."[69] Calvin takes the author of Hebrews to be describing the Law as the shadow outline of Christ, whereas the Gospel is the living icon of Christ painted to the life.[70] The same person is being represented in both forms of art, but the *eikon* is a much fuller image of the person than is the *skiagraphia*.

Like the comparison between Christ seen in the distance before sunrise and Christ seen before our eyes at noonday, the distinction between the Law as the shadow outline of Christ and the Gospel as his living icon reveals that the same Christ is being manifested in both the Law and the Gospel, while that manifestation itself is becoming increasingly clear, and the one being manifested is coming increasingly near. Indeed, in his discussion of the shadow outline and the living image, Calvin injects the spatial relationship as well, showing the proximity of this model to that of the sunrise. "It is to be noticed that the things which were shown to them from a distance are the same as those which are now set before our eyes. Both are shown the same Christ, the same justice, sanctification, and salvation. Only in the manner of the painting is there difference."[71]

5. THE LAW AS FIGURES DRAWN IN CONFORMITY TO THE ARCHETYPE

Calvin turned to another model of visual representation in describing the relationship of the ceremonies of the Law to Christ himself, that being the distinction between an image and the archetype it is meant to represent. Calvin first uses this model in his discussion of the death of Christ in the 1539 edition of the *Institutes*. Speaking of the way the Law speaks of the sacrifice for sin as sin itself, Calvin says it was called sin because it took on itself the curse due to sin. He then claims that Christ is the archetype that was being represented in all the figures of the sacrifices of the Law. "What was figuratively represented in the Mosaic sacrifices is manifested in Christ, the archetype of the figures."[72] This description of representation and archetype strongly echoes Plato's description of an *eikon* in the *Sophist*. "One art . . . is the making of likenesses (*eikastike*). The perfect example of this consists in creating a copy that conforms to the proportions of the original in all three dimensions and giving moreover the proper color to every part. . . . The first kind of image, then, being like the original, may fairly be called a likeness (*eikon*)."[73]

The claim that the Law of Moses figuratively represents the archetype, Christ, is based on the way Acts 7:44 and Hebrews 8:5 interpret Exodus 25:40, "And you shall make them according to the pattern for them, which is being shown you on the mountain." According to Calvin, the apostle in Hebrews 8:5 claims that the heavenly pattern that was sketched in the earthly tabernacle is Christ, and Calvin takes Stephen to be making the same point in Acts 7:44, namely, "that the whole of legal worship was nothing more than a picture which adumbrated the spiritual in Christ."[74] The whole of the cultic life of Israel, therefore, was meant to be a painting that corresponds to the archetype, Christ. The close proximity of this model to the previous one based on two modes of painting is revealed by an addition Calvin makes in the 1559 *Institutes*. Just after his claim from the 1536 edition that the aim of the sacraments of both the Law and the Gospel is to represent Christ and show him forth, one as awaited, the other as present and revealed, Calvin adds the sentence, "To this pertains that heavenly pattern of the Tabernacle and of worship under the law, which was put before Moses on the mountain."[75]

Calvin appeals to Christ as the archetype being represented in the Law to explain how Christ could say that Moses wrote about him (John 5:46). Calvin knows that Jesus Christ is not in fact mentioned in any passage of the Law of Moses, but he insists that unless Christ is the archetype being portrayed in the ceremonies of the Law, the meaning of the Law itself evaporates.[76] The importance of this claim for Calvin is revealed by the way he prefaces his whole discussion of the Law of Moses in the 1559 edition of the *Institutes*—by stating that without the reference to the archetype, the whole worship life of Israel would be ridiculous. "For if something spiritual had not been set forth to which they were to direct their course, the Jews would have frittered away their effort in those matters, just as the Gentiles did in their trifles."[77] Without such correspondence to Christ, there is no way to answer the mocking of profane people—whose criticism Calvin seems to appreciate—that the whole mass of ceremonies of the Law is nothing more than child's play. "That is, they do not pay attention to the purpose of the law; if the forms of the law be separated from its end, one must condemn it as vanity."[78]

6. The Symbols of Obligation and Bondage;
Symbols of Freedom

In the first edition of the *Institutes,* Calvin developed his understanding of
the power of the Law to reveal sin. He describes the Law as a mirror in
which we can behold our sin and the curse of God upon us, by means of the
obligation that it reveals we owe to God.[79] In the second edition of 1539, Calvin extends this function of the Law to the ceremonies of the Law as well, in
his attempt to give the proper understanding of the statement in Colossians
2:14, which speaks of God canceling the written bond that was against us in
the decrees. Calvin disagrees with those who apply this statement to the
moral law, agreeing instead with those like Augustine who apply it primarily
to the ceremonial rites of the Law, namely, that "in the Jewish ceremonies
there was confession of sins rather than atonement for them."[80] Considered
in themselves, and not as representations of Christ, the ceremonies of the
law, like the naked commandments themselves, simply represent to us our
obligation and sin. "What else did the Jews accomplish with their sacrifices
than to confess themselves guilty of death, since they substituted purification
in place of themselves? What else did they accomplish with their cleansings
but confess themselves unclean? They thus repeatedly renewed the 'written
bond' of their sin and impurity."[81]

Calvin uses this understanding of Colossians 2:14 to establish his fourth
distinction between the Law and the Gospel in the 1539 *Institutes.* The Old
Testament is one of bondage and fear because in it is manifested our obligation, sin, and guilt; whereas the New Testament is one of freedom and peace
because God has nailed the written bond of obligation to the cross. Calvin is
aware that such a dichotomy threatens the unity of the Old and New Testaments that he is trying so hard to preserve. He insists that the fathers under
the Law experienced the same grace of Christ as we do now, but they did not
receive that grace from the ceremonies of the Law when considered in themselves. "We hold that ceremonies, considered in themselves, are very appropriately called 'written bonds against' the salvation of men."[82] According to
Calvin, even though the fathers under the Law enjoyed the same freedom in
Christ that we do after the exhibition of Christ, their freedom was nonetheless hidden under the appearance of obligation and bondage created by
the ceremonies of the Law. "They were compelled to observe those ceremonies punctiliously, symbols of a tutelage resembling bondage [cf. Gal. 4:2–3];

and the written bonds [see Col. 2:14], whereby they confessed themselves guilty of sin, did not free them from obligation."[83]

In his commentary on Galatians of 1548, Calvin explicitly links the Law as the mirror of sin with the ceremonies of the Law as the confession of sin in his interpretation of the Law as "the disciplinarian until Christ came" (Gal. 3:24). "This was the aim of all the ceremonies: for why were there sacrifices and washings except that men might continually consider their pollution and condemnation? When a man sees his uncleanness before his eyes, and the innocent animal is held out as the image of his own death, how can he indulge in sleep?"[84] Calvin expands on the image of our death in sacrifices in his comments on Colossians 2:14 of the same year, focusing on the substitution of the innocent for the guilty. "For when they substituted in their place an innocent animal, they confessed that they were themselves deserving of that death. In short, all these ceremonies were exhibitions of human guilt and hand-writings of obligation."[85] Given the image of their sin and death in the ceremonies of the Law, the Israelites' freedom from sin in their consciences was concealed under the appearance of bondage. "To the outward eye appeared nothing but slavery."[86]

However, Calvin knows that an inward freedom in Christ hidden beneath the appearance of slavery in ceremonies will not ultimately suffice, since he also claims repeatedly that the ceremonies of the law shadow forth and represent the spiritual benefits of God in Christ. The ceremonies of the Law must therefore have a twofold referent, simultaneously representing to the Israelites their sin and death and their redemption from sin and death by the future work of Christ. "And certainly ceremonies had the power not only of alarming and humbling consciences, but of exciting them to faith in the coming Redeemer. In the whole solemnity of the ceremonial everything that was presented to the eye had impressed on it, as it were, the marks of Christ."[87] No matter how much obligation and sin might be manifested in the legal ceremonies, they refer those confessing their sins to the coming redemption of Christ, which they also represent before their eyes.[88] The coming of Christ has the twofold effect of fulfilling the representations of his redemptive work in the Law and of bringing the ceremonial acknowledgment of sin to an end, so that "no monument of obligation might remain."[89] In the time of the Gospel, our freedom is not hidden under an appearance of bondage, but is rather manifested in the symbols of the Gospel.[90]

7. The Symbols of Separation Dividing Jew and Gentile

Calvin's attention to the meaning and signification of the ceremonies of the Law led him to be especially sensitive to the surprising development of the inclusion of the Gentiles in the covenant made with Israel. Before the ascension of Christ, God separated the Israelites from the rest of the nations, thereby manifesting their exclusive election. Calvin makes this characteristic of the Law his fifth distinction between the Old and New Testaments in the 1539 *Institutes*. "The fifth difference, which may be added, lies in the fact that until the advent of Christ, the Lord set apart one nation within which to confine the covenant of his grace."[91] Calvin does not ascribe this exclusivism to narrowness of mind or arrogance on the part of the Jews, but rather to the explicit plan of God to elect Israel alone over against all the other nations. "Israel was honored with God's presence; the others excluded from all approach to him."[92]

According to Calvin, not even Jesus questioned the exclusive call of Israel, claiming that he came not to the Gentiles but to the lost sheep of the house of Israel [Matt. 15:24], and explicitly telling his disciples not to preach and minister to the Gentiles [Matt. 10:5]. Hence the will of God revealed after the ascension of Jesus to include the Gentiles equally with the Jews was shocking even to the apostles. "And no wonder! For it seemed completely unreasonable that the Lord, who for so many ages had singled out Israel from all other nations, should suddenly change his plan and abandon that choice."[93] However, it gradually became clear to them, in spite of their shock, that God had in Christ broken down the dividing wall between Jews and Gentiles, and now offered reconciliation to both in the preaching of the Gospel. According to Calvin, "The calling of the Gentiles, therefore, is a notable mark of the excellence of the New Testament over the Old."[94]

In his commentary on Ephesians of 1548, Calvin claims that the separation of the Jews from the Gentiles was symbolized by the ceremonies of the Law for "ceremonies were symbols of this separation, which openly testified to it."[95] The "dividing wall" between Jews and Gentiles spoken of in Ephesians therefore refers to the ceremonies of the Law, whereby "the Gentiles were excluded from the Kingdom of God."[96] The ceremonies manifested to the Jews the exclusive claim God had on them, distinguishing them visibly from the other nations and setting them apart.[97] The inclusion of the Gentiles by the preaching of the Gospel therefore necessitates the abolition of the ceremonies of the Law, for one of their primary purposes was to reveal the divinely sanctioned division between Jews and Gentiles.[98] Just as the legal ceremonies symbolize the separation of the Jews from the Gentiles, so the abolition of the ceremonies visibly manifests the inclusion of both Jews and Gentiles in Christ.

8. THE VEILED FACE OF MOSES; THE UNVEILED FACE OF CHRIST

Calvin develops two further distinctions between the Law and the Gospel after the 1539 edition of the *Institutes,* both of which trade on the contrast between being veiled and being unveiled. The first contrast is drawn in his commentary on 2 Corinthians of 1546, in light of Paul's comparison in chapter 3 between the veiled face of Moses and the unveiled face of Christ. The second is developed in his commentary on Hebrews of 1549, drawing on the contrast between the veiled face of God in the holy of holies before the coming of Christ and the unveiled face of God after the rending of the veil of the temple after the death of Christ.

In his comparison of the glory of the Law and the glory of the Gospel in 2 Corinthians 3, Paul states that the glory of the Law was manifested in the light that shone from Moses's face, which was so bright that the people could not look upon it. In spite of this glory, Paul claims that it is now set aside by the glory of the ministry of the Spirit (2 Cor. 3:7–8). This passage leads Calvin to remark on the very real glory of the Law of Moses. "The Law was adorned with many miracles but Paul here mentions only one of them, the brightness that shone in the face of Moses so as to dazzle the eyes of all. That brightness was a symbol of the glory of the Law."[99] According to Calvin, the superiority of the Gospel over the Law is revealed by the way the Gospel sets aside the glory of the Law. "Arguing from the lesser to the greater, he now declares that it is fitting that the glory of the Gospel should shine with an even greater brightness, since it is by far superior to the Law."[100] This contrast is reminiscent of that between what can be seen before dawn and what can be seen after the sun has reached its zenith at noon. There is light in both situations, but the Gospel is distinguished from the Law by the greater degree of light it manifests. In his comments on 2 Corinthians, Calvin contrasts the Law and the Gospel by means of a comparison between the light of the moon and stars and the light of the sun. "It follows that we cannot sufficiently prize or hold in reverence the glory of Christ which shines in the Gospel, just as the brightness of the sun shines forth in its rays."[101]

However, Paul not only contrasts the degree of light between the Law and the Gospel but also contrasts the quality of the light of each. The people at the time of Moses could not bear to gaze upon his face, but asked him to veil his face whenever the glory of God shone from it. The first thing this suggests to Calvin is that the glory of the Law is dazzling and even terrifying, whereas the light of Christ is so clear and alluring that we can look at it without an intervening veil. "He now openly rejoices that the majesty of the Gospel is not terrifying but gentle, not hidden but intimately accessible to all."[102] The Law is bright, but its light stuns the eyes of those who gaze upon it, so that they can only look upon it when it is veiled. The brightness of the Gospel, on the other hand, is not dazzling but clear, and can be beheld without an intervening veil. In his commentary on Hebrews of 1549, Calvin extends the veiling of Moses to the whole dispensation of the Law: it manifests Christ to Israel, but in such a way that the manifestation is veiled. "Moses kept the people under a veil: that since the reality was not yet shown forth he presented a foretaste of Christ in types and shadows: that he adapted himself to convince the ignorant people and did not rise above the childish elements."[103] Calvin even appeals to the veiled manifestation of Christ in the Law to explain why it does not explicitly mention Christ.[104] The veiling of Christ in the Law is yet another way of highlighting the relative obscurity of the manifestation of Christ in the Law.

The veil not only represents the dazzling and hidden light of the Law but also symbolizes the future blindness of the Jews, who will not be able to see that Moses bears witness to Christ, as Paul suggests in 2 Corinthians 3:12–16.[105] According to Paul, the veil is only taken away by Christ. Calvin takes this to mean that one only clearly reads the Law of Moses when Christ manifests himself in it. "The Law is in itself full of light but we appreciate its clarity only when Christ appears to us in it. The Jews turn their eyes as far away from Christ as they can, so that it is not surprising that they should see nothing when they refuse to look at the sun."[106] Moses really does point us to the self-manifestation of Christ, but our attention to the veil keeps us from seeing Christ in the Law.

9. THE DISTANT AND VEILED FACE OF GOD;
APPROACHING GOD FACE-TO-FACE

The second contrast Calvin develops on the basis of the veil has to do with the veil concealing the holy of holies that is torn when Christ dies, which Calvin first develops in his Hebrews commentary of 1549. According to Calvin, Christ opens access to God for us so that we can now approach God intimately and face-to-face, no longer at a distance and behind a veil.[107] The abolition of the high priesthood and the sanctuary symbolizes our more intimate access to God. "But now that the tabernacle has been abolished God admits us into his intimate presence, from which the fathers were prohibited."[108] Unlike all previous comparisons of the Law and the Gospel, the comparison based on the veil in the sanctuary has to do with the clarity and intimacy of our ability to approach God rather than the increasing clarity of the approach of Christ to us. Under the Law, the people stood at a distance, and only the priest entered behind the veil. "But now that we rely on Christ the Mediator, we enter by faith right into heaven, because there is no longer any veil to obstruct us. God appears to us openly, and invites us lovingly to meet him face to face."[109]

Calvin appeals to the veiled presence of God among the Jews to explain how it is that the Gospel of John can say that no one has ever seen God (John 1:18). According to Calvin, John is referring to the superior revelation of God in Christ compared to the self-revelation of God to the fathers under the Law. "Paul treats this more fully in 2 Cor. 3 and 4, declaring that there is no longer any veil, as under the Law, but that God is openly beheld in the face of Christ."[110] As this passage makes clear, Calvin can apply the veil of Moses, symbolizing the hiddenness of Christ in the Law, to the lack of the face-to-face vision of God by the fathers. What, then, of those fathers who spoke of having seen God face-to-face? "If any object that even then God was seen face to face, I say that that sight was not at all comparable to ours; but since God used at that time to show himself obscurely and from afar, those to whom he appeared more clearly said that they saw him face to face. They speak relatively to their own time."[111] For instance, Jacob exclaims that he has seen God face-to-face at Peniel (Gen. 32:30). According to Calvin, this is true, but relative to the time in which he lived.[112] The same may be said of the vision of God by Moses, in which he arrived at the clearest view of the nature of God of any of the fathers.[113] God only appears to us unveiled and face-to-face when he appears to us in Christ.

Calvin also interprets the veil of the sanctuary to indicate the obscurity of the manifestation of God in the ceremonies of the Law. When Moses is commanded to make a veil for the tabernacle, Calvin says, "But by the veil the obscurity of the shadows of the law was principally denoted."[114] Once again, we can see the way the veil of the temple blends into the veil on the face of Moses in Calvin's mind, as both indicate the distant and veiled presence of God under the Law, compared to the intimate and face-to-face vision of God in the Gospel. Since the ceremonies present a veil to keep the people from the presence of God, when the veil of the temple is torn from top to bottom, this signifies the end of the ceremonies so that we might have intimate access to God.[115] According to Calvin, the reintroduction of the ceremonies of the Law under the papacy has the effect of once again veiling God, thereby preventing us from intimately and boldly approaching God. "It is easily seen from this how horrible confusion rages in the Papacy. An immense heap of ceremonies exists there. Why is that, except that instead of one veil of the old temple, they may obtain a hundred?"[116]

As the discussion of the veil of Moses and of the temple indicates, the models Calvin develops by which to distinguish the Law from the Gospel mutually interpret and reinforce one another. The fundamental claim in all nine models is that the Law and the Gospel both manifest Jesus Christ, with the difference between the two lying in the clarity of the manifestation. Speaking of his own analysis of the Law and the Gospel compared to Augustine's, Calvin says, "Ours distinguishes between the clarity of the gospel and the obscurer dispensation of the Word that had preceded it."[117] The same figure is being represented, but more obscurely in the Law than in the Gospel. The Law represents in figures and shadows the reality and body of Jesus Christ. The Law represents in earthly symbols and types the spiritual blessings of God in Christ. The fathers under the Law saw the distant figure of Christ in the shadows of the early dawn, whereas we now see him before our eyes in the clear light of noon. The Law represented the absent Christ in a shadow outline, whereas the Gospel represents Christ to the life in an icon of full and living color. The freedom of Christ is hidden under the appearance of obligation and sin in the Law, whereas freedom is clearly manifested in the Gospel. The light of Christ illumined only the Jews under the Law but now shines upon all nations in the Gospel. The light clearly beheld in the unveiled face of Christ now eclipses the light of the Law hidden under the veil of Moses. The presence of God hidden at a distance behind the veil of the sanctuary may now be approached intimately, so that we see God face-to-face.

One may see the way each visual model reinforces the others in a striking paragraph added to the discussion of the Law in the 1559 *Institutes*. Calvin is discussing the end of the ceremonies of the Law and begins with a reference to the relationship between images and the archetype they represent: "the ceremonies would have provided the people of the Old Covenant with an empty show if the power of Christ's death and resurrection had not been displayed therein." He then turns immediately to the dichotomy between the shadow and the body in Colossians 2:17. "Consequently Paul, to prove their observance not only superfluous but also harmful, teaches that they are shadows whose substance exists for us in Christ [Col. 2:17]." He then introduces the figure of the veil of the temple, which he interprets by means of the shadow outline of the Law discussed in Hebrews 10:1. "Thus we see that in their abolition the truth shines forth better than if they, still afar off and as if veiled, figured the Christ, who has already plainly revealed himself. At Christ's death 'the veil of the temple was torn in two' [Matt. 27:51] because now the living and express image of heavenly blessings was manifested, which before had been begun in indistinct outline only, as the author of the Letter to the Hebrews states [Heb. 10:1]." Calvin then refers to the distant figure glimpsed in the shadowy distance to illustrate our clearer vision of Christ. "Not that the holy patriarchs were without the preaching that contains the hope of salvation and eternal life, but that they only glimpsed from afar and in shadowy outline what we see today in full daylight." Finally, Calvin combines the representation of God's blessing in earthly symbols with the relationship between the shadows of the Law and the substance of Christ. "For even though atonement for sins had been truly promised in the ancient sacrifices, and the Ark of the Covenant was a sure pledge of God's fatherly favor, all this would have been but shadow had it not been grounded in the grace of Christ, in whom one finds perfect and everlasting stability."[118] The fluidity with which Calvin moves from one model to another, often in the same sentence, should keep us from separating the models too rigidly from one another, even though they are distinct from one another.

Lying behind all the differences between the Law and the Gospel is the economy of manifestation instituted by God, which is adapted to the capacities of the Church as it grows and develops from infancy to adolescence.

"Paul likens the Jews to children, Christians to young men [Gal. 4:1 ff.]. What was irregular about the fact that God confined them to rudimentary teaching commensurate with their age, but has trained us through a firmer and, so to speak, more manly discipline?"[119] The differences between the representations of Christ in the Law and in the Gospel do not reflect a change in the nature of God, as the Manichaeans and Marcion supposed, but rather reflect God's accommodation to the differing capacities of humanity over time.[120] As we have seen, Calvin distinguishes at least three periods of human development in the history of the Church: the time of the fathers, the time of the Law of Moses, and the time of the apostles. However, he can also distinguish between the time of the tabernacle and that of the temple, a crucial distinction to which he thinks the Samaritans should have attended. "Where the Samaritans went wrong was that they did not take into account how much the manner of their own time differed from Jacob. The patriarchs were allowed to erect altars everywhere because the place that the Lord afterwards chose had not yet been appointed. But from the time that God ordered the temple to be built on Mount Zion their former freedom ceased."[121] We will see a similar distinction of times created by the destruction of the temple in Jerusalem and the return of the Jews from Babylon, which begins the restoration of all things in Christ. In each period of development, Calvin claims that the manifestation of Christ becomes more clear, more detailed, and more luminous.[122]

However, the increasing manifestation of Christ in accommodation to the increasing capacities of humanity in general, and the Jews in particular, raises an acute problem for the whole model, of which Calvin seems to have been fully aware. If the Israelites alone were educated by God in the coming of Christ from the time of Adam to the entrance of Jesus into Jerusalem, why then did the Jews of his day fail to recognize him as the one increasingly represented to them in the Law? Indeed, of all the Jews at the time of Jesus, one would think that those in Jerusalem would be the most able to recognize the truth of the figures when he appeared in their midst, for all the types and figures of the Law that represented Christ to the people were present in Jerusalem. "They had daily sacrifices; the Temple was ever before them, and should have kindled in their hearts a desire to seek God; the chief teachers of the Church were there, and there, too, was the sanctuary of the divine light. Their ingratitude was therefore utterly base; they had been steeped in these exercises from their childhood, and yet they reject and neglect the Redeemer promised to them."[123] The problem becomes even more acute when the Gospel is preached to the Gentiles, after the Jews had rejected it. Even though they had not been trained in the types and figures of the Law at all, the Gentiles readily and willingly embrace the very same Gospel that had been rejected by the Jews, even though it was allegedly the reality being figured in the whole of their life under the Law. "It was certainly very strange, that the Jews, peculiarly chosen and illumined by the doctrine of the Law, so presumptuously polluted God's worship, as though they despised him, and that the Gentiles, being novices, rendered obedience to God as soon as they tasted the truth of religion, so that his glory became through them illustrious."[124] Calvin thinks that it is this absurdity which created the pain in Paul's heart of which he speaks in his letter to the Romans. "There was no one who would not automatically entertain the thought, 'If this is the doctrine of the law and the prophets, how does it happen that the Jews so obstinately reject it?'"[125]

Calvin attempts to solve this problem by accusing the Jews of ingratitude, as well as of blindness, veiling their minds when they read Moses so that they do not see Christ. "Therefore, they read Moses and continually ponder his writings, but they are hampered by a veil from seeing the light shining in his face [2 Cor. 3:13–15]. Thus, Moses' face will remain covered and hidden from them until it be turned to Christ, from whom they now strive to separate and withdraw it as much as they can."[126] However, this does not completely solve the problem. Imagine I am a teacher who accommodates my teaching to the capacities of my students, and teach them about a certain subject from the time they are infants until the time they are adolescents, gradually clarifying the subject matter in proportion to their capacities. If, on the day of the final exam, when I will see if they have learned their lessons well, I test them on the subject matter about which I had been teaching them their whole lives, and they fail, whereas those who had not even been taught by me pass the exam easily, does it really suffice to blame the students for their ingratitude and blindness? Does it not really suggest that the whole experience in the classroom was futile, if those never taught a day in their lives immediately pass the test that my students fail? Since the fault cannot lie in the teacher (who would represent God), then the thought must necessarily arise that the subject matter on the exam had nothing to do with the lessons that were taught previously.

It is to Calvin's credit that his careful and sustained attention to the whole economy of the manifestation of the Law in the history of Israel makes him aware of this problem, for it is all too easily missed by most

Christians. The failure of the Jews to recognize Jesus as the one manifested to them throughout the whole course of the Law calls into question the truth of the Gospel. The answer to this problem is a mystery lying in the heart of God, as Paul himself acknowledges; but it would be very helpful if instead of vilifying Jews for their blindness and ingratitude, as Calvin does, Christians were profoundly humbled, and even anguished, by the failure of the Gospel among the Jews and the success of the Gospel among the Gentiles. "For I could wish that I myself were accursed and cut off from Christ for the sake of my own people, my kindred according to the flesh. They are Israelites, and to them belong the adoption, the glory, the covenants, the giving of the law, the worship, and the promises; to them belong the patriarchs, and from them, according to the flesh, comes the Messiah, who is over all, God blessed forever. Amen" (Rom. 9:3–5).

CHAPTER 5

Visual Confirmation of the Covenant of Adoption

Calvin's distinction between the Law and the Gospel led him to reflect on the distinctive ways God both revealed the Law to the Israelites and confirmed its revelation to them. Since Calvin understands the Law primarily in light of the covenant of adoption, founded on the mercy of God in Jesus Christ, the revelation of the Law really begins with Abraham, although the promise of Christ extends all the way back to Adam. The Law revealed to Moses is seen by Calvin as a renewal and confirmation of the covenant made with Abraham, although it also includes the addition of the Law in its conditional sense, which acts as a mirror to reveal sin. Since Calvin views the prophets as interpreters of the Law of Moses who apply it vigorously to the people of their time, the distinctive mode of the revelation of the Law would extend from the time of the patriarchs through the time of the prophets. Calvin's reflection on the revelation and confirmation of the covenant of adoption leads him to reflect directly on the essential relationship among visions, signs, and symbols, on the one hand, and oracles, doctrine, and the Word of God, on the other. He will often include in his discussion of the confirmation of the Law an explicit critique of the understanding of the sacraments in the Roman Church (at least as he understood it), thereby demonstrating that he thinks about the revelation and confirmation of the Law in an explicitly sacramental way.

I begin my examination of the revelation and confirmation of the covenant of adoption by examining the central role played by visions and dreams
for the patriarchs, Moses, and the prophets. The visions and dreams serve
two functions: they reveal the hidden things of God to the fathers under the
Law, and they confirm that revelation both for themselves and the Church,
by manifesting its divine origin. I then turn to a consideration of the visual
confirmation of the Law in miracles, the exodus, experience, and individual
members of the Church. I trace the development of each of these themes in
Calvin's writings and organize the discussion of each theme chronologically,
according to the order by which it emerges in Calvin's writings.

1. The Self-Manifestation of God in Visions and Dreams

Calvin first addresses the distinctive nature of God's self-revelation in the
Law in the 1536 *Institutes*. He argues that although God has never revealed
Godself to anyone other than through the Son, the manifestation of the Son
took diverse forms before the coming of Christ.[1] However, he does not specify the specific nature of the diverse forms of divine self-manifestation to the
fathers and prophets. In the second edition of the *Institutes* of 1539, Calvin for
the first time introduces the two forms of self-manifestation in oracles and
visions. "But whether God became known to the patriarchs through oracles
and visions or by the work and ministry of men, he put into their minds what
they should then hand down to posterity."[2] The addition of human ministry
to oracles and visions may reflect the influence of Martin Luther. Luther was
highly suspicious of divine self-manifestation by interior visions, insisting in
his argument with Karlstadt that the Word of God always comes to us externally, through the ministry of other people. It is remarkable, given Luther's position, that Calvin allows for the possibility that God revealed Godself to the patriarchs by oracles and visions. However, the visions are not yet
seen as confirming the divine origin of the oracles; rather, God gives such
confirmation in their hearts.[3]

By the time of the 1543 edition of the *Institutes,* Calvin made an addition
to the discussion of the self-manifestation of God through the Son, which
further clarifies the unique nature of divine self-manifestation to the fathers
and prophets: "For this Wisdom has not always manifested itself in one way.
Among the patriarchs God used secret revelations, but at the same time to
confirm these he added such signs that they could have no doubt that it was

God who was speaking to them. What the patriarchs had received they handed on to their descendants."[4] The reference to the role of human ministry in divine self-revelation that was present in 1539 drops out of consideration, being given the subsidiary role of the transmission of divine revelation to others. Moreover, Calvin adds the confirming role of signs in the giving of divine oracles, and does not appeal to inward confirmation, as he did in 1539. His position in 1543 is that God revealed Godself to the patriarchs by secret revelations and confirmed those revelations by signs. If we take secret revelations to mean oracles, then by 1543 the essential relationship between oracles and signs is already established.

Calvin returns to the role of visions in his commentary on Hebrews of 1549. In his discussion of the "many and various ways God spoke to the fathers," Calvin says, "We are better off, too, in the manner of revelation, for the diversity of visions and of other dispensations which existed in the Old Testament was evidence that there was not yet a firm and stable order of things such as is proper when everything is perfectly settled."[5] Here the identifying characteristic of divine self-manifestation to the prophets is that it takes place primarily by visions but also by other means.

Later in the Hebrews commentary, Calvin will specify the nature of two such visions, showing how they confirm the truth of the oracles being manifested to the fathers under the Law. The first vision is discussed in Calvin's interpretation of the statement made by Hebrews that Moses "persevered as though he saw him who is invisible" (Heb. 11:27). Calvin interprets this passage as referring to Moses' vision of the burning bush, which was revealed to Moses to strengthen him for the coming conflict with Pharaoh.[6] The vision of God gave Moses the confidence to endure the trials he experienced in the struggle to free the Israelites from Egypt, for it encouraged him to lift his eyes to God alone whenever dangers threatened to overwhelm him.[7] The second vision is one experienced by all the people at the base of Mount Sinai, when they heard the words of the Law spoken by God out of the fire on the mountaintop. According to Calvin, these signs were given so that the people might know that the whole of the Law proceeded from God alone.[8] Thus the Hebrews commentary confirms the tendency in Calvin to identify the distinctive mode of revelation to the fathers and prophets with visions, and to see such visions as confirming both the faith of the fathers and the divine origin of the Law.

Calvin further clarifies the distinctive mode of revelation to the fathers in his commentary on Acts of 1552. In his interpretation of Peter's sermon on

Pentecost, Calvin uses Peter's citation of Joel 2:28 to discuss the usual modes of divine self-revelation to the prophets. "By 'prophesy' he means to indicate a gift of intelligence of a rare and singular kind. The sentence immediately following is to the same effect, 'Your young men shall see visions, and your old men shall dream dreams.' These were the two normal means by which the Lord usually revealed himself to the prophets, as we learn from Numbers 12:6. For in that passage the Lord separates Moses from the normal run of the prophets, by saying, 'I appear unto my servants by a vision or by a dream, but with Moses I speak face to face.'"[9] The text from Numbers 12:6, suggested to Calvin by the reference to visions and dreams in Joel, gives him a succinct description of the usual mode of divine self-revelation to the fathers and the prophets, one that will continue to appear in subsequent commentaries. God manifests Godself to the prophets by dreams and visions, but to Moses God speaks face-to-face.

Calvin also gives a new interpretation of Moses' vision of the burning bush on Mount Sinai in his interpretation of Stephen's sermon. As in his Hebrews commentary, Calvin sees the vision of the burning bush as confirming the call of Moses to be the liberator of his people. However, he is much more interested now in how the sign of the burning bush itself confirms the faith of Moses. In his previous interpretation of this vision, Calvin said, "In short, God showed himself to Moses in such a way as to leave room for faith, and Moses beset on all sides by many terrors turned all his attention to God. He was certainly helped to do so by that vision of which we have spoken, but he saw more in God than the visible sign contained."[10] The important thing here is not the sign of the burning bush but the vision of God. In his commentary on Acts, however, Calvin seeks to draw out the meaning of the vision itself, by means of the analogy between the vision and the reality it signifies. "It remains to say something about the burning bush. It is a commonplace that God accommodates signs to realities by some sort of analogy (*similitudine*), and this is a quite common procedure with the sacraments."[11] According to Calvin, the reality being signified is the endurance of affliction by the people, sustained in their affliction by the presence of God in their midst.[12] The sign itself, not the vision of God beyond the sign, is therefore accommodated to strengthen the faith of Moses.[13] Since the Church is never completely free of affliction, the image of the Church depicted in the vision of the burning bush can strengthen the faithful in every age, including Calvin's day.[14]

Calvin appealed to the analogy of the sign to the thing signified in his discussion of baptism in the 1536 *Institutes*. "For this analogy or similitude is the surest rule of the sacraments: that we should see and ponder spiritual things in physical. For the Lord was pleased to represent them by such figures."[15] He emphasized the role of analogy in the sacraments by referring to it in the chapter on the sacraments in the 1539 edition. "Indeed, the believer, when he sees the sacraments with his own eyes, does not halt at the physical sight of them, but by those steps (which I have indicated by analogy) rises up in devout contemplation to those lofty mysteries which lie hidden in the sacraments."[16] The application of the principle of analogy between the sign and the reality signified in the interpretation of the vision of Moses means that by 1552 Calvin sees the visions and dreams of the prophets as having a sacramental role, which can confirm the faith of the Church not only at the time of Moses but also in Calvin's day. From this point onwards, Calvin will be very concerned to discern the meaning of every vision and dream revealed to the prophets—even the most obscure, as in the visions of Ezekiel—by means of the analogy between the sign and the reality signified.

If visions are confirming signs analogous to sacraments, then it becomes imperative to discern the difference between a genuine vision of God and a delusion brought about by Satan. "For in what other way could the oracles of God, in which the covenant of eternal life is contained, be guaranteed?"[17] The danger with regard to the illusions wrought by Satan is very real for Calvin, for he sees it as lying behind all the false doctrine of the pagans, the Papacy, and the Anabaptists.[18] The possibility of such satanic deception is the primary reason Luther wanted believers to rely only on the truth of the Word of God and not on visions or dreams, for only the Word brings certainty. Calvin cannot make this move, because for him the visions confirm the divine origin of the oracles of God.

Calvin therefore needs to provide criteria by which to discern true from false visions without undermining the significance of the visions themselves. He does so by appealing yet again to the category of "distinguishing marks." "Therefore the only remedy is for God to distinguish the visions that he grants with certain characteristics."[19] Calvin arrives at four distinguishing marks by which the fathers under the Law knew that the visions they beheld came from God. First, the vision brought about a clear awareness of God's majesty and presence.[20] Second, the Lord opens the eyes of the faithful so that they know that the signs they see are not hallucinations.[21] Third, the

Lord engraves the certainty of the symbols in the hearts of the faithful so that they might be certain that the vision is from God: "the Holy Spirit engraves marks and symbols of the divine presence in our hearts, so that no doubt may remain."[22] Fourth, the true visions of God are always given in conjunction with the oracle or Word they are meant to confirm, whereas false visions lack such a word. "Now we see why the vision was presented to Moses—so that its authority would rest in the Word of God. For bare visions would be of little use without the addition of teaching. But it is added not as the inferior part, but as the cause or end of all visions."[23] Calvin will appeal to these distinguishing marks of divinely inspired visions in his writings after 1552, in conjunction with his use of Numbers 12:6 to describe the usual manner by which God revealed Godself to the fathers and prophets. Thus, by the time of the Acts commentary in 1552, Calvin has clarified most of the distinctive features of God's self-manifestation to the fathers and the prophets under the Law. Let us now turn to examine the self-revelation of God to the patriarchs and prophets in visions and dreams, to see how Calvin describes the confirming nature of such visions, in conjunction with the oracles they are meant to confirm.

The Visions and Dreams of the Patriarchs: Abram

Calvin continues to refine his reflections about the visions and dreams of the patriarchs in his commentary on Genesis of 1554. My discussion begins with the vision presented to Abram after he rescued Lot from King Chedorlaomer and his allies. Calvin realizes the difficulty the timing of the vision presents, for God usually manifests Godself to the patriarchs and prophets in times of affliction, to strengthen and confirm them. Why, then, does God appear to Abram in a vision after a success? Calvin suggests that it is the victory itself that creates anxiety in Abram, because of the enmity it might have created in his neighbors. It could also be that Abram might be tempted by his success to secure a comfortable life for himself, and forget the promise made to him by God.[24] The way God recalls Abram to Godself is of particular interest to Calvin, for the text says, "the word of the Lord came to Abram in a vision" (Gen. 15:1). Calvin takes this to mean, "some visible symbol of God's glory was added to the word, in order that greater authority might be given to the oracle."[25] In other words, the vision is given to confirm the truth of the oracle, according to the usual manner of God's self-revelation to the prophets.[26]

Abram responds to the word in the vision by saying, "O Lord God" (Gen. 15:2), indicating to Calvin that he was able to distinguish this vision from a satanic delusion, because "some special mark of divine glory was stamped upon the vision, so that Abram, having no doubt respecting its author, confidently broke out in this expression."[27] As in the commentary on Acts, God inscribes certain marks on the visions God presents, especially the mark of God's glory, so that the vision might confirm the oracle and not be doubted as an illusion of Satan. Calvin adds a new concern to his discussion of visions, however, by insisting that the vision of God is accommodated to Abram's capacities, and does not reveal God as God truly is.[28] From this point onwards, Calvin will always add his concern that visions of God are accommodated to the capacity of the prophet, although he will also insist that the prophet's capacity for the vision of God increases over time, as discussed in the previous chapter.

In the vision, Abram expresses his anxiety that he remains childless, in spite of God's promise of offspring. God responds to his anxiety with a vision of the stars, which is meant to confirm Abram's faith. "For the Lord, in order more deeply to affect his own people, and more efficaciously to penetrate their minds, after he has reached their ears by his word, also arrests their eyes by external symbols, that eyes and ears may consent together."[29] The vision of the stars confirms Abram's faith by means of the analogy that Calvin thinks he must have drawn between the appearance of the stars and the oracle of God, that the God who made the whole host of heaven could replenish his desolate house with offspring.[30] However, Calvin is careful to remind his readers that the sight of the stars takes place in the vision of God that Abram is having, making it a vision within a vision, "which would manifestly reveal hidden things to him."[31]

God then repeats the promise to give Abram the land to possess it. When Abram asks how he is to know he will possess it, God commands him to bring a heifer, a goat, a ram, a turtledove, and a pigeon, and to divide the animals. Calvin interprets this ceremony as an "ancient rite in forming covenants," in which God intended to reveal to Abram that God creates the Church out of nothing, and raises it from the dead.[32] While Abram is chasing away the birds of prey, and the sun begins to set, he falls into a deep sleep, which for Calvin takes place while Abram is still in the vision from God, thereby combining the two modes of revelation found in Numbers 12:6.[33] In a dream within his vision, "a deep and terrifying darkness" descended upon Abram. According to Calvin, this darkness served two purposes: first, "that

Abram might know that the dream is not a common one, but that the whole is divinely conducted;" and second, that "it has, nevertheless, an analogy with the oracle then present," namely, that Abram's seed will be oppressed aliens and slaves for four hundred years in a land not theirs, after which they shall come out. "Thus here, not a mute apparition is presented to the eyes of Abram, but he is taught by an oracle annexed, what the external and visible symbol meant."[34] The dream of thick darkness makes the oracle more vivid, even as the oracle provides the analogy that gives the meaning of the dream.

Once the sun is down and it is dark, God adds a new vision to the dream, one in which "a smoking fire pot and flaming torch passed between the pieces." According to Calvin, this vision is meant to confirm Abram in his hope for future deliverance. To defend this interpretation, Calvin claims, "An analogy is always to be sought for between signs, and the things signified, that there may be a mutual correspondence between them. Then, since the symbol, in itself, is but a lifeless carcass, reference ought always be made to the word which is annexed to it. But here, by the word, liberty was promised to Abram's seed, in the midst of servitude."[35] According to Calvin, this vision in a dream in a vision not only represents the descendants of Abram but also vividly portrays the condition of the Church in every age, including his own.[36]

The overall vision ends with God making a covenant with Abram. Calvin interprets this to mean that the covenant was ratified by the rite of the divided animals, for the text says, "on that day the Lord made a covenant with Abram, saying, 'To your descendants I give this land.'" Calvin interprets this solemn rite of covenantal ratification in a sacramental way: "the word is always to be joined with the symbols, lest our eyes be fed with empty and fruitless ceremonies. God has commanded animals to be offered to him; but he has shown their end and use, by a covenant appended to them. If, then, the Lord feeds us by sacraments, we infer, that they are the evidences of his grace, and the tokens of those spiritual blessings which flow from it."[37] The covenantal rite gives visual confirmation of the promise of the land to Abram, about which Abram had questioned God earlier in the vision. And the rite itself takes place in a vision.

The visions and dreams of Abram offer a very rich and complex picture of how Calvin sees God communicating with the patriarchs. The vision of God that begins the whole narrative is meant to confirm the faith of Abram in light of the enmity of his neighbors. The sight of the stars, which is a vision within the vision, confirms his faith in the ability of God to provide him offspring. The rite of dividing the animals, which takes place in the vision, is meant to portray the affliction and deliverance of the Church. The dream within the vision, in which thick and terrifying darkness descends upon Abram, is meant to portray the coming bondage and oppression of his descendants. The new vision in the dream within the vision, of the smoking fire pot and burning torch passing between the pieces of animals, is meant to confirm the promise of deliverance from the coming bondage and oppression. Finally, the symbol of the covenantal rite, which is seen in the vision, is meant to confirm Abram's faith that God will give him and his descendants the land. All these visions, dreams, and symbols have an analogy with the reality they are portraying, one that can only be drawn by attending to the oracles that are appended to each vision, dream, and symbol, so that both Abram's eyes and his ears are confirmed in the truth God is revealing.

The Visions and Dreams of the Patriarchs: Isaac

The vision of Isaac is related in a very short passage in Genesis: "And that very night the Lord appeared to him and said, 'I am the God of your father Abraham; do not be afraid, for I am with you and will bless you and will make your offspring numerous for my servant Abraham's sake'" (Gen. 26:24). In spite of the brevity of this passage, Calvin expands on it considerably in order to make several observations about the nature and role of visions. First, he claims that the vision is a symbol of God's presence given to prepare Isaac to listen more attentively to God.[38] Second, to confirm the truth of the word, the vision has to be inscribed with certain marks by which Isaac can distinguish it from the delusions of Satan, namely, that it manifests the glory and majesty of God.[39] Third, God did not appear to Isaac in God's full glory but rather accommodated Godself to Isaac's capacities, "for, as the majesty of God is infinite, it cannot be comprehended by the human mind, and by its magnitude it absorbs the whole world."[40] Fourth, the vision was not mute, and hence without meaning, but rather had an oracle annexed to it, "which confirmed, in the mind of Isaac, faith in gratuitous adoption and salvation."[41] These extensive comments on one verse of Scripture not only reveal Calvin's intense interest in the mutual relationship between oracle and vision in the faith of the patriarchs but also confirm the criteria Calvin uses to assess the meaning and function of visions.

The Visions and Dreams of the Patriarchs: Jacob

The first vision given to Jacob comes in a dream he has when fleeing from his brother Esau to go to the land of Haran. According to Calvin, the vision was given to alleviate Jacob's troubles and anxieties, which were almost unbearable. Once again, Calvin points out that visions and dreams were the customary mode of divine self-manifestation to the fathers.[42] He insists that the dream must have been sealed with distinguishing marks disclosing the majesty of God, which distinguished it from other dreams.[43] He is particularly interested in the form of the vision in the dream, "namely, that God manifested himself as seated upon a ladder, the extreme parts of which touched heaven and earth, and which was the vehicle of angels, who descended from heaven upon earth."[44] Calvin considers and rejects the interpretation of the ladder by some rabbis, that it is a figure of Divine Providence. However, he does not turn to the oracle that follows the vision to draw the analogy between the sign and the thing signified but rather to his theological conviction that the covenant of adoption is grounded in Jesus Christ, the eternal image of the Father.[45] The ladder is a symbol of the way the Mediator connects heaven and earth, restoring the blessings of God to sinners alienated from God. This interpretation of the ladder is confirmed by the words of Christ in John 1:51, but for Calvin the most compelling reason for the truth of his interpretation is the fitting analogy it draws between the sign of the ladder and the reality of Christ. "For the similitude of a ladder well suits the Mediator, through whom ministering angels, righteousness, and life, with all the graces of the Holy Spirit, descend to us step by step. We also, who are not only fixed on earth, but plunged into the depths of the curse, and into hell itself, ascend even unto God."[46] The symbol of Christ was also the most fitting for the confirmation of Jacob's faith in his hour of greatest anxiety and trial.[47] Once again, the ladder as a symbol of Christ confirms the faith not only of Jacob but also of the Church after him, including in Calvin's day.[48]

Calvin highlights the conjunction of the oracle with the vision of the ladder in the dream, even though the analogy between the ladder and the reality it signifies is not drawn in conjunction with this oracle. "Mute visions are cold; therefore the word of the Lord is as the soul which quickens them."[49] The word gives life to the symbol, even as the symbol gives greater clarity and authority to the word. The description of the word as the soul animating the vision is one we will continue to see in Calvin's writings. The sacramental nature of the vision of Jacob is confirmed by the way Calvin uses the conjunction of word and symbol to criticize the understanding of the sacraments in the Roman Church, which he claims are mute. "We may therefore observe, that whenever God manifested himself to the fathers, he also spoke, lest a mute vision should have held them in suspense."[50] The dreams and visions of the fathers give Calvin one of his clearest examples of the mutual relationship between manifestation and proclamation in the self-revelation of God, over against what he takes to be the exclusive focus on manifestation in the Roman Church.

Calvin repeats this point at length in his discussion of the final vision of Jacob, which takes place as he is on his way to join Joseph in Egypt. Noting the way the text says, "God spoke to Israel in visions of the night" (Gen. 46:2), Calvin claims that there can be no living image of God without the word being present at the same time. "Wherefore, in all outward signs, let us ever be attentive to his voice, if we would not be deluded by the wiles of Satan."[51] The vision, on the other hand, gives the word or oracle of God greater clarity, energy, vividness, and authority, so that it penetrates more deeply into the heart. "Let this mutual connection, then, be observed, that the vision which gives greater dignity to the word, precedes it; and that the word follows immediately, as if it were the soul of the vision."[52] Calvin again criticizes the Roman Church, not only for severing the word from the symbol, making the sacraments "lifeless phantoms which draw away deluded souls from the true God," but also for inventing symbols on its own, which "exhibit nothing else than the empty pomps of a profane theater."[53]

The vision of God that was the most celebrated by Jacob took place as he was returning from Haran to confront Esau. Jacob was left alone at night by the river Jabbok, and he had a vision in which he wrestled with a man. Calvin takes this to be a figure of the trials he experienced at the hands of God, and immediately applies the figure to the faithful of every age.[54] Calvin insists that the primary opponent who wrestles with the faithful is not Satan but God, to test their strength. "This, though at first sight it seems absurd, experience and reason teaches us to be true."[55] The vision of Jacob wrestling with the Lord at night is such a vivid image of the experience of all the faithful that Calvin interprets this vision as a visible example of a universal experience in the Church, "namely, that in their temptations, it is necessary for them to wrestle with God."[56]

However, Calvin is also aware that Jacob is located in a particular time in the economy of divine self-manifestation that distinguishes him from us.

This distinctiveness of Jacob is revealed when God refuses to grant his request to reveal his Name to him, "because the time of full revelation was not yet completed."[57] In spite of the fact that Jacob sees God in the twilight of morning, he nonetheless confesses that he has seen God face-to-face. Calvin thinks that this is true when one sees the statement in the context of the patriarchs' own experience; but Moses saw God more clearly, even though he was only allowed to see his glory from behind; and the apostles saw God more clearly still, by the glory that shone on them in the face of Christ.[58]

The Visions and Dreams of the Patriarchs: Joseph

When we come to Joseph, we encounter an example of the other form of revelation God used to manifest hidden things to the fathers, namely, dreams. "Now since the Lord was, at that time, wont to reveal his secrets by two methods—by visions and by dreams—one of these kinds is here noted."[59] The problem with revelation by dreams is not, as in the case of visions, satanic deception but rather the question of how to distinguish a dream that reveals the hidden things of God from the dreams we ordinarily have. Once again, Calvin claims that divinely sent dreams are inscribed with certain marks whereby we can recognize them to be oracles of God.[60] Calvin does not, however, specify what these certain marks might have been.

The one element lacking in dreams that Calvin considered essential to visions is the word or oracle of God annexed to them. The dream does not make the oracle more vivid or clear but rather is itself the oracle God means to reveal. In other words, dreams, unlike visions, are exactly the kind of "mute visions" Calvin appears to reject in his discussion of visions. They are oracles in the form of images, with no verbal oracle appended to explain their meaning. Calvin's willingness to embrace their divine origin and authority shows that he is willing to consider divine self-revelation by manifestation apart from proclamation. "Thus Joseph, being certainly persuaded that he had not been deluded by an empty specter, fearlessly announced his dream as a celestial oracle."[61]

The first dream of Joseph portrays his brothers' sheaves bowing down to his sheaf. This symbol does not seem entirely apt to Calvin, since Joseph and his brothers were shepherds and not farmers. However, upon hearing the proclamation of the dream, Joseph's brothers immediately grasp its meaning but reject the possibility that it is a divine oracle, "because it was repugnant to their wishes."[62] The second dream has the same purpose, but it is more clearly of divine origin, since "the Lord now calls upon them to look towards heaven, where his august majesty shines forth."[63] When his father hears of the dream, he rebukes Joseph, which creates a serious problem for Calvin. Given Jacob's experience with visions in dreams, should he not have been able to see the dream as a divine oracle? Calvin thinks that he did but that he dissembled in rebuking Joseph in order to quell the strife his dreams were creating in his family. Calvin faults him for this, claiming that he should have said, "'If this is a common dream, let it be treated with ridicule rather than with anger; but if it has proceeded from God, it is wicked to speak against it.'"[64] However, even his brothers show that they acknowledge the authenticity of the dreams, for they would not have been stirred to such a pitch of animosity against Joseph if they thought that his dreams were merely fables.[65] Thus all people, whether pious or pagan, have the capacity to recognize dreams as divine oracles, even though they have no word of God annexed to them. In spite of the animosity created by Joseph's dreams, God revealed them to Joseph to make known to him in advance the goal to which God's providence was leading him.[66]

The Visions and Dreams of the Prophets: Moses

As we have seen, Calvin places Moses between the patriarchs and the apostles. Moses and the prophets see God more clearly in their visions than did the fathers, but they do not see God as clearly as do the apostles. I want to consider four visions of God presented to Moses, all of which appear on Mount Sinai: the burning bush (Exod. 3); the voice of God giving the Law from the fire atop the mountain (Exod. 19); the vision of God seen on Sinai by Moses and the elders (Exod. 24); and the vision of God seen by Moses which renews the covenant broken by the apostasy of the people (Exod. 33–34). Moses both participates in the economy of visions and dreams used by God for the patriarchs and prophets and transcends this economy by his ability to see and speak with God more openly and intimately.

I have already considered Calvin's interpretation of the vision of the burning bush displayed to Moses. His interpretation of the vision in his commentary of 1563 on the last four books of Moses builds on his previous discussions in the Hebrews and Acts commentaries. The vision is meant to confirm his calling to be the liberator of his people, and the symbol of the burning bush is meant to represent the afflictions of the people in Egypt, which will not consume them because the Lord is with them. Calvin adds that this vision is similar to the one seen by Abram, as both show the preservation of the people in the midst of affliction.[67] Unlike the Acts commentary, however, here Calvin does not raise the issue of how Moses knew he was not deluded by the delusions of Satan but rather commends Moses for turning aside to look at the burning bush, even though he was as yet unaccustomed to such visions. "In this, too, we must observe his tractableness, in turning aside to learn. For it often happens that God presents himself in vain, because we presumptuously reject such great mercy."[68] Just as Moses showed himself to be teachable by turning aside to behold the vision whose meaning he did not yet understand, so all the godly should attend to the signs that God might manifest to them.[69] Finally, Calvin draws attention to the voice of God annexed to the vision, which gives the vision its power to encourage Moses.[70]

The next vision of God on Sinai takes place during the promulgation of the Law to the Israelites. According to Calvin, the Law is primarily given to renew the covenant of adoption made with Abraham. "To this end, then, it was engraved upon the tables of stone, and written in a book, that the marvelous grace, which God had conferred on the race of Abraham, should never sink into oblivion."[71] The Law also contains conditional promises, which threaten the disobedient with the curse of God, but for Calvin this conditional covenant is embraced within the covenant of gracious adoption.[72] So that the people might know that the Law came not from Moses but from God, Moses is told that God will speak to him from a thick cloud, as a symbol of God's glory and presence, in order that the people might believe Moses forever.[73] According to the account of this vision in Deuteronomy, God spoke with the people out of the fire "face to face" (Deut. 5:4). "To speak 'face to face' is equivalent to discoursing openly and familiarly; and in point of fact God had spoken with them, as mortals and friends communicate with each other in their mutual dealings."[74] The fire, thunder, lightning, thick cloud, and trumpet on Mount Sinai were meant to vindicate the authority of the Law, and also to express the nature of the conditional Law, that it creates terror.[75] "Hence it follows that they were convinced, by a sense of the divine glory and majesty, that it was not allowable for them to doubt the authority of the Law."[76] According to Calvin, the glory that adorned the giving of the Law from Sinai should still be seen by the godly whenever they read Moses, so that they submit to his authority.[77]

To prepare the people for the reception of the written tables of the Law, God commanded Moses to bring Aaron, Nadab, Abihu, and seventy of the elders of Israel up Mount Sinai. They were to approach God, but not as closely as Moses. In this way, the unique authority of Moses would be vindicated by witnesses. When they were on the Mount, "they saw the God of Israel" (Exod. 24:10), "that they might afterwards relate to the people what they had seen, and thus that the thing, being proved by competent witnesses, might obtain undoubted credit."[78] Calvin reminds his readers that the elders did not see God as God is but rather "in accordance with the mode of dispensation which he thought best, and which he accommodated to the capacity of man."[79] He points out that the form of God is nowhere described, only the nature of the pavement that formed the footstool of the Lord. "The color of sapphire was presented to them, to elevate their minds in its brightness above the world."[80] In other words, they saw a symbol that represented to them the transcendent majesty of God, which would both ravish them with astonishment by its beauty and humble them with its majesty.[81] The symbol of the footstool of sapphire both elevates their minds above the world by its beauty and reveals that God cannot be comprehended by the human mind. That the elders beheld God, and ate and drank, is attributable to the mercy of God for Calvin, for the sight of God should destroy us.[82] That after this vision Moses ascends even higher to the presence of God reveals to the elders the greater authority that he has, which they can then attest to the people. The vision of God by the elders therefore supports the vision of the people when they saw God face-to-face out of the fire on Mount Sinai, thereby confirming the authority of Moses and the Law.

The final vision of God on Mount Sinai takes place after Moses broke the two tables of the Law in light of the apostasy of the people. Moses successfully intercedes with God on behalf of the people, and God forgives them their sin, and agrees to go with them to the land that God has promised them. Moses, however, wants to know for certain that God's presence will go with them, which Calvin takes to mean that he seeks "the manifest token of God's presence."[83] God agrees to this, as such a self-manifestation would renew the covenant that had been broken by the sin of the people. However, God does not accede to Moses' request that God show him the perfection of his glory, but he does agree to show him God's beauty, in which God "carries his manifestation of himself to its very utmost."[84] The superlative nature of this vision is seen in the way it is depicted in the Name of God, revealing that in the vision "there was then exhibited to the holy prophet, as it were, a living representation of God."[85]

In conjunction with the vision of God's beauty, God also promises to proclaim his Name. Once again, Calvin points out the essential conjunction between the vision and the word. Since "true acquaintance with God is made more by the ears than by the eyes," it follows that "speechless visions would be cold and altogether evanescent, did they not borrow efficacy from words." For Calvin, this means that "The soul of a vision is the doctrine itself, from whence faith takes its rise."[86] This does not mean that the vision of God is without significance, for the fact that Moses beholds God more fully than any other human after the apostasy of the people has the effect of confirming the renewal of the covenant of adoption.[87] However, even though Moses is granted the most intimate vision of the beauty of God, he is still told that he shall not see God's face, but only God's back, in accommodation to the capacities of Moses.[88] Calvin takes the example of the accommodated vision of God by Moses to be true for all the godly, to whom God "manifests himself as far as is expedient" and "assumes the face which we are able to bear."[89]

Although Moses is like all the godly in the way the self-manifestation of God is accommodated to his capacity, he surpasses both the patriarchs before him and the prophets after him by the clarity and intimacy of his vision of God. God is said to have spoken to Moses "face to face" (Exod. 33:11), which Calvin takes to mean "that God appeared to Moses by an extraordinary mode of revelation."[90] Thus, when Aaron and Miriam challenge the superiority of Moses, asking "Has the Lord spoken only through Moses? Has he not spoken through us also?" (Num. 12:2), God vindicates the unique authority of Moses by pointing out the singular mode of revelation he received, as distinct from all other patriarchs and prophets. "With him I speak face to face—clearly, not in riddles; and he beholds the form of the Lord" (Num. 12:8). By saying that God spoke face-to-face with Moses, Calvin thinks that a "more intimate and interior communication is denoted."[91] Such communication is not only more intimate and familiar, it is also more clear. Whereas the visions of the prophets are enigmas and similitudes, God speaks to Moses by "actual sight."[92] Calvin makes the same point in his comments on Deuteronomy 34:10. "Moses was distinguished from the other prophets, that God spoke to him face to face," so that "in comparison with others, he went beyond them all."[93] It is significant that Calvin locates the unique authority of Moses in the degree to which he was allowed to behold God.[94]

The Visions and Dreams of the Prophets: Isaiah

In his interpretation of Numbers 12:6, Calvin describes the visions and dreams of the prophets as "seals for the confirmation of prophecies; so that the prophets, as if sent from heaven, might with full confidence declare themselves to be God's lawful interpreters. For visions had their own peculiar marks, to distinguish them from phantoms and false imaginations; and dreams were also accompanied by signs, in order to remove all doubt of their authenticity."[95] Visions and dreams were not only authenticated by certain marks to show their divine origin; they also gave divine authority and credibility to the oracles of God they accompanied. Visions were "some visible appearance, which confirms and ratifies the truth of his oracles to the eyes and all the senses. Thus has God often appeared to his servants, so that his majesty might be inscribed upon his addresses to them."[96]

The vision of God granted to the prophet Isaiah is one of the most vivid and memorable among all prophetic visions, even though it would not, in Calvin's mind, equal or eclipse the singular visions of Moses. Since Calvin interprets visions in large part as confirming prophets in their calling when they are afflicted by trials, he does not think it likely that Isaiah saw his vision of God in the Temple at the beginning of his ministry, but only after he had performed the office of a teacher long enough to experience the apparent futility of his work, which might have induced him to give up his ministry.[97] Calvin explains the fact that Isaiah appears to have forgotten he was a prophet as being the effect of the overwhelming experience of beholding the glory and majesty of God. "And it is necessary that the godly should be affected in this manner, when the Lord gives them tokens of his presence, that they may be brought low and ravished outside themselves."[98] It was both useful and necessary for Isaiah to feel the dreadful majesty of God, as he was sent to announce divine judgment upon the people.

The first aspect of the vision Calvin addresses is Isaiah's bold claim, "I saw the Lord." If God is Spirit, bodily eyes cannot see God; and the boundless altitude of God prevents God from being seen in a bodily shape. Calvin responds to these objections by claiming that Isaiah did not see God as God is, but rather in a form accommodated to human capacity. Such accommodation would involve taking on a form that earthly and temporal human beings can behold, and "thus he attributes to God a throne, and robe, and a bodily appearance."[99] Even though God does not in fact have a bodily form, the figure beheld by Isaiah is not an illusion but is truly a symbol of the presence of God.[100] In the same way, when John the Baptist saw the dove, he claimed to see the Spirit; not that the Spirit can be seen in its essence, but rather because "in the representation there was no deception."[101]

The form adopted by God in the vision of Isaiah is that of a judge seated upon a throne. Calvin thinks that this description is the most apt for the circumstances of Isaiah's ministry, since he was to summon the Jews to the judgment seat of God. However, the description is not one invented by Isaiah (Plato's *phantasm*), but is rather an accurate description of the form of God's self-manifestation to Isaiah (Plato's *eikon*). "But lest we should suppose that the Prophet contrived the manner in which he would paint God, we ought to know that he faithfully describes the very form in which God was represented and exhibited to him."[102] The representation of the seraphim standing over the throne is also of significance for Calvin, especially the description of the positions of their six wings.[103] The wings with which they fly signify their ready obedience to God, whereas the wings veiling their faces show us the limits of our ability to behold God, since not even the angels can look at God with unveiled faces. Though the wings covering their feet are not as easy to decipher, Calvin takes them to signify the difficulty of viewing God. If we cannot gaze directly upon angels, it is even more the case that we cannot see God as God is.[104]

The smoke that fills the Temple is a "common and ordinary symbol" that has a twofold meaning: to restrain human curiosity, and to inspire terror.[105] The overall effect of the vision is terrifying to Isaiah, leading him to cry out that he is undone, for "he was so terrified by seeing God, that he expected immediate destruction."[106] Both the vision and the experience of terror it awakens confirm Isaiah in his ministry, and also confirm the message of Isaiah for the Jews.[107] God responds to the terror of Isaiah by sending the seraphim to purify his lips with a burning coal. As in the case of Abram, this ceremony takes place in the vision itself, to further strengthen Isaiah in his calling, for "by the aid of the outward sign God assisted the Prophet's understanding."[108] Though the burning coal has no intrinsic ability to purify his lips, by telling Isaiah that his lips are in fact clean, the angel confirms the truth of the sign, showing that the reality is given with it.[109] The conjunction of the word of the angel with the sign of the burning coal confirms Calvin's conviction that the word is an essential part of the sacrament, over against the silent sacraments of Rome, "where the sacraments are turned into stageplays."[110] The sacrament of the burning coal, presented to Isaiah in his vision, has the same effect as the vision itself, which is to confirm Isaiah in his calling, so that nothing may prevent him "from appearing as God's representative."[111] Finally, God speaks to Isaiah, to reveal to him the purpose of the vision, namely, that he was called "to deliver an incredible message about blinding the Jews."[112] Isaiah needed to be confirmed in his prophetic calling because God knew that his ministry would meet stiff resistance not only initially, as Isaiah had already experienced, but also for the length of his ministry among the Jews.[113] The vision, and the sacrament of purification within the vision, was necessary to confirm Isaiah in the legitimacy of his ministry in spite of its clear lack of results, which might have led him to despair.

Calvin's attention to every detail of Isaiah's vision is remarkable. He finds meaning in every figure and symbol, from the figure of the judge to the smoke filling the Temple. Even though there is no word or oracle to establish the analogy between the signs and the realities they represent, Calvin finds it quite easy and natural to draw such analogies, seen with special clarity in the way he interprets the meaning of the wings of the seraphim. The visions described by the prophets may be accommodated to their capacities, but the figures shown them by God are not empty or deceptive. Hence Calvin thinks it imperative to interpret the meaning of every detail of the vision, as it pertains not only to Isaiah and the people of his day but also to the Church in every age, especially in Calvin's, when the ministry of the evangelicals seemed to meet with so much opposition.[114]

The Visions and Dreams of the Prophets: Ezekiel

If the vision of Isaiah is one of the most memorable of the prophetic visions, the vision of Ezekiel is one of the most obscure. In light of the claim made by the Jews that the vision was so obscure that it should not be explained, Calvin says that it is absurd to suppose that God would appear in vain. He does not, however, deny the difficulties presented by the vision, "but yet into what God has set before us, it is not only lawful and useful but necessary to inquire."[115] In light of the obscurity of the vision, Calvin seems to be the most comfortable when he speaks about the nature of the vision itself, and less sure of himself when he interprets the various figures of the vision. For instance, when Ezekiel says that he saw the vision when "the heavens were opened," Calvin says that it would not be enough for God to part the heavens without at the same time giving the prophet a new power of vision by which to see.[116] When Ezekiel says, "I saw visions of God," Calvin thinks that this was necessary to confirm him in his prophetic office, in light of the incredibility of God appearing and speaking in Babylon. "This would never have been believed unless the calling of God had been marked in some signal and especial manner."[117] And when Ezekiel describes the vision of the whirlwind out of the north, with fire, Calvin states that the intention of the vision was "to invest his servant with authority, and then to inspire the people with terror."[118] The formidable form of the whirlwind corresponds well to the message of judgment Ezekiel was called to pronounce upon the Jews in Babylon.[119]

Calvin is especially attentive to those features of Ezekiel's vision that manifest the glory and majesty of God, thereby authenticating its divine origin.[120] Thus, when the prophet sees the color of amber with the appearance of fire within it, Calvin notes, "But then its color was remarkable, because it not only attracted the eyes of the prophet but dazzled them with its splendor, so that he acknowledged it as celestial and divine."[121] On the other hand, when the prophet says that he "saw the likeness of an appearance of a man above it," Calvin takes this as being a warning against using the vision as a warrant to say that God can be seen in visible and bodily form, as Ezekiel is only seeing forms and appearances.[122] The same point is made by Ezekiel when he says, "this was a vision of the likeness of the glory of Jehovah" (Ezek. 1:28). According to Calvin, this is a reminder that the whole vision is accommodated to the capacities of the prophet. "The glory of God is so beheld by the prophet, that God did not appear as he really is, but as far as can be beheld by a mortal man."[123] However, the accommodated self-manifestation of God is not delusive, for God is really seen in the vision, even if God is not seen as God truly is, for "he has so appeared, as to leave no doubt in the minds of his servants as to their knowing they have seen God."[124] Finally, Calvin directs our attention to the voice of God that is addressed to Ezekiel after the vision. Without this word being added to the vision, Ezekiel would not be certain that God had called him. "But when God confirmed the vision by his word, the prophet was enabled to say with advantage, I have seen the glory of God."[125] Both the vision and the word were needed to confirm Ezekiel in his calling, given the stiff resistance he would meet from the Jews in Babylon.[126]

The Visions and Dreams of the Prophets: Daniel

Calvin returns to the mode of divine self-manifestation in dreams in his lectures on Daniel of 1561. Calvin is especially interested in the way Nebuchadnezzar seems to recognize the dream he has as being of divine origin, given that he summons the magicians, astrologers, and sorcerers to narrate and interpret his dream (Dan. 2:2). To account for this possibility, Calvin turns to profane authors to see if they recognize the possibility of the divine inspiration of dreams. He knows it would be absurd to claim this for every dream, since most dreams arise from different causes, such as daily thoughts. "If I have meditated on anything during the day-time, something occurs to me at night in a dream."[127] Other dreams are caused by various affections, as we learn by experience.[128] Yet other dreams are caused by the body, so that fevers produce one kind of dream, thirst yet others, and drunkenness induces a state of frenzy.[129] In spite of the many natural causes of dreams, Calvin thinks that "it is sufficiently evident that some dreams are under divine regulation."[130] To make this case, Calvin surveys classical literature on this subject. Aristotle, for one, denied that dreams come from God, even though he ascribes to some of them a sort of divination. Cicero discusses dreams at great length, and makes the claim that "if there is any divination in dreams, it follows that there is a Deity in heaven; for the mind of man cannot conceive of any dream without divine inspiration."[131] Homer also agrees that dreams can be divinely inspired, since his heroes are divinely admonished in their sleep. On the basis of this evidence from classical authors, Calvin concludes that "the opinion concerning some kind of divine agency in dreams was not rashly implanted in the hearts of all men."[132]

Even though the ungodly recognize the divine agency in dreams, and may even receive divinely inspired dreams, their dreams do not have the same clarity as those of the godly. Calvin sees this as the case with regard to the king of Babylon, who knew he had a divinely inspired dream but could not remember it. "We perceive, then, that God reveals his will even to unbelievers, but not clearly; because seeing they do not see, just as if they were gazing at a closed book or a sealed letter."[133] Thus, even though God revealed his will to the king, he could not by himself understand what was revealed to him in the dream. "His dream would have been of no use to him, unless, as we shall see, Daniel had been presented to him as its interpreter."[134] One would think that Calvin would contrast the obscurity of the dreams of the unbelievers with the clarity of the dreams of someone like Joseph, who fearlessly announced his dream as an oracle. However, he claims that divine self-manifestation in dreams is usually obscure, taking place through figures and enigmas. "And this occurs in the case of the profane as well as of the servants of God."[135] Joseph knew that his dreams had been divinely inspired, and announced them to his brothers as divine oracles; but he had no idea what the dreams actually meant. "Hence God speaks in enigmas by dreams, until the interpretation is added."[136]

Thus, when Daniel has his own visions in his dream, he, like Joseph, not only recognizes the dream as an oracle but also delivers the vision to others, unlike King Nebuchadnezzar, who saw the vision vaguely, only to have it slip from his memory.[137] However, the vision leaves Daniel troubled and unable to understand it, until he asks an angel who appears to him what the dream might mean. "But we ought to understand how God opens up to Daniel, his servant, and to us by his assistance and ministry, these mysteries which cannot be otherwise comprehended by our human senses."[138] Because dreams do not have an oracle appended to them, the meaning of the dream cannot be understood by the one who dreams it; rather, another must interpret it to him. The essential combination of vision and oracle is repeated in the essential combination of dream and interpretation, except that the person having the dream knows only that it is divine, and must depend upon another to interpret its meaning.

2. Miracles as Confirming Signs

Calvin demonstrated an interest in miracles as signs confirming the truth of the Word of God as early as the first edition of the *Institutes* in 1536. He considers miracles a form of the sacraments God uses to confirm the truth of God's promises. "The term 'sacrament' as we have previously discussed its nature so far, embraces generally all those signs which God has ever signaled to men to render them more certain and confident of the truth of his promises. He sometimes willed to present these in natural things, at other times set them forth in miracles."[139] Among the sacraments set forth in miracles, Calvin includes the dew on the fleece confirming the promise of victory for Gideon (Judg. 6:37–38) and the withdrawal of the sun dial by ten degrees to promise safety to Hezekiah (Isa. 38:7). "Since these things were done to support and confirm their feeble faith, they were also sacraments."[140] Since this passage remains unchanged from the 1536 edition through the 1559 edition, we may safely conclude that the role of miracles as sacramental confirmation of God's promises was decided very early in Calvin's theological career.[141]

Calvin also thought that miracles gave confirmation to the truth of the Law delivered by Moses. In an addition to the *Institutes* made in 1550, Calvin states, "Now these very numerous and remarkable miracles which he relates are so many confirmations of the law that he has delivered, and of the doctrine he has published."[142] This idea could have been suggested to Calvin by his observation a year earlier in his Hebrews commentary that the fire, blackness, and darkness on Mount Sinai were "signs which God manifested to provide trustworthiness and reverence for his Law."[143] These miracles would include Moses being on the mountain for forty days; the lightning, thunder, and trumpet on Mount Sinai; the radiance of his face; and the death of Korah, Dathan, and Abiram. "By these was not God, from heaven, commending Moses as his undoubted prophet?"[144] Calvin claims that this is not disputable by the fact that Moses is the one narrating the miracles, since others who were contemporary with the events would have contradicted his narration had he invented it. The reliability of the miracles of Moses is so important to Calvin that he adds a whole section in 1559 dedicated to vindicating the reliability of the historical witness to these miracles.[145] The argument Calvin makes here is remarkably similar to the one that will be advanced by John Locke more than a century later. The authority of Moses is established by the miracles that he performed, and the authenticity of the miracles is validated by the historical accuracy of the accounts narrating the miracles.

The use of miracles as sacramental signs confirming the promise of God may be seen in the confrontation between Isaiah and King Ahaz. Isaiah tells Ahaz that God promises him victory over the alliance of Aram and Israel against him. Isaiah then commands Ahaz to ask for a sign from God. Calvin interprets such a sign in light of the distinction he made in the 1536 *Institutes* between natural and miraculous sacraments.[146] The purpose of the extraordinary sign is the same as the ordinary sign, namely, to confirm faith in the promise of God. The difference is that the work of the Holy Spirit is not seen in the ordinary sacraments, whereas it is in miracles.[147] God commands Ahaz to ask for a sign because he sees that Ahaz doubts the truth of the promise made to him through Isaiah. The sign allows Ahaz to see the truth with his eyes that he also heard with his ears, so that the promise might be confirmed. "For whenever God sees that his promises do not satisfy us, he adds helps to them suitable to our weakness; so that we not only hear him speak, but likewise behold his hand displayed, and thus are confirmed by an evident proof of the fact."[148] The miraculous sign therefore has an essential connection to the word whose truth it is given to confirm, as is also the case with ordinary sacraments, "for miracles added to the word are seals."[149]

Even though both miraculous and ordinary sacraments confirm faith in the word of promise, Calvin wants the godly to remain satisfied with those natural signs God has given for the benefit of the whole Church. They should not follow the example of Ahaz or Hezekiah in praying to God to have their faith confirmed by a miraculous sacrament.[150] Hezekiah prayed for a sign that would confirm the promise that he would not die of the illness from which he suffered, but Calvin thinks he did so by the secret impulse of the Holy Spirit. However, the sign that God granted to him, the turning back of the shadow of the sun by degrees, has, like all other sacraments, an analogy to the reality it is being given to confirm, "for it is as if he had said, 'As it is in my power to change the hours of the day, and to make the sun go backwards, so it is in my power to lengthen thy life.'"[151] Calvin is not interested in the number of degrees the sun goes back. For him, "it is enough if there is a manifest analogy and similitude."[152]

In his harmony of the last four books of Moses of 1563, Calvin notes how the faith of Moses was strengthened by the bestowal of three signs. The first sign would confirm that the Lord had sent Moses when the people returned to Mount Sinai to worship the Lord there. According to Calvin, this sign must be seen in conjunction with the Word of God that promised the deliverance of the people from Egypt.[153] The second sign was the staff of Moses that would become a serpent, which was meant to confirm the authority of Moses both in the eyes of his own people and in the eyes of Pharaoh. The third sign was the creation and removal of a skin disease when Moses would put his hand into his cloak. According to Calvin, the addition of sign to sign reveals God's concern to strengthen the faith of Moses, "from whence Moses might attain full confidence, and that no further hindrance should oppose his pious desires."[154]

The essential relation between the Word of God and miracles becomes especially pressing given that false prophets seem to have the ability to work signs of their own, by which to turn the hearts of the godly to false deities. Calvin thinks that the miracles that confirmed the Law could not be mistaken for the false signs of wonder workers, in spite of the way the Egyptian magicians and others can ape miraculous signs. "Thus in the miracles, whereby the Law was ratified, the glory of God so shone forth that they might obtain credit without any hesitation," for like the miracles confirming the Gospel, "they present evidences inscribed upon them by God."[155] Once the Law had been ratified by miracles, it should be used to test all alleged prophetic revelations certified by signs of their own. "In order, therefore, that we may duly profit by signs, an inseparable connection must be established between them and doctrine."[156] The Law that is confirmed by miracles becomes the criterion by which to reject all alleged miracles done by false prophets.

The essential connection between word and sign also prevents miracles alone from leading those who witness them to true faith and piety. King Nebuchadnezzar may have blessed the God of Shadrach, Mesach, and Abednego after their miraculous deliverance from the fiery furnace, but such a blessing did not come from true faith, according to Calvin, for a miracle "is not sufficient for solid piety, unless instruction is added, and occupies the first place."[157] Miracles may prepare one to believe the Word of God, or may confirm faith in the word; but they do not have the ability to create faith on their own. "But faith cannot be acquired by any miracle, or any perception of the divine power; it requires instruction also. The miracles avail only to the preparation for piety or for its confirmation; they cannot themselves bring men to worship the true God."[158]

3. THE EXODUS AS THE ARCHETYPE AND PLEDGE OF THE GRACE OF GOD

The miracles God performs are seen by Calvin as extraordinary sacraments, confirming the pious in the truth of the promises. Calvin claims that miracles are helps added to the word of God to address our weakness and infirmity, and must never be severed from the word or doctrine God is confirming by the miracle. There is, however, one miracle that not only confirms the truth of the promise but also itself reveals the grace and love of God for the Israelites, and that is the exodus from Egypt. Calvin develops this insight in his commentary on Psalms of 1557. According to Calvin, just as miracles confirm the truth of the promise, so every subsequent work of deliverance performed by God for the Israelites is an appendage to the original work of liberation in the exodus. The exodus is the "most remarkable instance of the goodness of God towards the children of Israel, as if it were the archetype or original copy of the grace of God."[159] The exodus itself, however, is seen as the confirmation of the covenant of adoption established with Abraham and his descendants, as "the chief and lasting pledge of the divine favor."[160] In particular it shows that "the divine goodness is principally displayed in the Church, which God has selected as the great theater where his fatherly love may be manifested."[161] This is the reason why the godly appeal to this event so often, for it is the most vivid confirmation of their adoption in Abraham, and the clearest pledge and symbol of the love of God.[162] Whenever the godly celebrate any subsequent deliverance by God, they often remind the people of the exodus, as the foundation of all subsequent works of salvation, "for on that occasion God made a remarkable display of the boundless treasures of his grace in establishing his Church, and left out no proof of his kindness, in order to make known the happiness of that nation."[163]

Calvin is especially struck by the clarity of the miracle performed in the exodus, as if the hand of God appeared visibly from heaven. The reality of the miracle is especially evident in the two contrasting fates of the Israelites and the Egyptians. The water through which the Israelites passed in safety is the same water in which Pharaoh and his army drowned. "The distinction made a conspicuous display of God's mercy in saving his people."[164] The Israelites at the time saw this most vividly, for they looked back at the sea through which they had passed safely and saw the dead bodies of the drowned Egyptians lying on the shore, which clearly revealed to them both the power and the love of God.[165] The clarity of the power and favor of God make it unnecessary to do more than simply narrate the event without literary embellishment, for the event itself strikes us with astonishment.[166] The clarity with which the event itself reveals the love, power, and mercy of God for the children of Abraham is not lost on Rahab, the prostitute in Jericho, who had heard the report of it. "The passage of the sea was a full and irrefragable proof, as much so as if God had stretched forth his hand from heaven."[167]

As the archetype of the grace and favor of God for the children of Israel, the exodus reveals in a paradigmatic way the nature of God in relation to the Church. "From this one example we ought to consider how God will be to us, so as to draw this conclusion, that in the future God will always be like himself."[168] Thus, when God threatens to destroy the people after they refuse to enter into the promised land, Moses appeals to the exodus itself as the basis on which to ask for forgiveness, for by delivering the people God had committed Godself to be their perpetual Savior.[169] So also, when Daniel prays for God's mercy on Jerusalem from his exile in Babylon, he appeals to the exodus as the primary evidence of God's grace that can give his heart the confidence it needs to call on God.[170] Even the return from Babylon itself, as astonishing as it was, is described analogously to the exodus from Egypt. "It amounts to this, that when God shall bring back the Church from captivity in Babylon, the deliverance will be of a kind not less striking and magnificent than when, in an early period, the nation went out of Egypt."[171]

4. THE WORK OF GOD CONFIRMS THE WORD OF GOD

The exodus confirms the covenant of adoption made with Abraham, and thereby confirms the adoption of Abraham's children. As the exemplary work of deliverance, it confirms the promise that God will in fact be with Abraham and his descendants. According to Calvin, what God does on the scale of the Church, God also does in the lives of each of the pious: God confirms by God's work what God promises in God's Word. Calvin first develops this form of confirmation in his commentary on the Psalms of 1557. When David prays that God not hide God's face from him (Ps. 27:9), Calvin describes the face of God as the visible manifestation of the favor of God, "as if it had been said, Lord, make me truly to experience that thou hast been near to me, and let me clearly behold thy power in saving me."[172] The faithful first know of the grace and mercy of God through the Word of God; but the mercy of which they are told in the word they come to experience in actual fact by the work of God. "We must observe the anagogy between the knowledge of grace from the Word of God and from experience (as it is called). For as God shows himself present to us in operation (as they usually speak), he must first be sought in his Word."[173]

The faith of the godly therefore rests on a twofold foundation: the Word of God that they hear and the work of God that they see and experience, even though "the contemplation of the works of God would not kindle this light within us, unless God, illuminating us by his word, should show us."[174] In other words, faith is truly established when it is founded not only on the proclamation, but also on the manifestation, of God's grace and favor, whereby "he confirms with his own hand what he had previously uttered with his lips."[175] The pious will always begin with the Word of God, and turn to the work of God to confirm the truth of the word in their own experience. The ungodly, on the other hand, will not believe the word of promise unless they first see the work of God's favor.[176] The godly will rely on the truth of the word even "though the effect does not immediately appear; for it is the peculiar excellence of faith to hold us dependent on the mouth of God."[177] The godly know that there will be times when the mercy of God is known only by proclamation and not by manifestation, yet that will not lead them to call into question the truth of God's favor towards them.

Nonetheless, Calvin insists that if the mercy of God were only to be made known to us by proclamation, and it were never to be manifested to us in our lives by the work of God, the lack of manifestation would undermine the truth of proclamation. When the author of Psalm 119 prays to God, "Let your steadfast love become my comfort according to your promise to your servant," Calvin interprets this to mean that "all our hope would end in mere disappointment, did not God at length appear as our deliverer."[178] The lack of the manifestation of God's mercy would undermine the truth of the Word of God to which the faithful cling; "for when God only speaks, and the thing itself does not appear, his word seems in a manner to lie dormant and to be useless,"[179] and God's promises of mercy "appear to be dead and void."[180] The work of God therefore seals the truth of the Word of God by manifesting the mercy that the word proclaims. "Thus it is proper to join doctrine with experience; for since the sight of God's works would produce little impression on us, he first enlightens us by the torch of his word, and next seals the truth of it by the actual accomplishment."[181]

Calvin sees the work of God as a secondary but essential confirmation and seal of the truth of the mercy of God. Given the weakness and infirmity of the pious, God intends both God's Word and God's work to found and strengthen faith in God's favor. "For that which God promises us in his word he seals by act, and as often as he exhibits to us manifestations of his grace and might, he intends them to be so many confirmations of what he has spoken, and so many helps tending to support all our doubts."[182] What we hear in God's Word may be the proclamation of what God has done for the Church in the past, such as the exodus from Egypt. When God would act the same way in the lives of those who heard these reports, "they also felt by actual experience, yea, even saw with their own eyes, what they knew before by hearsay, and the report of their fathers."[183] Because God always remains like Godself, the pious are confident that God will act in their own lives in a way that corresponds to and confirms the way God has acted in the past. Or what we hear in the word may be the promise of God's mercy and love, which we believe even when we do not see its effects. Were God to act in a way that confirmed the word of promise, then "what the faithful had before only heard of was now exhibited before their eyes. As long as we have only the bare promises of God, his grace and salvation are as yet hidden in hope; but when these promises are actually performed, his grace and salvation are clearly manifested."[184]

The goodness of God manifested to the pious in their own experience should lead them to seek God from the inmost affection of their hearts, "under the alluring influence of his goodness."[185] Such meditation is especially necessary when we pray to God, which is why the godly in the Psalms spend so much time contemplating the goodness of God manifested both to their ancestors and to themselves, in confirmation of God's promise, and "as so many testimonies of his electing love."[186] The godly ought never to fear that such testimonies of God's love will be lacking either in their own lives or in the lives of all the faithful, for "God had wrought on behalf of his chosen people many deliverances, which were as open and manifest as if they had been exhibited on a conspicuous theater."[187]

5. Grace Manifested to One Is a Pledge of Grace to All

The manifestation of God's grace in the lives of the faithful not only confirms the truth of the promise of God for them; it also gives living testimony to all the faithful that God will likewise manifest God's favor towards them. Calvin develops this insight in his commentary on the Psalms. God wants us to "take encouragement and comfort from whatever blessings he confers upon our neighbors, since by these he testifies that he will always be ready to bestow his goodness upon all the godly in common."[188] Thus, when David exhorts the godly in the Psalms to rejoice with him because of the favor God has manifested towards him, Calvin does not take this to be an invitation to sympathy but rather claims that David is holding out his own experience as a testimony that God will act towards all the faithful as God has acted towards him.[189] The exhibition of God's grace that seals the truth of the word for ourselves in turn becomes a seal and confirmation of the promise for all the godly, for "all the instances in which God attests his succor to his servants are so many seals, by which he confirms and gives us assurance of his goodness and grace towards us."[190]

When God saved David from affliction, God was giving a token or pledge to all the godly that God will likewise free them from their affliction, for God always remains like Godself.[191] The godly will rejoice at the deliverance of David from affliction, therefore, because the experience of David is a God-given pledge that God will act the same way to all members of the Church, even if they are currently suffering under affliction.[192] Just as the exodus as the archetype of grace is a pledge to us that God will always deliver the Church, so also the experience of one of the faithful is a confirmation that God will be merciful towards all the faithful. "God is presented to our view as merciful and kind to others, that we may assure ourselves that he will be the same towards us."[193] The goodness of God manifested to others, like the goodness revealed in the Church and in their experience, confirms the promise of mercy made to the faithful, making it possible for them to taste the full sweetness of God's goodness. "The remembrance of God must be sweet to us, and fill our hearts with joy, or rather ravish us with love to him, after he has caused us to taste of his goodness."[194]

CHAPTER 6

Symbols and Types of Christ in the Law

The covenant with Abraham, and the renewal of that covenant in the Law of Moses, is confirmed by many visible signs and symbols, which confirm the faithful in the divine origin and truth of the covenant, especially in times of trial. Calvin understands some of these forms of visual confirmation, such as visions and miracles, in an explicitly sacramental way, though all forms exhibit the mutual relation of sign and word that Calvin takes to be essential to any living icon of God. The word is the soul animating the visual representation, even as the visual representation gives force, clarity, and vividness to the word. Both image and word confirm that the Law is indeed the self-manifestation of God to the Israelites. However, the Law also contains within itself images, symbols, and types of the Christ who is yet to come. Understood in a vertical way, the Law is the progressive self-revelation of God, culminating in the self-manifestation of God in Christ. Understood in a horizontal and temporal way, the Law is the progressive self-manifestation of Christ, culminating in the exhibition of Christ in the flesh.

I now turn to a consideration of the self-representation of Christ in the images, symbols, and types of the Law. Since most of these images and types are what Calvin terms "ordinary signs," in contrast to extraordinary signs such as miracles, I attend in particular to the economy or dispensation followed by God in the institution of sacraments for the Israelites. This economy has three major periods: the time of the patriarchs before Moses; the time of the tabernacle from Moses through David; and the time of the Temple from Solomon to the death of Christ. However, Christ is also manifested to the Israelites in various people, especially the priests and kings of Israel, whom Calvin understands to be types of Christ. Thus Jerusalem, with its kings, priests, temple, and sacrifices, will be for Calvin the most vivid and complete representation of Christ to the Israelites, and later to the Jews.

I first examine the development of Calvin's understanding of the sacraments of the Law, since it underlies his understanding of the way Christ represents himself to the Israelites, and then turn to an examination of each of the symbols and types of Christ, according to the time of their appearance in the dispensation of God, from Adam until the coming of Jesus. The development of each of the symbols in Calvin's theology is considered as it arises within this dispensation, but the order of topics in the chapter follows the order of the economy of the self-manifestation of Christ as understood by Calvin.

1. The Sacraments of the Law in Relation to Christ

The representation of Christ in the sacraments of the Law was a central theological issue for Calvin throughout his career. In his first writing as an evangelical, he states that before the promised Christ appeared to the Israelites, God confirmed them in their hope in every possible way, "by providing them with his written law, containing numerous ceremonies, purifications, and sacrifices, which were but the figures and shadows of the great blessings to come with Christ, who alone was the embodiment and truth of them."[1] The question is, did the Law only *represent* Christ, or did it also *present* and offer Christ and his benefits to the Israelites, to be enjoyed by them? Calvin's answer, drawn in large part from Hebrews, seems to suggest that the Law represented, but did not present, Christ. "For the law was incapable of bringing anyone to perfection; it only presented Christ, and like a teacher spoke of and led to him, who was, as was said by Saint Paul, the end and fulfillment of the Law."[2] It is difficult to be certain from such a short passage, but the reference to Hebrews about the limitation of the ceremonies of the Law—that they could not per se bring anyone to perfection—combined with the statement that the Law only presented Christ, suggests that the ceremonies of the Law are not understood as offering Christ and his benefits to the Israelites.

Calvin returns to this question in the first edition of the *Institutes*. Over against the ambiguity of the 1535 preface, Calvin leaves no doubt that the sacraments of the Law have the same purpose as the sacraments of the Gospel, namely, to represent Christ. "Yet those ancient sacraments looked to the same purpose to which ours now tend: to direct and almost lead men by the hand to Christ, or rather, as images, to represent him and set him forth to be known."[3] The only difference between the two is the way Christ is represented in each. "There is only one difference: the former foreshadowed Christ promised while he was as yet awaited; the latter attest him as already given and revealed."[4] Calvin insists that this difference in the way that Christ is represented in no way detracts from the spiritual efficacy of the sacraments of the Law. Drawing on Augustine to make this point, Calvin affirms that "the sacraments of the Jews were different in their signs, but equal in the thing signified; different in visible appearance, but identical in spiritual power."[5] Calvin does acknowledge the diversity of the sacraments within the Law itself, for new sacraments are given over the course of the history of Israel, whereas the Gospel only sets forth Baptism and the holy Supper of the Lord as sacraments.[6] Such diversity over time was meant to disclose to the Israelites that the reality portrayed by their sacraments had not yet arrived.[7]

In the second edition of the *Institutes,* Calvin intensifies his insistence that the sacraments of the Law have the same spiritual power and efficacy as do the sacraments of the Gospel, to counter the claim made by the Anabaptists that the promises made to the Jews were only temporal and earthly. Calvin bases his claim on 1 Corinthians 10:3–4, in which Paul says that the Israelites "all ate the same spiritual food, and all drank the same spiritual drink. For they drank from the spiritual rock that followed them, and the rock was Christ." According to Calvin, this passage means that "the Lord not only provided them with the same benefits but also manifested his grace among them by the same symbols."[8] The Jews were baptized by their crossing of the sea and in the cloud, and ate and drank Christ in the manna and water flowing from the rock. Calvin returns to 1 Corinthians 10 to refute the Scholastic understanding that the sacraments of the Law foreshadowed grace but did not offer it. "Who dared treat as an empty sign that which revealed the true communion of Christ to the Jews?"[9]

Calvin bolsters his claim that the sacraments of the Law have the same efficacy as the sacraments of the Gospel in his commentary on Romans of 1540. Paul's description of the sign of circumcision as the seal of the righteousness of faith allows Calvin to draw a general conclusion concerning the efficacy of sacraments in general. "These are seals by which the promises of God are in a manner imprinted on our hearts, and the certainty of grace is established for us. Although apart from the Spirit they profit nothing, yet by them, as instruments, God distributes the power of his Spirit."[10] The benefit of this passage, unlike 1 Corinthians 10, is that it allows Calvin to speak of the efficacy of the regular sacraments of the Law, such as circumcision, without appealing to the exodus as the baptism of the Israelites.

In the 1543 edition of the *Institutes,* Calvin appeals to Romans 4:11 to bolster the case he made against the Scholastic understanding of the sacraments in the 1539 edition. Calvin uses Paul's description of circumcision to insist that the sacraments of the Law offered Christ and his benefits to the fathers. "They felt the same power in their sacraments as we do in ours; these were seals of divine good will toward them, looking to eternal salvation."[11] Calvin realizes that both Colossians and Hebrews may be used against this interpretation—the very passages to which he appealed in 1535—because they suggest that the sacraments of the Law are only figures lacking reality and therefore do not perfect the consciences of the people under the Law. Calvin responds by distinguishing between the mode of representation and the efficacy of the sacraments of the Law and the Gospel. "For until Christ was manifested in the flesh, all signs foreshadowed him as absent, however much he might make the presence of his power and himself inwardly felt among believers."[12] Even though the sacraments of the Law represent Christ as absent and yet to come, they nonetheless present both Christ and his benefits to the Israelites under the Law, to be felt and enjoyed by them.

Calvin reiterates this point in his commentary on 1 Corinthians of 1546. Interpreting Paul's statement that the Israelites ate the same spiritual food, Calvin claims that "he first of all gives a hint of what the power and efficacy of the sacrament is; and secondly shows that the old sacraments of the Law had the same power as ours have today."[13] Since the sacraments of the Gospel offer and present the reality they represent, the same must be true of the sacraments of the Law. "For God is not so deceitful as to nourish on empty appearances."[14] Even though the sacraments of the Law represent Christ as yet to come, they nonetheless truly offer the reality of Christ to the people under the Law, for "we have no right to separate the reality and the figure which God has joined together."[15]

Calvin is aware, however, of the difficulty of this position, for it assumes that the people of Israel would have known that the sacraments in which they participated were really both representing and offering Christ to be en-joyed by them. The problem is, how would they have known this? Calvin first addresses this problem in his commentary on John of 1553. Commenting on the statement of Jesus that Moses wrote about him (John 5:46), Calvin says, "I allow, of course, that there are few places where Moses openly pro-claims Christ; but what was the point of the tabernacle, the sacrifices and all the ceremonies, except as figures drawn in conformity to that first pattern which was shown him on the mountain? Therefore, without Christ, the whole ministry of Moses vanishes."[16] Since both Stephen in Acts 7 and the Epistle to the Hebrews tell us that the exemplar on the mountain was Christ, without Christ the whole sacramental economy of the Law would be mean-ingless. Calvin thought this answer strong enough to place at the beginning of his discussion of the Law in the final edition of the *Institutes*.[17]

However, this answer does not address the problem of how the people under the Law knew that the archetype Moses saw was in fact Jesus Christ. Such a position is intelligible from a retrospective point of view, but how did people at the time know that the sacraments of the Law were figuring the coming Christ, since the Law says nothing about him? Calvin addresses this question in the second part of his Acts commentary of 1554, when interpret-ing Paul's claim before King Agrippa that the death and resurrection of Christ fulfilled "what the prophets and Moses said would take place" (Acts 26:22). "But since no clear and, as they say, literal evidence (*testimonium*) of his death and resurrection exists in the Law, there is no doubt that they had teaching handed down by the fathers, from which they learned to refer all figures to Christ."[18] Since Calvin thinks that the first sacrament of Christ is the tree of life in the Garden of Eden, the oral tradition of which Calvin is here speaking must arise at the time of Adam, and last until the coming of Christ in the flesh. Even though Calvin thinks that the prophets more plainly predict the coming of Christ, they nonetheless base their teaching solely on the Law of Moses, acting as its interpreters, for "they convinced their own generation that they were teaching nothing new or different from Moses."[19] This will not be the only time Calvin will appeal to an oral tradition to ex-plain the meaning of a figure or ceremony, but it is remarkable that the only way he can show that the people under the Law, from Adam to John the Baptizer, knew that the sacraments of the Law referred to Christ was by means of an oral tradition handed down to them from the fathers.

Let us now turn to the specific sacraments, symbols, and types of Christ under the Law, beginning with the tree of life and culminating with both the kings and the priestly sacrifices in the Temple in Jerusalem. The order of my presentation follows the order of the economy of manifestation as Calvin describes it, and the development of each symbol of Christ in Calvin's thought is discussed as it arises in this economy. As indicated above, the three major periods of this sacramental economy are the symbols of Christ before the Law, the symbols of Christ revealed to Moses, and the symbols of Christ appearing in David and Jerusalem.

2. The Symbols of Christ for the Fathers before the Law

The Tree of Life

The first symbol of Christ appears in the tree of life in the Garden of Eden, before the fall into sin. Calvin first discusses the tree of life in the 1536 *Institutes,* in a passage that remained unaltered through the 1559 edition. The tree of life is the first example Calvin gives of the sacraments God institutes by means of "natural things."[20] In his commentary on Genesis of 1554, Calvin notes that the tree received its name not because it had the ability to bestow life on its own "but in order that it might be a symbol and memorial of the life which he received from God. For we know it to be by no means unusual that God should give us the attestation of his grace by external symbols."[21] The tree of life reveals to Calvin that human nature even in its original state could not ascend directly to God but had need of "monitory signs" to be led to the knowledge of God's grace. Thus divinely ordained symbols are given in accommodation to the limitations of human nature, by means of which God "stretches out his hand to us, because, without assistance, we cannot ascend to him."[22] Moreover, even though they do not yet need him as their Redeemer, Calvin thinks that the orthodox fathers such as Augustine are right to see the tree of life as a symbol of Christ, "inasmuch as he is the eternal Word of God; it could not indeed be otherwise a symbol of life, than by representing him in figure."[23] Adam was thereby reminded by the symbol of the tree of life that he received his life freely as a gift of God, and that he should seek for life in the Son of God, and not in himself.

Sacrifices of Expiation and Thanksgiving

When Adam and Eve fall into sin, God casts them out of the Garden, and in particular "excommunicates" them from the tree of life. As God always joins the reality signified to the sign, the loss of the tree of life reveals to Adam and Eve that they have lost the gift of life that was originally bestowed upon them, and must henceforth seek it from another source.[24] According to Calvin, Adam and Eve had to look to the death of Christ as the source of their life, and to represent the death of Christ to them in symbolic form God instituted sacrifices.[25] As Adam and Eve had forfeited the possibility of passing to eternal life with God without death, so by the symbol of sacrifices they were taught that they could only have life through death, namely, the death of the Redeemer.

One problem with Calvin's understanding of the replacement of the tree of life with sacrifices is that God nowhere directly institutes sacrifices for Adam and Eve. Since Calvin insists on the mutual relation of word and sign in every living image of God, one would think that the lack of a commanding or promising word in conjunction with sacrifices would keep him from introducing them at this point. Calvin is aware of this difficulty, and tries to establish his case by means of the sacrifices offered by Cain and Abel. He claims that both sons had been well instructed by their father, again appealing to a form of oral tradition. "The rite of sacrificing more fully confirms this; because it proves that they had been accustomed to the worship of God."[26] Hence the father must have delivered the divinely instituted rite of sacrificing to the sons, even though Scripture says nothing of this. "For we must remember, that the custom of sacrificing was not rashly devised by them, but was divinely delivered to them."[27] To make this case in the absence of any specific textual evidence, Calvin first cites the statement in Hebrews that "by faith Abel offered to God a more acceptable sacrifice than Cain's" (Heb. 11:4). According to Calvin, Abel would not have offered the sacrifice in faith if he had not had a command of God. Second, since obedience is better than sacrifice, it follows that Abel had been taught to sacrifice by God. Third, as God always remains like Godself, and God does not delight in sacrifices offered apart from faith in God's mercy, Abel must have looked to the goodness and beneficence of God as represented to him in the sacrifice.[28]

Having established by circumstantial evidence that Abel and Cain had a divine command to sacrifice, unlike the Gentiles who sacrificed without the command of God, Calvin claims that there were two reasons God instituted sacrifices: first, as an act of thanksgiving; and second, as a reminder that they need an act of expiation in order to be reconciled to God.[29] Calvin first makes the distinction between sacrifices of thanksgiving and of expiation in the first edition of the *Institutes,* echoing the discussion of this issue in the Apology of the Augsburg Confession of 1531.[30] Cain and Abel appear to have offered both kinds of sacrifice, as Cain offers the fruit of the land, while Abel sacrifices the firstlings of the flock of sheep.

As the sacrifice of Noah illustrates, the same sacrifice may symbolize both gratitude and expiation by blood, reminding the fathers that even their gratitude will not be accepted by God without the reconciliation offered by the Mediator.[31] However, the sacrifice of Noah after the flood poses the same problem for Calvin as the sacrifices of Cain and Abel, for Scripture does not mention a command to Noah to offer a sacrifice.[32] Calvin again solves the problem by appealing to the context and circumstances surrounding the sacrifice. In particular, the setting apart of clean animals to sacrifice reveals that God commanded Noah to offer the sacrifice. "But it was useless to set apart animals for sacrifice, unless God had revealed this design to holy Noah, who was to be the priest to offer up the victims."[33] Moreover, God's acceptance of the sacrifice reveals that it must have been offered by faith in the command of God. "Let us therefore know, that the altar of Noah was founded on the word of God."[34] The lack of an appeal here to the tradition of the fathers means that Calvin thinks that God directly revealed the command to offer the sacrifice to Noah, even though Scripture is silent about such a command.

Melchizedek

The mysterious figure of Melchizedek appears to Abram after his victory over King Chedorlaomer and his allies. "And King Melchizedek of Salem brought out bread and wine; he was priest of God Most High" (Gen. 14:18). Calvin links the appearance of Melchizedek to Abram with the oath sworn in Psalm 110, "You are a priest forever, according to the order of Melchizedek" (Ps. 110:4), which the Epistle to the Hebrews claims has been fulfilled in Christ (Heb. 5:6, 10; 7:17, 21; 9:11; 10:21). Calvin finds Melchizedek a critically important figure of Christ, whom he enlists in his ongoing criticism of the Roman priesthood and its offering of the sacrifice of the Mass. He first discusses Melchizedek in the first edition of the *Institutes,* in his description of the sacrifice of the Mass as an unutterable blasphemy against the priesthood and sacrifice of Christ. According to Calvin, Christ does not need any priests to succeed him, nor does his sacrifice need to be offered more than once, since he is the eternal priest. "Therefore, the Father designated him 'priest forever, according to the order of Melchizedek,' so that he should discharge an everlasting priesthood."[35]

Calvin returns to consider Melchizedek in his commentary on Hebrews of 1549. He first appeals to Melchizedek in an attempt to prove to the Jews that Jesus is the one whom God has made priest forever according to the order of Melchizedek. According to Calvin, aside from King Melchizedek himself, God made no one else besides Christ both priest and king. "Melchizedek therefore provides a pattern of the Messiah."[36] As we shall see, the clearest portrait of Christ appears in Jerusalem, where we see the conjunction of priests and kings, typifying Christ. However, Melchizedek as both priest and king is a clearer type of Christ, as Christ will be Priest and King in one person as well.

Calvin expands on Melchizedek as a type of Christ in his comments on Hebrews 7:1–10, as he thinks the Holy Spirit here is teaching the Church the meaning of the mystery of the king of Salem. Once again, the typology is established on the basis of Melchizedek being both king and priest. "It was certainly necessary that everything excellent should be found in the one who was a type of the Son of God."[37] Given the importance of Melchizedek as a type of Christ, Calvin is aware of the temptation to draw too detailed a comparison between the two, to which he thinks many of the orthodox fathers succumbed. Rather, he wants his readers to follow the analogy between the sign and the reality signified as set forth by the author of Hebrews. Thus, when Hebrews says that Melchizedek was "made like unto the Son of God" (7:3), Calvin interprets this to mean, "That is, as far as the mode of signification required: for the analogy between the reality and the sign must always be kept in mind."[38] Thus one should not look for every detail of Christ to be found in this image but must rather compare the two, as one would compare a living man to a portrait painted of him. "It is enough that we see the lineaments of Christ in him, just as the form of a living man can be seen in a painting, and yet the man himself is different from his picture."[39] It is enough if the image of Christ in Melchizedek directs us to Christ himself, without having Melchizedek represent everything we can see in Christ.

Calvin thinks that Hebrews sets forth five points of similarity between Melchizedek and Christ. First, since he is called King of Righteousness, this manifests the way Christ communicates his righteousness to us both by free reconciliation and by regeneration.[40] Second, since he is also called King of Peace, this represents the peace of conscience we can only find once Christ reconciles us to God.[41] Third, that Scripture fails to mention either his birth or his death makes him a type of the eternal nature of Christ, without making the comparison between the two overly detailed. "What was foreshadowed in Melchizedek, was shown in reality in Christ. We ought therefore to be content with this moderate knowledge that in showing us Melchizedek as one who was never born and never died, Scripture is setting forth in a picture the truth that for Christ there is neither beginning nor end."[42] Fourth, by presenting Melchizedek with tithes, Abram reveals his superiority both over himself and over the Levites, since they are descendants of Abram.[43] Fifth, Melchizedek's superiority over Abram is confirmed by the fact that he blesses him, since "this blessing of which the apostle speaks is the symbol of greater power."[44]

Calvin does not want any further comparisons to be drawn, since all of the analogies between Melchizedek and Christ should be drawn from the explicit statements of Scripture and not from our own conjecture.[45] This should give us both moderation and restraint, so that we do not find comparisons between Christ and Melchizedek that are not found in the scriptural accounts of Melchizedek.[46] However, this also means that we should not look for points of comparison between the two beyond the five that Calvin sees being set forth in the letter to the Hebrews, for the same Holy Spirit who teaches us about Melchizedek in Genesis 14 and Psalm 110 is the one who shows us how he is a type of Christ in Hebrews 7. Calvin uses this criterion to eliminate the analogy drawn by the orthodox fathers between the bread and wine offered to Abram by Melchizedek and the offering of the Eucharist as a sacrifice by priests. "They speak like this—Christ is a high priest according to the order of Melchizedek. Melchizedek offered bread and wine. Therefore sacrifices of bread and wine are symbols of the priesthood of Christ."[47] According to Calvin, this is not an analogy drawn by the author of Hebrews; and since the author of Hebrews is ultimately the Holy Spirit, by adding this comparison the fathers of the Church were basically accusing the Spirit of forgetfulness or negligence in teaching.[48] Why, then, does Scripture mention that Melchizedek offered Abram bread and wine? According to Calvin, it was a royal act to offer refreshment to those who were tired after battle. "If there is any mystery about the offering, it is only fulfilled in Christ inasmuch as he feeds us when we are hungry and tired out with weariness."[49]

In his commentary on Genesis of 1554, Calvin again asks "how Melchizedek bore the image of Christ, and became, as it were, his representative."[50] Calvin turns immediately to Psalm 110:4, and sees the analogy in the way kingship and priesthood is united in one person: "we hence infer that the image of Christ was presented to the fathers in his person."[51] The question is, how did David know that Melchizedek was the type of Christ, and that the one to come would be both like and yet superior to Melchizedek? Once again, Calvin appeals to an oral tradition handed on from Abram to David that set forth the analogy between Melchizedek and the Messiah, for "it is not to be doubted that the same truth had been traditionally handed down by the fathers."[52]

Calvin does not go on to detail all five analogies between Melchizedek and Christ that he drew out of Hebrews but rather mentions that Hebrews does not set forth an analogy drawn on the basis of the offering of bread and wine.[53] The silence of Hebrews on this issue not only refutes "the fictions of the ancients" but also shows how "utterly ridiculous are the Papists, who distort the offering of bread and wine to the sacrifice of their mass."[54] In contrast to the Hebrews commentary, Calvin here sees no typological meaning in the offering of the bread and wine, but only in the fact that Melchizedek blesses Abram. By blessing Abram, Melchizedek acts as priest, and foreshadows the blessing that Christ would bring, which is fulfilled when Christ lifts his hands and blesses his disciples after his resurrection (Luke 24:51).[55] However, the offering of bread and wine belongs to his office as king, and has no meaning beyond the fact that "he refreshed a wearied and famished army with royal liberality."[56] Calvin reiterates this point in the last edition of the *Institutes,* to refute the defense of the Mass as a sacrifice on the basis of the bread and wine offered by Melchizedek as a symbol of priesthood. "Melchizedek gave bread and wine to Abraham and his companions to refresh them, wearied by their journey and battle. What has this to do with a sacrifice?"[57]

Circumcision

When Abraham was ninety-nine years old, the Lord appeared to him and established a new covenant with him. "This is my covenant with you, which you shall keep, between me and you and your offspring after you: Every male among you shall be circumcised. You shall circumcise the flesh of your foreskins, and it shall be a sign of the covenant between me and you" (Gen.

17:10–11). The theme of circumcision arises in the 1536 edition of the *Institutes* to illustrate the diversity of the sacraments given by the Lord to Israel. "For circumcision was enjoined upon Abraham and his descendants [Gen. 17:10]. To it were afterward added purifications and sacrifices from the law of Moses. These were the sacraments of the Jews until the coming of Christ."[58] Calvin also appeals to circumcision to demonstrate how the sacraments of the law acted as images to represent Christ and to set him forth to be known.[59] He appeals to Paul in Romans 4:11 to establish this claim that circumcision was a seal of their faith in the coming seed of Abraham who would make them righteous.

Calvin also discusses circumcision in his brief defense of infant baptism. Since circumcision has been replaced by baptism, baptism must signify the same reality as circumcision, namely, that God will be our God and the God of our offspring. Since this promise applies to infants as well as adults, they should both be baptized.[60] Calvin expands on the relationship between circumcision and baptism at considerable length in the 1539 edition of the *Institutes,* in an attempt to address the rejection of infant baptism by the Anabaptists. He establishes what he calls an anagogic relationship (*anagoge*) between circumcision and baptism by showing that they represent the same reality, and differ only in the mode of their representation.[61] Remarkably, even after the replacement of circumcision with baptism, Calvin denies that the reality attested by circumcision is taken away from the Jews, even after the Gospel moves from them to the Gentiles. "Yet, despite the great obstinacy with which they continue to wage war against the gospel, we must not despise them, while we consider that, for the sake of the promise, God's blessing still rests among them. For the apostle indeed testifies that it will never be completely taken away: 'For the gifts and the calling of God are without repentance' [Rom. 11:29]."[62]

In his commentary on Genesis of 1554, Calvin is especially struck by the way God describes circumcision as his covenant (Gen. 17:9). He interprets this statement in light of the way human covenants are often engraved in brass or sculptured on stones to attest the memory of them. "So in the present instance, God inscribes his covenant in the flesh of Abraham."[63] Since the covenant is itself understood to be the word of promise, circumcision may therefore be said to be the "visible word, or sculpture and image," of the covenant with Abraham, "which the word more fully illustrates."[64] Circumcision thus demonstrates the mutual relation between image and word that Calvin sees in all forms of divine self-manifestation: "let us know, that as soon as the sign itself meets our eyes, the word ought to sound in our ears."[65] Once again, Calvin appeals to the word as the soul of the image to criticize what he takes to be the mute images of the Roman Church. "Since the promise is the very soul of the sign, whenever it is torn away from the sign, nothing remains but a lifeless and vain phantom."[66]

Calvin acknowledges that it may strike many as odd, if not foolish, to make a covenant in the foreskin of the people. In spite of its apparent foolishness, he seeks for the meaning of the sign itself by means of the analogy between the sign and the thing signified.[67] He returns to the two analogies he drew as early as 1536: on the one hand, circumcision signifies the pollution of human nature, making it a sign of repentance; on the other, it signifies the coming blessing promised to the seed of Abraham, making it a sign of faith.[68] Calvin maintains this twofold analogy throughout his life, as can be seen in his lectures on Jeremiah of 1563. "For circumcision, while a testimony of free salvation in Christ, at the same time initiated the Jews into the worship and service of God, and proved the necessity of new life; it was in short a sign both of repentance and of faith."[69]

Christ Appears to the Fathers as an Angel

After God made the covenant of circumcision with Abraham, he appeared to him in the plains of Mamre, but in the form of three men. According to Calvin, the three men were really angels. At times all three angels speak to Abraham, while at other times only one speaks to him. According to Calvin, this is done in order to reveal that all three angels represent the one God, and that one angel is the eternal Son of God, "who is the living image of the Father."[70] As we can see in this passage, Calvin can often refer the same manifestation either to God or to Christ. Thus, when the text says that Abraham stood before the face of the Lord even though he appeared to be standing before a man, Calvin says that by faith he looked upon God. "Whence we infer, that we act preposterously, if we allow the external symbols, by which God represents himself, to retard or hinder us from going directly to him."[71] On the other hand, Calvin will interpret all three men as the more intimate self-manifestation of Christ to Abraham, in contrast to the more obscure manifestation of Christ to Lot.[72]

Calvin first develops his understanding of angels as the self-manifestation of Christ in his commentary on 1 Corinthians of 1546. Speaking of the rebellious character of many of the Israelites in the wilderness during the exodus, Paul says, "We must not put Christ to the test, as some of them did, and were destroyed by serpents" (1 Cor. 10:9). According to Calvin, this passage reveals that it was Christ who was leading the Israelites from Egypt to the promised land.[73] When the angel of the Lord appears to Moses in the burning bush, Calvin first notes how the angel is the self-manifestation of God, appearing in a form accommodated to Moses' capacities.[74] However, Calvin goes on to agree with the orthodox fathers of the Church that the angel is in fact Christ, appearing in his office as Mediator.[75] The same may be said of the angel that God promises to send before Moses and the people after the apostasy of the golden calves.[76] On the other hand, that Christ often appeared to the fathers not only as an angel but also in human form is taken by Calvin to be a prelude to his appearance in the flesh, as when he appeared to Joshua as the commander of the army of the Lord. "We must beware, however, of imagining that Christ at that time became incarnate."[77]

In the final edition of the *Institutes*, Calvin appeals to the appearance of Christ as an angel to the patriarchs both to prove the eternal divinity of Christ and to refute the claim made by Servetus that God never manifested Godself to the fathers under the Law. Over against the Jewish denial of the divinity of Christ, Calvin says, "To the holy patriarchs an angel is said to have appeared, claiming for himself the name of the Eternal God."[78] Over against the claim made by Servetus that God never appeared to the patriarchs, Calvin juxtaposes the teaching of the orthodox fathers of the Church. "But the orthodox doctors of the Church have rightly and prudently interpreted that chief angel to be God's Word, who already at that time, as a sort of foretaste, began to fulfill the office of Mediator."[79] The self-manifestation of God in Christ in the form of an angel is therefore an essential element in Calvin's understanding of the eternal deity of Christ, as well as his claim that Christ manifested himself to the people under the Law. "It is not then to be wondered at, if the Eternal Word of God, of one Godhead and essence with the Father, assumed the name of 'the Angel' on the ground of his future mission."[80]

The Rite of Burial as a Symbol of the Resurrection

When Sarah died, Abraham bought the field of Machpelah from Ephron the Hittite and buried his wife in the cave facing Mamre (Gen. 23:17–20). Calvin thinks that Abraham's concern to bury Sarah has to do with the way the rite of burial symbolizes the hope of the resurrection. Calvin first develops his understanding of burial as a symbol of the resurrection and future life in his 1543 *Inventory of Relics*. He appeals to the practice of burial as observed by the fathers to argue that even in the period of ornate and elaborate ceremonies, the dead were buried in graves, not left unburied to be venerated as relics. "More ceremonies were then appointed by God than it becomes us to observe in the present day. Nay, even burial itself required more show than it now does, because by its figures it represented the resurrection, which was not so clearly revealed to them as it has been to us. But do we read that the saints were ever dug out of their graves, in order that they might be converted into a kind of puppets for children?"[81] The dead should be left in their graves to await the resurrection, not exhumed to be venerated as holy objects.

Even though the mention of the rite of burial arises in a polemical context, in subsequent references to the issue Calvin does not use it to critique the Roman veneration of relics but rather highlights the way it portrays the hope of a resurrection to the Israelites long before the reality of the symbol is exhibited in the resurrection of Christ. When Calvin writes in his Acts commentary of 1552 of the concern the apostles exhibited to bury Stephen after he was stoned to death, he draws attention to the way burial represents the resurrection. "For the rite of burial looks to the resurrection hope, since God ordained it for this purpose from the beginning of the world."[82] Calvin admits that the symbol of burial primarily benefits the living rather than the dead, but burial also honors the body of the deceased due to the pledge of future life.[83]

The rite of burial often included the washing of the body before burial, as in the case of Tabitha. "At that time she became ill and died. When they had washed her, they laid her in a room upstairs" (Acts 9:37). According to Calvin, this was passed down from the patriarchs "as if by hand, continuously through the generations, so that in death itself some visible representation might lift up the minds of the godly to a good hope."[84] He thinks that this rite was added to burial to compensate for the obscurity of the resurrection hope at the time of the fathers, whereby "contrary appearances should be adduced to represent life in death."[85] The rite of washing the dead had another signification as well, one common to all forms of washing under the Law, namely, to symbolize the need to be cleansed of all filthiness before we can please God.[86] Calvin knows that the Gentiles also observed the custom of washing the dead, but he believes they were aping the rites of the fathers without understanding their meaning.[87]

The Jews not only washed the bodies of the dead but also anointed them with oil. Commenting on the anointing of Jesus in his John commentary of 1553, Calvin sees this rite as increasing the vividness of the resurrection hope for the Jews before the resurrection of Christ. "Therefore believers needed such aids, which directed them to Christ who was still absent."[88] Calvin also comments on the elaborate rites carefully observed in the burial of Jesus. "They took the body of Jesus and wrapped it with the spices in linen cloths, according to the burial custom of the Jews" (John 19:40). According to Calvin, these customs were much more elaborate than those practiced after the resurrection of Christ, again to make up for his absence.[89] Once again, Calvin knows that the Gentiles also observed elaborate burial rituals with great care and ascribes this to their aping of the fathers without understanding the meaning of the ceremony.[90] The reason the Gentiles did not understand the meaning of their burial rites is that they lacked the word of promise that God appended to the rite of burial for the Jews. "For God's promise and Word is like the soul which gives life to ceremonies. Take away the Word, and all rites which men observe, although apparently belonging to the worship of the godly, are nothing but decaying or silly superstition."[91] This statement, however, begs the question: where is the promise or Word of God that God appended to the rites of burial that reveals that their meaning lies in setting before the eyes of the Israelites the coming resurrection? Calvin had previously appealed to the oral tradition of the fathers to account for the source of this custom. It seems that he now regards the oral tradition as handing down the divine promise of resurrection with the burial ceremonies. However, he gives no textual evidence for this claim.

When Calvin turns to his interpretation of the burial of Sarah in his Genesis commentary of 1554, he seems to acknowledge the difficulty of locating the authorization of such a rite either in an oral tradition or in a word of promise that is nowhere mentioned in Scripture. According to Calvin, Abraham was concerned to bury Sarah not because of an oral tradition or a word of promise but because "it has been divinely engraved on the minds of all people, from the beginning, that they should bury the dead; whence also they have ever regarded sepulchres as sacred."[92] Unlike his previous discussions of burial rites, he does not attempt to distinguish the rite of burial by the fathers from that practiced by the Gentiles but rather insists that both the Gentiles and the patriarchs followed this practice because God had inscribed it in their minds. According to Calvin, the rite of burial is a symbol of the resurrection, which God wished to be placed before the eyes of both the Israelites and the Gentiles, even though the Gentiles did not understand that it was a symbol of resurrection and an image of the future life.[93] This still begs the question of how Abraham and his descendants knew that burial rites were a symbol of the coming resurrection of Christ, a question that Calvin does not at this point answer. He does, however, see the translation of Enoch as both a "specimen of immortality" and "a sort of visible mirror of a blessed resurrection" for the patriarchs, which may have reinforced their understanding of burial as a symbol of the resurrection, although Calvin does not explicitly draw such a connection.[94]

The embalming of Jacob by the physicians of Egypt, which took place over a forty-day period (Gen. 50:2–3), prompts Calvin to compare the burial practices of the patriarchs with those of the Egyptians. The elaborate embalming ritual leads him to observe that "we know that among the Egyptians there was greater expense and pomp than among the Jews. Even the ancient historians record this among the most memorable customs of that nation."[95] Rather than attribute this custom to the divine engraving on the minds of all, Calvin returns to his claim that "the sacred rite of burial descends from the holy fathers, to be a kind of mirror of the future resurrection," and explains the elaborate embellishment of this rite by the Egyptians as due to their hypocrisy. "It happens that they who have declined from the true faith, assume a far more ostentatious appearance than the faithful, to whom pertain the truth and the right use of the symbol."[96] Calvin speculates that Joseph followed the Egyptian practice rather than the less ostentatious ceremony followed by his ancestors either through fear of seeming to condemn their practice or from unconsidered imitation. "But it would have been better, had he confined himself to the frugal practice of his fathers."[97]

Calvin returns to this question in his harmony of the three Gospels of 1555, with regard to the anointing of Jesus for burial. Once again, Calvin attributes the practice to the tradition handed down from the fathers "to foster them in the faith of a resurrection," and contrasts the right use of anointing with the practice of the Egyptians.[98] By contrast, "In this sacred symbolism God showed the Jews the image of life in death, that out of the decay and the dust they might hope to receive new vigor."[99] However, Calvin does not appeal to a word of promise to make this case, as he did when he discussed the anointing of Jesus in his commentary on John three years earlier.

In his commentary on the Psalms of 1557, Calvin observes that the lack of burial is of itself a sign of the curse of God, a theme that will consistently emerge in subsequent commentaries as well. When the psalmist laments that the enemies of Jerusalem "have given the bodies of your servants to the birds of the air for food, the flesh of your faithful to the wild animals of the earth" (Ps. 79:2), Calvin takes this as a double indignity, "God having intended that, in the burial of men, there should be some testimony to the resurrection at the last day."[100] Although the godly suffer the same curse that God threatens to the ungodly, Calvin thinks that the issue (*exitu*) of the punishment is different, "for God converts that which in itself is a token of his wrath into the means of salvation of his own children."[101] The refusal to bury one's enemies, on the other hand, is the sign of unspeakable barbarity, and to keep this from emerging among the Israelites, God commands them to bury the bodies of those they have rightly executed by hanging them from a tree. "And surely the body of a man suspended on a cross is a sad and hideous spectacle; for the rights of sepulchre are ordained for man, both as a pledge and symbol of the resurrection, and also to spare the eyes of the living, lest they should be defiled by the sight of so horrible a thing."[102] If the lack of burial is a sign of the curse and wrath of God, then burial must be a symbol of the love and favor of God. When God threatens the Israelites that if they disobey the Law their bodies shall be food for the birds and animals (Deut. 28:26), Calvin notes that "it is ignominious to be deprived of burial, and justly reckoned among the curses of God; while it is a sign of his paternal favor that we should be distinguished from the brutes, inasmuch as the rites of burial arouse us to the hope of resurrection and eternal life."[103]

In his lectures on Jeremiah in 1563, Calvin claims that the rite of burial symbolizes three distinct but related realities. First, burial is a symbol of the love of God and "a testimony of God's favor."[104] Second, burial after death is a sign or mark given by God to distinguish human beings from the rest of the animals. "In death there is no difference; the death of a man and the death of a dog, have no certain marks to distinguish one from the other."[105] Thus burial is a "mark to distinguish us from brute animals even after death."[106] Since the excellence of humanity lies in their having been created in the image of God, the rite of burial is a symbolic acknowledgment of that excellence.[107] Third, since the meaning of the image of God is to orient us towards eternal life with God, the rite of burial must also be a symbol of the future and immortal life pledged to humanity, "for when man's body is laid in the earth, it is, as it were, a mirror of the future life."[108] Since the land of Canaan was also a symbol of the future life in the Kingdom of God according to Calvin, burial in the land of Canaan would be a pledge of future life as well as a pledge of one's adoption by God, "as though all the children of Abraham were gathered in his bosom until they arose into a blessed and immortal life."[109]

In spite of the rich symbolic meaning Calvin comes to see in the rite of burial by 1563, he no longer appeals to the word or promise of God, or even the tradition of the fathers, to account for the divine institution of this rite but rather roots it in the law of nature known by all human beings, Jews and Gentiles alike. "But this is to be referred to the common law of nature, of which we have spoken elsewhere; for it is a sad and disgraceful thing, nay, a horrid spectacle, when we see men unburied; indeed the sense of nature dictates this, that when men are dead, they are to be buried; and the duty of burial has from the beginning of the world lived in human hearts; and burial is an evidence of a future resurrection."[110] Calvin appeals to the same sense of nature in his discussion of the resurrection in the 1559 edition of the *Institutes*. "But in order that this gross ignorance might not excuse anyone, unbelievers have always by natural instinct had before their eyes an image of the resurrection."[111] Since Calvin insists that it is the word alone that gives life to the symbol, one is left to wonder how it is that the Israelites recognized the rite of burial as a symbol of God's love, their superiority over the animals, and their future immortality and resurrection, if they were only taught about this rite from the law or instinct of nature they shared with the Gentiles.

The Land of Canaan as a Symbol of Adoption

When Jacob deceives his father, Isaac, into giving him the blessing that rightly belongs to his brother Esau, Isaac's blessing seems to be limited only to earthly benefits. "'May God give you of the dew of heaven, and of the fatness of the earth, and plenty of grain and wine'" (Gen. 27:28). Over against the Anabaptists, who took this blessing to indicate that the covenant with Abraham was not spiritual in nature, Calvin insists that such earthly blessings were signs of God's favor, and therefore helps by which the fathers might elevate from earthly to spiritual blessings. In particular, Calvin notes that "he appointed the land of Canaan as a mirror and pledge to them of the celestial inheritance."[112] Calvin first described the land of Canaan as a type and symbol of the eternal inheritance in the *Institutes* of 1539. Over against the Anabaptists, who thought that the hope of the fathers was confined to the land of Canaan, Calvin responds, "We contend, on the contrary, that, in the earthly possessions they enjoyed, they looked, as in a mirror, upon the future inheritance they believed to have been prepared for them in heaven."[113]

According to Calvin, the fathers knew that they were to ascend from the image of the land to God, for Abraham was taught that his real inheritance was God alone. "Then he adds the promise of the land, solely as a symbol of his benevolence and as a type of the heavenly inheritance."[114] To demonstrate that this is not groundless speculation on Calvin's part, he appeals to the testimony of David that God is his portion forever to illustrate that this was the experience of the fathers all along.[115] Thus, when God appears to Jacob in a vision as he sets out to Egypt to join Joseph, God promises to bring Jacob's descendants back to the land as a pledge of God's favor and love for Jacob, for "the possession of the land of Canaan was the symbol of the Divine favor, of spiritual blessings, and of eternal felicity."[116]

As a symbol of God's love and favor, the land of Canaan is also a symbol of the adoption of Abraham and his descendants, a theme Calvin begins to develop in his harmony of the last four books of Moses in 1563. God forbids the Israelites to sell any of the land in perpetuity, even after it has been allotted to them by tribe (Lev. 25:23), because "the land of Canaan was an earnest, or symbol, or mirror of the adoption on which their salvation was founded."[117] When Moses is told that he shall die before entering the land of Canaan, God alleviates the bitterness of this punishment by allowing him to see the land from the top of Mount Nebo (Deut. 34:1). The visible sight of the land confirms the sight of it he had already obtained from the promise of God, and thereby confirmed his faith.[118]

In his lectures on Jeremiah of 1563, Calvin interprets the land of Canaan both as a symbol and pledge of God's love and as a symbol of the adoption of the children of Abraham. When the Israelites are promised that if they obey the Law, God shall be their God and will give them "a land flowing in milk and honey" (Jer. 11:5), Calvin takes this to be a symbol of God's love accommodated to the capacities of the people, "that they might see by their eyes, exhibited to them even in this world and in this frail life some evidence of that favor, which far surpasses all that can be desired in the world."[119] The opulence of the land was meant by God to make it "a most excellent theater" in which they might behold the fountain of every good thing flowing to them, "so that the very sight of it ravished them with admiration."[120] The sight of the land should lead the people to submit to God out of gratitude, being drawn to love God by their awareness of God's goodness, which is why in Deuteronomy Moses keeps reminding the people of the land they are about to enter.[121] Thus Jeremiah promises the people that if they repent and return to the Lord, God will allow them to remain on the land God had promised them (Jer. 25:3–5), "for the land was as it were the pledge of their adoption; and the Jews, while they dwelt there, might have felt assured that God was their Father."[122]

Given that the land of Canaan is understood by Calvin to be a visible symbol of the eternal inheritance of the Israelites, as well as a symbol of God's love and a pledge of their adoption, it is odd that he never links the image of the land with the word of promise in order to see the land of Canaan as a sacrament for the Israelites. Given that the adoption of the Israelites is ultimately founded on the mercy of God in Jesus Christ, it is also noteworthy that Calvin does not attempt to understand the land of Canaan as in any way referring to the Christ who is to come. The land of Canaan symbolizes the love of God for the Israelites, and confirms their adoption, without reference to Jesus Christ at all.

3. The Symbols of Christ Revealed to Moses

We turn now to consider those signs, symbols, and sacraments of Christ revealed by God to Moses, including the feasts to be observed in memory and celebration of the exodus, as well as the forms of worship surrounding the tabernacle, priests, and sacrifices revealed to Moses on Mount Sinai. As we shall see, the feasts have both a retrospective and a prospective reference: they remind the Israelites of the exodus itself, which for Calvin is the archetype of God's grace, while also referring them to the coming redemption in Jesus Christ. Calvin understands the sacrifices of the Law as being either expiatory or eucharistic, with the former referring the Israelites to the sacrifice of Christ. The priests themselves are types of Christ, and the tabernacle is a representation of Christ corresponding to the archetype shown to Moses on Mount Sinai.

The Passover

The festival of the Passover is instituted by God through Moses and Aaron on the night that God struck down the firstborn of the Egyptians. Calvin first discusses the Passover in his commentary on 1 Corinthians of 1546.

Commenting on Paul's statement, "For our paschal lamb, Christ, has been sacrificed. Therefore let us celebrate the festival" (1 Cor. 5:7–8), Calvin notes how the Passover itself has a double reference: it not only serves as a memorial for the past redemption of the Israelites, but it is also a sacrament of the coming Christ.[123] When he turns to consider the institution of the Passover in his harmony of the last four books of Moses in 1563, Calvin begins by making the same distinction. On the one hand, the Passover is "a solemn symbol of their redemption" from captivity and death in Egypt. Since the exodus is itself the archetype of the grace of God, in the Passover, God, "as in a glass or picture, represented to their eyes his grace; and desired that they should on every succeeding year recognize what they had formerly experienced, lest it should ever depart from their memory."[124] The Passover is thus a symbol of thanksgiving, for "the Passover was instituted in token of their gratitude."[125] On the other hand, even the exodus was a sign or type of a higher redemption yet to come in the future, and hence the Passover festival "was the symbol of the future redemption as well as that which was past," a claim that Calvin establishes by reference to Paul's statement that Christ our Passover is slain.[126] Therefore, "the Passover not only reminded them of what God had already done for them, but also of what they were hereafter to expect from him."[127]

The Passover was as much a symbol of spiritual grace for the Israelites as was circumcision, "and so it has an analogy and resemblance to the Holy Supper, because it contained both the same promises, which Christ seals to us in that, and also taught that God could only be propitiated towards his people by the expiation of blood."[128] The expiation in blood is set forth in the sacrifice of the paschal lamb, which for Calvin is a type of Christ's sacrifice.[129] God commanded the people to sprinkle their doorposts and lintels with blood in order to teach them by this sign "that the sacrifice would profit none but those who were stained and marked with Christ's blood."[130] Since the Passover is a sacrament, Moses is very concerned to remind the Israelites to teach their children the meaning of the festival, "since, without the aid of this teaching, it would have been an unmeaning and useless spectacle. For doctrine may justly be called the life of the sacraments, without which no vigor remains in them, so far are they from imparting to us any life."[131]

The Cloud, the Sea, Manna, and the Water from the Rock

Paul's description of the exodus and the manna and water in the wilderness as being the Baptism and Supper of the Israelites plays a large role in the development of Calvin's argument that the sacraments of the Law convey the same reality as the sacraments of the Gospel, even though they represent this reality differently. However, when Calvin interprets these events in his subsequent commentaries, he does not stress their meaning as sacraments. For instance, when Psalm 78 speaks of the Israelites eating the "bread of heaven" in the wilderness, Calvin acknowledges that Paul takes it to be "a figure and symbol of Christ" but denies that this is what it means in the psalm.[132] In his discussion of God's provision of manna in his harmony on the last four books of Moses in 1563, Calvin again notes that Paul takes the manna to be "a type of the flesh of Christ, which feeds our minds unto the hope of eternal life," but he does not think that meaning applies to the incident in the wilderness as narrated by Moses but rather stresses the miraculous nature of the appearance of the bread.[133] Calvin does think that the Israelites drank spiritual, not just physical, drink in the water flowing from the rock, which made their ingratitude for such an exceptional gift all the more inexcusable.[134] However, he still does not describe the water as a sacrament of Christ, as he did in the 1536 *Institutes* and in the 1546 commentary on 1 Corinthians, in which he explicitly states, "[Paul] says that in the manna and the water flowing out of the rock, there was a sacrament, which corresponded to the holy Supper."[135] It appears that by 1557 Calvin began to downplay the sacramental nature of the exodus, the cloud, the manna, and the water, to highlight the correspondence between Baptism and Circumcision, and the Supper and the Passover.

The Sabbath

God instituted the Sabbath when God spoke to the Israelites out of the fire and smoke atop Mount Sinai. Calvin addresses the meaning of the Sabbath in the 1536 edition of the *Institutes*. He notes that since the Sabbath is found in the first table of the Law, having to do with piety and the worship of God, "the Lord has never enforced anything more strictly than this."[136] Following Colossians 2:16–17, he interprets the Sabbath as the shadow and figure of the body and truth that is found in Christ. In particular, the Sabbath represents in an external way the spiritual rest from all our works that God desires from us, so that God might work in us alone. "This moreover is the true Sabbath, whose type and, as it were, shadow, that Jewish Sabbath was."[137] The reality of the Sabbath is eschatological in nature, as indicated by the perfect number seven, and will not be fulfilled in us until the time "when God will be all in all [1 Cor. 15:28]."[138] The Sabbath is also given for the sake of the Church, so that it might gather once a week for prayers and praises of God, to hear the Word of God, and to use the sacraments. However, this day is not intrinsically holy, for "it is not by religion that we distinguish one day from another, but for the sake of common polity."[139] Finally, the Sabbath was instituted to give rest both to servants and to animals, lest their masters overwork them.[140]

In his *Catechism* of 1538, Calvin reiterates the three purposes of the Sabbath, namely, to rest from our own works, to gather together to hear the Law and carry out the ceremonies, and to give rest to servants and others under authority. However, he no longer describes the reality signified by the shadow of the Sabbath as the work of the Holy Spirit within us but rather as our participation in the death of Christ. "On this account Paul declares that the Sabbath was the shadow of the reality to come. The truth of this he explains elsewhere, when he teaches that we have been buried with Christ in order that through his death we may die to the corruption of our flesh."[141] Calvin still notes how the reality signified will only be fulfilled in us at the end of time, when, "utterly dead to ourselves, we become filled with God's life."[142]

In the second edition of the *Institutes* of 1539, Calvin appeals to the reality signified by the Sabbath to account for the importance of the Sabbath for the Israelites. He notes that God "bestows the highest approbation on its observance. Hence also, believers greatly esteemed the revelation of the Sabbath among the other oracles," so that "it is held in singular esteem among all the precepts of the law."[143] According to Calvin, the Sabbath has primacy over all other precepts because it is "a sign whereby Israel may recognize that God is their sanctifier [Ezek. 20:12]. If our sanctification consists in mortifying our own will, then a very close correspondence appears between the outward sign and the inward reality."[144] As in the *Catechism*, Calvin correlates the shadow and type of the Sabbath with the body and truth of our participation in the death and resurrection of Christ.[145] In the 1543 edition of the *Institutes*, Calvin explains the substitution of the Lord's Day for the Sabbath in terms of the exhibition in Christ of the reality signified by the Sabbath.[146]

In his interpretation of the Sabbath in his harmony of the last four books of Moses of 1563, Calvin defends the importance of the Sabbath against those who have traduced it, for "God indeed would have it to be a notable symbol of distinction between the Jews and the heathen nations."[147] This can only be done if we "remember the spiritual substance of the type," namely, that in the Sabbath God "placed before their eyes as the perfection of sanctity that they should all cease from their works."[148] This is why strangers in Israel were to observe the Sabbath with the Israelites, "so that wherever the Israelites turned their eyes, they might be incited to the observance of the Sabbath."[149] Over against those who mock the Sabbath as giving the Jews an opportunity for sloth, Calvin insists that we do well "to remember its analogy and conformity with the thing that it signifies; i.e., that the Jews might know that their lives could not be approved by God unless, by ceasing from their own works, they should divest themselves of their reason, counsels, and all the feelings and affections of the flesh."[150] Calvin then reiterates the claim that the reality signified by the Sabbath is our participation in the death and resurrection of Christ.[151]

If the Sabbath is a divinely instituted ceremony that represents the death and resurrection of Christ by means of the analogy between the sign and the reality signified, does this mean that the Sabbath is itself a sacrament? Calvin draws this conclusion in his lectures on Ezekiel of 1564, published after his death in 1565. In one of his last lectures, Calvin reflects on the meaning of the Sabbath in light of Ezekiel's description of it as a sign given to Israel by which they might know that the Lord sanctifies them (Ezek. 20:12). Since "the grace of regeneration was promised to the ancient people when God consecrated the seventh day," Calvin concludes from this that the Sabbath was in fact a sacrament for the Israelites. "He shows them that it was only an outward symbol, and that it contained a spiritual mystery. It now follows . . . that the Sabbath was a sacrament, since it was a visible figure of an invisible grace."[152] The Sabbath therefore offered the reality of sanctification that it represented, for God "promises in return what he witnesses and prefigures by an outward sign."[153]

The Blood of the Covenant

Moses built an altar at the base of Mount Sinai, and offered sacrifices of oxen. He then splashed half of the blood on the altar, and, after having read the book of the Law to the people, splashed the other half on them, saying, "See the blood of the covenant that the Lord has made with you in accordance with all these words" (Exod. 24:4–8). In his comments on this passage in 1563, Calvin notes that the blood that sealed the covenant was in fact "the blood of Christ in type and shadow," even as Christ sealed the new covenant with his blood in the holy Supper, "for it is obvious that Christ compares with the figure the truth which was manifested in himself."[154] Calvin clearly takes the blood of the covenant to be a sacrament, for he uses the conjunction of the reading of the Law with the splashing of the blood to highlight the mutual relationship between symbol and doctrine in any sacrament. "The context here shows us the true and genuine nature of sacraments, together with their correct and proper use; for unless doctrine precede them to be a connecting link between God and man, they will be empty and delusive signs, however honorable may be the encomiums passed on them."[155] Calvin makes a similar observation in his Hebrews commentary of 1549, in light of the apostle's reference to this ceremony on Sinai. "We see that the symbol was added only when the Law had been expounded. What kind of a sacrament would it be unless the Word preceded it? Hence the symbol is a kind of addition to the Word."[156]

The Tabernacle

After reading the covenant to the people, and sealing the covenant by sacramentally anointing the people with blood, Moses ascended Mount Sinai, and the glory of the Lord settled on Sinai like a devouring fire. While on the mountain, the first thing that God commanded Moses to do was to ask the people for an offering of the materials that will be necessary to build the tabernacle for the Lord. "And have them make me a sanctuary, so that I may dwell among them. In accordance with all that I show you concerning the pattern of the tabernacle and of all its furniture, so shall you make it" (Exod. 25:8–9). Calvin first addresses the meaning of the tabernacle in his commentary on Hebrews of 1549. The author of Hebrews focuses on the relationship between the pattern shown to Moses on the mountain and the tabernacle made in correspondence to that pattern. "They offer worship in a sanctuary that is a sketch and shadow of the heavenly one; for Moses, when he was about to erect the tabernacle, was warned, 'See that you make everything according to the pattern that was shown you on the mountain'" (Heb. 8:5). Calvin interprets this passage to mean that the tabernacle is a shadowy representation of Christ, who is the original to which the picture corresponds. "God orders that all the parts of the tabernacle should correspond to the original pattern that had been shown to Moses on the mountain. If the form of the tabernacle referred to something else, the same must be true of the rites and the whole priesthood."[157]

The author of Hebrews also describes the tabernacle as a "parable" (Heb. 9:9). Calvin takes this to mean that it is an antitype that refers one to the archetype, in the same way that the image of a person refers one to the actual person. "He means that the second tabernacle was a pattern corresponding with the first; for the likeness of a man ought so to compare with the man himself that by looking at it our minds are immediately directed to the man."[158] However, in the case of the tabernacle, the one being represented by the antitype cannot be seen, thereby making it the visible representation of something unseen. "Greek writers sometimes use the word [*antitupon*] when they discuss our sacraments, and they do so intelligently and fittingly because every sacrament is the visible image of invisible things."[159] In his commentary on the first part of Acts in 1552, Calvin insists that the visible representation truly corresponds to the unseen reality, since it was shown to Moses on the mountain. "In saying that Moses saw a figure the Spirit of God means that we are not allowed to invent figures, but that all our senses must be turned intently on the figure shown by God, so that the whole of religion may be regulated by it."[160]

When Calvin interprets the significance of the tabernacle in his harmony of the last four books of Moses in 1563, he clearly follows the lead of Hebrews 9 and Acts 7. "Stephen and the Apostle, therefore, are our best expositors, that the tabernacle, the altar, the table, the Ark of the covenant, were of no importance except in so far as they referred to the heavenly pattern, of which they were the shadows and images."[161] God did not intend the minds of his people to stop at the external representation but rather intended the image to act as steps by which the people might elevate their minds to the spiritual reality being represented.[162] Ultimately, the reality being represented in the tabernacle was Christ himself.[163] However, Calvin warns his readers not to seek to discover spiritual mysteries in every detail of the tabernacle's construction, "since it was by no means the intention of God to include mysteries in every hook and loop."[164] Instead of speculating about the meaning of every detail, Calvin wants to follow the lead of the author of Hebrews, who establishes the analogy between the tabernacle and Christ by treating the main points of comparison, much as we saw in the comparison of Melchizedek and Christ.[165] Thus the candlestick in the sanctuary symbolizes that the power of God's Spirit alone avails for the preservation of the Church, as is also suggested by the vision of the candlestick by Zechariah.[166] The making of the veil manifested to the people that the reality signified by the tabernacle was as yet hidden, and far off.[167] The main point that the Jews are to remember is that the tabernacle is made after the heavenly archetype seen by Moses, so that they do not cling to the representation but ascend from the figure to the reality it figures. "The best method of correcting gross error among the Jews was not to let them stop at the visible tabernacle and the sacrifices of beasts, but to set Christ before their eyes and make them look up to him."[168]

The Priesthood

After Moses is given divine instructions regarding the construction of the tabernacle, he is told to bring Aaron and his sons to the Lord to serve as priests, and is then told to make vestments for them and to perform ceremonies of consecration for their ordination to the priesthood (Exod. 28–29). After the dedication of the tabernacle, God commands Moses to set aside the tribe of Levi in order to appoint them over the tabernacle and all its equipment (Num. 1:47–54). Calvin first addresses the nature of the Israelite priesthood in the 1536 edition of the *Institutes,* in his polemic against the Roman view of priests who offer the sacrifice of the Mass. They claim that they have received their anointing from the sons of Aaron, "but meanwhile they do not notice, when they profess themselves successors of the sons of Aaron, that they do wrong to Christ's priesthood, which alone was foreshadowed and prefigured by all the ancient priesthood."[169]

Calvin treats the ways in which the Levitical priests foreshadow Christ in his commentary on Hebrews of 1549. He notes five points of comparison between the priests of the tabernacle and Christ. First, the priests were taken from among men; second, they acted for the whole people; third, they appeased God with sacrifices; fourth, they shared in our infirmities to help in our troubles; and fifth, they were elected and approved by God in this office. The thrust of these five points is to make it clear that the priesthood is a type and figure of Christ and that it therefore comes to an end once Christ comes to offer himself as the sacrifice for sin. "What is clearer than that the truth which is in Christ, is being compared with its types, which were prior to it in time and have now ceased?"[170]

Calvin expands on his understanding of the way the priests represent the person of Christ in his harmony of the last four books of Moses in 1563. At times, Calvin seems to make no distinction between the Aaronic and Levitical priesthood, following the lead of Numbers 17:1–11. "Now it is unquestionable, that the Levitical priests were the representatives of Christ; since, with respect to their office, they were even better than the very angels; which would by no means be reasonable, unless they had been the type of him, who is himself the head of the angels."[171] By the fact that only the priests could serve in the tabernacle, the Israelites were shown that they could not approach God on their own, "so that there was need of an Intercessor to propitiate him."[172] On the other hand, by the fact that the priests were taken from among the people, and had need of purification themselves, the people were directed from the type and figure to the reality yet to come.[173]

The garments of the priests therefore reveal that they represent something spiritual that is not yet present in their persons. "But God would show by this symbol the more than angelic brightness of all the virtues which was to be exhibited in Christ."[174] Sewn into the garments of the priests were twelve stones representing the twelve tribes of Israel, symbolizing "that, however vile and abject we may be in ourselves, and so altogether worthless refuse, yet inasmuch as Christ deigned to engraft us into his body, in him we are precious stones."[175] The high priest also bore the names of the tribes engraved on his shoulders, to exhibit to the people the need for Christ to bear them up to heaven, since they lack the strength to do so themselves.[176] The Urim and Thummin were worn by the priests to represent the person of Christ, who is the self-manifestation of the hidden God.[177] The bells and pomegranates hanging from the garment of the priest signify that we are foul before God until we are covered with the sweetness of Christ, and that the sound of the Gospel must ring out for us to have favor with God. "In this allegory there is nothing too subtle or far-fetched: for the similitude of the smell and the sound naturally leads us to the honoring of grace, and to the preaching of the gospel."[178]

The elaborate garments worn by the priests were not for the sake of ostentation but rather, "since Christ was vividly represented in the person of the high priest, this was a most important part of the legal service," for it had the "purpose of placing before men's eyes all that faith ought to consider in Jesus Christ."[179] The very fact that the priest had to be separated from the people by special garments manifested to the people that he was representing a person other than himself who would himself be free from all impurities.[180] The ablutions and sacrifices of purification for the priests added to this representation of Christ, for "the principal design of God was to set forth the image of perfect holiness which was at length beheld in Christ."[181] The same might be said of the Nazarites, who were set apart in a particular and special way from the rest of the people. "For the nearer any one under the Law approached to God, the more did Christ shine forth in him."[182]

Although Calvin at times seems to combine the Aaronic and Levitical priesthood, he nonetheless thinks that the distinction between the two orders of priests is significant as well, for it manifests important aspects of Christ's priestly work. By placing the Levites over the management of the tabernacle, God reveals the inability of the people to approach God on their own.[183] On the other hand, by elevating Aaron and his sons above the Levites, God directed the people to the coming of one Mediator, through whom alone they would have access to God.[184] The ratification of Aaron's calling by God in the miracle of the sprouting staff also manifested the ratification of the priesthood of Christ.[185] Because they truly represented Christ, the priests of Israel truly conveyed the blessing and grace of God to the people, even though the source of that grace was Christ. Thus the blessing of the people by the priests "was an efficacious testimony of God's grace" (Num. 6:22), even as the truth of the blessing was only exhibited when Christ lifted up his hands to bless his disciples after he was raised from the dead (Luke 24:50). Just as Moses would be consoled by the sight of the land of Canaan as the pledge of God's favor and adoption before he died, so God had Aaron's son Eleazar accompany Aaron up Mount Hor before he died, so that he might be consoled by the sight of his son. "For it was exactly as if the image of the Mediator was visibly set before his eyes."[186]

The Sacrifices of the Law

After the dedication of the tabernacle, God instituted the sacrifices the priests were to offer to God. Calvin first addressed sacrifices in the first edition of the *Institutes*, in his discussion of the way the sacraments of the Law were images that represented Christ. "Sacrifices made them aware of their unrighteousness and, at the same time, taught them that some satisfaction must be paid to God's justice. They were therefore taught that there should be some high priest, a mediator between God and men, to make satisfaction to God's justice by the shedding of blood and by the offering of a sacrifice to be received for the forgiveness of sins."[187] Calvin distinguishes between sacrifices of expiation, which are offered to "appease God's wrath, to satisfy his justice, to wash sins, and to implore grace and salvation," and sacrifices of thanksgiving, by which we dedicate ourselves to God, and in which are included "all our prayers, praises, thanksgivings, and whatever we do for the worship of God."[188]

Calvin expands on the way the sacrifices of expiation are patterned after the archetype of the sacrifice of Christ in the 1539 edition of the *Institutes*. "What was figuratively represented in the Mosaic sacrifices is manifested in Christ, the archetype of all the figures."[189] The priestly sacrifices therefore figuratively represented the sacrificial death of Christ to the Israelites, so that "there might be set before the people's eyes a likeness of the sacrifice that was to be offered to God in expiation."[190] In his commentary on Hebrews of 1549, Calvin insists that even though the sacrifices of the Law are figurative representations of the sacrifice of Christ, they nonetheless truly offer the sacrifice of Christ and its benefits to the people of Israel. "As the eternal salvation of the soul is in Christ so these were true evidences of this salvation."[191] However, the daily and yearly repetition of the sacrifices reveals that the truth of the sacrifices has not yet been exhibited. "Therefore God was not satisfied, guilt was not removed and consciences were not appeased; otherwise there would have been an end to sacrifice."[192] By their mode of representation the sacrifices reveal that Christ is to be expected in the future, even as they offer the sacrifice of Christ and its benefits to the Israelites.

Calvin expands upon the meaning of sacrifices of thanksgiving in his commentary on the Psalms of 1557. The purpose of such sacrifices was to magnify and celebrate the goodness of God that had been experienced by the one offering the sacrifice.[193] The eucharistic sacrifice is therefore only rightly offered when it comes forth from a heart that has surrendered to God out of love for the goodness of God it has experienced.[194] The animals offered in eucharistic sacrifices are therefore "the outward symbols of thanksgiving."[195] However, the sacrifice of animals also had another referent, namely, to the sacrifice of expiation offered by Christ, which must purify our gratitude so that it might be acceptable to God. "However we might propose to ourselves to praise the name of God, we could only profane it with our impure lips, had not Christ offered himself up a sacrifice, to sanctify both us and our services" (Heb. 10:7).[196]

Sacrifices of thanksgiving cannot therefore be separated from sacrifices of expiation, even if they are distinct. In his lectures on Hosea in 1560, Calvin reiterates the point made in the 1536 *Institutes*, that sacrifices of expiation have a twofold reference. On the one hand, they represent to us our sin and guilt, and the death which should fall on us as sinners. "God had instituted sacrifices for this end, that whoever sinned, being reminded of his guilt, might mourn for his sin, and further, that by witnessing that sad spectacle, his conscience might be more wounded; when he saw the innocent animal slain at the altar, he ought to have dreaded God's judgment."[197] Thus God will reject sacrifices that are offered "as false veils to cover their sins."[198] On the other hand, sacrifices of expiation figure and present the sacrifice of Christ for the forgiveness of sin, so that "the sinner, being reminded by the sight of the victim, might confess himself to be worthy of eternal death, and thus flee to God's mercy, and look to Christ and his sacrifice; for in him, and no where else, is to be found true and effectual expiation."[199]

In his harmony of the last four books of Moses, Calvin notes that the rite of sacrifice was not first instituted by Moses but had been practiced by the fathers before the giving of the Law. "Nor can there be any doubt but that by the sacred inspiration of the Spirit, the holy fathers were directed to the Mediator."[200] With regard to the ubiquitous observance of sacrifices among the Gentiles, Calvin claims that they derived this practice from the patriarchs, but did not preserve the double reference to their guilt and the sacrifice of Christ.[201] By giving the Law, God gathered together more clearly and more fully all the different kinds of sacrifices that had been corrupted by the Gentiles, and "left out no part of them at all which might afford a profitable exercise for believers."[202]

The care and scrupulousness God required in the observance of various sacrifices should have disclosed to the Israelites that something spiritual was being represented in their sacrifices, "so that under the external images the spiritual truth might meet their eyes."[203] Thus the morning and evening sacrifices should have reminded the Israelites of their guilt at the beginning and end of the day, so that they might continually flee to God's mercy for refuge.[204] On the other hand, the sacrifice of Yom Kippur, taking place only once a year for the sins of the whole people, more clearly represented the one perpetual sacrifice offered by the Son of God.[205] The addition of fire to the sacrifices represented the efficacy of the Holy Spirit, "on which all the profit of the sacrifices depends; for unless Christ had suffered in the Spirit, he would not have been a propitiatory sacrifice."[206] The sacrifices appointed for voluntary offenses reveal that there is forgiveness of sin for such sin in the Gospel as well as under the Law, for "there ought to be a mutual agreement between the external representation of grace under the Law, and the spiritual effect which Christ brought in."[207]

Unlike the sacrifices of the fathers, which had no clear Word of God appended to them, the sacrifices of the law have the promise of forgiveness added to them, "[t]hus the priest shall make atonement on his behalf for his sin, and he shall be forgiven" (Lev. 4:26). According to Calvin, "pardon was truly promised to the fathers, who reconciled themselves to God by the offering of sacrifices, not because the slaying of beasts expiated sins, but because it was a certain and infallible symbol, in which pious minds might acquiesce, so as to dare to come before God with tranquil confidence."[208] Thus pardon is not only represented to the people under the Law by their sacrifices but also truly offered to them, "else would these ancient figures be more than delusive, which had no other object than to be testimonies and mirrors of the grace which was finally manifested to us in Christ."[209] The sacrifices atone for sin and offer pardon in a sacramental way, by which what belongs to Christ and his sacrifice is transferred by metonymy to the figures and symbols of Christ under the Law, "yet in such a way that the similitude should be neither empty nor inefficacious, for in so far as the fathers apprehended Christ in the external figures, atonement was truly exhibited in them."[210] Sacrifices are no more delusive or empty symbols than is baptism, which is also said to wash away sins, but in a sacramental way. The only difference is not the efficacy of the sacraments but the way they represent Christ, "since baptism sets Christ before us as if he were present, whilst under the Law he was only obscurely typified."[211]

Rites of Purification

Among the sacrifices of the Law, God instituted specific rites of purification, over and above the rites of expiation (Lev. 12). Calvin notes the addition of these rites to the initial rite of purification in circumcision in the first edition of the *Institutes,* to highlight the progressive economy of the bestowal of the sacraments on the Israelites.[212] According to Calvin, the rites of purification symbolized to the Jews their own uncleanness, and set forth figuratively the cleansing power of the blood of Christ.[213]

In his commentary on John of 1553, Calvin notes that the water and the blood that flowed from the side of Jesus on the cross exhibited the true atonement for and cleansing from sin attained in his death. "For forgiveness of sins and righteousness and purity of the soul were prefigured in the Law by the two symbols of sacrifices and ablutions."[214] At times Calvin can appear to identify washing with the expiation for sins achieved in the death of Christ. When David asks God to purge him with hyssop (Ps. 51:7), Calvin takes this washing to be a means of expiation referring him to the blood of Christ.[215] Hyssop is therefore an outward symbol of expiation, and by asking to be purged with hyssop, David is asking that the reality signified by the hyssop be given to him.[216] However, in his harmony of the last four books of Moses of 1563, Calvin notes that the rites of purification after childbirth symbolize the cleansing we need due to our corrupt natures, as does circumcision.[217] Similarly, the purification required after a nocturnal emission reminded the Israelites of the corruption inherent in our nature. "In the ablution the remedy of the evil was proposed, since the mark of ignominy induced them to repentance."[218]

The Bronze Serpent

When the people complained against God and Moses in the wilderness about the lack of food and water, God sent poisonous serpents among the people. When the people repented of their sin, the Lord commanded Moses to make a bronze serpent and set it upon a pole, so that whoever looked to the figure when bitten by a serpent might live (Num. 21:4–9). According to Calvin, the apparent absurdity of this cure was intended by God to make the power and goodness of God more conspicuous. This becomes even more clear when we compare the figure with the reality it represents, for Christ compares himself to the bronze serpent in the Gospel of John (John 3:14). "And, surely, unless the brazen serpent had been a symbol of spiritual grace, it would not have been laid up like a precious treasure, and diligently preserved for many ages in God's sanctuary."[219] Calvin claims that the analogy between the sign of the bronze serpent and the reality of Christ is perfect, since Christ saves us from sin by coming in the likeness of sinful flesh, and this appears to be folly to people. "If, then, we desire to obtain salvation, let us not be ashamed to seek it from the curse of Christ, which was typified in the image of the serpent."[220] Calvin makes the same point in his comments on John 3:14 ten years earlier. "The similitude is not inappropriate or farfetched. Even as it was only a serpent in outward appearance, and had no infection of poison, so Christ put on the form of sinful flesh which was nevertheless pure and free from sin, to cure in us the deadly wound of sin."[221] However, Calvin goes on to note that Christ is not only making a comparison here, but is also saying that it was a sacrament in the same way that manna was, according to 1 Corinthians 10:3, "until it was changed into an idol by the people's superstition."[222] Calvin's statement in 1563 that the bronze serpent is a "symbol of spiritual grace" may mean that he still thinks of it as a sacrament, but he does not explicitly say so, nor does he insist on this being the case even in 1553: "If anyone thinks differently, I shall not argue the point."[223]

4. THE SYMBOLS AND TYPES OF CHRIST UNDER THE DAVIDIC MONARCHY

Calvin thought that Melchizedek was a singular type and symbol of Christ because he was a priest and king in one person. We have already seen how for Calvin the priests were types of Christ, but we do not get the full image of Christ in Israel until we come to the establishment of the Davidic monarchy. However, the claim that David and his kingdom is a type and image of Christ and his kingdom is a theme that only gradually begins to emerge in Calvin's writings, until it emerges with full clarity in 1557 in his commentary on the Psalms. David also marks the transition from the worship of God in the tabernacle to the Temple in Jerusalem. Moreover, God unconditionally promises never to remove God's love from the son of David, and promises Solomon that God has chosen to dwell in the Temple forever. Given the presence of both the king and the Temple within its walls, the city of Jerusalem itself becomes an especially vivid image of Christ as priest, king, and the one in whom God dwells fully.

David and His Kingdom as an Image of Christ and His Kingdom

Calvin first describes David as a type of Christ in his commentary on Romans of 1540, in reference to the way Paul quotes verses from the Psalms to describe sinful human nature. "In other Psalms he complains of the wickedness of his enemies, foreshadowing in himself and his descendants a type of the Kingdom of Christ."[224] Calvin returns to this idea in his commentary on the first half of Acts in 1552, with regard to the prayer of the apostles that the Lord spoke by the Holy Spirit through their ancestor David (Acts 4:24–25). He acknowledges that when David asked why the nations rage and rulers plot against the Lord and his anointed (Ps. 2:1–2), David is thinking of Saul and the Philistines. "Yet because his kingdom was established to be an image of the Kingdom of Christ, David does not remain in the shadow but grasps the solid form; indeed, the Holy Spirit, as the apostles here remind us, reproves the absurd folly of the world which dares to invade the Kingdom of Christ which God had established as much in the person of David as of Christ himself."[225] The kingdom of David is not only the image and type of the Kingdom of Christ but also the beginning of the Kingdom of Christ.

Calvin can therefore take the historical circumstances of David's life with full seriousness, for he not only prefigures Christ and his Kingdom but also actually inaugurates the Kingdom of Christ. When Paul says that the saying of God to David, "You are my Son; today I have begotten you" (Ps. 2:7), has been fulfilled in Jesus, Calvin notes first of all that all kings are generally called "sons of God" (Ps. 82:6). Hence the Word of God in Psalm 2 must elevate David above the ranks of all other kings as being by way of eminence the Son of God.[226] However, this does not mean that David himself was not begotten as the Son of God, which Calvin takes to mean manifested to others as the Son; for God clearly established the kingdom of David so that all could see the hand of God in choosing and elevating him.[227] David is singled out above all other kings because he is the image of Christ, yet he is also truly begotten of God in the divine establishment of his rule, even as his rule is an image of the Kingdom of Christ. The same relationship can be seen in the way Calvin describes the sufferings of David as both real in themselves and typifying the sufferings of Christ. In his commentary on John of 1553, Calvin notes how when David said that for his thirst he was given vinegar to drink (Ps. 69:21), he was speaking metaphorically. However, to show that he was also the type of the Christ who was to come, Christ drinks real vinegar on the cross.[228]

Calvin develops the variety of ways in which David represents Christ in his commentary on the Psalms of 1557. As we have already noted, David is an image of Christ in the way he is exalted by the calling of God above all other rulers. According to Calvin, David knew he was king primarily as an image and type of Christ, in whom was to be found the solid truth of the kingdom foreshadowed in himself.[229] Thus, when David is manifested to Israel as their king by the appointment of God, he is begotten as the Son of God in a pre-eminent way, but only insofar as he is the type of Christ.[230] However, David was truly exalted as the Son of God in his own life, "for as soon as it became known that he was made king by divine appointment, he came forth as one who had been lately begotten of God, since so great an honor could not belong to a private person."[231] All kings are called the sons of God because they are God's representatives, "but they are not clothed with that sacred majesty by which David was honored to be an image of God's only begotten Son."[232] The manner of his manifestation as king is also an image of Christ, for David is manifested to be king after he had been pursued out of the land of Israel by Saul, foreshadowing the manifestation of Christ as king after his abasement on the cross and in the grave.[233] Hence David could be said to be the stone the builders rejected that has now been made the cornerstone, even as he is also the type of Christ. "In short, all that is here stated properly related to the person of Christ; and that which was dimly adumbrated in David was brightly represented and fulfilled in Christ."[234]

David is also an image of Christ in the way he was manifested to be king by triumphing over the opposition of his enemies.[235] When David sings of the way the help and protection of God helped him to attain victory over his enemies, he is speaking of the real victories he won.[236] At the same time, by proving himself victorious over all his enemies, he is acting as the image or type of Christ.[237] David also had to fight against the enemies who rose up within his kingdom, which is yet another way in which "the kingdom of David was a type under which the Holy Spirit intended to shadow forth (*depingat*) to us the Kingdom of Christ," for enemies of Christ manifest themselves in the Church from the beginning.[238]

Both David and his kingdom are types of Christ and his Kingdom.[239] In particular, the victories of David and the extent of his kingdom typify the way Christ will extend his dominion throughout the world.[240] Calvin thinks that the evanescent character of David's kingdom revealed to the Israelites that it was the type of the coming Christ, for it never truly lived up to the promises of God made to David, as when Balaam prophesies that a scepter will come out of Israel and crush the borderlands of Moab and the territory of all the Shethites (Num. 24:17). "I admit, indeed, that some beginnings existed in the person of David, but they were very far from exhibiting the fulness of the reality."[241] The prophecy is in fact partially fulfilled in David, or else his kingdom would not be an image of Christ's; but his kingdom did not fulfill the promises, either in its extent or in its duration, thereby directing the people of Israel to Christ as the one who will fulfill the promises.[242]

The promise given to David that his throne would be established forever (2 Sam. 7:16) also reveals that David is a type and image of Christ.[243] Calvin thinks that he can establish this point without any reference to the testimony of Christ and the apostles but merely by examining the history of the Davidic monarchy. "If we set Christ aside, where will we find that everlasting duration of the royal throne of which mention is here made? The second from David, in the order of succession, was despoiled of the greater part of the kingdom, so that out of twelve tribes he retained scarcely one tribe and a half."[244] After the loss of the northern kingdom, the kingdom of Judah was subject to endless calamities, until it was at length dragged off to captivity in Babylon. "And I pray you to consider where was the dignity of the throne, when the king, after his sons were put to death before his eyes, was himself treated as a criminal (2 Kings 25:7). The Jews were indeed afterwards permitted to dwell in their own country; but it was without the honor and title of a kingdom."[245] The only conclusion Calvin thinks we can draw from this history is either that the promise of God falls to the ground concerning the perpetuity of David's throne or that it is only fulfilled in Christ.[246]

This does not mean that every prophecy regarding the restoration of the kingdom of David has to be referred immediately to Christ. For instance, when Isaiah tells Jerusalem, "Your eyes will see the king in his beauty" (Isa. 33:17), Calvin takes this as referring to Hezekiah. However, given the partial fulfillment of this prophecy in Hezekiah, he himself must be set forth by Isaiah as a type or image of Christ, who alone fulfills the prophecy.[247] Calvin denies that such an interpretation is an allegory, since it takes seriously the partial fulfillment of the prophecy in Hezekiah. However, even if we take Hezekiah seriously, the lack of stability in his kingdom leads us to Christ. "But, because in Christ alone is found the stability of that frail kingdom, the likeness which Hezekiah bore leads us to Christ, as it were, by the hand."[248]

David is also an image of Christ by the sufferings he endured, which adumbrate the sufferings of Christ. The locus classicus of this foreshadowing is found in Psalm 22. Calvin takes the psalm to be a sincere expression of the severe trials experienced by David. As David himself is an image of Christ, his sufferings also set forth a type of the sufferings of Christ.[249] However, David is not only a type of Christ, but he is also an exemplar for all those who are in Christ, both before and after he was manifested in the flesh. Thus the sufferings of David refer us to Christ, and through him to ourselves as members of Christ. When David laments that even his bosom friend whom he trusted, who ate of his bread, has lifted up his heel against him (Ps. 41:9), Calvin takes this both to typify Christ and to exemplify the conflicts within the Church that all the godly will experience, "in order that each of us may prepare himself for the same condition."[250]

When God promises to restore the people of Israel, God sets forth David and his kingdom as a pledge and symbol of that restoration and salvation. When the people of Israel cry, "Give victory to the king, O Lord; answer us when we call" (Ps. 21:9), Calvin observes that it is not odd that the king should be linked to the answering of prayer so long as we see the king as a type of Christ.[251] God encouraged the people to turn to the king as "the minister of God's saving grace" in order to lead them by the image of the king to the saving help of Christ, the Mediator. "Their king will be as it were a mirror in which they may see reflected the image of God."[252] David himself appeals to the Mediator of whom he is the type and image when he prays to God for favor. When he asks God to "look on the face of your anointed" (Ps. 84:9), Calvin thinks that he is seeking "to obtain the divine favor through the intervention of the Mediator of whom he was the type."[253] Thus both the people and David himself know that David and his kingdom are pledges of the grace and favor of God, since they are images of Christ the Mediator. When Jeremiah promises the people of Jerusalem that they shall see the return of the kings who sit on the throne of David (Jer. 17:25), Calvin takes this to mean that "thus they saw as it were with their own eyes the favor of God present with them, inasmuch as David and his posterity were visible pledges of God's favor."[254] The one way in which David is not an image or type of Christ is that Christ is the Son of God, namely, God manifested in the flesh. "At that time God ruled over his chosen people by the hand of David, but after the coming of Christ he began to reign by himself, that is, in the person of his only-begotten Son, who was truly God manifested in the flesh (1 Tim. 3:16)." Nonetheless, in the flesh Christ is still the son of David, even if God reigns in person in him.[255]

The figure of David as a type of Christ takes on a very prominent role in the final edition of the *Institutes*. In the chapter in which Calvin makes the transition between the knowledge of God the Creator and the knowledge of God the Redeemer, he appeals repeatedly to David to demonstrate that God never showed Godself to the ancient people of Israel apart from the Mediator. "And there is no doubt that our heavenly Father willed that we perceive in David and his descendants the living image of Christ."[256] David was set forth by the prophets as the one from whom they should expect the restoration of the people.[257] The person of David therefore becomes the crucial figure who demonstrates, according to Calvin, that since "God cannot without the Mediator be propitious toward the human race, under the law Christ was always set before the holy fathers as the end to which they should direct their faith."[258]

The Temple in Jerusalem as the Representation of Christ

Calvin applied the same understanding he had developed regarding the tabernacle—that it was a portrayal of the exemplar seen by Moses on the mountain, namely, Christ—to the Temple in Jerusalem. In his commentary on the first half of Acts in 1552, Calvin notes how the opponents of Stephen see him as speaking against both the Temple and the Law of Moses. "But the great value of the temple and the usefulness of the ceremonies consists rather in their being ascribed to Christ, as to their original pattern."[259] However, in his commentary on John of 1553, Calvin notes the distinctive place that the temple had in the economy of divine self-manifestation to the Jews, especially with regard to the mobility of the tabernacle versus the location of the temple in Jerusalem. "The patriarchs were allowed to erect altars everywhere because the place which the Lord afterwards chose had not yet been appointed. But from the time that God ordered the Temple to be built on Mount Zion their former freedom ceased."[260] Jesus himself honored the importance of the Temple and its ceremonies for the people of his time. Calvin attributes Jesus' going into the Temple to teach (John 7:14) to the fact that he wanted to add the Word of God to the ceremonies of the Temple, for the Word alone makes such ceremonies into living images of God. "But because the priests were then almost dumb and the scribes adulterated pure doctrine with their leaven and false inventions, Christ undertook the teaching office."[261]

In his commentary on the Psalms of 1557, Calvin observes that the beauty and stability of the Temple were meant to elevate the minds of the people from the Temple to the exemplar that it represented. When the psalm says that God built his sanctuary like the high heavens and like the earth that God founded forever (Ps. 78:69), Calvin insists that the beauty of the Temple ought to be referred to Christ. "It was not the will of God that the minds of his people should be entirely engrossed with the magnificence of the building, or with the pomp of the outward ceremonies; but that they should be elevated to Christ, in whom the truth of the figures of the former economy was exhibited."[262] The same must be said about the stability ascribed to the Temple. Lest any object that the Temple was in fact destroyed by the Babylonians, Calvin responds by insisting that "the stability celebrated consists in Christ alone."[263] This is the reason why God, through the prophet Haggai, was so concerned that the Temple be rebuilt after the return from the Babylonian exile, not that the Temple per se was of importance, but because it was a visible representation of the coming Christ.[264] The promise of God through

Haggai that "the latter glory of this house shall be greater than the former" (Hag. 2:9) was meant to refer the Jews to the glory of the coming Christ and not to the building of the Temple per se.[265] Calvin denies that this promise was at least partially fulfilled when Herod reconstructed the Temple; rather, he thinks that the Herodian Temple was built to turn the hopes of the people away from Christ. "That they might not look to Christ, this delusive and empty spectacle was presented to them, so as to astound them."[266] Only in Christ, Calvin claims, do we find a glory that will never perish, even as in him we find the king who will reign forever, "for though they were to gather the treasures of a thousand worlds into one mass, such a glory would yet be corruptible; but when God the Father appeared in the person of his only Son, he then glorified indeed his Temple; and his majesty shone forth so much that there was nothing wanting to complete perfection."[267]

The Sacrificial Offerings in the Temple

According to Calvin, the sacrifices offered by the priests in the Temple had the same meaning as those that were offered in the tabernacle. The sacrifices of expiation were meant to represent to the people their sin and the death that is rightfully theirs, so that they might flee to the mercy of God in the sacrifice of Christ.[268] The death of the animal on the altar therefore represented to the people in a visible image the death to which they themselves should be subject, to induce repentance; and the death that Christ would undergo for their sakes to expiate their sins, to foster faith.[269] The sacrifices of thanksgiving, on the other hand, were meant to represent that as all good things come freely from God, so the people who receive such benefits offer themselves and all they have freely to God.[270]

Even though the Gentiles also had their temples in which sacrifices were offered, they did so without the command or promise of God, and hence their sacrifices were entirely futile, no matter how much outward splendor they might have had. Even though the sacrifices of the Jews did not appear to be different from those of the Gentiles, they were offered in obedience to and trust in the command and promise of God, and hence were living images of Christ. "We must therefore hold, that sacraments at first sight appear trifling and of no moment, but their efficacy consists in the command and promise of God."[271] Nonetheless, God reminded the Jews that even when sacrifices are offered in true faith, repentance, and gratitude, in accordance with the command and promise of God, they still belong to a particular stage of the divine economy that is destined to come to an end. David acknowledges this limitation when he says, "Sacrifice and offering you do not desire. . . . Burnt offering and sin offering you have not required" (Ps. 40:6). Calvin claims that David means that "the rudiments which God had enjoined upon his ancient people for a time had some other end in view, and were like infantile instructions designed to prepare them for some higher state. But if their truth and substance are contained in Christ, it is certain that they have been abolished by his coming."[272]

The Image of Christ in the Kings and Priests in Jerusalem

In his commentary on Psalms of 1557, Calvin sees an essential connection between the promise of God to establish the throne of David forever and the promise of God to dwell in the Temple forever.[273] On the one hand, the choice of David and Zion confirms the love of God for the people of Israel, and itself becomes a symbol of that love. On the other hand, the presence in the same city of the priests and kings of Israel sets forth the image of Christ as priest and king.[274] David himself, according to Calvin, describes Jerusalem as the place where both the place for the invocation of God and the thrones of David are to be found (Ps. 122:4–5). "The sanctuary erected on Mount Zion was intended to keep their faith fixed upon the spiritual priesthood of Christ; and in like manner, by the kingdom of David, there was presented to their view an image of the kingdom of Christ."[275] Calvin makes the same point in the final edition of the *Institutes*: "From this it follows that both among the whole tribe of Levi and among the posterity of David, Christ was set before the eyes of the people as in a double mirror."[276]

In his lectures on Jeremiah of 1563, Calvin describes the priests and kings in Jerusalem as the symbols of the temporal and eternal happiness of the Israelites, "for both the king and the priests were images of Christ. For as by the priesthood they knew that God was propitious to them, they being reconciled to him by sacrifice, and as by the kingdom they knew that God was the protector and guardian of their safety, so these two things constituted a real and complete happiness."[277] The Israelites ought therefore to have ascended by analogy and anagogy from the temporal kingship and priesthood of Jerusalem to the coming spiritual kingship and priesthood of Christ.[278] Jerusalem therefore represents the final phase in the development of the self-manifestation of Christ to the Israelites and the Jews, until the manifestation of Christ in the flesh, which itself culminates in the city of Jerusalem.

CHAPTER 7

Symbols of the Presence of God to Israel

In the Law, God not only institutes living images and symbols that refer the Israelites and Jews to the manifestation of Christ in the flesh but also creates symbols and signs of the presence of God, so that the Israelites and Jews might know that God is near to them and indeed dwells among them. If the living images of Christ refer the Jews to the future manifestation of Christ in the flesh, the living symbols of the presence of God refer the Jews upwards from the visible sign to the invisible God in heaven. We have already seen one set of such symbols in the visions seen by the patriarchs and prophets. For instance, when Isaiah says that he saw God in the Temple, Calvin says, "Here we learn a profitable doctrine, that whenever God grants any sign of his presence, he is undoubtedly present with us, for he does not amuse us with unmeaning shapes, as men wickedly disfigure him by their contrivances. Since, therefore, that exhibition was no deceitful representation of the presence of God, Isaiah justly declares that he saw him."[1] As this passage indicates, in the symbols of God's presence, the invisible God becomes somewhat visible, which is why Calvin includes visions in this category.

I now turn to Calvin's understanding of the symbols of God's presence that are created by the works of God and then those employed by God during the exodus, including both the pillar of fire and the cloud and the tabernacle and the ark of the covenant, culminating in the symbols of God's presence in Jerusalem, including the temple and the city itself, as well as in

205

the prophets. I conclude with an examination of Calvin's understanding of false symbols of God's presence, which are always on his mind even as he is discussing the true symbols of God's presence. Calvin thinks that one of the crucial issues of his day is the proper way to understand the symbols of God's presence, over against what he took to be the abuse of such symbols in the Roman Church, not only in their use of images in worship but also, especially, in their adoration of the eternal Son of God in the reserved host of the Eucharist. Calvin carefully studied the dynamic of the symbols of God's presence in the history of Israel in order to try to come to the right understanding of the symbols of God's presence in the Christian Church.

1. Symbols of God's Presence in the Works of God

According to Calvin, God can use ordinary phenomena to manifest God's presence to people. In his Genesis commentary of 1554, Calvin describes the breeze in the Garden of Eden as both a natural phenomenon and a symbol of the presence of God, to awaken Adam and Eve to the sin into which they had fallen.[2] As in the case of visions, Calvin understands such symbols as the self-manifestation of God, by which the invisible God becomes somewhat visible. "For, since he is in himself incomprehensible, he assumes, when he wishes to manifest himself to men, those marks by which he may be known."[3] Similarly, when Jacob returns in trepidation to Esau, only to discover that his brother embraces him with favor, he describes seeing the face of Esau as seeing the face of God, "that is, as if God had given some sign of his presence."[4]

God can also manifest signs of God's presence when God acts in judgment, distinguishing between the godly and the wicked. In his commentary on Isaiah of 1559, Calvin interprets the threat that the hand of God would be turned against Jerusalem in this way. "Besides, the turning of the hand of God denotes generally a sign of his presence, as if he should say, I will display my hand. This he is wont to do in two ways; either by chastising the wicked, or by delivering believers from their distress."[5] Similarly, when Isaiah speaks of the day of visitation, Calvin describes this as the manifestation of either the mercy or the judgment of God. "Both kinds of visitation have the same object in view, for we do not see the Lord but in his works; and we think that he is absent unless he gives us some sign of his presence."[6] Thus, when God delivers the people in an extraordinary way, God is said to rend the heavens, for the work manifests the presence of God to us, "because otherwise we think that he is a great distance from us."[7] As we can see, the works of God manifest the presence of God to us when God approaches either in mercy or in judgment, when we had thought that God did not regard us or was absent from us.

2. SYMBOLS OF GOD'S PRESENCE IN THE CLOUD AND THE PILLAR OF FIRE

Calvin first discusses the cloud and the pillar of fire as symbols of the presence of God in the 1539 edition of the *Institutes*. He appeals to these symbols because they both manifest and conceal God, thereby demonstrating that the God who becomes somewhat visible in such symbols nonetheless remains invisible and incomprehensible. "God, indeed, from time to time showed the presence of his divine majesty by definite signs, so that he might be said to be looked upon face to face. But all the signs that he ever gave forth clearly told men of his incomprehensible essence. For clouds and smoke and flame [Deut. 4:11] restrained the minds of all, like a bridle placed on them, from attempting to penetrate too deeply."[8] In his commentary on 1 Corinthians of 1546, however, Calvin stresses the way the cloud was truly the self-manifestation of God to the Israelites during the exodus, to show that the cloud represented the eternal blessings of God in Christ. "His main purpose however was to bear witness to himself, and reveal himself, as their God, and eternal salvation is included under that. Throughout the Scriptures the cloud is called the sign of his presence."[9] These two passages reveal one of the central dynamics at work in Calvin's discussion of symbols of God's presence: the symbol truly reveals the presence of God with the people, even as God is hidden by the symbol in order to remain incomprehensible.

In his discussion of the cloud and the fire in his commentary on the Psalms of 1557, Calvin highlights the way God was truly present with the people by means of these symbols. The presence of God with the people in the wilderness confirms their adoption as much as did the exodus, since God revealed that God was willing to lead the people to the land of Canaan even as God delivered them from the land of Egypt.[10] Because God was truly present with the people by means of these symbols, the sin of the people in the wilderness is all the more serious, for "they had every day full in their view signs of the presence of God, and even necessity itself should have constrained them to yield a true and holy obedience."[11] The continual manifestation of God's presence throughout the journey in the wilderness revealed to later generations that God would also be present with them, even though these particular signs of God's presence were temporary.[12] The people of Israel continually recalled the symbols of God's presence in the cloud and the fire to assure themselves by these signs of God's presence in their own day, even when such signs were absent.[13]

In his discussion of the cloud and the fire in his harmony of the last four books of Moses in 1563, Calvin reaffirms the point he made in his commentary on 1 Corinthians, that God is truly present in the symbol of God's presence, even as God transcends the limitations of the symbol. When Moses says that the Lord went before the people in the cloud, Calvin notes that "we must observe the sacramental mode of speaking, wherein God transfers his name to visible figures; not to affix to them his essence, nor to circumscribe his immensity, but only to show that he does not deceitfully expose the signs of his presence to men's eyes, but that the exhibition of the thing signified is at the same time conjoined with them."[14] According to Calvin, the true presence of God must not be confused with the local presence of God. The presence of God is truly exhibited by the symbol, even as God is not attached to or confined within the symbol. "Therefore, although Moses states that God was in the cloud and the pillar of fire, yet he does not wish to draw him down from heaven, nor to subject his infinite glory to visible signs, with which his truth may consist without local presence."[15]

When the people rebel against God in the wilderness, Calvin again points out that they do so before the God who appears to them in these symbols.[16] God is present in the cloud, even though God is truly present in heaven and does not descend from heaven to be confined in the symbol. Thus, when Moses says that God descended in the cloud and stood before him on Mount Sinai, Calvin takes this to refer not to God's immensity, which is universally diffused, but to human perception, "because under the appearance of the cloud God testified that he met with Moses."[17]

Finally, Calvin notes the way the cloud appears to be identified with God's word of command (Num. 9:18), revealing that the cloud is a visible word of God. "I do not doubt that the name of word, was given to the sign, inasmuch as God speaks as much to the eye by outward signs as he does to the ears by his voice. Still, from this mode of expression we may gather that the use of signs is perverted and nullified, unless they are taken to be visible doctrine, as Augustine writes."[18] It is noteworthy that this is the only place in which Calvin highlights the mutual relation between symbol and Word when speaking of the cloud and the pillar of fire. In all other instances, the cloud is taken strictly as a visible symbol, which truly exhibits the presence of God without either dragging God down from heaven or confining the essence of God within the symbol.

3. The Tabernacle as the Symbol of God's Presence

The Israelites should have learned from the cloud and the pillar of fire that God is present with them even when these symbols, which were temporary, were no longer seen by them.[19] However, God did not leave the Israelites without any further signs of God's presence but rather instituted the tabernacle as the symbol of God's presence that would be with them until the dedication of the Temple in Jerusalem. Calvin first discusses the tabernacle in the 1539 edition of the *Institutes,* with regard to the cherubim that adorned the ark of the covenant. He makes the same point regarding the angels that he did with regard to the cloud: they manifest God's presence even as they disclose that God remains hidden. "The mercy seat from which God manifested the presence of his power under the law was so constructed as to suggest that the best way to contemplate the divine is where minds are lifted up above themselves with admiration. Indeed, the cherubim with wings outspread covered it; the veil shrouded it; the place itself deeply enough hidden concealed it [Exod. 25:17–21]."[20] Calvin elaborates on this function of the tabernacle in his discussion of the cherubim who guard the Garden of Eden in his commentary on Genesis of 1554. According to Calvin, the representation of angels as cherubim was designed with the needs of the tabernacle in mind, "for God designed, that what he knew would prove useful to the people, should be revealed in the sanctuary."[21] The cherubim, like the rest of the tabernacle, were shown to the people to aid their ascent to God, due to their infirmity. Without such helps, the ascent to God would not be possible. Thus they act as ladders and vehicles, by which we might climb from the visible symbols on earth to the invisible God in heaven. "Moreover, I call them vehicles and ladders, because symbols of this kind were by no means ordained that the faithful might shut up God in a tabernacle as in a prison, or might attach him to earthly elements, but that, being assisted by congruous and apt means, they might themselves rise to heaven."[22]

In his commentary on the Psalms of 1557, Calvin shows how David reveals to us the proper way to use the tabernacle. On the one hand, David knows he can still call on God even in exile from the tabernacle, as God is not confined to that symbol.[23] On the other hand, David directs his prayers towards the tabernacle, thereby viewing it as a true symbol of God's presence.[24] This attitude discloses for Calvin the ideal mean with regard to the use of the tabernacle: it is a true symbol of the presence of God, to which God is not confined. "By these words he intimates that he kept a middle way, inasmuch as he neither despised the visible sign, which the Lord had appointed on account of the rudeness of the times, nor by attaching a superstitious importance to a particular place, entertained carnal conceptions of the glory of God."[25]

Even as the nature of God is not bound or confined to the visible tabernacle, so the senses and thoughts of the people should not be bound to the visible symbol, but should rise from the symbol to the invisible God as on a ladder.[26] This does not mean that God is not truly present in the tabernacle, however, for David says that he loves the house where God dwells, the place where God's glory abides (Ps. 26:8). These expressions bear witness to the fact that the tabernacle is a true symbol of the presence of God, by which to give confidence to the prayers of the faithful, "that they might not think that they sought him in vain."[27] Since the tabernacle truly assures the people of the presence of God, it is the living image or mirror in which the invisible God may be beheld.[28]

Thus, when David asks when he shall come and behold the face of God (Ps. 42:2), Calvin claims that he turns to the tabernacle, to see in that image the God who cannot be seen, for "it behooved the faithful in seeking to approach God, to begin by those things. Not that they should continue attached to them, but that they should, by the help of these signs and outward means, seek to behold the glory of God, which of itself is hidden from sight."[29] On the other hand, David says that he longs for the courts of the Lord so that he may enjoy the living God (Ps. 84:2), revealing that he seeks to rise from the visible symbol of God's presence to the God represented therein for he "knew that the visible sanctuary served the purpose of a ladder, because, by it the minds of the godly were directed and conducted to the heavenly model."[30] To accentuate the way the tabernacle helps us to ascend to God, Calvin will describe God as coming down to "stretch out his hand to us, so to speak, in order to lift us up to himself."[31]

In his description of the tabernacle in his harmony of the last four books of Moses of 1563, Calvin accentuates the way God descends to the Israelites to appear to them in the living image of the tabernacle, to lift them up to Godself in heaven. The people are meant to feel near to God in the sanctuary, not to shut up God in the tabernacle or affix their minds to the visible symbol. "He descends to them, therefore, not to occupy their minds with a gross superstition, but to raise them up by degrees to spiritual worship."[32] The visible beauty of the tabernacle was meant to draw the minds of the people from the visible symbol to the beauty of the invisible God who was therein represented.[33] The oil with which the tabernacle is anointed is also meant to direct the minds of the people from the symbol to the reality it represents, "for we have already often seen that there had been set before this rude people a splendor in sacred symbols, which might affect their external senses, so as to uplift them as it were by steps to the knowledge of spiritual things."[34]

On the other hand, the tabernacle truly is the symbol of the presence of God, by means of which God may be truly said to dwell among God's people. When God tells the Israelites that God will dwell in their midst and will walk among them (Lev. 26:11–12), Calvin takes this to mean that the truth represented by the tabernacle is truly exhibited by that symbol.[35] The promise of God to dwell in the tabernacle is visibly confirmed when the tabernacle is dedicated, for the cloud, itself a symbol of the presence of God, covers the tent.[36] Even though God cannot be confined to the tabernacle, the presence of God in the tabernacle must nonetheless be real, or else the worship of the Israelites would be in vain.[37] Thus the presence of the cloud over the tabernacle has the effect of assuring the Israelites that God hears them when they pray to God, and that God will be "nigh to his people by the presence of his power and grace, whenever he was invoked by them."[38] However, the most vivid confirmation that the tabernacle is the house in which God dwells comes from the presence of the ark of the covenant within it. "But, although the tabernacle was called God's house, yet there was a more express image of his glory in the Ark of the Covenant; because the Law, whereby God bound the people to himself, was there deposited."[39]

4. THE ARK OF THE COVENANT AS THE SYMBOL OF GOD'S PRESENCE

Calvin first discusses the ark of the covenant as the symbol of God's presence in his commentary on Romans of 1540. He interprets Paul's statement that to the Jews belong "the glory" (Rom. 9:4) as referring above all else to the ark of the covenant. "Besides many signs of his presence, he formerly exhibited a singular proof of it in the ark, from which he gave both answers and heard his people, in order to put forth his power in helping them."[40] In contrast to the tabernacle, which he viewed primarily as a vehicle or ladder by which the pious were to ascend as if by steps to God, Calvin interprets the ark of the covenant as the means by which God descends to the Israelites, becoming somewhat visible in the living image of the ark, so that the Israelites might feel and experience the presence of God, especially God's grace and power.

This trajectory becomes especially clear in his commentary on the Psalms of 1557. When David prays to God, "Thy face, O Lord, so I seek" (Ps. 27:8), Calvin interprets this to refer "to the mode of manifestation in which God was wont to render himself in some degree visible," in particular to the symbol of God's presence in the ark, which, "without any impropriety, everywhere denominated his face."[41] Though it is true that God is essentially invisible, it is also true that the invisible God becomes somewhat visible in the ark of the covenant, as in a mirror darkly.[42] Though Calvin reminds his readers that they should ascend from the visible symbol to God, he still emphasizes the descent of God to the ark to appear to the Israelites therein, "furnishing us on earth with an image of his heavenly glory."[43] In striking contrast to his understanding of the use of the tabernacle, to which the Israelites were not to confine their senses or thoughts, Calvin admonishes his readers to attend very carefully to the images in which God appears to us, in contrast to the false images created by human beings. "But as it is according to his sovereign pleasure that God vouchsafes us to look upon him (as he does in Word and sacraments), it becomes us steadily to fix our eyes on this view."[44] Calvin wants us to ignore images of God painted by the human imagination, so that we might direct our eyes intently to the images in which the invisible God becomes somewhat visible to us. "The ark is also termed the beauty of God; because being in himself invisible, he made it a symbol of his presence, or, as it were, a mirror in which he might be seen."[45]

The descent of God to the ark of the covenant is especially necessary if the godly are to call upon God with confidence that God is near to them and will hear their cries. "Although, therefore, he does not thereby change place himself, he is felt by us to draw sensibly nearer."[46] When the ark of the covenant is moved from the tabernacle to the Temple, the people ascend Mount Zion in order to behold the face of God in the ark of the covenant, and "genuine worshippers found from experience, that by this means they were greatly aided in approaching him."[47] According to Calvin, God did indeed answer the prayers of the godly from the ark of the covenant, for "God exhibited himself to his saints in the ark of the covenant, and thereby gave them a certain pledge of speedy succour whenever they should invoke him for aid."[48]

The godly experience the presence of God in the ark because by means of it God manifests to them his power and grace.[49] Thus, when the pious are exhorted to seek the face and strength of God, they are directed to seek the face of God in the ark of the covenant in particular, for there they experience the present help of God.[50] Thus God may be said to come to God's people when God displays God's power by means of the ark. "Hence it is called the Ark of his strength, not a mere idle shadow to look upon, but what certainly declared God's nearness to his Church."[51] When God wants to reveal to the Israelites that God is no longer present among them to help them, God has the ark carried away from them. "It is indeed very obvious, that God was not fixed to the outward and visible symbol; but . . . in suffering it to be carried away, he testified, that he himself had also departed from them."[52]

However, as Calvin notes in his commentary on Isaiah of 1559, God is not truly carried away when the ark is taken away. The ark of the covenant is distinguished from the idols of the Gentiles because the Israelites were to ascend from the visible symbol to God, whereas the Gentiles focused all their attention on their idols.[53] Calvin makes the same point in his harmony of the last four books of Moses of 1563. When Moses says to the ark, "Rise up, Lord, and let thine enemies be scattered" (Num. 10:35), Calvin points out that Moses does not confine the power of God to the ark but rather thinks of it sacramentally, as the living image of God's power and glory.[54] Even the way in which the ark was carried among the people is for Calvin a reminder that the ark is the true pledge of the grace and power of God, even as God is not confined to the ark. The long interval God commanded the people to leave between themselves and the ark "had the effect of exercising their faith by preventing them from confining the grace of God within too narrow limits, and reminding them, that though they were far distant from the ark, the divine power was ever near."[55]

Though Calvin does not explicitly relate the symbol of the ark with the Word of God, which he terms the soul of living images, he nonetheless implicitly links the symbol of the ark with the Word of God by means of the tables of the Law that are deposited in the ark. As we have seen, Calvin claims that there "was a more express image of his glory in the Ark of the Covenant; because the Law, whereby God bound the people to himself, was there deposited."[56] Calvin considered the Law the renewal of the covenant God made with Abraham and Sarah, and thought that God had written the Law on the two tablets of stone so that there might be a perpetual memorial of this renewal.[57] Calvin can therefore speak of the tables of the Law themselves as signs of the presence of God, or even as the face of God, as when Moses encounters the Israelites in the midst of their idolatrous worship of the golden calves.[58] Calvin can even understand the tables of the Law that are deposited in the ark of the covenant as being the self-representation of God. "The tables were actually deposited in the Ark of the Covenant, and by them God represented himself, so that without them the tabernacle was in a manner empty."[59] However, Calvin never explicitly says that the tables of the Law are the word or doctrine that gives life to the symbol of God's presence in the ark of the covenant.

5. The Temple in Jerusalem as the Symbol of God's Presence

The tabernacle was replaced as the symbol of God's presence when Solomon built the Temple in Jerusalem, and the ark of the covenant was carried into the Temple, after which the cloud of the glory of the Lord filled the Temple (1 Kings 8:1–13). Calvin first addresses the Temple as a symbol of the presence of God in his discussion of Stephen's sermon in his commentary on Acts of 1552. He is especially interested in the apparent contradiction between the statement made by Stephen, that "the Most High does not dwell in houses made by human hands" (Acts 7:48), supported by Isaiah 66:1–2, and the promise that God would dwell in the Temple forever (Ps. 132:14). According to Calvin, the two statements can be reconciled if we remember that the symbols of God's presence are misused when we seek to tie God down to them, and it is this abuse that Stephen and Isaiah were denouncing. "Therefore the Israelites were wrong when they fixed their attention on the symbols, and fabricated an earthly god for themselves."[60] Calvin therefore understands the Temple according to the same dynamic we saw with regard to the tabernacle: God descends in the symbols of God's presence so that the people might ascend by these steps to God.[61] God is present in symbols only to the godly who seek God in a spiritual way by means of such symbols and do not confine God to the symbol.[62] He strengthens this position by insisting that God is only present for us in such symbols if we reach out to God in heaven by faith, for "if we do not reach up to him in faith, he will not be present for us. From this it is easy to conclude that, when he dwells in the midst of his people, he is neither fixed to the earth, nor contained in any place, seeing that they seek him spiritually in heaven."[63] The logic of this position seems to be that God is only present in symbols of God's presence if the godly do not see them as symbols of God's presence at all but rather seek God only in heaven, not in the symbol.

Calvin returns to the question of the presence of God in the Temple at the time of Jesus in his commentary on John of 1553. He thinks that the pool by the Sheep Gate in which invalids sought to be healed was within the Temple itself. According to him, God healed the people in this pool in order to attest God's presence in the Temple during a time when there were no longer signs of God's presence, especially since the cessation of prophecy. "And since various temptations pressed on them from every side they needed this extraordinary aid, lest they should think God had entirely deserted them and so be discouraged and fall away."[64] By healing the people in the Temple, God confirmed that the worship that God had instituted in the Temple was not in vain, as God was still present in the Temple.[65] God therefore made the Temple into "a most noble theater" in which both Jews and foreigners could see the goodness of God manifested in the healing of those afflicted by disease.[66] Far from being present only for those who seek God in heaven by faith, God is concerned to manifest God's presence in the Temple in every age, including the time of the manifestation of God in the flesh. This impression is reinforced later in the commentary when Calvin discusses the way the Jews, including Greek-speaking Jews, went up to the Temple to worship during the Passover. "For although religion and godliness were not confined to the Temple, yet they were nowhere else allowed to offer sacrifices to God, nor had they anywhere else the Ark of the Testimony, the symbol of the divine presence."[67]

In the second part of his commentary on Acts of 1554, Calvin returns to the question he addressed in the sermon of Stephen, for Paul reiterates Stephen's claim that God does not dwell in temples made by human hands (Acts 17:24). How can this be, if God describes the Temple as God's eternal resting place? "I reply that as he was not tied to one place, so the last thing he intended was to tie down his people to earthly symbols. On the contrary he comes down to them, in order to lift them up on high to himself."[68] The Temple is abused, therefore, when the descent of God to it is not followed by the corresponding ascent of the pious to God. Calvin associates the upward direction of the godly to the guidance of the Word of God that is heard in the Temple, "because men always incline downward to understand God in a carnal way, but God raises them up on high by the guidance of his Word. He merely uses symbols as intermediaries with which to introduce himself in a familiar way to slow men, until, step by step, they ascend to heaven."[69] God therefore distinguishes the Jews from all other nations by promising to be present to them in the Temple.[70]

In his commentary on the Psalms of 1557, Calvin claims that the superiority of the Temple over the tabernacle did not consist primarily of the excellent materials out of which it was constructed but rather in the promise of God to dwell in the Temple forever (Ps. 132:14).[71] This promise is related to God's choice of Mount Zion to be the place of God's dwelling, in contrast to the tabernacle, which never had a fixed place in which to reside.[72] Calvin sees the stability of the resting place of the symbol of God's presence in the ark to confirm the godly that they also will stand firm.[73] The promise of God to dwell forever in the Temple could therefore be said to be the true foundation on which the Temple rested, not only before it was built, but also, even more, after it was destroyed by the Babylonians, for "the glory of the Lord returned to it once more, and remained there up to the advent of Christ."[74]

This is not to say, however, that the beautiful materials out of which Solomon constructed the Temple play no part in its superiority over the tabernacle. Calvin thinks that this is why David longed to have the Temple built, though it was only Solomon who would do so.[75] The splendor of the Temple makes it a more vivid representation of the glory and power of God for the Jews than the tabernacle had been.[76] The vision of the Temple was therefore intended by God to elevate the Jews by its astonishing beauty, for "the faithful in times past were affected with the outward splendor of the temple, when, besides attracting the eyes of men, it had the power to ravish with admiration all their senses."[77] The glorious materials used in the sanctuary had the same effect, and also encouraged the Jews to dedicate everything precious to God.[78]

Because of its beauty and splendor, Calvin thought that the Temple in Jerusalem was nothing short of "an image of heaven."[79] This image is an expression of the incomparable goodness of God, for it gives people confined on earth a vision of the heavenly dwelling place of God.[80] In Psalm 20, God is said to send help from Zion, as well as from heaven. For Calvin, the former is said to reinforce the reality of the Temple as the image of heaven, while the latter is said to keep the godly from confining God to that image.[81]

The image of heaven therefore represents the loving intimacy of God with the Israelites, even as the heavenly dwelling of God manifests God's majestic transcendence. "By looking to the heavens, then, they were to discover the power of God—by looking to Zion, his dwelling-place, they were to recognize his fatherly love."[82] To accentuate the heavenly referent of the Temple, Calvin will often claim that the beauty of the Temple lay in the heavenly archetype of which it was the representation.[83] He does not relate this prototype to Christ but rather says that the form of the Temple was "an image of spiritual things," over against those who wanted to use such splendor to defend the presence of "pictures and idols" in places of worship.[84]

The beauty of the Temple not only ravished the Jews with admiration and lifted their hearts and minds to the heavenly dwelling place of God of which it was the image but also was a true symbol and pledge of the presence of God in their midst. When they worshiped there "according to the appointment of his word, they stood as it were in his presence, and actually experienced that he was near them."[85] On the one hand, as we saw in the commentary on Acts 7, Calvin will closely link the presence of God in the Temple with the right worship of God that uses earthly means to ascend as by steps to God. When the godly lift up their hearts to God, they experience the presence of God in their midst, according to God's promise, "In all places where I record my name, I will come unto thee, and I will bless thee" (Exod. 20:24).[86] According to this model, when the people ascend to God, God descends to dwell among them.

On the other hand, Calvin will stress the descent of God to dwell in the Temple, which makes possible the ascent of the people to God. For instance, when the prophet says that the Lord has gone up with the sound of a trumpet, Calvin claims that this "was not a mere empty sound which vanished away in the air; for God, who intended the ark of the covenant to be a pledge or token of his presence, truly presided in that assembly."[87] In his commentary on Isaiah of 1559, Calvin insists that "the Temple is called God's rest, because he gave the sign of his presence in the temple; for he had chosen it as the place where men should call on him, and from which he would give a display of his strength and power."[88] The manifestation of God's presence in the Temple would then make possible the corresponding ascent of the people to God: "reminded by the outward signs of God's presence, they might raise their minds higher and rise to heaven."[89] In his commentary on the minor prophets of 1560, Calvin even describes the Temple as the image of God, in which the invisible God becomes somewhat visible; "it was also a sign and symbol of religion, where the face of God shown forth."[90] The appearance of God in the Temple did not mean that God left heaven but rather that God had accommodated Godself to the capacities of the people, "for he could not in himself be known, but in a certain way appeared to them in the temple."[91] For this reason, Jonah directs his prayer to the holy temple, "for that was a visible symbol, through which the Jews might understand that God was near to them."[92]

In his harmony of the last four books of Moses of 1563, Calvin again accentuates the self-manifestation of God in the Temple, which makes possible the more intimate approach of the people to God, for "they placed themselves nearer, and in some special manner in his sight, when they approached his sanctuary."[93] The Temple is not called the place where God puts God's name to enclose God within the Temple, to circumscribe God's infinite essence, or drag God down from heaven, but is rather called this "with reference to man; whilst, in deference to their ignorance, he sets before their eyes a visible symbol of his presence." However, even though God "allows himself to be invoked on earth, yet he would not have the minds of men rest there, but rather lifts them up on high as if by steps."[94]

In his lectures on Jeremiah of the same year, Calvin claims that Jeremiah called Jerusalem the throne of God's glory because the Temple was chosen as the dwelling place of God, "for the presence of his power and grace was evidenced by the clearest proofs."[95] The enormity of Hananiah's deception is accentuated in that it was perpetrated before the face of God, "for God was by that symbol in a manner visible, when he made evident the presence of his power and favor in the Temple."[96] If Hananiah stands in the presence of God, even though he is ungodly, then the presence of God must not in this instance be predicated on the prior ascent of the godly to heaven but must rather be the condition that makes such ascent possible, thereby exacerbating the crime of his deception.

To account for the simultaneous presence of God within the Temple and the need for the godly to ascend to God in heaven, Calvin employs the description of the Temple as both the dwelling place and the footstool of God. Calling the Temple the dwelling place or house of God accentuates the reality of the presence of God manifested therein, "that all the faithful might have boldness to draw near unto God freely, whom they beheld coming to meet them of his own accord."[97] On the other hand, describing the Temple as God's footstool directed the people from the presence of God in the Temple to the presence of God in heaven, so that they would not think that God was confined within or affixed to the Temple. "For God desired to dwell in the midst of his people in such a manner, as not only to direct their thoughts to the outward temple and to the ark of the covenant, but rather to elevate them to things above."[98] Calvin is especially fond of the description of the Temple in Psalm 132:7: "'Let us go to his dwelling-place; let us worship at his footstool.'" As the dwelling place of God, the Temple confirms the faith of the pious that God is truly near them and hears their prayers.[99] As the footstool of God, the people are directed to lift their gaze from the Temple to the presence of God in heaven "and fix their contemplations with due reverence upon God himself."[100] However, this elevation from the Temple to God is made possible by the experience of the real presence of God in the Temple. "While God dwells in heaven, and is above all heavens, we must avail ourselves of helps in rising to the knowledge of him; and in giving us symbols of his presence, he sets, as it were, his feet upon the earth, and suffers us to touch them."[101] The description of the Temple as both dwelling place and footstool creates the dynamic Calvin sought with regard to any symbol of God's presence: God truly manifests God's presence in the Temple, but only so that we might seek God in heaven by means of God's presence in the Temple, rather than seek to confine God within the Temple.[102]

According to Calvin, the people of Israel made the mistake of confining God within the Temple, as though the promise made by God that the Temple would be God's dwelling forever (Ps. 132:14) meant that the people could sin with impunity and never fear the departure of God from their midst. "Under the influence of this spirit of vain confidence they proceeded to such inconceivable lengths in shedding innocent blood."[103] This vain confidence is what Jeremiah deplored in his prophecy in the Temple, deriding the triple rampart the Jews thought the Temple gave them against the judgment of God. "'We are invincible; how can enemies come to us? How can any calamity reach us? God dwells in the midst of us, and here he has his habitation, and not one and single fort, but a triple fort; he has his court, his Temple, and his Holy of Holies.'"[104] The promise of God to dwell in the Temple should have encouraged the people to seek God in heaven; but when the people sought to confine God within the Temple, God departed from the Temple. This is rather vividly described in Ezekiel's vision of the glory of God departing over the threshold of the Temple, which "is just as if he should extinguish the splendor of his glory by which the temple was adorned, and transfer it elsewhere."[105] The departure of the presence of God from the Temple is confirmed by the subsequent destruction of the Temple by the Babylonians. "Hence it was necessary to persuade the faithful that God no longer dwelt in the Temple, but that it remained only an empty spectacle, because he had taken away his glory since the place was corrupted by so many defilements."[106]

The destruction of the Temple, however, did not mean that the promise of God to dwell in the Temple forever was proven to be false or unreliable. I mentioned earlier that Calvin sees the promise of God in Psalm 132:14 to be the foundation of the Temple even before it was built. This is even more true for Calvin after the devastation of the Temple by the Babylonians. "The visible appearance of the temple was taken away, but meanwhile, since the temple was founded on the promise of God, it stood among the ruins."[107] This is why Daniel prays in the direction of the Temple even when it has been destroyed, and Haggai and Isaiah can speak of a second Temple more glorious than the first.[108] All this is made possible by the promise of God, "'This is my resting-place forever; here I will reside for I have desired it'" (Ps. 132:14). "It was eventually seen, in a very striking manner, that this was the promise of an infallible God, when, after the Temple had been overthrown, the altar cast down, and the whole frame of the legal service interrupted, the glory of the Lord returned to it once more, and remained there up to the advent of Christ."[109]

6. Jerusalem as the Theater of God's Glory

The promise of God to dwell in the Temple forever elevates the city of Jerusalem itself to a symbol of the presence of God. In his commentary on the Psalms of 1557, Calvin develops his understanding of Jerusalem as the theater of God's glory. Just as the universe is the theater of God's glory because of the powers of God that are displayed therein, the same holds for the city of Jerusalem.[110] The reason God is more vividly represented in Jerusalem has to do with the presence of the ark of the covenant in the Temple, which "was established there by the commandment of God as a symbol or token of his singular grace."[111] For this reason, God may be described as dwelling in Jerusalem, not merely in the Temple. "He was there as to the sense of his grace, experience showing, that while his majesty is such as to fill heaven and earth, his power and grace were vouchsafed in a peculiar manner to his own people."[112]

The presence of God in the city meant that God would be the protector of the city. This was manifested to the Jews by means of the physical appearance of the city, including its towers and ramparts, for "in these external things the blessing of God in some respect shone forth."[113] As we have repeatedly seen with symbols of the presence of God, the walls and towers are signs that should elevate the minds of the pious to God in heaven. "In making mention here of her towers and walls, we are not to suppose that he would have the minds of the faithful rest in these things. He rather sets them before us as a mirror which represents the face of God."[114] The same should be said of the palaces of Jerusalem, and its citadels, for "by the aid of these outward things they should elevate their minds to the contemplation of the glory of God."[115]

The protection of God was also manifested to the Israelites by the mountains of Jerusalem, in accommodation to their capacities, "in which they may see, beyond all doubt, that the Church is well defended from all perils, as if it were surrounded on all sides with like walls and bulwarks."[116] Once again, the Jews were to elevate their minds and hearts from the visible sight of the mountains to the heavenly protection of God.[117] Even the fertility of the lands around Jerusalem was meant to be an image to the Israelites of the grace and favor of God, as though it were "the most beautiful part of a theater, which attracted all eyes towards it, and moved all minds to admiration."[118] In sum, the whole appearance of the city of Jerusalem, from its palaces and walls to its mountains and environs, was a living image of the favor and protection of God. "God would have them behold, as it were, the marks of his grace engraven wherever they turned themselves, or rather, recognize him as present in these marks."[119]

Just as the sight of the city gave confidence and hope to the Israelites, so the appearance of the city cast the enemies of Jerusalem into consternation and dismay. "It is related of Caesar in ancient times, that when speaking of the ease with which he subdued Egypt, he made use of the laconic saying, 'I came, I saw, I conquered;' but the prophet here states the contrary, that the ungodly were struck with amazement at the mere sight of the city, as if God had dazzled their eyes with the splendor of his glory."[120] God also manifests God's grace and favor by defending the city of Jerusalem by miraculous intervention, without any assistance from human defenders, to reveal that the safety of the city lies in the power of God. "It is therefore asserted, that the glory of God was conspicuously displayed when the enemies of Israel were discomfited by such a miraculous interposition."[121]

God made Jerusalem a theater of God's glory both by adorning it with many gifts and by defending it from its enemies by God's power alone. This is what made the devastation of the city under the judgment of God all the more striking and alarming, when God departed from the Temple and the city before the Babylonian exile.[122] Even as the city had once been the theater of God's grace, power, and glory, so it would become the theater of God's wrath and vengeance, as when Lamentations describes Jerusalem as the refuse in the midst of the people, "as though God had erected a theater in Judea, and there exhibited a remarkable and unusual example of his vengeance."[123] As with the Temple, the destruction of the city had the effect of calling into question the truth of the covenant God made with Israel, "for no one thought that any memorial of God's covenant could flourish when that city was extinct."[124] Nonetheless, even in exile in Babylon, the Jews looked to Jerusalem as the pledge of God's grace and protection, the very sight of which would stimulate the earnestness of their prayers, as in the case of Daniel. "For when praying for the liberation of his people, he directed his eyes towards Jerusalem, and that sight became a stimulus to inflame his mind to greater devotion."[125]

7. Prophecy as the Sign of God's Presence

Calvin viewed the presence of prophets among the people as a sign or symbol of the presence of God. In his commentary on John of 1553, Calvin makes this point with regard to the presence of God in the Temple at the time of Jesus. "Because the Holy Spirit who dwelt in the prophets was a completely sufficient witness of the divine presence, religion needed no other confirmation then."[126] Calvin reiterates this understanding of prophecy in his harmony of the last four books of Moses in 1563, with reference to the promise of God to send to the people a prophet like Moses. "Hence it follows that God, by a certain symbol of his presence, declares his favor towards us as often as he enlightens us with the gifts of his Spirit, and raises up true and faithful teachers."[127] This holds true even when the prophets are sent to proclaim the wrath of God against the people, for the presence of this word is still a sign of the presence of God. "Whenever, then, the prophetic word is announced, we have a sure and clear evidence of the presence of God, as though he wished to be connected with us."[128] Thus, when the people tire of the judgment of God against them, and wish God to be silent, God declares that the people will be forsaken. "Therefore God says, 'You cannot bear my word, by which symbol I show that I am present with you; I will forsake you.'"[129] The greatest calamity that the people of God can experience is the absence of the word of God in their midst, for it manifests that they have been abandoned by God.[130]

This means that the prophetic Word of God not only gives life to the other symbols of God's presence but also is itself a mirror in which we may behold the face of God. "For God was never willing to be disjoined from his word, because he himself is invisible, and never appears otherwise than in a mirror. Hence God's glory, and sanctity, and justice, and goodness, and power, ought to shine forth in the gift of prophecy."[131] The Word of God delivered by the prophets not only manifests the presence of God in our midst but is also the guide that leads us by steps to the heavenly presence of God.[132] Calvin will even say that the conjunction of the prophetic Word with the sacraments of the Law together bring us to the true recognition of God. "Just as men reveal themselves by their appearance and speech, so God utters his voice to us by the voice of the prophets, and in the sacraments puts on, as it were, a visible form, from which he can be known according to our small capacity."[133]

8. False Symbols of the Presence of God

Calvin contrasts the real presence of God in the divinely instituted symbols of God's presence with the carnal presence of God in signs of God's presence invented by the human mind. In the first edition of the *Institutes,* Calvin ascribes the creation of false images and idols to the desire to have God physically present before us. Even though both Jews and Gentiles thought that the God they worshiped through images truly dwelled in heaven, "they did not believe God present to them, unless he showed himself physically present. In obeisance to this blind longing, they raised up signs, wherein they believed God was set before their physical eyes. Since they thought God saw himself in these, they also worshipped him in them. Finally, all men, having fixed their minds and eyes upon them, began to grow more brutish and to be overwhelmed with admiration for them, as if something of divinity inhered in there."[134] The proof that they regard God as carnally present and visible within their images appears when they prostrate themselves before their images and pray to them as though to the ears of God, which Calvin terms their "carnal veneration."[135]

Calvin expands on this passage in the 1539 edition of the *Institutes*. Appealing to the creation of the golden calves by the Israelites in the wilderness, Calvin contrasts the symbols of God's presence in the miracles God wrought in the exodus with the desire to have God present in physical symbols, for "they did not trust that he was near them unless they could discern with their eyes a physical symbol of his countenance."[136] The issue in both passages seems to be the desire to transform God into the likeness of the flesh, that is, "some figment like itself," in which fleshly eyes can recognize the carnal presence of God in a corporeal image of God's countenance. Since both the image and the presence of God within the image are conceived in a fleshly and carnal way, there is no upward dynamic at work in the image, leading the worshiper from the earthly symbol to the throne of God in heaven. Rather, the attention of the worshiper is affixed to the image, and God is worshiped in the image. Calvin accentuates this point in a passage added to this section of the *Institutes* in 1550. "For just as soon as a visible form has been fashioned for God, his power is also bound to it. Men are so stupid that they fasten God wherever they fashion him; and hence they cannot but adore."[137]

Calvin expands on the desire to seek the presence of God in a carnal way in images in his commentary on the first part of Acts in 1552. When Peter chastises the people of Jerusalem for thinking that he made the lame man walk by his own power or piety (Acts 3:12), Calvin says that all people have the tendency to take what belongs to God alone and ascribe it to creatures. "Thus we see the Papists locating the power of God in the saints; they even enclose his divine presence in a stone or a stump of wood, as soon as the statue is consecrated to Barbara or Chrysogonus."[138] Calvin is especially interested in Stephen's discussion of the creation of the golden calves by the Israelites in the wilderness. As in the *Institutes*, Calvin ascribes the creation of such idols to the human desire to have God present in a way that fits the capacities of the flesh.[139] This, however, raises a very serious issue for Calvin, since God manifests God's presence to the Israelites in symbols that are accommodated to their ignorance, infirmity, and carnality. "Yet God certainly does accommodate himself to our ignorance to this extent, that he allows us to see himself after a fashion under figures. For under the Law there were very many symbols to testify his presence."[140] The central question will therefore be how to distinguish true symbols of God's presence from false symbols of God's presence, so that the rejection of the latter does not undermine the reality of the former.

Calvin sets forth two criteria by which to distinguish true versus false symbols of God's presence. First, he insists that only God has the right and ability to institute symbols of God's presence, for "there can be no true image of God except as he himself has ordained."[141] Human beings do not need to create new symbols of God's presence, for God has already ordained and instituted such symbols, which in the Law extend from the cloud and the fire in the wilderness to the Temple in Jerusalem at the time of Jesus. "Therefore whatever things are contrived contrary to his Word by the will of men are false and counterfeit."[142]

Second, Calvin asserts that the human attempt to create images without the ordination and institution of the Word of God founders on the carnality of human nature. Human beings are incapable of creating images of God's presence that do not subject God to the capacities of the flesh, for "as the human mind conceives nothing about God except what is crass and earthly, so it transfers all signs of the divine presence to the same materialism."[143] In other words, symbols of God's presence created by human ingenuity reverse the dynamic at work in divinely instituted symbols: rather than raise the worshiper from the symbol to heaven, the false symbol drags God down from heaven and confines God to the symbol. So great is this downward impulse that it even corrupts the divinely instituted symbols of God's presence, as we have repeatedly seen. "God does indeed come down to us, as I have said, but for this purpose, that he might lift us up to heaven. But we who are attached to the earth, wish to have him similarly on the earth."[144] This corruption of divinely instituted symbols of God's presence is most vividly revealed for Calvin in the Roman doctrine of transubstantiation. "[M]en superstitiously create a worldly and carnal God for themselves, a God who comes down to them so that they may remain firmly bound to the earth and not aspire to heaven."[145] According to this criterion, the attachment of God to a symbol demonstrates that the conception of God is itself carnal, for otherwise it would be unthinkable to affix the presence of God to the image.

Calvin returns to the question of false symbols of God's presence in the second half of the Acts commentary of 1554. He increases the degree of difficulty of his rejection of humanly manufactured symbols of God's presence by allowing that the conception of God in those making such images is not necessarily carnal. "It was easy to object that statues and images are placed in temples to testify to the presence of God, and indeed no one was so stupid that he did not know that God fills all things."[146] Calvin replies by accusing those who use images in this way with contradicting themselves. If God fills all things, then why do they address their prayers to their images? And why do they expect help from them? And why do they think one temple is holier than another, as though it were nearer to God? "They used to run to Delphi, to seek for the oracles of Apollo there. Minerva used to have her seat and dwelling at Athens."[147]

The problem with this criticism of false symbols of God's presence is that it undermines everything Calvin has said about the true symbols of God's presence. The Israelites were given signs of God's presence so that they might know that God was near them and heard their prayers. Moreover, the Temple in Jerusalem, and Jerusalem itself, was a symbol of God's presence making it more sacred than any other temple, to which the Jews both near and far would travel to worship before the face of God that was visible in the ark of the covenant. Calvin is aware of this problem, and responds to it in the following two ways. The first is clearly to distinguish God from every created thing, and to set God above the world, so that we refuse to measure God by our own mental capacity or imagine God according to our own carnal sense. This will keep us from seeking to transform God into the likeness of our own fleshly capacities. "For as they are carnal and earthly they wish to have one who corresponds to their own nature. Secondly, in conformity with their audacity they make him of such a nature as they can grasp."[148] We can only rightly contemplate a symbol of God's presence if we have already clearly distinguished God from all creation, including the particular created form God uses to manifest God's presence.

The refusal to distinguish God from the world afflicted the Gentiles, who "dragged God off his heavenly throne, and made him part and parcel with the elements of the world."[149] However, the same thing happened with the Jews in relation to the Temple, which was a true symbol of God's presence. The Jews would have denied that they confined God to the Temple, but again they contradict themselves by their devotional life, in which "they tie God to the temple just like a mortal man."[150] Maintaining the proper distinction between God and creation keeps us from attaching or confining God to the symbol of God's presence. However, it does not itself undermine the credibility of humanly devised images, since the failure to distinguish God from the world also perverts the right use of true symbols of God's presence. This criterion therefore addresses the right use of symbols but does not distinguish between the temple of Minerva in Athens and the Temple of God in Jerusalem.

To address this question, Calvin returns to his earlier criterion of divine institution versus human invention. The true symbols of God's presence are those instituted by the Word of God, whereas false symbols have no such Word. However, Calvin links the Word to the symbol not primarily to authorize the creation of the symbol, but because it is the Word in particular that gives to the symbol its upward dynamic, leading the godly from the contemplation of the symbol to God in heaven. "We see from this that there was a great difference between the symbols of God's presence, which men thoughtlessly devised for themselves, and those which God ordained, because men always incline downwards to understand God in a carnal way, but God raises them up on high by the guidance of his Word."[151] If maintaining the proper distinction between God and creation keeps us from affixing or confining God to the symbol of God's presence, then the Word of God conjoined to the symbol guides us step by step from the visible symbol to the invisible God in heaven, so that the symbol serves its proper purpose.[152] Calvin makes the same point in his commentary on Genesis of the same year. "For as superstitious men foolishly and wickedly attach God to symbols, and, as it were, draw him down from his heavenly throne to render him subject to their gross inventions: so the faithful, piously and rightly, ascend from earthly signs to heaven."[153]

Calvin continues to accentuate the categorical distinction between God and creation in his commentary on Psalm 115 of 1557. Referring to the way Cicero describes the Gentiles as praying before their gods, Calvin says that he would not have spoken this way had they not held the notion that they were approaching nearer to their gods by addressing prayers to their brass, silver, or marble figures.[154] The dynamic at work here appears to be dragging God from heaven in order to confine God to the figure or image that represents God. "Averse to seek God in a spiritual manner, they therefore pull him down from his throne, and place him under inanimate things."[155] In the final edition of the *Institutes,* Calvin intensifies the dialectical distinction between God and the created world in order to undermine all human attempts to make symbols of God's presence for themselves.[156] The spiritual nature of God makes it impossible for God to be affixed to earthly realities. The immensity of God makes it impossible for God to be contained or confined within earthly images. And the incomprehensibility of God forbids us from ascribing any local presence whatever to God.

However, Calvin seems to extend his criticism beyond the attempt to drag God down from heaven to affix and confine God to the symbol, since after all this can also be done with true symbols of God's presence. Rather, he insists that God cannot manifest God's presence or powers in anything made of "dead materials" such as wood, brass, or stone. "But it still remains true, that workmen by their skill make gods of lifeless things to which no honor can belong."[157] He even goes so far as to deny that such "dead materials" can manifest God's presence even when God is not confined to them; nor can they be used as steps or means by which to rise from the visible, temporal world to the invisible, eternal God. "In this sense they called the images of the gods their gods; because they thought they could not ascend to the heights in which the Deity dwelt, unless they mounted by these earthly means."[158]

The criticism of confining God to the image is certainly familiar, but Calvin's claim that God cannot draw near or manifest God's presence in stone, wood, brass, or silver appears to undermine his insistence that the tabernacle, the Temple, and especially the ark of the covenant were symbols of God's presence, in which the invisible God became somewhat visible. Moreover, Calvin insists that God manifested God's presence in the tabernacle and the Temple precisely so that the Israelites and Jews would be able to draw near unto God, so that they might be assured that their prayers would be heard. To cite but one example, Calvin says, "although believers are taught that always, wherever they dwell, they walk before God; yet they placed themselves nearer, and in some special manner in his sight, when they approached his sanctuary."[159] Finally, Calvin's explanation of the right use of such earthly symbols of God's presence is that they should be means by which believers on earth ascend to the heavenly throne of God. "But although he allows himself to be invoked on earth, yet he would not have the minds of men rest there, but rather lifts them up on high as if by steps."[160] Calvin's attempt to undermine any and every symbol of the presence of God crafted by human ingenuity would end up, if taken on its face, undermining everything he says about the self-manifestation of God in the divinely instituted symbols of God's presence. Indeed, he sounds very much like the position he elsewhere refutes, as in this passage from the final edition of the *Institutes*: "Yet Xerxes, when he on the advice of his wise men rashly burned or destroyed all the temples of Greece, thought it absurd for gods, who ought to have free access to all things, to be shut up within walls and roofs. As if it were not in God's power somehow to come down to us, in order to be near us, yet without changing place or confining us to earthly means; but rather by these to bear us up as if in chariots to his heavenly glory, a glory that fills all things with its immeasurableness and even surpasses the heavens in height!"[161]

Calvin argues much more consistently and effectively when he illustrates the futility of humanly devised symbols, given the abundance of divinely ordained symbols before our eyes, as when the Israelites ask Aaron to make them "a dead idol" to go before them, despite the "illustrious and living image of his glory and power" in the cloud and the pillar of fire that continually accompanied them.[162] The issue here is not the impossibility of the manifestation of God's presence in earthly reality—for after all clouds and fire are earthly things—but rather the folly of searching for the presence of God in products of the human imagination when God surrounds us with innumerable, true, and certain symbols of God's presence. "Yet, accounting as nothing all these true, and sure, and manifest tokens of God's presence, they desire to have a figure which may satisfy their vanity. And this was the original source of idolatry, that men supposed that they could not otherwise possess God, unless by subjecting him to their own imagination."[163] The problem is that the human imagination cannot represent God in a way that leads the viewer upwards, as God does, but rather has the effect of dragging God down from heaven and confining God to the limitations of all human knowledge.[164] Only God can accommodate Godself to human capacities without becoming subject to the limitations of those capacities.[165]

The mutual relation between symbol and Word is a distinguishing mark of true symbols of God, according to Calvin. If the force of the symbol brings God nearer to us, the force of the Word leads us from the visible symbol to God in heaven.[166] For this reason, Calvin seems to prefer at times speaking of the Word itself as the descent of God to us, accompanied by the sacred signs, since the Word for him preserves this upward trajectory. "Men wish to enjoy the presence of God and this is the beginning and source of idolatry; for God is not present with us by an idol, but by his word and by the power of his Spirit; and although he holds out to us in the sacraments images both of his grace and of spiritual blessings, yet this is done with no other intention than to lead us upwards to himself."[167]

Due to the upward trajectory Calvin sees in the Word of God, reinforced by his agreement with Luther that faith comes from hearing the

Word of God, Calvin will develop a third criterion by which to argue against the possibility of devising symbols of God's presence, namely, that God reveals Godself to us by the Word alone, without any accompanying symbols at all. Calvin appeals to Moses's statement in Deuteronomy to support this position. "Since you saw no form when the Lord spoke to you at Horeb out of the fire, take care and watch yourselves closely, so that you do not act corruptly by making an idol for yourselves" (Deut. 4:15–16). Calvin appeals to this text when interpreting the voice of God that speaks to the disciples during the transfiguration. "It is noteworthy that God's voice sounded out of the cloud; his body or his face was not seen."[168] Calvin knows that God does in fact appear to people in Scripture, yet he claims that the forms chosen by God prevented people from seeking to represent God in those forms.[169] By taking this approach, Calvin appears to privilege the Word of God alone as the way by which God reveals Godself to humanity. "For God cannot be apprehended by human senses, but he must be manifest to us by his own word; and he descends to us, so that we might be raised to heaven."[170]

Calvin reiterates this emphasis on the Word alone in his interpretation of Deuteronomy 4:15. "It is a confirmation of the second commandment, that God manifested himself to the Israelites by a voice, not in a bodily form; whence it follows that those who are not contented with his voice, but seek his visible form, substitute imaginations and phantoms in his place."[171] Once again, Calvin notes that both the patriarchs and Moses not only heard God speaking but also saw visions of God, "and he also manifested himself to the prophets under visible figures."[172] He acknowledges that this appears to contradict the prohibition against images based on divine self-manifestation by Word alone, "when, on the other side, it is easy to object that visible forms have often been exhibited, wherein he testified his presence."[173] Calvin attempts to solve this contradiction in two ways. First, the self-revelation of God through the exhibition of forms was specific to each context, and a "temporary symbol," and is not the general rule for divine self-revelation.[174] Second, the visions of the patriarchs were testimonies of heavenly glory intended "rather to elevate men's minds to things above than to keep them entangled amongst earthly elements."[175] Thus the visions and exhibitions of God's presence to the patriarchs and prophets do not contradict the statement made by Moses that God only reveals Godself to humanity in the Word of God. "This conclusion, therefore, always remains sure, that no image is suitable for God, because he could not be perceived by people otherwise than in a voice."[176] According to this model, the Word of God alone is the living image of God, making it impossible for us to seek any visible image of God in conjunction with the Word. God "had exhibited the living image of his glory in the doctrine itself. Hence we may conclude that all those who seek for God in a visible figure not only decline, but actually revolt, from the true study of piety."[177]

The insistence that God only manifests Godself to us by the Word we hear, not by any image we see, is impossible to reconcile with Calvin's ubiquitous insistence that the self-manifestation of God takes place by means of the mutual relation between Word and image. Calvin's claim that the signs of God's presence revealed to the fathers and prophets were only "temporary" does not address the symbols of God's presence in the tabernacle, Temple, and ark, which accompany the people from Sinai until the coming of Christ. "God then says that he had sworn by the sanctuary, because he himself is invisible, and the temple was his living image, by which he exhibited himself as visible."[178] When combined with his claim that God's presence cannot be manifested under "dead materials," Calvin's rejection of humanly devised symbols of God's presence renders any visual self-manifestation of God impossible. Such claims by Calvin will always be available to support the interpretation that the Word alone has priority, not the living images of God in various signs and symbols instituted by God. It is not at all clear how Calvin can make such categorical statements about the impossibility of the visual self-manifestation of God without realizing how threatening they are to his theological approach of always combining what we hear with what we see.

CHAPTER 8

The Manifestation of Judgment
and Restoration in the Prophets

The prophets are for Calvin the most vocal critics of the human attempt to repre-
sent God according to the carnal human imagination, or to confine God to
the symbols of God's presence that God sets in our midst. The prophets
emerge in a critical time in the life of Israel, announcing that Israel stands
under the judgment of God, culminating in the Assyrian and Babylonian
captivities. However, the prophets also proclaim the coming deliverance of
the people of God from captivity and the restitution of the kingdom of David
and the Temple. Both messages are delivered at a time when they seem incredible. The message of judgment comes when Israel and Judah seem to be
the most successful, whereas the message of redemption is delivered when
the situation seems hopeless, given the destruction of the Temple and Jerusalem and the captivity of the people in Babylon. Moreover, the true prophets of God must compete for a hearing with the false teachers and prophets
who emerge at the same time. According to Calvin, there must be marks by
which the godly can distinguish between true and false prophets; and the
prophets themselves must be able to speak in a vivid and gripping way in
order to gain a hearing from a presumptuous or despairing people. I first examine the question of how to discern the true prophets of God and then turn
to Calvin's understanding of the distinctive nature of prophetic speech, including the use of accommodation, vivid verbal representation (*hypotyposis*),

and even symbols, to reveal to the people realities that are otherwise hidden from their view.

1. THE DISTINGUISHING MARKS OF TRUE PROPHETS

The question of discerning the true prophets of God is of immediate urgency for Calvin, given his own situation of supporting the evangelical teachers over against the allegedly false teachers of the Roman Church. In the first edition of the *Institutes*, Calvin claims that the distinguishing mark of true prophets is that the whole of their ministry and authority is located in the Word of God that they are called faithfully to deliver. "The Lord willed Moses be heard as the first of all the prophets. But what could he command or announce at all, except from the Lord? Nor could he do anything else."[1] What was true for Moses also applied to all the other prophets: their only authority and power came from the Word of God. "For none of the prophets opened his mouth without the Lord anticipating his words."[2] Moreover, none of the prophets had the ability to speak the Word of the Lord without first being made instruments of the Spirit by God.[3] The prophet is therefore forbidden from adding anything to the Word of God from his own thoughts but is faithfully to deliver to the people only what he receives from God.[4]

In the 1543 edition of the *Institutes*, Calvin adds that the prophets who faithfully hand on what they first receive from God are adorned by God with power and various titles.[5] Moreover, in 1543 Calvin accounts for the priority of Moses over the subsequent prophets by describing the prophets as interpreters of the Law, which had come to them in written form. "As for doctrine, they were only interpreters of the law and added nothing to it except predictions of things to come."[6] Thus the prophets not only deliver the Word they hear from the Lord, but this Word can be verified as a true interpretation of the Law of Moses. That the prophets themselves are appended to the writings of the Law does not mean they have equal status with the Law.[7]

The ability of the prophets to predict the future, which is the one gift added to them over and above their pure exposition of the Law, is made one of the criteria for verifying the truth of Scripture in the 1550 edition of the *Institutes*. In particular, the fulfillment of prophecy by subsequent historical events proves that the prophets spoke by the Spirit of God. For instance, "when Jeremiah, some time before the people were led away into exile, set the duration of the captivity at seventy years, and indicated the return and liberation [Jer. 25:11–12; 29:10], must not his tongue have been under the guidance of the Spirit of God?"[8] The fulfillment of prophecy therefore vindicates the credibility of the written records of the prophetic oracles.[9] Not surprisingly, in subsequent commentaries Calvin will describe the fulfillment of prophecy as the divine confirmation of the prophecy. In his commentary on Isaiah of 1559, Calvin calls the fulfillment of prophecy "a seal to authenticate the prophecies that might otherwise have been called in question."[10] Thus, when Sennacherib is defeated in his attempt to take Jerusalem, Calvin describes this as the divine proof that Isaiah is a true prophet called by God, "since God had given so splendid an attestation of his doctrine from heaven."[11] The event not only confirmed the truth of Isaiah's prophecy for other believers but also "manifestly sealed" his calling as a prophet, giving him greater confidence in his ministry.[12] The same dynamic is revealed when Jeremiah describes the fall of Jerusalem at the hands of King Nebuchadnezzar of Babylon, for it "seals his previous prophecies," and also gives "proof of all his former doctrine," for "he brings before us the reality, and shows that whatever he had predicted was accomplished by God's hand, and in a manner almost incredible."[13] Such confirmation may also be given not only by other prophets but also by unbelieving historians, as happened with Jeremiah's description of the destruction of Babylon. Both Daniel and Xenophon attested the truth of the prophecy by the events they narrated and thereby "sealed, by a public testimony, what had been divinely predicted by Jeremiah."[14] According to Calvin, "no mortal, had he been a hundred times endowed with the spirit of divination, could ever have clearly expressed a thing unknown," so that the actual destruction of Babylon confirms for later generations that Jeremiah was "of a certainty the instrument of the Holy Spirit."[15]

The calling of the prophet by God is also confirmed by visions, as discussed above. According to Calvin, Isaiah was granted the vision of God in the Temple after his ministry had met with stiff resistance in Jerusalem.[16] However, the vision may also seal the truth of the prophecy for those to whom it is delivered, as when Jeremiah saw the two baskets of figs placed before the Temple of the Lord (Jer. 24:1). "God indeed often spoke without a vision; but we have stated elsewhere what was the design of a vision; it was a sort of seal to what was delivered; for in order that the prophets might possess greater authority, they not only spoke, but as it were sealed their doctrine, as though God had graven on it, as it were by his finger, a certain mark."[17] The prophet Ezekiel was granted his elaborate and vivid visions of

God in Babylon to confirm both for himself and for others that God could indeed call a prophet in that alien place.[18]

God may also exhibit other distinguishing marks by which to manifest to others the calling of a prophet. For instance, Daniel is described by Calvin as having "sure and striking marks by which he could be recognized as God's prophet, and his calling be rendered unquestionable," both for the Jews and for the Babylonians.[19] Although Daniel and his companions acquired a remarkable aptitude in the science and literature of the Babylonians, only Daniel was given the gift of the interpretation of dreams and visions. Consequently, all could recognize "by marks impressed for many years how to distinguish him from the common order of men."[20] Similarly, Ezekiel was engraved with distinguishing marks when he was completely governed by the Spirit, which would lift him up and take him away. "He understands that visible marks were graven upon him, which obtained for his doctrine authority with all the people," for God thereby separated him from others so "that he should represent something celestial."[21] Moses was also endued with preeminent gifts by which all might recognize him as a prophet; however, Calvin does not want the gift of prophecy to be tied to such gifts so that it cannot appear in their successors, such as Joshua.[22]

The visual confirmation of the prophet and his message is necessary if the prophet is to carry out his ministry faithfully in light of the intense opposition he will inevitably face. When Isaiah boasts that the one who vindicates him is near, so that he will not be disgraced (Isa. 50:7), Calvin says that he "paints as in a picture the condition of all the ministers of the word; that, by turning aside from the world, they may turn wholly to God and have their eyes entirely fixed upon him."[23] The prophet needs to turn his eyes to God alone, but he also needs to turn his eyes away from the splendor of those whom he opposes, for it can otherwise dazzle his eyes and turn him from faithfully following his calling. Thus, when Pashur of the Temple police has Jeremiah placed in stocks and then released, only to be directly rebuked by Jeremiah, Calvin observes that "God's prophet here closes his eyes to the splendor of the priestly office, which otherwise might have hindered him to denounce God's judgment."[24] Finally, the prophet must make sure that he, like Jeremiah, has "eaten" the words of God, so that they do not proceed from the tip of the tongue, like an actor on the stage, but from the depths of his heart.[25]

God confirms the prophets in the face of such opposition because ultimately God is representing and manifesting Godself to the people in their ministry. In a section added to the final edition of the *Institutes* in 1559, Calvin says that the Temple was the dwelling place of God because it was the locus of the teaching of heavenly doctrine.[26] Calvin describes opposing the prophets as being "like blotting out the face of God which shines upon us in teaching."[27] As Calvin had previously described the Temple, especially the ark of the covenant, as "the face of God," so now he describes the teaching of the prophets in the same manner. "Believers were bidden of old to seek the face of God in the sanctuary [Ps. 105:4], as is oftentimes repeated in the law for no other reason than that for them the teaching of the law and the exhortations of the prophets were a living image of God."[28]

When Haggai says that the Jews "feared the Lord" because of his message to them, Calvin says that they acted as if "the majesty of God had openly appeared to them," though there was "no visible appearance of God" in the prophecy. "We may then conclude from these words, that the glory of God so shines in his word, that we ought to be so much affected by it, whenever he speaks by his servants, as though he were nigh to us, face to face, as Scripture says in another place."[29] This is why Calvin describes prophets as symbols of the presence of God, as discussed in chapter 7, for God represents Godself to us in their ministry.[30] Thus, when the people see the great work that God did in freeing them from the Egyptians, they are said to believe in the Lord and in his servant Moses (Exod. 14:31), for "those who faithfully deliver his commands must be as much attended to as if he himself openly descended from heaven."[31]

2. Divine Self-Accommodation in Prophetic Speech

Since God represents Godself to us through the ministry of the prophets, God employs human language to depict God's nature and work to us. According to Calvin, God does this in order to accommodate God's self-representation to the limited capacities of human beings.[32] The language of the prophets therefore cannot be taken univocally, for this would make God into a temporal and worldly reality; nor can the language be equivocal, since then it would not convey any true meaning. It must instead be both analogical, having a similarity amid difference with God, and anagogic, elevating us from the temporal and earthly to the eternal and spiritual. According to Calvin, God uses human language in the prophets to express God's relationship to us, and also to depict the Kingdom of Christ.

Calvin first addresses the accommodated speech of God in the 1539 edition of the *Institutes,* when speaking of the way Scripture describes God as repenting, for instance, when God is said to have repented having made Saul the king of Israel (1 Sam. 15:11). "Now the mode of accommodation is for him to represent himself to us not as he is in himself, but as he seems to us."[33] The repentance of God does not describe how God is in Godself but rather how God appears to us. God *in se* does not repent, even though God appears to repent in what we see and experience of God's works. Thus this expression, like those expressing God's anger, is "taken from our own human experience."[34] Calvin makes the same claim in his commentary on Genesis of 1554, in his interpretation of the statement that God repented of making humanity. "The repentance which is here ascribed to God does not properly belong to him, but has reference to our understanding of him. For since we cannot comprehend him as he is, it is necessary that, for our sake, he should, in a certain sense, transform himself."[35] So also, in his commentary on Jonah of 1560, Calvin appeals to divine self-accommodation to interpret the way God is said to repent of the calamity God was going to bring upon the Ninevites.[36]

In the 1543 edition of the *Institutes,* Calvin again appeals to divine self-accommodation to explain how God can appear to change, only now in reference to the differences between the Law and the Gospel. According to Calvin, God's self-manifestation is accommodated to human capacities that develop and strengthen over time, as humanity comes to maturity. Hence God's mode of manifestation in one age will appear to be different from that of another, without any difference in the reality being manifested. "Rather, he has accommodated himself to men's capacity, which is varied and changeable."[37] The appeal to divine self-accommodation is therefore central to Calvin's claim that the Law and the Gospel manifest the same God, and reveal the one Jesus Christ, in spite of their obvious differences.[38] In his commentary on 1 Corinthians of 1546, Calvin claims that it is the mark of a skilled and wise teacher not to teach the same thing in the same way to everyone but rather to teach the same thing in different ways and forms, in accommodation to the differing capacities of the students.[39] Since God is the wisest of all teachers, it is only fitting that God should accommodate God's teaching to the varying capacities of God's people over time. As Calvin notes in 1554, we should embrace the accommodated form of divine self-revelation, realizing that God descends to our level in this manner in order to raise us up to God. "For he does not speak in this earthly manner, to keep us at a distance from heaven, but rather by this vehicle, to draw us up hither."[40]

Calvin is especially impressed by the way the prophets use figures of speech and similitudes when speaking about God to the people. Divine self-accommodation in the prophets means that God uses various figures by which to manifest Godself to us, in ways accommodated to our capacities, to move us more deeply.[41] In the words of the prophets, God does not appear as God is in God's self but rather takes on different forms by which to manifest Godself to us, to penetrate more deeply into our hearts, "for the Scriptures set before us various representations, which show to us the face of God."[42] Such images and figures should not be taken as a precedent for making images of God in worship, as Calvin thinks Rome falsely concluded, but rather show us that we cannot know God in any other way than by comparison with what we as humans know.[43] Even though we should not use such figures to make images of our own, Calvin nonetheless insists that God's accommodated speech in the prophets is vividly iconic and pictorial, for "as we cannot understand, according to our capacities, the celestial mysteries of God, it is necessary that such representations should be set before our eyes."[44]

The most prevalent figures and similitudes used in the prophets are those that transfer human affections and experiences to God. We have already seen one such form in the language that speaks of God's repentance. According to Calvin, "This figure, which represents God as transferring to himself what is peculiar to human nature, is called *anthropopatheia*."[45] Calvin appeals to this kind of figure in his commentary on the Psalms of 1557, to understand how God can be described as standing far off from the cries of the psalmist. "Nothing can be hid from his eyes; but as God permits us to speak of him as we do to one another, these forms of expression do not contain anything absurd, provided we understand them as applied to God, not in a strict sense, but only figuratively, according to the judgment which mere sense forms from the present appearance of things."[46] The same may be said of the way God is said either to forget or to remember the faithful: these speak of God as the pious experience God, not as God is in Godself.[47]

God uses many different figures in order to convey God's judgment of and wrath against sin. God is said to be angry with sinners but not because God experiences anger in God's nature; such expressions are accommodated to our capacities in order to reveal to us how much we ought to detest sin.[48] The prophets also refer to God's wrath as a devouring fire, and thereby "represent it by external symbols, because it cannot be perceived by the eyes, or by any other sense."[49] God may even compare Godself to a bear robbed of her cubs, or as a lion, who will come to rend the people with no one to spare them. Such harsh expressions are required, for we are asleep in our sins and need to be awakened by various striking figures. "For the same purpose are those metaphors respecting the eternal fire and the worm that never dies."[50] The metaphors and figures used by the prophets are not only accommodated to our finite and earthly capacities; they are also meant to awaken us from our slumber in sin.

The figures that call forth the most comment from Calvin are those meant to express the love and care of God for Israel. For instance, in order to manifest with what tender love God regards Israel, God will assume the character of a shepherd. "As this is a lowly and homely manner of speaking, he who does not disdain to stoop so low for our sake, must bear a singularly strong affection towards us."[51] What is significant about these figures of speech is that, unlike the figures of God's wrath, Calvin does not deny that God experiences such affection but rather insists that God's affection of love far outstrips the ability of any human language to express it. So, when God adopts the persona of a husband burning with the greatest love for his wife, Calvin admits that this does not sound suitable for God's majesty but allows it as yet another inadequate but necessary way by which to express the depth of God's love.[52] This does not mean that God experiences love the way a husband does for his wife, but this is not because God experiences no love at all (as Calvin says of the affection of wrath) but rather because God's love far outstrips a husband's love. "Whatever is calculated to set forth the love of God, does not derogate from his glory; for his chief glory is that vast and ineffable goodness by which he has once embraced us, and which he will show us to the end."[53]

One of the more common metaphors God uses to express God's love is by adopting the persona of a father. On the one hand, God uses this metaphor to express God's distress in light of the sins of the people, "not that he is subject to human passions, but because he cannot otherwise express the greatness of the love which he bears towards us."[54] Once again, Calvin denies that God experiences human passions, such as sighing and groaning, but all for the sake of expressing the greatness of God's love. The advantage of the figure of a father, over and above that of a husband, is that the father will continue to love his children even in the midst of wrath against them for their sin, even as God is said to remember mercy in the midst of wrath (Hab. 3:2), "because he cannot bear that the fruit of his own body should be torn from him."[55] The figure of a father is used by God so that we will be drawn to God, allured by the sweetness of God's love and goodness, which we know from our own experience to be stronger than wrath. "In order to move us more powerfully and draw us to himself, the Lord accommodates himself to the manner of men, by attributing to himself all the affection, love, and compassion which a father can have."[56]

Even though the figure of a father is quite frequently used to express God's love, and is Calvin's usual way to express the goodness and love of God, he acknowledges that the figure of a mother is even better at conveying the depth of God's love for us. When God compares Godself to a woman in labor, Calvin says, "By this metaphor he expresses astonishing warmth of love and tenderness of affection; for he compares himself to a mother who singularly loves her child, though she brought him forth with extreme pain."[57] Once again, Calvin notes the apparent inadequacy of the metaphor, not because God really does not experience the affection of love, but because the metaphor is inadequate to express the greatness and depth of God's love: "for God loves very differently from men, that is, more fully and perfectly, and, although he surpasses all human affections, yet nothing that is disorderly belongs to him."[58] If any object that the metaphor of father is more appropriate to God, Calvin responds by highlighting the limitations of both metaphors as expressions of God's love, "so that, if all that can be said or imagined about love were brought together into one, yet it would be surpassed by the greatness of the love of God. By no metaphor, therefore, can his incomparable goodness be described."[59] Calvin therefore has no problem combining both figures, to show how the Jews should have known that God "has manifested himself to be both their Father and their Mother."[60]

In spite of the limitations of both metaphors, Calvin nonetheless thinks that the metaphor of a mother more fully expresses the love of God for Israel. When God cries out, "Shall a woman forget her child!" Calvin says that this is an apt similitude, for a mother's "love toward her offspring is so strong and ardent, as to leave far behind it a father's love."[61] The metaphor of a mother is therefore better than that of a father "to express his very strong affection."[62] Calvin sees this on the human level in the way mothers abandon themselves to the care of their children out of strong affection for them. "What amazing affection does a mother feel toward her offspring, which she cherishes in her bosom, suckles on her breast, and watches over with tender care, so that she passes sleepless nights, wears herself out by continues anxiety, and forgets herself!"[63] However, he is aware of the difference between mothers and God, since there are mothers who do not experience such love but rather exhibit cruelty towards their children. "The affection which he bears towards us is far more ardent and vehement than the love of all mothers."[64]

The rule governing the interpretation of metaphors expressing God's love and goodness is found for Calvin in Jesus' statement, "If you, then, who are evil, know how to give good things to your children, how much more your heavenly Father?" (Matt. 7:11). The similarity is found in giving good things, whereas the difference is found in our being evil. Moreover, the love of God greatly surpasses the love of human parents, both because God has no evil and because God is not a creature. "Although therefore it should happen that mothers (which is a monstrous thing) should forsake their own offspring, yet God, whose love toward his people is constant and unremitting, will never forsake them."[65] Therefore, it is impossible for any human metaphor to express the depth and steadfastness of God's love for Israel, since God's love vastly transcends human love. "And yet in human affairs it is impossible to conceive of any sort of kindness or benevolence which he does not immensely surpass."[66]

The prophets also adopt figures to express the care and protection of God. For instance, God may be described as armed with a shield. Though this is inappropriate for God, it is done in accommodation to our need, for "when troubles and dangers arise, when terrors assail us on every side, when even death presents itself to our view, it is difficult to realize the hidden and invisible power of God, which is able to deliver us from all fear and anxiety."[67] To reassure us of God's protection in spite of what we see, God is described as armed for our protection, "for the purpose of impressing more effectually upon our hearts the conviction that God is present to help us."[68] Calvin thinks that an even more beautiful and alluring figure of God's protection is found when God describes Godself as a hen or bird, protecting the faithful under God's wings.[69] The figure is not apt if we think of the nature of God in itself, but it is presented to us in accommodation to our infirmity, so that we might be allured to God by the beauty and goodness of the image.[70] The alluring beauty of the image facilitates the anagogic movement from the image to God, so that the faithful "may ascend by degrees to God."[71]

Finally, the prophets adopt metaphors and figures in order to describe Christ and his Kingdom to the Israelites. Calvin first notes this prophetic mode of expression in the 1539 edition of the *Institutes*, calling it the key that will open up the reading of the prophets regarding Christ: "the better to commend God's goodness, the prophets represented it for the people under the lineaments, so to speak, of temporal benefits."[72] The prophets followed this procedure not to confine the minds of the Israelites to the earth, as the Anabaptists taught, but rather to elevate them by steps from the image of earthly happiness to the inconceivable happiness of eternal life.[73] This form of accommodation is particularly suited to what Calvin calls the childlike capacities of the Israelites. "The same church existed among them, but as yet in its childhood. Therefore, keeping them under this tutelage, the Lord gave, not spiritual promises unadorned and open, but ones foreshadowed, in a measure, by earthly promises."[74]

Calvin uses this key of interpretation to explain the way the prophets speak of the Kingdom of Christ, as well as Christ the King. When Isaiah prophesies the restoration of the Kingdom after the exile, he describes it in terms of an abundance of rain, grain, cattle, oxen, and donkeys (Isa. 30:23–25). According to Calvin, this is a customary way of speaking for the prophets, "for the true happiness of the children of God cannot be described in any other way than by holding out the image of those things which fall under our bodily senses, and from which men form their ideas of a happy and prosperous condition."[75] Since we have no direct knowledge of spiritual life and happiness, we must form our conception of such happiness from those things that we do know.[76]

One reason the prophets use such images is out of accommodation to our limited human capacities, which can only know the unknown eternal life by means of the known earthly happiness. When Jeremiah portrays the restoration of the people in terms of grain, wine, oil, flocks, and herds, Calvin says that he does this in accommodation to the inherent limitations of finite existence. "As, then, the kingdom of Christ is spiritual and celestial, it cannot be comprehended by human minds, except he raises up our thoughts, as he does, by degrees."[77] This is even more true for the Israelites, who represent the childhood of human development for Calvin. Even those like David who knew that the Kingdom of Christ was spiritual, represented that Kingdom to the people under the external images of earthly blessings, "for he knew that God intended so to rule at that time his Church, as that manner of teaching should be suitable to children."[78] Such earthly images were necessary for this stage of human development, "because spiritual truth, without any metaphor, could not have been sufficiently understood by a rude people in their childhood."[79] The goal, as we have seen, was to raise the children up by degrees from the images of earthly things to the spiritual realities they represented, "according to the condition and comprehension of childhood."[80]

However, another reason the prophets use such external images to describe Christ's Kingdom is related to the way the blessings of this Kingdom are hidden under realities that appear to contradict them. "Nothing is more contrary to our natural judgment than to seek life in death, riches in poverty and want, glory in shame and disgrace—to be wanderers in this world, and at the same time its heirs! Our minds cannot naturally comprehend these things."[81] Understood in this way, the images the prophets use to describe Christ's Kingdom are as necessary for us as they were for the Israelites in the state of childhood, for this contradiction will remain for all the faithful until Christ comes on the last day.[82] The faithful after Christ, just like the pious before Christ, must follow the anagogy from the visible image to the invisible reality, to rise by degrees from the earthly to the spiritual. "For while we only hope, our happiness is concealed from us; it is not perceptible by our eyes or by any of our senses."[83] Such images are therefore as useful for the Christian Church suffering affliction in this life as they were for the Jews suffering during the Babylonian exile.

Since David himself is a type of Christ, it is not surprising that the prophets depict Christ to the Israelites under the figure of an earthly king. For instance, when Jeremiah promises that God will raise up for David a righteous Branch, who shall rule wisely and execute justice and righteousness in the land, Calvin thinks that this is a fitting image of Christ, accommodated to the earthly capacities of the Israelites.[84] On the one hand, even though the figure is inadequate fully to represent the reality of Christ, it still bears an analogy and similarity to him, and hence is fitting.[85] On the other hand, while holding to the analogy between earthly kings and Christ, we must also remember to follow the anagogy from earthly realities to the spiritual realm, "for though he is compared to them, yet there is no equality; after having contemplated in the type what our minds can comprehend, we ought to ascend further and much higher."[86] Thus the proper way to contemplate the images of Christ in the prophets is to hold at one and the same time to the analogy and the anagogy between earthly kings and Christ, so that we discern the similarity amid difference between the two, and also elevate from the earthly figures and images to the spiritual reality of Christ.[87]

3. The Iconic Language of the Prophets (*Hypotyposis*)

The prophets not only accommodate their teaching to the finite and child-like capacities of the Israelites and Jews, but they must also adjust their teaching due to the profound resistance their message arouses in their audience.

This resistance arises either from the refusal to see themselves as sinners under radical judgment before God or from the apparent impossibility of their deliverance and restoration by God once God's judgment and wrath has fallen upon them. According to Calvin, the prophets cannot adequately address the obstacle that either presumption or despair creates for their message simply by teaching and asserting their message, even if it is the Word of the Lord. Rather, the prophets must develop vivid and gripping ways of speaking that can more effectively rouse sinners from their slumber or despair, and place the reality of their message before the very eyes of the people, as in an image or a picture. They must, in other words, use their language to create visual images of the truth they are proclaiming to the people, so that they are brought into the presence of the reality they proclaim, even if that reality is otherwise hidden from view. The rhetorical device they use most often, according to Calvin, is *hypotyposis,* in which, as he says, "the thing itself is not only set forth in words, but is also placed, as it were, before their eyes in a visible form."[88]

Calvin demonstrated an interest in this form of teaching in his earliest writing, his commentary on Seneca's *De Clementia.* Seneca bids Nero to "consider this city in which the throng that streams ceaselessly through its widest streets is crushed to pieces whenever anything gets in its way, to check its course as it streams like a rushing torrent." Calvin claims that Seneca here is using the rhetorical device of "description," which in Greek is called "*enargeia,* which conceives images of things as here as if before our eyes Seneca represents a populous city."[89] In his work *Ad Herennium,* which Calvin cites in this context, Cicero defines this rhetorical device as follows: "It is ocular demonstration when an event is so described in words that the business seems to be enacted and the subject to pass vividly before our eyes."[90] Cicero thinks that such a device is especially suited to appeal to affections like pity, "for it sets forth the whole incident and virtually brings it before our eyes."[91] Seneca also speaks of the power of figurative representations, not for the sake of applause, like the poets, but because they are necessary "as props to our feebleness, to bring both speaker and listener face to face with the subject under discussion," a thought that will occur with great frequency in Calvin.[92]

Calvin highly prized the ability to use language to set the reality under discussion before the eyes of the reader, considering it the primary goal of a teacher. In one of his first writings as an evangelical, the *Psychopannychia* of 1534/36, Calvin opens the treatise by stating that "the best method of pressing an enemy and holding him fast so that he cannot escape, is to exhibit the controverted point, and explain it so distinctly and clearly, that you can bring him at once as it were to close quarters."[93] Calvin's high valuation of the ability of teachers to use language in this way is disclosed in his praise of Philip Melanchthon, when he tells him, "you are pleased by an unembellished and frank clarity which, without any concealment, sets a subject before the eyes and explains it."[94] When Paul tells Timothy to "hold the pattern of sound words (*hypotyposis*) which you have heard from me" (2 Tim. 1:13), Calvin thinks that Paul is exhorting Timothy to hold both to the substance and to the form of expression of the teaching he heard from Paul. "For *hypotyposis,* the word used here, means a vivid picture, as if the object concerned were actually before our eyes."[95] Thus for Calvin the best form of teaching renders the subject visible, as if before the eyes of the reader.

The prophets use the device of *hypotyposis* to place before the eyes of the Israelites and Jews realities they would much prefer to ignore. For instance, rather than simply tell the people that they are sinful, Isaiah uses all his skill to compose a poem, in which the people of Israel are portrayed as a vineyard, in which he tries "to present a striking and lively picture of their wickedness."[96] Again, rather than simply teach the people that they are wicked, Isaiah tells them that all their tables are covered with filthy vomit (Isa. 28:8), by which he "draws, as it were, a picture of what usually happens to men who are given up to drunkenness, for they forget shame, and not only debase themselves like cattle, but shrink from nothing that is disgraceful."[97] To reveal to the people of Israel the full extent of their infidelity to God, Hosea tells them that the Lord commanded him to marry a wife habituated to adultery and whoredom, and to have children by her. According to Calvin, the people knew that he did not actually do this but rather intended to paint a vivid picture of their betrayal of the Lord. "It is, in short, an exhibition, in which the thing itself is not only set forth in words, but is also placed, as it were, before their eyes in a visible form."[98] When the people refuse to listen to the prophets, Jeremiah says that they think that the prophets are nothing but wind, utterly lacking the Word of the Lord (Jer. 5:13), which paints a living image of the perversity of the people, "for there is here a vivid description, by which he sets as it were before our eyes how impious the Jews had become."[99]

The prophets knew that the people were not only blind to their sin and faithlessness but also oblivious to the threat of God's vengeance under which their sin placed them. Rather than simply tell the people that the threat of vengeance was upon them, and hastening towards them, the prophets painted pictures of the coming wrath with their words. "It is customary with the prophets, when they threaten sinners, with the view of producing terror, to add lively descriptions, as if for the purpose of bringing those matters under the immediate view of men."[100] To strike the people with the imminence of the vengeance of God, the prophets will often speak of future events in the past tense, as when Isaiah tells them that hell has enlarged his soul (Isa. 5:14): "for he intended to bring them immediately before the people, that they might behold with their eyes what they could not be persuaded to believe."[101] Similarly, Isaiah is commanded to name his child "the spoil speeds, the prey hastens" (Isa. 8:1–4), in order to represent the matter by a symbol, "that it might make a deeper impression on their minds and be engraven on their memory."[102]

The prophets may also use hyperbole to make the threat of God's vengeance more vivid. For instance, Isaiah describes a day when the sun and stars will not give their light in order to "place the anger of God, as it were, before their eyes, and affect all their senses."[103] However, such hyperbolic expressions still do not adequately convey the actual experience of God's wrath, for "it is impossible to exhibit an image of the judgment of God so alarming that the reality shall not be felt to be the more revolting and terrible."[104] The prophets use hyperbole "to represent vividly the dreadful nature of the judgment of God, and to make an impression on men's hearts that were dull and sluggish."[105] Since the people are deaf to the truth that the prophets proclaim, the prophets must add visual images of the coming vengeance to penetrate more effectively into the hearts of their audience. "Thus the prophet, as the Jews were deaf, exhibited to their view what they would not hear."[106] However, unlike rhetoricians, who use such expressions "only to catch the applause, or to fill men with empty fear or joy," the prophets use such rhetorical devices "to teach, to exhort, to reprove, to threaten, in a way calculated to be effectual," seeing that "men are very inattentive to God's judgments."[107]

The coming vengeance and wrath of God means that the people of Israel are threatened with calamity and destruction. To strike the hearts of the Israelites with the consequences of their sin, the prophets will often "exhibit graphically and as if in a painting such overwhelming distress that, wherever you turn your eyes nothing is to be seen but frightful desolation."[108] Such graphic representations are necessary because we are not at all touched by an awareness of the coming disaster, "for we need to have a representation made to us which is fitted to impress our minds, and to arouse us to consider the judgments of God, which otherwise we despise."[109] The use of *hypotyposis* is also adapted "to touch the feelings, when the event itself is not only narrated, but placed as it were before our eyes."[110] Thus Jeremiah portrays the imminence of the coming destruction from Babylon before it occurs by describing a voice crying out from Dan, "They are here!" (Jer. 4:15–16). By doing so, Jeremiah uses language in a visual way, by giving "a lively representation of the ruin which was at hand" which "sets before our eyes what could not be fully expressed in words."[111]

To move the people more effectually, especially in light of their insensitivity, the prophets will even represent in themselves a visual image of the affective response the people should be having to the coming calamity. For instance, Micah says, "For this I will lament and wail" (Mic. 1:8), for he knew that the torpor of the people made it "necessary that they should be brought to the scene itself, that, seeing their destruction before their eyes, they might be touched with both grief and fear."[112] To have the same effect, the prophet Jeremiah calls for the professional mourners to come and raise a dirge over the people (Jer. 9:17–18), which "gives a lively description of what takes place in times of mourning."[113] Jeremiah will also present the image of such mourning in himself, when he asks that his eyes run down with tears day and night (Jer. 14:17). "It was necessary that this coming calamity should be set before their eyes, in the person of Jeremiah, as in a mirror, in order that they may at length learn to fear."[114] Jeremiah even represents Rachel as returning from the dead to mourn over the devastation of her children (Jer. 31:15). According to Calvin, this figure is a "personification (*prosopopoeia*)," which has "far more vehemence" than a simple narration, "for rhetoricians mention personification among the highest excellencies, and Cicero, when treating the highest ornament of oration, says, that nothing touches an audience so much as when the dead are raised up from below."[115]

Once the calamity and devastation depicted by the prophets actually comes upon the people, the prophets will confront a new but equally difficult problem, that of restoring a devastated people to hope. Once again, the prophets will resort to the device of *hypotyposis*, to represent before the eyes of the people the truth of God's promised deliverance and restoration, so that "in the destruction of the city, in their captivity, and in what appeared to be their utter destruction, they may behold the light of God."[116] When Isaiah prophesies about the coming destruction of Babylon, he describes the noise of the army the Lord is mustering for battle, which according to Calvin is "a still more lively representation" placing the event of their deliverance before the eyes of the Jews. "Words uttered plainly, and in the ordinary manner, do not strike us so powerfully or move our hearts so much as those figures which delineate a living image of the events."[117] Similarly, the description of God commanding the north and the south to give God's people up "is far more forcible" for it allows "the people to view the event as if it had actually happened."[118] When Isaiah says that he will give thanks to God for the deliverance that as yet was only promised to the people, Calvin regards this as an *hypotyposis,* "by which the thing itself is, as it were, painted and laid before the eyes of men, so as to remove all doubt."[119] Habakkuk has the same end in view when he describes God as rendering Godself "somewhat visible" from Mount Paran, for it is "a living picture, as it were, set before the eyes of the faithful, in order to strengthen them in their adversity, and to make them assured that they shall be safe through God's presence."[120]

The Jews in captivity knew all too well the power and pride of their enemies, and were tempted to despair of the help of God. The prophet Isaiah therefore portrays God as going to war against the enemies of the Jews such as Edom, so that they might have confidence in the power of God to deliver them.[121] Joel intends to inspire the same confidence when he portrays God as gathering all the nations to be punished in the valley of Jehoshaphat. The use of *hypotyposis* gives greater efficacy to the word of consolation than would a bare promise of deliverance. "The faithful, then, not only hearing by mere words that this would be, but also seeing, as it were, with their eyes what the Lord set forth by a figure, and a lively representation, were more effectually impressed, and felt more assured, that God would at length become their deliverer."[122] Zechariah uses the device of personification to attain the same end, representing the Lord as standing on the Mount of Olives, to do battle against all the nations, "for the object of such personification is no other but that the faithful might set God before them as it were in a visible form."[123] Even though God invites us to Godself with a clear voice, we are too entangled with earthly thoughts and considerations to follow. "The prophet, then, in order to aid our weakness, adds a vivid representation, as though God stood before their eyes."[124] Only in this way can the prophets confirm the Jews in their hope for deliverance, for the bare word without these living images would not be sufficient to reveal to them what would otherwise be hidden from view.[125]

Just as the prophets represented to the people the weeping they should have done, to awaken them from their senselessness, so the prophets represent to the people the weeping their enemies will do, to give them hope that God will triumph over all their power and pride. For instance, at a time when the Moabites appeared to be in a period of profound peace and prosperity, Isaiah represents them as howling and weeping, to confirm the truth of his prophecy, "that they might see almost with their own eyes those events which appear to be incredible."[126] To make the image more vivid, Isaiah assumes the character of a Moabite in mourning, "to exhibit their condition, as it were, on a stage," in order that the Jews might more readily believe the coming calamity.[127] The very language of the prophets, therefore, with its use of *hypotyposis, prosopopoeia,* and hyperbole, combines proclamation and manifestation, so that the Jews not only hear of the coming judgment or deliverance but also see these realities before their eyes, as in a living image or painting.

4. The Symbolic Representations of the Prophets

The prophets not only use language in a way that visually manifests the reality of which they are speaking, they also add external symbols to their words, to make their message more compelling. Calvin first addresses the use of symbolic representation by the prophets in his Acts commentary of 1554. While Paul is staying at Caesarea, a prophet named Agabus came and bound his hands and feet with Paul's belt, saying, "This is the way the Jews in Jerusalem will bind the man who owns this belt and will hand him over to the Gentiles" (Acts 21:10–11). According to Calvin, Agabus is following a long precedent of prophetic activity, for "it was common for the prophets to give a symbolic representation of what they were saying."[128] Calvin claims that they confirmed their message with signs only by the leading of the Spirit. Thus Isaiah was ordered to go about naked (Isa. 20:2), Jeremiah was told to wear stocks around his neck and to buy and sell a field (Jer. 27:2, 32:7), and Ezekiel secretly dug a hole through the wall of his house and carried his luggage out of it by night (Ezek. 12:7). Though the people may have thought such actions absurd, "the same Spirit who made the symbols suit his words, used to touch the hearts of the godly within, as if they were already being confronted with the actual situation."[129] Calvin notes that the false prophets used symbols in a similar way, as Satan always apes God, as when Hananiah broke Jeremiah's yoke as a false symbol of liberation (Jer. 28:2), but they were only able to deceive the reprobate. "But since there was no underlying efficacy of the Spirit, their deception did no harm to the faithful."[130] Finally, Calvin observes the mutual relation of symbol and word, since Agabus not only makes a symbol with Paul's belt, but also speaks, "by which he teaches the faithful the value and purpose of the ceremony."[131] Thus the prophets use symbols to confirm the truth of their prophecies but only at the instigation of the Holy Spirit, who adapts and conjoins the symbols to the words in order to strengthen the faithful while at the same time touching them within. The goal of such symbols is the same as for *hypotyposis,* that is, to set the reality of which they speak before the eyes of their audience.[132]

To demonstrate to the Jews the futility of their hope in Egypt and Ethiopia, Isaiah is commanded to walk about among the people naked and barefoot.[133] Once again, we see that the prophet performed the external symbol by the command of the Lord, and not at his own instigation, and that this symbol "is fitted to excite admiration and to strike awe."[134] Moreover, the symbol is not a mute one, but the Lord adds the word that reveals the design of the symbol, namely, that the hope in Ethiopia and Egypt will be futile (Isa. 20:3–6). Calvin considers the option that this might be a *hypotyposis,* as was the marriage of Hosea to the unfaithful woman, but he insists instead that Isaiah actually walked about naked whenever he prophesied for a period of three years. "He places himself in the midst between God and his countrymen, so as to be the herald of a future calamity, not only in words, but likewise by a visible symbol," though, according to Calvin "he uncovered those parts which could be beheld without shame."[135] Calvin again observes that the false prophets also use symbols "to dazzle the eyes of the multitude, and gain credit to themselves; but these symbols are worthless, because God is not the author of them."[136] Since, according to Calvin, the Roman sacraments lack both the command and the doctrine of God, they are worthless ceremonies, not real sacraments.[137]

Jeremiah is commanded to hide the loincloth he is wearing under a rock by the Euphrates, and to retrieve it many days later, only to find it ruined (Jer. 13:1–7). According to Calvin, this was done in light of the recalcitrance of the Jews to his message, making it "necessary to reprove their torpidity by an external symbol."[138] Prophetic symbols are therefore made necessary by the stubborn refusal of the Jews to believe the Word of God proclaimed by Jeremiah, much as we saw with regard to *hypotyposis.* Had God merely told them that they had been God's precious possession, but now were being cast off due to their rottenness, this would not have been enough, for "in the state of security and dullness in which we know the Jews were, such a simple statement would not have so effectually penetrated into their hearts, as when this symbol was presented to them."[139] The addition of the symbol gives more effectiveness to Jeremiah's message, so that the people felt the force of it in their souls when "they saw that the judgment of God was at hand."[140]

Calvin makes the same point with regard to the command of God that Jeremiah not marry or have children, for "his celibacy might have been intended to be, as it were, a living representation, in order to produce more of an effect on the Jews."[141] So also, when Jeremiah is commanded to go to the potter's house, he does this to show the Jews their own situation more vividly, because of the greater efficacy of visual representation.[142] Jeremiah was commanded to break an earthenware jug in the presence of witnesses from Jerusalem in order to seal his prophecy that Jerusalem would be destroyed, because only in this way could God break through the resistance of the people to this message.[143] God appends to this symbol the word that shows its meaning, which Calvin uses to demonstrate once again "that signs are wholly useless when the word of God does not shine forth, as we see that superstitious men always practice many ceremonies, but they are only histrionic acts. But God never commanded his prophets to show any sign without adding doctrine to it."[144]

The mutual relation of prophetic word and symbol is even more clearly set forth in Calvin's discussion of the yoke worn by Jeremiah to represent the coming captivity of the people to the Babylonians (Jer. 27:1–5). On the one hand, "a visible symbol was added in order to confirm the prediction" by which God "teaches not only our ears, but also our eyes and all our senses."[145] This is why Calvin will say that mere doctrine without the addition of an external symbol would have been "frigid" and thus ineffectual. On the other hand, Calvin will also say that the symbol itself would be "frigid" and ineffectual if doctrine had not been added to it, "for we know that all signs are as it were dead, except life is given them by the word."[146] Thus, just as naked doctrine and the mere Word of God would not have enough force to touch the hearts of the people without the addition of the prophetic symbol, so the symbol itself would be frigid and even dead without the addition of the Word of God that animates it. "God, therefore, has ever added doctrine to his signs, which may therefore be truly compared to the soul, which gives life to the body, that would otherwise be without motion or strength."[147]

Calvin makes the same point with regard to the paving stones Jeremiah lays in Egypt for the king of Babylon (Jer. 43:8–10). On the one hand, the proclamation of God's vengeance needs to be confirmed by a visible symbol to arouse unbelieving people. "For so great was their stupidity, that unless

God aroused all their senses, they would never have attended: they were deaf. Then the Lord set before their eyes what they were unwilling and refused to hear."[148] On the other hand, had God not added doctrine to the symbol of the stones, they would have been without benefit, "for all signs we know are frigid and without importance without the word. It is God's word, then, that in a manner gives life to the signs, and applies them for the benefit and instruction of men."[149]

Since prophetic symbols have a mutual relationship with the Word of God, by which they confirm the word and are given life by the word, Calvin thinks that they are in fact sacraments, but only temporary ones.[150] As sacraments, prophetic symbols are given in accommodation to our infirmity, "to secure faith to doctrine," so that "the promises may be more fixed and ratified in our hearts."[151] Not surprisingly, Calvin appeals to the prophetic symbols to ground his criticism of the "mute ceremonies" of the Roman Church. Thus, when Ezekiel is commanded to represent the siege of Jerusalem by means of a brick set before him (Ezek. 4:1–3), Calvin says, "This had been a childish spectacle, unless God had commanded the prophet to act so. And hence we infer, that sacraments cannot be distinguished from empty shows, unless by the word of God."[152] This, however, is what makes the actions of the prophet Hananiah so troubling. He should have known that the wooden yoke on Jeremiah's neck "was like a sacrament; for it was a visible sign to establish the credit of his message."[153] However, to confirm the truth of his prophecy that the people would be freed after only two years of captivity, Hananiah added his own symbol by breaking the yoke of Jeremiah and casting it away, and then added doctrine to explain the meaning of this symbolic action.[154] How, then, are the Jews to discern whether Hananiah is a true prophet? He appeals to the Name of God for his action, and he joins the symbol with the doctrine. Calvin replies by claiming that "God ever supplies his own people with the spirit of discernment, provided they humbly pray to him."[155] However, Calvin notes that Jeremiah says nothing against Hananiah or his action until the Word of God comes to him again, though he thinks he is simply waiting until the time is right to confront him. He also observes that Jeremiah refers to Hananiah as a prophet. It is significant, however, that Hananiah fulfills all the criteria Calvin establishes for true prophetic symbols: he joins the symbol to doctrine and claims God as the author of both. Only when the Word of God comes to Jeremiah, confirmed by the symbol of an iron yoke to replace the wooden yoke, is it clear that Jeremiah, not Hananiah, is the true prophet of God.[156]

5. The Appearance of Things Unseen

The prophets need to employ the visually gripping language of metaphor and *hypotyposis,* as well as add external symbols to their teaching, because they are called by God to make known to the people of Israel realities that cannot otherwise be seen. Calvin thinks that this is the reason they are often called "seers" in Scripture, for "they were enlightened by God, who opened their eyes to perceive things which otherwise they would not of themselves have been able to perceive."[157] In particular, the prophets are given the ability to see the coming judgment and redemption of God, which is hidden from view from all others, as though they were placed on a watchtower.[158] In spite of their dullness and even willful blindness, the people cannot see what the prophets see because their vision transcends the limitations of all forms of human knowledge. "He did not see then what ordinary men might behold, but God showed in a vision things which no mortal senses could apprehend."[159]

Although the prophets are given the ability to see the approach of both judgment and redemption, Calvin focuses in particular on their ability to see restoration where everyone else can see only ruin and devastation. For instance, once the Temple in Jerusalem is destroyed, Isaiah nonetheless tells the people that the mountain of the Temple shall be the highest of the mountains, to which all nations shall stream, even though at the time "a disgraceful solitude made it almost an object of detestation, since it had lost its former splendor in consequence of having been forsaken by God."[160] Isaiah therefore paints a picture of the restored Temple with his words, so that the godly might look to his vision of the future and not at the present devastation that surrounded them.[161] The godly are to form their judgments not according to the present appearance of things but according to the images of a future reality portrayed before them in the words of the prophets, which they are not otherwise able to behold, so "that they might cherish good hopes when things were at their worst."[162]

The prophets will even use language to make the future sound present, as though what they promise has already been accomplished, for they know how hard it is to console a people with no apparent cause for hope. While the people are still in Babylon, Isaiah sings for joy that the Lord has comforted his people (Isa. 49:3), by which "he places the subject almost before their eyes, that they may be fully convinced that they shall have the most abundant cause of rejoicing; though at the time they saw nothing but grief and sorrow."[163] However, the Jews confront the same difficulty once they return from Babylon to Jerusalem and begin to rebuild the Temple. They are told of the glorious restoration of both the Temple and the kingdom, but "the kingdom was as yet nothing; and the Temple was more like an ignoble shed than what might have been compared in glory to the previous Temple."[164] Haggai meets this objection by urging the people "to overlook the present appearance, and to think of the glory which was yet hidden."[165] The same trial confronted the faithful yet again under Antiochus IV Epiphanes, when he sets up the desolating abomination in the Temple. "The prophet urged the pious to look upon God's power with the eye of faith, although it was then hidden from their view, and was trampled under foot by the impious in the pride of their audacity."[166] The prophets need to portray the reality of God's promised future "with greater beauty and copiousness, and paint in lively colors, those things which exceed the capacity of our reason,"[167] so that the Jews might judge the future not by present appearances but by the promises of God.[168]

The godly, however, do not entirely transcend the limitations of their own times. Even though they are given the ability to see things in the word of the prophets that are otherwise entirely hidden from view, they also see what lies before their eyes. Thus they will alternate between expressions of hopelessness, based on present appearances, and expressions of hope, based on what they cannot see but by the eyes of faith. Thus Jerusalem in Lamentations says that she has no hope, but yet she does not despair. "And this mode of speaking ought to be borne in mind; for hope sees things which are hidden. But at the same time the faithful speak according to the common appearance of things, and when they seem to despair, they regard what falls under their own observation and judgment."[169] Even the prophets alternate between the view of reality given to their earthly eyes and the hidden reality only disclosed in the mirror of the Word of God. Thus Jeremiah awakens in hope, even before the exile has begun, for he looks to the hidden things of God that are revealed only in the mirror of God's Word.[170] This also explains how Habakkuk could celebrate the triumph over the Babylonians long before it appeared in history, for he, like Jeremiah, saw the reality hidden in the future in the mirror of the Word of God.[171] What is true for Habakkuk should be true for all the godly: they should behold the hidden realities revealed in God's promises as though they have already been accomplished, no matter how impossible that might appear to the eyes of the flesh.[172] Thus, in

Psalm 137, the psalmist celebrates the destruction of Babylon with the same certainty that Habakkuk had, for he, like all the godly, looks not to present appearances but to the mirror of the Word of God. "He calls upon all God's people to do the same, and by faith from the elevation of heaven's oracles, to despise the pride of that abandoned city."[173]

Ultimately, the hidden reality set forth in the mirror of the prophetic Word is Jesus Christ, according to Calvin, for this is the only reality that can truly give hope. "For they must have a hundred times succumbed under their evils, had they not Christ before their eyes; not indeed in a carnal manner, but in the mirror of the word; as the faithful see in that what is far distant and even hidden from them."[174] The prophets therefore direct the eyes of the people away from the present appearance of things to the as yet hidden coming of Jesus Christ, for in him alone is to be found the restoration of the glory of both the Temple and the kingdom.[175] This does not mean that the return from Babylon and the restoration of the Temple and Jerusalem are not themselves blessings promised to the Jews in the mirror of the prophetic Word. On the contrary, Calvin insists that "the return of the Jewish people from the Babylonian captivity, having been a miracle of such splendor as was sufficient to swallow up and confound all the thoughts of men, . . . compels us to own that it was a signal work of God."[176] When Isaiah prophesies that in plain sight the sentinels of Jerusalem see the return of the Lord to Zion (Isa. 52:8), Calvin insists that this promise began to be fulfilled with the restoration of Jerusalem after the exile. "For, when he restored the Jews to liberty, and employed the ministry of Zerubbabel, Ezra, and Nehemiah, these things were fulfilled."[177] Similarly, when God promises through Zechariah that God will come and dwell in the midst of the Jews (Zech. 2:10), Calvin points out that this was fulfilled when the Temple was rebuilt.[178]

However, Calvin does not want the fulfillment of the prophetic promises to be confined to the restoration of the Temple and Jerusalem after the Babylonian captivity but rather sees this restoration as the beginning of the restoration of all things in Christ, "for we must begin with the deliverance which was wrought under Cyrus (2 Chron. 36:22–23), and bring it down to our own time."[179] Rather than separate the return from Babylon from the redemption in Christ, Calvin combines them, so that they are both part of one redemptive act, "for it ought to be considered one and the same favor of God, that is, that he brought back his people from exile, that they might at length enjoy quiet and solid happiness when the kingdom of David shall again be established."[180] Similarly, the Jews had in truth been given signs of the presence of God in the rebuilt Temple, but the promise of God to dwell in the midst of them would ultimately be fulfilled by the appearance of Christ, who is God manifested in the flesh.[181] Therefore, even though the Temple had been rebuilt, the promise of Haggai that the glory of the second Temple would be greater than the first would only be fulfilled "when God the Father appeared in the person of his only Son, [for] he then glorified indeed his Temple; and his majesty shone forth so much that there was nothing wanting to a complete perfection."[182]

CHAPTER 9

The Living Image of God in Jesus Christ

Calvin understands Jesus Christ to be the fulfillment of the Law and the Prophets.
Understood in a horizontal and temporal sense, Christ is the reality that is
represented and portrayed to the Israelites in the symbols and sacraments of
the Law. Understood in a vertical and transcendental sense, Christ is the
completion of the symbols of God's presence to the Israelites, for "in him the
whole fullness of deity dwells bodily" (Col. 2:9). Finally, Christ is the fulfillment of the promises of God in the prophets, for he is the fulfillment of the
restoration of the Kingdom and the Temple that began after the liberation
and return of the Jews from Babylon. Even as Calvin thinks it impossible to
understand the Law and the prophets without reference to Jesus Christ, so
he also thinks it impossible to understand Jesus Christ without seeing him in
the context of the history of God's self-manifestation to Israel and the Jews.
"It yet greatly assists our faith to compare the reality with the types, so that
we may seek in the one what the other contains."[1]

I. JESUS CHRIST AS THE LIVING IMAGE OF GOD

To accentuate the consummate role Jesus Christ plays in manifesting God to
both Jews and Gentiles, Calvin will describe Christ as "the living image of
God," who is the source and meaning of all other living images of God.[2] In
contrast to all other living images, Jesus Christ is the one in whom God fully

represents and communicates Godself to us. In his preface to the French New Testament of 1535, Calvin describes Christ as "God's true and glorious image, in whom he fully represents himself to us."[3] By this, Calvin means that in Jesus Christ alone are to be found all the good things that we lost in Adam, and of which we are otherwise destitute. Even though creation is also the living image of God, the universe does not offer us anew the good things we lost in Adam, nor does it remove all the evil that we brought upon ourselves that separates us from God. The good things that we desperately need in order to be reunited to God are only found in Jesus Christ. Calvin makes this point succinctly at the beginning of his discussion of prayer in the 1536 edition of the *Institutes*. "The Lord willingly and freely reveals himself to us in his Christ. For in Christ he offers all happiness in place of our misery, all wealth in place of our neediness: in him the Lord opens to us the heavenly treasures that our whole faith may contemplate that beloved Son of his, our whole expectation depend upon him, and our whole hope cleave to and rest in him."[4] Christ is distinguished from all other living images of God by the fact that he alone removes the evil that alienates sinful humanity from God, and lavishly bestows on them the good things they lack that can unite them to God.

In his *Catechism* of 1538, Calvin associates the living image of God with the second person of the Trinity. "Our understanding cannot conceive of the Father without including the Son at the same time, in whom his living image shines; and the Spirit in whom his might and power are visible."[5] In the second edition of the *Institutes* of 1539, Calvin combines this insight with the self-manifestation of God in Christ, thereby setting forth a Trinitarian understanding of God's self-revelation, over against the Scholastic position that makes God simply the object of faith. "It has been said that we must be drawn by the Spirit to be aroused to seek Christ; so, in turn, we must be warned that the invisible Father is to be sought solely in Christ, his image."[6] To support this claim, Calvin appeals to Hebrews 1:3, which describes Christ as the splendor of the Father's glory and the express image of his substance.[7] Thus Christ the Son of God is the living and express image of the Father, who can only be known by the illumination of the Holy Spirit. Calvin builds on this insight in the next edition of the *Institutes* in 1543, to support his claim that the sinful person cannot come to the knowledge of God without the grace of the Holy Spirit.[8]

Calvin continues to stress this Trinitarian self-manifestation of God in subsequent biblical commentaries. For instance, in his commentary on John of 1553, Calvin insists that "these two things must be joined: there can be no knowledge of Christ until the Father enlightens by his Spirit those who are blind by nature; and yet it is useless to seek God unless Christ leads the way, for the majesty of God is higher than men's senses can reach."[9] Similarly, in his harmony of Matthew, Mark, and Luke of 1555, Calvin claims that even as we only know Christ by the illumination of the Holy Spirit, so we only know God in Christ, the living image of God.[10] The central role of the Holy Spirit in opening our minds to see the living image of God in Christ indicates that there is a hiddenness to the self-manifestation of God in Christ that needs to be surmounted, which lies primarily in the lowliness and weakness of his humanity.

Even though Calvin will associate the living image of God with the eternal Son and Word of God, he is critical of the orthodox fathers for their association of the image of God with the divinity of Christ per se. Calvin does not think that the language of image refers primarily to the essence of the Son of God but rather to the way the Son manifests God to us.[11] In particular, in Jesus Christ, the God who is essentially invisible becomes somewhat visible. "The Father is called invisible because he himself is not apprehended by the human mind but shows himself to us by his Son and thus makes himself in a manner visible."[12] Jesus Christ is therefore the self-manifestation of God the Father, for "he is the image of God because he manifests to us things in his Father that would otherwise remain hidden."[13] This is why Hebrews calls Christ the image of the substance of the Father (Heb. 1:3), "because the majesty of the Father is hidden, until it shows itself impressed on his image."[14]

On the one hand, Calvin will attribute the hiddenness of the Father to the fact that God dwells in light inaccessible, which would blind our minds if we looked at it directly. "It follows from this that we are blind to the light of God unless it illuminates us in Christ."[15] The light of the Father, which would otherwise blind us, can safely be beheld in Jesus Christ, the image of the Father. "This is coming to the light which is otherwise justly called inaccessible."[16] On the other hand, Calvin will say that God is hidden in darkness unless God's light shines on us in Christ. "Apart from Christ there is no light, but unbroken darkness. Since God is the only light by which we must all be illumined, so this light is shed on us (so to speak) only by such irradiation."[17] For both reasons, Calvin insists that any attempt to seek to know God apart from Christ can only end in futility. "God is not to be sought after in his inscrutable majesty (for he dwells in light inaccessible), but is to be known in so far as he reveals himself in Christ."[18] Jesus Christ is the one in whom God the Father manifests himself fully and completely, for Christ "is an express image which represents God himself," so that "whatever is peculiar to the Father is also expressed in Christ."[19] Calvin claims that this "should be reckoned among the first axioms of our religion," namely, that "the Father, who is otherwise invisible, has revealed himself in his Son alone."[20] Since God is the fountain of every good thing, it follows that the self-manifestation of God in Christ is something to be both experienced and enjoyed. "We should learn the excellency of Christ by a true sense of faith and by our own experience,"[21] for "God has given himself to us to be enjoyed wholly in Christ."[22]

According to Calvin, the self-manifestation of God in Christ is total and complete.[23] The degree to which God manifests and communicates Godself distinguishes Jesus Christ from all other living images of God. "For God has often exhibited himself to men, but only in part. In Christ, however, he communicates himself to us totally. He has also manifested himself, but in figures, or by power and grace. In Christ, however, he has appeared to us essentially."[24] Because God manifests Godself to us essentially in Jesus Christ, we should not seek to know anything about God apart from Christ.[25] Because God offers Godself completely in Jesus Christ, we should enjoy God in Christ alone.[26] In particular, this means that Jesus Christ represents the powers of God to us in a way that reveals the complete presence of God in him. "For in Christ he shows us his righteousness, goodness, wisdom, power, in short, his entire self."[27] The powers of God are manifested in all of God's works, but these works reveal that they are not the source of these powers. Jesus Christ, on the other hand, is the source of the powers we behold in him, making him the express image of God the Father. "For Paul is not concerned here with those things which by communication belong also to creatures, but with the perfect wisdom, goodness, righteousness, and power of God, for the representing of which no creature would suffice."[28] The self-communication of the Father takes place by means of the powers that we see in Christ, which have their ultimate source in the Father.[29] The divine essence of Christ is therefore rightly and necessarily to be inferred from the powers of God that are represented in him, for only God can manifest God's powers so entirely and completely. "As, then, God is known by his powers, and his works are witnesses of his eternal divinity (Rom. 1:20), so Christ's divine essence is rightly proved from Christ's majesty, which he possessed equally with the Father before he humbled himself."[30] Calvin appeals to this manifestation of powers in the 1539 *Institutes,* as one of the proofs establishing the divinity of Christ. "Moreover, if apart from God there is no salvation, no righteousness, no life, yet Christ contains all these in himself, God is certainly revealed."[31]

The self-manifestation of God is total and complete in Christ, but it is also accommodated to the finite and even sinful capacities of human beings. The reason God manifests God's powers in Christ is to bestow what we lack, so that we might be reunited to God.[32] We need a Mediator to manifest the powers of God to us, for otherwise God's majesty is too great for us to comprehend.[33] We are not capable of ascending on high to God unless God appears to us in a manner that is accommodated to our limited capacities. "For the majesty of God in itself is too high for men to mount up to it. Therefore unless Christ the Mediator comes to meet us, all our senses fade away to nothing in the search for God."[34] By manifesting Godself fully in Christ, God descends to our level in order to manifest God's nearness to us. "But since all our senses fail as soon as we wish to rise to God, Christ is set before our eyes as the visible image of the invisible God."[35] For this reason, Calvin endorses the statement of Irenaeus that in Christ the infinite God became finite, out of accommodation to our capacities.[36] The descent of God in Christ, in turn, makes possible our ascent to God, which is otherwise impossible. "For how can mortal man ascend to the height of God unless he is raised on high by his hand? God in Christ descended to the lowliness of men to stretch out his hand to them."[37]

Compounding the difficulty of ascending to God is our sin, which makes God terrifying to us.[38] Our sin will therefore keep us from approaching near to God, out of the justifiable fear we might be destroyed.[39] Christ the living image of God not only brings God down to our level but also manifests the favor of God that alone can allow us to approach God with confidence. "It is evident from this that we cannot believe in God except through Christ, in whom God in a manner makes himself little, in order to accommodate himself to our comprehension, and it is Christ alone who can make our consciences at peace, so that we may dare to come in confidence to God."[40] To emphasize the way the living image of God is accommodated both to our capacity and to our sinful condition, Calvin also describes Christ as "God manifested in the flesh," following 1 Timothy 3:16. "The difference between God and man is very great, and yet in Christ we see God's infinite glory joined to our polluted flesh so that the two become one."[41] The living image of God must therefore be seen not only in the divinity of Christ but also, especially, in his humanity and flesh, if he is to reveal God to finite and sinful people.

"Christ is not only, as the eternal Word of God, his lively image, but even on his human nature, which he has in common with us, the imprint (*effigies*) of his Father's glory has been engraved, that he might transform his members to it."[42]

Christ will only fully and completely manifest and communicate God to us if he both removes from us the evil that separates us from God and bestows on us all the good things of which we are otherwise destitute.[43] Because he removes our sin by taking it upon himself, with all its consequences, the blessings of God in Christ will be hidden under an appearance that increasingly conceals them, and will only be fully manifested in the resurrection and ascension of Christ. "He says, however, that the treasures are hidden, because they are not seen shining brightly, but rather, as it were lie hidden under the contemptible humility and simplicity of the cross."[44] As we shall see, Calvin will be especially attentive to the dialectic of the manifestation and concealment of God in Christ throughout his discussion of the life and work, death, resurrection, and ascension of Christ. "It is true that at first sight Christ seems to be low and abject, but his glory appears to those who have the patience to pass on from the cross to the resurrection."[45]

2. GOD HIDDEN AND REVEALED IN CHRIST

In his early theological writings, Calvin appeals to the miracles of Christ as the clearest evidence of his divine nature. For instance, in his preface to the French New Testament of 1535, Calvin says, "By his power, he has given life; in his name, the works he has had given to him to do were sufficient witnesses to him (John 10:25)."[46] Similarly, by showing his power over the wind, the waves, the fish, and even the sun, all the elements and all creatures give witness to the divine power of Christ.[47] Calvin demonstrates the same confidence in the revelatory power of the miracles of Christ in the second edition of the *Institutes*. "How plainly and clearly is his deity shown in his miracles?"[48] The miracles so clearly attest Christ's divine power, according to Calvin, that "Christ offered his miracles to confound the unbelief of the Jews, inasmuch as these were done by his power and thus rendered the fullest testimony of his divinity [John 5:36; 10:37; 14:11]."[49]

In subsequent biblical commentaries, however, Calvin becomes much more aware of the dialectic of the revelation and concealment of the divinity of Christ, due to an increasing emphasis on the self-emptying of the Son of

God in Christ. In his commentary on Philippians of 1548, Calvin accentuates the concealment of the divine nature of Christ during the entirety of his earthly ministry. "Christ, indeed, could not renounce his divinity, but kept it concealed for a time, that under the weakness of the flesh it might not be seen."[50] The living image of God still appears in Christ, but in the context of this concealment, which increases in intensity until his death on the cross. "In fine, the image of God shown forth in Christ in such a manner that he was nevertheless abased in outward appearance and brought to nothing in the estimation of men."[51] The miracles of Christ still reveal the glory of his divinity, but they do not entirely remove the hiddenness of the divinity of Christ in his lowly humanity, as Calvin notes in his commentary on John of 1553. "It was indeed hidden under the lowliness of the flesh, yet so that it still sent forth its glory."[52]

Moreover, Calvin distinguishes between two functions of miracles. On the one hand, miracles demonstrate the presence of the power of God working through the ministry of Jesus. In his commentary on the first part of Acts of 1552, Calvin notes that "Jesus of Nazareth was a man approved by God by manifest testimonies so that he could not be despised as some base or obscure person."[53] According to Calvin, Peter calls the miracles of Jesus "proofs whereby they set a thing before men's eyes," so that "the miracles that God wrought through him had the effect of bringing him honor and glory."[54] In his commentary on John, Calvin sees this divine approbation as being given initially in the baptism of Jesus by John and the descent of the Holy Spirit upon Jesus in the form of a dove.[55] The Holy Spirit is visibly given to Christ in order that we may know that "in Christ dwells the abundance of all gifts of which we are destitute and empty," whereas the Spirit is given in the form of a dove because "God wished to represent openly that gentleness of Christ which Isaiah 42:3 praises: 'The smoking flax he shall not quench, and a bruised reed he will not break.'"[56] However, the miracles of Christ also reveal that God is at work in him, as attested by the confession of Nicodemus.[57] In this understanding of miracles, it is the power of God that is displayed, not the power of Christ per se.[58] In this way, the miracles God does through Jesus serve the same purpose as the miracles of Moses and the prophets, namely, to confirm the truth of Christ's teaching. "Thus Paul glories that his apostleship was confirmed by signs and wonders."[59] Even though Satan may ape such miracles in order to lead astray those who deserve to be deceived, "Yet when eyes are opened and the light of spiritual wisdom shines, miracles are strong enough attestation of the presence of God, as Nicodemus here declares."[60]

In his harmony of Matthew, Mark, and Luke of 1555, Calvin ascribes the power of God at work through Christ to the Holy Spirit.[61] At times, the power of God at work in Christ can change the attitude of the people witnessing the miracles from hostility to admiration, which Calvin thinks happens when Jesus heals the blind and mute demoniac (Matt. 12:22–23).[62] However, not all were made docile by the miracles of Christ so as to submit to his teaching, for some still demanded a sign from heaven (Luke 11:16). "What they wanted to see was some heavenly phenomenon in which God should in some way appear visibly."[63] The desire to see the power of God in miracles even led some, like Herod, to ignore the teaching of Christ altogether, so that God might perform like an actor for their amusement.[64] In sum, the miracles that God does through Christ should have the effect of confirming that his teaching is of divine origin, as is the case with the other prophets. They do not, however, demonstrate the divine power of Christ himself.

On the other hand, the miracles of Christ are seen to reveal his own power and glory, even if the blindness of most prevents them from seeing it. "The gist of it is that Christ was recognized as a man who showed in himself something far greater and more sublime."[65] In the Gospel of John, the miracles are described as manifesting the glory of Christ, so that they, along with the baptism, inaugurate the time of his public manifestation.[66] However, the manifestation of his divine glory takes place within the concealment of Christ's divinity in his human nature. In order rightly to understand the miracles, one must use them to ascend from the humanity of Jesus that one sees to his unseen divinity. "The issue revolved around this: they fixed on the sight of flesh and despised Christ; and so he commands them to rise higher and look at God."[67] Thus, in spite of the concealment of his divinity beneath his humanity, Calvin insists that the miracles of Christ would be sufficient to reveal his divine glory, if our blindness did not prevent us from ascending from the humanity we see to the divinity concealed within him.[68] This is why the last miracle Jesus performs in John is the raising of Lazarus, to manifest his divinity before it is increasingly concealed under the weakness and affliction of his suffering and death.[69] However, even the miracles that manifest Christ's own glory and power must be joined to his teaching in order to bear proper fruit, as happened with those who believed after Jesus raised Lazarus. "Hence, by the word believe we must only suppose he means a teachableness in embracing Christ's teaching," for "miracles have a two-fold use. Either they prepare us for faith, or confirm us in the faith."[70]

In his harmony of the Gospels of 1555, Calvin interprets the miracles of Jesus in an analogic and anagogic way, to encourage his readers to ascend from the visible miracles they see to the invisible spiritual healing that Christ was sent to bring to us. He takes his cue from the way Matthew describes the miracles of healing that Jesus did as fulfilling the prophecy of Isaiah, "he took our infirmities and bore our diseases" (Isa. 53:4). "This is the analogy we must follow: whatever benefits Christ bestows on men in their flesh, we must relate to the aim which Matthew sets before us, that he was sent by the Father to relieve us from all our ills and woes."[71] Thus, when Christ reaches out his hand to cleanse the leper, Calvin interprets this act almost exclusively in light of the power of Christ to cleanse us from our spiritual infirmities. Calvin will interpret the symbols Christ uses in performing miracles in the same analogical way, so that they manifest his power to heal our spirits.[72]

Calvin also locates the miracles of Christ in the context of his concealed divinity. Indeed, he discerns a certain economy of self-manifestation in the Gospels, disclosed to him by Jesus' repeated command not to make his miracles known to others. "Little by little, and by steady degrees, he came out into the light. And he was only revealed as the one he was to the extent that the time ordained by the Father allowed."[73] Because the miracles are done by one who nonetheless appears to have no glory or power, Calvin thinks that Matthew points us to Isaiah so that we might not misunderstand the coincidence of the revelation and concealment of divine power and glory in Christ. "By this circumstance he wanted to show that the glory of Christ's divinity is to be estimated none the less because it is revealed under the phenomenon of weakness."[74] The coming suffering, abandonment, and death of Jesus will be of such magnitude as to entirely remove from the minds of even the faithful the proofs of his divinity given in his miracles. In spite of their ability to manifest the divine power of Christ even in the midst of his self-emptying and humiliation, the coming scandal of the cross will necessitate another more powerful witness to the divinity of Christ than that afforded by his miracles alone.

3. The Coming Scandal of the Cross

As indicated above, Calvin increasingly interpreted the whole of Jesus' life and death under the rubric of the self-emptying and self-humbling of the Son of God as delineated in Philippians 2:6–8. Beginning with the 1539 edition of the *Institutes*, Calvin begins to emphasize the fact that the divinity of Christ was hidden and concealed beneath the appearance of his lowly and suffering humanity. According to Calvin, when Paul says that Christ was found in the form or fashion of a human, he did not mean that Christ was not truly human, as Marcion thought. "Rather, although Christ could justly have shown forth his divinity, he manifested himself as but a lowly and despised man."[75] Calvin intensifies this interpretation in the 1543 edition of the *Institutes* by speaking of the humanity of Christ as a veil that hides his divinity. "He took the image of a servant, and content with such lowliness, allowed his divinity to be hidden by a veil of flesh."[76] In his commentary on Philippians of 1548, Calvin reiterates this understanding of the humanity of Christ as a veil concealing his divinity but now in light of the objection that the miracles of Christ seem to contradict this concealment.[77] Calvin responds by insisting that the humble flesh of Christ was like a veil hiding his divinity, and pointing to the resurrection, and not the miracles or even the transfiguration, as the ultimate declaration of his divinity.[78]

In his commentary on Hebrews of 1549, Calvin explains why Christ emptied himself in this way, that is, to become as like us in our infirmities as possible, so that we might know how much he loves us, and not fear approaching him.[79] Were Christ not to have experienced any of our infirmities, and were he incapable of suffering, then his likeness to us would be placed in jeopardy. "But when we hear that he too endured the bitterest agonies of spirit, the likeness to us is clear."[80] The flesh of Christ must veil his divine glory in this way in order for him to be our Redeemer, for otherwise he would have been incapable of bearing our infirmities. "From this fact it is clear that our faith is confirmed and his honor undiminished because he bore our ills."[81] Calvin reiterates the theme that the humanity of Christ conceals his divinity like a veil, even as it is also the way and the door to heaven for us, "since it is that which directs us to the enjoyment of all God's benefits."[82] To draw near to us, Christ must become as like us as possible, in order thereby to open the way to eternal life for us. This means that he must hide his divinity from us during the days of his flesh, so that he can take upon himself all of the infirmities that afflict us. "Although the flesh of Christ was unpolluted by any stain, it had the appearance of being sinful, since it sustained the punishment due to our sins, and certainly death exerted every part of its power on the flesh of Christ as though he were subject to it."[83]

In his commentary on John of 1553, Calvin combines the concealment of the Son of God in his self-emptying with the manifestation of the Son of

God in his miracles. Thus, when the Jews are said to have complained about Jesus, Calvin says, "the divine majesty of Christ was not so concealed under the contemptible and lowly appearance of the flesh that it did not send forth beams of his manifold brightness."[84] Nonetheless, Calvin will emphasize the way Christ accommodates himself to our capacities not only by concealing his divinity but also by ascribing all divinity to the Father, so as to appear to us as a fellow human being. "By accommodating himself to men's capacity, he will at one time assert his divinity and claim for himself what is of God, and at another time will be satisfied with bearing a human character and give the whole glory of divinity to the Father."[85] According to Calvin, Christ does this so that we might gradually be led from his humanity to his divinity, as we are incapable of ascending to God without the mediation of his humanity.[86]

However, before we can move from the humility of the human Jesus to the divine majesty of the Son of God, we must first pass through the scandal of the crucifixion, in which Christ's divine majesty will be completely hidden from our view.[87] Because he knows that this hour is coming, which his followers will not be able to withstand on their own, Christ does all he can before his death to prepare the disciples to withstand this dreadful trial, according to Calvin. Thus, when Christ enters into Jerusalem, he accepts the acknowledgment of the people that he is their promised King, even as "he openly acknowledges that his reign is inaugurated by his marching to death."[88] Once he is in Jerusalem, he tells his disciples that the hour has come for him to be glorified, even though he knows that before then he must be crucified. Calvin takes this glorification to be the preaching of the Gospel to the whole world that will take place after his death. "Again, in case this contemplation of his glory should quickly vanish away when he was condemned to death, hung on the cross and then buried, he anticipates and warns them in good time that the ignominy of his death does not obstruct his glory."[89] However, shortly after he tells them this, he also says that his soul is troubled. According to Calvin, this can only happen if the divinity of Christ is not only hidden in his flesh, but if it is also at rest, no longer active in his life. "For his divinity was hidden, did not put forth its power and, in a sense, rested, that an opportunity might be given for making expiation."[90]

Since Christ knows his divinity will be completely hidden and at rest when he suffers and dies, he not only points the disciples to the glory that will follow his crucifixion but also points to the glory of the crucifixion itself. In spite of all appearances to the contrary, the cross will be the victory of

Christ over Satan, sin, and death, and will therefore be the hour in which the Son of God is glorified. "Might not a sight so sad and ugly have overwhelmed them a hundred times? Christ therefore forestalls this danger and recalls them from the external aspect of his death to its spiritual fruit."[91] For the same reason Christ asks that their hearts not be troubled, and points them to faith both in God and himself as the sole remedy for the trials that await them. "For it was an extraordinary temptation that soon they would see him hanging on the cross, a sight that would cause them nothing but despair."[92] Only by means of faith in the humble and weak Christ will we truly be able to rise to the true knowledge of God in Christ. "But faith will never reach heaven unless it submits to Christ who appears as the God lowly in aspect; nor will it be firm unless it seeks a foundation in the weakness of Christ."[93]

Calvin knows that the same trial and temptation that confronted the apostles still confronts all of us now when we read the accounts of the trial, torture, suffering, and death of Jesus in the Gospel of John. As early as the 1536 edition of the *Institutes,* Calvin developed an anagogic reading of the passion narrative, so that readers might be led from the apparent sight of weakness, suffering, and defeat to the true spiritual account of the transfer of our sin and death from us to the Son of God. "He suffered, moreover, under Pontius Pilate, condemned indeed by the judge's sentence, as a criminal and wrongdoer, in order that we might, by his condemnation, be absolved before the judgment seat of the highest Judge."[94] Calvin encourages his readers to follow the same anagogic method when they read the account of the passion in John's Gospel. "But when we realize that our condemnation is blotted out by Christ's, because it pleased the heavenly Father thus to reconcile mankind to himself, we are raised on high by this alone and boldly and without shame glory even in Christ's ignominy."[95] Such consideration even takes away the scandal we might all confront by seeing the Son of God executed in a forsaken place called "the place of the skull." When we realize that "in no other way could our guilt be removed than by the Son of God becoming an outcast for us," a scene of apparent evil and malediction becomes "an inestimable example and pledge of the divine power, wisdom, righteousness, and goodness."[96]

In his harmony of the Gospels of 1555, Calvin frames the whole of the life of Jesus in light of the apparent contradiction between the heavenly glory and earthly humiliation of Christ. For instance, the shepherds are sent to behold the King of the Jews who has been born, but what they see contradicts any expectation they might have had. "What is more pathetic than believing one to be King of the whole people, who is not ranked worthy of even the lowest place in the crowd? And to hope for a restoration of the kingdom, for salvation, from one who for his poverty and lack of support is turned out into a stable?"[97] Only by holding firmly to the Word that they had heard could the shepherds so easily "overcome by their deep faith whatever in Christ struck them as lacking in glory and honor."[98] Calvin describes the divinity of Christ as being hidden throughout his earthly life, so that he might as a true human undertake all that was necessary for our salvation. Asking how Luke could say that Jesus grew in knowledge, Calvin says, "We must not imagine that he was two-faced about this: though he was one person *God* and *man,* it does not follow that his human nature was given anything that was properly divine, but as far as concerned our salvation, the Son of God kept his divine power as it were concealed."[99]

Moreover, Calvin appeals to the idea he derives from Irenaeus—that the divinity of Christ was at rest in his suffering and death—to understand the whole of Christ's earthly life, not only his suffering and death. "In short, unless we wish to deny that Christ was made true man, we shall not be ashamed to admit that he freely took what cannot be separated from human nature."[100] Calvin will use this understanding of Christ's divinity at rest to explain how Christ can at times ascribe all divinity to God, while acting only as a human being in his own person, as when Jesus prays that the storm be stilled. "In this respect his divine majesty was in a sense quiescent, although at last in its own order it came forth."[101] Calvin is quite clear that the divine power of Christ remains hidden and at rest throughout his life and death and only truly exhibits itself in his resurrection and ascension. This is why Jesus tells his followers not to tell anyone of the glory of his transfiguration until after he has been raised from the dead, for only then will they see that his divinity was present all along, even though it was hidden and at rest in his life and death.[102] Perhaps under the influence of Irenaeus, in the final edition of the *Institutes* of 1559, Calvin describes the self-emptying of the Son of God in such a way that only his humanity was manifested, without any divine glory shining at all.[103]

As in the Gospel of John, Calvin interprets the entrance into Jerusalem as the ceremonial inauguration of his Kingdom. However, in the harmony Calvin again emphasizes the way the entrance manifests the self-emptying of Christ. "To claim royal honor, Christ entered Jerusalem riding on an ass. Magnificent splendor indeed!"[104] The solution to the scandal created by this scene is to robe Christ in the prophecy of Zechariah, that their king would come to the Jews in this way.[105] Just as Christ, in the Gospel of John, shows forth his divine power before his death by raising Lazarus, so in the synoptic Gospels Christ manifests his divinity by giving his disciples the sign of a man carrying a water pot as they seek a place to celebrate the Passover.[106] Calvin appeals to his own readers to see in this sign a way to overcome the offense that they might experience in his day upon reading the account of Christ's suffering and death, revealing that the scandal of the cross confronts every generation of believers and not just the original disciples. "It is worth our while today to overcome the scandal of the cross to know that as the very hour of death was upon him, the glory of Godhead appeared in Christ along with the weakness of the flesh."[107] In the Last Supper, Christ attempts to strengthen his disciples to withstand the coming trial of his death by pointing them to the resurrection that will follow upon his death, when he promises them he will not drink of the fruit of the vine until he drinks it new with them in his Father's kingdom (Matt. 26:29). "They had to be guided to Christ's death that they might use it as a ladder to ascend to heaven, so now, because Christ died and was received into heaven, by looking at the cross we should be led up to heaven, that his dying and life restored should hold together."[108]

As in the commentary on John, Calvin explains the genuine reality of Christ's grief and agitation in Gesthemane (Matt. 26:37) by appealing to the divinity that remained at rest within him, so that he might do all that was necessary to save us.[109] And as in John, Calvin directs the reader to surmount the offense of the arrest and trial of Jesus by reading the narrative anagogically. "First, to remove the scandal of the cross, look at the benefit Christ gives us in his self-emptying: thus will the incomparable goodness of God and the efficacy of grace dispel by their own light whatever is ugly and shameful in the scene."[110] Thus, in spite of the degrading appearance of the Son of God being arrested, bound, and restrained, we should realize that in this way we are loosed from the power of the devil and from the guilt that held us captive before God. When we do so, "not only is that stumbling-block removed upon which our faith might have struck, but there follows in its place a great wonder at the immense grace of God, who reckoned our deliverance so precious that he handed over his only-begotten Son to be bound by the wicked."[111]

So also, to remove the offense of Jesus being tried by Pilate, we should see in this scene the heavenly tribunal before which Christ takes our place.[112] Pilate's declaration of the innocence of Christ is likewise intended to show us that Christ is exchanging places with us before God, which alone can remove the offensiveness of the scene. "The ugliness of this scene might at first sight greatly agitate men's minds unless the thought came to us that the penalty that was due to us was laid on Christ: now, with the guilt removed, let us not hesitate to advance in the sight of the heavenly Judge."[113] Calvin therefore asks that the water that once washed Pilate's hands now be used "to clear our eyes of all that hinders us from seeing lucidly, in the midst of condemnation, the righteousness of Christ."[114]

The derision Christ experienced from the onlookers while hanging on the cross manifests to us both our own condition before God and the amazing extent of the self-emptying of the Son of God. "This was the hardest part of all his pains, that all should have treated him as a man cast off and forsaken by God, with vexation, spite, and insult."[115] The full extent of his self-emptying is reached when Christ cries out in agony that God has forsaken him.[116] Calvin insists on the necessity of this aspect of Christ's sufferings from the first edition of the *Institutes* onward, namely, that he "experienced all the signs of a wrathful and avenging God, so as to be compelled to cry out in deep anguish, 'Father, Father, why hast thou forsaken me?' [Ps. 22:1; Matt. 27:46]."[117] Calvin accounts for Christ's ability to experience the trial "that he was now against God and doomed to ruin" by appealing to the way "the Godhead yielded to the infirmity of the flesh, in the interests of our salvation, that Christ might fulfill the whole role of Redeemer."[118] Thus the full extent of the self-emptying of the Son of God is reached when Christ dies "as though under the wrath of God," and hence as if "he were cast into the labyrinth of evil."[119] Those asking him to prove that he is the Son of God by coming down from the cross simply do not realize that he shows himself to be the Son of God by emptying himself out to this extent on the cross.[120] However, his death on the cross hides his divine nature completely from view. "For by dying in this way he was not only covered with ignominy in the sight of men, but also accursed in the sight of God."[121]

To support us through the trial created by the death of the Son of God, when "God's Son lay in disgrace and shame, and (as Paul says) was emptied out," God manifests signs of the divinity of Christ in the hour of his death, in anticipation of the coming resurrection. "To the majesty of Christ, came superb testimony of the sun's eclipse, the earthquake, the cloven rock, the tearing of the veil, just as if heaven and earth gave their due service to their Maker and Designer."[122] In contrast to the apparent blindness of the Jews, "the very natural senses compelled outsiders, even soldiers, to confess what they had learned neither from the Law nor from teachers," so that the centurion at the foot of the cross became "a momentary herald of the Deity of Christ."[123] Finally, that Christ's dead body was not cast into a pit but rather buried with honor points us to the coming glory of the resurrection, for burial itself is a pledge of the resurrection.[124] The burial of Christ attests the reality of his death, as well as his taking on himself the curse that lay on us. Because the divine power of Christ was deeply concealed in this death, "God meant this [burial] as a kind of foreshadowing of what he would shortly bring to pass, the he would raise his Son in splendor and victory, above the heavens."[125]

4. Christ Declared the Son of God in the Resurrection

The self-emptying of the Son of God unto death on the cross means that the divinity of Christ must be hidden beneath the veil of a humble and apparently powerless human being, and that it must remain as if quiescent so that Christ can take on himself the full extent of human infirmity, sin, and malediction. In spite of the various manifestations of his divine power in miracles and in the transfiguration, the scandal of the cross is sufficient of itself to remove all such demonstrations of divinity from our view. If Christ is to show himself the living image of God, to bestow on needy sinners all the good things they need for eternal life, he must clearly exhibit to our view his divinity, so that our faith might rest in confidence on him alone. In the 1536 *Institutes* Calvin saw the resurrection primarily in terms of the human nature of Christ. "He rose again to life, a true man, yet now not mortal, but incorruptible, glorified by receiving body and soul."[126] However, by the second edition of 1539 he located the manifestation of Christ's divine glory in his resurrection from the dead, which was necessary to surmount the appearance of weakness in his death on the cross. "For as he, in rising again, came forth victor over death, so the victory of our faith over death lies in his resurrection alone."[127]

Calvin clarifies this manifestation of the divine power in his commentary on Romans of 1540. "He says that Christ had been declared with power, because there was seen in him the power which properly belongs to God by his resurrection."[128] The divine power in particular was that of the Spirit, which, although it is ascribed to God by accommodation, also properly belongs to Christ.[129] Calvin makes the same point in his commentary on 2 Corinthians in 1547, in light of Paul's statement that Christ was crucified in weakness but yet lives by the power of God (2 Cor. 13:4). "It is as if he had said, 'Will you esteem Christ less because he showed his weakness in his death, as though the heavenly life that he lived after his resurrection were not a clear token of his divine power?'"[130]

In his commentary on Acts of 1552, Calvin shows how faith in Christ depends on the establishment of the resurrection of Christ beyond any doubt, as Luke indicates when he says that Christ showed himself alive after his passion by many proofs (Acts 1:3).[131] The many proofs are understood by Calvin to involve the forty days he showed himself to the apostles before his ascension, with such "proofs" being understood via Aristotle as "the necessary element in signs."[132] By raising Christ from the dead, God has "begotten" Christ as the Son of God, even as David was begotten as Son on the day his kingdom was established by God.[133] The apostle Paul establishes that Christ was begotten as the Son of God, and made the express image of God, in his resurrection.[134] "And when Psalm 2:7 says, 'Thou art my Son: this day I have begotten thee,' the resurrection is established as a proof for the acknowledgement of Christ's glory and his ascension into heaven was the complement of that glory."[135] To accentuate this point, Calvin strengthens his discussion of the resurrection in the final edition of the *Institutes* in 1559 by pointing to the resurrection as the central testimony to the divine Sonship of Christ, "because then at last he displayed his heavenly power, which is both the clear mirror of his divinity and the firm support of our faith."[136]

Thus, to surmount the scandal presented by the weakness of Christ in his death and burial, we must pass on from the cross to the resurrection. "In this way nothing will prevent his glory from shining everywhere."[137] That Christ has been raised from the dead removes the stumbling block from the appearance of his death, but it does not remove the necessity of passing through his cross and death before moving on to the resurrection.[138] In the same way, we ought to begin with the humanity of Christ, in whom divinity was hidden and at rest, in order from there to pass on to his divinity. "Now when Christ is truly known, the glory of God shines in him, so that we may know for certain that our faith in him does not depend on man, but is founded on the eternal God; for it rises from Christ's flesh to his divinity."[139] We must follow the order established by the self-emptying of the Son of God, for it manifests God to us in accommodation to our capacities, and makes necessary our vision of humility before leading us on to divine power and glory: "apprehending Christ on earth, born in a stable and hanging on a cross, it goes on to the glory of his resurrection and then at length to his eternal life and power, in which shines his divine majesty."[140] Only when we have passed from the cross to the resurrection, and from the suffering humanity to the glorious divinity of Christ, can we truly know Christ as the living image of God the Father.[141]

5. "God Has Made Him Both Lord and Christ": The Ascension into Heaven

According to Calvin, the glory and power of God revealed in the resurrection of Christ is but the beginning of his self-manifestation as the Son of God. Even though Christ emerges victorious over sin, death, and the wrath of God in his resurrection, he does not truly inaugurate his reign as Lord and King until the ascension into heaven, to sit at the right hand of God the Father. In the first edition of the *Institutes,* Calvin says, "We believe likewise that just as he was manifested in the flesh 'he sits there at the Father's right hand.' By this is meant that he has been appointed and declared King, Judge, and Lord over all."[142] Just as Christ in his death takes upon himself all the evil that separates us from God, so it is only when he ascends to the right hand of God in heaven that Christ lavishes upon us all of the good things he receives from the Father to bestow on us.[143] However, the ascension into heaven means that the dialectic of revelation and concealment that accompanied his earthly life is again reintroduced, together with another dialectic of physical absence and spiritual presence. "Therefore, although, lifted up into heaven, he has removed the presence of his body from our sight, yet he does not refuse to be present with his believers in help and might, and to show the manifest power of his presence."[144] Calvin reiterates these points in his Catechism of 1538, but adds that in his ascension Christ receives the Spirit, by which he then bestows every good thing on his believers.[145]

In the second edition of the *Institutes,* Calvin combines the resurrection and ascension as together overcoming the scandal created by the weakness of Christ on the cross, and inaugurating the full power of the Kingdom of Christ. "Now having laid aside the mean and lowly state of mortal life and the shame of the cross, Christ by rising again began to show forth his glory and power more fully. Yet he truly inaugurated his Kingdom only at his ascension into heaven."[146] Calvin reiterates this point in his commentary on Hebrews of 1549: "the apostle harks back to his ascension, by which not only the offence of the cross was removed, but also that humbling and inglorious condition which he took upon himself along with our flesh."[147] Calvin again highlights the dialectic of absence and presence, by insisting that Christ showed himself present with power more fully, and bestowed his benefits more effusively, when he was absent bodily than when he walked on earth. "Indeed, we see how much more abundantly he then poured out his Spirit, how much more wonderfully he advanced his Kingdom, how much greater power he displayed both in helping his people and in scattering his enemies."[148] In the 1543 edition of the *Institutes,* Calvin supports this claim with several passages from Augustine, which show that the bodily absence of Christ leads to a more intimate spiritual presence of Christ. "For the church had him in his bodily presence for a few days; now it holds him by faith, but does not see him with the eyes.'"[149] Calvin emphasizes this point again in his commentary on John of 1553. "For the chief glory of Christ's Kingdom is that he governs the Church by his Spirit. But he entered into the lawful and, as it were, ceremonial possession of his Kingdom when he was exalted to the right hand of the Father. So there is nothing surprising in his delaying the full manifestation of his Spirit until then."[150]

One of Calvin's favorite texts for establishing the dialectic of absence and presence is Ephesians 4:10, "He who descended is the one who ascended far above all the heavens, so that he might fill all things." In his commentary on Ephesians of 1548, Calvin addresses directly the apparent contradiction that this passage presents, that the one who is beyond the spheres of the heavens nonetheless fills all things by his power. "But Paul tells us that he is removed from us in bodily presence in such a way that he nevertheless fills all things, and that by the power of his Spirit."[151] Calvin agrees with Luther that the right hand of God means the present power of God, but he insists that the power of Christ is present by the Spirit (and not only by his divine nature), even though Christ is absent in terms of his embodied human nature. "Wherever the right hand of God, which encompasses heaven and earth, is displayed, the spiritual presence of Christ is shed abroad and he is present by his boundless power; although his body must be contained in heaven, according to the statement of Peter (Acts 3:21)."[152]

Calvin emphasizes the visibility of Christ's ascension into heaven in his commentary on Acts of 1552, which was clearly attested by both apostles and angels, in order to convince his readers that Christ is absent from us in his embodied humanity.[153] According to Calvin, the reason a cloud hides Jesus after his ascension is to keep his followers from seeking him by the eyes of the flesh any longer.[154] The resurrection alone would not be enough to take away from us the desire to see Christ with our eyes, which is why Peter tells the Jews that heaven must receive Christ until the time of universal restoration (Acts 3:21). "It follows that they must raise their minds on high to seek Christ with the eyes of faith, although in respect of distance he is infinitely removed from them, and although he dwells outside the world in heavenly glory."[155] Calvin thinks that this is the reason Jesus forbids the women to touch him after he has been raised from the dead, lest they think he has risen to reign on earth.[156]

However, even as he emphasizes the absence of the body of Christ to focus our attention on the presence of Christ by the Spirit, Calvin increasingly focuses on the humanity of Christ, especially his body, as being the source of all the blessings that Christ bestows on us after his ascension. In the second edition of the *Institutes* in 1539, Calvin insists that Christ enriches us with the life of God through the bestowal of this life on his flesh, even though it did not have this power of itself. "Nevertheless, since it is pervaded with fullness of life to be transmitted to us, it is rightly called 'life-giving.'"[157] Calvin reiterates this point in his commentary on John of 1553. "Christ, inasmuch as he is a man, was appointed by the Father to be the Author of life, that we should not have to seek it afar off."[158] Even though the humanity of Christ is absent from us spatially, the fact that God bestows the life we need on his humanity and even his flesh brings that life much nearer to us, so that we may seek it in a fellow human being. "What had been hidden in God is revealed to us in Christ the man, and life, formerly inaccessible, is now close at hand."[159] Calvin makes the same point with regard to the Lordship and rule of Christ. By raising Christ to his right hand, God now rules over heaven and earth by means of the human Jesus, to whom we should look for help and protection from all that afflicts us. "Of course we acknowledge that God is the Ruler, but his rule is actualized in the man Christ."[160] By receiving all power and blessing from God the Father, the human Christ brings these blessings near to us, for they are found in one like us, even if he is no longer to be seen among us, and is absent as to his bodily presence.

6. The Cross as the Brightest Image of the Love of God

The manifestation of the divine power and glory of Christ in the resurrection and ascension not only directs the faithful to the reign of the human

Christ in heaven but also causes the light of the love of God to radiate from the death of Christ on the cross. This is a theme that begins to emerge with increasing intensity in the commentaries from 1548 onwards. By clearly demonstrating his divinity after his death, Christ reveals that his death was freely undertaken out of love for sinners, and represented the self-emptying of the eternal Son of God on our behalf. Calvin is especially concerned to stress this point over against the teaching of some Scholastics that the obedience of Christ unto death on the cross merited his exaltation to the right hand of the Father. "For the Holy Spirit wants us in the death of Christ, to see, taste, reckon, feel, and acknowledge only God's unmixed goodness, and Christ's great and inestimable love towards us, that, regardless of himself, he spent himself and his life for our sakes."[161] Calvin illustrates this point by means of one of his favorite metaphors, the mirror. Just as the brightness of a mirror does not benefit itself, but the others who see its light, so Christ's death was of no benefit for him, but represented his desire to benefit others.[162] The journey of Christ to the cross, culminating with his cry that God had abandoned him even while his enemies mocked him, is for Calvin the brightest mirror of the selfless love of God we can behold. "The fact that the Son of God suffered himself to be reduced to such ignominy, yea, descended even to hell, is so far from obscuring, in any respect, his celestial glory, that it is rather a bright mirror from which is reflected his unparalleled grace towards us."[163]

If the power and glory of God are manifested in the resurrection and ascension of Christ, then the goodness and love of God are exhibited on the cross, making the cross the clearest and most certain pledge of the love of God for sinners. "The true looking of faith, I say, is placing Christ before one's eyes and beholding in him the heart of God poured out in love. Our firm and substantial support is to rest on the death of Christ as its sole pledge."[164] According to Calvin, the goodness of God shines forth more brightly in the cross than in the whole of creation, because the cross represents the restoration of the creation that had been lost to sin. "For in the cross of Christ, as in a splendid theater, the incomparable goodness of God is set before the whole world. The glory of God shines, indeed, in all creatures on high and below, but never more brightly than in the cross, in which there is a wonderful change of things—the condemnation of all men was manifested, sin blotted out, salvation restored to men; in short, the whole world was renewed and all things restored to order."[165]

Understood in this way, the glory of God not only shines in the resurrection and ascension of Christ, but also in the apparently shameful death of

Christ itself, for it was there that the enemies of God and humanity were defeated. "And this was accomplished: for in the death of the cross which Christ suffered, so far from obscuring his honor, there shines the brightest, since there his incredible love to mankind, his infinite righteousness in atoning for sin and appeasing the wrath of God, his wonderful power in overcoming death, subduing Satan, and, indeed, opening up heaven, put forth it full brightness."[166] The light of God's love and goodness that shines from the cross reveals that the real victory was won not in the resurrection but in the death of Jesus, even though it appeared that he had been horribly defeated in such a death.[167] Indeed, by bearing our sin, death, and curse away from us, Christ discloses more of the glory and majesty of God on the cross than he does seated at the right hand of the Father in heaven, in spite of the apparent malediction that appears on the cross. "And this fruit swallows up all the ignominy of the death of Christ, that his majesty and glory may be more clearly seen than if we beheld him sitting in heaven; for we have in him a striking and memorable testimony of the love of God, when he is so insulted, degraded, and loaded with the utmost disgrace, in order that we, on whom had been pronounced a sentence of everlasting destruction, may enjoy along with him immortal glory."[168]

Calvin is aware that the offensive appearance of the cross of Christ is not removed from those who lack faith, as the power of his resurrection is revealed to us by the Holy Spirit.[169] To those who do not believe, Christ still appears as the crucified one who was condemned by both human and divine authority. "Although Christ rose from the dead, yet the Jews always regarded him as a person who had been crucified and disgraced, in consequence of which they haughtily disdained him."[170] This is why, according to Calvin, so many seek to know God apart from Christ, for they cannot believe that the glory and majesty of God can be known through a condemned, forsaken, and executed man. "This foolish desire is bred from contempt of Christ's humility, and it is a very great injustice, for in that aspect he represents the infinite goodness of the Father."[171] Although the faithful see the cross as the clearest mirror of the glory of God's love and goodness, this glory is hidden from the ungodly by the offensive appearance of the cross. "In the death of Christ we see a boundless glory which is concealed from the ungodly."[172] Calvin knows that in his own day the faithful are mocked by those who do not believe, for the apparently absurd desire to seek life and blessing from a dead and cursed human being.[173] According to Calvin, the way to overcome our repulsion from the scandal of the cross is to descend within ourselves to come to a serious awareness of our sin. In that way, we will recognize our likeness in the death of Christ, which will open the way for us to see the grace of God shining forth in his death.[174]

Once we have been brought to the perception of the goodness and love of God in the death of Christ, our awareness of such goodness should ravish our minds and hearts with greater admiration than any other form of beauty can enkindle. "Now, it must be that the grace of God wholly draws us to himself and inflames us with the love of him by whom we obtain a serious awareness of it. If Plato affirms this of his Beautiful, of which he saw only a shadowy idea from afar, this is much more true with regard to God."[175] This is especially true if we are first aware of our own misery, for the death we experience in ourselves will cause us to seek the life manifested in Christ from the depths of our hearts. "As it is an incomparable blessing, it ought to carry us away and inflame all our senses with a wonderful desire and love for it."[176] The appearance of the life of God in the death of Christ makes our experience of this gift all the more astonishing to us, for we can see our death in his, even as he offers his life to us. "This might indeed, at first sight, appear to be absurd, that the death of Christ is the cause and source of our life; but, because he bore the punishment of our sins, we ought therefore to apply to ourselves all the shame that appears on the cross. Yet in Christ the wonderful love of God shines forth, which renders his glory visible to us; so that we ought to be excited to rapturous admiration."[177]

Calvin does not want us to ignore all the other pledges of God's goodness and love that we experience in this life, especially the good things of creation we should contemplate every day. "For if it is asked why the world was created, why we have been put in it to have dominion over the earth, why we are preserved in this life to enjoy innumerable blessings and are endowed with light and understanding, no reason can be given but the free love of God towards us."[178] However, the sending of the eternal Son of God to die for us so that we might live is for Calvin the chief representation of God's love that transcends all others, for it reveals not only that God loves us but also that God is love itself. "For it was not only the infinite love of God which did not spare his own Son, that by his death he might restore us to life, but it was a more wonderful goodness which ought to ravish our minds with amazement. Christ is such a shining and remarkable proof of the divine love toward us that, whenever we look at him, he clearly confirms the doctrine that God is love."[179]

7. "It Is Finished": Christ Is the End of the Law

The manifestation of Jesus Christ in his life, death, resurrection, and ascension brings to fulfillment the representation of Christ to the Israelites in the types and figures of the Law and the prophets. Along with the miracles, resurrection, and ascension of Christ, the testimony of the Law and the prophets constitutes one of the essential demonstrations that Jesus is the Christ, Lord, and Redeemer of the Jews, and also of the Gentiles.[180] According to Calvin, the Jews should have been able to identify Jesus as the promised Messiah and Redeemer from the distinguishing marks set forth in the Law and the prophets.[181] Because the Law represents Christ as in a shadow outline of a painting, the Jews should have been able to recognize the Christ even before he was manifested in the flesh, and should have been referred to him by the portrait that represented him. "Thus the Jews should have had an idea of Christ from the prophets before he was manifested in the flesh."[182] Calvin includes in this representation both the verbal promises of God and the visual symbols, ceremonies, and sacraments of the Law, for together they should lead to the recognition of Jesus Christ, even as we recognize other people by seeing their faces and hearing their voices. "Just as men are known by their appearance and speech, so God utters his voice to us by the voice of the prophets, and in the sacraments puts on, as it were, a visible form, from which he can be known according to our small capacity."[183]

Even though Christ is portrayed in the Law, only God the Father can remove the veil that blinds our eyes so that Christ is manifested to us in the Scriptures.[184] We should therefore come to the recognition of Jesus Christ from the Scriptures, namely, the Law and the prophets, so that we might behold him rightly. "Hence we are taught that we must not judge the glory of Christ by human view, but must discern by faith what is taught us concerning him by the holy Scriptures."[185] Once the Father manifests Christ to us in the Scriptures, Christ will reveal the Father to us, and lead us to him. "If one were to sift thoroughly the Law and the Prophets, he would not find a single word which would not draw and bring us to him."[186]

Even though the proper recognition of Christ depends on seeing him in light of the Law and the prophets, without which we cannot rightly appraise his glory, Calvin subsumes the fulfillment of prophecy to the resurrection and ascension of Christ as the primary demonstration of his Sonship. For instance, Calvin insists that Jesus really does fulfill the prophecy of Zechariah by riding into Jerusalem on a donkey. However, he thinks that the Jews misunderstand the nature of Christian faith when they challenge this as a proof that Christ is the Son of God. "When we say that Jesus is the Christ, we do not start out from his entry into Jerusalem sitting on an ass"; rather, "it was in his resurrection that his divine power especially shown forth."[187] Even though the Jews should in principle have been able to recognize Jesus as the Christ and Son of God from the testimony of the Law and the prophets, it is only in the resurrection that anyone can come to the true recognition of him as the Son of God, God manifested in the flesh. However, once we attain to this recognition, the fulfillment of prophecy is a necessary confirmation of his Sonship. "Yet we should not despise this confirmation, that by his wonderful providence God showed in that entry, as in a theater, the fulfillment of Zechariah's prophecy."[188]

In his commentary on Zechariah, Calvin acknowledges that the description of the king riding on the donkey is metaphorical, and is meant to be an image of humility. However, he thinks that by actually entering Jerusalem on a donkey, Jesus means to demonstrate that he is the reality being foreshadowed by this figure, even if it was not meant to be a literal prophecy of the coming King.[189] Calvin makes the same point with regard to the way Christ drinks vinegar on the cross. When David says, "For my thirst they gave me vinegar" (Ps. 69:21), Calvin acknowledges that he meant this metaphorically. But to show that he is the reality being typified by David, Jesus literally drinks vinegar on the cross. "For from it we perceive more fully how much the truth differs from figures, when the things which David suffered only figuratively appear openly and, as it were, in substance in Christ."[190]

There are times, however, when Jesus truly fulfills what the prophets foretell in a nonmetaphorical way. For instance, the prophets acknowledge that David and his descendants reign as kings over Israel, but they also foretell a day when God alone will reign over Israel. According to Calvin, this could only be fulfilled by Christ, who is both the Son of David and God manifested in the flesh. Thus, when Micah prophesies that "Jehovah himself shall reign over them" (Mic. 4:6), Calvin says, "And this was really and actually fulfilled in the person of Christ. Though Christ was indeed the true seed of David, he was yet at the same time Jehovah, even God manifested in the flesh."[191] Christ also really fulfills the prophecy of the suffering servant in Isaiah, according to Calvin, in a way that could only point to him as being the one foretold. When Isaiah says that many will be astonished at him, Calvin turns directly to Christ as providing the meaning of this prophecy. "He came into the world so as to be everywhere despised; his glory lay hid under the humble form of the flesh; for though a majesty worthy of 'the only-begotten Son of God' (John 1:14) shone forth in him, yet the greater part of men did not see it, but, on the contrary, they despised that deep abasement which was the veil or covering of his glory."[192]

Christ also manifests himself as the reality that was foreshadowed in type by David and the other types of Christ, such as the king, priests, and sacrifices. For instance, both David and Jesus show themselves to be the stone the builders rejected (Ps. 118:22), with David being the one who dimly foreshadows the reality that is clearly manifested in Christ.[193] Similarly, when the priests lifted up their hands to bless the people, this was in fact an efficacious testimony to the blessing of God. However, the reality of this figure was fulfilled when Jesus was raised from the dead.[194] Finally, to show that his death was the reality foreshadowed by the sacrifices of the Law, it was ordained that Jesus die during the Passover, to show that he is the true victim who bears away our sin. "God who had appointed him as Victim for the expiation of sin chose that very day to bring into contrast the body and the shadow."[195]

The appearance of Christ not only manifests the reality that had been foreshadowed by the kings, priests, and sacrifices of the Law, but it simultaneously brings the figures of the Law to an end by replacing them with their reality. For instance, under the Law the Jews observed many ceremonies that were filled with much pomp and splendor. According to Calvin, such opulence was necessary in order to compensate the Israelites for the absence of Christ. However, once Christ appears, he not only brings to light the reality foreshadowed by the ceremonies but also brings the ceremonies of the Law to an end.[196] Calvin interprets the last words of Jesus in the Gospel of John, "It is finished" (John 19:30), to mean not only that his death is the completion of our salvation but also that it therefore brings to an end the whole economy of the Law. "Christ contrasts his death with the ancient sacrifices and figures; as if he said, 'Of all that was practiced under the Law, there was nothing that could of itself atone for sins, appease the wrath of God and obtain justification. But now the true salvation is shown and exhibited to the world.'"[197] The water and blood that flow from the side of Christ after his death exhibit to us that the reality foreshadowed by the rites of purification and expiation in the Law have been fulfilled by the death of Christ, and therefore must come to an end.[198] The appearance of the reality brings the shadows to an end, and the manifestation of the truth brings the figures to an end.

However, before Christ fulfills the truth of the symbols of the Law, he also fully participates in them. This is especially true regarding the burial rites of the Jews and the worship of God in the Temple in Jerusalem. As we have seen, Calvin understood the rite of burial to be a symbol of the resurrection. For this reason, Calvin commends the disciples of John for coming to get his body after Herod beheaded him, even though John was the last of the prophets who pointed to Christ in the flesh.[199] Since the reality of the rite of burial would not appear until Christ was raised from the dead, Christ himself participated in the burial rites of the Jews, which is why he commended so highly the woman who anointed him for his burial. "Accordingly, the anointing of Christ was not superfluous then; for he was soon to be buried, and was anointed as if to be laid in the tomb."[200] This is also why the body of Jesus was wrapped with spices in linen cloths (John 19:40).[201] Because he had not yet been raised from the dead, even Christ needed to be anointed and embalmed for burial according to the custom of the Law. However, once he was raised from the dead, and exhibited the reality foreshadowed in these burial rites, the ceremonial burial practices of the Jews should come to an end.[202] Thus, even though Jesus himself was anointed for burial, after he is raised from the dead such anointing should no longer be practiced. "The resurrection of Christ had reached into all the tombs with its life-giving perfume, to breathe life upon the dead. Hence these outward ceremonies are now abolished."[203] Those who continue such practices, like the monks in the Roman Church, are actually denying the reality of the resurrection of Christ, according to Calvin, "for his resurrection abolished those ancient ceremonies."[204] Calvin claims that such ceremonies and rites were accommodated to the childish capacities of the Israelites and the Jews but are no longer suitable for those who have come to increasing maturity.[205] However, since Christ himself was properly buried according to the burial rites of the Jews, the time of the childhood of the Israelites must have come to an end on the day that Christ was raised from the dead.

Jesus Christ is the reality and archetype that was figured to the Jews first in the tabernacle and then in the Temple in Jerusalem. However, Jesus also worshiped in the Temple, and even performed miracles there. The relationship of Jesus to the Temple is therefore quite complex. Moreover, Calvin's representation of this relationship appears to change over time. In his commentary on John of 1553, Calvin clearly indicates that the Temple is as much a symbol of the presence of God at the time of Jesus as it was when it was first built. Due to the lack of prophets at the time of Jesus, God performed miracles of healing in the pool by the Sheep Gate, so that the Jews might know that God still approved the worship that took place in the Temple.[206] Far from challenging the need to exhibit signs of God's presence in the Temple, Jesus performs a miracle of healing there himself, thereby making the Temple a theater of God's glory.[207] Jesus also teaches in the Temple (John 7:14), which he did in order that the ceremonies of the Law might be made living images by the addition of the Word of God, thereby supporting and vivifying the worship of God in the Temple.[208] Finally, as the Temple was the living symbol of the presence of God even in his day, Jesus joined all the Jews near and far in going to Jerusalem to worship before the face of the Lord, and to observe the sacrifices of the Law.[209] Thus, in the commentary on John, Calvin depicts both God and Jesus as being deeply concerned to manifest signs of the presence of God in the Temple to confirm the legitimacy of the worship and sacrifices offered there, and Jesus himself both vivifies the ceremonies of the Law by teaching in the Temple and journeys to Jerusalem during the different feasts to worship before the face of God in the Temple. Calvin does not contrast the Temple as shadow to Christ as reality, or suggest that the Temple must be destroyed now that Christ has appeared.

In his harmony of Matthew, Mark, and Luke of 1555, by contrast, Calvin begins by noting how the Temple as a symbol of God's presence is a shadowy figure of the reality of Christ, in whom the fullness of God dwells bodily. "But in Christ the presence of God was tangibly displayed, no longer in shadows."[210] The implication of this passage seems to be that once Christ emerges as the true Immanuel, God with us, the symbols of the presence of God in the Temple come to an end. The relentlessly negative picture of Temple worship that Calvin portrays in the harmony reinforces this impression. For instance, when Mary enters the Temple in Jerusalem to offer the sacrifice of purification for her firstborn son, Jesus, she meets Simeon and Anna. Calvin takes this opportunity to paint a relentlessly negative image of worship in the Temple at the time of Jesus. "This episode is given to show us that, though practically the whole people had turned to irreligion in a wicked contempt for God, there yet remained a few who worshipped him, and that Christ was known by them from his earliest infancy."[211] Calvin claims that all the scribes and priests in the Temple were devoid of the Spirit of God except Simeon and Anna.[212] When Jesus later is found by his parents in the Temple speaking with the teachers of the Law, Calvin interprets his saying that he must be in his Father's house to refer not to the Temple but to his own lofty vocation.[213]

Not surprisingly, when Jesus enters the Temple in the last days of his life, Calvin describes the Temple as being completely polluted with superstition and abuse. He poses the question as to why Jesus should chastise the moneychangers in the Temple "when the temple was so chock-full of superstition."[214] Calvin responds by saying that Jesus wanted to show by a symbolic action how the whole Temple was corrupted by abuse, and "that Christ had no intention of restoring all the ancient ceremonies."[215] The bitterness of Jesus' attack on moneychanging is due to "the well-known fact that the practice had been introduced by the priesthood with a greedy eye on discreditable gain."[216] Unlike the commentary on John, where Calvin sees the Temple as still being the face of God before which the Jews were required to worship, in the harmony Calvin claims that God had already departed from the Temple by the time Jesus entered it in the last days of his life. By telling the Jews in Jerusalem, "See, your house is left to you, desolate" (Matt. 23:38), Jesus is telling them that the promise of God to dwell in the Temple forever has come to an end, due to the intolerable sin of the Jews. "Christ contends that they vainly boast themselves of God's presence, for their crimes have driven him away."[217]

According to Calvin, therefore, the Temple is to be destroyed, and the whole people of the Jews brought to utter ruin, not because of the appearance of the reality typified by the Temple but because of the intolerable sins of the Jews, which had driven God out of the Temple before Jesus even came to Jerusalem. Indeed, according to Calvin, the appearance of Christ as God manifested in the flesh would have brought an end to the Temple as the dwelling place of God but would not at all have entailed its destruction. "The temple had been erected with the view that it would cease to be God's abode and dwelling-place at the coming of Christ: yet it would have stood as a notable monument to the continuing grace of God had it not been ruined by the sin of the people."[218] That God wills the Temple to be destroyed represents the vengeance of God against the sins of the Jews, which at this point cannot be related to the fact that Jesus is executed in Jerusalem. "He proclaims the razing of the temple and the ruin of the whole people."[219] Thus, when Jesus leaves the Temple, his disciples realize that he is saying farewell to it for the last time, to erect a more splendid Temple in himself. "He had nothing more to do with the temple where everything was contrary."[220]

However, neither the disciples nor any Jew living near or far could believe that the Temple could be destroyed, both because of the promise of God to dwell there forever and because of the scale and opulence of the

Temple being constructed by Herod.[221] The opulence of the Temple there-fore formed an obstacle to prevent the eyes of the Jews and even the disciples from being raised to the greater glory of the Temple in Jesus Christ and his Kingdom. To remove this obstacle, Calvin thinks Jesus predicts the destruc-tion of the Temple, to free the Jews once and for all from the childish cere-monies that come to an end in his death and resurrection. "The destruction of the temple helped the Jews not to be overly-addicted to earthly elements in their cult of shadows."[222] However, the primary reason the Temple had to be destroyed was to punish the Jews for their rejection of Christ and not, as above, for the accumulation of their sins up to the time of Christ. "But there was a particular reason that God determined by a terrible example to be avenged on that race that had rejected his Son and despised the grace he offered them."[223]

In spite of his claim that the coming of Jesus Christ need not entail the destruction of the Temple itself, Calvin develops three reasons why it was necessary for it to be destroyed by divine decree. First, God had already de-parted from the Temple by the time Jesus arrives in it, due to the presump-tuous sin of the people who "were so blinded with a perverse confidence in the outward cult and the temple that they believed they had a hold on God."[224] Second, both the Jews and the disciples were too attached to the beauty of the Herodian Temple to "believe that the magnificent splendor of the present temple would give place to Christ," and so the destruction of the Temple was necessary to remove this obstacle.[225] Third, the destruction of the Temple symbolized the destruction of the whole race of the Jews by God, in vengeance for the intolerable crime of executing the Son of God sent to them. "So having steeped themselves in sacrilege beyond all wicked-ness they continued with crime after crime to bring on themselves every ground for final annihilation."[226] Unlike either the Babylonian captivity or the oppression and defilement under Antiochus IV Epiphanes, the sin of putting Jesus to death means that the Jews "break God's covenant," which means that they in turn are "rejected by God."[227] "The reason for this fearful vengeance was that the desperate wickedness of the people had come to its culmination."[228] Given Calvin's insistence that Jesus Christ is the substance and reality of the covenant made by God with the Jews, it is astonishing to see him describe it as "broken," and the Jews themselves as "rejected by God" and subject to "final annihilation."

Moreover, Calvin thinks that Daniel prophesied this final destruction of the Temple, Jerusalem, and the Jews themselves. Calvin thinks that Daniel speaks of two abominations that cause desolation, the first under Antiochus IV Epiphanes (Dan. 9), and the second after the crucifixion of Jesus (Dan. 12). There is hope for restoration after the first abomination, but there will be no hope for restoration after the second. Calvin thinks that Christ is speaking about this second abomination in his prophecy about the fall of Jerusalem and the Temple. "Christ chose only what suited his purpose: that the end of sacrifices was at hand, and that the abomination was to be placed in the temple, which would be a sign of final desolation."[229] According to Calvin, Titus was sent by God to fulfill this prophecy made by Daniel, of which Jesus had reminded the Jews of his day. "Christ declares that as soon as it is surrounded by its enemies it will be all over, for it is wholly deprived of help from God."[230]

The sacrifices in the Temple are brought to an end by the death of Christ, which is the real sacrifice represented in a shadowy way by the Temple sacrifices. The end of these sacrifices is symbolized by the rending of the veil in the Temple. "Even if the building of the temple were to stand, there could no longer be any service of God there under the accustomed rite, for now, as the substance of the shadows and the reality was fulfilled, all legal types were transformed into spirit."[231] However, it is hard to see how the Temple could stand without undermining the prophecy of Daniel, in Calvin's reading of it, for the cessation of the sacrifices by the death of Christ sets in motion the events leading up to the complete destruction of the Temple, Jerusalem, and the Jews by Titus. Calvin makes this very point in his lectures on Daniel in 1561. "For while Christ passed through the period of his life on earth, he did not put an end to the sacrifices; but after he had offered himself up as a victim, all the rites of the law came to a close."[232] Since the death of Christ fulfills the symbolic sacrifices of the Law, the Temple must be destroyed to free the Jews from their attachment to these childish ceremonies, for "unless God had openly demonstrated it before their eyes, they would never have renounced their sacrifices and rites as mere shadowy representations."[233] Following the end of the sacrifices comes the ultimate profanation of the Temple, after which it and the people will be destroyed beyond any hope of recovery.[234] The reason this destruction was prophesied by Daniel, according to Calvin, was to console the godly after the death of Jesus at the hands of the Jews that one would soon be sent to destroy the Jews to punish them for this crime. Titus again fulfilled this. "Without the slightest doubt, he here signifies that God would inflict dreadful vengeance upon the Jews for their murder of his Christ."[235] The godly are warned that this leader should be in a deluge in order to warn the godly to separate from the Jews at this time, for Titus "should overthrow the city and national polity, and utterly put an end to the priesthood and the race, while all God's favors would at the same time be withdrawn."[236]

The city of Jerusalem, with its mountains, walls, palaces, and Temple, and especially the ark of the covenant, was the most complete and vivid symbol of the presence of God among the Jews, setting before them a living image of Christ in whom the fullness of God dwells bodily. However, when Jesus comes to Jerusalem, he proclaims that God has abandoned the city and the Temple to complete and hopeless destruction, and has withdrawn his presence forever from the Jews. The sacrifices of the Law, from Abel to the time of Jesus, set the death of Jesus before the Jews as the sole source of their access to God. However, the actual death of Jesus in Jerusalem unleashes the eternal wrath of God against the Jews, entailing their complete rejection by God. How can the symbols of the coming Christ give hope to the Jews, when the reality of Christ necessarily entailed their utter and final annihilation? How can Jesus Christ be the substance of the covenant made with Israel, when his appearance brings to fruition the breaking of that covenant? Having worked so hard to establish the correspondence between the symbols and types of Christ in Israel, and the reality of Christ in the flesh, it is astonishing to see Calvin turn Jesus Christ completely against the people to whom he was so vividly represented and exhibited as their only hope and salvation. According to Calvin, by sending Titus to utterly destroy Jerusalem and the Temple, "God determined to make an exceptional impression on our memory in the case of the Jews, that the coming of Christ might shine with clearer light for generations to come."[237] Is this really light? Or does it not cast a shadow over the whole of Calvin's claim that Jesus Christ always was, and always will be, the one hope and source of salvation for the Jews?

CHAPTER 10

The Gospel as the Living Portrait
of Jesus Christ

The glorification of the crucified and buried Jesus Christ begins with his resurrection from the dead and culminates in his ascension into heaven, and his session as King at the right hand of the Father. Even as the suffering and death of Christ represent for Calvin the way Jesus Christ becomes like us so that he can take from us all the evil that separates us from God, so his resurrection and ascension exhibit the way God lavishes upon his humanity everything we lack, so that he might freely bestow these gifts on us. Christ reveals to us his glory, and offers to us all the gifts he has received from the Father, in the Gospel. Even though the Gospel is the Word of Christ that gives rise to faith by hearing (Rom. 10:17), Calvin increasingly describes the Gospel itself as being the visual self-manifestation of Christ and all his benefits. Moreover, given the mutual relation between Word and sign, God appends to the Gospel many forms of visual confirmation, in terms of miracles, visions, and other people as exemplars of grace, as well as the sacraments. All these forms of visual confirmation reinforce Calvin's description of the Gospel as a mirror or living portrait in which Christ exhibits and offers himself to us with all his benefits.

1. The Exhibition of Christ in the Mirror or Portrait of the Gospel

In his preface to Olivetan's New Testament of 1535, Calvin describes the Gospel as the joyful news of our adoption as children of God in Jesus Christ.[1] In particular, the Gospel reveals to us that the powers of God that we lost in Adam are now offered to us for our salvation in Jesus Christ. "Thus, he is our only Savior, to whom we owe our redemption, peace, righteousness, sanctification, salvation, and life."[2] The presence of these benefits in Christ also fulfills the shadows, figures, and types of the Law, which exhibited Christ and his powers to the fathers under the Law. The Gospel is therefore the presentation and exhibition of all of these blessings in the person of Jesus Christ himself.[3] This description of the Gospel as the fulfillment of the shadows of the Law and the presentation and exhibition of all the blessings of God in Christ is echoed in the *Psychopannychia* of 1534/36, in Calvin's description of how Christ made a proclamation to the spirits in prison (1 Pet. 3:19), for "the virtue of the redemption obtained by Christ appeared and was exhibited to the spirits of the dead."[4]

In the *Institutes* of 1536, Calvin reinforces this understanding of the Gospel as the visual exhibition of otherwise hidden blessings by turning to the description of faith in Hebrews 11:1: "Now faith is the assurance of things hoped for, the conviction of things not seen." According to Calvin, this is as if to say that faith "is the vision of things which are not seen, the perception of things obscure, the presence of things absent, the proof of things hidden. For God's mysteries pertaining to our salvation are of the sort that cannot in themselves and by their own nature (as is said) be discerned; but we gaze on them only in his Word."[5] This passage from Hebrews allows Calvin to introduce one of his favorite dialectical relationships—that in the word of the Gospel faith beholds the invisible gifts of God in Jesus Christ. In his Catechism of 1538, Calvin describes the Gospel as the way God the Father offers Jesus Christ to us, in whom, in contrast to the Law, God appears gracious towards us.[6] Calvin will therefore describe faith as the perpetual gaze of the faithful on Christ alone.[7]

In the *Institutes* of 1539, Calvin describes the Gospel as the way God offers Christ to us, as the fountain of every good thing.[8] Calvin makes the same point in his Reply to Sadoleto of the same year, when the pastor testifies before God that he had only tried to fully display the virtue and blessings of Christ.[9] Because Christ is the living image of God the Father, faith beholds the face of God graciously inclined towards us, even as that vision of God becomes clearer and closer over time.[10] Calvin echoes this point in his commentary on Romans of 1540. "When we first taste the Gospel we do indeed see the countenance of God turned graciously towards us, but at a distance. The more our knowledge of true piety increases, we see the grace of God with greater clarity and more familiarity, as though he were coming nearer to us."[11] Faith therefore beholds the gracious face of God in the Gospel of Jesus Christ, in whom we find the treasure of every good thing God wishes to give to needy sinners.

To support his claim that faith is the increasingly clear and more intimate vision of the face of God, Calvin turns to Paul's description of faith in 2 Corinthians 3:18, "when he declares that through the gospel, with uncovered face and no veil intervening, we behold God's glory with such effect that we are transformed into his very likeness."[12] In light of this passage, Calvin begins to describe the Gospel as the mirror in which we behold the face of God in Jesus Christ, by which we are increasingly transformed into the image we are contemplating. He uses this passage to show how faith necessarily leads to regeneration and newness of life by the re-creation of the image of God within the faithful.[13]

Along with the transforming contemplation of the mirror of the Gospel, Calvin turns to Galatians to describe the Gospel as the visual portrayal of Christ crucified. He allows that the Supper may in this sense be called a sacrifice, because it, like the Gospel, represents the cross of Christ before our very eyes. "Nevertheless, we do not deny that the sacrifice of Christ is so shown there that the spectacle of the cross is almost set before our eyes—just as the apostle says that Christ was crucified before the eyes of the Galatians when the preaching of the cross was set before them [Gal. 3:1]."[14] In the third edition of the *Institutes* in 1543, Calvin again turns to Galatians 3:1, to show how the faithful should see Christ crucified in the preaching of the Gospel and not in images of the cross made by human beings: "But whence, I pray you, this stupidity if not because they are defrauded of that doctrine which alone was fit to instruct them? Paul testifies that by the true preaching of the gospel 'Christ is depicted before our eyes as crucified.'"[15] By understanding the Gospel as the living portrayal of Christ, Calvin increasingly shifts the focus from the exhibition of the power and benefits of Christ to the self-representation of Christ himself. When Paul speaks of the Gospel as "concerning his Son" (Rom. 1:3), Calvin remarks, "In this important passage Paul teaches us that the whole Gospel is contained in Christ. To move even a step from Christ means to withdraw oneself from the Gospel."[16]

In his commentary on 2 Corinthians of 1546, Calvin continues to develop the idea of the Gospel as a painting that depicts Christ. He describes false ministers as those who paint Christ in various shapes and colors. Some "present Christ in different shapes at different times, like Proteus," whereas others, "to please men, present Christ under different disguises."[17] In opposition to these distorted representations of Christ, Paul claims that Christ must always be represented in terms of the Yes of God that appears in him.[18] In his commentary on Galatians of 1548, Calvin compares the clarity and forcefulness of the Gospel to a living portrait of Jesus Christ himself. "Therefore he tells them that his teaching was so clear that it was not so much naked teaching as the living and express image of Christ."[19] The Gospel Paul preached to the Galatians was like a portrait of Christ crucified painted in exact correspondence to his appearance.[20] Consequently, they should have been as moved and affected by his preaching as they would have been had they witnessed the crucifixion in person.[21] According to Calvin, such a forceful and vivid representation is not due to the rhetorical ability of Paul but rather to the power of the Holy Spirit in his preaching.[22] All preachers are called to paint Christ crucified before the eyes of their congregations, so that they also become eyewitnesses of his death.[23] As he had in the 1543 *Institutes,* Calvin contrasts the vividness of such preaching with the human desire to make representations of Christ crucified in crucifixes, statues, and paintings. "When the Church has such painters as these she no longer needs wood and stone, that is, dead images, she no longer needs any pictures."[24] Calvin ascribes the emergence of pictures, statues, and other images to the decline in the forcefulness of preaching, which no longer vividly portrayed Christ crucified, leaving the congregations to look elsewhere.[25]

Calvin continues to describe the preaching of the Gospel as the portrait of Christ in commentaries after Galatians. For instance, in his comments on Colossians of the same year, he says that the best way of retaining proper doctrine "is to set Christ before our eyes, just as he is with all his blessings, that his power may be truly perceived."[26] To know Christ rightly, he advises his readers to observe carefully "in what colors Paul depicts Christ to us."[27] When Hebrews speaks of the confirmation of the covenant by the sprinkling of blood on the people, Calvin hearkens back to the portrait of the crucifixion in the Gospel to claim that the promises of God are similarly sealed for us "when we not only hear God speaking but see Christ offering himself as a pledge of what is said," so that "when the Gospel is preached his sacred blood falls on us along with the words."[28] Calvin also interprets the saying of Jesus in the Gospel of John, that the Son of Man must be lifted up as was the bronze serpent in the wilderness, with reference to the way Christ is publicly portrayed as crucified in the proclamation of the Gospel.[29] Thus, when Paul tells us that the sole object of our knowledge is to know "God's love which is exhibited to us in Christ," and that "all the treasures of wisdom and knowledge are hidden in Christ, he does not invent some unknown Christ but one whom by his preaching he portrayed to the life, so that, as he says in Gal. 3:1, he is seen as it were crucified before our eyes."[30]

Since the preaching of the Gospel portrays Christ crucified to the life before the eyes of the faithful, Calvin does not think that the saying of Jesus to Thomas, "Blessed are they who have not seen and yet believe" (John 20:29), can be taken so as to exclude all seeing from faith, for Christ also blesses the eyes that see what they see (Matt. 13:16). According to Calvin, those who see Christ in the preaching of the Gospel see him more clearly and more vividly than did those who saw him in person. "For today we behold Christ in the Gospel no less than if he stood with us. In this sense Paul tells the Galatians that he was crucified before their eyes."[31] In the preaching of the Gospel, faith sees the Christ who cannot be seen. If we wish to discern his presence among us, and to see him with profit, we must turn to the Gospel that portrays him to us and not to paintings or other images.

Calvin even uses the metaphor of painting to describe the way the four Gospels themselves represent Christ to us. First of all, the proper representation of Christ will combine his words and his works in an inseparable relationship, as Luke indicates when he says that in his gospel he "wrote about all that Jesus did and taught from the beginning" (Acts 1:1). "From this we must note that those who simply know the bare history have not the Gospel, unless there is added a knowledge of his teaching, which reveals the fruit of the acts of Christ. For this is a holy knot, which may not be dissolved."[32] Even as the acts of Christ seal the truth of his teaching, so also the teaching of Christ reveals the meaning of his miracles, death, and resurrection.[33] Moreover, Calvin distinguishes between the representation of Christ's body in the Synoptic Gospels and the exhibition of his soul in the Gospel of John. He advises his readers to begin with the Gospel of John before reading the other Gospels. "For whoever grasps the power of Christ as it is here graphically portrayed, will afterwards read with advantage what the others relate about the manifested Redeemer."[34]

Taken together, all four Gospels form the full and complete representation of Christ as the Redeemer: "it is right and proper to use the word Evangelist of those who represent before our eyes Christ, sent by the Father, that our faith may recognize him the author of the life of blessedness."[35] The advantage of the Synoptic Gospels is that they hold together the portrayal of Christ's life with the foreshadowing of that life in the Law and the prophets, which forms as inseparable a relationship in the portrayal of Christ as does his words and works.[36] Since the Evangelists were interested above all else in setting forth an accurate and vivid portrayal of Christ, the reader should not be surprised to find events narrated in one place in Luke that are found at another time in Matthew. "The Evangelists had no intention of so putting their narrative together as always to keep the exact order of events, but to bring the whole pattern together to produce a kind of mirror or screen image of those features most useful for the understanding of Christ."[37]

Calvin also elaborates on the way in which the image of Christ is beheld in the mirror of the Gospel for our contemplation. In his commentary on 2 Corinthians of 1546, Calvin interprets Paul's description of our transformative contemplation of Christ in the mirror of the Gospel in the following way. "He uses the similitude of the image in the mirror to make three points: first, that we need not fear obscurity when we approach the Gospel, for in it God shows his unveiled face; second, that this should not be a dead and fruitless contemplation, for through it we should be transformed into God's image; third, that neither of these things happen all at once, but by continual progress we increase both in the knowledge of God and in conformity to his image."[38] If the Gospel as a living portrait emphasizes the way Evangelists and preachers accurately depict Christ to the life, the Gospel as the mirror in which the image of Christ may be contemplated emphasizes the Gospel as the self-manifestation of Christ. When Paul speaks of the blindness of whose who do not rightly behold the light of the Gospel, Calvin paraphrases Paul as saying, "'For nothing,' he says, 'appears in it but Christ and he does not appear obscurely but shines forth clearly.'"[39] Paul describes the Gospel as the glory of Christ because it is "the Gospel in which Christ's glory shines."[40]

The description of the Gospel as the manifestation of the glory of Christ also allows Calvin to emphasize the transforming power of the Gospel when it is properly contemplated.[41] This allows him to speak of two forms of the self-manifestation of Jesus Christ, the first in his flesh as he walked on earth and the second in the Gospel. It is only the second that has the power to transform lives into the image of God that they behold in the Gospel.

Hence, when Paul speaks of when the goodness and loving-kindness of God our Savior appeared (Titus 3:4), Calvin insists he is speaking of the self-manifestation of Christ in the Gospel. "Paul is not speaking as usual of that manifestation of Christ when he came as man into the world, but of his manifestation in the Gospel, when he offers and reveals himself in a special way to the elect. At Christ's first coming Paul was not renewed."[42]

Moreover, Calvin also speaks of two forms of contemplating Christ in the mirror of the Gospel, one of which is superficial, the other of which is transformative. When James speaks of hearers of the Law who are not doers as those who look into the mirror but then forget what they saw, Calvin interprets the mirror as the Gospel, along the lines of 2 Corinthians 3:18. "Certainly the teaching of heaven is like a looking-glass in which God allows us to gaze upon himself—but in such a style that we are transfigured into his likeness [cf. Paul at 2 Cor. 3:18]."[43] The person who is not transformed by this contemplation of God in the mirror does not allow what he sees to penetrate into the affections of the heart.[44] On the other hand, when James speaks of the one who looks into the perfect Law, Calvin takes this to mean "the perception which searches the depths, and transforms us into the likeness of God."[45] To show how the contemplation of the glory of Christ in the Gospel should transform us in the affections of our hearts, Calvin draws a parallel from Plato's description of the contemplation of the Beautiful. "Granted that Plato was groping in the darkness; but he denied that the beautiful, which he imagined, could be known without ravishing a man with the admiration of itself—this in *Phaedrus* and elsewhere."[46] Since the glory of Christ shines in the Gospel, and manifests to us his love and goodness, Calvin thinks that it is impossible that we should not only be enlightened in our minds but also transformed in our affections.[47]

Because of its transformative power, Jesus Christ manifests himself more effectively in the Gospel than he did when he was on earth, accenting again Calvin's dialectic of physical absence with spiritual presence and power. For instance, when five thousand believe the preaching of the apostles in the Temple even though the apostles were arrested for preaching it (Acts 4:4), Calvin says, "By the effectiveness of this teaching Christ showed that he was alive more clearly than if he had offered his body to be handled and to be seen by the eyes of men."[48] This is why, according to Calvin, Jesus told his disciples that when he leaves them they will do greater works than he did when he was among them (John 14:12). "Now Christ's ascension was soon followed by the wonderful conversion of the world, in which his divinity was displayed more powerfully than when he lived among men."[49] Calvin makes a similar observation when Simeon looks on Christ and says that his eyes have seen the salvation of God (Luke 2:30). According to Calvin, Christ may be seen better by us now that Christ is absent from us in the body and is seated at the right hand of the Father.[50] Thus, when Jesus pronounces the eyes that see what they see blessed, Calvin thinks he is not speaking of fleshly vision but of the perception of the glory of God in Christ, "because the lively image of God shines upon them, and in it they perceive their salvation and full blessedness."[51] Since the living image of God in Christ appears before us in the mirror of the Gospel, our eyes also may be blessed by beholding Christ, for "the perfection of wisdom, righteousness and life which was once revealed in him shines constantly in the Gospel."[52]

Since we behold Christ, as it were, face-to-face in the Gospel, it is not only possible for us to look upon and contemplate Christ in this mirror, but Calvin also suggests that it is possible, and in fact necessary, for Christ to look back upon us. Calvin notes the way Peter did not return to himself after having denied Christ until Christ looked upon him. "So he had to meet Christ's eyes to come to himself."[53] According to Calvin, this experience is not unique to Peter but is shared by all the godly. "Which of us does not neglect with deaf ear and unconcern—not the many and various songs of birds (and yet they incite us to glorify God)—but the actual voice of God, which in Law and Gospel clearly and distinctly resounds for our learning?"[54] Hearing the Law and the Gospel does not have the power to awaken us from our stupor, which, according to Calvin, goes "on and on, until he grants us a sight of himself. This alone converts the hearts of men."[55] Thus not only for Peter, but for everyone, "repentance starts from the look the Lord gives."[56]

Ultimately, according to Calvin, the transformative contemplation of Christ in the mirror of the Gospel, as well as Christ's transformative beholding of us, depends not only on the clarity of the self-manifestation of Christ in the Gospel but also on the interior illumination of the Holy Spirit. Paul says as much when he says of the transformative vision of Christ in the Gospel, "for this comes from the Lord, the Spirit" (2 Cor. 3:18). According to Calvin, Paul means to remind us "how the whole power of the Gospel depends upon its being made life-giving to us by the power of the Holy Spirit."[57] Calvin therefore distinguishes between two forms of the manifestation of the glory of Christ, one in the Gospel and the other by the power of the Spirit: "in our redemption he shines forth upon us in the person of his Son by the Gospel, but that would be in vain, for we are blind, unless he were also to illuminate our minds by his Spirit."[58] Calvin claims that this is why Paul went blind after his vision of the glory of Christ, so that he might learn that his power to see comes from Christ and not from himself.[59] This explains why the faithful can see Christ now, even though he is absent from them in terms of his body, for the spiritual life of Christ lives in them. "But as soon as a man begins to live by the Spirit, he is at once given eyes to see Christ."[60]

The same blindness afflicted those who beheld Christ in the body, according to Calvin. The problem for them was compounded by the offensive appearance of Christ, as his divinity was deeply hidden and as it were at rest beneath the weakness of the flesh. Therefore, those who rightly beheld the glory of Christ, such as Simeon, did so only by being given the eyes of faith by the Holy Spirit. "So the Spirit of God illuminated his eyes by faith, that he might perceive the glory of the Son of God, in the miserable and unworthy appearance."[61] This is why Jesus tells Peter that flesh and blood could never have revealed to him that he is the Christ, the Son of the living God (Matt. 16:17), for "all human senses fail in this respect until God opens our eyes to see his glory in Christ."[62] According to Calvin, the most astonishing example of the illumination of the Spirit takes place during Luke's portrayal of the crucifixion. As Jesus is about to die, with his divinity completely at rest and deeply concealed by the weakness of his suffering and deeply afflicted humanity, one of the thieves nevertheless recognizes him as his King and Savior. According to Calvin, even if the thief had followed Christ before this time, so that he had faith in him due to his teaching and miracles, the offensive appearance of his death would have erased the efficacy of such faith, leaving him unable to behold the glory of Christ at this moment.[63] However, this thief, who by a career of killing had attempted to extinguish his conscience, suddenly penetrates beneath the contrary appearance of Christ to see the glory and power beneath his ignominy and humiliation, "and proclaims him author of life in the hour of dying."[64] According to Calvin, this should make all of us feel deeply ashamed for being so slow to see the glory of Christ, for this thief lacked all the manifestations of his glory we now enjoy in the resurrection, ascension, and Gospel.[65] The thief on the cross is therefore one of the most vivid examples of the illuminating power of the Spirit of which Calvin knows: "so much the more admiration is due to the grace of the Holy Spirit that gave such a shining illustration of itself."[66]

2. The Visual Confirmation of the Gospel in Miracles

The confirmation of the truth of the Gospel by miracles is initially addressed by Calvin in the context of the demand by their Roman opponents that the evangelicals produce miracles to prove the truth of their Gospel. In his preface to the 1536 edition of the *Institutes,* Calvin addresses this demand directly. "In demanding miracles of us, they act dishonestly. For we are not forging some new gospel, but are retaining that very gospel whose truth all the miracles that Jesus Christ and his disciples ever wrought serve to confirm."[67] Calvin would hold to this position for the rest of his theological career. The evangelicals do not need to produce miracles to confirm their teaching, for they are simply trying to recover the Gospel that has already been confirmed by the miracles of Christ and the apostles. The implication is that those who produce new miracles are also inventing new teaching, which they seek to establish over and above the Gospel by such prodigies. "But, compared with us, they have a strange power: even to this day they can confirm their faith by continual miracles!"[68] According to Calvin, whenever miracles are produced to establish doctrine that goes beyond the Gospel, they are not the work of God but rather the deceitful tricks of Satan, set forth to deceive the simple-minded and unlearned.[69] Miracles must therefore be assessed according to the Word of God and not according to their apparent power or significance.[70]

In his commentary on 1 Corinthians of 1546, Calvin notes how the Jews kept demanding signs, even though Christ and the apostles had already confirmed the truth of the Gospel by the miracles they performed. "For there were no bounds to their curiosity, and their persistent demanding; and as often as they had obtained miracles, they were none the better for them."[71] In his commentary on Hebrews of 1549, Calvin claims that the Gospel was in fact confirmed by the miracles of Christ and the apostles, as though God had set God's seal on the truth of their preaching. "Those, therefore, who do not reverently receive the Gospel, commended as it is by such evidences, do wrong not only to the Word of God, but also to his works."[72] The sight of miracles is meant to confirm the message of the apostles that we hear, "since God's miracles as it were harmonize with the voice of men by their complementary evidences."[73] Once again, Calvin contrasts the right use of miracles, which is "to serve the establishing of the Gospel," with the alleged miracles of Rome, "by which they distort their own fictitious miracles to weaken the truth of God."[74] According to Calvin, "in the miracles which God displays there is sure enough corroboration both of the doctrine and of the ministry if only our eyes are open to see."[75] If we are fooled by the false miracles of Satan, the fault is not with God but with our own blindness. "But whoever has a pure heart perceives God with the purity of inward vision as often as he shows himself."[76]

Since miracles are performed by God to establish the truth of the Gospel, the perception of a miracle per se does not profit the beholder but can lead him or her to stupefied confusion. Commenting on the "wonder and amazement" experienced by those who saw the lame man walk at the word of Peter, Calvin says, "Let us therefore learn reverently to consider the works of God, that our wonder at them may serve as an entrance for doctrine."[77] There is therefore an inseparable and mutual relationship between miracles and doctrine. The miracle prepares for or confirms faith in the doctrine, even as the doctrine reveals to us the meaning and purpose of the miracle. "In brief, the one is not to be separated from the other. Experience is rich in evidence to this."[78] This is why, according to Calvin, Luke says that the Lord "testified to the word of his grace by granting signs and wonders to be done through them [the apostles]" (Acts 14:3). "Hence Luke says at this point that the Gospel was established by miracles, not that some confused religion might possess the minds of men, but that through the teaching of Paul they might be brought to the pure worship of God."[79]

Calvin does allow that God could in fact work miracles disjoined from the teaching of the Gospel. However, even were this to happen, "in the first place it was a rare occurrence, and secondly a very meager result followed from them. For the most part, however, God has wrought miracles, so that by them the world might know him, not simply or in his bare majesty but in the Word."[80] It is hard to discern if Calvin is speaking hypothetically, or if he has particular miracles in mind. Calvin does not identify Rome with the performance of bare miracles, though, but with the attempt to establish new doctrine not found in the Gospel with their miracles more recently performed. Now that the Gospel has been established by miracles, we should judge all subsequent miracles by the doctrine they are said to confirm. "Now we must see whether the Gospel commands us to invoke the dead, to burn incense to idols, to transfer the grace of Christ to alleged saints, to undertake votive pilgrimages, to devise profane acts of worship, of which there is never a mention in the Word of God. Yet there is nothing less consonant with the Gospel than that these superstitions should have place."[81]

Calvin is well aware, however, that some of the miracles done by the apostles do in fact seem to support one of the devotional practices of the Roman Church, namely, the veneration of relics as possessing unusual spiritual power. "God did extraordinary miracles through Paul, so that when the handkerchiefs or aprons that had touched his skin were brought to the sick, their diseases left them, and the evil spirits came out of them" (Acts 19:11–12). According to Calvin, God did this "in order that the authority of his teaching might be more certain," so that "those who had never seen the man [Paul], might reverently embrace his teaching, even though he was not on the spot."[82] Calvin does not challenge the ability of God to show God's power through inanimate objects that had been touched by people with spiritual power, which is one of the claims lying behind relic veneration, but rather rejects the purpose to which the Roman Church puts such objects. "That is why the Papists are all the more absurd, when they twist this verse in favor of their relics, as if Paul in fact sent his handkerchiefs so that men might venerate and kiss, as in the Papacy men reverence Francis' shoes and breeches, Rose's girdle, Saint Margaret's comb, and similar trifles."[83] Calvin does not address the question that begs to be asked at this point, however, which is whether the power that is said to reside in such objects might be used to confirm the truth of the Gospel in Calvin's own day, even as the handkerchief of Paul did in his day.

Since Calvin claims that the purpose of miracles is to confirm the truth of the Gospel, he clearly seems to prefer that miracles come to an end once the truth of the Gospel has been established. This is not due to a metaphysical claim that God cannot act directly in the world, for, as we have seen, Calvin thinks that countless miracles take place under our eyes every day, beginning with our birth. Rather, it reflects Calvin's suspicion of the uses to which the Roman Church put the miracles it claimed had been performed since the time of the apostles, to give divine support for devotional practices to which Calvin strenuously objected as contradicting the Gospel. Thus, when Jesus tells his disciples after the resurrection, "And these signs will accompany those who believe" (Mark 16:17), Calvin ponders whether Jesus meant this for perpetuity, or for a definite time. "Though Christ does not say exactly whether he wished this to be an occasional gift, or one to abide in the Church forever, yet it is more likely that miracles were only promised for that time, to add light to the new and as yet unknown Gospel."[84] Calvin thinks that the gift of performing miracles might have been lost as punishment for human ingratitude, but thinks it more likely that "the real purpose for which miracles were appointed was to give enough assurance for the Gospel teaching at the outset."[85] He supports this claim by an empirical and historical observation regarding the gradual disappearance of miracles, without citing sources in support of this observation.[86] The purpose of the cessation of miracles soon becomes clear: it allows Calvin to distinguish between the legitimate and divine miracles of the apostles and the deceptive and satanic delusions of the Roman Church.[87] Calvin does not seem to be able to conceive of a miracle after the time of the apostles that could confirm the Gospel, as he identifies them entirely with the attempt of the Roman Church to give divine sanction to devotional practices that cannot be found in Scripture.

3. TEMPORARY SIGNS OF PERPETUAL GRACE

Calvin thought that God exhibited unusually vivid signs of God's grace at the time of the emergence of the Gospel that were meant to reveal to the Church the perpetual gifts God would bestow upon it, without the signs themselves being perpetual. In a way, the miracles that confirm the Gospel could be included within this class of temporary signs, as they visually manifest the divine sealing of the truth of the Gospel for all generations, and hence do not need to be repeated. Another of these signs is the visible manifestation of the Holy Spirit on the apostles at Pentecost. The appearance of the Spirit in cloven tongues of fire was meant to stir up the senses of the disciples, but again "it was not so much for their benefit as for ours, even as the appearance of the cloven and fiery tongues had its meaning rather for us and for the universal Church than for them."[88] Following the analogy of the sign to the thing signified, Calvin claims that the tongues of fire appeared on the apostles "to show forth the working of the Holy Spirit in the apostles which afterwards followed," whereas the fire itself symbolized "the efficacy which the word of the apostles would carry."[89] The sign itself was not meant to accompany the preaching of the Gospel from thenceforth. Rather, "the Lord gave the Holy Spirit once to his disciples in visible shape, that we may be assured that the Church will never lack his invisible and hidden grace."[90] Similarly, when the apostles prayed to the Lord for the requisite boldness to proclaim the Word of God, the place where they were gathered was shaken (Acts 4:31). According to Calvin, this was a sign that had the "effect in letting the faithful know the presence of God is with them. It is nothing else than a symbol of the presence of God."[91] Calvin acknowledges that such symbols are rarely given to confirm prayer, but this one was "a sign of the perpetual benefit of prayer, set before us as an example."[92]

One of the most prominent temporary signs given at the dawn of the Gospel was the visible bestowal of the Holy Spirit on those who were baptized. "Because the sending of the Holy Spirit in so spectacular a manner was a symbol of the hidden grace wherewith the Lord continuously imparts his elect," Calvin thinks that it was not shown for the benefit of the apostles alone, but for the benefit of all the faithful, for "there was revealed as in a mirror the universal grace of Christ towards his Church, while he poured forth the gifts of his Spirit in full measure."[93] Moreover, the visible bestowal of the Spirit by the laying on of hands was meant "to establish forever the authority of his Gospel, and at the same time to testify that the Spirit will always be the Governor and Director of the faithful."[94] The visible bestowal of the Spirit was also necessary to confirm the calling of the Gentiles, which took even the apostles by surprise.[95] Even though the preaching of the Gospel is no longer established by such visible signs, "this visible symbol represents to us, as if in a picture, how effective the preaching of the Gospel is as an instrument of the divine power."[96]

Calvin is aware that the apostles were able to see many different things that no longer appear to those who follow them, but again, this is to give us a visible sign of a perpetual gift in the Church. For instance, we no longer see angels, nor can we see Christ ascending into heaven, as did the apostles. However, for Calvin, these appearances were meant to be signs that the Kingdom of heaven has been opened for all the faithful in Christ, especially for those who no longer see such realities. "But all the signs by which God shows himself present with us relate to this opening of heaven, especially when God communicates himself to us to be our life."[97] The gift of prophecy, in terms of predicting future events, also emerged during the time of the apostles, only to disappear again, in order to reveal that the emergence of the Gospel begins the period of the restoration of all things, and was thus "a sign of a more complete situation."[98] Finally, the saints who were raised from their graves at the death of Jesus were only alive on earth for a short while, "that as in a mirror or picture they should manifest the power of Christ. Since God wished in their person to confirm among the living the hope of life in heaven, there should be nothing strange if once they had performed this task they had again rested in their tombs."[99]

4. Confirmation of the Gospel in Visions

Calvin describes visions and dreams as the usual mode of divine self-revelation in the Law and the prophets, following Numbers 12:6. One would think, therefore, that this mode of revelation would come to an end in the new economy of the Gospel. However, Calvin speaks of God confirming faith in the Gospel by visions in a way that directly echoes his discussion of the Law, without any observation about the difference between the two economies of divine self-manifestation. For instance, when the Lord speaks to Ananias "in a vision" (Acts 9:10), Calvin makes the following observation: "Vision here means some symbol that was placed before his eyes to testify to the presence of God. For the use of visions is duly to confirm the majesty of the Word so that it might obtain credence among men."[100] Calvin observes how this mode of visual confirmation was also used with the prophets, without distinguishing between the prophets and the Gospel.[101] The only qualification Calvin makes is to distinguish the visions of God from the delusions of Satan, as he did with prophetic visions.[102]

God uses visions not only to confirm the Word of God but also to reveal new truths to the disciples. Thus, when God wills that the Gospel be preached to the Gentiles, Peter is shown a vision three times of unclean animals, which he is told to kill and eat (Acts 10:9–16). According to Calvin, God does this to overcome the understandable resistance that Peter, a devout Jew, would have to eating unclean food.[103] This vision is significant not only for Peter but also for those following him, as the inclusion of the Gentiles in the Church is one of the great mysteries of the Gospel. "For when it teaches that the separation between Jews and Gentiles was only temporary, it is just as if God proclaimed from heaven that he is gathering all peoples of the world into his grace, so that he may be God of all."[104] However, even though Peter is shown the vision three times, and is taught by the Word from heaven to kill and eat, Calvin claims that the meaning of the vision and teaching were not clear until the Spirit interpreted their meaning to him.[105] Moreover, once Peter goes to Cornelius the next day, he learns that Cornelius also had been shown a vision while he had been praying the previous day. Calvin thinks that the mind is less disposed to hallucinations while fasting and praying than it otherwise might be, which enhances the reliability of the vision.[106] The visions of Peter and Cornelius therefore both reveal and confirm, both for themselves and for us, that the calling of the Gentiles to join the Jews in the fellowship of the Gospel in fact comes from God and not from human opinion. Visions therefore seem to play as crucial a role in the confirmation of the Gospel as they did in the confirmation of the Law and the Prophets.

Paul himself has a vision in the night in which he receives a call to go to Macedonia (Acts 16:9). Calvin notes the way that God uses different forms of revelation in accommodation to the situation at hand, making it clear that visions are an acceptable form of revelation in the time of the Gospel.[107] This observation sounds as though Calvin thinks that visions take place after the apostolic period, including possibly in his own day, or even in his own experience. Calvin notes that the vision was clearly distinguished from the delusions of Satan, for Paul immediately took the vision to be a calling from God, without any adjoining Word. Visions from God have the distinguishing marks of the Spirit, whereas those from Satan lack these.[108] According to Calvin, Satan used such a naked vision to deceive Brutus, showing that visions are an issue outside of the economy of the Law and the Gospel.[109] On the other hand, Calvin narrates the account given in Josephus of a vision of the high priest in Jerusalem shown to Alexander the Great, which kept him from destroying Jerusalem once he saw the high priest in person for "he was struck as if he had seen God appearing to him from heaven."[110] The apostles also held out the legitimate possibility of such visions, for when Jesus appeared to them in Jerusalem, they thought they were seeing a vision of the resurrection and not the risen Lord himself.[111] God also spoke with Paul in a vision while he was in Corinth.[112] However, Calvin notes that "it was not an everyday experience for Paul to have visions."[113]

Faith may also be confirmed by visions of Jesus Christ himself. The most vivid example of such confirmation comes during the stoning of Stephen. When it is clear that he is going to be put to death for his profession of faith, he turns his eyes away from the appearance of death that surrounds him and directs them intently to heaven. According to Calvin, Christ appears to him at once, so that, "trusting to a vision of Christ, he composes himself, and in dying triumphs in a splendid victory over death."[114] Calvin does not think that the ability to see Christ this way is limited to the time of the apostles, for he tells his readers that "since we are bound too much to the earth, it is no wonder that Christ does not show himself to us."[115] Stephen does not see Jesus by the power of his natural vision but is rather given "other than earthly eyes" to penetrate all the way to the glory of God. Calvin takes this as an indication that all of us could attain to this sort of vision were we intent enough on directing our eyes to heaven.[116] We may not necessarily be given a vision of Jesus at the right hand of the Father, but we will in fact be given a vision of the presence of Christ within us. "And this way of seeing ought to be enough for us, since by his power and grace God not only shows that he is near us, but also proves that he dwells within us."[117] However, not even Stephen saw Jesus in his true glory, "but only as much as the capacity of man could bear. For that immensity cannot be comprehended by the measure of a created being."[118]

Paul is also given a vision of the glory of Christ, but again in accommodation to his limited human capacities, so that he might know that in Christ he had to do with God.[119] When Paul narrates the account of this vision to King Agrippa, he says that it happened at midday, to remove the suspicion that it might have been an apparition. "For although he was overcome by fear and fell to the ground, yet he hears a voice distinctly, he asks who is speaking, he understands the reply that is given; and these are signs of a mind in good order."[120] For Calvin, visions of Christ played a crucial role both in confirming the faith of Stephen before his death and in calling Paul to faith in the Gospel. Far from being limited to the mode of revelation under the Law, Calvin holds out to his readers the hope that Christ will also appear within them when they to turn their eyes and hearts to heaven with as much intensity as they can.

5. INDIVIDUALS AS EXEMPLARS OF GRACE TO ALL

In his commentary on 1 Timothy of 1548, Calvin notes how Paul supports his claim that Jesus Christ came into the world to save sinners by holding himself up as the foremost of sinners. Calvin thinks that "by giving in Paul a pledge of his grace, Christ has called all sinners to a sure expectation of obtaining forgiveness."[121] The change of Paul from a ferocious enemy of the Gospel to one of the foremost apostles should give all sinners confidence that Christ is willing to do the same for them.[122] God wanted to display the example of grace in Paul as widely as possible, to exhibit a visible example of the power of grace to be found in Christ "as though on an illustrious and elevated theater, so that no one should doubt that if only he comes to Christ in faith, he may obtain pardon. All our distrust is removed when we see in Paul a visible type of that grace which we seek."[123]

Calvin sees a similar example of grace in the Samaritan woman by the well. Like Paul, the woman does not exhibit any signs of godliness when

Christ approaches her, but rather seems to be living a life of manifest sinfulness.[124] Calvin sees in this woman a mirror held before all of us, which should manifest to us the fact that God does not call us based on any prior worthiness on our part.[125] The same kind of example is set before our eyes by the calling of Matthew, the tax collector.[126] In concert with Paul and the Samaritan woman, "Matthew is a witness and preacher of the grace revealed in Christ, and also a testimonial and example of it."[127] The vision of such examples confirms before our eyes that Christ does not call the worthy, but rather the greatest of sinners, so that we might approach the throne of grace with more confidence.

6. CONFIRMATION OF THE GOSPEL IN THE SACRAMENTS

The primary visual confirmation of the Gospel is to be found in the sacraments, according to Calvin. Calvin first addresses the meaning and use of the sacraments in the first edition of the *Institutes*. Calvin defines a sacrament as "an outward sign by which the Lord represents and attests to us his good will toward us to sustain the weakness of our faith. Another definition: a testimony of God's grace, declared to us by an outward symbol."[128] A sacrament is therefore the visual representation of the grace and favor of God in an external symbol. Moreover, according to Calvin, a sacrament is always joined to a preceding promise, as subsequent confirmation of the promise, "to make it as it were more evident to us."[129] A sacrament therefore gives visual and symbolic testimony to the grace of God that has already been declared to us in the promise. The visual representation of grace is necessary given the ignorance and infirmity that afflicts the faithful, and represents the accommodation of God to our earthly and finite capacities.[130] To accentuate the confirming function of sacraments, Calvin will call them "seals" that confirm the truth of the Word for us and "symbols of the covenant" that give visual ratification to the covenant.[131] As such, they are "exercises which make us more certain of the trustworthiness of God's Word."[132]

Sacraments are therefore visual images and representations of the invisible spiritual realities offered to us in the promises of God, by which the Lord descends to our capacity in order to lead us back to God. Calvin endorses Augustine's description of a sacrament as "'a visible word' for the reason that it represents God's promises as painted in a picture and sets them before our sight, portrayed graphically and in the manner of images."[133] Calvin adopts another visual metaphor to describe the way sacraments represent the grace of God before our eyes, by calling them "mirrors in which we may contemplate the riches of God's grace, which he lavishes upon us."[134] As visual words or mirrors of God's abundant grace, the sacraments set before our eyes the same grace and mercy that the promise declares to our ears, to establish us in faith. The created realities by which God represents God's grace do not have this representational capacity of themselves but only as the Word of God marks them out as proofs and seals of the promise.[135] Since Calvin is especially interested in the "sacraments which the Lord willed to be ordinary in his church," he claims that such sacramental representation is given in ceremonies, "Or (if you prefer) the signs here given are ceremonies."[136]

Calvin acknowledges that neither the promise nor the sacraments are efficacious without the illumination of the Holy Spirit, but he denies that this makes either the Word or the sacraments superfluous.[137] According to Calvin, we cannot be established in faith until we not only hear the grace of God with our ears but also see the grace of God with our eyes, even though neither hearing nor seeing is of any use without the illumination of the Holy Spirit. Since sacraments are intended to lead us back to God, Calvin claims that the illuminating power of the Spirit is not bound to the symbols, but rather "God uses means and instruments which he himself sees to be expedient."[138] Thus, when the sacraments "set God's promises before our eyes to be looked upon," we should not confine our attention to them, but rather, "laying aside all things, both our faith and our confession ought to rise up to him, the author of the sacraments and all things."[139]

Both the Word and the sacraments have the same purpose, namely, "to offer and set forth Christ to us, and in him the treasures of heavenly grace."[140] Over against those who contrast the efficacy of the sacraments of the Gospel with those of the Law, Calvin insists that the sacraments of the Law set forth and offered Christ, even if they did so with different symbols. "Yet those ancient sacraments looked to the same purpose to which ours now tend: to direct and almost lead men by the hand to Christ, or rather, as images, to represent him and set him forth to be known."[141] As we have seen, the sacraments of the Law foreshadow Christ as yet to come, while those of the Gospel attest Christ as already revealed. For this reason, the sacraments of the Gospel present Christ more clearly, even though the sacraments of the Law also presented Christ. To illustrate this point, Calvin turns to the water and blood that flowed from Christ's side in the Gospel of John. According to Calvin, water and blood were symbols of purification and satisfaction under the Law.

By flowing from Christ's side, they reveal that the same benefits of Christ's death that were offered to the Israelites are now fulfilled in the death of Christ, and that these benefits are now to be offered through Baptism and the eucharistic Supper. "For this reason, Augustine has called it the well-spring of our sacraments."[142]

In his *Catechism* of 1538, Calvin repeats the definition of a sacrament that he gave in the first edition of the *Institutes,* namely, that "it is an outward sign by which the Lord represents and attests to us his good will toward us," or, more succinctly, "a testimony of God's grace, declared to us by an outward sign."[143] Calvin also accentuates the role of sacraments as exercising our faith, for in them the Lord accommodates himself to our capacity.[144] The sacraments exercise faith by acting as visual confirmation of the preceding Word of promise.[145] As in the *Institutes,* the symbols themselves only have the capacity to represent the promises "because they have by the Lord's Word been marked with this signification."[146]

In the second edition of the *Institutes,* Calvin accentuates the role of the sacraments in confirming faith. According to Calvin, "the clearer anything is, the better fitted it is to support faith."[147] Since the sacraments represent the promises of God graphically and visually, they are therefore the best suited to support faith. "But the sacraments bring the clearest promises; and they have this characteristic over and above the word because they represent them for us as painted in a picture from life."[148] For this reason, Calvin assigns the ministry of confirming and increasing faith particularly to the sacraments.[149] However, the sacraments confirm faith not by confining our attention to them but by raising our minds from the visible symbols we see to the hidden mysteries that they represent. "Indeed, the believer, when he sees the sacraments with his own eyes, does not halt at the physical sight of them, but by those steps (which I have indicated by analogy) rises up in devout contemplation to those lofty mysteries which lie hidden in the sacraments."[150] The sacraments are the clearest promises because they paint the promises of God to the life before our eyes, and raise us by analogy from the sacraments that we see to the mysteries of grace that we do not see.

To keep his readers from confining their minds to the contemplation of the signs themselves, as though they were of themselves efficacious, Calvin introduces a distinction in 1539 between the ministry of the sacraments and the efficacy of the Holy Spirit.[151] Thus, as he had in 1536, Calvin claims that in spite of the mutual confirmation of ears and eyes by the Word and the sacraments, neither form of manifestation confirms faith without the interior operation of the Holy Spirit. However, the Spirit does not replace the confirmation provided by the Word and especially the sacraments, but rather seals their confirmation on our souls. "Therefore, Word and sacraments confirm our faith when they set before our eyes the good will of our Heavenly Father toward us, by the knowledge of whom the whole firmness of our faith stands fast and increases in strength. The Spirit confirms it when, by engraving this confirmation in our minds, he makes it effective."[152]

For this reason, Calvin is increasingly critical of the Scholastic view that the sacraments are efficacious provided that no obstacle of mortal sin intervenes. This teaching confines the attention of the faithful to the symbols themselves, as though they were efficacious of themselves, "so that they repose in the appearance of a physical thing rather than in God himself."[153] To guard against this error, Calvin insists that the enjoyment of the reality symbolized by the sacraments is not bound to participation in the sacraments. Even though it is the chief office of the sacraments to confirm faith, Calvin cautions his readers nonetheless that "assurance of salvation does not depend upon participation in the sacrament, as if justification consisted in it."[154] On the other hand, one may participate in the symbols without enjoying the grace they represent.[155] By distinguishing between the ministry of the sacraments and the efficacy of the Spirit, Calvin hopes to give the sacraments their due without confining the power of God to them alone. Even though the sacraments are suited to confirm faith because they offer the clearest promises, their efficacy lies not in the vividness of their visual representation but in the inner power of the Holy Spirit.

In the 1543 edition of the *Institutes,* Calvin is especially interested in enlisting the support of the fathers, especially Augustine, for his interpretation of the sacraments. Augustine, unlike Calvin, defines a sacrament as "a visible sign of a sacred thing," or "a visible form of an invisible grace." However, Calvin claims that his own definition explains Augustine's teaching more clearly, which is obscure due to its brevity.[156] Calvin explains how the fathers developed the term "sacrament," by taking the Latin Vulgate translation of *mysterion* and applying it "to those signs which reverently represented sublime and spiritual things."[157] He also brings in Chrysostom to support his understanding of divine self-accommodation in the sacraments. "Now, because we have souls engrafted in bodies, he imparts spiritual things under visible ones."[158]

However, in 1543 Calvin is especially critical of the Roman practice of the sacraments, in which the Word added to the sacrament is viewed as a magical incantation mumbled inaudibly over the sacramental symbols.[159]

Moreover, even if the people had been able to hear the priest, they would not have understood anything, "for they spoke everything in Latin among unlearned men."[160] Although Calvin agrees with his opponents that "a sacrament consists of a word and the outward sign," he appeals to Augustine to insist that the sacramental word is not to be mumbled, or hoarsely whispered, but clearly and audibly proclaimed to the people.[161] The proclaimed word is necessary for the sacrament to confirm faith, as it is the word or doctrine of the sacrament alone that directs the people from the outward sign to the reality it represents. "Accordingly, when we hear the sacramental word mentioned, let us understand the promise, proclaimed in a clear voice by the minister, to lead the people by the hand wherever the sign tends and directs us."[162]

Calvin also appeals extensively to Augustine in order to clarify the distinction between the sacraments and the reality they represent. Calvin cites Augustine to support his claim that people may participate in the sacraments without participating in Christ. "Hence that distinction (if it be duly understood), often noted by the same Augustine, between a sacrament and the matter of the sacrament."[163] Calvin takes this distinction to mean that even as one joins the reality and the sacrament, one must also distinguish between them, so that one does not transfer the reality represented by the sacraments to the sacraments themselves. According to Calvin, the reality is truly received when we apprehend the word of the sacrament by faith. For those who lack faith, "a sacrament is thus separated from its truth by the unworthiness of the recipient, so that nothing remains but a vain and useless figure."[164] Since Christ is the matter and substance of all the sacraments, their efficacy is dependent on the way they "foster, confirm, and increase the true knowledge of Christ in ourselves" in order to "possess him more fully and enjoy his riches."[165] Augustine, in Calvin's view, wants to distinguish between the sacrament and the reality of the sacrament so that we neither disdain the sacrament as a worthless and empty sign nor pervert the sacrament "by not lifting our minds beyond the visible sign, to transfer to it the credit of those benefits which are conferred on us by Christ alone. And they are conferred through the Holy Spirit, who makes us partakers in Christ."[166]

In the *Catechism of the Church of Geneva* of 1545, Calvin again defines a sacrament as "an outward attestation of the divine benevolence towards us, which represents spiritual grace symbolically, to seal the promises of God in our hearts, by which the truth of them is better confirmed."[167] Calvin gives even greater emphasis to the role of the Holy Spirit in confirming faith than he did in the *Institutes* of 1539, calling the sacraments "secondary instruments" of the Spirit.[168] Given that the efficacy of the sacraments lies wholly in the Spirit, why then does God choose to confirm faith by means of the sacraments? Once again, Calvin appeals to God's self-accommodation to carnal human capacities. "But as we are surrounded by this gross earthly body, we need symbols or mirrors, to exhibit to us the appearance of spiritual and heavenly things in a kind of earthly way."[169] Calvin also repeats the distinction between the sacrament and the reality of the sacrament that he introduced in the 1543 edition of the *Institutes*. The right way to participate in the sacraments is to seek Christ alone and his grace in them, for "we are to regard the sign in the light of an aid, by which we may be directed straight to Christ, and from him seek salvation and real felicity."[170] Even though faith is needed to use the sacraments rightly, there is nothing absurd in seeking in the sacraments the "nourishment, strengthening, and furtherance" of faith, for Paul tells us they are given for the sealing of God's promises.[171] It would therefore be arrogance to think that we could do without the sacraments, given the infirmities that are always to be found in the faithful.

In his response to the Adultero-German Interlude of 1549, Calvin emphasizes the way that sacraments are meant to correspond to the reality that they represent. "Unless the sign correspond to this the nature of the Sacrament is destroyed."[172] By means of the correspondence or analogy between the symbol and the reality symbolized, the sacraments are meant to raise us from bodily perception to intellectual comprehension.[173] The understanding mind, in turn, is to be led by the sacrament to seek the reality it symbolizes in heaven. To illustrate this upward movement, Calvin endorses the view that describes the sacraments as "ladders" helping us to climb from earth to heaven. "Christ invites us to himself. As we cannot climb so high, he himself lends us his hand, and assists us with the helps which he knows to be suited to us, and even lifts us to heaven, as it is very appropriately expressed by those who compare the sacraments to ladders."[174] The metaphor of the hand reaching down from heaven, in tandem with the image of a ladder, emphasizes the upward dynamic that sacraments are meant to facilitate, over and above the clarity with which they represent the promises of God that Calvin had emphasized earlier in his career. Calvin contrasts his view of the sacraments as ladders to Christ in heaven with the Roman view that confines Christ within the sacraments themselves.[175] Whereas in 1543 Calvin described the uncomprehending gaze of the congregation that lacked the proclaimed word when they saw the sacrament, Calvin now describes the congregation as gazing stupidly on the sign and neglecting to seek Christ in heaven.[176]

In his *Exposition of the Heads of Agreement of the Zurich Consensus* of 1554, Calvin accentuates the upward thrust of the sacraments by means of the relationship between the pattern seen in the tabernacle and the heavenly exemplar after which it was fashioned. "So in the present day we should be intent on that spiritual archetype, and not delude ourselves with empty shows."[177] Calvin combines the appeal from the earthly type to the heavenly archetype with the metaphor of ladders, to show that our attention should not be confined on earth, for the symbol we see is intended to lead and guide us to Christ in heaven.[178] According to this model, faith receives the reality exhibited by the sacraments because it uses the helps of the sacraments to mount up to Christ in heaven as on ladders. "But if faith must intervene, no man of sense will deny that the same God who helps our infirmity by these aids, also gives faith, which, elevated by proper ladders, may climb to Christ and obtain grace."[179] The sacraments are helps to faith not because they are the clearest promises of God, representing them before our eyes as in a painting from life, as in 1539, but rather because they are ladders by which faith is helped to climb from the world to heaven, to seek Christ there.

Calvin repeats this claim in his *Second Defense of the Sacraments against Westphal* of 1554/5. Just as David looked to the face of God in the ark of the covenant so that he might climb to heaven to seek God there, so also Calvin turns the faithful to the Word and the sacraments, so that they do not "fail to climb up to heaven by those ladders which were not without cause set up for us by God."[180] In his *Last Admonition to Joachim Westphal,* Calvin combines the metaphor of ladders with vehicles, to demonstrate how the sacraments are intended to carry us from earth to heaven. "And to what end did Christ institute the Supper and Baptism, but just in accommodation to our weakness, to raise us upwards to himself by the vehicles of types?"[181] Up until 1545, Calvin describes the self-accommodation of God in the sacraments in terms of the manifestation of hidden spiritual realities in creaturely images and symbols, to confirm our faith more effectively. Beginning in 1549, Calvin describes such accommodation in light of the helps God gives the faithful in the ladders or vehicles of the sacraments, by which they can ascend from earth to heaven. This does not mean, however, that Calvin neglects the role of sacraments as giving visual confirmation to our faith in Christ. In his commentary on Jonah of 1559, Calvin claims that when all access to God seems to be closed up, we should recall that we have been adopted from infancy, and that God "has also testified his favor by various signs, especially that he has called us by his Gospel into a fellowship with his only-begotten Son, who is life and salvation; and then, that he has confirmed his favor both by Baptism and the Supper. When, therefore, these things come to our minds, we may be able by faith to break through all impediments."[182]

To discern Calvin's understanding of the different sacraments of the Church, I begin by discussing his evaluation of those sacraments inherited from the Roman Church that Calvin denied were ordinary sacraments of the Church. I then turn to a discussion of Baptism and the holy Supper of the Lord, to develop Calvin's understanding of the dynamic of the true sacraments of the Church. As we shall see, Calvin's understanding of Baptism creates a tension regarding the relationship of the sign with the thing signified. On the other hand, his understanding of the Supper will create a tension regarding the relation of the descent of Christ to us in the sign and our use of the sign as a ladder by which to climb up to Christ in heaven.

7. The Laying on of Hands

The laying on of hands is a symbol that arises in four different contexts for Calvin. The first has to do with its use in ordaining presbyters and deacons for the office of ministry. The second has to do with the confirmation of those who had been baptized in infancy and now come to the profession of faith after catechesis. The third has to do with the bestowal of the visible gifts of the Holy Spirit in the apostolic age. The fourth has to do with the public restoration of the penitent to full communion with the Church, and is explored below in the discussion of whether penance is a sacrament. For the sake of clarity, each of these issues is discussed separately, as Calvin's position on each is distinctive and tends to develop dramatically over time, especially with regard to the issue of ordination.

Calvin first discusses the laying on of hands for ordination in the 1536 edition of the *Institutes*. He is especially concerned with the Roman view that the sacrament of ordination of itself bestows the Holy Spirit on those who receive it, while the oil of ordination bestows an indelible character on the souls of those who receive it. Calvin discerns three rites in the Roman sacrament of ordination. The first is insufflation, by which the bishop breathes on the ordinand and says, "Receive the Holy Spirit" (John 20:22). According to Calvin, Christ was not instituting a sacrament when he breathed on his apostles after the resurrection but rather "used it as a symbol of a particular miracle."[183] By falsely imitating what Christ alone could do, the bishops act "like apes, which imitate everything wantonly and without any discrimination," while they also "mock Christ," for "they are so shameless as to dare affirm that they confer the Holy Spirit."[184] The second rite is anointing with oil, in imitation of consecration to the Aaronic priesthood. According to Calvin, such priestly consecration is an explicit denial of the sole Priesthood of Christ, and reflects the way the Roman Church tends "to shape one religion out of Christianity and Judaism and paganism by sewing patches together."[185]

The third rite of ordination is the laying on of hands. Calvin admits that this symbol is in a different class from the others, as it was the practice of the apostles.[186] Calvin acknowledges that this rite was of Hebraic origin, by which the Israelites "presented to God by the laying on of hands that which they wished to be blessed and sanctified."[187] Calvin claims that the apostles adopted this practice without returning to the shadows of the Law, and more important, without the superstition that he thinks infects the Roman practice. "For they laid hands upon those for whom they prayed the Holy Spirit to come from the Lord, and they administered him by this sort of symbol, in order that they might teach that he comes not from them but descends from heaven."[188] The key for Calvin comes in the prayer for the Holy Spirit that accompanied the laying on of hands, for it reveals that the apostles did not think that the symbol itself conferred the Holy Spirit, over against the Roman view.[189]

The question for Calvin is, "was it thenceforth continuously held to be a sacrament?"[190] According to him, the laying on of hands is no more a sacrament than is the lifting up of hands to pray, which the apostles also practiced. "In the end, all the gestures of the saints would turn into sacraments."[191] Therefore, Calvin categorically denies that the laying on of hands is a sacrament, even though it was a Hebrew custom also followed by the apostles, since there is no promise of God attested by the sign, which for Calvin is the definition of a sacrament.[192] However, so long as there was no expectation that the Holy Spirit is being given, Calvin would allow for the installation of a bishop by the laying on of hands.[193]

The *Institutes* of 1539 preserves this discussion of the laying on of hands from the first edition, including the categorical denial that it is a sacrament.[194] Moreover, the *Draft Ecclesiastical Ordinances* of 1541 seem to set forth a similar understanding, allowing for the practice if it is not viewed as a sacrament conveying the Holy Spirit, but denying its use due to the superstition surrounding it.[195] In the version of the article officially received by the magistrates of Geneva, all mention of the laying on of hands is removed.[196] Clearly, even as late as 1541, Calvin is so concerned with the Roman view that the Spirit is given with the ceremony of the laying on of hands that he will not allow it even when this belief does not accompany it.

However, in the third edition of the *Institutes* of 1543, Calvin completely changes his position on the symbol of the laying on of hands. In his discussion of the orders of ministry in the Church, Calvin describes the rite of ordination in terms of the laying on of hands. "It is clear that when the apostles admitted any man to the ministry, they used no other ceremony than the laying on of hands."[197] Calvin repeats the 1536 discussion of the Hebraic roots of this rite; but far from denying its value as a sacrament, he claims that even its lack of clear dominical institution does not prevent it from being considered as commanded by God. "Although there exists no set precept for the laying on of hands, because we see it in continual use with the apostles, their very careful observance ought to serve in lieu of a precept."[198] Calvin also denies that the laying on of hands is "an empty sign," provided it is restored to its true origin. "For if the Spirit of God establishes nothing without cause in the Church, we should feel that this ceremony, since it has proceeded from him, is not useless, provided it may not be turned into superstitious abuse."[199] The uniform practice of the apostles therefore takes the place of an explicit Word instituting the rite of the laying on of hands, so that it can be considered to have proceeded from the Holy Spirit. Calvin accentuates this claim for authority in *The Necessity of Reforming the Church* of the same year. "It is absurd, therefore, to trouble us about the form of ordination, in which we differ neither from the rule of Christ, nor from the practice of the apostles, nor from the custom of the ancient Church."[200] Calvin also suggests that the Holy Spirit is conferred through this ceremony, by means of his paraphrase of 2 Timothy 1:6, in which Paul asks Timothy to rekindle the gift of God he received through the laying on of hands. "It is as if he said, 'See to it that the grace which you received by the laying on of hands, when I created you presbyter, is not void.'"[201]

In his discussion of the sacraments in 1543, Calvin indicates his willingness to consider the laying on of hands a sacrament, though it is not an "ordinary sacrament" for the confirming of the faith of all believers, as are Baptism and the holy Supper of the Lord.[202] Therefore, in his discussion of the "false sacraments" of the Roman Church, Calvin willingly allows a place for the laying on of hands among the sacraments of the Church. "For in it there is a ceremony, first taken from Scripture, then one that Paul testifies not to be empty or superfluous, but a faithful token of spiritual grace [1 Tim. 4:14]. However, I have not put it as number three among the sacraments because it is not ordinary or common with all believers, but is a special rite for a particular office."[203] Calvin is aware that his Roman opponents will celebrate this complete reversal of his previous position as a vindication of their ministry, but he adds the qualification that ministers are to be ordained as pastors to preach the Gospel, not to be consecrated as priests to offer the sacrifice of the Mass.[204] He also removes entirely his sarcastic mockery of the apish imitation of every gesture of the apostles as constituting a sacrament, and replaces it with this terse statement. "There remains the laying on of hands. As I concede that it is a sacrament in true and lawful ordinations, so I deny that it has a place in this farce [of Roman ordinations], where they neither obey Christ's command not consider the end to which the promise should lead us."[205] Thus, by 1543, Calvin allows that the laying on of hands is a sacrament, with both a dominical institution (inferred from universal apostolic practice) and the efficacy of the Spirit bringing the reality of the sign, even though it is not numbered among the ordinary sacraments of the Church.

Calvin reinforces his understanding of the laying on of hands as a sacrament in his commentary on 1 and 2 Timothy of 1548. Calvin highlights Paul's statement that Timothy received the gift through the laying on of hands, noting that it was not an empty symbol, but that the Spirit effected the reality signified by the symbol. "For we gather that the ceremony was not in vain, since God by his Spirit effected that consecration which men symbolized by the laying on of hands."[206] Calvin addresses his concern that the Spirit not be seen as automatically given with the symbol by accentuating the role of prayer in the ceremony.[207] However, he denies that this makes the ceremony itself meaningless, for it "was a faithful token (*tessera*) of the grace they received from God's own hand."[208] This is not to say that Timothy had no gift of the Spirit before the laying on of hands, "but rather that it shone forth more brightly when the teaching office was laid upon him."[209]

In his *True Method of Giving Peace* of 1549, Calvin explicitly allows that the laying on of hands is a sacrament, as it is understood to be by the Roman Church.[210] However, he denies that the Roman practice of consecrating priests to offer the sacrifice of the Mass is a sacrament, and denies that the Spirit works through this symbol.[211] On the other hand, when laying on of hands is performed according to the purpose for which it was instituted, and is accompanied by the prayers of the community, the Spirit does work through the ceremony to join the reality with the symbol, to effect inwardly what the rite outwardly represents. "We gather from this that the laying on of hands is a rite consistent with order and dignity, seeing that it was used by the apostles; not of course that it has any efficacy or virtue in itself, but its power and effect depend solely on the Spirit of God."[212]

The laying on of hands also plays a role in the controversy over whether confirmation ought to be considered a sacrament. In the first edition of the *Institutes* of 1536, Calvin denies that the laying on of hands as practiced by the apostles was anything more than a rite of consecration.[213] He is especially bothered by the Roman teaching that the grace of baptism is incomplete without the increase of grace in confirmation.[214] According to him, this is a diabolical teaching that has the effect of leading the faithful away from the truth of their baptism.[215] He again denies that the laying on of hands is a sacrament, as the ancient writers of the Church only mention two sacraments. "The ancients speak of the laying on of hands, but do they call it a sacrament? Augustine openly affirms that it is nothing but prayer."[216] Calvin does wish that the ancient practice of catechizing those baptized as infants could be restored, so that at the age of ten they could be examined about their faith before the whole congregation, and be taught anything about which they were still ignorant. But he does not mention the laying on of hands in this regard.[217]

In the third edition of the *Institutes* in 1543, Calvin gives a fuller description of the practice of catechesis in the ancient church, to indicate that it formed the completion of infant baptism by giving a fuller confession of faith.[218] He also notes the more essential role of the rite of the laying on of hands in this ceremony. "Thus the youth, once his faith was approved, was dismissed with a solemn blessing."[219] Calvin notes that it was customary, but not necessary, for the bishop to bless the child by the laying on of hands. "Therefore, I warmly approve such laying on of hands, which is simply done as a form of blessing, and wish that it were today restored to pure use."[220] However, he reiterates his objection to calling this form of the laying on of hands a sacrament, for to do so would denigrate the power of baptism.[221]

Calvin reiterates this position in his commentary on Hebrews of 1549. He thinks that Hebrews is referring to the rite of blessing catechumens when it speaks of "the teachings of baptisms, and of laying on of hands" (Heb. 6:2). He claims that the passage shows that this rite came from the apostles, even though it was perverted by the Roman Church when it was defined as a sacrament that confers the spirit of regeneration, thereby mutilating baptism. "They intended by this sign to confirm the profession of faith which adolescents make when they pass from their childhood, but they have planned nothing less than the destruction of the force of baptism."[222] However, in spite of this perversion of making the laying on of hands into a sacrament, Calvin still wants to restore its proper use as a solemn prayer of confirmation.[223] He continues to endorse the laying on of hands in confirmation in his commentary on Acts of 1554.[224] Once again, however, he denies that the laying on of hands in confirmation can be considered a sacrament without blaspheming against the power of baptism.[225]

Finally, the laying on of hands plays a role in the controversy over the manifestation of the visible gifts of the Holy Spirit in the Church. One of the central texts thought to give authoritative warrant to the sacramental view of confirmation comes in the Book of Acts, when Peter and John were sent from Jerusalem to Samaria to pray for those who had accepted the Word of God. However, the Holy Spirit had not yet come upon these Samaritans, for they had only been baptized in the name of Jesus. "Then Peter and John laid their hands on them, and they received the Holy Spirit" (Acts 14:14–18). In the first edition of the *Institutes* of 1536, Calvin denies that this event has to do with a fuller grace than is given in baptism, as his Roman opponents claim. Rather, it has to do with the manifestation of the visible gifts of the Spirit that accompanied and confirmed the preaching of the Gospel in the apostolic period.[226] However, Calvin claims that the visible gifts of the Spirit ceased being given at the time of the apostles.[227] Since the visible gifts are the reality signified by the laying on of hands, the cessation of the reality makes the continuance of the symbol absurd in Calvin's eyes. "But since that grace has ceased to be given, what purpose does the laying on of hands serve?"[228]

Calvin consistently maintains this understanding of the laying on of hands for the rest of his theological career, indicated by the fact that this section of the *Institutes* remains unedited from 1536 through 1559.[229] In his commentary on Acts of 1552, Calvin repeats his claim that the visible presence of the Spirit was only manifested for a time to confirm the authority of the Gospel. Since God no longer gives the reality, it makes no sense to continue the rite of the laying on of hands for this purpose. "This is not to be tolerated now, because they have made a permanent principle in the Church, out of what was a temporary sign, as if the Holy Spirit was at their disposal."[230] Calvin notes that even the apostles prayed in order to show that they did not give the Spirit themselves, even though God nonetheless used this symbol as an instrument by which to bestow the visible grace of the Spirit.[231] For this reason, Calvin is willing to consider the laying on of hands in the apostolic period a sacrament, but only a temporary one, since the reality it attests is no longer being given. "For when all agree that it was a temporary grace, that was exhibited by the symbol, it is perverse and ridiculous to retain a sign, when the reality has been removed."[232] Thus the laying on of hands is not a false sacrament but rather a temporary one, which becomes an empty symbol once the reality is no longer given through the sign.[233]

8. Anointing the Sick with Oil

In the first edition of the *Institutes,* Calvin rejects the Roman claim that extreme unction is a sacrament. He acknowledges that there appears to be a scriptural basis for the sacrament, in terms of both the ceremony and an attached promise, in the epistle of James. "Are any among you sick? They should call for the elders of the church and have them pray over them, anointing them with oil in the name of the Lord. The prayer of faith will save the sick, and the Lord will raise them up; and anyone who has committed sins will be forgiven" (James 5:14–15). However, Calvin denies that this passage constitutes the institution of a sacrament, claiming instead that it is no different from the practice of the disciples in the Gospel of Mark. "They cast out many demons, and anointed with oil many who were sick and cured them" (Mark 6:13). According to Calvin, both the apostles and Jesus were rather free in their use of such symbols and ceremonies, as when Jesus at times uses dust and spittle, at other times just a touch, or the apostles heal by word or touch, as well as by oil. For this reason, Calvin claims that the anointing of which James speaks "is not an instrument of healing, but only a symbol, by which the unschooled in their ignorance might be made aware of the source of such great power, that they might not give the credit for it to the apostles. It is a well-known commonplace that by oil the Holy Spirit and his gifts are signified [Ps. 45:7]."[234]

However, like the other visible gifts of the Spirit mentioned above, the gift of healing was temporary, lasting only as long as the apostles in order to confirm the Gospel.[235] Thus, even were he to concede that the anointing of which James speaks is a sacrament, it no longer applies to us, since the reality is no longer being given.[236] Calvin does not, however, appear to be willing to concede that it was a sacrament, for he asks why Rome does not make sacraments out of the bathing pool of Siloam, or why they do not lie on dead people to raise them, or any of the other symbols employed by the apostles when they healed people. When his opponents object that James commands this symbol to be used, Calvin replies, "That is, James spoke for that time when the church still enjoyed such a blessing of God. Indeed, they affirm that the same force inheres in their anointing, but we experience otherwise."[237] Since the gift of healing has long since departed from the Church, the continuing use of this symbol is as much a foolish aping of the apostles as is the laying on of hands after the visible gifts of the Spirit have ceased.[238] Thus Calvin categorically denies that extreme unction is a sacrament, "for neither is it a ceremony instituted by God, nor has it any promise."[239] Yet even if it did meet these criteria, Calvin denies that the promise, and hence the symbol, applies to us, for "even they themselves make clear by experience" that the gift of healing is no longer present in the Church.[240]

In *The True Method of Giving Peace* of 1549, Calvin changes his understanding of the anointing of the sick, claiming that in the apostolic period it was in fact a sacrament. "As we acknowledge the Anointing which the Apostles used in Curing the Sick to have been a Sacrament, so we deny that it belongs to us, because, like the grace to which it was subservient, it was temporary."[241] Calvin appeals to the ancient histories of the Church to support his claim, which he takes to be widely acknowledged.[242] Since the grace represented by the symbol of anointing ceased being given long ago, it is meaningless to keep using the symbol as though it were a sacrament.[243] His Roman opponents may claim that the passage from James supports their understanding of anointing the sick as a sacrament, but Calvin says in response, "I deny it to have been his intention to prostitute what he knew to be an efficacious sign representing divine grace, to a frigid imitation."[244]

Calvin supports this understanding of anointing the sick in his commentary on James of 1550. He concedes that it was viewed as a sacrament in the apostolic period, and that it was an instrument that God used for healing.[245] His argument now is that since the reality signified is no longer being given, it is wrong to keep using the sign as though it were a sacrament. "This is really quite evident: there is nothing more absurd than to call something a Sacrament which is empty, and does not truly offer us the matter signified."[246] Since "God withdrew from the world fourteen hundred years ago" the reality signified, the Roman theologians are not imitators of the apostles, but "apes," when they consider such anointing a sacrament today.[247] Thus unction, like the laying on of hands for visible gifts, is not a false sacrament invented by the human imagination but is rather a temporary sacrament through which God has ceased to work.[248]

Calvin also seems to deny that the sacrament spoken of by James was identical to the occasional anointing practiced by the disciples, over against his position in 1536. In his harmony of the Gospels of 1555, Calvin says, "Therefore I consider this to have been a visible symbol of spiritual grace which testified that the healing of which they were ministers came from the secret power of God."[249] However, in spite of these clear changes in his interpretation of apostolic anointing, Calvin makes no major changes in the discussion of unction in the *Institutes* from 1536 to 1559, except to note that the gift of healing was a temporary gift that "quickly perished partly on account of men's ungratefulness."[250]

It is puzzling that Calvin does not see any use at all for the practice described by James, even if he no longer considers it a sacrament. Just as he denied that the laying on of hands in confirmation was a sacrament, but rather a useful form of prayer, he could have accentuated the way James seems to ascribe the efficacy of anointing the sick to the prayer of faith. After all, Calvin insists that "the Lord is indeed present with his people in every age; and he heals their weaknesses as often as necessary, no less than of old."[251] The danger of viewing such anointing as a sacrament would be no greater in this instance than in the laying on of hands in confirmation. The one reason that may have kept Calvin from adopting this position was his aversion to oil, the use of which he categorically rejects in the Roman rites of baptism, confirmation, and ordination.

9. PENANCE

Calvin engages in a lengthy discussion of the Roman teaching on penance in the first edition of the *Institutes*, especially the definition of penance as contrition, confession, and satisfaction. More germane to our concerns, he explicitly denies that it is a sacrament, for it lacks both a ceremony instituted by God and a promise to which it is appended as confirmation.[252] If his opponents do not like his definition of a sacrament, he is willing to turn to the definitions provided by Augustine, all of which indicate that visual manifestation is essential to a sacrament, which is lacking in penance. "He says, 'Visible sacraments were instituted for the sake of carnal men, that by the steps of sacraments they may be transported from things discernable by the eyes to those understood.' What similar thing do they themselves see or can they show others in what they call 'the sacrament of penance?'"[253]

However, were the Roman Church to define the sacrament in terms of the priest's absolution, Calvin thinks that a better case could be made for it being a sacrament. "For it was easy to say that it is a ceremony to confirm our faith in forgiveness of sins, and has 'the promise of the keys,' as they call the statement, 'Whatever you bind or loose on earth will be loosed and bound in heaven' [Matt. 18:18; cf. 16:19]."[254] In spite of this concession, Calvin denies that penance could ever be considered a sacrament, for "no promise of God—the only basis of a sacrament—exists," and because "every ceremony displayed here is a mere invention of men, although we have already proved that the ceremonies of sacraments can only be ordained by God."[255] For Calvin, as for Luther before him, baptism is the sacrament of penance, to which sinners return once they repent.[256]

In the second edition of the *Institutes*, Calvin moves his discussion of contrition, confession, and satisfaction to a new chapter devoted entirely to penance.[257] In his discussion of penance as a sacrament, he confirms his description of baptism as the sacrament of penance by appealing to a work ascribed to Augustine.[258] In the third edition of the *Institutes*, Calvin makes a considerable addition to the beginning of his discussion of whether penance is to be considered a sacrament, by presenting a lengthy discussion of the practice of public or canonical penance under the bishops in the early Church. "The ancients observed this order in public repentance, that those who had discharged the satisfactions enjoined upon them were reconciled by the solemn laying on of hands. That was a symbol of absolution by which the sinner himself was raised up before God with assurance of pardon, and the church admonished to expunge the memory of his offense and receive him kindly into favor. Cyprian very often calls this 'giving peace.'"[259] Calvin acknowledges that the laying on of hands was often done by bishops, as is also reflected in several canons of provincial synods.[260] By the time of Gratian, this practice was combined with private reconciliation, which became normative by Calvin's day. Although Calvin does not reject the efficacy of private reconciliation, he clearly wishes for the restoration of the laying on of hands in a public symbol of absolution.[261] However, he acknowledges that this symbol of absolution is of human invention, and is therefore neither a sacrament nor a necessary rite, only a desirable one from his point of view.[262]

The laying on of hands in public reconciliation would therefore be similar to the laying on of hands in confirmation, which Calvin also wants to be restored in 1543.

10. Marriage

In the first edition of the *Institutes*, Calvin acknowledges that marriage has been instituted by God but denies that it is a sacrament. "All men admit that it was instituted by God; but no man ever saw it administered as a sacrament until the time of Gregory. And what sober man would ever have thought it such?"[263] According to the definition of a sacrament advanced by Calvin, it lacks an outward ceremony instituted by God to confirm faith in a promise. Calvin denies that the statement of Paul in Ephesians 5:28 is the institution of marriage as a sacrament. Calvin admits that it is an apt comparison to view the union of husband and wife as representative of the mystery of the union of Christ and the Church. However, the ignorance of Greek in Roman theologians misled them, so that they did not understand why the Old Vulgate translated *mysterion* as *sacramentum*.[264] Calvin never changed his position on marriage from this point on, and never edited this passage of the *Institutes* from 1536 to 1559. Indeed, he repeats his position in the commentary on Ephesians of 1548. "But the present question is whether marriage has been appointed as a solemn symbol of the grace of God, to declare and represent to us something spiritual, such as Baptism or the Lord's Supper. They have no ground for such an assertion, unless it be that they have been deceived by the doubtful signification of the word, or rather by their ignorance of the Greek language."[265]

11. Baptism as the Symbol of Adoption

In the first edition of the *Institutes*, Calvin claims that baptism shows the faithful three things to confirm their faith. The first thing signified by baptism is the forgiveness of sin.[266] According to Calvin, the water is not an instrument of our cleansing and forgiveness, but rather the sacrament of baptism gives us the certain knowledge of our forgiveness, by sealing the message of forgiveness. The forgiveness symbolized in baptism is not just for sins committed prior to baptism but covers the whole life of the faithful.[267] Baptism therefore comforts those who groan under the burden of their sins, so that they are not reduced to despair. The second thing signified by baptism is the mortification and vivification of the godly in Christ.[268] According to Calvin, this takes place not by our imitation of the death and resurrection of Christ by our putting sin to death within ourselves but rather by the participation in Christ through baptism.[269] Both mortification and forgiveness were foreshadowed to the people of Israel in the cloud and the sea (1 Cor. 10:2). Just as Pharaoh and his army were drowned in the sea, so in baptism the faithful are shown by a sign that the power of sin has been vanquished, even if it continues to vex them. Just as the cloud sheltered the Israelites from the heat of the sun in the wilderness, so the blood of Christ protects the faithful from the fire of the wrath of God by the forgiveness of sin.[270]

Finally, baptism bears testimony to the unity with Christ that the faithful enjoy, together with all his blessings.[271] The right way to receive baptism is therefore to realize that "it is God who speaks to us through the sign," so that we see God as the one forgiving and renewing us, and uniting us with Christ and all his blessings.[272] The best way to come to the confirmation offered by baptism is by following the analogy between the sign and the thing signified. "These things, I say, he does for our soul within as truly and surely as we see our body outwardly cleansed, submerged, and surrounded with water."[273] However, Calvin once again denies that baptism itself is an "organ or instrument" by which the gifts of God are bestowed upon us; it is rather a pledge by which the will of the Lord is attested to us.[274]

In the *Catechism* of 1538, Calvin reverses the order of the gifts represented by baptism to place the primacy on participation in Christ, from which follows the grace of forgiveness and regeneration.[275] Calvin denies that the grace of forgiveness or regeneration inheres in the water, "but only that the knowledge of such gifts is received in this sacrament when we are said to receive, obtain, get what we believe to have been given us by the Lord."[276] The confirmation of faith provided by baptism has to do solely with our clearer awareness of the grace of God in Christ and not with the actual bestowal of that grace upon us in baptism.

Calvin adds a lengthy appendix to his discussion of baptism in 1539 in the second edition of the *Institutes* to defend the practice of infant baptism against the objections of "certain frantic spirits" who have disturbed the Church over the issue.[277] He argues that the foundation of the proper understanding of baptism is grounded in the promise that the sacrament represents and confirms.[278] Since the promise and spiritual reality represented in baptism is, as we have seen, forgiveness and regeneration, Calvin argues that there is an anagogic relationship between circumcision and baptism, since circumcision figured the same realities for the Jews. The only difference between the sacraments lies in the external ceremony of each.[279] Since the covenant with the Jews included their descendants, and was sealed on their male infants by circumcision, it follows that the infants of the pious are members of the covenant with their faithful parents, and should therefore not be deprived of the seal of the covenant in baptism.[280] Were Christian parents to be denied this sealing of the covenant on their children, they would have less assurance of the abundant mercy of God than did the Jews, which for Calvin is unthinkable, for it would mean that "Christ's coming would have the effect of making grace more obscure and less attested than it had previously been for the Jews."[281] It is clear, therefore, that the baptism of infants is meant primarily to be a confirmation of the faith of the parents, and only secondarily to be of benefit to the infants themselves.[282]

The mere promise of mercy would not be enough to confirm the faith of parents, for they need to see the sealing of the promise on their children to confirm for them that the promise is extended to them. "Accordingly, let those who embrace the promise that God's mercy is to be extended to their children deem it their duty to offer them to the church to be sealed by the symbol of mercy, and thereby to arouse themselves to a surer confidence, because they see with their very eyes the covenant of the Lord engraved upon the bodies of their children."[283] The visual confirmation of the promise of mercy and goodness to their children is the chief comfort offered by the sacrament of infant baptism, confirming the parents' knowledge of God as the abundantly flowing fountain of every good thing. "For how sweet is it to godly minds to be assured, not only by word, but even by sight of the eyes, that they obtain so much favor with the heavenly Father that their offspring are within his care?"[284] The children who are baptized also receive the benefit of knowing that their adoption as children of God was sealed on their bodies while they were yet infants.[285] However, baptism itself does not incorporate them into the covenant or make them children of God, any more than the lack of baptism necessarily means the damnation of infants.[286]

Calvin is very concerned not to ascribe to the water of baptism that which can only be attributed to the blood of Christ. The water is a symbol of forgiveness and mortification, but the blood of Christ is the reality that is attested by the water, and it alone cleanses our souls.[287] Calvin continues this line of thought in his commentary on Romans of 1540. He interprets Paul to be saying that circumcision becomes uncircumcision when the Jews attend only to the sign and neglect what the sign signifies.[288] Calvin thinks that the same mistake can be made with regard to baptism.[289] Baptism seals the grace of God offered to us in the promise, and therefore the reality signified by baptism is only obtained by faith in the promise. Calvin makes the same point when discussing the meaning of baptism as being buried with Christ in his death (Rom. 6:4). This is only true for those who have faith in the promise, for they alone receive the reality that is attested and sealed by baptism.[290] The sacrament of baptism represents and attests the grace of Christ offered to us in the promise, to be received by faith. However, at this point in his career, baptism does not offer what it represents, nor does God act through baptism as through an instrument to effect in us what baptism represents and offers to us.

In the third edition of the *Institutes,* Calvin accentuates the ecclesial nature of baptism. He inserts the ecclesial and corporate significance of baptism into the opening sentence of the discussion of baptism. "Baptism is the sign of the initiation by which we are received into the society of the church, in order that, engrafted in Christ, we may be reckoned among God's children."[291] From this point onwards, Calvin will always combine the theme of our engrafting into Christ with the theme of our initiation into the society of the Church. We cannot become members of Christ without becoming members of the body of Christ, nor can we be adopted as children of God without being initiated into the whole family of God. In his treatise *The Necessity of Reforming the Church* of the same year, Calvin repeats his criticism of those who ascribe the whole benefit of baptism to the water, and do not raise their minds to the blood of Christ that alone cleanses us from sin. "For in the schools as well as in sermons, they so extolled the efficacy of signs, that, instead of directing men to Christ, they taught them to confide in the visible elements."[292] Calvin also criticizes the lack of the explanation of baptism in the Roman Church, by means of the proclaimed word that should always accompany baptism.[293]

In the *Catechism of the Church of Geneva* of 1545, Calvin accentuates the ecclesial nature of baptism seen in the 1543 *Institutes,* by describing baptism as "a kind of entry into the Church. For in it we have a testimony that we, while otherwise strangers and aliens, were received into the family of God, so that we are reckoned among his household."[294] Calvin repeats his concern not to have the sign of baptism eclipse the reality signified, which is the blood of Christ applied to us by the Holy Spirit.[295] However, for the first time in his discussion of baptism, Calvin nonetheless insists that the reality signified by the water of baptism is truly offered by it, and is to be attached to it. "M: But do you attribute nothing more to the water than to be a mere symbol of ablution? C: I think it to be such a symbol that reality is attached to it. For God does not disappoint us when he promises us his gifts. Hence both pardon and newness of life are certainly offered to us and received by us in Baptism."[296] Thus, unless we block the reception of these benefits, the water of baptism truly offers to us the reality it signifies, so that "we are fed with Christ and granted his Spirit."[297] From this time forward, Calvin will be concerned to emphasize the way the water of baptism, in conjunction with the Word, truly exhibits and offers the reality it symbolizes and represents.

In his commentary on 1 Corinthians of 1546, Calvin highlights the way Paul describes believers as all being baptized into one body, further emphasizing the meaning of baptism as incorporation into the society of the Church. "Paul says: 'By baptism we are engrafted into the body of Christ, so that we are bound together, joined to each other as members, and live the one life.'"[298] Calvin also emphasizes the way the efficacy of baptism lies not in the water but in the power of the Holy Spirit.[299] However, unlike the Romans commentary, which ascribed the presence of the reality of baptism to faith in the promise, Calvin here insists on the willingness of God actually to carry out everything that God represents to us in baptism.[300] Thus God not only represents our engrafting into the body of Christ in baptism but also actually carries this out through baptism. "However, so that no one might suppose that this is effected by the outward symbol, Paul adds that it is the work of the Holy Spirit."[301]

In his *Acts of the Council of Trent with the Antidote* of 1547, Calvin finally describes baptism as "the ordinary instrument" through which God freely works to wash and renew us. "The only exception we make is, that the hand of God must not be tied down to the instrument. He may of himself accomplish salvation."[302] Calvin is still concerned not to identify the efficacy of baptism with the water, but he no longer denies that the sacrament is an instrument that God ordinarily uses to confer grace upon us, even though God may give that gift without the sacrament. Calvin addresses this issue in even greater detail in his commentary on the Pauline epistles of 1548. In light of Paul's statement that as many as were baptized have put on Christ (Gal. 3:27), Calvin raises the objection that both Scripture and experience seem to confute the conjunction between the symbol of baptism and the Spirit.[303] In response, Calvin says that Paul speaks of the sacraments in a twofold way. "When he is dealing with hypocrites who boast of the bare sign, he then proclaims the emptiness and worthlessness of the outward sign, and strongly attacks their foolish confidence."[304] The reason for this is that they corrupt the ordinance of God, and thus sever the reality from the sign by their presumption. "When, however, he addresses believers, who use the signs properly, he then connects them with the truth which they figure. Why? Because he reveals no deceitful display in the sacraments, but what the outward ceremony figures he exhibits in fact. Thus, in agreement with the divine appointment, the truth becomes joined to the signs."[305] God truly offers the reality figured in baptism to all who are baptized. Those who lack faith and repentance divorce the reality from the sign, whereas those who receive the sacrament with faith also receive what it figures.[306] In this way, Calvin thinks that he can prevent believers from binding the grace of God to the sacrament while nonetheless viewing the sacrament as truly presenting and offering the reality it represents and figures.[307]

Calvin returns to this issue when interpreting Paul's statement to the Ephesians that Christ has cleansed the Church by the washing of water in the word (Eph. 5:26). Calvin is concerned to interpret this saying with care, "lest, as has often happened, men in their perverted superstition make an idol out of the sacrament."[308] However, he responds to this concern by repeating that God actually performs what the sacrament figures, for otherwise it would be a fallacious sign.[309] Calvin knows that there are some who think that this still gives too much credit to baptism, and might lead people away from the work of God alone. He addresses this concern by describing baptism as an instrument that God uses in accommodation to our capacities, so that we may acknowledge that it is God who truly cleanses, without denying the proper role of baptism in figuring this cleansing to us. "Not that the power of God is shut up in the sign, but he distributes it to us by this means on account of the weakness of our capacity."[310] The efficacy of the sign comes from the Spirit, by which God accomplishes in the soul what God represents by the symbol. This does not tie the Spirit to the sacrament, for God can also act without the sacrament. "Nothing more is attributed to the sign than to be an inferior instrument, useless in itself, except so far as it derives its power from elsewhere."[311] In order that too much might not be ascribed to the sign, the Word of promise is also necessary in baptism, "which explains the force and use of the sign," for otherwise people are "bemused by signs" because "their minds are not directed to the Word, which would lead them to God."[312]

Calvin reinforces his understanding of baptism as symbolizing our in-corporation into the body of Christ in his commentary on Titus of 1550. When Paul says that we are saved through the washing of regeneration (Titus 3:5), Calvin interprets this statement in a corporate and communal way. "The train of the thought of the passage is this: 'God saves us by his mercy and he has given us a symbol and pledge of this salvation by baptism, by admitting us into his Church and engrafting us into the Body of his Son.'"[313] According to Calvin, Paul links the symbol of baptism with the thing signified in order to highlight the fact that "God does not play games with us with empty figures but inwardly accomplishes by his own power the thing he truly shows by the outward sign."[314] Baptism is only rightly under-stood when we join the thing signified with the sign, while leaving to God the task of accomplishing in us what the sign represents to our eyes.[315] Thus our awareness that the Spirit of God regenerates us should not lead us to ne-glect the symbol of baptism, which offers the invisible Spirit to us by means of a visible sign.[316]

In his commentary on 1 Peter of 1551, Calvin is as troubled by those, like Schwenkfeld, who take all the power and effect away from baptism, as he is with those like the Roman theologians who stop at the outward sign of bap-tism and fix all their hope of salvation there.[317] To preserve the power and ef-ficacy of baptism, it ought always to be combined with its reality, so that we "learn then not to divorce the thing signified from the sign."[318] To keep from ascribing too much power and efficacy to the water of baptism, on the other hand, we ought to "leave to Christ and also to the Holy Spirit each his own honor, so that no part of our salvation should be transferred to the sign."[319] Baptism truly figures and offers forgiveness and mortification of sin, but only Christ by the Holy Spirit exhibits the truth that the sacrament figures, "that the reality may be conjoined with the sign."[320] Because Christ truly effects what the sacrament represents, we may seek in the symbol of baptism all that we need in order to be adopted as children of God by being engrafted into the body of Christ.[321]

In the final edition of the *Institutes* in 1559, Calvin makes several addi-tions in order to clarify his understanding of the sacrament of baptism as an instrument God uses to distribute to us the grace of Christ, by performing and exhibiting the truth that is represented by the sign. Calvin had in 1536 di-rectly denied that baptism was an instrument or organ of grace in this sense. "For the Lord was pleased to represent [spiritual things] by such figures—not because such graces are bound and enclosed in the sacrament or because the sacrament is an organ and instrument to confer them on us."[322] Calvin dropped the denial that baptism is an organ or instrument of grace in the 1539 edition of the *Institutes,* but he did not replace it with a claim that God actually performs what the sacrament figures until the final edition of the *Institutes.*[323] "And he does not feed our eyes with a mere appearance only, but leads us to the present reality and effectively performs what it symbolizes."[324] Moreover, whereas in 1536 Calvin interpreted the baptism of Paul as simply assuring him his sins had already been forgiven, without baptism offering him forgiveness, Calvin adds in 1559, "Yet it is not my intention to weaken the force of baptism by not joining the reality and truth to the sign, in so far as God works through outward means."[325] The sign must never be divorced from the reality, even though it is God alone who can exhibit and effect the reality that the sacrament represents, acting through the sacrament as through an instrument.

The one point of tension left unresolved by Calvin concerns the reason the thing signified is divorced from the sign in the ungodly. On the one hand, to emphasize the fact that God truly offers and effects what baptism symbolizes and represents, Calvin will claim that it is the ungodliness of the recipient that divorces the reality from the sign, and prevents it from being received with the sign.[326] On the other hand, to show that the Spirit of God is not bound to the sign, Calvin will insist that only the elect are given the reality represented in baptism, while it is withheld from the reprobate. "Besides, many receive the sign who are not made partakers of grace; for the sign is common to all, to the good and bad alike; but the Spirit is bestowed only on the elect, and the sign, as we have said, has no efficacy without the Spirit."[327] By claiming that God does not in fact offer to all what the sign represents, but only truly offers it to the elect, Calvin seems to undermine his insistence that baptism does not mock the eyes with a delusive symbol, but that God truly offers what the sacrament represents.[328]

12. THE HOLY SUPPER OF THE LORD

The holy Supper of the Lord shares with baptism the role of being an exercise of faith that protects, arouses, and increases it throughout the life of the godly. In the first edition of the *Institutes,* Calvin determines the meaning and purpose of the Supper by turning to the promise that it attests. Whereas the third benefit symbolized by baptism was our engrafting into Christ himself with all his benefits, Calvin makes our engrafting into Christ the primary benefit attested by the Supper, "so that whatever is his we are permitted to call ours, whatever is ours to reckon as his."[329] The Supper is a proof and witness of the exchange Christ has made with us, which becomes effective in us when we are engrafted in him. Christ takes upon himself our sin, guilt, poverty, weakness, and mortality, in order to pay our debt for us, and bestow on us his wealth, power, and immortality.[330] "All of these things are so perfectly promised in this sacrament, that we must consider him as truly shown to us, just as if Christ himself present were set before our gaze and touched by our hands."[331] In particular, the bread and wine of the Supper represent to us the body and blood of Christ that were given for us, so that we may learn that they are the life and food of our soul. Such recognition takes places by means of the analogy between the sign and the thing signified: "as bread nourishes, sustains, and keeps the life of our body, so Christ's body is the food and protection of our spiritual life."[332] However, Calvin does not at this point say that the signs of bread and wine actually offer the body and blood of Christ to us in the Supper.

The purpose of the Supper is therefore to "seal and confirm" the promise of Christ to be the food and drink of our soul unto eternal life (John 6:55). "And to do this, the Sacrament sends us to the cross of Christ, where that promise was indeed performed and in all respects fulfilled."[333] According to Calvin, we should attend to the question of how we "possess the whole Christ crucified, and to become a participant in all his benefits," and not to the question of how his body is devoured by us. We should seek Christ in the Supper as food and drink for our souls, and thereby readily understand "how the body of Christ is offered to us in the sacrament, namely, truly and effectively. And he will not be at all anxious over the nature of the body."[334] Calvin then expends a great deal of energy showing that the body of Christ has ascended to heaven, and as it is a true human body, it has a fixed dimension and is contained in a place.[335] Christ can still show his presence in power and strength in order to live in the faithful to sustain, strengthen, quicken, and keep them, even though his body is present only in heaven.[336] This is what Calvin means by saying that Christ is shown forth truly and effectively in the Supper, namely, that the presence of the body "manifests itself here with a power and effectiveness so great that it not only brings an undoubted assurance of eternal life to our hearts but also assures us of the immortality of our flesh."[337] In this way, Calvin hopes to avoid resurrecting Marcion's teaching that the body of Christ is present wherever the divinity of Christ is present, while also avoiding making the sacrament into an idol to be adored as God.

The sum of Calvin's teaching at this point in his career seems to be that the Supper of the Lord represents, attests, and exhibits the life we receive from Christ crucified, to remind us of the reality of our union with Christ and of our redemption by his death on the cross.[338] Calvin supports this position by appealing to Paul's statement that in the Supper we "declare the Lord's death" (1 Cor. 11:26). "Here again the purpose of the Sacrament is made clear, that is, to exercise us in the remembrance of Christ's death."[339] Calvin claims that the Roman teaching that the Mass is a sacrifice for sin "weakens and destroys the sacrament by which the memory of his death was bequeathed to us."[340] On the other hand, Calvin teaches that the Supper should be celebrated frequently, at least once a week, for "it was ordained to be frequently used among all Christians in order that they might frequently return in memory to Christ's Passion, by such remembrance to sustain and strengthen their faith, and urge themselves to sing thanksgiving and to proclaim his goodness."[341] Indeed, Calvin claims that the Lord has "engraved and inscribed the remembrance of his Passion" in the Sacred Supper.[342] Thus in 1536 Calvin views the holy Supper of the Lord as a witness and proof of the promise of our engrafting in Christ so that all that is ours is his, and all that is his is ours, and also as the remembrance of Christ's death as being our life. It exhibits Christ to us as though he stood before us, but it does not offer what it represents, even though Calvin says that it offers the body of Christ truly and efficaciously.[343]

In the *Two Discourses on the Lausanne Articles* of 1537, Calvin cites patristic authorities to support the claim of Farel and Viret that the body of Christ is in heaven. Hence, neither the natural body nor the blood of Christ is offered to the faithful in the Supper. Rather, the Supper is "a spiritual communication by which he makes us truly participant of his body and his blood, but wholly spiritually, that is by the bond of his Spirit."[344] Calvin reinforces the nature of this spiritual communication in the *Confession of Faith concerning the Eucharist* of the same year, signed by Calvin, Farel, Viret, Bucer, and Capito. The confession begins by noting the way the faithful receive eternal life from the vivifying body of Christ through the Spirit, so that the faithful commune with the whole Christ, his body and blood as well as his Spirit. Even though the true body of Christ is in heaven, "the efficacy of his Spirit is limited by no bounds, but is able really to unite and bring together into one things that are disjointed in local space."[345] The faithful by the Spirit really do experience communion with the life-giving flesh of Christ, even if that flesh is in heaven. "This communion of his own body and blood Christ offers in his blessed Supper under the symbols of bread and wine, presenting them to all who rightly celebrate it according to his own proper institution."[346] This terse sentence seems to indicate that more is being offered in the Supper than a memorial of the death of Christ and a testimony to the promise of Christ to become one with the faithful, as in the first edition of the *Institutes*.

Calvin repeats his understanding of spiritual communion with the heavenly body and blood of Christ in his *Catechism* of 1538.[347] Once again, the Holy Spirit is the bond that unites believers on earth with the body and blood of Christ in heaven, so that the power of his life might feed believers.[348] However, it appears that the *Catechism* primarily echoes the understanding of the Supper in the first edition of the *Institutes*, for it claims that the Supper is given as proof of the spiritual communion we have with Christ, in which "Christ with all his riches is shown to us, just as if he, present, were set before our gaze," in order to remind believers of the benefits they receive from their spiritual communion with Christ.[349] "Accordingly, body and blood are represented under bread and wine, so that we may learn not only that they are ours, but that they are life and food for us."[350] The analogy of bread and body, and wine and blood, should lead us to reflect on the benefits we receive from our spiritual communion with Christ, but they do not offer this communion to us.[351]

In the second edition of the *Institutes*, Calvin accentuates the way all of our life is to be sought from the life-giving flesh of Christ. The Word of God is the ultimate source of our life, but in order that this life might be manifested to perishing sinners, the Word became flesh and manifested its life in flesh like ours.[352] The flesh of Christ is therefore the rich and inexhaustible fountain from which we ourselves must seek all life, even as that flesh receives its life from God.[353] In the Supper, Christ testifies to this life-giving communion of his body and blood and "truly offers and shows it to all who sit at that spiritual banquet, although it is received by believers alone, who accept such great generosity with true faith and gratefulness of heart."[354]

It soon becomes clear that Calvin no longer understands the testimony, offer, and exhibition in the Supper to represent the communion with Christ that believers always enjoy. Instead, he claims that God is not a deceiver, and thus does not set forth an empty symbol before us. Thus, even though "the breaking of the bread is a symbol; it is not the thing itself," Calvin nevertheless insists that "by showing the symbol the thing itself is shown."[355] To support this claim, Calvin appeals to Paul's statement that in the bread and cup we have a participation in Christ's body and blood (1 Cor. 10:16). The bread and wine of the Supper not only represent and figure the life-giving body and blood of Christ, but they also present and exhibit them. "Therefore, if the Lord truly represents the participation in his body through the breaking of bread, there ought not to be the least doubt that he truly presents and shows his body."[356] Even as the godly ought to distinguish the symbol from the reality symbolized, so they ought always to join the reality to the symbol, for it is truly presented by the symbol. "But if it is true that a visible sign is given us to seal the gift of a thing invisible, when we have received the symbol of the body, let us no less surely trust that the body itself is also given to us."[357]

From this point on, Calvin insists that what God represents (*repraesentat*) in the symbol of the Supper God simultaneously presents (*exhibeat*) in reality. This is the reason the symbol is given the name of the thing symbolized, for it not only represents the thing itself by analogy but also truly exhibits and presents the reality it represents.[358] Calvin notes that this is done even with regard to symbols devised by humans, which can only be "images of things absent rather than marks of things present."[359] How much more ought this to be the case with symbols instituted by God, which "have the reality joined with them?"[360]

However, Calvin also insists that the reality represented and exhibited by the Supper is present in heaven, and must be sought there, and not in the symbols of the body in the bread and wine.[361] Even though Christ's body and blood are in heaven, we enjoy true participation in them through the bond of the Holy Spirit.[362] Nonetheless, Calvin admits that he does not have the capacity to express the way that God offers us the reality when God shows us the symbol, and urges his readers to be ravished with wonder before the mystery rather than to try too hard to express everything in words. "Therefore, nothing remains but to break forth in wonder at the mystery, which plainly neither the mind is able to conceive nor the tongue to express."[363]

In the *Short Treatise on the Holy Supper of Our Lord and Only Savior Jesus Christ* of 1541, Calvin claims that even though the Gospel offers the same participation in the life-giving flesh of Christ as does the Supper, God instituted the Supper out of accommodation to our weakness and infirmity.[364]

The need for the visible representation of the promises becomes especially clear when we descend into ourselves and see how destitute we are of every good thing, and how full of sin and evil we are. "Now our heavenly Father, to succor us from [the feeling of such misery], gives us the Supper as a mirror in which we contemplate our Lord Jesus Christ crucified to abolish our faults and offenses, and raised to deliver us from corruption and death, and restoring us to a heavenly immortality."[365] This mirror confirms our faith more fully than would the preaching of the Gospel, even though both offer the same grace of Christ.[366]

Since every good thing we lack can only be ours when we are joined with Christ, the Supper represents two things to us in particular: "Jesus Christ as source and substance of all good; and second, the fruit and efficacy of his death and passion."[367] Since our communion with Christ takes place especially by means of his flesh and blood, these are set before us in the symbols of the bread and wine. As in the second edition of the *Institutes,* Calvin notes that the symbols take the name of the thing they symbolize, but now the reason given is that the bread and wine are "the instruments" by which Christ distributes the reality of his body and blood to us.[368] Once again, this takes place out of accommodation to our infirmity, by showing us a visible representation of our invisible communion with Christ.[369]

However, the symbol not only represents the invisible reality to us but also offers us the reality with the symbol.[370] Even as the reality ought to be distinguished from the symbol that represents it, so the reality ought always to be joined to the symbol, for God does not deceive with empty appearances. "If God cannot deceive or lie, it follows that he performs all that it signifies. We must then really receive in the Supper the body and blood of Jesus Christ, since the Lord there represents to us the communion of both."[371] Thus the bread and wine not only represent the reality of the body and blood of Christ and our communion with them but also actually offer them to us so that we may participate in them.[372] The Supper is therefore a symbol that represents and exhibits the body and blood of Christ to us, and also an instrument through which God distributes the body and blood of Christ to us.[373] Nonetheless, Calvin cautions his readers that even though the reality is offered with the symbols of the Supper, it is not to be sought in the symbols themselves, but in heaven, even as it is made present to the faithful by the bond of the Spirit.[374] Calvin claims that this interpretation is not new with him but is rather reflected in the eucharistic liturgy of the early Church. "Moreover, the practice always observed in the ancient Church was that, before celebrating the Supper, the people were solemnly exhorted to lift their hearts on high, to show that we must not stop at the visible sign, to adore Christ rightly."[375]

In the *Manner of Celebrating the Lord's Supper* of 1542, Calvin combines the themes we have seen in the *Short Treatise* of 1541. On the one hand, he reminds the congregation that Christ does not deceive us with empty signs but will perform in our souls all that he represents to our eyes in the symbols of bread and wine.[376] Christ represents both himself and all his benefits to us in the Supper, in order that he might exhibit and present this reality to all who participate, "for, in giving himself to us, he bears testimony to us that all he has is ours."[377] On the other hand, Calvin encourages the congregation to lift up their minds and hearts to heaven, so that they seek the reality joined to the signs in heaven and not in the signs themselves.[378] The faithful are to be guided by the word of God, which has an inseparable relationship to the symbols of bread and wine, to seek Christ in heaven so that they might be nourished by his vivifying flesh. "Let us be contented, then, to have the bread and wine as signs and evidences, spiritually seeking the reality where the word of God promises that we shall find it."[379] Christ will perform in our souls what the symbols represent to us—"to make us partakers of his own body and blood, in order that we may possess him entirely in such a manner that he may live in us and we in him"—only if we on our part seek Christ not in the symbols of bread and wine but in heaven.[380]

In the third edition of the *Institutes*, Calvin emphasizes the theme of accommodation to our weakness that he incorporated into his discussion of the Supper in 1541. "Since, however, this mystery of Christ's secret union with the devout is by nature incomprehensible, he shows its figure and image in visible signs."[381] Calvin makes it clear that the analogy of the sign to the thing signified not only represents the spiritual blessings the faithful always enjoy in Christ but also communicates those blessings to us in the Supper.[382] Moreover, he accentuates the offer of communion with the life-giving flesh and blood of Christ in the Supper, over and above the offer we receive in the Gospel.[383] He makes it clear that Christ not only offers himself and his benefits to us in the Supper but also inwardly accomplishes what the Supper outwardly exhibits.[384]

Calvin claims that the Church has always taught his distinction between the signs and the reality signified, as well as the need to see the reality offered and exhibited in the signs that represent it, thereby claiming catholicity for his teaching on the Supper.[385] However, he shows a willingness to allow for different ways of expressing the mystery he is describing, so long as such teaching "may neither fasten [Christ] to the element of the bread, nor enclose him in the bread, nor circumscribe him in any way (all which things, it is clear, detract from his heavenly glory); finally, such as may not take from him his own stature, or parcel him out to many places at once, or invest him with boundless magnitude to be spread through heaven and earth."[386] So long as Christ is not dragged out of heaven to be confined under the physical symbols of his body and blood, and his human nature is rightly understood as being in heaven, then Calvin is willing to "accept whatever can be made to express the true and substantial partaking of the body and blood of the Lord, which is shown to believers under the symbols of the Supper—and so to express it that they may be understood not to receive it solely by imagination or understanding of the mind, but to enjoy the thing itself as nourishment of eternal life."[387]

As in 1539, Calvin reiterates his inability to express this mystery in words, pointing to the experience of the reality in the Supper instead of to his own teaching.[388] However, essential to the right experience of this mystery is the need to seek the life-giving flesh and blood of Christ in heaven and not in the symbols of bread and wine. Indeed, God gives us these symbols in accommodation to our weakness, to give us the assistance we need to seek Christ in heaven. "For in order that pious minds may duly apprehend Christ in the Supper, they must be raised up to heaven."[389] Once again, Calvin claims that this upward ascent is reflected in the eucharistic liturgy of the early Church. "And for the same reason it was established of old that before the consecration the people should be told in a loud voice to lift up their hearts."[390] In order that the people might rightly be directed to Christ in the celebration of the Supper, Calvin insists that the Word explaining the promise and meaning of the sacrament must be loudly and intelligibly declared to the congregation, as opposed to the private whispering of Roman priests during the words of consecration. "Silence involves abuse and fault. If the promises are recited and the mysteries declared, so that they who are about to receive it may receive it with benefit, there is no reason to doubt that this is a true consecration."[391]

In the *Catechism of the Church of Geneva* of 1545, Calvin consolidates all of the themes we have discerned in the development of his teaching on the Supper. He notes that although Christ is offered to us in the Gospel and

Baptism, the Supper is still necessary, for by it "the communion of which I have spoken is confirmed and increased in us. For though both in Baptism and in the gospel Christ is exhibited to us, yet we do not receive him wholly but only in part."[392] Calvin insists that the body and blood of Christ are not simply represented in the Supper but are also exhibited and presented in the bread and wine.[393] This is done not by dragging the body and blood of Christ from heaven, but by the Spirit of Christ, which joins us to the reality of the symbols.[394] To enjoy the reality that is represented and exhibited to us in the Supper, we must not seek the body and blood of Christ in the symbols of bread and wine. "Rather, I think that in order to enjoy the reality of the signs we must be raised to heaven where Christ is and whence we expect him to come as judge and redeemer."[395]

In his commentary on 1 Corinthians of 1546, Calvin clarifies the distinction between representation and exhibition that is crucial for his understanding of the veracity of the symbols of the Supper. As we have seen, the bread and wine not only figure but also exhibit the reality they represent. This is why the symbol is called by the name of the thing it signifies.[396] In the 1539 *Institutes* Calvin thinks that humanly devised symbols cannot exhibit the reality they represent, for they are only "images of things absent rather than marks of things present."[397] He clarifies this point in the commentary on First Corinthians. The bread and wine are not called the body and blood of Christ in the same way that we call a statue by the name of the person it represents. "The statue of Hercules is called 'Hercules'; but it is nothing but a bare, empty representation."[398] The sacraments are in a different category of representation, because they exhibit the reality they figure. "Therefore the bread is the body of Christ, because it bears indubitable witness to the fact that the very body, which it stands for, is held out to us; or because, in offering us that symbol, the Lord is giving us his body at the same time."[399] Human symbols can only be bare and empty representations of absent realities. Only God can create symbols that not only represent and figure a reality but also present and exhibit that reality to us. Therefore, when we see the symbols of bread and wine, we should be certain that the Lord will give us the reality they symbolize. "You see the bread, and nothing else, but you hear that it is a sign of the body of Christ. Be quite sure that the Lord will really carry out what you understand the words to mean: that his body, which you do not see at all, is spiritual food for you."[400] However, the Lord will only do this if we at the same time seek him not in the symbols of bread and wine but in his glory in heaven.[401] Christ can communicate himself to us in this way not by changing the nature or location of his life-giving flesh but by the power of the Holy Spirit.[402]

The most significant development that takes place in Calvin's understanding of the holy Supper of the Lord after 1539 regards his increasing emphasis on the Supper as a means by which to elevate the faithful from earth to heaven where Christ dwells in glory. Already in 1543, Calvin describes the chief purpose of the Supper as being a help by which we might raise our minds to heaven, in contrast to the Roman teaching of transubstantiation.[403] Calvin also describes the Supper as an accommodation to our weakness, whereby we are given the assistance we need to raise our minds and hearts to heaven.[404] He highlights the upward dynamic of the Supper, again in contrast to the Roman doctrine of transubstantiation, in *The True Method of Giving Peace, and of Reforming the Church* of 1549.[405] To accentuate the purpose of the Supper in raising us to heaven, Calvin describes it both as a hand stretched out by Christ to lift us up to heaven and as a ladder that Christ gives us so that we might ascend to him in heaven. "Christ invites us to himself. As we cannot climb so high, he himself lends us his hand, and assists us with the helps which he knows to be suited to us, and even lifts us to heaven, as it is very appropriately expressed by those who compare the sacraments to ladders."[406] In the Supper Christ reaches his hand down to us to draw us upwards to himself, and assists our weakness by giving us ladders to climb to him. If we seek Christ in the symbols of bread and wine, we totally thwart this purpose.[407] Calvin uses the preface to the eucharistic prayer in the Roman Church against what he takes to be the earthbound attention directed to the sign of the bread. "And what meaning will there be in the ancient preamble, 'Sursum Corda,' which the Papists still chant in their masses, if our worship cleaves to the earth?"[408]

In his interpretation of the sermon of Stephen in his commentary on Acts in 1552, Calvin seeks to combine the downward thrust of the Supper, by which it represents and exhibits the body and blood of Christ, with the upward dynamic of the Supper, by which it helps to lift us up to heaven. On the one hand, God does in fact descend to us in the sacraments, by becoming somewhat visible, in accommodation to our weakness.[409] On the other hand, the reason God comes down to us is not to leave us clinging to earth, so that we might confine the presence of God here, but rather so that we might have the means by which to ascend to God. "God does indeed come down to us, as I have said, but for this purpose, that he might lift us up to heaven."[410] Calvin thinks that Stephen reminds the Jews that the tabernacle was made after the heavenly archetype seen by Moses on Mount Sinai in order that the Jews might lift their minds from the earthly sign of God's presence to the spiritual reality it signifies in heaven.[411] Thus God testifies to God's presence in the Temple, as we have seen, so that the Jews might seek God in heaven by means of that symbol.[412] In a similar way, God descends to us in the sacraments so that we might ascend to him in heaven by faith. "In a word, the promise accepted by faith brings it about that God listens to us, and gives out his power in the sacraments, as if he were present; but if we do not reach up to him in faith, he will not be present for us."[413]

After this commentary, Calvin will use the symbols of God's presence in Israel both to critique the attempt to affix God to earthly symbols, as in the doctrine of transubstantiation, and to provide a model for the right way to understand the sacrament of the Lord's Supper. In his commentary on Genesis of 1554, Calvin describes all the symbols of God's presence among the Israelites as "ladders and vehicles," by the help of which they might ascend from earth to heaven.[414] In the following year, in his defense of the Zurich Consensus, Calvin appeals to the archetype Moses saw on Mount Sinai, as discussed in Acts and Hebrews, as providing the key for the right approach to the holy Supper of the Lord.[415] The Supper therefore invites us, not to confine our attention to the earthly signs, but to climb as by a ladder from the sign to the reality of Christ in heaven, "for nowhere else is Christ to be sought, and nowhere are we to seek rest than in him alone."[416]

Just as the representation and exhibition of the reality represents the descent of God to us in accommodation to our weakness, so also the setting up of symbols as ladders are aids for us, without which we would never be able to ascend to God and obtain grace.[417] Indeed, in his second defense of the orthodox faith concerning the sacraments against Westphal, Calvin combines the descending nature of the representation and exhibition of Christ in the Supper with the ascending nature of the ladder by which we climb from earth to heaven, by means of the role of anagogy. "For to what end does Christ hold forth a pledge of his flesh and blood under earthly elements unless it be to raise us upwards? If they are helps to our weakness, no man will ever attain to the reality, but he who thus assisted shall climb, as it were, step by step from earth to heaven."[418]

Calvin never seems to be aware of the irreducible tension that these two claims create in his doctrine of the holy Supper of the Lord.[419] On the one hand, he insists that the Lord not only represents and figures but also exhibits and presents the body and blood of Christ in the bread and wine of the Supper. Moreover, the Lord, by the power of the Spirit, inwardly effects what the sacrament outwardly represents, so that as we eat and drink the bread and wine, we are fed by the Spirit on the heavenly flesh and blood of Christ. "For Christ is neither a painter, nor an actor, nor a kind of Archimedes who presents an empty image to amuse the eye; but he truly and in reality performs what by external symbol he promises."[420] On the other hand, Calvin insists that Christ is not to be sought in the symbols of bread and wine but in heaven. Christ gives us the symbols as vehicles or ladders to help us in our weakness, so that we might ascend from earth to heaven, to seek the reality symbolized there. If we do not mount up to heaven on these ladders, the reality simply will not be given to us.[421] In the first model, the initiative lies entirely with Christ, who exhibits and effects by his Spirit the communication of his body and blood that is represented to us in the sacrament of the Supper. In the second model, the initiative lies with the godly, who use the Supper as the means of their anagogic ascent from the earthly symbol to the heavenly reality, to attain their communion with the body and blood of Christ. "In order to drink the blood of Christ by faith, the thing necessary is not that he come down to earth, but that we rise up to heaven, or rather the blood of Christ must remain in heaven in order that believers may share it among themselves."[422]

The same tension is introduced into the final edition of the *Institutes*. On the one hand, against his opponents who think that he is shaping his teaching according to the dictates of reason, Calvin insists that the heart of his teaching comes from faith in this mystery. "We say that Christ descends to us both by the outward symbol and by his Spirit, that he may truly quicken our souls by the substance of his flesh and his blood."[423] On the other hand, Calvin claims that the Lutheran teaching, that Christ is presented "under the bread," frustrates the whole design of God in the Supper, which is to raise us to Christ in heaven. "Moreover, since it is God's plan (as I often reiterate) to lift us to himself, by appropriate vehicles, those who call us indeed to Christ, but to Christ hidden invisibly under the bread, wickedly frustrate his plan by their obstinacy."[424] Calvin seeks to resolve this tension by claiming that the descent of Christ to us both by the symbols and by the Spirit takes place so that we might thereby ascend to Christ in heaven. "For they think they only communicate with [the body of Christ] if it descends into the bread; but they do not understand the true manner of descent by which he lifts us up to himself."[425] In this way, the presence of Christ exhibited by the symbols makes possible our ascent to Christ in heaven, as in Calvin's image of the Supper as the hand of Christ reaching down to pull us up to himself. Such an interpretation is supported by the way it appears to echo Calvin's description of the presence of God in the Temple. "The last thing he intended was to tie down his people to earthly symbols. On the contrary he comes down to them, in order to lift them up on high to himself."[426]

CHAPTER 11

The Manifestation of Piety in the Church

The Gospel and the sacraments foster, strengthen, and confirm faith and piety by manifesting Jesus Christ and the fountain of every good thing set forth in him by God the Father. Faith is confirmed both by hearing the promises in the Gospel and by seeing them portrayed and represented before our eyes in the sacraments, even though the Holy Spirit is necessary for both to bear fruit in our minds and hearts. The Gospel and the sacraments are therefore central to the worship life of the Church. However, Calvin insists that the piety fostered in the inmost affection of our hearts would seek to manifest itself to others, both in the language we use and in the bodily gestures we employ, including those codified in the rites and ceremonies of worship. Indeed, even though the primary purpose of the sacraments is to represent and exhibit Christ and his benefits to us, their secondary purpose is to bear witness to our faith and gratitude to others. Even though piety, like other affections of the heart, remains hidden from the view of others, it becomes somewhat visible in our words and gestures. According to Calvin, such verbal and visual expressions of piety have the ability to stimulate piety in oneself as well as in others, making the mutual communication of piety one of the central purposes of worship in the Church. However, human beings, unlike God, can use words and actions to conceal their thoughts and affections from others. The very words and gestures that should reveal piety to others may in fact mask the lack of piety in our hearts. Thus Calvin is very concerned that there be a correspondence between the hearts of the godly and the language and gestures they employ. Calvin also develops an extensive criticism of humanly devised images based on his understanding of the proper purpose of public worship, as this is the central issue in his rejection of the use of such images.

I. The Purpose of Public Worship

Calvin's thoughts about the purpose of public worship are quite rudimentary in 1536, and clearly develop in light of his experience in the pastorate in Geneva, Strasbourg, and again in Geneva. In the 1536 *Institutes,* Calvin discusses the nature of public worship in the context of his discussion of prayer, which for him is the central act of worship. Even though the pious are exhorted to pray at all times, Calvin thinks that it is still useful for believers to gather together at agreed upon times and places to pray, hear the Gospel, and partake of the sacraments.[1] He is especially concerned that the godly not think that such places of worship are holy or bring them nearer to God, since Paul tells the faithful that they are the true temples of God. "Let those who wish to pray in God's temple, pray in themselves."[2]

In spite of this qualification, Calvin thinks it is useful for the pious to gather together to pray, to hear preaching, and to celebrate the sacraments together. However, even as he is concerned that we not think such places of worship are holy, he is also concerned that we not consider the arrangements of the worship of the community to be binding on conscience, as they are instead governed by the rules of decorum.[3] According to Calvin, the primary elements of communal worship consist of public prayer, the sermon, and the Supper, as well as the singing of psalms and hymns, baptisms, and the discipline of excommunication. However, it is clear that in 1536 Calvin is primarily concerned with avoiding the errors of the Roman Church, with its view of consecrated spaces of worship and holy days of obligation, and not with the positive meaning of public worship per se.

In the second edition of the *Institutes* of 1539, Calvin gives greater emphasis to the usefulness of public worship, given the temptation some might feel to pray alone in secret, after the counsel of Jesus in the Sermon on the Mount.[4] Calvin is concerned that the faithful truly express in their prayers what lies in their hearts, but with this proviso he insists that the godly cannot neglect gathering together to worship and pray. "For he, who promises that he will do whatever two or three gathered together in his name may ask [Matt. 18:19–20], testifies that he does not despise prayers publicly made, provided ostentation and chasing after paltry human glory are banished, and there is present a sincere and true affection that dwells in the secret place of the heart."[5] Calvin reiterates his concern that the faithful not see such places of public prayer as intrinsically holy, though now with reference to the new economy of the Gospel, which is different from that of the Law.[6] Christ brings the time of the Temple to an end, and the pious are now commanded to worship God in spirit and in truth, even when they gather for public prayers.

Calvin expands on his understanding of public worship in his commentary on First Corinthians of 1546. When Paul chastises the Corinthian Church for their divisive behavior when they come together to worship, Calvin observes, "We know what the Church ought to meet together to do; to hear teaching; to pour out prayers and sing hymns to God; to celebrate the mysteries; to make confession of our faith; to take part in religious rites and other godly exercises. Anything else that is done there is out of place."[7] Calvin makes two key additions to preaching, prayers, hymns, and the sacraments. On the one hand, the community gathers to confess its faith, which became increasingly important to Calvin given his controversy with the "Nicodemites" in France during this time. On the other hand, Calvin adds "pious rites and other pious exercises" to the elements of worship, indicating the increasingly important role given to the rites and ceremonies of worship, which is discussed more fully below. It is clear that by 1546 one of the essential roles of public worship is to manifest our piety to others in the confession of faith and other rites, so that the piety of the community might be both expressed and stimulated thereby.

Moreover, Calvin describes the preaching, sacraments, and rites of the Church in public worship as the mirror of which Paul speaks, in which we now see God enigmatically. "For God, who is otherwise invisible, has appointed these as means for revealing himself to us."[8] Calvin notes that Paul says the same thing about the universe itself, in which the glory of God shines out for all to see.[9] The invisible God becomes somewhat visible in the public worship of the Church, even as the invisible God appears to us in the mirror of the created world. Calvin contrasts the way we see God in the mirror of "preaching, or other inferior aids, or sacraments," with the way angels see God face-to-face, without the need of a mirror. "But we, who have not scaled such heights, look upon the image of God in the Word, in the sacraments, and, in short, in the whole ministry of the Church."[10]

Calvin continues to develop the visibility of God in the ministry of the Church in subsequent commentaries. Even though the angels see God face-to-face, they did not know of the mystery of the calling of the Gentiles until they saw the wisdom of God manifested in the mirror of the Gospel.[11] Calvin claims that God appears in the sacraments and the Gospel in a manner similar to the way God appeared to the Israelites in the symbols of God's presence in the Law, in accommodation to our ignorance.[12] For this reason, the ministry of the Church offers the same access to heaven that Jacob enjoyed in his vision of the ladder joining heaven to earth.[13] However, Calvin also acknowledges the accommodated mode of this divine self-manifestation, appearing in forms that might seem inappropriate or even absurd. "He promises spiritual righteousness, and sets a little sprinkling of water before our eyes. He seals the promise of the soul's eternal life with a morsel of bread and a sip of wine."[14]

To describe the purpose of such accommodated forms of manifestation in worship, by 1554 Calvin begins to describe the Gospel, sacraments, and rites of the Church as "aids" to assist us in our infirmity and weakness. These aids were given both to the Israelites and to the Christian Church to lead us to the spiritual worship of God. "The faithful never based the worship of God strictly on ceremonies, but thought of them merely as aids, with which to discipline themselves on account of their weakness."[15] Whereas the ungodly think that God is properly worshiped by the splendor and ostentation of ceremonies per se, the godly know that God offers such ceremonies to us as helps to unite us to God, both before and after the coming of Christ.[16] Whereas the ungodly use the ceremonies of public worship to conceal themselves from God and others, the godly use them as helps by which to seek God, "and the advantage which they derive from them creates love to them in their hearts, and longings after them."[17]

For this reason, Calvin insists that the "temples" in the Christian Church have the same kind of alluring beauty as did the Temple in Jerusalem, by which to draw our affections. "The Word, the sacraments, public prayers, and other helps of the same kind, cannot be neglected, without a wicked contempt of God, who represents himself to us in these ordinances, as in a mirror or image."[18] Christians could even worship in this way in the Temple in Jerusalem, so long as they did not seek sacrifices of expiation there, and did not view it as being the face of God.[19] The ceremonies of worship are therefore the means by which God allures us to Godself, in order to raise us up to God, for "they are exercises of piety which we cannot bear to want by reason of our infirmity."[20] We should follow the example of David, who did not rest in such ceremonies but "made use of them as a ladder, by which he might ascend to God, finding he had not wings with which to fly thither."[21] Such exercises of piety become so important to Calvin that by 1557 he begins to list them at the head of the purposes of public worship, ahead of preaching. "Whenever true believers assemble together at the present day, the end which they ought to have in view is to exercise themselves in true piety—to call to remembrance the benefits which they have received from God—to make progress in the knowledge of his word—and to testify the oneness of their faith."[22] Indeed, in the final edition of the *Institutes,* Calvin begins his discussion of the Church with our need for the accommodated helps and aids of piety God provides for us in the public worship of the Church, which are made necessary due to "our ignorance and sloth."[23]

When the exercises of piety are removed from us, or we are taken away from them, we should still recall them in our minds, in order to be helped by them even in their absence, even as David called to mind the ceremonies of worship in his exile.[24] Those in Calvin's day, such as the evangelicals in France, who are deprived of the holy Supper of the Lord, should nonetheless recall it to mind, in order to rise to the contemplation of God.[25] By keeping the exercises of piety in mind, we can pray to God by their help at all times, even when we, like Daniel, are separated from the rites of piety for a lengthy period. "If any one in these days is cast into prison, and even prohibited from enjoying the sacred Supper to the end of his life, yet he ought not on that account to cast away the remembrance of that sacred symbol; but should consider within himself every day, why the Supper was granted to us by Christ, and what advantages he desires us to derive from it."[26]

Since the rites and ceremonies of worship help us in our weakness and infirmity to be increasingly united to God and to one another, we ought to value the benefit of public worship above all other gifts of this life, along with the sacraments. "By these, and our common sacraments, the Lord, who is one God, and who designed that we should be one in him, is training us up together in the hope of eternal life, and in the united celebration of his holy name."[27] Calvin makes the same point in the final edition of the *Institutes,* in light of David's lament over being separated from the tabernacle. "Surely, this is because believers have no greater help than public worship, for by it God raises his own folk upward step by step."[28] On the other hand, there can be no worse calamity in this life than when the rites and ceremonies of public worship are taken away from us, as happened to the Israelites under the Assyrians. "It would therefore be better for us to be deprived of meat and drink, and to go naked, and to perish at last through want, than that the exercises of piety, by which the Lord holds us, as it were, in his own bosom, should be taken away from us."[29]

2. Language Is the Image of the Mind

One of the central ways the faithful manifest and express their piety to others is through language, both spoken and sung. In the first edition of the *Institutes,* Calvin locates the worship of God not only in the heart but also in the tongue and the entire body. Thus, when God commands, "You shall have no other God before me" (Exod. 20:3), Calvin says, "This we must do not only to declare, by tongue and bodily gesture, and by every outward indication, that we have no other God; but also with our mind, whole heart, and all our zeal, show ourselves as such."[30] The chief place that the godly are to do this is in their prayers. On the one hand, Calvin is concerned that the language and songs of prayer truly express the inmost affection of the heart.[31] On the other hand, when language and song do express the heart's affection, they exercise the mind in thinking about God.[32] However, given the danger of hypocrisy, Calvin tends to prefer silent prayers, as these more clearly manifest the affections of the heart before God. "Lastly, the tongue is not even necessary for private prayer: the inner feeling would be enough to arouse itself, so that sometimes the best prayers are silent ones."[33]

The same emphasis on the inner affection of the heart may be seen in the *Catechism* of 1538. The tongue may contribute something to prayer, but "the Lord through his prophet has declared what value this has when mindlessly expressed, when he lays the greatest vengeance upon all who, estranged from him in heart, honor him with their lips."[34] However, in *Articles concerning the Organization of the Church and of Worship at Geneva* of 1537, Calvin indicates that the use of the tongue in singing might in fact influence the affections of the heart by awakening in them a more ardent desire to praise God. Calvin claims that singing the Psalms was the practice both of Paul and of the early Church, but that experience itself confirms its usefulness. "Certainly as things are, the prayers of the faithful are so cold, that we ought to be ashamed and dismayed. The psalms can incite us to lift up our hearts to God and move us to an ardor in invoking and exalting the praises of his Name."[35] One can see in this observation that Calvin's experience as a pastor was decisive in leading him to search for ways to incite and stimulate the piety of the congregation in their prayers, given his impression of the frigidity of prayer life in Geneva. Even though Calvin will continue to root the genuine meaning of language and song in the affections of the heart it ought to express, he will increasingly describe the way such language inspires and stimulates one's own piety as well as the godly affections of others.

In the second edition of the *Institutes,* Calvin qualifies his statement that the best prayers are silent ones by describing the way the affection of the heart will be aroused by the language of prayer or will of itself be of such strength and vehemence that it will spontaneously seek to express itself in language. "For even though the best prayers are sometimes unspoken, it often happens in practice that, when feelings of mind are aroused, unostentatiously the tongue breaks forth into speech."[36] The language of prayer not only erupts from the affection of the heart, but it can also awaken the affections of the heart so that it is aroused to pray. Moreover, Calvin continues to describe the way sung language in particular has this power to stimulate the heart. In his *Draft Ecclesiastical Ordinances* of 1541, Calvin says, "It will be good to introduce ecclesiastical songs, the better to incite the people to prayer and to praise God."[37]

Calvin defends the apostolic and patristic warrant for such congregational singing in the third edition of the *Institutes.* "It is evident that the practice of singing in the church, to speak also of this in passing, is not only a very ancient one but also was in use among the apostles."[38] Calvin cites both 1 Corinthians 14:15 and Colossians 3:16 to demonstrate that Paul encouraged such singing. "For in the first passage he teaches that we should sing with voice and heart; in the second he commends spiritual songs, by which the godly may edify one another."[39] In particular, such singing has the effect of arousing the affections of the congregation so that it prays with more intensity.[40] In his commentary on 1 Corinthians of 1546, Calvin appeals to Pliny to support his claim that singing was a rite practiced by the earliest Christians that was adopted from the rites of the Jews.[41] He also appeals to Plato in support of his claim that music has the greatest power to move the affections of the human heart, which is confirmed by experience.[42] Thus, by 1546, Calvin is thoroughly convinced that the rite of singing is the most powerful way the godly can both give expression to their piety, and also awaken and incite the hearts of others to do the same.

In his commentary on 1 Corinthians, Calvin describes language as the image of the mind. "For since speaking is the image of the mind men convey their thoughts and feelings to each other, so that they come to know each other's minds well."[43] Calvin ascribes this description to a proverb but also claims that Aristotle supports it. "Our speech ought to be the reflection of our minds; not only as the proverb observes, but as Aristotle teaches at the beginning of his *On Interpretation*."[44] I have been unable to identify the source of the proverb, but it does resemble statements made by Plato. For instance, in the *Theaetetus*, Socrates describes the various meanings of "an account," which when added to true belief yields knowledge in its most perfect form. "The first will be giving an overt expression to one's thought by means of vocal sound with names and verbs, casting an image of one's notion on the stream that flows through the lips, like a reflection in a mirror or in water," to which Theaetetus responds by saying, "We certainly call that expressing ourselves in speech."[45] In the *Republic*, Socrates seeks to come to a clear understanding of justice "by fashioning in our discourse a symbolic image of the soul, that the maintainer of the proposition may see precisely what it is that he was saying."[46] The description of language by Aristotle is similar to those given by Plato. "Spoken words are the symbols of mental experience and written words are the symbols of spoken words. Just as all men have not the same writing, so all men have not the same speech sounds, but the mental experiences, which these directly symbolize, are the same for all, as also are those things of which our experiences are the images."[47] Finally, Horace, in his *Ars Poetica*, speaks of the way language is the image of the mind, in the course of discussing how poetry can be a painterly art giving an accurate representation of reality.

Calvin uses the proverb regarding language to interpret what the Gospel of John means by calling the eternal Son of God the Word of God. "For just as in men speech is called the expression of the thoughts, so it is not inappropriate to apply this to God and say that he expresses himself to us by his Speech or Word."[48] Calvin is concerned to point out one of the major differences between human and divine speech, however, which is that God always discloses God's heart to us in the Word, whereas humans often conceal themselves behind their language.[49] Since the Gospel in particular expresses the love of God for us, it is a true image of the love in the heart of God.[50] Thus we never have to worry if Christ's testimony of love is deceiving us in the Gospel, as we do when we speak with others.[51] Calvin makes the same point about the Word of God spoken by the prophets, when Jeremiah describes his prophecy as the thoughts of God's heart (Jer. 23:20). "It hence follows that there is nothing deceptive, as they say, in God's word; for he here declares that whatever he had committed to his servants were the thoughts of his heart."[52]

The prayers and confessions of the faithful are at their best when they correspond to the truth of the Word of God in their own expressions, for when this happens "no sweeter symphony can be imagined."[53] However, even though human beings are often deceptive in their language, and hide the thoughts of their hearts behind the words that they use, God will often bring it about that they will betray the affections of their hearts in their speech. "Yet what Christ says here is proved by common use, 'out of the abundance of the heart the mouth speaks.'"[54] Calvin qualifies this statement by noting that this rarely happens with regard to good and kind words, but rather takes place when the evil affections of the heart are betrayed in language. "Moreover, although good words do not always flow from the inmost heart but are just born on the tip of the tongue, as they say, yet it is on the other hand true that evil words are always witnesses to an evil heart."[55]

Given the propensity of human beings to deceive others when they speak, Calvin endorses David's exhortation that we keep our tongues from evil and our lips from speaking deceit (Ps. 34:13), so that "our speech may be a true representation of our hearts."[56] On the other hand, to indicate the integrity and sincerity of his speech, David describes it as being spoken in the heart (Ps. 15:2), which "denotes such agreement and harmony between the heart and tongue, as that the speech is, as it were, a vivid representation of the affection or feeling within."[57] The ability to speak in and from the heart is especially necessary for those called to teach and preach in the Church, for they should only say to others that which the Lord has revealed in the inmost affections of their own hearts. Thus Calvin says of David that "he speaks from his personal feeling and experience as a believer. This is very necessary in one who would be a teacher; for we cannot communicate true knowledge unless we deliver it not merely with the lips, but as something which God has revealed to our own inmost hearts."[58] However, this kind of integrity should be found in all the godly, for their personal confession of faith should spring from and accurately express the thoughts and feelings of their own hearts, "for many talk inconsiderately and utter what never entered into their hearts."[59]

On the other hand, Calvin insists that faith cannot remain hidden in the heart but must manifest itself in language.[60] Calvin was especially concerned about the self-manifestation of faith in confession in light of the evangelicals in France, who could be tempted to keep their faith in their hearts given the dangers to which an open confession would expose them. Calvin denied that true faith could remain hidden in the heart without manifesting itself in speech, "for they who sincerely worship God ought not to be dumb, but to testify both by actions and by words what they carry inwardly in their hearts."[61] Just as our language ought to be an accurate representation to others of the inward affections of our hearts, so the affections of our hearts must express themselves in language to others. "In short, we see that there is no true religion in the hearts of men, except a confession is made, for there ought to be a consent between the heart and the tongue."[62]

The language we use to express our faith not only reveals our inmost thoughts and affections to others but also has the effect of further stimulating faith within us. This is especially true of the language of prayer. Calvin makes this point in his *Catechism* of 1545. "M: But do you mean that no use is to be made of the tongue in prayer? C: No indeed. For often it is of assistance for the elevating of the mind and preventing it from so readily straying from God."[63] Even though Calvin was initially suspicious of any language that did not spring from the affection of the heart, even favoring silent prayers to spoken prayers, he gradually came to see that the language of prayer has the effect of awakening the affections of the heart, even as it also expresses those affections. "I admit that the heart ought to move and direct the tongue in prayer, but, as it often flags or performs its duty in a slow and sluggish manner, it requires to be aided by the tongue."[64] If our hearts are cold in prayer, the very language of prayer can stimulate and intensify our affections, even as that language also expresses those affections. "There is a reciprocal influence. As the heart, on the one hand, ought to go before the words, and frame them, so the tongue, on the other, aids and remedies the coldness and torpor of the heart."[65] Such language need not be especially eloquent to be powerful. Indeed, Calvin thinks that hypocrites excel at the eloquent rhetoric of prayer, whereas the godly utter broken and ecstatic cries to God.[66] Such ecstatic language arouses the affections not only of the one praying but also of the ones hearing such prayer, thereby intensifying the fervor of their prayer and "inflaming others to the same ardor."[67] Indeed, the language of prayer is the most effective when the affections it expresses transcend the ability of language to represent them.[68] The godly are not discouraged by this, however, for they know that God sees their hearts long before they are manifested in speech, and thus sees the affections that cannot be expressed in language.[69]

3. The Solemn Act of Public Thanksgiving and Praise

Although all the affections of the heart ought to break forth in the language of prayer, Calvin was especially concerned that expressions of gratitude and praise should sound forth in the public worship of believers. This is especially true with regard to the holy Supper of the Lord, which ought to be a public testimony to the gratitude of the congregation.[70] However, the testimonies of gratitude ought not to be limited to the celebration of the Eucharist, even if that is the central memorial of our redemption by the death of Christ. Rather, each believer ought to bear witness to the gratitude they feel in their hearts towards God.[71] The purpose of such public manifestations of gratitude is again to invite and incite the congregation to feel and express the same gratitude themselves "that they may encourage one another to act in the same manner."[72] Thus the gratitude we feel in our hearts towards God must be expressed not only in private but especially in public worship, in order to edify the whole community of the faithful, as Calvin thinks was done in Israel in the Psalms of thanksgiving.[73]

The public act of thanksgiving will only have the ability to invite and stir up others to do the same when it springs from the genuine affection of the heart.[74] The godly can only rightly express their gratitude to others when they have first experienced the goodness of God for themselves. "David not only asserts that God is good, but he is ravished with admiration of the goodness which he had experienced. It was this experience, undoubtedly, which caused him to break out into the rapturous language of this verse."[75] Language is unable to express the full extent of our gratitude, because our experience of the powers of God overwhelms us. "We only praise God aright when we are filled and overwhelmed with an ecstatic admiration of the immensity of his power."[76] The experience of the powers of God, especially of God's goodness, is essential if our expressions of gratitude are to have any meaning before God and others.

According to Calvin, we must give thanks to God in our hearts, and by ourselves, before we testify to that gratitude before others.[77] The failure of such gratitude to emerge in language would indicate that our gratitude is not in fact lively and forceful enough, for "it would be an indication of great coldness, and of want of fervor, did not the tongue unite with the heart in this exercise."[78] Such individual and private expressions of gratitude are necessary if we are to be of benefit to the community in the public act of thanksgiving.[79] However, such private acts of thanksgiving are not enough, for we must also testify to our gratitude before the whole congregation, "so that we may mutually stimulate one another."[80] Just as the tongue must be joined to the inward affection of the heart, so our private thanksgiving must be joined to the public act of gratitude.

Calvin identifies two specific ceremonies as acts of thanksgiving made by individuals: the making of vows and the celebration of birthdays. Calvin first discusses vows in the third edition of the *Institutes* of 1543. According to Calvin, one of the legitimate purposes of vows is to "attest our gratitude to God for benefits received," making them "exercises of thanksgiving."[81] Calvin gives as examples the vow Jacob makes should he be led home unharmed from exile (Gen. 28:20–22), as well as the vows spoken of in the Psalms (i.e., Ps. 22:25). He claims that vows as acts of gratitude are not limited to the Law but are also useful under the Gospel. "For it is not inconsistent with the duty of a pious man to consecrate to God a votive offering as a solemn symbol of recognition, lest he seem ungrateful toward his kindness."[82] Calvin repeats this understanding of vows in his interpretation in 1559 of the vows made by the sailors after they cast Jonah into the sea. Their godly intent was "to bind themselves to God, and also to express their gratitude, and to make it evident that they owed to him both their life and every favor bestowed on them."[83] Once again, Calvin insists that vows as actions and testimonies of gratitude belong both to the Law and to the Gospel, which also prescribe what is legitimate for us to vow unto God.[84] Calvin accuses the Roman Church of violating both aspects of legitimate vows, accusing them of vowing things not commanded by the Law or Gospel and seeking to bind God to themselves.

With regard to the celebration of birthdays, Calvin notes that this custom is common to average people as well as to rulers such as Pharaoh (Gen. 40:20). "Nor is the custom to be condemned, if only men would keep the right end in view; namely, that of giving thanks unto God by whom they were created and brought up, and whom they have found, in innumerable ways, to be a beneficent Father."[85] Calvin makes the same point in response to the way Jeremiah sins by cursing the day on which he was born, "for a man must be in a state of despair when he curses the day in which he was born. Men are, indeed, wont to celebrate their birth-day; and it was a custom which formerly prevailed, to acknowledge yearly that they owed it to God's invaluable goodness that they were brought forth into vital light."[86] Calvin thinks that most people pervert the proper purpose of birthday celebrations by indulging in drunken excess. "In short, they keep up the memory of God, as the Author of their life, in such a manner as if it were their set purpose to forget him."[87]

The person accustomed to thank God in her heart and in private expressions of gratitude will act in an exemplary way in the congregation, inviting and arousing others to follow her example.[88] By giving public expression to our gratitude, we inflame the feeling of gratitude in our own hearts, even as we excite others to follow our example, "for to be lukewarm, or to mutter, or to sing, as the saying is, to themselves and to the muses, is impossible for those who have actually tasted the grace of God."[89] Thus, even though we ought to experience and ponder the goodness of God in our hearts every day, and to give thanks to God in private, we are also to give thanks to God in public worship, for "the solemn profession of piety, by which every man stimulates not only himself but others to the performance of their duty, is far from being superfluous."[90]

One of the essential purposes of the public worship of the Church is that the worshiping community might give voice to the praises of God that silently sound forth from all creatures.[91] Since the godly have been given the ability to see, feel, and enjoy the powers of God set forth in God's works as in a painting, they ought to testify to these powers in their language of worship.[92] The Church exists to give thanks to God for God's overwhelming goodness, and to sing the praises of the powers of God on behalf of the whole creation. "Nothing more frequently meets us than this teaching—that we have been redeemed by God that we may celebrate his glory; that the Church was planted that in it he may be glorified, and we may make known his powers."[93]

4. The Manifestation of Piety in Gestures, Rites, and Ceremonies

Calvin insists that the piety of believers should manifest itself not only in their speech but also in their bodily gestures. In the first edition of the *Institutes*, Calvin includes such gestures in his description of how we demonstrate that we have no other God. "This we must do not only to declare, by tongue and bodily gesture, and by every outward indication, that we have no other God; but also with our mind, our whole heart, and all our zeal, to show ourselves as such."[94] Piety is not only rooted in the heart, but it also comes to expression in language and gesture. Calvin makes the same point with regard to the way that baptism serves our confession of faith before others.[95] On the other hand, Calvin is from the beginning of his career especially suspicious of the uses to which the Roman Church put rites and ceremonies. For instance, he is caustically dismissive of the claim that many Roman rites and ceremonies come from an unwritten apostolic tradition. "In fact, children and jesters so aptly mimic these that they might seem to be the most suitable officiants of such holy rites!"[96]

Since the danger always exists that the godly might think "the worship of God to be the better for a multitude of ceremonies," Calvin advises the simplifying of worship, and thinks that "it may be a fitting thing to set aside, as may be opportune in the circumstances, certain rites that in other circumstances are not impious or indecorous."[97] This simplification is especially necessary in the celebration of the sacraments, for Calvin thinks these had become buried in an accumulated mass of unnecessary rites and ceremonies, so that "there is no consideration or mention of God's Word, without which even the sacraments themselves are not sacraments."[98] Given this situation, Calvin advises the elimination of as many ceremonies as possible, even those that in other circumstances could be considered godly and useful.[99] Thus, even as he insists that piety must be manifested in the gestures of the body as well as in the soul, in 1536 Calvin has little positive to say about the use of such gestures, rites, and ceremonies.

Calvin begins to reconsider the importance of bodily gestures in worship in his discussion of evangelical participation in Roman rites in 1537. Calvin was concerned with the claim of some evangelicals in France that they could still safely participate in Roman rites, such as the Mass or the veneration of images, since they possessed true faith in Christ in their hearts and consciences. He categorically rejected such a disjunction between the inward conscience and the outward gestures of a person.[100] He will not accept the claim that one could reject belief in images in one's conscience while venerating an image with one's bodily gestures, such as prostrating oneself before them, bending the knee, or uncovering one's head.[101] Calvin was especially distressed that any of the godly could think that they could participate in the Mass with their bodies while believing in Christ in their hearts. The altar and priest declare that a sacrifice is being offered, which is a direct affront to Christ. The priest then, by gestures and inaudible words, claims to draw Christ down from heaven into the bread and wine, and acts in his person by offering the sacrifice of Christ for the benefit of humanity. "These acts you see received by the whole multitude, with the same veneration as those mentioned above; you shape your features to imitate them, when they ought visibly to have expressed the utmost abhorrence!"[102] The same may be said of the veneration of the reserved host, which the Roman Church takes to be the same as venerating the eternal Son of God. Calvin equates such veneration with the worship of idols in ancient Israel.[103] Such veneration not only calls into question the veracity of the faith of the participant, but it also sets a disastrous example for the weak in faith, who think it safe to combine faith in Christ with the worship of idols.[104] For Calvin, it is not enough to believe in Christ in one's conscience, or even to confess such faith in one's speech, if one does not manifest such faith in one's bodily gestures as well. "Wherefore, it behooves every man who possesses a pure zeal for piety, not only to refrain his tongue from impious words, but keep every part of his body untainted by any sacrilegious rite."[105] To do otherwise is to risk removing faith from one's heart, for the bodily veneration of idols cannot but have a negative impact on such faith.[106]

If the practice of ungodly gestures can have a negative impact on the faith of the heart, then it stands to reason that the observance of godly gestures and rites should have a strengthening effect on faith. Thus, in the second edition of the *Institutes* of 1539, Calvin adds to his discussion of prayer the way that the affections of the heart are both expressed in and strengthened by bodily gestures. "As for the bodily gestures customarily observed in praying, such as kneeling and uncovering the head, they are exercises whereby we try to rise to a greater reverence for God."[107] Calvin elaborates even more fully on the positive use of ceremonies and rites in the third edition of the *Institutes* of 1543. On the one hand, Calvin insists that the new economy of the Gospel means that there are fewer, simpler, and clearer ceremonies than in the economy of the Law. "Accordingly, to keep that means, it is necessary to keep fewness in number, ease in observance, dignity in representation, which also includes clarity."[108] Calvin accuses the Roman Church of ignoring this difference in economies, thereby obscuring Christ by the multiplicity of ceremonies.[109]

On the other hand, Calvin insists that ceremonies are nonetheless useful exercises for piety, provided that the simpler economy of the Gospel is observed. "Therefore, God has given us a few ceremonies, not at all irksome, to show Christ present."[110] According to Calvin, the rites that strengthen godliness are part of the decorum that Paul commands the churches to observe in their public worship.[111] To strengthen piety, such rites must reveal Christ. "Now ceremonies, to be exercises of piety, ought to lead us straight to Christ."[112] In contrast, the excessive ceremonialism of the Roman Church violates decorum and obscures the manifestation of Christ. "We see such an example in the theatrical props that the papists use in their sacred rites, where nothing appears but the mask of useless elegance and fruitless extravagance."[113]

Calvin continues to develop a positive understanding of rites and ceremonies as expressions and exercises of piety even as he maintains his harsh criticism of the ceremonialism of the Roman Church. He thinks that the abundance of ceremonies in the Roman Church directly violates the distinctive pedagogy of the Gospel, thereby returning the Church to the earlier economy of the Law. He takes Paul's statement that the time of childhood is past (Gal. 4:1) as being an effective weapon against the pomp of ceremonies in the Roman Church, which he claims "dazzles the eyes of the simple so that they admire the dominion of the Pope."[114] The Roman Church cannot claim that such ceremonies are necessary for the ignorant and weak, for God has determined that the pedagogy of the Law has come to an end with the coming of Christ.

Moreover, Calvin is convinced that excessive attention to ceremonies is always an indication of the lack of piety in the heart. "The reason is that they imagine God is like them, when they are carnal and devoted to the world."[115] Those who superstitiously confine God to the outward signs of God's presence, as Calvin thought Rome did in the doctrine of transubstantiation, will also think that God is pleased with the outward performance of beautiful and elaborate ceremonies.[116] Calvin therefore applies the saying of Isaiah, that the people worship God with their lips but not with their hearts, to the Roman Church, implying that attention to ceremonies betrays a lack of worship in the heart. "If we do not begin with [worship in the heart], all that men profess by outward gestures and attitudes will be empty display."[117] Calvin does not even consider the possibility that such ceremonies could both express and strengthen piety—the very enumeration of them is sufficient to show their futility. Thus he urges his readers to search their hearts to make sure they worship God there, so that the truth might be joined to their ceremonies.[118] No matter how much the eyes of human beings may be dazzled and even blinded by the splendor of ceremonies, God sees the heart, and is primarily interested in being worshiped there.[119]

On the other hand, Calvin continues to insist on the necessity of worshiping God not only in the heart but also in the gestures, rites, and ceremonies of the body. In his commentary on 2 Corinthians, Calvin uses the statement of Paul that we should avoid all defilement of body and of spirit to support his criticism of the evangelicals who hide their piety behind Roman ceremonies. "For if any man shows any appearance or indication of idolatry at all or takes part in wicked and superstitious rites, even if in his soul he is perfectly upright—which is impossible—he will still be guilty of having defiled his body."[120] Since piety is hidden in the heart of the believer, it can only be manifested by the gestures and signs of the body, along with language.[121] Thus the worship of God in the heart can never be disjoined from the worship of God in the body, for in this way we not only devote our bodies as well as our souls to God but also strengthen the piety within us.[122] According to Calvin, the gestures, rites, and ceremonies of the godly serve two necessary purposes: they are exercises of piety, and they are also expressions of the worship of God in body as well as in soul, for "it is right, that not the mind only, but the body also, should be employed in the service of God."[123]

5. The Gestures and Rites of Prayer

Kneeling

In his treatise against participating in the rites of the ungodly in 1537, Calvin claims that Scripture describes the worship of God by the distinguishing mark of bending the knee, as when Elijah is told that there are some in his day whose knees have never bent to Baal (1 Kings 19:18).[124] Calvin therefore rejects the claim that one can have true faith in God while bending the knee in veneration of the reserved host.[125] Thus it is not at all surprising that he should give a positive role to the gesture of bending the knee in his discussion of prayer in the second edition of the *Institutes* of 1539. "As for the bodily gestures customarily observed in praying, such as kneeling and uncovering the head, they are exercises whereby we try to rise to a greater reverence for God."[126] In the third edition of 1543, Calvin uses the rite of bending the knee in prayer to illustrate how a church regulation can be both divine and human. "It is of God in so far as it is a part of that decorum whose care and observance the apostle has commended to us [1 Cor. 14:40]. But it is of men in so far as it specifically designates what had in general been suggested rather than explicitly stated."[127] Thus, by 1543, Calvin sees bending the knee as a useful exercise of piety and reverence, which adds decorum to worship but which is not per se commanded or instituted by God.

In his commentary on the Pauline Epistles of 1548, Calvin repeats the claim made in 1537 that bending the knee is one of the central symbols of the worship of God in Scripture, for "God is to be worshipped, not only with the interior affection of the heart, but also by outward profession, if we would render him what is his own."[128] Because the gesture is used both in civil society as a sign of respect for authority and in worship as a primary symbol of the adoration of God, Calvin is very concerned to distinguish between the two uses of the gesture. For instance, when Cornelius falls at Peter's feet and worships him (Acts 10:25), Calvin considers whether he was using the symbol in a civic or a religious way.[129] According to Calvin, Cornelius was guilty of excess in making this gesture, for he did so as a sign of divine and not civic veneration. "Here Cornelius is not greeting his Proconsul or the Emperor with a political rite, but having been struck with admiration at the sight of Peter he confers honor on him as though he were in the presence of God."[130]

Calvin accuses the Roman Church of ignoring this distinction, and of introducing a false distinction between the kinds of divine veneration we can display. "And they certainly claim *latria* for God alone, as if they were saying, that the adoration of worship is due only to him. They make the adoration of *dulia* common to the dead and their bones, to statues and pictures. They assign *hyperdulia* to the Virgin Mary and the cross on which Christ hung."[131] Calvin admits to having shown the adoration of *dulia* for the relics of Anna, the mother of the Virgin Mary, when he was a child. "Among others, I remember having myself, long ago, kissed a portion of it at Ursicampus, a monastery in the vicinity of Noyon, where it was held in great reverence."[132] Calvin rejects this distinction, since anything other than civic adoration must be directed to God alone.[133]

Thus, when Abraham bows before the Hittites in his desire to procure a burial plot for Sarah, Calvin excuses his act as one of civic adoration, and notes that the Mediterranean region is more given to such rites, as Aristotle himself noted.[134] Calvin interprets the way the leper kneels before Jesus in the same manner (Matt. 8:2). "We know that such adoration was a common thing with the Jews, as the Eastern peoples are more inclined to such ceremonies."[135] On the other hand, the veneration shown to Jesus by the man born blind is religious in nature, even if it does not reach to the full measure of faith.[136] Finally, when the Israelites are exhorted to worship, fall down, and kneel before the Lord, Calvin states that the "three words which are used imply that, to discharge their duty properly, the Lord's people must present themselves as a sacrifice to him publicly, with kneeling, and other signs."[137]

The symbol of kneeling not only expresses the adoration that we should offer to God in our bodies, but it also stimulates various affections that are necessary in prayer. Thus kneeling is a useful rite of prayer, even if it is not per se necessary, "because this sign of reverence is commonly employed, especially where prayer is not perfunctory, but serious."[138] In particular, kneeling helps both to express and to foster humility in the one praying, since "the outward exercise of the body helps the weakness of the mind."[139] Calvin is concerned, however, that the humility being symbolized in the gesture is truly present in the heart.[140] He thinks that kneeling awakens the fervor of the one praying, and also excites the same devotion in those who witness the gesture, to the mutual edification of the worshiping community.[141] Thus, even though bending the knee is not necessary, Calvin thinks that it is a very useful help in prayer. "First of all, it reminds us of our inability to stand before God, unless with humility and reverence; then, our minds are better prepared for serious entreaty, and this symbol of worship is pleasing to God."[142]

A more dramatic symbol of humility is the gesture of prostration. Calvin thinks that the man born blind may initially have worshiped Christ by bending the knee, but he ends up prostrating himself before Christ, "carried away in wonder as if he were out of his mind."[143] Similarly, when the Israelites worshiped before the face of the Lord, Calvin takes this to mean that they prostrated themselves before the ark of the covenant.[144] To express the full extent of his suffering on our behalf, and the intensity of his prayer to God, Jesus threw himself on the ground in the Garden of Gesthemane. "Christ lies full on the earth as a Suppliant and places himself in the lowest attitude for the greatness of his grief."[145] Calvin interprets the way Ezekiel falls upon his face upon seeing the destruction of Jerusalem in the same manner, as a symbol of his great distress as well as his humility.[146] However, Calvin never discusses the usefulness of prostration, and hence does not see it as a gesture of prayer that is as useful as bending the knee in his own day.

Lifting up the Hands

Calvin first discusses lifting up the hands to pray in his discussion of false sacraments in the first edition of the *Institutes*. He sees the laying on of hands by the apostles as being no different from the fact that they prayed on bended knee and facing to the east.[147] Calvin does not mention lifting up the hands in prayer in a positive way until his commentary on 1 Timothy of 1548. When Paul says that he desires that in every place people should pray, lifting up holy hands, Calvin thinks that this gesture is so widespread that it must be taught by nature.[148] Calvin claims that the ceremony itself is congruent with true piety, provided that the truth it represents also accompanies it. "Firstly, knowing that God is to be sought in heaven, we should form no carnal or earthly conception of him, also that we should lay aside fleshly affections so that nothing may prevent our hearts from rising above the world."[149] By lifting up our hands in prayer, we signify that we do not confine God to this world but instead lift up our minds and hearts to seek God in heaven. Idolaters, who confine God to the images they create, testify against themselves by using this ceremony.[150] In his commentary on the Psalms of 1557, Calvin views the lifting up of hands not only as symbolizing the raising of our hearts to heaven but also as an aid to the same.[151] In his commentary on Isaiah two years later, he ascribes the rite of lifting hands not only to the teaching of nature but also to divine inspiration.[152]

Calvin comes to see this rite not only as encouraging and stimulating the godly to seek God in heaven but also as a symbol of confidence, expressing their hope in God alone, "for except this ceremony were to raise up our minds, (as we are inclined by nature to superstition), every one would seek God either at his feet or by his side."[153] The rite of lifting up our hands in prayer encourages us not to confine God to the images of God in the world but to seek God in heaven. The ceremony also incites us to deny our own desires that keep us clinging to this world, so that we are able to rise to God in the inmost affections of our hearts "and to go forth, as it were, out of ourselves whenever we call on God."[154] Calvin is concerned that the godly not bear testimony against themselves by using this ceremony, and thus encourages them to lift up their hearts even as they raise their hands. "It is, then, the right way of praying, when the inward feeling corresponds with the external gesture."[155]

It is significant that Calvin never qualifies his endorsement of raising up our hands with the proviso that it is not necessary in prayer, as he does with regard to kneeling. Given that God inspires the use of this rite through the teaching of nature, Calvin may take this to be a divinely instituted rite. According to the account of at least one visitor to Geneva in Calvin's day, the congregation raised their hands when they sang the Psalms.[156] The godly are therefore to kneel when they pray to represent and awaken their humility, and are to raise their hands so that they might lift their hearts to God in confidence. "But just as the lifting up of the hands is a symbol of confidence and longing, so in order to show our humility, we fall down on our knees."[157]

Lifting up the Eyes to Heaven

Related to the raising of our hands in prayer is the gesture of raising our eyes to heaven. Calvin first discusses this rite in the commentary on John of 1553, with reference to the prayer of Jesus. When Jesus lifts up his eyes to pray at the tomb of Lazarus, Calvin takes this to be "the sign of a mind truly prepared for prayer."[158] The usefulness of this gesture is similar to that of raising the hands: it encourages us to leave earth behind so that we seek God in heaven.[159] However, unlike the raising of hands, Calvin does not claim that this rite is either taught by nature or inspired by God, and adds the qualification that it is not necessary in all prayer. "For the publican, praying with his face cast to the ground still reaches heaven by his faith."[160] Nonetheless, the ceremony is a useful one, for it can incite the godly to seek God more ardently, even as it may also express the vehemence of their affections in prayer.[161]

Along with the lifting of our hands, lifting our eyes to heaven can be a useful exercise whereby we are led to raise our hearts to God, "for men are indolent and slow by nature and tend downwards by their earthly spirit and need such arousing or rather vehicles to raise them to God."[162] Thus, even though the gesture is not necessary in all prayer, it is still a useful help in our weakness, so that we are raised up to God in our hearts and minds.[163] This is especially true since for Calvin, as for Cicero, the eyes are the keenest of all the senses, and lead the heart in the direction to which they are looking. This is why David says that his eyes are always directed to the Lord.[164] Calvin is concerned, however, that the godly not be overly concerned with the use of the external gesture to the neglect of their internal affections. The best rule to follow in prayer is to let the inward affections shape and frame the gestures of the body.[165] The godly will express their affections with different gestures at different times, as was the case with the prayers of David.[166] When Christ lifted his eyes to heaven, he did so guided by the vehemence of his affections. "By this gesture, Christ declared that in his mind's affections he was in heaven rather than on earth, so that he left men behind him and talked intimately with God."[167] However, in spite of Calvin's proviso that this gesture is not necessary in prayer, it is clear that he favors it for its usefulness in raising our hearts and minds to heaven, in conjunction with the lifting up of our hands. When he discusses the prayer of the publican, he notes the legitimacy of the gesture he uses, but does not see such a gesture as useful in prayer. "He was merely using this as a sign of humility which he commends to his disciples."[168]

Fasting as Preparation for Prayer

Given Calvin's concern that we deny our earthly affections and raise our hearts and minds to God in prayer, it is not surprising that he begins to see the usefulness of fasting as preparation for prayer. He first discusses the use of fasting in this manner in the third edition of the *Institutes* of 1543. He links the discipline of fasting in particular with solemn public prayers in light of momentous events either in the Church or in society as a whole, and sees such a practice as coming from the Law and the prophets as well as from the apostles. "This is a holy ordinance and one salutary for all ages, that pastors urge the people to public fasting and extraordinary prayers."[169] Calvin appeals to examples from Acts in which fasting is joined to prayer when the apostles are appointing ministers to the churches (Acts 13:3, 14:23). The purpose of such fasting, like raising the hands in prayer, is to direct the affections of the godly to God. "Surely we experience this: with full stomach our mind is not so lifted up to God that it can be drawn to prayer with a serious and ardent affection and persevere in it."[170] Since the discipline of fasting in preparation for serious prayer is found in the Law, the prophets, and the apostles, as well as in the early Church, it is clear that Calvin does not think that this is an optional ceremony, although it is limited to those times when serious and solemn prayer is required of the Church. Calvin thus exhorts all believers to prepare for both public and private prayers with fasting.[171]

Calvin repeats his insistence on the need for fasting in his commentary on 1 Corinthians of 1546. When Paul tells the faithful to abstain from sexual relations for a time for the sake of prayer, Calvin refers this to the kind of fasting "by which believers prepare themselves for prayer or before undertaking some serious affair. Similarly he means the kind of prayer which requires a deeper and more concentrated mental effort."[172] Once again, Calvin limits the need for such fasting to the occasions that make such prayer necessary, "for example, when some disaster is threatening us, which appears to be a sign of God's wrath; or when we are struggling with some difficulty; or when something very important has to be carried out, such as the appointing of pastors."[173] In his commentaries on the Hebrew Scriptures, Calvin notes the way the Israelites not only fasted but also clothed themselves in sackcloth and ashes in preparation for such prayer.[174] The Israelites therefore used such practices as helps to increase their ardor in praying, for "it stirred them up more eagerly to the desire to pray."[175] Calvin distinguishes between the wearing of sackcloth and ashes, which belongs to the past economy of the Law, and fasting, which remains in force among believers after Christ.[176] The godly need the stimulus of fasting to aid them in their solemn prayers, for "when fasting is joined to prayer, then prayer becomes more earnest."[177] However, Calvin is always concerned to avoid the superstition that he thought accompanied fasting, for the Roman Church had viewed it as both necessary and meritorious. To counter this danger, Calvin insists that fasting is not perpetually necessary, "but when any great necessity presses upon us, that exercise is added by way of help, to increase the alertness and fervor of our minds in the pouring forth of prayer."[178] It is significant that Calvin successfully instituted a weekly day of prayer for the sake of the calamities that afflicted the Church, especially in France, but he was not successful in instituting a general fast on such days to aid in the earnestness of their prayers.[179]

Praying over Others

One of the ceremonies used by the prophets, Christ, and the apostles was that of praying over others. Calvin makes note of this rite in his commentary on James of 1550. When James tells the elders to pray over the sick (James 5:14), Calvin says, "The object of the rite of praying over a man was, as it were, to set him in the presence of God, for when circumstances are brought home to us, we find a greater warmth in our prayers."[180] Calvin makes the same point when he discusses the way Paul lies on the young man who died by falling out of a window (Acts 20:10). "But I think the only reason why Paul now laid himself on top of the young man was to stimulate himself to the effort of prayer."[181] Calvin notes that Elijah did the same thing to raise a dead person but claims that Paul is not imitating Elijah but is rather stirring himself up to pray in earnest for the young man's life, and "is indicating by this gesture that he is offering it to God to be restored to life."[182] However, in spite of the exhortation of James, and the vivid examples of the prophets, Christ, and Paul, Calvin does not seem to think that this ceremony would be of particular use in his own day, though he does not forbid the practice. However, he may be thinking of the stimulus of praying over others when he seeks to have the laying on of hands as a form of prayer restored both in confirmation and in the restoration of the penitent to the community.

Praying in Private

Given Calvin's deep suspicion of the hypocrisy of Roman ceremonies, it is not surprising that in the first edition of the *Institutes* he seems to favor private prayer over all forms of prayer. He joins his understanding of prayer as an emotion of the inmost heart to Jesus' injunction that we pray to God in secret in our bedroom (Matt. 6:6). "For he did not mean to deny that it is fitting to pray in other places, but he shows that prayer is something secret, which is both principally lodged in the heart and requires a tranquility far from all our teeming cares."[183] Even though Calvin has increasingly stressed the importance of public prayer, he did not deny that solitude is a useful stimulus to genuine and heartfelt prayer. When he comments on the injunction to pray in secret in 1555, Calvin first adds the qualification that Christ did not want us to avoid the public prayers of the Church. "Christ is not taking us away from such efforts, but only warning us to keep God before our eyes whenever we settle ourselves for prayer."[184] Thus Christ, according to Calvin, is not telling us that the only legitimate prayers are those we say in secret but is rather telling us that "whether one is alone or in company at prayer the attitude to adopt is to think of God as one's witness, as though shut off in an inside room."[185]

However, Calvin does not deny the usefulness of praying alone without any witnesses, even if this is not the sole meaning of Christ's words. "And it is useful for the faithful, in order to pour out their prayers and their appeals more freely in God's sight, to withdraw from human gaze. There is another advantage in a quiet place, that we may have our minds more free and unburdened of any outside calls."[186] Thus, when Christ withdraws from his disciples to pray alone, Calvin notes the usefulness of this practice, both for Christ and for all believers. "Since prayer's fervor flows more freely in solitude, it is useful to pray alone."[187] Calvin makes the same observation with regard to the prayer of King Hezekiah, after Isaiah tells him he will not recover from his illness. Even though he is not alone, he turns his face to the wall so that he might focus all his attention on God in his prayers.[188] Calvin does not think that the external gesture is as significant as is his desire to set God alone before his eyes.[189] The faithful pray more freely and ardently when they withdraw from the view of others, so that they may pour out their hearts freely before God. "What, then, is it to make known our cause to God? It is to do this when no one is witness, and when God alone appears before us."[190]

Thus, although the pious are to have God as the witness of their hearts whenever they pray, they are not to neglect the aid to prayer provided by solitude, for in this way they become accustomed to pouring out their hearts to God in a manner not otherwise possible.

6. Signs of Piety and Impiety

Calvin exhibits a keen interest in the ways in which piety manifests itself in the words and actions of the characters portrayed in Scripture. For instance, Ananias demonstrates the piety in his heart by going to Saul even as he tells the Lord that Saul is responsible for much evil against the saints in Jerusalem.[191] Calvin thinks that prompt and willing obedience, especially in light of certain danger, is an especially clear sign of piety. For instance, the prompt dedication of Lydia in the Book of Acts and the hospitality she shows to Paul are notable for Calvin, for "her holy zeal and piety reveal themselves in the fact that she dedicates her household to God at the same time."[192] Piety may be revealed in the silent gestures people make, without any words being added. For instance, Calvin thinks that the people who saw Zechariah emerge from the Temple know that he has seen a vision of the Lord, even though he was unable to speak. "When he comes out, he shows by gestures and by signs that he has been made dumb. We may well believe that fear showed on his face. They infer that God has revealed himself to him."[193]

Related to the manifestation of piety is the exhibition of a teachable spirit, for this is the precondition for piety. Calvin sees signs of such teachableness in the people who follow Christ out into the wilderness, even though he was trying to get away from them.[194] Such a teachable disposition is especially notable in those who forget about how they appear to others so that they might draw near to Christ. Thus, when Zachaeus climbs the sycamore tree to see Jesus, Calvin sees this as evidence of the seed of piety, since "rich men are usually proud and want to appear serious."[195] When Christ sees such zeal, even though he has secretly inspired it in Zachaeus, he reveals himself to him.[196] Christ responds in the same manner to the scribe who agrees with his summary of the Law: "because he showed himself willing to learn Christ stretches out his hand to him and teaches us by his example that we should help any in whom the first glimmer of docility and a right mind appears."[197] Piety is also manifested when those who had initially disagreed in matters of faith immediately cease contention when the truth is revealed to them, as happened with the disciples in Jerusalem who initially objected to Peter going to the Gentiles.[198]

Piety manifests itself in the ceaseless prayers of the godly, even when God seems deaf to their prayers. Even though their prayers may be disturbed by violent passions and assailed by doubts, the fact that a person does not stop calling upon God is a clear sign of piety, as in Psalm 88.[199] Piety also reveals itself in those Gentiles who ascribe to God all dominion and divinity, in spite of the fact that they dwell in a land that worships idols, as in the case of Rahab.[200] Rahab demonstrates the character of true faith when she gives possession of the land of Canaan to the Israelites simply on the basis of the promise made to Abraham. "Moreover, in the language of Rahab, we behold that characteristic property of faith described by the author of the Epistle to the Hebrews, when he calls it a vision or sight of things not appearing."[201] Calvin sees the same kind of piety manifesting itself in King Nebuchadnezzar, in his response to Daniel's interpretation of his dream, "when he prostrated himself before God and his prophet."[202] This is especially true since kings are usually blinded by their own splendor, and given the fact that the dream reveals the judgment of God on the pride of Nebuchadnezzar.[203] On the other hand, when King Darius tells Daniel that the God he serves faithfully will deliver him, Calvin refuses to see this as evidence of the king's piety; rather, "he thus wished to adorn himself in the spoils of deity."[204]

Calvin is also attentive to any signs of impiety that might manifest themselves. Just as the revelation to Zechariah was manifested on his face without any speech accompanying it, so Calvin thinks that impious pride betrays itself on the face.[205] This is why Isaiah says that the eyes of the haughty shall be brought low (Isa. 2:11). "When he speaks of lofty looks and loftiness, he employs an outward gesture to denote the inward pride of the mind; for sinful confidence almost always betrays, by the very looks, a contempt of God and of men."[206] Even though the impious may seek to hide their true affections beneath a mask of piety, their true state of mind will appear on their faces when their impiety reaches its full strength, as happened in the day of Ezekiel. "But the prophet here signifies that the Israelites were so immersed in impiety, that they displayed themselves as the open enemies of God on their very countenances."[207]

Impiety also manifests itself in the indifference or hostility shown to public worship. For instance, when the people return from Babylon and attend only to the building of their own houses, this is a sign of their impiety.[208] Similarly, the absence of the princes from the Temple when Jeremiah prophesied there revealed their impious contempt of the worship of God.[209] Impiety also betrays itself when the ungodly openly resist the manifest works of God. Thus, when Pharaoh asks his magicians to perform the same works performed by God through Moses, Calvin thinks that his impiety, hitherto hidden in his heart, breaks forth into open view. "For he was sufficiently instructed in the wonderful power of God had not iniquity urged him onwards into desperate madness."[210]

Calvin discusses two symbols that were used by Jesus and the apostles when they met with such manifest impiety: shaking off the dust of the feet and rending one's garments. Jesus tells his followers to shake the dust off their feet when they meet with manifest contempt for the Word and work of God. Calvin interprets this gesture as a widely known symbol of cursing among the Jews, "as though they made testimony that the inhabitants of the spot were so foul that their contagion infected the earth whereon they stood."[211] The symbol reveals that the impiety of the inhabitants is of such a degree that the godly do not wish to be contaminated by it, as when Paul and Barnabas shake off the dust of their feet at the people of Antioch (Acts 13:51).[212] Given that Jesus commands the observance of this symbol, and the apostles actually practice it, it is odd that Calvin apparently sees no use for it outside of its original Jewish context. The same may be said of the ritual of rending one's garments when one hears blasphemy. According to Calvin, "it is quite clear from other passages in Scripture that this was a custom and rite commonly used by Easterners, whenever they wished to express, by an outward gesture, either great sorrow or detestation."[213] In spite of its presence not only in Jewish but also in apostolic practice, Calvin sees no use for this rite outside of the eastern context from which it arose.

7. Testimonies of Repentance

Calvin thinks that repentance, like piety, is something deeply hidden in the heart of the penitent, which nonetheless must manifest itself to others. In the second edition of the *Institutes,* Calvin considers the ceremonial forms by which repentance was attested in the Scriptures. Unlike those who thought that weeping, fasting, and ashes were the chief elements of repentance, Calvin teaches that they are used to manifest sorrow for sin in special occasions. Even though the Jews observed these practices under the Law, Calvin claims that they are still of use in his own day "whenever the Lord seems to threaten us with any ruin or calamity."[214] Indeed, Calvin thinks that it would be a very beneficial practice were pastors of the Church in his day to call for a time of fasting and weeping in light of an approaching calamity, even if this would not include the wearing of sackcloth and ashes, provided "they always urge with greater and more intent care and effort that 'they should rend their hearts and not their garments' [Joel 2:13]."[215]

Calvin reinforces his desire to see times of public and communal fasting and weeping in the third edition of the *Institutes*.[216] He explicitly removes the wearing of sackcloth and ashes from the ceremonies to be observed at such times, thereby distinguishing the practice from that of the Israelites and Jews. "But there is no doubt that meeting and weeping and fasting, and like activities, apply equally to our age whenever the condition of our affairs so demands. For since this is a holy exercise both for the humbling of men and for their confession of humility, why should we use it less than the ancients did in similar need?"[217] Calvin explicitly rejects the objection that the calling of such a public fast is part of the shadows of the Law that has passed with the dawning of the Gospel.[218] Calvin appeals to the words of Christ, that the time will come when his disciples will fast (Matt. 9:15), to support the use of this ceremony in the age of the Gospel. Given that Calvin institutes a weekly day of special prayer in light of the appearance of "Pestilence, War, and other calamities" in 1542, it is clear that he also desired this day to be such a time of fasting and weeping, although he was never successful in achieving this goal.[219]

Calvin directly laments the failure to institute such a fast in Geneva in his commentary on Joel of 1559. In light of Joel's command to blow the trumpet in Zion to proclaim such a fast, Calvin insists that the Gospel has not in fact abolished such a ceremony.[220] Calvin laments his inability to institute such a time of public fasting and penance in Geneva, insisting that the refusal of the people to tolerate such a ceremony shows how they do not understand any of the major topics of Christian doctrine: "as they know not commonly what repentance is, so they understand not what the profession of repentance means; for they understand not what sin is, what the wrath of God is, what grace is."[221] The failure of the Church to institute a time of communal fasting and weeping calls into question the entirety of its faith in the Gospel, according to Calvin.

In his commentary on Isaiah of the same year, Calvin returns to the question of whether the wearing of sackcloth and ashes is common to both the Law and the Gospel, as are fasting and weeping. Calvin gives two reasons for why this aspect of the day of fasting is no longer necessary. On the one hand, sackcloth and ashes belong to the ceremonies of the Law.[222] On the other hand, such rites are to be ascribed to the excessive ceremonialism of eastern people, noted previously by Aristotle, which is not as fitting for people in the cooler climes. "If we wished to imitate the former, it would be nothing else than to enact the part of apes, or of stage-players."[223] In spite of these two qualifications, Calvin does not think it would be a bad idea for those observing public acts of penitence to wear penitential clothing. "Yet there is nothing to hinder those who intend to confess their guilt, from wearing soiled and tattered garments, after the manner used by supplicants."[224] Given Calvin's strong aversion to luxurious and opulent clothing, it is quite possible that the weekly day of weeping and fasting he wished to institute would also have included wearing such clothing.

Calvin does not limit the ritual symbols of repentance to public times of fasting and weeping, however, but thinks they should be used whenever serious sins emerge in the Church. In light of Paul's commendation of the godly grief that was manifested in the one who did wrong among the Corinthians, Calvin says, "He speaks of signs of repentance and among these there is this special sign whereby by punishing sins we in a way anticipate God's own judgment, as he teaches elsewhere, 'If we judged ourselves, we should not be judged of the Lord' (1 Cor. 11:31)."[225] Calvin does not think that the manifestation of repentance is necessary for private sins, but only when the sin is known publicly.[226] He makes the same point regarding the words of Jesus that Tyre and Sidon would have repented with sackcloth and ashes in light of his deeds of power (Matt. 11:21). "The outward profession of penance is only called for when men turn to God for some serious defection. And, indeed, sackcloth and ashes are signs of guiltiness, for appeasing the anger of the judge. Therefore they properly apply to the beginning of conversion."[227]

As we have seen, one of the manifest signs of repentance for Calvin is weeping, which is all the more truthful when it takes place without witnesses, as in the case of Peter.[228] Calvin acknowledges that repentance does not always require tears, "but in the graver sins it is too stupid and unfeeling not to be wounded with grief and sorrow to the point of shedding tears."[229] Clearly, then, weeping would be one of the signs of repentance that Calvin would want the pastors and elders to see before restoring a penitent to full communion with the Church. "But whenever a sinner gives a probable sign of conversion, Christ wants him to be admitted to reconciliation and not to be broken or lose heart by being repulsed."[230]

Calvin could not imagine that repentance for sin could be serious without it being manifested to others in the signs of repentance.[231] He constantly cites the saying of Joel that we rend our hearts and not our garments (Joel 2:13), for the ceremonies of repentance are meaningless without the inward affection of the heart they are meant to reveal. However, when there is true repentance in the heart, the signs of repentance have the same reciprocal relationship that we have seen with the gestures and language of prayer: they both express and further incite the feelings of repentance. "They are causes, because the marks of our guilt, which we carry about us, excite us the more to acknowledge ourselves to be sinners and guilty; and they are effects, because, if they were not preceded by repentance, we would never be induced to perform them sincerely."[232] Calvin continues to acknowledge that the pious no longer use sackcloth and ashes to attest and incite their repentance, but it is clear that he does think that weeping and fasting are still useful signs of conversion, as may be inferred from the signs of obstinacy he describes, such as feasting and luxury.[233] Thus the penitent in Calvin's day should publicly weep and fast, and even wear penitential clothing, even as the Jews did in the days of the Law, in order to manifest and stimulate their own repentance.

Calvin is aware, however, of how deceptive the signs of repentance and conversion can be. For instance, King Nebuchadnezzar seems to be making a genuine confession of faith when he confesses the Lord to be the God of gods (Dan. 2:47), but as we know his conversion was ephemeral.[234] Since the signs of repentance are to be seen by others, the danger exists that they may be manifested solely for the eyes of the spectators, not for the eyes of God, who sees the heart. Such was the case with the false repentance of the king's counselors in Jeremiah's day, who looked to their king and not to God.[235] In spite of his desire to see the institution of both communal and individual weeping and fasting to manifest and stimulate repentance, Calvin knows that the only reliable signs of repentance are the works that we do over time, especially towards our neighbors. "Besides, works are the only testimonies to real repentance; for it is a thing too excellent to allow its root to appear to human observation."[236]

8. The Prohibition of Human Images
from Places of Public Worship

As we have seen, Calvin's understanding of the proper meaning and use of the gestures, rites, and ceremonies of worship seems to have been decisively shaped by his controversy with the evangelicals in France who wished to participate in external Roman rites while nourishing their faith and piety within their hearts. Calvin had insisted in the first edition of the *Institutes* of 1536 that the worship of God entails both the body and the soul, but his criticism of the "Nicodemites" highlighted the significance of bodily gestures for the worship either of the true God or of idols. Calvin denies that one can have true piety in the heart and conscience while framing one's body in a gesture of adoration before what one believes to be an idol.[237] Not only does Calvin reject the external veneration of such images, such as statues, paintings, crucifixes, or altars; but he also points to the way that these images have been consecrated by a special ceremony to be made integral to the worship of the Roman Church.[238] Knowing the role such images are intended to have in worship, the godly should withhold viewing them in the same way, either in the thoughts of their hearts or in the gestures of their bodies, following the example of Paul in Athens.[239] Both aspects of images—their dedication and consecration in places of worship and their veneration and adoration by the gestures of worshipers—were central to Calvin's concern to have them removed from orthodox and evangelical churches.

Calvin directly addresses the location of human images in public places of worship in the third edition of the *Institutes* of 1543. He allows for the legitimacy of sculpture and painting as human arts, following his endorsement in the 1539 edition of all the liberal and manual arts as gifts of the Holy Spirit for the benefit of this life.[240] "But because sculpture and painting are gifts of God, I seek a pure and legitimate use of each, lest those things which God has conferred upon us for his glory and our good be not only polluted by perverse misuse but also turned to our destruction."[241] Calvin claims that painting and sculpture are legitimate only when they represent what can be seen by the human eye, thus apparently endorsing Plato's view of artistic representation and rejecting any depictions of God or Christ. "Within this class some are histories and events, some are images and forms of bodies without any depicting of past events."[242] Thus both historical events and human figures such as portraits are legitimate forms of artistic expression, according to

Calvin. He thinks that depictions of historical events "have some use in teaching or admonition," whereas portraits have "no value for teaching," claiming, "I do not see what they can afford other than pleasure."[243] However, he does not reject artistic depictions of the human body, except those that encourage licentiousness, something he thought all too common in the art-work of his age.[244] He therefore endorses the use of painting and sculpture to portray both historical events and the human body and figure, provided that the latter are done with decency and sobriety. To reject the gifts of painting and sculpture would be an act of ingratitude against the Spirit of God, from whom all such gifts flow.[245] "It is no wonder, then, that the knowledge of all that is most excellent in human life is said to be communicated to us through the Spirit of God."[246]

The question, therefore, is whether "it is expedient to have in Christian temples any images at all, whether they represent past events or the bodies of men."[247] This question is distinct from the issue of the representation of God, which Calvin categorically rejects as violating both the nature of God and the legitimate use of the visual arts, which are limited to what we can see. Calvin's first answer to this question is to point to the early Church, when Christian temples were commonly empty of images. His second response is to point to the danger of inflaming human superstition by placing images in Christian temples. However, even if one allowed for the legitimacy of such artwork in Christian temples, Calvin still thinks that its presence is at odds with their purpose. "But even if so much danger were not threatening, when I consider the intended use of temples, somehow or other it seems to me un-worthy of their holiness for them to take on images other than those living and symbolical ones which the Lord has consecrated by his Word. I mean Baptism and the Lord's Supper, together with other rites by which our eyes must be too intensely gripped and too sharply affected to seek other images forged by human ingenuity."[248] Since Christian temples contain living im-ages that represent both Christ and his benefits, as well as arouse symbols of piety, gratitude, and repentance, the presence of painting and sculpture would distract the eyes of the worshipers from these living images. Dead human images that represent absent realities have no place in Christian temples, in which living images truly exhibit and offer the realities they represent and figure.

Calvin considers both the veneration and the location of human images in his commentaries after 1543. In his commentary on 1 Corinthians of 1546, Calvin applies Paul's injunction to flee from idolatry (1 Cor. 10:14) to the ven-

eration of human images by bodily gestures of adoration, and directs it especially against the "Nicodemites" in France. "For, just as God is said to be
worshipped by kneeling and other signs of reverence, whereas the fundamental and true way to worship him is in our hearts, so it is the case of idols,
the same principle applying to opposites."[249] In other words, idolatry consists
not only in the thought of the mind and heart that affixes God to the image
and confines God there but also in the acts of bodily veneration that manifest the thoughts of the heart. The person may protest that she is not worshiping the image in her heart, but her body is saying the opposite. "For in
view of the fact that God ought to have not only the inward love of our
hearts, but also our outward devotion, the man who gives a token of outward
worship to an idol is to that extent depriving God of his due."[250] It is clear
that Calvin thinks it next to impossible to split the affections of the heart
from the adoration of the body in this way, but even were it possible, God is
still being deprived of the gestures of adoration being shown to an idol.[251]

Calvin uses a similar argument against the use of images in Roman worship. He rejects the distinction that Roman theologians draw between the
adoration of images and the adoration of idols. "Because they deny that the
images and statues which they worship are idols, they say that the worship . . . is *eikonodouleia,* but not *eidolodouleia.*"[252] According to Calvin, God
rejects "adoration of any kind" that is directed towards an image.[253] The same
may be said of the use of images in pagan worship. Calvin realizes that pagan
worshipers would claim that they are not worshiping God in their images,
for "they are persuaded that God is in heaven," and is merely "represented
under these signs."[254] He refutes this claim not by showing how images nonetheless contradict the nature of God but rather by appealing to the devotional rites and gestures of the pagan worshipers in relation to these images.
By directing their supplications to images, they betray their conviction "that
in approaching these images the gods were nearer to them."[255]

That the heathens really did confine God to their images is revealed by
their devotional life, which contradicts their claim that they worship God in
heaven. One cannot worship God in heaven, and direct one's prayers and
supplications to an image. In light of the objection that "all superstitious persons confessed that God is in heaven, and did not openly ascribe divinity to
wood or stone," Calvin responds: "when they flee to statues and images and
perform vows to them, they undoubtedly ascribe to them what belongs to
God."[256] The ascription of divinity to the images is also manifested by the
gestures the ungodly make before their images, for they imagine "that they

cannot reach the hand or ear of God without bowing down before these images to utter their prayers."[257] Idolaters need never verbally ascribe divinity to their images of wood and stone, for their prayers and gestures of adoration reveal that they think God is present in visible form, in spite of what they say.[258] The use of images, statues, and paintings in the devotional life of the community reveals that people think that God is present in these images, no matter how much they protest that God is in heaven.[259]

The other reason images are problematic in Christian temples has to do with the rites of dedication used to introduce the images into places of worship. In light of the dedication of the image by King Nebuchadnezzar (Dan. 3:1–7), Calvin notes that such ceremonies of dedication take place whenever images are incorporated into the worship life of a community. "With respect to the dedication, we know it to have been customary among the profane nations to consecrate their pictures and statues before they adored them."[260] Such ceremonies of consecration lead directly to the bodily adoration of the images, since no one would think of adoring a statue or image before it was consecrated. "For as long as the images remain with the statuary or painter, they are not venerated; but as soon as an image is dedicated by any private ceremony (which the papists call a 'devotion'), or by any public and solemn rite, the tree, the wood, the stone, and the colors become a god! The papists also have fixed ceremonies among their exorcisms in consecrating statues and pictures."[261] The solemn rite of consecration and dedication integrates the image into the worship of divinity in the community, and leads directly to its veneration by prayers, prostration, and other bodily gestures.

This phenomenon holds true not only for images of deity, as in the case of Nebuchadnezzar, but also for statues and paintings of visible realities, which are themselves legitimate objects of artistic representation.[262] When people see such paintings or statues outside the temple, they are not inclined to adore them. "If the painter's workshop is full of pictures, all pass them by, and if they are delighted with the view of them they do not show any sign of reverence to the paintings."[263] However, once the painting is transferred from a painter's workshop to the temple, its significance changes dramatically by its association with divinity, so that it comes very quickly to be venerated and adored. "But as soon as the picture is carried into another place, its consecration so blinds and so stupefies them that they do not remember that they had already seen the picture in a profane workshop."[264] Calvin makes this point specifically with regard to statues of the saints, which would be one form of legitimate artistic expression according to his criteria. "Thus we see the papists locating the power of God in the saints; they even enclose his divine presence in a stone or a stump of wood, as soon as the statue is consecrated to Barbara or Chrysogonus."[265]

For Calvin, the decisive issue is the placement of statues, paintings, and other images in Christian temples, along with the ceremonies of consecration and dedication by which they are introduced into the temples. "This is therefore the reason why God did not admit any pictures into his Temple, and surely when the place is consecrated, it must surely happen that the image will astonish men just as if some secret divinity belonged to it."[266] Once images are dedicated and consecrated in temples, the ceremonial veneration and adoration of the images by invocation, prostration, genuflection, and so on, is bound to follow, thereby depriving God of half the worship that we owe. Calvin does not object to the visual arts of painting and sculpture but rather sees them as gifts of God given for the good of humanity and the glory of God. He only objects to their placement in Christian temples, for this represents a fundamental misuse and perversion of their purpose.

Moreover, Christian temples should be filled with living images of Christ and vivid symbols of piety, which exhibit and offer the realities they represent and figure. Painting and sculpture, on the other hand, can never be more than "images of things absent rather than marks of things present."[267] No matter how much they are fashioned to the life, they cannot offer the reality that they represent. "The statue of Hercules is called 'Hercules'; but it is nothing but a bare, empty representation."[268] Calvin therefore claims that they have no place in the worship life of the Christian community.[269]

CHAPTER 12

The Revelation of the Thoughts of the Heart

Human language and gestures not only disclose and incite the piety that lies hidden in the human heart, but they also reveal a full range of affections related to human society. Since language is the image of the mind, it is also the bond of society, bringing people into communication with one another. Gestures and other ceremonies are also able to convey our affections, such as love, modesty, grief, and mourning, as well as hatred, pride, and despair, to others. Due to the tenderness of the sense of sight, the signs of affection we see from others can draw our affections to them, leading us to be tempted towards ostentatious display, in order to draw the eyes of others to ourselves so that they might be ravished with admiration for us. Since such display may mask the true thoughts and affections of our hearts, Calvin is ever attentive to the danger of hypocrisy, by which we create an image in our language and gestures that conceals our true thoughts and feelings. Since other human beings are unable to see into the recesses and dark places of our hearts, the only cure for hypocrisy is to remember that whereas human beings judge by appearances, God sees the heart, and has no need of human language or gestures to know our thoughts and affections. The godly therefore live as though in a theater, beheld at all times by God and the angels even when there are no human witnesses. Only when we are constantly aware that God sees the inmost affections of our hearts are we able to use both language and other signs and gestures in a way that reveals, and does not conceal, the hidden thoughts of our hearts.

1. Language as the Chief Bond of Society

Since language is the image of the mind (*character mentis*), it is one of the principal means of human communication and therefore of social interaction and communion. "For since speaking is the image of the mind, men convey their thoughts and feelings to each other, so that they come to know each other's minds well."[1] Until we reveal our thoughts and feelings to one another by language, they remain hidden in the inmost affection of the heart, known only to ourselves. "The inner thought of a man, of which others know nothing, is clear to him alone."[2] This remains true even after we have expressed our thoughts in language, not only when our expressions fail to describe accurately our thoughts, but also when we do express ourselves clearly.[3] The self-revelation of the thoughts of the heart in language is central to Calvin's understanding of interpretation, for he seeks to reveal the mind of the author by the way the sense or meaning of the author emerges naturally from the language the author uses. However, this also discloses the limits of interpretation, for only the one speaking really knows the thoughts and feelings that come to expression in language, and there is always a degree to which one's thoughts and feelings remain ineffable, known to oneself alone. We have seen this ineffability in particular in terms of Calvin's inability fully to articulate or even to understand his experience of communion with the body and blood of Christ in the holy Supper of the Lord. "Therefore, nothing remains but to break forth in wonder at the mystery, which plainly neither the mind is able to conceive nor the tongue to express."[4]

In spite of Calvin's awareness of the limitations of human language, he nonetheless insists that people must strive to give an accurate representation of their thoughts and affections in their language, for this is central to the establishment and maintenance of community. Calvin therefore agrees with Paul that it is a perversion of the holy assembly of the worshiping community when people speak in a tongue unknown to others. "It is therefore pointless and absurd for a man to speak to a gathering of people, when the hearer understands not a word of what he says, and cannot even catch the slightest sign, to show him what the speaker means."[5] By speaking to others in an unknown tongue, we make ourselves barbarians to one another, and therefore separate ourselves from the fellowship of the Church.[6] Since the fellowship of the Church is rooted not merely in human communication but also in our communion with Christ, when we are gathered together in worship our language ought to be a clear and full manifestation of our inmost affections, as though we were speaking with our dearest friends.[7]

However, Calvin is of course painfully aware that the human race is not united in its language. After all, he did not know the German language, and hence was not able freely to communicate with his friends and colleagues such as Martin Bucer, Philip Melanchthon, and Heinrich Bullinger, even if they were able to express themselves to one another in Latin. According to Calvin, this situation is the direct result of the perversion of human nature by sin, for the original plan of God was that human beings were to be united in the sacred bond of language, and thereby united in society and piety.[8] The loss of a common language is therefore an accidental violation of human nature itself, to be ascribed to the divine punishment of humanity. "For as language is the image of the mind, how does it come to pass, that men, who are partakers of the same reason, and who are born for social life, do not communicate with each other in the same language?"[9] According to Calvin, the punishment matches the crime, for since "unity of language ought to have promoted among them consent of piety," the use of language to wage war on God brought about the horrible diversity of languages that we now experience.[10]

In spite of the punishment of God, Calvin sees the goodness of God shining forth in three ways with regard to human speech. First, in spite of their divergent languages, nations still manage to communicate with each other.[11] Though Calvin does not explicitly say so, one imagines that he is thinking of transnational languages such as Greek and Aramaic at the time of the apostles, or Latin in his own day. Second, through the Gospel God is now invoked as Father in all languages on earth. "Whence it has come to pass, that they who before were miserably divided, have coalesced into unity of the faith."[12] Third, Calvin celebrates with gratitude the recovery of Hebrew, Greek, and classical Latin in his own day, which allows teachers of the Church to discover the mind of the authors of Scripture by means of their original languages.[13]

Since we communicate not only our thoughts but also our affections to others by means of language, Calvin calls language both the image of the mind and the bond of society. This role of language is most clearly revealed in the experience of being among people who speak an unknown language. "Language being, as it were, the image and mirror of the mind, those who cannot employ it in their mutual intercourse are no less strangers to one another than the wild beasts of the forest."[14] The inability to communicate is especially distressing in a situation of hostility, for language in particular is of great usefulness in mediating between hostile parties and in moving enemies to compassion.[15] Language is what makes us human, for otherwise we would be utterly unable to have communion or communication with one another. "By language, we know, not only words, but also feelings are communicated. Language is the expression of the mind, as it is commonly said, and therefore it is the bond of human society. Had there been no language, in what would men differ from brute beasts? One would barbarously treat another, there would indeed be no humanity among them."[16] This is what made both the Assyrian and the Babylonian invasions so terrifying, for the Israelites and the Jews did not know the language of their conquerors, and therefore lacked all bonds of society with them, and all means of conciliating them or moving them to pity.[17]

In light of the obstacles to community created by the diversity of human languages, the unity of people in spite of such differences can only be ascribed to the miraculous grace of God, as when Zechariah promises that ten men from every language and nation shall seek to be taught by a Jew (Zech. 8:23).[18] The same may be said when the people are delivered safely from captivity by a people of an unknown language.[19] On the other hand, this is also what makes the perversion of language through deceit and falsehood so dangerous, for it directly violates the God-given purpose of language to be the image of the mind, and therefore clearly threatens to undermine the sacred and principal bond of human society.[20] We are given language so that we might reveal our hidden thoughts and affections to others, and thereby create and foster community with one another, as well as conciliate those who have fallen into enmity with each other. The use of language to deceive others, so that we conceal our true thoughts and affections, is therefore a serious threat to the human community in general, and to the Church in particular, as Calvin is all too well aware.[21]

2. The Manifestation of Affections in Gestures and Signs

The thoughts and affections of human beings are not only revealed in language, but they also disclose themselves in their bodily gestures, which function for Calvin as signs of their affections. Since the communication of affections is the sacred bond of society, the most important affection we can manifest to others is love. The greatest demonstration of love we can show to others is our willingness to suffer death for their welfare. Paul demonstrates the proof of such love when he tells the Church in Rome that he would be willing to suffer both temporal and eternal death for the sake of the Jews, who are his own people and the chosen people of God. "It was, therefore, a proof of the most fervent love that Paul did not hesitate to call on himself the condemnation which he saw hanging over the Jews, in order that he might deliver them."[22] In a similar though less dramatic way, Paul tells the Corinthians that he is willing to spend not only everything he has, but his very life, for their welfare and salvation.[23] Love also manifests itself by the alms we freely give to others, as these take their name from the affections they are meant to reveal. "Since the word alms is properly speaking mercy, an inner feeling of the heart, it has been transferred to the outward services by which we help the poor."[24] To assure others that such alms come from sincere affection, we ought at the same time to take their own miseries and concerns into our own hearts as though they were our own, as David relates in his prayers.[25]

Finally, love comes to be represented in certain rites and ceremonies by which it is both symbolized and nurtured. For instance, Calvin has no doubt that the early Christians, from the apostles through the fathers, practiced common meals that they called love feasts (*agapas*), "because they symbolized their brotherly love, and consisted of what they contributed."[26] However, in spite of the ancient foundation of this rite in the Jewish, apostolic, and patristic community, Calvin expresses no interest in restoring this rite to the Church of his own day. The reason may lie in the fact that for Calvin the holy Supper of the Lord is the primary expression and stimulus of love in the Christian community, "which can more forcefully than any means quicken and inspire us to love, peace, and concord."[27] The unity of believers in the Supper is rooted in the self-communication of Christ to them, making them all one in him. This unity is symbolized by the bread that is made of many grains, which represents that "we should be joined and bound together by such great agreement of hearts that no sort of disagreement or division may intrude."[28] The self-communication of Christ both furnishes believers with the most powerful example of love and unites them more powerfully than any other social union by means of their participation in Christ, "inasmuch as he makes himself common to all, also makes us one in himself."[29] For this reason, Calvin urged the frequent celebration of the Supper, for as often as we receive the symbols of the Lord's body and blood, "we reciprocally bind ourselves to all the duties of love in order that none of us may permit anything that can harm our brother, or overlook anything that can help him where necessity demands."[30]

Calvin also notes the way Paul tells his congregations to greet each other with a holy kiss (Rom. 16:16; 1 Cor. 16:20). Again, Calvin shows his keen interest in the origins of this apostolic custom. "A kiss, as we see from many passages of Scripture, was a frequent and quite customary symbol of friendship among the Jews. This custom was, perhaps, less frequent among the Romans. It was not, however, unusual, although only relatives were allowed to kiss women."[31] Calvin makes a similar point in relation to the Greeks.[32] According to him, this Jewish custom came very early to be associated with the holy Supper of the Lord, by which the pious would attest their love for one another. "After this they offered their alms to prove in deed and effect what they had represented by the kiss, as we see in one of the homilies of Chrysostom."[33] The kiss was therefore one of the solemn ceremonies of worship adopted by the apostles from Jewish custom, and made an integral part of their celebration of the Supper.[34] Thus, according to Calvin, Paul is enjoining the Church in both Rome and Corinth to manifest their love for one another when they gather in worship, not only in word and deed, but also by means of the symbol of mutual love in the kiss.[35]

Calvin explains the disappearance of this custom by means of the aversion, or even abhorrence, Greeks and Romans felt towards kissing. "But among the nations who had no wish at all to adopt the practice of kissing, there crept in its place, the custom of kissing the paten."[36] Calvin notes with harshness how such ceremonial kissing in the Roman liturgy appears to contradict the nature of both the Supper and the symbol of love.[37] However, in spite of the Jewish, apostolic, and patristic observance of the holy kiss in association with the worship of the community, especially during the celebration of the Supper, Calvin has no desire to restore this rite to the evangelical and orthodox Church of his day, over against its alleged perversion in the Roman liturgy. "Paul, however, does not appear to be enjoining a ceremony of any kind, but simply exhorting them to cherish brotherly love, which he distinguishes from the unholy friendships of the world."[38] One reason for Calvin's reluctance to see this symbol as a perpetual rite of the Church is his sense that the lusts of the people of his day are more unruly than they were at the time of the early Church, so that "the intercourse between men and women is seldom conducted with modesty."[39] Calvin therefore removes the symbol of the kiss entirely from the ceremonies and rites of the worshiping community.

Jesus also presents a symbol of love to the apostles by washing their feet, saying that by doing so he has given them an example, that they should do the same (John 13:14). Calvin sees this act as a demonstration of the depths to which we should go to serve one another in love, assuming a willing slavery in the service of our neighbor. "For there is no love where there is not a willing slavery in assisting a neighbor."[40] He also sharply criticizes the annual ceremony of foot washing in the Roman Church as lacking the affection attested in this rite. "Every year they hold a theatrical feet-washing, and when they have discharged this empty and bare ceremony they think they have done finely and are then free to despise their brethren."[41] Calvin seems to be especially vexed by the persecution of the evangelicals by the Roman hierarchy, in contradiction to the love symbolized in this rite.[42] However, he does not argue for the correct observance of this ceremony, so that it really does represent the self-denying service we should show to one another, but rather claims that Christ did not at all intend to institute a perpetual ceremony in this act, in spite of his clear command that we should do likewise. "At any rate, Christ does not enjoin an annual ceremony here, but tells us to be ready through our life to wash the feet of our brethren."[43] Calvin therefore removes entirely from the ceremonies of the Church the rite of foot washing.

People also show their hatred of others in the gestures and signs they use. For instance, Paul is concerned that the Corinthians not think that his admonitions to them spring from hatred, since "a desire to reproach is a sign of hatred."[44] On the other hand, by casting his eyes down to the ground, Jesus manifested his contempt for those who wished to stone to death the woman caught in adultery. "By this gesture he showed that he despised them."[45] Similarly, by drawing in the dirt while they were speaking to him, Jesus disclosed that he did not think they were worth hearing.[46] Other signs of hatred are hissing and gnashing the teeth, by which people taunt their enemies, "for he who gnashes with his teeth shows the bitterness of his mind, and even fury; for to gnash with the teeth is what belongs to a wild beast."[47] Finally, one may tear one's garments in order to reveal that one holds another in complete abhorrence, as was especially common in eastern cultures, according to Calvin, "for these nations, having much greater warmth of temperament than we have who inhabit cold countries, display a greater vehemence in gesture, deportment, dress, and other outward signs."[48]

Pride may also manifest itself in our gestures and deportment, even if we utter not a word. When David says that the eyes of the wicked stealthily watch for the helpless (Ps. 10:8), Calvin says he is "giving a beautiful and graphic description of the very mien or gesture of such wicked men, just as if he had set before our eyes a picture of them."[49] Calvin thinks that pride reveals itself in particular in the eyes, in which the feelings of the heart may be seen, as in Isaiah's description of the king of Assyria.[50] The haughty betray their hidden pride especially in the way they regard the poor and afflicted Church that they oppress, because "the luster of their honor and power dazzles their eyes, so that they make no account of God's spiritual kingdom."[51] However, pride and arrogance may also be revealed in the way people carry themselves, including the way they walk in public. "For as it is a sign of modesty to have a cast down look (as even heathen writers have declared), so to have excessively high looks is a sign of arrogance; and when a woman lifts up her head it can betoken nothing but pride."[52]

Calvin is especially interested in the various signs of grief that are manifested in the lives of the godly, in large part to counter the claim of those who think that Stoic apathy is essential to piety. To counter this claim, Calvin points to the example of Paul, who tells the Corinthians that he wrote to them with many tears (2 Cor. 2:4). According to Calvin, tears "in a brave and courageous man are a sign of great distress."[53] Paul testifies to his tears, and hence to his grief, to show that he was afflicted with grief before he admonished the Corinthians.[54] Paul also appeals to his tears when he speaks of the enemies of the Church, to show the Philippians that he is not motivated by hatred, "but by godly zeal, inasmuch as he sees that the Church is miserably destroyed by such pests."[55] According to Calvin, all the godly, especially the pastors, should manifest grief in the same way when they behold the calamity of the Church.[56] Similarly, the groaning and tears of Jesus at the tomb of Lazarus testify to the legitimacy of the passions, so long as they are not disordered (*ataxia*), for such signs of grief testify to the profound sympathy Jesus has for our afflictions.[57]

Calvin is especially drawn to the psalms, which he calls "An Anatomy of All the Parts of the Soul," for they portray in a vivid way the various forms of grief that afflict the hearts of the godly. "Or rather, the Holy Spirit has here represented to the life all the griefs, sorrows, fears, doubts, hopes, cares, perplexities, in short, all the distracting emotions with which the minds of men are wont to be agitated."[58] Calvin notes the way grief is wont to manifest itself on the faces of those who are suffering, "for terror or alarm, like other passions, makes itself visible in the face. The countenance itself speaks, and shows what are our feelings."[59] For instance, the author of Psalm 88 speaks of the way his eye mourns because of his affliction, "a plain indication of the low condition to which he was reduced."[60] The body itself may manifest signs of grief in the sounds that emerge from it, showing the great distress of the person.[61] The person in grief may also extend her arms, in order to move others to pity for her sorrow, "for when we wish to move men to pity, we stretch forth our arms."[62]

The most common signs of grief are of course crying and weeping. Even though grief is rooted in the affections of the heart, when it reaches its full strength it will of its own manifest itself in weeping. "Silence is a token of patience; but when grief overcomes one, he, as though forgetting himself, necessarily bursts out into crying."[63] Grief may manifest itself to others in groans, even when we try to hide it by suppressing our cries. "This happens when we endeavor to restrain our grief, and yet cannot prevent the outward signs of grief from breaking out in spite of us."[64] According to Calvin, we tend to restrain our weeping in the presence of others, especially if they are our enemies, "for an enemy would deride our weeping in misery."[65] However, when grief is strong enough it breaks through the inhibitions of fear and shame to manifest itself even before the eyes of our enemies.[66] The extremity of grief is reached when our weeping, far from giving us relief from our sorrow, actually inflames our sorrow all the more. "But when we weep and our eyes shed tears, and when the mind in a manner exhausts itself, it is a sign of the greatest grief."[67] When grief reaches such an extremity, it may no longer be possible to represent it to others either in language or in weeping. This is why, according to Calvin, Moses says nothing about the grief of Jacob when he is told that Reuben lay with his concubine, "because his grief was too great to be expressed. For here Moses seems to have acted as did the painter who, in representing the sacrifice of Iphigenia, put a veil over her father's face, because he could not sufficiently express the grief of his countenance."[68] However, the extremity of grief may also change our affections themselves, so that we no longer care for those who are our own flesh and blood.[69]

Closely related to grief are the signs and ceremonies of mourning, in response to the death of those whom we love. Calvin is very concerned with the proper expression of mourning, for he is convinced that people tend to excess at such times, verging on despair. On the one hand, Calvin does not deny the legitimacy and necessity of rites of mourning, for these are expressions of our God-given affections. Thus, when Paul urges us not to mourn as those who have no hope (1 Thess. 4:13), Calvin says, "He does not, however, forbid us to express any grief at all, but calls for restraint in sorrow, for he says that ye sorrow not, even as the rest, which have no hope."[70] Once again, Calvin denies that we are called to "a Stoic indifference."[71] However, as those who believe in the resurrection, our expressions of grief must be moderated by our hope, so that our uncontrolled mourning does not lead us into despair. "It is, therefore, unfitting that we, who have been fully grounded in the resurrection, should express our grief unduly."[72]

Calvin is aware that each nation and culture has distinctive rites of mourning to observe the death of loved ones. Once again, Calvin distinguishes between western and eastern cultures in this regard. "The Italians and other western nations allow their hair and beard to grow when they were in mourning; and hence arose the phrase, to lengthen the beard. On the other hand the eastern nations shaved the head and beard, which they reckoned to be ornamental; and when they reversed their ordinary custom, that was a token of mourning."[73] As we have seen before, Calvin highlights the way Eastern nations in warmer climes are more expressive in their external manifestation of affections than are northern Europeans like himself.[74] He is therefore well aware that certain expressions of mourning may seem excessive to northerners that are nonetheless legitimate and moderate forms of expression in Eastern cultures, such as crying out, "Alas! Lord, our king is dead!" (Jer. 34:5). "The warmer the climate the more given to gestures and ceremonies the people are. In these cold regions gesticulations and crying out, 'Alas! Lord, alas! Father,' would be deemed impertinent and foolish gesticulations."[75] Eastern peoples also pull out their hair and tear open their skin as they cry aloud in mourning.[76] They would also change their clothing as a sign of mourning, putting on sackcloth and ashes.[77]

Even though Calvin attempts to place such gestures and rites of mourning in their cultural context, he nonetheless thinks that such eastern practices are excessive. For instance, he thinks that the use of sackcloth for mourning, common to both believers and unbelievers, threatens to empty the ceremony of its penitential meaning.[78] When the reference to God is removed from the ceremony, the danger is very great that it will be used in an ostentatious display of mourning, so that "he who mourned might appear miserable to others, and make a display of his weeping and tears."[79] Nonetheless, Calvin thinks that the use of sackcloth as a sign of mourning is something innate in human nature.[80] On the other hand, he thinks that other gestures of mourning, such as self-mutilation, are not legitimate signs of mourning, as they go against human nature, "for it is not agreeable to humanity to pull off the beard, to make bald the head, or to tear the hands and the face with the nails."[81] This is why God prohibited such practices in the Law. "You are children of the Lord your God. You must not lacerate yourselves or shave your forelocks for the dead" (Deut. 14:1). Acording to Calvin, "that was preposterous affectation. And we know that men are ambitious in grief. Hence that God may impose restraint upon sorrow, he forbids his people to cut the skin, or to produce baldness."[82]

Calvin thinks that such restraint is necessary due to the way people try to outdo one another with expressions of grief, which has more to do with human ambition than with genuine mourning and grief. "But we see that men vied with one another in lamenting for the dead; for it was deemed a shame not to show grief at the death of their friends."[83] Calvin is aware that his own culture has its share of excessive rituals of mourning, as when women strike themselves or raise their hands in a gesture of extreme despair.[84] The same may be said of mourning for excessive lengths of time, as when Israel mourns the death of Aaron for a month (Num. 20:29), "for men are naturally only too much inclined to excessive grief, even although they do not indulge it; and besides, the hope of a better life avails to mitigate sorrow."[85]

In spite of the dangers of excess and ambition that haunt rituals of mourning, Calvin still insists that they are necessary expressions of pious affections. "When any one dies, friends and neighbors meet, and show respect to his memory."[86] The purpose of such gatherings is not only to show signs of mourning but also to hear words of comfort from those who love us, "as when relatives, and friends, and neighbors meet together for the purpose of mourning; they hear lamentations, and add some signs in agreement."[87] Calvin gives two reasons in particular why "this solemn mourning has not been unreasonably received as a general custom" by the godly, namely, "to exercise themselves both in the fear of God, and in the hope and desire of the future resurrection."[88] To begin with, since death is a sign of the curse of God on humanity, it is profitable to use the occasion of the death of a loved one to humble ourselves before God.[89] Second, we should use the custom of mourning to reflect on the unity of the living with the dead, as we share with them the hope of a future life, "so that in death itself the communion of the new and immortal life shines forth."[90] The rites of mourning are rightly observed if they are used to meditate on our common participation in the curse of God revealed in death, and on our communion in eternal life with all the godly.

3. The Eyes Manifest and Guide the Affections

The visible signs and expressions of human affections are so powerful because they appeal to the eyes, which for Calvin are the most keen and tender of the senses. "The eyes are, as it were, the guides and conductors of man in this life, and by their influence move the other senses hither and thither."[91] On the one hand, the affections of the heart reveal themselves primarily in the eyes. "For we know that the eyes are the principal outlets to the affections; for when the affections burst forth in the eyes, and are conspicuous there, it is not surprising if all our desires are marked by this form of speech."[92] It is in this sense that the eyes are the guides of our lives, in that they direct our path in the direction of our affections. "Hence they seize their way, as it were, with their eyes."[93] The eyes therefore urge us on by their gaze to the objects of our affections, until we attain what we desire.[94] For instance, Eve had looked on the tree of the knowledge of good and evil many times without desiring it; but once she became convinced in her heart that it was good to acquire such wisdom, she looks on the tree in a different way, "whereas before she had passed it by a hundred times with an unmoved and tranquil look."[95]

Once the eyes are directed by the affections towards the object of their desire, they further inflame such affections by the beauty that they behold. When Potiphar's wife is led from looking upon Joseph to casting her eyes upon him, she not only regards him differently than before but is further inflamed by what her eyes see. "Thus we see that the eyes were as torches to inflame the heart to lust."[96] The same phenomenon may be observed in those who join the affection of the heart to their contemplation of false images in places of worship, as Ezekiel accuses the Jews of doing in the Temple, "not only because they were devoted to idols with all their heart, but also because they were drawn that way by their eyes, as if their eyes had been torches to inflame their mind."[97] The affections lead the eyes in the direction of their desire, while the eyes inflame the affections by contemplating the object of desire. When this happens, the eyes work together with the affections to override all sense of justice and equity in our minds, as when the children of Reuben and Gad cast their eyes on the land of Jazar and Gilead (Num. 32:1).[98] For this reason, Calvin urges the godly to guard the sense of sight above all others, for it is the sense that most deeply penetrates into the inmost affections of our hearts.[99]

On the other hand, the tenderness of the sense of sight may actually be a help in awakening and fostering humane and godly affections. For instance, even though physical beauty was the occasion for calamity in the case of Joseph, it was a benefit for Moses, for it induced those who saw him to care for him.[100] The sense of sight is also of great effectiveness in moving people to have mercy on those who are afflicted, "for there is in the eyes, we know, the tenderest sense."[101] The sight of the misery and suffering of others can move even enemies to have sympathy on those who are afflicted. "Hence it is, that even the most savage enemies are sometimes softened, for they are led by their eyes to acts of humanity."[102]

Since the sense of sight is the most tender of all the senses, Calvin also thinks that the power of sight is the principal part of human life. When Zedekiah has his eyes pulled out by the Babylonians, Calvin considers him to have been doomed to constant misery. "When the eyes are pulled out, we know that the principal part of life is lost."[103] For this reason, according to Calvin, the Jews thought that the power of life manifested itself principally in the eyes. "To enlighten the eyes signifies the same thing in the Hebrew language as to give the breath of life, for the vigor of life appears chiefly in the eyes."[104] The power of life revealed in the eyes, and their ability to influence the affections of the heart, also explains why magicians think their art lies principally in the eyes.[105]

For this reason, Calvin urges the godly to have God before their eyes at all times, for only in this way will the power of sight guide our lives in the right direction, and prevent us from being inflamed with sinful affections.[106] When the eyes are restrained and guided by the fear and love of God, they can look upon the splendor and apparent prosperity of the wicked without being tempted to follow their lead.[107] By keeping God before our eyes, we will not be misled, as was Lot, into thinking that life in Sodom is life in paradise.[108] Those who have their hearts and eyes directed to God, and to God's Kingdom, will not be allured and blinded by the passing splendor of the world with all its apparent glory. "Hence, although the mind of the flesh does not understand the excellence of the heavenly life, yet we do not consider it as it deserves unless we are ready for its sake to renounce those things that shine before our eyes."[109]

4. THE DANGER OF OSTENTATION

The keenness and tenderness of the sense of sight directly influences Calvin's understanding of the perversion of gestures, rites, and ceremonies by ostentation and pomp. Since the eyes are drawn to splendor, and the heart is en-kindled by what they behold, human beings are easily led to the opinion that their gestures and rites are the most holy and true when they are the most splendid and beautiful. Since the eyes of the pious ought ever to be directed to God, and guided by the fear of the Lord, Calvin held it to be axiomatic that those who delight in the external splendor of ceremonies are utterly lacking in integrity of heart. "To glory in appearance and not in heart, means to make outward show a disguise and to regard sincerity of heart as of no importance, for those who are really wise will never boast except in God. But where there is empty show, there is no sincerity and no uprightness of heart."[110]

Such ostentation may appear in the opulent and luxurious clothing we wear, by which we hope to draw the eyes of others to ourselves, thereby revealing our pride and ambition.[111] For this reason, those who seek glorious and expensive attire for themselves lack inward integrity of heart. "Where, indeed, is pure sincerity of heart found under splendid ornament?"[112] However, such ambition may also pervert the ceremonies and gifts that God gives to us in the Law and the Gospel. For instance, Calvin notes the way ambition turns the ceremony of cleansing into an ostentatious display. "Since superstition is ambitious, it undoubtedly led to ostentation."[113] Similarly, the gift of speaking in tongues was given as the visible confirmation of the truth of the Gospel. "But ambition afterwards corrupted this second use, when many carried over to ostentation and display, what they had received for illuminating the greatness of the heavenly wisdom."[114]

God deplores all luxury, ostentation, and pomp of both clothing and ceremonies, and commands us instead to exhibit our humility in simple gestures, rites, and ceremonies. "I have no doubt that he who is 'humble and contrite in spirit' is indirectly contrasted by him with the array, and splendor, and elegance of ceremonies, by which the eyes of men are commonly dazzled, so as to be carried away with admiration."[115] However, because the ostentation and pomp of ceremonies can both dazzle the eyes of worshipers and ravish them with admiration, hypocrites find them extremely useful as ways of deceiving the simple.[116] Such ostentation may also be found in those who have no solid doctrine to teach, preferring instead to ravish the minds of all by the splendor of their external rites. "This is the reason why men and women who intend to deceive, always heap together a number of ceremonies."[117]

Since hypocrites are able to dazzle the eyes of the simple with the pomp of their ceremonies, they conclude that they may also be able to dazzle and even blind the eyes of God.[118] Calvin thinks that the Roman Church in particular attempts to dazzle the eyes of people and of God in this way, for they "think that God is duly and in the best manner worshipped, when they accumulate many pompous exhibitions of ceremonies."[119] The Roman Church therefore thinks that God is rightly worshiped merely by the observance of their splendid and ornate ceremonies, regardless of the lack of piety and love in their hearts.[120] Such ostentation may even be seen in the vestments that the priests and bishops wear in the Roman Church, which they think essential to the right worship of God. "For they would think themselves to be doing great dishonor to God, or rather to their idols, were they not to adorn themselves when going to perform sacred duties."[121] For this reason, when Calvin and his colleagues in the evangelical and orthodox churches remove such ostentatious ceremonies and vestments, their Roman opponents accuse them of abolishing the worship of God. "The reason is, that in Popery everything had a dazzling appearance, and drew the admiration of men."[122] Calvin's concern to simplify the worship of God is directly related to his conviction that the ostentation and pomp of ceremonies both reveals and fosters the lack of integrity in the heart of the worshiper. Once again, it never occurs to him that such rites and ceremonies could in fact express and enkindle true faith and piety in the worshiping community, for he held it to be axiomatic that "where there is empty show, there is no sincerity and no uprightness of heart."[123]

5. HYPOCRISY

Calvin exhibits an interest in hypocrisy throughout the course of his writing career. In his commentary on Seneca's treatise *De Clementia* of 1532, Calvin traces the meaning of the term hypocrisy to the theater. "What Seneca previously called a 'goodness assumed for a time' he now calls, wearing a mask, a metaphor drawn from comedy and tragedy, in which masked persons act in the theater. Hence, 'to wear a mask' means to lay aside one's natural form. And we speak of a counterfeit and hypocritical man as 'masked.'"[124] Calvin then quotes Cicero with regard to the false glory attained by hypocrites, with their inane ostentation. "For if anyone thinks that he can win everlasting glory by pretense, by empty show, by hypocritical talk and looks, he is very much mistaken."[125] Calvin goes on to observe the way the same hypocrisy plagues his own day. "What? Are there not also in our own age 'monsters of men, dripping with inner vices,' yet putting forth the outward appearance and mask of uprightness?"[126] Thus, already in 1532, Calvin associates vain ostentation with hypocrisy and the false simulation of godliness and virtue, and points to the time when such actors will be unmasked.

In his writings as an evangelical, Calvin is constantly attentive to the various ways hypocrites use both works and ceremonies to hide the true affections of their hearts. "Hypocrites, though chargeable with the grossest faults, nevertheless deceive by wearing a mask of godliness."[127] The difficulty is that hypocrites hide their ungodliness from human eyes by means of this mask of piety, so that the real extent of their sin is not revealed.[128] Calvin sees such hypocrisy in the deliberations of the rulers of Jerusalem as they decide what to do about Jesus. "Their main object was, indeed, to show something like gravity, moderation, and prudence, so as to practice deception upon others."[129] Hypocrites may be so skilled at the deceptive appearance of virtue and piety that they may wind up fooling themselves as well as others, mistaking the mask they have created for the true affections of their hearts.[130] Since hypocrites are no different from actors, they no longer project the image of virtue and holiness once their audience is no longer present.[131] They act no differently when they feel that they are no longer in the presence of God, as in the case of Balaam, "for as soon as they can withdraw themselves, they revel like fugitive slaves."[132] However, despite their skill in hiding their true thoughts from others by their masks, God at times reveals the marks of their impiety on their very faces.[133]

One of the most effective ways hypocrites hide their lack of piety is by means of the external gestures, rites, and ceremonies of worship, for these may be easily performed without any corresponding inward affection of the heart. Calvin thinks that Jesus was the most critical of such ceremonial worshipers, and turns once again to classical sources to give a clear understanding of what Jesus means by hypocrisy. "In the profane writers, hypocrite was the name for a stage performer, who acted out, in theater and festival, fictitious roles, but Scripture transfers it to the two-faced personality, and the fake."[134] Jesus is especially concerned with those who pretend to be sincere worshipers of God while they only do so for selfish gain and reputation.[135]

Calvin claims that there is an essential relationship between hypocrisy and superstition. Just as the superstitious confine the reality represented in symbols to the symbol itself, in order to drag God down from heaven, so hypocrites confine the meaning of the worship of God to the external ceremonies themselves, thinking to put God in their debt by the mere performance of externals. "The result is that they are infatuated by visible signs, and then, neglecting piety, make a great commotion to put God in their debt with a childish method and things of no value."[136] Hypocrites thus think that their entire relationship with God may be safely managed by means of external symbols and ceremonies, by which they bind God to themselves and their desires, and by which they hide their hearts from God and one another. This is why Jeremiah tells the Jews of his day that it is vain for them to trust in the Temple of the Lord, for "in the regular way of hypocrites they turned truth into falsehood, making out that external ceremonies were all-sufficient for observance, and were content to use the Temple as an empty sham."[137]

Hypocrites not only hide from the eyes of others by their use of ceremonies, but they even think they can dazzle and blind the eyes of God.[138] This is the kind of hypocrite addressed in Psalm 50, "whose whole religion lies in the observance of ceremonies, with which they attempt to blind the eyes of God."[139] Far from pleasing God, Calvin claims that God brands "such a disjunction of the external signs of piety from faith and the sincere affection of the heart as sacrilege."[140] Calvin claims that the Roman Church is especially guilty of this kind of hypocrisy, by which they appear to approach God in ceremonies, all the while using ceremonies to flee and hide from God.[141] Calvin thinks that this is the behavior that Hosea describes as sowing the wind. "So also hypocrites have their displays, and set themselves in order, that they may appear wholly like the pious worshippers of God."[142]

However, as critical as Calvin remains of the Roman Church, with its ostentation and pomp of ceremonies, he is equally aware that hypocrites use the reformed worship of the evangelical temples to hide their impiety from God. "The hypocrites also among us boast of Baptism, and the holy Supper, and the name of Reformation; while, at the same time, these are nothing but mockeries, by which the name of God and the whole of religion are profaned, when no real piety flourishes in the heart."[143] Even though Calvin is scathing in his criticism of Roman worship as a haven of hypocrisy, he is equally convinced that the majority of worshipers in evangelical churches are hypocrites, in spite of their simpler ceremonies and rites. "Thus in all generations there have existed play-acting worshippers of God, whose total sanctity consisted in gesticulations and empty displays."[144] God is no less mocked when we use the divinely instituted ceremonies of worship to hide our impiety than when we create more glorious and splendid forms of worship by which to do the same, "for it was a vain display when there was no integrity within."[145]

Since hypocrites convince themselves and others that God is pleased by the performance of ceremonies alone, they become outraged when they discover that God detests such a form of worship, and betray the impiety they had attempted to mask by these ceremonies. Calvin thinks that this is why Cain became so angry once he discovered that God had not accepted his sacrifice. "When afterwards they see that they gain no advantage, they betray the venom of their minds."[146] Calvin thinks that this is why one so often finds in the prophets the statement that God does not accept or delight in the sacrifices offered by the Israelites, for in this way their hypocrisy betrays itself. "Thus hypocrites ever mock God with their fopperies and regard God as extremely cruel, when not satisfied with external display."[147] Since Calvin thinks that the members of his own congregations think that God is satisfied by their observance of external ceremonies, the pastors of his own day should relate the same message to their congregations, as he tirelessly did in his own sermons. "As then men deceive themselves with such trifles, it is necessary to show that all those things which hypocrites obtrude on God, without sincerity of heart, are frivolous trumperies."[148]

In spite of such prophetic and pastoral admonitions about the futility of hypocritical worship, Calvin is convinced that hypocrites so thoroughly delude themselves that not even these will bring the secrets of their hearts to light. God alone can do this.[149] Hypocrites hide their true affections so deeply beneath the false appearance of ceremonies and works that only the light of God can reveal them.[150] However, prophets and pastors know that the Word of God itself has the ability to penetrate beneath the mask worn by hypocrites to their deeply hidden affections (Heb. 4:12). "There is no thicker darkness than that of unbelief, and hypocrisy makes us blind in a terrifying way. The Word of God scatters this darkness, and puts hypocrisy to flight."[151] Just as doctors cannot discover a hidden ulcer without pressing down and probing into the recesses where it is hidden, so hypocrites will not betray themselves by the simple teaching of doctrine, unless that doctrine is brought to bear on the concrete circumstances of their lives.[152] When the people of Geneva objected to Calvin's sharp tone in his sermons, he more than likely took this as a sign that he was unmasking the ungodliness deeply concealed behind their masks of piety and love. "Hence it is that hypocrites become mad, when God summons them to judgment."[153]

6. Human Eyes See Appearances;
the Eyes of God See the Heart

Hypocrites think that they can blind the eyes of God by the splendor of their works and ceremonies, and hide their true affections behind their masks of piety and love, because they do not realize the qualitative difference between the eyes of God and the eyes of human beings. Hypocrites rightly know that they alone are the ones who know the true state of their thoughts and affections, and that these are hidden from other people until they decide to reveal them to others by their language and gestures. Even when language and gestures are used to manifest our thoughts and hearts to others, other people can only know them by working by analogy from the outward representation to the inner affection that still lies hidden within us, and remains truly known by ourselves alone. "The inner thought of a man, of which others know nothing, is clear to him alone. If later, he reveals it to others, that does not alter the fact that his spirit alone knows what is in him."[154] If hypocrites use language and gestures to conceal their real thoughts and affections, and do not betray them in any other way, then it is impossible for other human beings to know that they are being deceived.

Given their success in hiding from other human beings, hypocrites falsely conclude that they can deceive God in the same way, for they think that God also judges their thoughts and affections by beginning with the external representation of them in language and gestures. However, according to Calvin, God sees us in exactly the opposite way that others see us. Human beings judge our thoughts and affections by looking at their external manifestation, and inferring the affection within. God looks directly into the deepest recess of our hearts, and sees it more clearly than we ever will. "For not only are our words and outward works open to him, but the inmost recesses of our heart and deepest thoughts of our mind are better and more clearly revealed to him than to ourselves."[155] The more successfully we deceive others, the more we condemn ourselves before the eyes of God.[156] If we wish to win the approval of God, we must begin with the hidden affections of our hearts, and then make sure that what we say and do corresponds to those affections, in order that they might truly be revealed to others.[157] Human beings can only see the external revelation of our affections, and then judge the thoughts of our heart on that basis, knowing they may be deceived. God sees directly into the inmost thoughts and affections of our hearts, and then looks to see if our language and gestures correspond to and reveal these thoughts and affections.

Calvin tirelessly appeals to the qualitative difference between the eyes of God and the eyes of human beings in order to show the futility of hypocrisy. Thus, in his commentary on Romans of 1540, Calvin thinks that Paul's description of the judgment of God as "according to truth" (Rom. 2:2) is meant to illustrate this difference between divine and human modes of judgment.[158] The judgment of God begins with the hidden affections of the heart, and only accepts our external works if they are rooted in godly affections. "It follows from this that a mask of a feigned piety will not prevent him from punishing secret wickedness with his judgment."[159] This is why, according to Calvin, Paul exhorts us continually to have our praise not of other human beings but of God. "Because the eyes of men are fixed on mere appearances, he denies that we ought to be satisfied with what is commended by human opinion. This is often deceived by external splendor. We should, rather, be satisfied with the eyes of God, from which the deepest secrets of the heart are not hidden."[160]

Calvin sees the same ability to see into the human heart in Jesus Christ. When many came to believe in him during the Passover festival, "Jesus on his part would not entrust himself to them, because he knew all people" (John 2:24). Even though such demonstrations of faith might fool other people, they cannot deceive Christ, for "he estimates according to their hidden source, that is, according to the inmost affection of the heart, the things which dazzle our eyes with their false brilliance."[161] This is why Jesus tells the Pharisees that they are content to justify themselves in the sight of others, but God knows their hearts (Luke 16:15). "Men applaud outward shows; at God's judgment the sincere heart alone is approved."[162]

The difference between human eyes and the eyes of God also lies behind the statement made in the New Testament that God is no respecter of persons. The judgment of human beings is all too often swayed by external matters such as beauty, rank, wealth, and friendship, in a way that perverts a just accounting. "A regard to persons blinds our eyes, so as to leave no room for right or justice; but Paul affirms that it is of no value in the sight of God."[163] God does not pay any attention to such appearances but rather looks directly into the heart to see if it has faithfulness and integrity.[164] No matter how much we may win the support and approval of others by the persona we so effectively create, it is of no use before God, for God pays no attention to such externals, "for he is not a mortal man whom outward appearance pleases, but he reads us for what we are inwardly in our hearts."[165]

To accentuate the difference between the eyes of God and the eyes of human beings, Peter describes God as the one "who knows the human heart" (Acts 15:8), in order to encourage the Church in Jerusalem not to judge holiness of life on the basis of external appearances.[166] Jeremiah means to point to the same distinction between the eyes of humans and the eyes of God when he asks, "O Lord, do not your eyes look for truth?" (Jer. 5:3). "He intimates that the eyes of God are different from those of mortals; men can see a very little way, hardly three fingers before them; but God penetrates into the inmost and the most hidden recesses of the heart."[167] Calvin thinks that the difference between human and divine perception was not unknown to the pagans, for their "poets, when they speak with a sober and well-regulated mind of the worship of God, require both a clean heart and pure hands."[168] Thus, in spite of the fact that each person has his or her unique ways of seeking to conceal their affections from God in deeply hidden recesses of their hearts, God sees through all such attempts, rendering them futile in God's eyes, for "the eyes of God cannot be dazzled and darkened."[169] One of the cleverest stratagems hypocrites use to hide themselves from God is by calling God to witness of their account. Emboldened by their success in deceiving others, they think that they can deceive God in this manner. "Thus they would represent the character of God to be different than what it is, as if by their deceptions they could dazzle his eyes."[170] The true character of God is best described by "the knower of hearts," something hypocrites would do well to remember.[171]

Calvin appeals to the distinction between God's vision and ours in order to account for the often perplexing and even vexing judgments of God on people whom we cannot help but admire and approve.[172] When we are told that those who have not the Son have not the Father also, this does not seem fair or just to us, for we can think of many people in the history of the world who appeared to live upright and heroic lives. "For we are satisfied with external appearances, because the filthiness of the heart is hidden from us. But God sees that underneath lies the foulest filth."[173] The same question arises with regard to original sin, which condemns even newborn infants to destruction. Calvin knows that to the human eye nothing appears in infants but innocence, but he claims that God's eye sees the defilement due to original sin that otherwise escapes our eyes.[174] Finally, Calvin will appeal to the eyes of God to explain why one person is punished for doing something for which another was spared. When Zechariah asks how he is to know what he is told about his son is true, he sounds no different to us than do Gideon or Mary, who were not punished for asking such questions. "This does not appear from their words. The understanding must be God's, for his eyes pierce to the very fountain of the heart."[175]

According to Calvin, the Gospel has the power to reveal the secret thoughts and affections otherwise hidden under masks of piety and love. When Isaiah says that there will come a time when a fool will no longer be called noble, or a villain regarded as honorable (Isa. 32:5), Calvin says that God does this by means of the Gospel. "And this is the reason why the gospel is so much hated by the world; for no man can patiently endure to have his 'hidden thoughts' and concealed baseness revealed."[176] In particular, the "inner thoughts of many are revealed" (Luke 2:35) by the persecutions that accompany faith in the Gospel.[177] The thoughts and affections of the heart are also manifested to others by means of dissention and disagreement about the Gospel in the Church. At such times, those who pretended to be faithful are unmasked, whereas the integrity and faithfulness of the pious are revealed.[178] Since the power of hypocrisy is so great that it can delude the most discerning person into thinking he or she is truly pious, Calvin wants his readers to meditate continually on the Gospel, and to be aware at all times of the persecution and strife that it will bring, so that when these come to us we do not fall away.[179] Such trials are good for the pious and for the Church, for they bring before our eyes those thoughts and affections that had previously been known to God alone.[180]

Were people to remember that God sees their hearts more clearly than they do, they would at the very least be restrained from giving in to sinful impulses, thinking they can elude the eyes of all witnesses. "Were the truth graven upon men's hearts that they cannot elude the eye of God, this would serve as a check and restraint upon their conduct."[181] The pious, on the other hand, have been awakened by the light of God in Christ, and know that even when there are no human witnesses, their hearts, thoughts, and actions are as manifest to God and the angels as if they were in a theater.[182] Once God reveals Godself to the godly, they realize that their hearts and thoughts are revealed to God. "Wherefore, let us know, that God manifests himself to the faithful, in order that they may live as in his sight; and may make him the arbiter not only of their works, but of their thoughts."[183]

The faithful know that God is the one true witness of their thoughts and works, even when there are no other witnesses to behold them, and that

God sees the most secret aspects of our hearts. Calvin thinks that this is why Jesus speaks of the Father seeing in secret (Matt. 6:4), "for the theater of God is in the hidden corners, and it is a splendid cure he applies for healing the disease of ambition, to recall us to the power of God's vision, who can make all the vain-glory vanish from our hearts, and disperse it altogether."[184] Content with the eyes of God upon their hearts, the pious will be able to withstand even the false accusations of their enemies, for they know that God sees their integrity though it be hidden under the reproaches of others.[185] The faithful will therefore consider their obedience to God primarily in light of the submission of their hearts and minds to God.[186] Above all, the pious will hold in abhorrence any disjunction between their inward affections and outward speech and gestures. "When the heart does not correspond to the outward life, and harbors any secret evil intent, the fair exterior appearance may deceive men, but it is an abomination in the sight of God."[187]

CHAPTER 13

The Distinguishing Marks of the Children of God

The self-manifestation of piety and love in the language, symbols, and gestures of the Christian community has the effect of manifesting to the world the adopted children of God, who are gathered out of and distinguished from the reprobate. Calvin is therefore concerned to set forth the distinguishing marks by which the adopted children of God might be identified by others. "The elect cannot be recognized by us with assurance of faith, yet Scripture describes certain sure marks to us, . . . by which we may distinguish the elect and children of God from the reprobate and the alien, insofar as he wishes us so to recognize them."[1] Since no one can be adopted as a child of God without being made a member of the body of Christ, Calvin first of all needs to identify the distinguishing marks of the Church, over against the claim of Rome to be the true Church of Christ. However, given the reality that hypocrites are highly skilled at concealing their impiety by means of the symbols and ceremonies of the Church, Calvin seeks to identify the signs by which the adopted children of God might be more confidently identified, especially by means of their love for one another. Since the purpose of adoption is the re-creation of the image of God, the restoration of the image of God becomes the most certain sign by which the children of God may be recognized. However, since the children of God are conformed to the image of the crucified Son of God, the lives of the godly should be a lively representation of Christ crucified, meaning that they suffer simply because they believe in him and bear witness to him. Moreover, if the godly are to be separated from the reprobate, it is necessary to set forth the signs by which the reprobate might be identified, so that the godly might not be misled by their example, which often presents an alluring attraction to them. To warn the godly from fellowship with the reprobate, God will set forth vivid examples of their punishment and destruction, not only in Scripture, but also in human history, from which the godly are to profit. The manifest destruction of the reprobate both fosters the fear of the Lord in the children of God and consoles them in light of the fact that the wicked appear to prosper in this life more than the children of God. The destruction of the reprobate, and the protection of the godly, forms yet another way by which God manifests the distinction between them.

I. The Certain Marks of the Church and Its True Beauty

Calvin was a member of what he called the evangelical and orthodox Church, which he claimed had emerged from the Roman Church just as the Jews had emerged from Babylon after their captivity. Since Calvin had concluded that the Roman Church was no longer the Christian Church, he was forced to confront two crucial questions: How could the Christian Church have disappeared from view during the ascendancy of the papacy? and, What are the distinguishing marks by which the true Church may be recognized when it appears? Calvin addresses both questions in his preface to Francis I that accompanied every edition of the *Institutes* from 1536 onwards. Calvin identifies the two most effective questions that the Roman theologians put to their evangelical opponents. "Our controversy turns on these two hinges: first, they contend that the form of the church is always apparent and observable. Secondly, they set this form in the see of the Roman Church and its hierarchy."[2] To counter these objections, Calvin must establish that the Church can in fact be hidden from view during certain times of its history, and that its identifying marks are not to be found in the Roman see and the bishops in communion with Rome. "Rather, it has quite another mark, namely, the pure preaching of God's Word and the lawful administration of the sacraments."[3]

The form of the Church is not to be found in the splendor of the Roman episcopacy but rather in the Word and the sacraments; and this form is at times not seen in the world, as Calvin thought was the case before the emergence of Martin Luther in 1520. To defend his claim that the Church can at times be hidden from view, Calvin appeals to the example of the Church during the time of the prophets. "What form do we think it displayed when Elijah complained that he alone was left [1 Kings 19:10 or 14]?"[4] To show that the Church is not to be identified with the splendor of bishops in synodical communion, Calvin turns to the trial of Jesus before the Sanhedrin. "Was not such pomp manifested in that council where priests, scribes, and Pharisees assembled to deliberate concerning the execution of Christ [John 11:47 ff.]?"[5] If the Church is to be identified with its external form, then both Elijah and Jesus must be guilty of schism.[6] On the other hand, if the certain marks of the Church are the pure preaching of the Word and the lawful administration of the sacraments, then the prophets and Jesus are members of the true Church even if its form was not visible in their day, and even if they were being persecuted and killed by those who claimed to represent the visible form and splendor of the Church.

In his subsequent biblical commentaries, Calvin attends to those places in which the true marks of the Church may be properly discerned. One vivid example is in the Book of Acts, when the faithful are said to devote themselves to "the apostles' teaching and fellowship, to the breaking of bread and the prayers" (Acts 2:42). "Do we seek the true Church of Christ? The image of it is here painted to the life."[7] On the other hand, Calvin uses the mark of preaching to show why the Roman bishop is no longer the legitimate successor to the apostle Peter. "That the Pope's court is at Rome is well enough known; but there they show no mark of the Church."[8] Calvin also highlights the times when those who represent the apparent form of the Church persecute and seek to destroy those who belong to the true but hidden Church, as at the trial of Jesus in Jerusalem. "Those who came to that Council represented the entire Church of God, yet they all conspired together to extinguish the one hope of salvation."[9]

Calvin is also interested in those times in its history when the Church begins to emerge from its hiddenness so that its form may begin to be discerned by others. For instance, after the murder of Abel and the banishment of Cain, Moses mentions the birth of Seth. "To Seth also a son was born, and he named him Enosh. At that time people began to invoke the name of the Lord" (Gen. 4:26). According to Calvin, this represents the emergence of the visible form of the Church in human history, for "the face of the Church began distinctly to appear, and that worship of God was set up which might continue to posterity."[10] Calvin claimed that the same thing was happening in his own day, with the emergence of the evangelical and orthodox Church from the Church of Rome.[11] He sees the face of the Church emerging yet again with the calling of Abram, after it was hidden by the scattering of humanity after the tower of Babel.[12]

On the other hand, Calvin thinks that the admiration of the disciples for the glory of the Temple can be seen in the attitude of his contemporaries towards the Roman Church. In both instances the true Church is almost completely hidden by the splendor, might, and magnificence of the false Church. "A similar sense of awe for the Papacy grips many simple people today; they see it supported by huge wealth and vast resources and at first gasp in amazement, so as to despise the Church whose face is ignoble and squalid."[13] Calvin is well aware that the believers of his day might be drawn to the appearance of splendor and wealth in the Roman Church, compared to the homeliness and poverty of the evangelical Church. He therefore warns his readers not to judge the Church by such splendor, lest they mistake the apparent Church for the true Church.[14]

Over against the appearance of such wealth and splendor in the Roman Church, Calvin points his readers to the true Church hidden under its very ordinary appearance.[15] He is well aware that the lowly appearance of the evangelical Church is one of the reasons that few in his day are attracted to it, whereas the power and glory of the Roman Church are very alluring. "And certainly, as things are today, there is no need to be surprised if such a deformed state of the Church is frightening them away, but the brilliance that shines in its opponents is blinding their eyes."[16] However, far from driving people away, Calvin insists that the lowly appearance of the Church should confirm the fact that it is the Church of Christ crucified, for "it is particularly reasonable that in the form of the Church the living image of Christ should appear as in a mirror."[17]

Calvin does not deny that the Church has its own beauty, but he wants to locate that beauty in the spiritual gifts that God bestows upon it.[18] He claims that such beauty can be manifested in the Church even if it has few members, as when a remnant of the Jews returned from Babylon, "because the excellence of the Church does not consist in multitude but in purity when God bestows splendid and glorious gifts of the Spirit of God on his elect."[19] This beauty was seen in the early Church, even though it was few in

numbers, and suffered under the cross of Christ. "At the time when she flour-
ished most, it was not purple, gold, and precious stones, which imparted to
her the splendor which invested her, but the blood of martyrs."[20] Calvin
contrasts the true beauty of the Church with the splendor exhibited by the
Church of Rome, which lies only in external images and artwork.[21] Far from
glorifying the Church, such attention to external splendor brought about the
loss of the true beauty of the Church.[22] However, Calvin also acknowledges
that the evangelical communities also bear responsibility for the lack of spiritual beauty in the Church, due to their ingratitude.[23]

Even though Calvin will often describe the Church of Rome as though
it were the antithesis of the true Christian and catholic Church, he also holds
that the true Church was hidden in the Roman Church, only to emerge
in his own day with the teaching of Luther.[24] This means that the Roman
Church contains within itself the true Church, since God remains faithful
even in spite of human faithlessness. "Hence it arises, that our baptism does
not need renewal, because although the Devil has long reigned in the papacy,
yet he could not altogether extinguish God's grace; nay, a Church is among
them; for otherwise Paul's prophecy would have been false, when he says that
Antichrist was seated in the temple of God (2 Thess. 2:4)."[25] Thus Calvin is
willing to grant to his opponents the truth of their claim that the Church of
God is with them, only he insists that it is hidden, and is not to be seen in
the public face of the Roman Church.[26] If one looks at the marks that Rome
holds out, namely, the historic episcopacy in communion with the Bishop of
Rome, then the Roman Church is opposed to the true Church of Christ.
However, if one looks at the true marks of the Church, such as baptism, then
God has in fact preserved the true Church in hiddenness in the Church of
Rome, for otherwise the Church of Christ would have perished. "For God
always preserves a hidden seed, that the Church should not be utterly extinguished: for there must always be a Church in the world, but sometimes it is
preserved miserably as in a sepulchre, since it is nowhere apparent."[27] The
appearance of the evangelical and orthodox Church in Calvin's day therefore
represents the emergence of the true Church from its time of hiddenness
within the Roman Church, and not the beginning of a new Church.[28] Now
that the true Church has emerged, however, Calvin wants the children of
God to judge it by its true and certain marks and not by the appearance of
splendor.[29] Wherever the marks of preaching and the sacraments are to be
seen, the godly are to embrace that community as the Church, regardless of
its otherwise lowly appearance.[30]

2. THE MARKS OF TRUE PASTORS

Related to the distinguishing marks of the Church are those signs by which the genuine pastors of the Church may be recognized. Calvin is especially attentive to these marks and signs in his interpretation of the letters of Paul. The first sign of a genuine pastor is the fact that his life conforms to the doctrine that he preaches and teaches.[31] Just as Paul sets himself forth as "a living picture of a good and faithful pastor," so every pastor and bishop should be able to set himself forth as an example to imitate.[32] "Doctrine will have little authority unless its power and majesty shine in the life of a bishop as in a mirror. Thus he tells the teacher to be an exemplar which his pupils can follow."[33] Pastors must always be careful, however, to make Christ the model that they imitate, to direct the faithful from themselves to Christ.[34]

The most powerful confirmation of doctrine is to be seen when the pastor is willing to suffer persecution and even death for the sake of his testimony to the Gospel. For this reason, Paul appeals to the marks in his body inflicted by his persecutors as his insignia, showing that he is a genuine and faithful pastor.[35] The clearest confirmation of the doctrine preached by a pastor is to be seen in his willingness to lay down his life for its sake. "How powerfully is the faith of the people confirmed, when a pastor does not hesitate to seal his doctrine by the surrender of his life!"[36] By acting in this way, pastors conform themselves to Christ, who laid his own life down for our sake.[37] The willingness of a pastor to suffer and die for the doctrine he preaches is related to the deep concern that the pastor should exhibit for his congregation. "It is right that every pastor should bear the concerns of the Church on his heart, should feel its ills as if they were his own, sympathize with its sorrows and grieve for its sins."[38] This concern must manifest itself by the care he exhibits for the congregation, not only in general, but also for each member in particular, so that he dedicates himself to healing and building up the body of Christ.[39] Calvin links the care a pastor should manifest for his congregation with the power of God that should shine forth in his ministry, again using Paul as his exemplar.[40] Calvin does not think this power has only to do with the success of Paul's preaching but also with "the efficacy of the Spirit, in which God manifestly showed himself."[41] The power of God may be seen in the care that the pastor has for his flock, as well as his willingness to lay down his life for their welfare. "Now such a manifestation of the divine power, as we have often seen, is like a seal to sign the certainty of, and to confirm, his teaching office."[42]

Calvin contrasts the marks of a true pastor with the form of ministry to be seen in the Roman Church, which he claims is given over entirely to its own interests so that it may tyrannically domineer over others.[43] Such selfish and tyrannical behavior on the part of bishops proves to Calvin that they are not in fact the genuine successors of the apostles, as they claim to be.[44] The bishops ignore the genuine marks of true pastors, according to Calvin, focusing instead on the external ornaments of their office. "They do not think that Episcopacy consists in anything but revenues, and also in vain insignia, such as to be mitred, to wear an episcopal ring, and to exhibit other like trumperies."[45] Calvin is concerned to set forth the marks of true pastors lest the people of his day be deceived by the splendor of the Roman episcopacy into thinking that it represents the true pastorate.[46] In spite of its splendid appearance, Calvin portrays the Roman hierarchy as the opposite of the true pastorate. "They no less abhor the true office of pastor than they strive greedily for their domination."[47]

3. The Signs of Adoption

Calvin is concerned to identify the distinguishing marks of the true Church and of true pastors because no one can be considered a child of God who is not engrafted into the body of Christ. On the other hand, those who share in the fellowship of the preaching and sacraments of the Church may be considered children of God. "And, since assurance of faith was not necessary, he substituted for it a certain charitable judgment whereby we recognize as members of the church those who, by confession of faith, by example of life, and by partaking of the sacraments, profess the same God and Christ with us."[48] However, Calvin is careful to point out that this judgment is made on the basis of love, not with the certainty of faith. Each of the faithful have the testimony to their adoption in themselves, by means of the Spirit of adoption, which leads them to cry out with confidence, "Abba, Father!" (Gal. 4:6).[49] This testimony takes root in the inmost heart of each child of God, and cannot, therefore, be seen by others.[50] However, the Spirit will in fact manifest its presence in the lives of the children of God, so that it can be discerned by others. "For the Spirit of God is a Witness to me of my calling, as he is to each of the elect. For others we have no testimony, except from the outward efficacy of the Spirit; that is, in so far as the grace of God shows itself in them."[51] When we see the manifestation of the Spirit in others, we may judge, on the basis of love, that they are children of God.[52]

The recognition of others as children of God is on the one hand rooted in the love that we ought to have for one another in the body of Christ. Those who belong to the true Church, identified by the distinguishing marks of preaching and the sacraments, ought to be regarded as our brothers and sisters.[53] This is especially true since the appearance of the gifts of the Spirit ought to bind us to one another more than any other social bond. "There is nothing, therefore, which ought to make us seek the friendship of men more than God's manifestation of himself among them through the gifts of his Spirit."[54] Since this is an aspect of love, not of faith, it makes no difference if some whom we acknowledge to be children of God in fact fall away.[55] On the other hand, the recognition of others as children of God is an essential aspect of our gratitude to God for all the gifts God so lavishly showers upon us. "It is our part to set so high a value upon the gifts of the Holy Spirit, that they shall be to us the seals, as it were, of his hidden election."[56] The godly should be alert to the manifestation of the Spirit wherever it appears, and should not refuse to acknowledge it where it appears. "For our understanding of the gifts of God is niggardly if we do not reckon as children of God those in whom there shine forth the true signs of piety, which are the marks by which the Spirit of adoption manifests itself."[57]

Sanctification and the Renewal of the Image of God

The first sign of adoption, as we have seen, is the call to the fellowship of the true Church. "God separates them from the rest of the world, which is the sign of election."[58] However, the separation of the children of God from the world is the beginning of their sanctification by the Spirit. Since God only sanctifies those whom God adopts, holiness of life is another sign of adoption.[59] The appearance of sanctification not only reveals to others that one is a child of God but also gives confirmation to one's assurance of adoption.[60] Since the call to holiness is inseparable from the call to fellowship with the Church, those in whom no sanctification appears ought not to be regarded as children of God. "For it is by this mark that they show they differ from the children of the devil."[61] As a consequence, those who do not live holy lives should not be allowed to remain in the fellowship of the Church.[62] Holiness of life is therefore the certain mark distinguishing the children of

God from the reprobate.[63] However, the full manifestation of the children of God will only take place on the last day, and is only provisionally manifested in this life. "All those, therefore, in whom the marks of adoption shine forth, let us reckon to be the sons of God until the books are opened which will thoroughly reveal all things."[64]

One of the most important ways that the sanctification of the Spirit manifests itself to others is in the love the children of God show to one another. Calvin is especially concerned to highlight the role of love, as it is the most effective way to unmask hypocrisy, which all too easily hides beneath the symbols and ceremonies of the Church.[65] Since God manifests Godself in others by means of the gifts of the Spirit, we ought to show that we love God by loving those in whom God manifests Godself to us. "God is invisible; but he represents himself to us in the brethren and in their persons demands what is due to himself. Love to men springs only from the fear and love of God."[66] God is said to care nothing for sacrifices to direct the godly to the manifestation of their adoption in the love they have for one another, and to call hypocrites to account.[67] Those who do not manifest love in their lives should not be viewed as children of God, for "any profession of faith which does not prove itself by a good conscience and manifest itself in love is insincere."[68]

The most certain mark by which the children of God manifest their adoption is by the re-creation of the image of God within them.[69] Beginning with the second edition of the *Institutes,* Calvin defines the purpose of sanctification as the renewal of the image of God within us. "Therefore, in a word, I interpret repentance as regeneration, whose sole end is to restore in us the image of God that had been disfigured and all but obliterated through Adam's transgression."[70] The restoration of the image of God is gradual, and takes place throughout the life of the children of God, fostered in large part by the transforming power of the Gospel, "because God makes his glory to shine in us little by little."[71] God sets forth the Law in order to reveal to the godly the archetype to which they should conform if they want to express the image of God in their lives. "For God has so depicted his character in the law that if any man carries out in deeds whatever is enjoined there, he will express the image of God, as it were, in his own life."[72]

The re-creation of the image of God means that the powers of God that were manifested in Adam now begin to be represented in the lives of the adopted children of God, "so that man represents as in a mirror the wisdom, righteousness and goodness of God."[73] Just as the Church is the place in which the powers of God are praised and glorified, so the powers of God ought to be manifested in the lives of the godly, to the glory of God. "It behooves us to declare these powers not only by our tongue, but also by our whole life."[74] As the nature of God is manifested in the powers set forth in the universe, so the lives of the godly manifest the nature of God by the appearance of the image of God in their lives. "Therefore, what God is in heaven, he bids us be in this world, that we may be reckoned his children. For when God's image appears in us, it is, as it were, the seal of his adoption."[75] The image of God may not only be seen by others, but Calvin also insists that God beholds God's image in us, leading to our further acceptance by God.[76] The renewal of the image of God means that the pious truly reflect the nature of God as in a mirror, so that God sees the reflection of God's face in their souls. "Since, therefore, whenever God contemplates his own face, he both rightly loves it and holds it in honor."[77] The adopted children of God should therefore resemble God in their lives, so that those who see them may see the powers and character of God reflected in their lives, the way children resemble their parents.[78]

Conformity to the Image of Christ Crucified

The image of God is restored in the godly not only by the power of the Spirit but also by their participation in Christ, who is himself the living image of God. "And to wake us more effectively, Scripture shows that God the Father, as he has reconciled us to himself in his Christ [see 2 Cor. 5:18], has in him stamped the image [see Heb. 1:3] to which he would have us conform."[79] Thus the children of God will not only represent the character of God as in a mirror, but they will also represent Jesus Christ. "For we have been adopted as sons by the Lord with this one condition: that our life express Christ, the bond of our adoption."[80] Christ is the living image of God not only in his divinity but also in his human nature. The restoration of the image of God in the children of God will therefore bring them into conformity with the human life of Jesus.[81] Thus, just as Christ suffered and died in humiliation and weakness before he was raised unto eternal glory, so all the children of God will suffer and die in Christ before inheriting eternal life with God.

On the one hand, our conformity to Christ will bring about the mortification of sin and the renewal of our spirit.[82] On the other hand, the conformity of the children of God to the image of Christ will necessarily entail suffering affliction for the sake of his name.[83] Calvin clearly distinguishes the suffering that conforms us to the image of Christ from the suffering that is common to all fallen humanity. Even though the godly suffer all the common afflictions of humanity, they are conformed to the image of Christ when they suffer solely for the sake of their faith in him. "I am speaking of the afflictions they have to bear for the testimony of Christ."[84] Calvin realizes that this kind of suffering catches many believers unprepared, for they are unaware that they must be conformed to Christ in this way. They delight in hearing about the suffering of Christ when it has to do with their reconciliation with God, "but when he appears with his cross, then, as though struck at its novelty, we either avoid or abhor him; and that not only in our own persons, but also in the persons of those who deliver to us the Gospel."[85] Calvin therefore encourages his readers to meditate on the cross of Christ throughout their lives, so that when Christ with his cross appears to them, they are not taken by surprise and offended.[86] When they do so, the children of God will learn that Christ was not raised to eternal life until he had first suffered and died. Therefore, the pious should expect their life on earth to express nothing but the image of the death of Christ.[87]

To console the faithful in their sufferings, Calvin points to the way their afflictions conform them to Christ, and so prepare them for the inheritance of eternal life and glory with him.[88] Just as the goodness of God was revealed when he raised Christ from the ignominy of the cross to the glory of his Kingdom, believers trust that the same goodness will be shown in those who are conformed to the image of Christ crucified. "The amazing goodness of God is especially seen in the fact that he desires his glory to be conspicuously displayed in us who are entirely covered with dishonor."[89] Even as passing on to the resurrection surmounts the scandal of the cross of Christ, so the godly ought in their afflictions to look to the glory for which they are being prepared.[90]

However, the primary consolation of the children of God lies in the fact that their afflictions allow them to represent the image of Christ crucified more fully in their lives, forming their chief glory in this life. "They endure insults and ignominies, but because they know that the marks of Christ have more value and merit in heaven than the empty and fading shows of earth, the more unjustly and abusively the world torments them, the richer grounds they have for glorying."[91] Even though the world regards the stigmata of

Christ as being disgraceful, to be avoided at all cost, the children of God embrace them as having more glory than all the insignia of earthly glory and power.[92] The suffering of the godly for the sake of Christ is therefore an essential sign of their adoption as children of God, for those adopted in the Son must represent the image of Christ in their lives. "For persecutions are seals of adoption to the children of God, if they endure them with fortitude and calmness."[93] Far from avoiding the afflictions brought on them for the sake of Christ, the godly ought to see them as their highest glory, "for in that case he decorates us with his insignia."[94]

To give the pious even more grounds for hope in their afflictions, Calvin points them to the example of others who have suffered for the sake of Christ. Calvin notes the power of examples in his Seneca commentary of 1532. "Before those whom we wish to arouse, as with spurs dug in, to virtue, we are accustomed to set great men for imitation. Hence Cicero [*De Orat.* 2.9.36] 'History is life's school-mistress'; in her, as in a mirror, we see our own life. We discern with our eyes what we are to avoid, what to follow."[95] When we see that the saints before us have suffered in the same way, and yet see that God has sustained and preserved them in the midst of their sufferings, "then relying on this, we ought to venture farther than we had been accustomed, having already a pledge of our victory in the persons of our brethren."[96] Such examples are to be seen not only in the Christian Church but also in the Church of Israel. For this reason, James points believers to consider the example of the suffering and patience of the prophets (James 5:10). "James is right to put their example before our eyes, so that we may learn to consider it in any time of trial when we lose patience or hope."[97] For example, Calvin directs his readers to the sufferings of the fathers in Genesis, who lived as a small band of exiles in an often hostile land, so that we might be exhorted "from the example of the Fathers, to constancy in enduring the cross."[98] He was personally drawn to the example of the sufferings of David, especially in the Psalms, stating in the preface to his commentary on the Psalms that "whatever that most illustrious king and prophet suffered, was exhibited to me by God as an example for imitation."[99] Calvin also directs his readers to the example of Jeremiah, who suffered great hardship and affliction solely for his proclamation of the Word of the Lord to the city of Jerusalem.[100] When we see the patient endurance of Abraham, David, and Jeremiah in their afflictions, we are given the courage to endure the cross when it appears in our lives. "If, then, we shudder at any time at the horrors of the cross, let us remember the example of the prophet."[101]

4. The Signs of Reprobation

Calvin was not only interested in the signs of adoption by which the children of God are made known to others, but he was also interested in the signs of reprobation, which reveal that a person or whole people are destined to eternal destruction. Given the centrality to adoption of being a member of the Church where preaching and the sacraments are present, it is not surprising to see that Calvin makes the explicit rejection of the preaching of the Gospel one of the signs of reprobation.[102] As we have seen, Calvin understands the Gospel to be a clear portrayal and manifestation of Christ with all his benefits. Those who reject the preaching of the Gospel therefore prove themselves to be reprobate. This is why Paul says that the Gospel is veiled for those who are perishing (2 Cor. 4:3). "It is exactly as if he had said, 'If anyone says that he does not acknowledge the manifestation of Christ of which I boast, by that very fact he clearly proves himself a reprobate, for the sincerity of my teaching is openly and clearly discerned by all who have eyes to see.'"[103] The rejection of the Gospel is a sign of reprobation even for those who otherwise live lives of apparent holiness.[104] The full extent of this sign of reprobation is reached when the rejection of the Word of God leads God to withdraw the Word entirely from the people, as Amos threatened God would do (Amos 8:11).[105]

A second sign of reprobation is the deliberate rebellion against the first table of the Law of Moses, for this reveals one's direct opposition to God. "Such a man does not err through weakness, but by rising up in rebellion against God gives a sure sign of his reprobation."[106] Over against those who say that penitence can obtain forgiveness for any sin, Calvin insists that the sin of blasphemy can never be forgiven, as it is the sin against the Holy Spirit of which Jesus speaks. "For blasphemy against the Spirit is a certain sign of reprobation. Hence it follows that whoever fall into it have been given a reprobate spirit."[107] Sinning against the Holy Spirit, like the rejection of the Gospel, reveals that one is so captive to Satan that the Spirit cannot enter.[108]

A third sign of reprobation appears when people no longer heed the voice of their conscience but rather rush headlong into manifest and grave sin. Paul appeals to such signs of reprobation in the opening chapter of Romans, "for the Lord punishes those who have alienated themselves from his goodness by casting themselves headlong into destruction and ruin of many kinds."[109] Persistence in such manifest forms of godlessness has the effect of numbing and deadening the conscience, so that one no longer has any re-morse for sin at all.[110] Not only is all remorse removed from the conscience, but so is the distinction between good and evil that the conscience is to hold before us, "and when we no longer distinguish between light and darkness, between white and black, it is a sign of ultimate reprobation."[111] Even though such security is a sign of reprobation, few of the reprobate actually manifest this sign, "lest the world should be embroiled in final confusion."[112] When those who have attained this form of security are confronted by the judg-ment of God, it leaves them completely unmoved, and hardens them in their sin. "When, therefore, all those things produce no effect on us, it is a sure sign of hopeless madness."[113] Such reprobation was seen in the Jews in Egypt at the time of Jeremiah, for they persisted in their sin even after the destruction of their nation by the wrath of God.[114]

Calvin thinks that the appearance of the signs of reprobation is rela-tively rare, and counsels pastors to hold out the hope of forgiveness to those who have fallen, for "the judgment of eternal death must not be rashly lev-eled against anyone."[115] Indeed, so strong is the hope of the godly in the goodness and mercy of God that they would try to reach those who have already been condemned to eternal destruction. "Accordingly, until even all the vicious give clear evidence of being reprobate, not one of them is to be handled too severely that the forgiveness of sins is not made plain to him at the same time."[116] However, Calvin does not want to deny that such manifest signs of reprobation can in fact appear, either in an individual or in a whole people, and when they do appear, he wants us to take them seriously. "Yet if the ungodliness of some does not seem otherwise than hopeless to us, as if the Lord had pointed it out with his finger, we should not contend against the just judgment of God or seek to be more merciful than he is."[117]

One example of the Lord pointing out the reprobate as by a finger oc-curs for Calvin in the case of the Jews. Calvin thinks that all the signs of rep-robation clearly appear in the Jewish people from the time of the crucifixion of Jesus onwards to his own day. To begin with, the Jews clearly and persis-tently reject the preaching of the Gospel and its manifestation of salvation in Jesus Christ alone. "This is the ultimate form of godlessness."[118] The Jews manifested their reprobation by both crucifying the Son of God and forbid-ding the Gospel to be preached to the Gentiles. By doing so, they placed themselves in direct opposition to God. "They wage war against God. They are universally hated by the world. They are opposed to the salvation of the

Gentiles. In short, they are destined for eternal destruction."[119] Moreover, the Jews remain unmoved by the judgment of God revealed against them for fifteen hundred years, in the destruction of Jerusalem and their dispersal throughout the world.[120] Their insensitivity to the judgment of God is therefore one more sign of their reprobation. "The one thing which caused their ruin was their despising of the divine judgment through their negligent disregard of the dignity which they had obtained."[121]

Calvin even sees signs of reprobation in the Jews he meets in his day, for their rejection of Christ reveals that they have lost the light of reason and common sense. "I have had much conversation with many Jews: I have never seen either a drop of piety or a grain of truth or ingenuousness—nay, I have never found common sense in any Jew."[122] He is convinced that this lack of reason is due to the fact that God has blinded the Jews "and delivered them up to a reprobate sense," so that they are not at all to be trusted beyond their understanding of Hebrew grammar.[123] The reprobation of the Jews is so obvious to Calvin that it can even be manifested in the way they interpret a single verse of Scripture. "Ravings so monstrous prove the authors of them to have been delivered over to a reprobate mind, as a dreadful example of the wrath of God."[124] Thus, even though Calvin holds out for the presence of an elect remnant among the Jews, of the whole people he can unequivocally say that "they have absolutely no hope, because they are vessels of the wrath of the Lord."[125]

5. Manifestations of God's Wrath against the Reprobate

To warn the children of God against following the example of the reprobate, Calvin claims that God often exhibits their destruction in a highly visible way, as in a living image or mirror. Calvin expresses interest in the exemplary punishment of the wicked in his commentary on Seneca of 1532. When Seneca speaks of punishing one to make the rest better, Calvin comments, "The Greeks call this sort of punishment *paradeigma*, the Latins *exemplum*, when the punishment of one is the fear of many, as Gratian and Valens [Code Just. 9.27.1] say, for which reason punishments are sometimes more severe than usual [Claud., Dig. Just. 48.19.16]."[126] Calvin claims that Paul appeals to the punishment of the Israelites in the wilderness for the same reason, to give a vivid representation of the punishment of sin to the adopted children of God. "These examples bring home to us, as if they were pictures painted by an artist what sort of judgment threatens idolaters, fornicators, and others who despise God; for these are living images representing God to us in his anger with sins like those."[127] The vivid representation of such punishment is meant to warn the children of God against following such examples.[128]

The exhibition of such punishment on the reprobate is a manifestation of the love that God has for God's children, for they are warned in a salutary way by the wrath shown to others. When Paul speaks of the wrath of God that comes upon the disobedient (Eph. 5:6), Calvin claims that "he is now addressing believers, not so much to frighten them with their danger, as to rouse them that they may learn to behold in the reprobate, as in mirrors, the dreadful judgments of God."[129] Such judgments are dreadful because they entail the eternal destruction of those upon whom they fall. God wishes God's children to see such judgments in others rather than to feel them in themselves. "In short, whenever God threatens, he shows his punishment indirectly, as it were, that, beholding it in the reprobate, we may be deterred from sinning."[130] To illustrate how such indirect punishment is a manifestation of God's love, Calvin appeals to the example of a father who severely punishes his servant for the correction of his son, which is "for the benefit of his son, that he may learn wisdom by what another suffers."[131]

Calvin thinks that Amos chastises the Israelites for not being warned from sinning by the manifest punishment of their neighboring nations, when he tells the Israelites to behold the Syrian and Philistine cities destroyed by the Assyrians (Amos 6:1–3). "By this representation Amos shows that there was no excuse for the Jews or Israelites for sleeping in their sins, inasmuch as they could see, as it were in a mirror, the judgments which God brought on the heathen nations."[132] Calvin highlights many such examples in history, beginning with those narrated in Scripture. Some examples have to do with individuals, such as Cain. "Moreover, in the first murderer, God designed to exhibit a singular example of malediction, the memory of which should remain in all ages," so that all ages might be admonished "by such examples that nothing can succeed when God is angry with and opposed to them."[133] Others have to do with entire peoples, as in the attempt to reach heaven by building the tower of Babel. "And this history shows that God will ever be adverse to such designs; so that we here behold, depicted before our eyes, what Solomon says: 'There is no counsel, nor prudence, nor strength against the Lord' (Prov. 21:30)."[134]

The most vivid and enduring depiction of such punishment is to be found in the account of the destruction of the cities of Sodom and Gomorrah. "This was such a notable example of divine vengeance that whenever Scripture speaks of the universal destruction of the ungodly, it refers to this as a type."[135] Thus even the apostles appeal to Sodom and Gomorrah when they wish to warn the godly by means of the punishment of the reprobate by God, "because it is an outstanding and living image."[136] The fire used to destroy Sodom is a visible image of the eternal fire that will consume the reprobate in hell, as it is described in Jude 7.[137] Thus, when Jeremiah wants to depict the destruction God will bring upon Edom, he appeals to the example of Sodom and Gomorrah. "God therefore designed to represent once for all, as in a mirror, how dreadful will be his vengeance on all the wicked."[138]

The children of God only truly profit from such examples, however, when they learn from Scripture how to discern such vivid examples of the punishment of the reprobate in other historical narratives, as well as in their own day. When Ezekiel blames the Jews for not learning from the vivid example of Sodom, Calvin says that "the remedy must be taken in time that we receive instruction from the examples of punishment which we read in Scripture, or in other histories, or such as we witness with our own eyes."[139] Once the godly have been given the eyes of faith and the spectacles of Scripture, they can begin to discern and profit from the punishment of the reprobate. "Thus it becomes the faithful to be employed in reflecting on the histories of all times, that they may always form their judgment from the Scripture, of the various destructions which, privately and publicly, have befallen the ungodly."[140] Such meditation is especially necessary given the fact that the ungodly and reprobate seem to attain more worldly power and glory in this life than do the godly, and thus present an alluring example they might be tempted to follow, to their ruin. This is why the godly are told that they "will look on the destruction of the wicked" (Ps. 37:34). "God would make us daily to behold such sights if we had eyes to behold his judgments."[141] Even though such manifest proofs of judgment are of no profit to the world, those in the Church should reflect on them to their benefit, "that we may seriously fear and not provoke his extreme judgments, and thus perish with the wicked."[142] Far from thinking that they will necessarily be spared such punishment themselves, they ought rather to reflect that it could easily come upon them were they not to anticipate it by judging and condemning themselves.[143]

The godly are not only warned by the destruction of the reprobate, but they are also comforted, for the prosperity of the wicked in contrast to the suffering of the faithful is a severe trial for the children of God.[144] The living images of the punishment of the reprobate assure the children of God that those who oppress them will indeed face a similar end, no matter how invincible they may appear to us to be.[145] However, the judgment of God is not exhibited the same way against the reprobate. At times, punishment and destruction fall upon them suddenly and dramatically, as in the case of Sodom and Gomorrah. At other times, the reprobate are spared for a long period, so that they might be a spectacle to all the world.[146] This is why, according to Calvin, David asks God not to slay the wicked right away, lest his people forget (Ps. 59:11). "But when God impresses a sign of his curse on the impious, and prolongs their life, it is the same as though he placed them in a theater to be looked upon leisurely and for a long time."[147] Whether they are destroyed suddenly or gradually, the vivid images of the punishment of the reprobate are of comfort to the children of God. This is why Nahum speaks of the news of the destruction of Ninevah as good tidings for the Jews (Nah. 1:15).[148] The visible destruction of the reprobate is therefore one more way by which God distinguishes the children of God from the ungodly, for the favor of God "is far more distinctly seen, when God allows the reprobate to perish, but preserves his own in safety."[149]

The destruction of the reprobate not only helps to warn and comfort the children of God, but it also glorifies God, by vividly manifesting God's justice and judgment. Calvin thinks this is why the prophets often compare the destruction of the reprobate to sacrifices, as when Isaiah says that the sword of the Lord is sated with blood and fat (Isa. 34:6), "for animals are slain in sacrifice for the worship and honor of God, and in like manner the destruction of this people will also tend to the glory of God."[150] In order that the children of God might not be repulsed by the revolting appearance of the blood of slaughter, Isaiah describes the blood that stains God's garments "to be highly beautiful and ornamental."[151] By describing the destruction of the reprobate as a sacrifice, and their blood as ornamental, the prophets show that God is as glorified by the exhibition of God's justice against the wicked as by the manifestation of God's goodness towards the children of God.[152] Calvin often sounds as though there is a symmetry of glory created by God's mercy and vengeance, as if they both equally manifested the beauty and glory of God. "We know that although the reprobate perish, the glory of God shines no less clearly in their destruction than in the salvation of the godly."[153] However, at other times, he clearly indicates that even though God's glory shines forth in God's judgments, the glory of God is primarily manifested in the mercy that God exhibits towards sinners in forgiveness and reconciliation. "God indeed manifests his glory both by his power and wisdom, and by all the judgments which he daily executes; his glory, at the same time, shines forth chiefly in this—that he is propitious to sinners, and suffers himself to be pacified; yea, that he not only allows miserable sinners to be reconciled to him, but that he also of his own invites and anticipates them. Hence it is evident, that he is the true God."[154]

CHAPTER 14

The Revelation of the Children of God

In spite of his concern to set forth the signs by which the children of God might be distinguished from the reprobate in this life, Calvin is clearly aware that the children of God are also hidden in this life, as they await the time of their revelation. On the one hand, the faithful increasingly express the image of Christ crucified in this life, meaning that their glory and life are hidden under the appearance of ignominy and death. On the other hand, the children of God are subjected to the discipline of their Father, who chastises them out of love. "For the Lord disciplines those whom he loves, and chastises every child whom he accepts'" (Heb. 12:6). The children of God may therefore look more afflicted than the reprobate, which can lead the world to think that they themselves are reprobate, as happened in the case of Job. Calvin encourages the faithful to look to the grace of God, and especially to the mirror of God's promises, so that they might endure such chastisement with patience and faith, in the hope that God will again show God's favor to them. Calvin thinks that God subjects the children of God to the darkness of affliction and death so that they might see the light of grace and life more clearly, leading them to see the light of God even in the darkness of death. Because the glory of the children of God is yet to be revealed, they look to the promises of God so that they might see in them the appearance of things unseen, even as they walk by faith and not by sight. The faithful behold God now in the promises and symbols of God's grace, as in a mirror enigmatically, even as they look forward in hope to the day when they shall see

God face-to-face. The life of the children of God is hidden in Christ, and will only be revealed when Christ appears in glory. The appearance of Christ will bring about the restoration of all things in the Kingdom of God, as well as the destruction of the kingdom of Antichrist, and the judgment of all people, which shall once and for all separate the children of God from the reprobate. Christ will then hand the kingdom over to the Father, so that God may be all in all, and so that the children of God may see God face-to-face, having been fully transformed into the image and likeness of God.

1. The Signs of God's Wrath upon the Children of God

The children of God are both manifested and hidden in this life. On the one hand, their participation in the body of Christ, their sanctification and renewal into the image of God, their love, and their representation of Christ crucified all present clear signs of their adoption for others to see. On the other hand, the children of God, like the prophets and apostles before them, are more often than not reviled by the world, and are treated as though they themselves were reprobate, as Paul describes the apostles as being a spectacle to the world (1 Cor. 4:9).[1] According to Calvin, this creates one of the severest trials for the children of God, for the world does not acknowledge them as such but rather reviles them as though they were condemned both by humanity and by God. "Hence it can hardly be inferred from our present state that God is our Father, for the devil so manages everything that he obscures this benefit."[2]

According to Calvin, the concealment of the children of God under an appearance of reprobation is the direct result of the fact that God manifests the same signs of wrath against them as against the reprobate. "God takes measures indiscriminately against both the reprobate and the elect, and his scourges declare his wrath more often than his love. Even Scripture speaks thus, and experience confirms it."[3] The difference is that these signs of wrath are for the chastisement and discipline of the children of God, and are therefore pledges of God's love for them.[4] The difficulty arises from the fact that no love can be seen in the signs of wrath that God uses to chastise God's children, since "the scourges of God are rightly reckoned in themselves to be signs of God's wrath."[5] The faithful must therefore believe that when they see such signs of wrath against themselves, they are in fact the manifestation of God's love and care for them, even though this love cannot be seen.[6]

In spite of such persuasion, the signs of wrath that they see cannot but cause sorrow and dismay in the godly. "Hence when things go wrong, sorrow takes possession of our minds, and drives away all confidence and consolation."[7] In this way, all the godly are conformed to the example of Joseph, who was beloved by God even as he was sold into slavery by his brothers and cast into prison by the Egyptians. "For, from the time Christ gathers us into his flock, God permits us to be cast down in various ways, so that we seem nearer hell than heaven."[8] In spite of their confidence that God loves them, the appearance of God's wrath is devastating to the children of God, and causes them great sorrow. "The whole strength of man fails when God appears as a Judge and humbles and lays them prostrate by exhibiting signs of his wrath."[9]

The sorrow of the godly is increased by the fact that the afflictions they suffer convince others that they are in fact reprobate, as happened to David.[10] The same thing happened in the case of Job, according to Calvin, since human beings cannot help judging someone to be reprobate who is afflicted so severely by God. "And it is certainly an error which is too common among men, to look upon those who are oppressed with afflictions as condemned and reprobate."[11] Indeed, since God tends to afflict the godly more than the reprobate, the world praises the reprobate as though they were the children of God, even as it reviles the children of God as though they were reprobate.[12] This is what led Cicero to condemn the religion of the Jews, according to Calvin, for he judged their worthiness by their appearance of malediction. "Lastly, he treats the numerous massacres to which the Jews were exposed, as a proof of their religion being hated by all the deities; and he thinks that this ought to be a sufficient sign of the detestable character of their religion."[13] The success and prosperity of the reprobate form yet another source of sorrow for the children of God, for it can appear that God in fact loves them.[14]

The inability of the world to distinguish the children of God from the reprobate is understandable, given that the signs of wrath shown against them are the same that God shows towards the reprobate.[15] The godly may therefore truly be said to be marked out by the signs of reprobation discussed in the previous chapter. "When Job was smitten with terrible ulcers, so as to become corrupt, he seemed for a time to present the marks of a reprobate person."[16] Moreover, Calvin thinks that such judgments spring from a proper sense of piety, found even in unbelievers.[17] Scripture reinforces this natural sense of piety by clearly stating that calamities such as scourges, the pestilence, the sword, and famine are signs of God's wrath.[18] "Then, when poverty, famine, diseases, and exile, and even death itself, are viewed in themselves, we must always say that they are curses of God, that is, when they are regarded in their own nature."[19] Thus Calvin does not fault the natives of Malta for thinking that Paul was a murderer when a poisonous viper came out of the fire and fastened itself onto his hand (Acts 28:1–5), for, as discussed in the previous chapter, Calvin exhorts the children of God to be attentive to the visible exhibitions of God's wrath against the reprobate. However, "seeing that God afflicts good and bad indiscriminately, yes, and even spares the reprobate and scourges his own with greater severity," Calvin urges caution in making such judgments. If iniquity is clearly apparent in those who are suffering, then "God is pointing out his judgment as if with his finger," but if no iniquity is seen, "the best thing is to suspend judgment about punishment." Also, we must not be precipitate in our judgments, but must wait to see the outcome, as when Paul survived the viper's bite; for "a different outcome makes it plain that those who seem to be sharing the same punishment in the eyes of men, are quite different in the eyes of God."[20]

The children of God are therefore afflicted by the same signs of wrath as are the reprobate, and at times are chastised more severely; but their confidence that God chastises those whom God loves leads them to view such afflictions as ways to exercise their faith and patience, even though the same afflictions are proofs of God's wrath against the reprobate.[21] However, Calvin does not seem comfortable leaving matters thus, for he goes on to suggest that God always mingles in signs of God's favor and blessing along with the signs of wrath towards God's children. After all, Joseph found the blessing of God even while he was in prison, for otherwise it might have entered his mind "that he was forsaken and abandoned by God, and was continually exposed to new dangers. He might have imagined that God had declared himself his enemy."[22] Thus, when the godly are tempted to think the same things in their affliction, Calvin says that they need the same discernment as Joseph "to enable them, with the eyes of faith, to consider those benefits of God by which he mitigates the severity of their crosses."[23]

God mitigates the sorrow of the godly by adding the sweetness of grace to their afflictions, and moderates their punishment by drawing back God's hand.[24] "But as God is never so severe towards his own people as not to furnish them with actual experiential evidence of his grace, it always stands true that life is profitless to men, if they do not feel, while they live, that he is their Father."[25] Calvin encourages the faithful to turn to the prophets in particular to learn to discern the sense of God's grace and love in their afflictions, as when Isaiah says that he was sent to comfort the afflicted people of God (Isa. 40). "From this passage we learn what we ought chiefly to seek in the prophets, namely, to encourage the hopes of godly persons by exhibiting the sweetness of divine grace that they may not faint under the weight of afflictions, but may boldly persevere in calling on God."[26] Calvin also encourages the children of God to confirm by their own experience the statement of David, that the anger of God is but for a moment, but God's favor is for a lifetime (Ps. 30:5).[27]

Calvin also teaches the children of God to look past their own experience of affliction, in which nothing but the wrath of God may appear, to the promises of God's mercy, which can comfort them in their affliction. "Let us learn, I say, to look to his mercy; and let us be convinced of this, that though signs of his wrath may appear on every side, yet the punishments we suffer are not fatal, but on the contrary, medicinal."[28] Without the word of promise, the signs of God's wrath might overwhelm the children of God with despair, even if they are being chastised out of love.[29] At such times, Calvin tells the godly to ignore what they see with their eyes, so that nothing will stand in the way of their confidence in the truth of the promise of God's mercy. "He testifies that he is propitious and benevolent towards us; yet outward signs threaten his wrath. What then are we to do? We must close our eyes, disregard ourselves and all things connected with us, so that nothing may hinder or prevent us from believing that God is true."[30] However, because they know the promise of mercy to be true, the children of God have patience in their afflictions, because they know that God will once again show them God's favor.[31]

2. The Light of Life in the Darkness of Death

God afflicts the children of God not only to chastise and discipline them but also to bring them to a clearer and more vivid vision of the life that comes from God. We should have a clear sense of God as the fountain and source of life from the day of our birth, for all people can feel within themselves the life that comes from God. However, such is the extent of human blindness that we do not see such life when it is clearly before us, but only after we have been confronted with a vision of death, as happened in the case of Paul. "Indeed, we felt we had received the sentence of death so that we would rely not on ourselves but on God who raises the dead" (2 Cor. 1:9). Calvin thinks that Paul's experience is paradigmatic for all the faithful. "Our dullness is such that the light of life often dazzles our eyes so that we have to look at death before we can be brought to God."[32] Calvin sees Christ following the same method in his healing work, as when the young man began convulsing and foaming at the mouth when he was brought to Christ (Mark 9:20). "The true beginning of our healing is when we are afflicted so profoundly that we are next door to death."[33] Since we do not see the light of life when it shines clearly before us, God consigns us to the darkness of death, that the light of God might be more clearly apprehended by us.

The vision and experience of the power of death is especially useful in bringing the godly to surrender their trust in all earthly aid and help. The godly may know in their minds that God alone is to be trusted for life, but this awareness only sinks into their hearts "when death comes to present itself before [their] eyes."[34] The darkness of death may also help us to see the abundant blessings of God that surround us at all times, to which we had previously been oblivious.[35] This is why God chose to deliver the Israelites by bringing them through the wilderness, so that they might better experience the sustaining power of God. "It was profitable for them to have set before their eyes how they had been extricated from the deep abyss of death, in order that they might more readily acknowledge this to have been, as it were, the beginning of their life."[36]

The children of God are consigned to the darkness of death so that they might by their own experience clearly apprehend the power of God to deliver them from death. Calvin sees this happening repeatedly in David's life, as that is expressed in the Psalms. "Now, the description of so miserable a condition illustrates the more strikingly the grace of God in the deliverance which he afterwards granted him."[37] The experience of deliverance from apparent death increases the confidence of the godly in the power of God to deliver them from all adversity.[38] God may even delay God's help, so as to appear to abandon God's children to death, in order to show them that God is nigh even in the darkness of death, and has the power to deliver them. "But by this means his power shines forth more clearly, when he raises us up again from the grave."[39]

The faithful learn by their own experience the work that is peculiar to God, namely, to bring light out of darkness and to raise the dead to life. The experience of the psalmist therefore mirrors the experience of Paul, when he says that the Lord upheld him when his foot was slipping (Ps. 94:18).

"The fact of the Psalmist having been delivered after he had been consigned to certain death, made the Divine interposition the more conspicuous."[40] The children of God only attain a vivid apprehension of God as the source of life when they themselves experience such deliverance from the darkness of death, when all help seemed to be lost.[41] When the children of God appear to be abandoned to the darkness of death, Calvin exhorts them to look to Christ; for he was abandoned in the grave for three days before he was raised from the dead. "When God thus intends that we should languish for a time, let us know that we are thus conformed to Christ our head, and hence let us gather materials of confidence."[42] Knowing that God brings light out of darkness, and restores the dead to life after having appeared to abandon them, the children of God can hope that God will again show tokens of God's grace and favor even when they languish in the darkness of affliction.[43]

The power of God to bring light out of darkness and life out of death reveals to Calvin that the light of God not only shines after we have been in the darkness of death, but that it also shines in the darkness of death itself, and "quickens even death itself."[44] Thus, in the midst of feeling that God had abandoned him to the darkness of death, David nonetheless apprehends the light of grace in the midst of the darkness. "Thus, it seemed to David, so far as could be judged from beholding the actual state of his affairs, that he was forsaken by God. At the same time, however, the eyes of his mind, guided by the light of faith, penetrated even to the grace of God, although it was hidden in darkness."[45] According to Calvin, this explains how David could call on God as his God, even as he cried out that God had forsaken him.[46]

The eyes of faith allow the children of God to see the life and favor of God where the eyes of the flesh tell them there is only the darkness of death and wrath. "This is faith's true office, to see life in the midst of death, and to trust the mercy of God—not as that which will procure us universal exemption from evil, but as that which will quicken us in the midst of death every moment of our lives."[47] Thus, before the faithful experience for themselves the power of God to deliver them from death, they behold by faith the mercy and compassion of God that are otherwise hidden from view, for "faith raises our hearts above this darkness, to behold God in heaven as reconciled to us."[48] This is why Hosea can say that the appearing of the Lord is as sure as the dawn, even when he was abandoned to the darkness of death (Hos. 6:3). "This is the true exercise of our faith, when we lift up our eyes to the light which seems to be extinguished, and when in the darkness of death we yet continue to promise ourselves life."[49] The hope of the faithful that God will again bring them to the experience of light and life is rooted in the way that the eye of faith sees the light of God even in the thickest darkness of affliction, "as when one is cast into a deep pit, by raising upward his eyes, he sees at a distance the light of the sun."[50] To help the faithful to see the light of life in the darkness of death, Calvin directs them to the promises of God, in which this light may be beheld as in a mirror.[51] Were no other light to be seen in our afflictions, the promises of God can nonetheless bring the light of God into the thickest darkness, and instill the children of God with hope, even when to all appearances their situation is hopeless. "For when any promise of God is set before us, it is like a small light kindled in darkness."[52]

3. The Appearance of Things Unseen

The ability of faith to see the light of life in the midst of death, and the favor of God in the midst of wrath, confirms the nature of faith as the "assurance of things hoped for, the conviction of things not seen" (Heb. 11:1). The eyes of faith see realities that are completely concealed from the eyes of the flesh. Calvin highlights this aspect of faith in the first edition of the *Institutes*.[53] Faith points us to the future for which we hope, which, as Paul reminds us, cannot be seen (Rom. 8:24); and yet faith nonetheless sees the realities for which we hope, by exceeding our natural capacity of sight. "While he calls it an indication and proof (in Greek *elenchus*, demonstration) of things not appearing, he is speaking as if to say that the evidence of things not appearing is the vision of things which are not seen, the perception of things obscure, the presence of things absent, the proof of things hidden."[54] Calvin ascribes the ability to see invisible things, and to perceive hidden things, to the Word in which they are manifested.[55]

Calvin continues to explore faith as the vision of things unseen in subsequent biblical commentaries. He is interested in the way Paul describes faith as looking upon that which cannot be seen (2 Cor. 4:18). "Note the expression, we look at things which are not seen; the eye of faith sees further than all man's natural senses and that is why faith is called 'the seeing of things which are invisible.'"[56] The eyes of faith look past the appearance of present things, which are temporary, to future things, which are eternal. Even when Paul opposes walking by faith to walking by sight (2 Cor. 5:6–7), Calvin still describes faith as the ability to see those things that cannot be seen. "Now faith is rightly opposed to sight because it perceives things that are hidden from men's senses and reaches forward to things future that do not appear."[57] As we have seen, the things that do appear in the faithful contradict the future realities for which they hope. "Believers are more like dead men than living, for they often seem to be forsaken by God and they always have the elements of death shut up within them."[58] Nonetheless, faith still sees these future realities that are hidden under a contrary appearance, for "faith is the manifestation of things which do not appear."[59] Thus, even though Paul rightly opposes faith to sight, faith is nevertheless able to see unseen reality because it beholds it in the mirror of the Word, even as it waits for the day when it shall see God face-to-face.[60]

Calvin continues to explore the paradoxical vision of faith in his commentary on Hebrews of 1549. "The Spirit of God shows us hidden things, the knowledge of which cannot reach our senses."[61] The contradiction is heightened by a consideration of the condition of the faithful, which stands in further contradiction to what they see by faith. "Eternal life is promised to us, but it is promised to the dead; we are told of the resurrection of the blessed, but meantime we are involved in corruption; we are declared to be just, and sin dwells within us; we hear that we are blessed, but meantime we are overwhelmed by untold miseries; we are promised an abundance of good things, but we are often hungry and thirsty; God proclaims that he will come to us immediately, but seems to be deaf to our cries."[62] Were faith not able to see the realities promised in the Word, even though they are hidden by the appearance that contradicts them, then the godly would be without hope and consolation in this life.[63]

Calvin applies this ability of faith to see that which cannot be seen to Peter's statement that the faithful love and believe in the one whom they have not seen (1 Pet. 1:8). On the one hand, faith does not attend to the visible, for all that can be seen contradicts the object of our faith and love.[64] On the other hand, faith has its own vision, by which it sees the invisible things for which it hopes in the mirror of the Word.[65] We see the same dynamic in Calvin's interpretation of the statement made by Jesus to Thomas that apparently contrasts faith to sight: "Blessed are they that have not seen, and yet have believed" (John 20:29). On the one hand, faith believes in those things that are necessarily hidden from human perception.[66] On the other hand, faith sees with its own eyes those things that are hidden from human powers of perception, allowing it to transcend the limitations of human sight. "This is why it is called a demonstration of things invisible and not apparent."[67] Finally, in an addition made in 1555, Calvin invokes the same paradox of seeing that which cannot be seen in his interpretation of Paul's statement that we hope for what we do not see (Rom. 8:24–25). "Since hope extends to things which we have not yet experienced, and represents to our mind the image of things which are hidden and far remote, anything that is either openly seen or grasped by the hand cannot be hoped for."[68] The vision of faith, seeing the image of remote and hidden things, takes place in spite of the actual appearance of misery, affliction, and death in the children of God.[69]

Faith not only beholds the hidden blessings of God but also sees the hidden judgment and wrath of God that has yet to come upon the world, since "there is nothing more incongruous than that we should measure the wrath of God by the suffering which we see in the world."[70] Calvin contrasts the way the children of God behold the hidden judgment of God as though it were already present with the way the ungodly want to banish the judgment of God to heaven.[71] He appeals to Noah as a particularly vivid example of this aspect of faith. "Noah paid such respect to the Word of God that he turned his eyes from the contemporary view of things and went in fear of the destruction which God threatened as though it were present to him."[72] The faithful may even profit from the chastisements God inflicts on them in this life to discipline them, which often appear to be greater than those seen in the reprobate; for in their afflictions, the godly see, as in a mirror, the hidden judgments that shall yet fall upon the ungodly, for "they are a certain proof or a lively exhibition of that judgment which the unbelieving fear not, but thoughtlessly deride."[73]

4. "For Now We See in a Mirror, Enigmatically; but Then Face to Face"

The ability of faith to see with its own eyes those realities that are deeply concealed from human perception depends on the manifestation and representation of those realities in the living images God creates for us on earth, by means of the inseparable conjunction of symbols and the Word. Thus, when Paul says that we now see in a mirror, enigmatically, Calvin interprets the mirror to be the self-representation of God both in the ministry of the Church and in the works of God in the universe. "For God, who is otherwise invisible, has appointed these as means for revealing himself to us."[74] However, in his commentary on John of 1553, Calvin suggests that yet another mirror given to us is found in the grace of the Holy Spirit within us, by which we may see Christ, who is otherwise absent from our sight. "For although he is not seen with the eyes, yet his presence is known by the sure experience of faith."[75] Thus the faithful in this life see God only in the mirrors of creation, the ministry of the Church, and the gifts of the Spirit, by which God represents Godself to them, even as they long to see God face-to-face.[76]

Calvin contrasts the self-manifestation of God in the mirrors of the Church and the universe with the way the angels behold God, suggesting that such mirrors are made necessary by the limitations of our embodied existence. "But we, who have not yet scaled such heights, look upon the image of God in the Word, in the sacraments, and, in short, in the whole ministry of the Church."[77] Calvin makes the same suggestion in his interpretation of the statement of Paul that God dwells in unapproachable light (1 Tim. 6:16). "Thus by faith we do enter into God's light, but only in part, so that it is still rightly said to be a light inaccessible to man."[78] In his interpretation of Peter's statement of the prophetic word as a lamp shining in a dark place (2 Pet. 2:19), Calvin notes that the darkness in particular is the reality of death that confronts us in this life.[79] Even the fathers, who were said to have seen God face-to-face, still saw only through the mirrors of symbols, which were made necessary by their embodied existence. "Hence the majesty of God, now hidden, will only then be seen in itself when the veil of this mortal and corruptible nature is removed."[80]

Calvin contrasts the vision of God in an obscure mirror with the face-to-face vision of God, which will take place on the Last Day. However, since the limitations of embodied existence make the self-revelation of God in images and mirrors necessary, then "even if fullness of vision will be delayed until the day of Christ, we will begin to have a closer view of God as soon as we die. Our souls will then be set free from our bodies, and we will have no further need of either the external ministry or other inferior aids."[81] Calvin appeals to this intermediate vision of God to argue against the invocation of the saints in his commentary on 1 Corinthians of 1546. Over against the Roman claim that the saints see the whole world in the reflected light that they have in the presence of God, which Calvin claims "smacks more of Egyptian theology than it agrees with Christian teaching," Calvin suggests that the children of God who have departed this life are "so gripped, and as it were absorbed, by the vision of God, that they can think of nothing else at all."[82]

There are therefore three distinct stages of the vision of God: through the mirror of creation, the ministry of the Church, and the gifts of the Spirit; the nearer vision of God without the need of a mirror after death; and the fullness of vision that will take place only on the Last Day. Even though the children of God who have died enjoy the nearer vision of God without aids, they still long for the full revelation of God on the Last Day, as Calvin points out in the *Psychopannychia* of 1534/36. "But if the eyes of the elect look to the supreme glory of God as their final good, their desire is always moving onward till the glory of the Lord is complete, and this completion awaits the judgment day."[83] However, in his commentary on 1 John Calvin is concerned to point out that even in the fullness of vision to be granted on the Last Day, the children of God will not see God completely, even if they will see God clearly, because there always remains a disproportion between them and God that cannot be surmounted. "But when the apostle says that we shall see him as he is, he refers to a new and ineffable mode of vision, which we have not now."[84]

If the vision of God is dependent upon the degree of proportion between the children of God and God, then the more the children of God are brought into conformity with God, the more clearly will they see God. The vision of God therefore depends directly on the renewal of the image of God within the faithful. Calvin first makes this point in his commentary on 1 Timothy of 1548. In light of Paul's statement that no human can see God, Calvin claims that "we must be renewed and made like God before it can be given to us to see him."[85] He makes the same point the following year, in light of the statement in Hebrews concerning "the holiness without which no one will see the Lord" (Heb. 12:14). "He says that no one can see God without sanctification since we shall only see God with eyes which have been renewed according to his image."[86] The renewal of the image of God brings us into greater correspondence with the inaccessible light in which God dwells, so that we may approach the light of God's glory without fear of being destroyed by it. "And now, indeed, God begins to restore his image in us: but in what small measure! Therefore, unless we are stripped of all the corruption of the flesh, we shall not behold God face to face."[87] During the time when the image of God is being renewed in us, "God presents himself to be seen now, not as he is, but as our little capacity can grasp."[88] However, the very Gospel that acts as a mirror in which we can now see God also transforms us more and more into the image of God, so that we might one day see God face-to-face.[89]

The renewal of the image of God that makes the vision of God possible also forms the bond of union uniting the children of God to God. "The highest human good is therefore simply union with God. We attain it when we are brought into conformity with his likeness."[90] As early as 1539, Calvin noted the presence of this idea in Plato, making him unique among the philosophers. "Plato meant nothing but this when he often taught that the highest good of the soul is likeness to God, where, when the soul has grasped the knowledge of God, it is wholly transformed into his likeness."[91] However, Calvin does not fully endorse Plato's position, as he observes in his commentary on 2 Peter of 1551. "This teaching was not unfamiliar to Plato, because he defines the highest human good in various passages as being completely conformed to God. But he was wrapped up in the fog of errors, and afterwards he slid away into his own invented ideas."[92] The re-creation of the image of God makes possible the participation of the children of God in the glory of God, which also includes the face-to-face vision of God.[93] The complete restoration of the image of God will also be the complete manifestation of the children of God, according to the statement of Jesus that they will be like the angels (Matt. 22:30): "it has not appeared what we shall be until we are transformed into his glory and see him as he is."[94]

5. "When Christ Who Is Your Life Is Revealed, You Also Will Be Revealed with Him"

In spite of the renewal of the image of God in the faithful, it remains nonetheless the case that their life is hidden under an appearance that contradicts it. "We are exposed to a thousand miseries and our souls to innumerable evils, so that we always find a hell within us."[95] Since their life is hidden with Christ in God, it will only be fully revealed when Christ himself appears in glory (Col. 3:3–4).[96] For now, the glory of the children of God can only be seen in Christ, as though in a mirror, so "that in him, as in a mirror, we may see the glorious treasures of divine grace, and the innumerable greatness of that power which has not yet been manifested in ourselves."[97] The children of God will only come into their own glory when Christ himself appears in glory, which may explain why Calvin reserves the fullness of the vision of God until that day. "For if our life is shut up in Christ, it must be hid until he appears."[98] Calvin links this understanding of the glory of the children of God with the renewal of the image of God, claiming that only those who are transformed into the image of God will be revealed in glory when Christ appears on the Last Day.[99]

The revelation of Jesus Christ will also bring about the complete restoration of the Kingdom of God, and the renewal of all things. "And he will appear to all with the ineffable majesty of his Kingdom, with the glow of immortality, with the boundless power of divinity, with a guard of angels."[100] According to Calvin, the death of Christ has already brought about such a renewal in principle, but it is not yet revealed in fact. "For as the Kingdom of Christ is only begun, the perfection of it deferred until the last day."[101] The renewal of all things can only take place when the enemies of Christ are defeated once and for all and the children of God are brought into the glory of the Kingdom.[102] The revelation of the Kingdom of God will bring about the manifestation of the powers of God throughout the world, after all that hides them has been destroyed. "How much greater will their wonder be at seeing the final display of divine justice, goodness, and wisdom, when the kingdom of Christ is completed."[103] This restoration will have an impact on the whole of creation and not only the children of God, "because God will restore the fallen world to perfect condition at the same time as the human race."[104] In particular, the restoration of the world will bring about the removal of all decay and corruption, "that no appearance either of deformity or of impermanence will be seen."[105]

The completion of the Kingdom of God will also mean the restoration of the disorder in the Church. To begin with, there are many hypocrites in the body of the faithful whose glory appears to eclipse that of the true children of God.[106] However, the disorder of the Church does not reach its apex until the appearance of the Antichrist within it, which Calvin, like Luther, thought had occurred in his day. Calvin claims that the marks of the Antichrist set forth by Paul in his letters can all be clearly discerned in the Church of Rome, especially in the papacy.[107] The appearance of the Antichrist in the Church therefore reveals to Calvin that he lives in the last time before the return of Christ. "We today must bestir ourselves and apprehend by faith the near advent of Christ when Satan causes confusion so as to disturb the Church. For these are the signs of the last time."[108] That the light of Christ is already emerging in Calvin's day to signal the end of the reign of the Antichrist is for Calvin further confirmation that the day of the restoration of all things is close at hand. When Paul says that the lawless one will be destroyed by the manifestation of Christ's coming (2 Thess. 2:8), Calvin says, "Paul indicates, however, that in the meantime Christ will scatter the darkness in which Antichrist will reign by the rays which he will emit before his coming, just as the sun, becoming visible to us, chases away the darkness of the night with its bright light."[109]

The day of the manifestation of Christ will also bring about the judgment of the world, which not only includes its restoration to the true order intended by God but also the disclosure of the inmost thoughts and affections of the heart. The world will be restored to order by Christ when the godly are vindicated over against those who afflicted and persecuted them (2 Thess. 1:5). "We are to remember the righteous judgment of God, which will raise us above this world. Death will thus for us be the image of life."[110] Christ will reveal the inmost affections and thoughts of the heart on the Last Day, when it will become clear that God sees the heart and not appearances. Those who think that they have hidden their thoughts from God simply because they are hidden from others will suddenly have these thoughts brought to light.[111] The judgment of Christ will therefore take place by shining the light of God from the inside out, so that everything that is now hidden will be revealed. "We shall then come forth into the light, whereas many now are hidden as though in darkness. For then the books that are now shut will be opened."[112] The judgment of Christ will therefore bring about the true revealing of the children of God, and their ultimate distinction from the reprobate.[113]

Finally, the appearing of Christ will bring about the abolition of all rule in heaven and on earth, other than the rule of God. There will no longer be temporal rulers, with their various degrees of honor and authority; nor will there be any degrees of authority within the Church, as in the offices of preachers and teachers, "so that God alone may exercise his own power and dominion through himself, not through the hands of men or angels."[114] Christ will also bring about the defeat of the last of his enemies, which is death itself, to be revealed in the resurrection of the body. "Believers should therefore take heart, and not lose hope, until all things which ought to come before the resurrection of the body are fulfilled."[115] Once all rule has been abolished, and death itself has been defeated, Christ will hand the Kingdom of God over to the Father, and subject himself to the Father, so that God will be all in all (1 Cor. 15:24–28). According to Calvin, this means that the children of God will no longer need the mediation of the humanity of Christ but will be able to behold God directly, "and the humanity of Christ will no longer be in between us to hold us back from the nearer vision of God."[116]

The mediation of Christ, including his role as the image of the invisible God, will come to an end when Christ brings us to the unmediated vision of God. "For he was not appointed our leader just to draw us to the sphere of the moon or the sun, but to make us one with God the Father."[117] Eternal life will therefore consist of the face-to-face vision of God, the fountain and author of every good thing, and union with God by means of the restoration of the image and likeness of God. "If the Lord will share his glory, power, and righteousness with the elect—nay, will give himself to be enjoyed by them and, what is more excellent, will somehow make them to become one with himself, let us remember that every sort of happiness is included under this benefit."[118]

Conclusion

"For now we see in a mirror, enigmatically; but then face to face" (1 Cor. 13:12).
As this study has shown, Calvin describes the self-manifestation of God in a
vast array of mirrors, living images, signs, and symbols, not only in the works
of God in the universe, but also in the works of God in Israel and the Christian Church. However, the pious long to see God more clearly than they can
in these mirrors and symbols, and press on to the face-to-face vision of God.
In one of his earliest writings, Calvin describes the peaceful longing of the
saints even in death for the face-to-face vision of God. "But if the eyes of the
elect look to the supreme glory of God as their final good, their desire is always moving onward till the glory of God is complete, and their completion
awaits the judgment day. Then will be verified the saying, 'I will be satisfied,
when I awake, with beholding thy countenance' (Ps. 17:15)."[1] In his comment
on this psalm verse twenty years later, Calvin will accentuate the vision of
God we do enjoy in this life in innumerable symbols that God places before
us, but he will still point out the longing of the pious for the face-to-face vision of God. "It is true, indeed, as Paul declares, that so long as we continue
in this state of earthly pilgrimage, 'we walk by faith, not by sight'; but as we
nevertheless behold the image of God not only in the glass of the gospel, but
also in the innumerable evidences of his grace which he daily exhibits to us,
let each of us awaken himself from his lethargy, that we may now be satisfied
with spiritual felicity until God, in due time, bring us to his own immediate

presence, and cause us to enjoy him face to face."[2] To see God face-to-face, the godly must be transformed more and more into the image of God, for they will only see God face-to-face when they are like God. "For we must be renewed and made like God before it can be given us to see him."[3] Beholding the living images of God outside of us, in order to be transformed into the living image of God ourselves, is therefore central to our relationship with God, according to Calvin, and embraces everything from the creation of the universe to union with God in eternal life.

Far from replacing images with words, Calvin combines image and word in all aspects of our lives with God and with others. We must hear the Word of God if we are rightly to behold the symbols in which the invisible God becomes somewhat visible; but we must also behold with our eyes the goodness of God that the Word declares to us, so that the truth of that Word might be confirmed for us. Calvin will accentuate the visibility of divine self-revelation by describing the Word of God itself as a living image of God, in which the hidden thoughts of God might be beheld, even as human thoughts are represented in the language we use. When Calvin encounters a symbol in Scripture to which no Word of God is attached, such as the sacrifices of the patriarchs, or burial rites, or the exodus itself, he will nonetheless uphold the meaning and necessity of these symbols, which the godly are to consider and contemplate. Unlike Luther, Calvin will exhibit no unease with the self-revelation of God in visions and dreams, not only to the prophets, but also to the apostles.

Calvin's concern to see the self-revelation of God in terms of the combination of the Word of God that we hear and the living images of God that we behold places him squarely within the broader catholic tradition from the time of the orthodox theologians of the early Church to his own day. Calvin combines proclamation and manifestation in an exemplary way, providing us with one model of how to fulfill David Tracy's call that we learn to combine the two in our day.[4] Calvin also holds together the revelation of God in the truth of the Word with the manifestation of the goodness of God in the beauty of God's works, in a way that anticipates Hans Urs von Balthasar's attempt to do the same in our own day.[5] We are led to union with the fountain of every good thing in God only when we hold together the proclamation of that goodness in the Word of God with the manifestation of that goodness in the beauty of the living images of God.

Moreover, one can discern what one might call an increasing catholicity in the development of Calvin's theology. The self-disclosure of God in the universe, which is initially interpreted as rendering all the Gentiles without excuse, is increasingly seen as an image that all the pious are to contemplate, once they have been given the eyes to see it by the Word and the Holy Spirit. The image of God in humanity, which Calvin initially describes as "obliterated and deleted" in Adam, is increasingly described as yet remaining in the "lineaments" of the image in the reason, understanding, and sense of divinity in all people. The laying on of hands, which Calvin caustically dismissed in 1536 as Rome's "aping" of the apostles, is described as a sacrament with regard to ordination, and a useful rite with regard to confirmation, by the third edition of the *Institutes* in 1543. The gestures of prayer, such as the uplifting of hands and eyes and the bending of the knee, are increasingly seen as both expressing and stimulating piety in ourselves and others. Calvin even recognizes the legitimacy of the pious use of the sign of the cross, though he thought that too much superstition was attached to it to restore it in his day.[6] His willingness to adopt and endorse sacraments and rites that he initially rejected has not been fully appreciated, and can serve as an important resource for ecumenical understanding.

Calvin exhibits a consistent tendency to distinguish between various living images of God, even as he holds them inseparably together in a mutually reinforcing way. He distinguishes between the mirror and theater of God in the universe, which reveals the goodness of God to us in this life, and the image of the invisible God in Christ, which reveals the goodness of God leading to eternal life. However, he increasingly insists that the pious need to contemplate both images of God throughout their lives, especially on Sunday, when they are to consider the works of God in the universe, even as they contemplate the living images of God in Christ in the Gospel, baptism, the holy Supper, and the various rites and ceremonies of worship. Calvin clearly distinguishes between the economy of divine self-manifestation in the Law and the Gospel, to argue, against Rome, that the economy of manifestation in the Law has come to an end now that the one portrayed therein has appeared. However, Calvin insists that the godly are continually to compare the types and shadows of the Law with the reality and light of the Gospel, to come to a fuller understanding of the self-revelation of God in Christ.

Calvin's continual coordination of the Law with the Gospel keeps the question of the meaning of the covenant with Israel always before the reader. Calvin has two distinct ways of viewing the symbols of divine self-revelation to Israel. On the one hand, the economy of the Law is seen as portraying in an increasingly clear way the Christ who is approaching from the future, until the day when the reality being portrayed finally appears. Once the reality is manifested, the shadows and types come to an end, making Christ the end of the Law. On the other hand, Calvin also sees the symbols of the Law as signs of the presence of God. Christ as God manifested in the flesh may be seen as the consummation of the symbols of God's presence, but this would not necessarily entail the termination of the symbols of God's presence given to the Israelites and Jews. This possibly accounts for the way Calvin will at one time vehemently deny that any meaning remains in the symbols of the Law, as in his discussion of the need for the Temple to be destroyed, and at another time claim that the symbols of the Law still retain their meaning, as in his claim that the Temple could have remained even after the resurrection of Christ as a monument to the grace of God. For reasons that are not entirely clear, Calvin increasingly turned to an understanding of the Jews as a people clearly and unequivocally rejected by God, and manifesting in themselves all the signs of reprobation, revealed in the destruction the Temple and the dispersion of the people. However, Calvin clearly leaves us with another alternative, one that sees the symbols and images of God's presence to the Jews as still conveying the reality they symbolize, even after the manifestation of God in the flesh. "Yet, despite the great obstinacy with which they continue to wage war against the gospel, we must not despise them, while we consider that, for the sake of the promise, God's blessing still rests among them. For the apostle indeed testifies that it will never be completely taken away: 'For the gifts and the calling of God are without repentance'" (Rom. 11:29).[7]

We have also seen that an unresolvable tension lies at the heart of Calvin's discussion of the living images of God. Calvin insists that the symbols instituted by God truly offer and present the reality that they represent, and are therefore the instruments God uses to descend to us. However, he also claims that the reality being represented in these symbols must be sought in heaven, and encourages the godly to use divine symbols as ladders and vehicles by which they might ascend to God. Calvin creates this tension in order to keep the godly from confining God to the symbols of divine self-manifestation, so that we might be led from the image that we see to the God whom we do not yet see. This tension is compounded by the various reasons Calvin gives for the rejection of images of human institution in the worship of God. On the one hand, Calvin contrasts the "dead images" that humans create, which are only the image of absent things, with the "living images" instituted by God, which truly present the reality they represent. On the other hand, Calvin rejects the use of images in worship on the basis of the invisible nature of God, which cannot be represented in any symbol or image. He can at times so insist on the essential invisibility of God that he appears to undermine his whole understanding of divine self-manifestation in symbols and living images. Again, he creates this tension in order to maintain the dialectical relationship between the visibility and invisibility of God, and the presence and absence of God, which he thinks is maintained by images of divine creation but not by images of human devising. This tension is meant to lead us from the vision of God in a mirror, enigmatically, to the beholding of God face-to-face, so that we never rest contented with the present state of our vision but press on to the clear vision we shall enjoy on the Last Day. "Let each of us awaken himself from his lethargy, that we may now be satisfied with spiritual felicity until God, in due time, bring us to his own immediate presence, and cause us to enjoy him face to face."[8]

Notes

Abbreviations

Calvin: Commentaries
Calvin: Commentaries. Translated and edited by Joseph Haroutunian. Philadelphia: Westminster Press, 1958.

Calvin: Theological Treatises
Calvin: Theological Treatises. Edited by J. K. S. Reid. Philadelphia: Westminster Press, 1954.

Catechism
Catechism or Institution of the Christian Religion, 1538. Translated by Ford Lewis Battles. In I. John Hesselink, *Calvin's First Catechism: A Commentary*. Louisville, KY: Westminster John Knox Press, 1977.

CNTC
Calvin's New Testament Commentaries. Edited by David W. Torrance and Thomas F. Torrance. 12 vols. Grand Rapids, MI: Wm. B. Eerdmans, 1959–1972.

CO
Ioannis Calvini opera quae supersunt omnia. Edited by Wilhelm Baum, Edward Cunitz, and Edward Reuss. 59 vols. *Corpus Reformatorum*, vols. 29–87. Brunsvigae: A. Schwetschke and Son (M. Bruhn), 1863–1900.

CTS
The Commentaries of John Calvin on the Old Testament. 30 vols. Edinburgh: Calvin Translation Society, 1843–1848.

Inst.
John Calvin, *Institutio Christianae religionis 1559.* Cited by book, chapter, and section, from OS III–V, followed in parentheses by references to *Calvin: Institutes of the Christian Religion,* 2 vols., edited by John T. McNeill and translated by Ford Lewis Battles (Philadelphia: Westminster Press, 1960).

OE
Ioannis Calvini Opera Omnia, Series II, Opera Exegetica Veteris et Novi Testamenti. Geneva: Librairie Droz, 1992– .

OS
Ioannis Calvini opera selecta. Edited by Peter Barth, Wilhelm Niesel, and Dora Scheuner. 5 vols. Munich: Chr. Kaiser, 1926–1952.

Romans
Ioannis Calvini Commentarius in Epistolam Pauli ad Romanos. Edited by T. H. L. Parker. Leiden: E. J. Brill, 1981.

Tracts and Treatises
John Calvin. *Tracts and Treatises.* Translated by Henry Beveridge. 3 vols. Grand Rapids, MI: Wm. B. Eerdmans, 1958.

Introduction

  1. Comm. Deut. 4:12, CO 24:384C; CTS 4:119.

  2. *Inst.* 1536, OS I.44; [21].

  3. Edward A. Dowey, *The Knowledge of God in Calvin's Theology* (Grand Rapids, MI: Wm. Eerdmans, 1994), pp. 3, 13.

  4. E. David Willis, *Calvin's Catholic Christology* (Leiden: E. J. Brill, 1966), p. 118.

  5. Thomas F. Torrance, *Calvin's Doctrine of Man* (London: Lutterworth Press, 1949), p. 37.

  6. Ibid., p. 31.

  7. Lucien Richard, *The Spirituality of John Calvin* (Atlanta: John Knox Press, 1974), p. 159.

  8. Alexandre Ganoczy, *The Young Calvin,* trans. David Foxgrover and Wade Provo (Philadelphia: Westminster Press, 1987), pp. 198, 199.

  9. Carlos N. M. Eire, *War against the Idols: The Reformation of Worship from Erasmus to Calvin* (Cambridge: Cambridge University Press, 1986), p. 316.

  10. Ibid., p. 224.

  11. Ibid., p. 230.

12. B. A. Gerrish, *Grace and Gratitude: Calvin's Eucharistic Theology* (Minneapolis, MN: Fortress Press, 1993), p. 108.

13. Dawn de Vries, *Jesus Christ in the Preaching of Calvin and Schleiermacher* (Louisville: Westminster John Knox Press, 1996), p. 15.

14. William Bouwsma, *John Calvin: A Sixteenth-Century Portrait* (New York: Oxford University Press, 1988), p. 158.

15. Bernard Cottret, *Calvin: A Biography,* trans. M. Wallace McDonald (Grand Rapids, MI: Wm. Eerdmans, 2000), p. 242.

16. Mary Potter Engel, *Calvin's Perspectival Anthropology* (Atlanta: Scholars Press, 1988), p. 53.

17. Susan Schreiner, *Where Shall Wisdom Be Found? Calvin's Exegesis of Job from Medieval and Modern Perspectives* (Chicago: University of Chicago Press, 1994), pp. 138, 148.

18. Philip Butin, *Revelation, Redemption, Response: Calvin's Trinitarian Understanding of the Divine-Human Relationship* (New York: Oxford University Press, 1995), pp. 3, 87.

19. Barbara Pitkin, *What Pure Eyes Could See: Calvin's Doctrine of Faith in Its Exegetical Context* (New York: Oxford University Press, 1999), p. 61.

20. Bouwsma, *John Calvin,* p. 72.

21. Eire, *War against the Idols,* p. 263.

22. T. H. L. Parker, *John Calvin: A Biography* (Philadelphia: Westminster Press, 1975), p. 42.

23. T. H. L. Parker, *Calvin's Doctrine of the Knowledge of God,* rev. ed. (Grand Rapids, MI: Wm. Eerdmans, 1959), p. 116.

24. Ibid., p. 51.

25. Edward Dowey, *Knowledge of God,* p. 95.

26. Ibid., p. 139.

27. Gerrish, *Grace and Gratitude,* p. 107.

28. Thomas Davis, *The Clearest Promises of God: The Development of Calvin's Eucharistic Teaching* (New York: AMS Press, 1995), p. 161.

29. Richard, *Spirituality of John Calvin,* p. 162.

30. *Inst.* I.xi.13, OS I.102.19–25; (1:113–114).

31. *Calvin's Commentary on Seneca's De Clementia,* trans. Ford Lewis Battles and Andre Malan Hugo (Leiden: E. J. Brill, 1969), pp. 22–23.

32. Ibid., pp. 50–51.

33. Ibid., pp. 122–123.

34. Ibid., pp. 304–305.

35. Ibid., pp. 30–31.

36. Ibid., pp. 80–81.

37. Ibid., pp. 52–53.

38. Ibid., pp. 50–53.

39. Ibid., pp. 52–53.

40. See in particular David F. Penham, "*De Transitu Hellenismi ad Christianismum*: A Study of a Little Known Treatise of Guillaume Budé followed by a Translation into English" (Ph.D diss., Columbia University, 1954).

41. Robert D. Cottrell, *The Grammar of Silence: A Reading of Marguerite de Navarre's Poetry* (Washington, DC: Catholic University of America Press, 1986), p. 98.

42. Ibid.

43. Ibid., p. 96.

44. Cicero, *De Oratore* II.lxxxvii.357.

45. *De Oratore* III.xl.161.

46. *De Partitione Oratoria* vi.20.

47. *Institutio 1536* IV.2, OS I.119; *Inst.* 1536:88.

48. *Institutio 1536* V.44, OS I.201; *Inst.* 1536:157.

49. *Enchiridion*, in *Collected Works of Erasmus*, vol. 66, *Spiritualia*, ed. John O'Malley (Toronto: University of Toronto Press, 1988), p. 41.

50. Ibid., p. 38.

51. Ibid., p. 72.

52. John C. Olin, ed., *Christian Humanism and the Reformation: Selected Writings of Erasmus*, 3d ed. (New York: Fordham University Press, 1987), p. 108.

53. *Enchiridion*, p. 74.

54. Ibid., p. 75.

55. Ibid., p. 86.

56. Ibid., p. 81.

57. Ibid.

58. Ibid., p. 84.

59. Paula Sommers, *Celestial Ladders: Readings in Marguerite de Navarre's Poetry of Spiritual Ascent* (Geneva: Librairie Droz, 1989).

60. Jean Boisset, *Sagesse et sainteté dans la pensée de Calvin* (Paris: Presses Universitaires de France, 1959), pp. 225–314.

61. *Inst.* III.ii.41, OS IV.51–52; (1:589).

62. Comm. 1 John 2:3, CO 55:311A; CNTC 5:245.

63. Comm. 1 Peter 2:3, CO 55:233B; CNTC 12:258.

64. CO 9:793C; *Calvin: Commentaries*, p. 59.

65. Comm. 1 Corinthians 1:21, CO 49:326C; CNTC 9:40.

66. *Institutio 1536* V.65, OS I.218; *Inst.* 1536:171; *Inst.* IV.iii.16, IV.iv.15, IV.xiv.20, 28.

67. Comm. 2 Timothy 2:17, CO 52:368B; CNTC 10:314.

CHAPTER 1. *The Universe as the Living Image of God*

1. *A Tous Amateurs de Iesus Christ et de son Evangile, Salut*, CO 9:793C; *Calvin: Commentaries*, p. 59.

2. Ibid.

3. CO 9:795A; *Calvin: Commentaries*, pp. 59–60.

4. Ibid.

5. Ibid.

6. CO 9:797A; *Calvin: Commentaries*, pp. 60–61.

7. Ibid.

8. *Institutio 1536* I.A, OS I.37; *Inst.* 1536:15.

9. *Institutio 1536* III.B.17, OS I.108; *Inst.* 1536:78.

10. *Institutio 1536* II.A.9, OS I.75; *Inst.* 1536:48.

11. *Institutio 1536* II.B.10, OS I.75–76; *Inst.* 1536:49.

12. *Catechismus, 1538*, CO 5:324C; *Catechism*, p. 8.

13. Ibid. Barbara Pitkin rightly notes the foundational role that Hebrews 11:3 will have for Calvin's discussion of the self-disclosure of God the Creator, but she dates the emergence of this text at 1549, when Calvin publishes his Hebrews commentary, whereas it first emerges in 1537, in the *Instruction in Faith*. See Pitkin, *What Pure Eyes Could See*, p. 82.

14. *Catechismus, 1538*, CO 5:324C; *Catechism*, p. 8.

15. Ibid., CO 5:325; *Catechism*, p. 9.

16. Ibid.

17. Ibid.

18. *Institutio 1539* I.11, CO 1:286; (1:52–53).

19. Comm. Romans 1:20, *Romans* 29:36–40; CNTC 8:31.

20. *Institutio 1539* I.11, 17; CO 1:286C, 291A.

21. *Institutio 1539* I.14, CO 1:289A; (1:62).

22. *Institutio 1539* I.15, CO 1:289C; (1:63).

23. "Plato inter omnes religiosissimus et maxime sobrius," *Inst. 1539* I.16, CO 1:290C.

24. *Institutio 1539* I.11, CO 1:286C.

25. *Institutio 1539* I.12, CO 1:286–287; (1:53).

26. Ibid.

27. Ibid.

28. Ibid.; (1:53–54).

29. *Institutio 1539* I.12, CO 1:287B; (1:59).

30. *Institutio 1539* II.35, CO 1:326B; (1:274).

31. *Institutio 1536* I.20, CO 1:292–293; (1:72–73).

32. *Institutio 1536* I.17, CO 1:291A; (1:68).

33. *Institutio 1539* I.37, CO 1:303A; (1:96).

34. *Institutio 1539* I.38, CO 1:303C; (1:97).

35. Ibid., CO 1:303–304; (1:97).

36. Ibid., CO 1:304A; (1:98).

37. *Institutio 1543* VI.46, CO 1:508A; (1:179).

38. *Institutio 1543* VI.47, CO 1:509A; (1:180).

39. *Institutio 1543* VI.47, CO 1:509B; (1:181).

40. *Institutio 1543* VI.48, CO 1:509C; (1:181).

41. *Institutio 1545* III.56, CO 1:405C; (1:400).
42. *Catechismus Ecclesiae Genevensis*, OS II.103.13–22; *Calvin: Theological Treatises*, p. 112.
43. Comm. 1 Corinthians 1:21, CO 49:326C; CNTC 9:40.
44. Ibid.
45. Ibid.
46. Comm. Hebrews 11:3, OE 19.184; CNTC 12:160.
47. Ibid.
48. Ibid.
49. Comm. Romans 1:19, *Romans* 29; CNTC 8:31.
50. Comm. Genesis Argumentum, CO 23:7–8A; CTS 1:59–60.
51. Ibid.
52. Ibid.
53. Ibid., CO 23:7–8C; CTS 1:60.
54. Ibid.
55. Ibid., CO 23:11–12; CTS 1:64.
56. Ibid., CO 23:9–10B; CTS 1:62–63.
57. Ibid.
58. Comm. Acts 14:17, CO 48:328C; CNTC 7:13–14.
59. Comm. Genesis 1:26, CO 23:25B; CTS 1:92.
60. Comm. Acts 17:27, CO 48:416B; CNTC 7:119.
61. Ibid., CO 23:9–10B; CTS 1:62.
62. Ibid.
63. Comm. Genesis 2:3, CO 23:33A; CTS 1:105–106.
64. Comm. Genesis 1:5, CO 23:18A; CTS 1:78.
65. Comm. Genesis 3:17, CO 23:73A; CTS 1:173.
66. Ibid.
67. Comm. Genesis Argumentum, CO 23:9–10C; CTS 1:63.
68. Comm. Acts 14:15, CO 48:326A; CNTC 7:10–11.
69. *Inst.* II.vi.1, OS III.320–321; (1:340–341).
70. Comm. Genesis Argumentum, CO 23:9–10C; CTS 1:63, my emphasis.
71. Comm. Genesis Argumentum, CO 23:11–12A; CTS 1:64.
72. Comm. 1 Corinthians 1:20, CO 49:325B; CNTC 9:38.
73. Ibid., CO 49:325C; CNTC 9:39.
74. Comm. 1 Corinthians 1:27, CO 49:330A; CNTC 9:44.
75. Comm. Psalm 19:1, CO 31:195A; CTS 8:309.
76. Comm. Psalm 19:4, CO 31:196–197; CTS 8:313.
77. Comm. Psalm 19:4, CO 31:197A; CTS 8:313.
78. Comm. Psalm 19:1, CO 31:194–195; CTS 8:309.
79. *Inst.* I.vi.1, OS III.60.25–30; (1:70).
80. Comm. John 7:15, OE 11/1.235; CNTC 4:185.
81. Comm. Psalm 29:5, CO 31:289B; CTS 8:479–480.
82. Comm. Genesis 1:6, CO 23:18C; CTS 1:79–80.

83. Comm. Psalm 29:5, CO 31:289A; CTS 8:479.

84. *Inst.* I.xiv.1, OS III.153.13–16; (1:160–161).

85. *Inst.* I.xiv.2, OS III.154.1–4; (1:161).

86. *Inst.* I.ii.1, OS III.35.2–3; (1:41).

87. Comm. Isaiah 40:26, CO 37:24–25; CTS 15:231–232. "I do not deny, indeed, that our outward form, in so far as it distinguishes and separates us from brute animals, at the same time more closely joins us to God. And if anyone wishes to include under 'image of God' the fact that, 'while all other living beings being bent over look earthward, man has been given a face uplifted, bidden to gaze heavenward and to raise his countenance to the stars,' I shall not contend too strongly" (*Inst.* I.xv.3, OS III.177.1–6; [1:186]). The quote is from Ovid, *Metamorphoses* I.84 ff.

88. *Inst.* I.v.3, OS III.46–47; (1:54).

89. In I.v.11 Calvin changes the phrase *mundi compositione* to *mundi fabricam et pulcherrimam positionem* (OS III.55.7), and in I.vi.3 he changes the phrase *effigiem suam in mundi compositione impressam* to *effigiem suam in pulcherrima mundi forma impressam* (CO 1:292C, OS III.63.23).

90. *Inst.* I.ii.1, OS III.34.21–25; (1:40). It seems to me that both Parker and Dowey are correct in their descriptions of the reason for the reorganization of the *Institutes*. The four books of the *Institutes* do reflect the four articles of the Creed having to do with God the Creator, Christ, the Holy Spirit, and the holy, catholic Church, as Parker suggests; whereas the distinction between the knowledge of God the Creator and the knowledge of God the Redeemer distinguishes the content of Book I from that of Books II through IV. See Parker, *Calvin's Doctrine*; Dowey, *Knowledge of God*.

91. Comm. Acts 14:15, CO 48:326A; CNTC 7:10–11.

92. *Inst.* I.vi.1, OS III.61.26–29; (1:71).

93. *Inst.* II.vi.1, OS III.320.29–33; (1:341).

94. Comm. Romans 1:20, *Romans* 29.33–40; CNTC 8:31.

95. Comm. Genesis Argumentum, CO 23:11–12B; CTS 1:64.

96. Comm. Genesis Argumentum, CO 23:7–8C; CTS 1:60.

97. Comm. Psalm 104:1, CO 32:85A; CTS 11:145.

98. Comm Genesis Argumentum, CO 23:7–8C; CTS 1:60.

99. Comm. Psalm 19:1, CO 31:194–195; CTS 8:309.

100. See Dowey, *Knowledge of God*, pp. 3 ff; and especially Ford Lewis Battles, "God Was Accommodating Himself to Human Capacity," *Interpretation* 31 (January 1977). For a discussion of the way in which Calvin relates divine self-accommodation to the self-manifestation of God in creation and Christ, see Randall C. Zachman, "Calvin as Analogical Theologian," *Scottish Journal of Theology* 51:2 (1998).

101. Comm. Psalm 86:9, CO 31:794C; CTS 10:386.

102. Comm. Isaiah 29:9, CO 36:490C; CTS 14:319.

103. Comm. Jeremiah 10:7, CO 38:67C; CTS 18:22.

104. Comm. Romans 1:19, *Romans* 29:33–35; CNTC 8:31.

105. *Inst.* I.v.3, OS III.47.3–6; (1:54).

106. Comm. Acts 17:27, CO 48:415–416; CNTC 7:118–119.
107. Comm. Psalm 103:8, CO 32:78B; CTS 11:133.
108. Comm. Hebrews 11:3, OE 19.184; CNTC 12:160.
109. Comm. Psalm 8:1, CO 31:88B; CTS 8:94.
110. Comm. 1 Corinthians 1:21, CO 49:326A; CNTC 9:39.
111. Comm. Genesis Argumentum, CO 23:7–8B; CTS 1:59–60.
112. Comm. Psalm 103:8, CO 32:78B; CTS 11:133.
113. Comm. Psalm 19:7, CO 31:199A; CTS 8:317.
114. *Inst.* I.vi.3, OS III.63.25–28; (1:73).
115. *Inst.* I.vi.1, OS III.60.29–30; (1:70).
116. Comm. Genesis Argumentum, CO 23:9–10B; CTS 1:63.
117. Comm. Isaiah 34:16.
118. Comm. Isaiah 52:6, CO 37:246C; CTS 16:98.
119. Comm. Habakkuk 2:20, CO 43:562B; CTS 29:130.
120. Comm. 1 Corinthians 1:21, CO 49:326C; CNTC 9:40.
121. *Inst.* I.v.14, OS III.59.5–7; (1:68).
122. Comm. Hebrews 11:3, OE 19.183.16–18; CNTC 12:159.
123. Comm. Genesis 2:3, CO 23:33A; CTS 1:105.
124. Comm. Exodus 20:8, CO 24:578–579; CTS 4:436–437.
125. Comm. Genesis 1:5, CO 23:18A; CTS 1:78.
126. Comm. Zechariah 12:1, CO 44:322B; CTS 30:341.
127. Comm. Psalm 19:1, CO 31:194; CTS 8:307.
128. Comm. Psalm 19:1, CO 31:194C; CTS 8:308–309.
129. Ibid.
130. Comm. Ezekiel 1:22, CO 40:49; CTS 22:90.
131. Comm. Psalm 19:1, CO 31:195B; CTS 8:309.
132. Comm. Isaiah 66:1, CO 37:436B; CTS 16:409–410.
133. Comm. Ezekiel 1:22, CO 40:49B; CTS 22:90.
134. Comm. Jeremiah 10:1–2, CO 38:59A; CTS 18:8.
135. "Hence Moses was instructed from his childhood in that art, and also Daniel among the Chaldeans [Acts 7:22; Dan. 1:17, 20]. Moses learned astrology as understood by the Egyptians and Daniel as known by the Chaldeans" (ibid.).
136. Comm. Jeremiah 10:12–13, CO 38:76–77; CTS 18:35–36.
137. Comm. Psalm 19:1, CO 31:195B; CTS 8:309.
138. "When the father and creator saw the creature which he had made moving and living, the created image of the eternal gods, he rejoiced, and in his joy determined to make the copy still more like the original, and as this was an eternal living being, he sought to make the universe eternal, so far as might be. . . . Wherefore he resolved to have a moving image of eternity, and when he set in order the heaven, he made this image eternal but moving according to number, while eternity itself rests in unity, and this image we call time" (Plato, *Timaeus* 37.c–d).
139. Comm. Jeremiah 51:15–16, CO 39:454C; CTS 21:220.
140. Comm. Psalm 147:4, CO 32:427B; CTS 12:294.

141. Comm. Isaiah 40:26, CO 37:25B; CTS 15:232.

142. Comm. Psalm 93:1, CO 32:16–17; CTS 11:6–7.

143. Comm. Jeremiah 51:15–16, CO 39:454–455; CTS 220–221.

144. Comm. Psalm 68:32, CO 31:635–636; CTS 10:43.

145. Comm. Psalm 96:5, CO 32:39A; CTS 11:52.

146. Comm. Isaiah 13:10, CO 36:263B; CTS 13:418.

147. Comm. Jeremiah 10:1–2, CO 38:58B; CTS 18:7.

148. *Advertissement contre L'Astrologie qu'on appelle Iudiciaire*, CO 7:513–542; "A Warning against Judiciary Astrology," trans. Mary Potter, *Calvin Theological Journal* 18:2 (1983): 183.

149. Comm. Genesis 1:14, CO 23:21C; CTS 1:85.

150. Ibid.

151. Comm. Jeremiah 51:15–16, CO 39:455B; CTS 21:221–222.

152. Comm Psalm 18:8, CO 31:174A; CTS 8:267.

153. Comm. Psalm 18:9, CO 175C; CTS 8:271.

154. Comm. Psalm 18:14, CO 31:177B; CTS 8:273–274.

155. Comm. Jeremiah 10:12–13, CO 38:77B; CTS 18:37.

156. Comm. Jeremiah 51:16, CO 39:455C; CTS 21:222.

157. Comm. Psalm 65:11, CO 31:609A; CTS 9:463.

158. Comm. Jeremiah 10:12–13, CO 38:77B; CTS 18:37.

159. Comm. Jeremiah 51:15–16, CO 39:454C; CTS 21:220.

160. Comm. Jeremiah 10:12–13, CO 38:76A; CTS 18:35.

161. Comm. Psalm 93:3, CO 32:17C; CTS 11:8–9.

162. Comm. Psalm 119:89, CO 32:253C; CTS 11:469.

163. Comm. Psalm 104:10, CO 32:89B; CTS 11:154.

164. Ibid.

165. Comm. Jeremiah 51:15–16, CO 39:454C; CTS 21:220.

166. Comm. Psalm 8:3–4, CO 31:91B; CTS 8:99–100.

167. Comm. Psalm 8:1, CO 31:87–88; CTS 8:93.

168. Comm. Psalm 104:31, CO 32:96C; CTS 11:169.

169. Comm. Psalm 104 Argumentum, CO 32:84C; CTS 11:143.

170. Comm. Psalm 115:16, CO 32:190B; CTS 11:355.

171. *Inst.* I.xiv.22, OS III.172–173; (1:182).

172. Comm. Psalm 104:31, CO 32:96C; CTS 11:169.

173. Comm. Psalm 118:1, CO 32:202C; CTS 11:378.

174. Comm. Psalm 145:7, CO 32:414B; CTS 12:274–275.

175. Comm. Psalm 8:1, CO 31:88A; CTS 8:94.

176. Comm. Psalm 104:29, CO 32:96B; CTS 11:168.

177. Comm. Psalm 18:47, CO 31:192A; CTS 8:303.

178. Comm. Jeremiah 10:10, CO 38:72; CTS 18:27.

179. Ibid.

180. Comm. Psalm 104:29, CO 32:95C; CTS 11:167.

181. Comm. Jeremiah 10:10, CO 38:72B; CTS 18:28.

182. Comm. Acts 17:28, CO 48:416C; CNTC 7:119–120.
183. *Inst.* I.v.10, OS III.54.24–29; (1:63).
184. Comm. Genesis 1:26, CO 23:25B; CTS 1:92.
185. Comm. Acts 17:27, CO 48:416B; CNTC 7:119.
186. Comm. Psalm 77:14, CO 31:718B; CTS 10:219.
187. Comm. Psalm 139:13, CO 32:381:B; CTS 12:214.
188. Comm. Psalm 139:13, CO 32:381B; CTS 12:315.
189. Comm. Psalm 111:2, CO 32:167–168; CTS 11:313.
190. Comm. Psalm 77:13, CO 31:717C; CTS 10:218–219.
191. *Institutio 1536* I.A, CO 1:27B; *Inst.* 1536:15.
192. Comm. Romans 1:21, *Romans* 30.69–71; CNTC 8:32.
193. Comm. Romans 1:21, *Romans* 30–31; CNTC 8:32.
194. Comm. Romans 1:23, *Romans* 31–32; CNTC 8:33.
195. Comm. Romans 1:23, *Romans* 32.20–24; CNTC 8:33–34.
196. CO 9:797A; *Calvin: Commentaries*, pp. 60–61.
197. Comm. Psalm 106:21, CO 32:124C; CTS 11:224.
198. Comm. Jeremiah 10:7, CO 38:67B; CTS 18:21.
199. Comm. Acts 17:24, CO 48:410C; CNTC 7:112–113.
200. Comm. Isaiah 44:15–17, CO 37:116C; CTS 15:375–376.
201. Comm. Acts 17:24, CO 48:411B; CNTC 7:113–114.
202. Comm. Psalm 136:1, CO 32:364A; CTS 12:183.
203. Comm. Exodus 20:4, CO 24:376–377; CTS 4:107.
204. Comm. Deuteronomy 4:19, CO 24:386C; CTS 4:122–123.
205. Comm. Isaiah 44:15–17, CO 37:115–116; CTS 15:374–375.
206. *Institutio 1536* I.E.10, CO 1:32C; *Inst.* 1536:20.
207. *Catechismus* 1538, CO 5:328A; *Catechism*, p. 12.
208. *Institutio 1539* III.24, CO 1:385B; (1:101).
209. Comm. 1 Corinthians 8:4, CO 49:430C; CNTC 9:174.
210. Comm. 1 Corinthians 8:4, CO 49:430C; CNTC 9:174.
211. Comm. Jeremiah 10:8, CO 38:69B; CTS 18:24.
212. Comm. Jeremiah 51:18, CO 39:457B; CTS 21:225.
213. Comm. Daniel 5:4, CO 40:698B; CTS 24:131.
214. Comm. Isaiah 40:18, CO 37:19B; CTS 15:222–223.
215. Comm. Habakkuk 2:19, CO 43:559B; CTS 29:125.
216. Comm. Exodus 32:4, CO 25:82–83; CTS 5:333–334.
217. Comm. Exodus 20:4, CO 24:376–377; CTS 4:107.
218. Comm. Exodus 20:4, CO 24:377B; CTS 4:108.
219. Comm. Genesis Argumentum, CO 23:7–8B; CTS 1:59.
220. *Institutio 1543* III.34, CO 1:391C; (1:112).
221. *Inst.* I.v.10, 11, OS III.54–55; (1:63).
222. Comm. Romans 1:19, *Romans* 29.34–35; CNTC 8:31.

CHAPTER 2. *Symbols of God's Goodness in the Present Life*

1. Comm. Acts 14:17, CO 48:328C; CNTC 7:14.
2. *Inst.* I.v.9, OS III.53.14–16.
3. *Institutio 1536* VI.5, CO 1:199C; *Inst.* 1536:180.
4. *Institutio 1539* XVII.26, CO 1:1144A; (1:713).
5. *Institutio 1539* XVII.28, CO 1:1145B; (1:714).
6. Ibid. (1:714–715).
7. Ibid.
8. Ibid.
9. *Institutio 1539* VII.10–22, CO 1:808–816; (1:436–448).
10. *Institutio 1539* VII.25, CO 1:818B; (1:450).
11. Ibid.
12. Comm. Psalm 112:2, CO 32:172B; CTS 11:322.
13. CO 9:797A; *Calvin: Commentaries,* pp. 60–61.
14. Comm. Genesis 26:28, CO 23:367–368; CTS 2:74.
15. Comm. Jeremiah 24:7, CO 38:462B; CTS 19:228.
16. Comm. Genesis 48:15, CO 23:584B; CTS 2:428.
17. Comm. Psalm 18:26, CO 31:183A; CTS 8:285.
18. Comm. Psalm 132:15, CO 32:350–351; CTS 12:158–159.
19. Comm. Psalm 22:10, CO 31:226A; CTS 8:369.
20. Comm. Psalm 71:6, CO 31:655–656; CTS 10:85.
21. Comm. Psalm 22:10, CO 31:226B; CTS 8:369.
22. Comm. Psalm 22:10, CO 31:226B; CTS 8:369. "When we are born into the world, although the mother do her office, and the midwife may be present with her, and many others may lend their help, yet did not God, putting, so to speak, his hand under us, receive us into his bosom, what would become of us? And what hope would there be of the continuance of our life? Yea, rather, were it not for this, our very birth would be an entrance into a thousand deaths" (Comm. Psalm 71:6, CO 31:355–356; CTS 10:85).
23. Comm. Psalm 22:10, CO 31:226B; CTS 8:369.
24. Comm. Jeremiah 20:17–18, CO 38:355B; CTS 19:49.
25. *Institutio 1539* VII.29, CO 1:1145–1146; (1:715).
26. Comm. John 6:11, OE 11/1.189.20–23; CNTC 4:146.
27. Comm. Jeremiah 9:13–15, CO 38:42C; CTS 17:485–486.
28. Comm. Psalm 8:8–10, CO 31:94–95; CTS 8:107–108.
29. Comm. Jeremiah 5:24, CO 37:634C; CTS 17:299–300.
30. Comm. Isaiah 28:29, CO 36:483–484; CTS 14:306.
31. Comm. Ezekiel 7:20, CO 40:168–169; CTS 22:264.
32. Comm. Ezekiel 7:20, CO 40:168–169; CTS 22:264.
33. Comm. Ezekiel 16:15, CO 40:348A; CTS 23:111.
34. Comm. Zechariah 9:16, CO 44:280C; CTS 30:270.

35. Comm. Psalm 109:8, CO 32:150A; CTS 11:277.
36. Ibid. "Besides, all this multitude of miseries does not destroy the chief blessing of life, viz., that men are created and preserved unto the hope of a happy immortality; for God now manifests himself to them as a Father, that hereafter they may enjoy his eternal inheritance" (Comm. Exodus 20:12, CO 24:604–605; CTS 5:10–11).
37. Comm. Romans 4:13, *Romans* 89–90; CNTC 8:91–92.
38. Comm. 1 Timothy 4:8, CO 52:300A; CNTC 10:244.
39. Comm. Psalm 23:1, CO 31:238A; CTS 8:391.
40. Comm. Isaiah 65:21–22, CO 37:431A; CTS 16:401.
41. Comm. Deuteronomy 6:10, CO 24:232–233; CTS 3:374.
42. Comm. Jeremiah 32:38, CO 39:37B; CTS 20:208.
43. Comm. Isaiah 65:10, CO 37:424A; CTS 16:389–390.
44. Comm. Psalm 71:15, CO 31:659A; CTS 10:91.
45. Comm. 1 Timothy 4:8, CO 52:300A; CNTC 10:244.
46. Comm. Hebrews 2:5, OE 19.33; CNTC 12:21.
47. Comm. Genesis 3:17, CO 23:73A; CTS 1:173.
48. Comm. Leviticus 13:58, CO 24:321C; CTS 4:18.
49. Comm. Genesis 36:1, CO 23:477B; CTS 2:252.
50. Comm. 1 Corinthians 7:31, CO 49:421A; CNTC 9:160.
51. Comm. Psalm 90:10, CO 31:838B; CTS 10:471.
52. Comm. Genesis 27:2, CO 23:373B; CTS 2:83.
53. Comm. Psalm 39:6, CO 31:399–400; CTS 9:78–79.
54. Comm. Psalm 90:3, CO 31:834C; CTS 10:464.
55. Comm. Micah 5:10–15, CO 43:380A; CTS 28:319.
56. Comm. Psalm 4:7, CO 31:64B; CTS 8:49.
57. Comm. Amos 8:3–4, CO 43:142C; CTS 27:361–362.
58. Comm. Deuteronomy 28:12, CO 25:18A; CTS 5:222–223.
59. Comm. Hosea 9:15, CO 42:405–406; CTS 26:345–346.
60. Comm. Joel 2:30, CO 42:571A; CTS 27:98–99.
61. Comm. Isaiah 32:20, CO 36:555B; CTS 14:426.
62. Comm. Jeremiah 5:25, CO 37:635C; CTS 17:301.
63. Comm. Psalm 25:13, CO 31:258C; CTS 8:429.
64. Comm. Acts 20:24, CO 48:465B; CNTC 7:179.
65. Comm. Genesis 38:7, CO 23:494B; CTS 2:279–280.
66. Comm. Romans 3:29, *Romans* 78.76–79; CNTC 8:80. This sentence was added in the 1556 edition.
67. CO 9:791B; *Calvin: Commentaries*, p. 58.
68. *Psychopannychia*, CO 5:180C; *Tracts and Treatises* III:423.
69. CO 5:181C; *Tracts and Treatises* III:424.
70. Comm. Genesis 5:1, CO 23:105B; CTS 1:227–228.
71. *Inst.* I.xv.1, OS III.173.27–29; (1:183).
72. *Institutio 1536* I.A, CO 1:27–28; *Inst.* 1536:15.
73. CO 1:28B; *Inst.* 1536:16.

74. Ibid.

75. *Catechismus,* CO 5:330A; *Catechism,* p. 14.

76. *Institutio 1539* XVII.10, CO 1:1131C; (1:696).

77. CO 1:1132A; (1:697).

78. Comm. James 3:9, CO 55:441B; CNTC 3:292.

79. Ibid.

80. Ibid.

81. Comm. John 13:34, OE 11/2.133.1–3; CNTC 5:70.

82. Comm. Isaiah 58:7, CO 37:330A; CTS 16:234.

83. *Inst.* III.vii.6, OS IV.156–157; (1:696).

84. Comm. Acts 17:28, CO 48:418B; CNTC 7:121.

85. Ibid. In his Genesis commentary of the same year, Calvin will speak of "some remnant (*aliquod residuum*) of the image of God" (Comm. Gen. 9:6, CO 23:147B; CTS 1:296).

86. Comm. John 1:4, OE 11/1.18.10–13; CNTC 4:11.

87. Comm. John 1:4, OE 11/1.18.13–16; CNTC 4:11.

88. Comm. Genesis 9:22, CO 23:151A; CTS 1:301.

89. Comm. Deuteronomy 29:20, CO 25:49C; CTS 5:277.

90. Comm. Genesis 2:16, CO 23:45C; CTS 1:127.

91. Comm. Genesis 5:5, CO 23:106C; CTS 1:229–230.

92. Comm. Numbers 19:11, CO 24:335B; CTS 4:42.

93. Comm. Psalm 8:5, CO 31:92B; CTS 8:102.

94. Ibid. This is a considerable expansion of the description of the light remaining in human beings given in his 1553 commentary on John. "There are two main parts in that light which yet remains in corrupt nature. Some seed of religion is sown in all: and also, the distinction between good and evil is engraven in their consciences" (Comm. John 1:5, OE 11/1.19.33–36; CNTC 4:12).

95. Comm. Psalm 8:8–10, CO 31:95B; CTS 8:108.

96. *Inst.* I.xv.4, OS III.179.25–27; (1:189).

97. *Inst.* I.xv.8, OS III.185.30–37; (1:195).

98. *Inst.* I.xv.6, OS III.183.7–8; (1:192–193).

99. *Inst.* I.iii.3, OS III.40.19–22; (1:46–47).

100. Comm. Genesis 9:6, CO 23:147A; CTS 1:295.

101. Comm. Jonah 1:13–14, CO 43:227C; CTS 28:60–61.

102. Mary Potter Engel has rightly called attention to the tension created by Calvin's claims that on the one hand the image of God has been entirely deleted from humanity by the fall of Adam, while on the other hand the lineaments of the image of God remain in all humans. She rightly explains this tension by means of the perspective Calvin has when he makes each kind of claim, and describes those perspectives as God as Father versus God as Judge (*John Calvin's Perspectival Anthropology* [Atlanta, GA: Scholars Press, 1988], pp. 42–57). However, it seems to me that the best way to describe these perspectives is with regard to the distinction Calvin makes between the blessings of this life and the blessings of eternal life. The image of God

remains in human beings in its lineaments with regard to the blessings of temporal life, even inducing God to care for humanity providentially. However, the lineaments of the image do not provide for us the powers by which we could be united with God in eternal life, and in this sense the image has been deleted, only to be restored in Christ.

103. Comm. Leviticus 24:22, CO 24:622B; CTS 5:36.

104. Comm. Habakkuk 1:14–15, CO 43:513C; CTS 29:49.

105. Comm. 1 Corinthians 11:7, CO 49:476B; CNTC 9:232.

106. Ibid.

107. Ibid.

108. Ibid.

109. Comm. 1 Corinthians 11:10, CO 49:476–477; CNTC 9:232.

110. Ibid.

111. Comm. 1 Corinthians 11:4, CO 49:475B; CNTC 9:231.

112. Comm. Genesis 1:26, CO 23:27B; CTS 1:96.

113. Comm. Genesis 2:18, CO 23:46C; CTS 1:129.

114. Comm. 1 Timothy 2:13, CO 52:277A; CNTC 10:217–218.

115. Ibid.

116. Comm. Genesis 2:18, CO 23:47A; CTS 1:129.

117. Ibid.

118. Comm. 1 Corinthians 11:11, CO 49:478A; CNTC 9:234.

119. Ibid.

120. Comm. Jeremiah 20:17–18, CO 38:355B; CTS 19:48.

121. Comm. Psalm 148:11, CO 32:436A; CTS 12:308.

122. Comm. Genesis 20:16, CO 23:294B; CTS 1:533.

123. Comm. Isaiah 4:1, CO 36:95A; CTS 13:150.

124. The disagreement between John L. Thompson and Jane Dempsey Douglass will play to a draw, because Douglass draws primarily from the commentary on 1 Corinthians, which makes the subordination of women a matter of decorum and civic polity, whereas Thompson deploys the writings from the later commentaries in which the subordination of women is rooted in the image of God itself. Calvin kept both claims in play, as the final edition of the commentary on 1 Corinthians was published in 1555, a year after the commentary on Genesis (Jane Dempsey Douglass, *Women, Freedom, and Calvin* [Philadelphia: Westminster Press, 1985]; John L. Thompson, *John Calvin and the Daughters of Sarah: Women in Regular and Exceptional Roles in the Exegesis of John Calvin* [Geneva: Librairie Droz, 1992]).

125. Comm. Acts 17:29, CO 48:418–419; CNTC 7:121–122.

126. Ibid.

127. Comm. Jeremiah 10:8, CO 38:69C; CTS 18:24.

128. Comm. Jeremiah 10:14, CO 38:79B; CTS 18:40.

129. Ibid.

130. *Psychopannychia*, CO 5:180C; *Tracts and Treatises* III:423.

131. *Inst.* I.xv.3, OS III.178.10–14; (1:188).

CHAPTER 3. *The Manifestation of the Providential Care of God*

1. *Calvin's Commentary on Seneca's De Clementia,* trans. Ford Lewis Battles and Andre Malan Hugo (Leiden: E. J. Brill, 1969), pp. 28–29.

2. Ibid., pp. 30–31.

3. CO 9:797A; *Calvin: Commentaries,* pp. 60–61.

4. *Institutio 1536* II.10, CO 1:63; *Inst.* 1536:49.

5. Ibid.

6. Ibid.

7. Ibid.

8. Ibid.

9. As we shall see throughout this chapter, Calvin never isolates the power of God from the other powers of God, but always associates it with goodness, wisdom, and justice, though the emphasis on these companion powers changes over time. It is simply not accurate to say of Calvin that "divine immutability and power made the doctrine of providence a source of comfort to the believer" (Susan Schreiner, *The Theater of His Glory: Nature and the Natural Order in the Thought of John Calvin* [Durham, NC: Labyrinth Press, 1991], p. 35). Calvin found the thought of God's immutability and power when taken in isolation to be terrifying. The same may be said of William Bouwsma's claim that "God, for Calvin, is identified with power" (*John Calvin,* p. 173). Schreiner is more accurate in her later work, when she notes that for Calvin the powers of God are inseparably united in the essence and nature of God; hence power is never isolated from justice, wisdom, or goodness (Schreiner, *Where Shall Wisdom Be Found?* p. 119). Mary Potter Engel rightly notes the way Calvin never treats the power of God in isolation from the other powers (*John Calvin's Perspectival Anthropology,* p. 131).

10. *Catechismus,* CO 5:324–325; *Catechism,* p. 8.

11. *Catechismus,* CO 5:325B; *Catechism,* p. 9.

12. Ibid. I have found no evidence for the presence of two distinct forms of faith in Calvin, as has been argued by Barbara Pitkin. "Providential faith is a knowledge of God through God's creative and providential works, as illuminated by the word of Scripture and as revealing Christ the eternal Son. Saving faith is a knowledge of God's redemptive works, as illuminated by the word of Scripture and as revealing Christ incarnate" (Barbara Pitkin, *What Pure Eyes Could See: Calvin's Doctrine of Faith in Its Exegetical Context* [Oxford: Oxford University Press, 1999], p. 161). Calvin does not root God's providence in the unincarnate Son or Logos of God, but in the powers of God that express God's nature and essence. The Word of God in Scripture teaches us about the creative and providential works of God, and about the redemptive works of God. Faith embraces both elements of divine teaching, because both lead us to the author and fountain of every good thing in God, both with regard to the good things of this life and with regard to the things that lead to eternal life. I agree with Pitkin that the contemplation of creation and providence should not be

collapsed into or replaced by the redemptive work of God in Christ, but I do not agree with the way she makes this case with regard to Calvin's theology.

13. *Catechismus,* CO 5:337–338; *Catechism,* p. 22.

14. Ibid.

15. *Institutio 1539* I.13, CO 1:287–288; (1:59–60).

16. *Institutio 1539* I.13, CO 1:288A; (1:60).

17. Ibid.

18. Ibid.

19. Ibid.

20. Ibid.

21. *Institutio 1539* I.15, CO 1:289B; (1:62).

22. *Institutio 1539* I.13, CO 1:288C; (1:61).

23. Ibid.

24. *Institutio 1539* I.16, CO 1:290A; (1:63–64).

25. *Institutio 1539* I.16, CO 1:290C; (1:64).

26. Comm. Psalm 8:2, CO 31:88C; CTS 8:95.

27. Comm. Psalm 8:2, CO 31:89A; CTS 8:96.

28. Comm. Isaiah 51:6, CO 37:230A; CTS 16:71.

29. Comm. Daniel 2:21, CO 40:577B; CTS 24:145.

30. Comm. Daniel 2:21, CO 40:576; CTS 24:143–144.

31. Comm. Psalm 107 Argumentum, CO 32:135B; CTS 11:245.

32. Comm. Psalm 107:10, CO 32:138A; CTS 11:251–252.

33. Comm. Psalm 107:23, CO 32:141A; CTS 11:257.

34. Comm. Psalm 107:10, CO 32:138A; CTS 11:251.

35. Comm. Amos 4:9, CO 43:62B; CTS 27:238.

36. Comm. John 9:3, OE 11/2.3.26–29; CNTC 4:239.

37. Comm. 9:29, CO 24:117B; CTS 3:191.

38. *Institutio 1539* I.17, CO 1:291A; (1:68).

39. Pitkin notes the importance of the eyes of faith with regard to Calvin's discussion of providence in the Psalms commentary but seems to miss its appearance in the 1539 edition of the *Institutes* (*What Pure Eyes Could See,* pp. 122–126).

40. Comm. Psalm 107:42, CO 32:144B; CTS 11:264.

41. Comm. Psalm 33:13, CO 31:331A; CTS 8:549.

42. Comm. Psalm 91:7, CO 32:4B; CTS 10:482–483.

43. Comm. Psalm 40:4, CO 31:407A; CTS 9:92.

44. Comm. Psalm 73:16, CO 31:682; CTS 10:142.

45. Comm. Psalm 73:16, CO 31:683; CTS 10:143.

46. Comm. Psalm 92:7, CO 32:12–13; CTS 10:498.

47. Comm. Genesis 18:18, CO 23:258B; CTS 1:480.

48. Comm. Habakkuk 2:1, CO 43:521B; CTS 29:61.

49. Comm. Psalm 73:16, CO 31:683; CTS 10:143.

50. Comm. Jeremiah 26:14, CO 38:526C; CTS 19:328. Susan Schreiner rightly draws attention to the ability of the eyes of faith to see what otherwise remains hidden with regard to God's providence (*Where Shall Wisdom Be Found?* p. 128).

51. *Inst.* I.xvi.2, OS III.189.8–11; (1:199); I.xvii.1, OS III.202.31–35; (1:211).

52. Comm. Psalm 107:42, CO 32:144B; CTS 11:265.

53. Comm. Psalm 91:7, CO 32:4B; CTS 10:482–483.

54. Comm. Psalm 116:7, CO 32:194C; CTS 11:363–364.

55. *Institutio 1539* IV.51, CO 1:511B; (1:197).

56. *Institutio 1539* IV.51, CO 1:511C; (1:197–198).

57. *Institutio 1539* IV.51, CO 1:5112A; (1:204).

58. *Institutio 1539* IV.27, CO 1:495–496; (1:200)

59. *Institutio 1539* VIII.38, CO 1:889B; (1:202).

60. Ibid.

61. Ibid.

62. *Institutio 1539* VIII.40, CO 1:890C; (1:207).

63. *Institutio 1539* VIII.40, CO 1:890–891; (1:207).

64. *Institutio 1539* VIII.41, CO 1:891B; (1:208).

65. Ibid.

66. *Institutio 1539* VIII.41, CO 1:891–892; (1:209).

67. *Institutio 1539* VIII.46, CO 1:895–896; (1:219).

68. *Institutio 1539* VIII.47, CO 1:896C; (1:220).

69. *Institutio 1539* VIII.49, CO 1:897C; (1:222).

70. *Institutio 1539* VIII.51, CO 1:899A; (1:224).

71. *Institutio 1539* VIII.49, CO 1:898A; (1:222).

72. Comm. Psalm 27:1, CO 31:271–272; CTS 8:451.

73. Comm. Jeremiah 46:3–5, CO 39:285B; CTS 20:576.

74. Comm. Jeremiah 51:15–16, CO 39:453C; CTS 21:219.

75. Comm. Daniel 4:17, CO 40:663C; CTS 24:265.

76. Comm. Psalm 109:26, CO 32:157A; CTS 11:291.

77. *Institutio 1539* VIII.45, CO 1:894C; (1:218).

78. *Institutio 1543* VI.49, CO 1:510C; (1:199).

79. Ibid.

80. Comm. Lamentations 3:37–38, CO 39:588C; CTS 21:428.

81. Comm. Psalm 105:17, CO 32:105C; CTS 11:185–186.

82. Comm. Psalm 147:7, CO 32:428B; CTS 12:297.

83. Ibid.

84. Comm. Psalm 107:43, CO 32:145A; CTS 11:266.

85. Comm. Daniel 11:27, CO 41:249A; CTS 25:314.

86. *Institutio 1539* VIII.45, CO 1:894C; (1:218).

87. *Institutio 1543* VI.50, CO 1:511A; (1:201).

88. *De aeterna Dei praedestinatione,* CO 8:351; *Concerning the Eternal Predestination of God,* trans. J. K. S. Reid (Louisville, KY: Westminster John Knox Press, 1997), p. 167.

89. Comm. John 7:15, OE 11/1.235.11–19; CNTC 4:185.

90. Comm. Psalm 9:1, CO 31:97A; CTS 8:111.

91. Comm. Exodus 8:19, CO 24:102–103; CTS 3:167.

92. Comm. Deuteronomy 8:3, CO 24:240A; CTS 3:385–386.

93. Comm. Psalm 65:9, CO 31:607B; CTS 9:460.

94. Comm. Isaiah 9:4, CO 36:193A; CTS 13:304.

95. Comm. Isaiah 26:10, CO 36:434B; CTS 14:224.

96. Comm. Isaiah 28:21, CO 36:479C; CTS 14:299.

97. *Inst.* I.xvi.2, OS III.190.2–8; (1:199).

98. *De scandalis*, OS II.179; *Concerning Scandals*, trans. John W. Fraser (Grand Rapids, MI: Wm. Eerdmans, 1978), p. 28.

99. Ibid.

100. *De scandalis*, OS II.179; *Scandals*, p. 29.

101. *De scandalis*, OS II.180–181; *Scandals*, p. 30–31.

102. *De scandalis*, OS II.181; *Scandals*, p. 31.

103. *De scandalis*, OS II.186–187; *Scandals*, p. 39–40.

104. *De scandalis*, OS II.189; *Scandals*, p. 43. Pitkin appears to date the appearance of this theme to the Psalm commentary of 1557 (*What Pure Eyes Could See*, pp. 118–122).

105. *De scandalis*, OS II.190; *Scandals*, p. 44.

106. *De scandalis*, OS II.192; *Scandals*, p. 48.

107. *Institutes 1539* VIII.45, CO 1:895A; (1:218).

108. *De aeterna Dei praedestinatione*, CO 8:349; *Concerning the Eternal Predestination of God*, p. 164.

109. *De aeterna Dei praedestinatione*, CO 8:349; *Concerning the Eternal Predestination of God*, pp. 164–165.

110. *Contre la Secte des Libertins*, CO 7:186–192; *Treatises against the Anabaptists and against the Libertines*, trans. Benjamin Farley (Grand Rapids, MI: Baker Book House, 1982), pp. 242–249.

111. *Inst.* I.xvii.1, OS III.202.11–14; (1:210).

112. Comm. Genesis 9:6, CO 23:147A; CTS 1:295. See also Comm. Jonah 1:13–14, CO 43:227C; CTS 28:60–61; Comm. Habakkuk 1:14–15, CO 43:513C; CTS 29:49; Comm. Leviticus 24:22, CO 24:622B; CTS 5:36.

113. Comm. Psalm 147:9, CO 32:428C; CTS 12:297.

114. Comm. Acts 14:17, CO 48:329A; CNTC 7:14.

115. Comm. Deuteronomy 28:12, CO 25:18A; CTS 5:222–223.

116. Ibid.

117. Comm. Psalm 148:14, CO 32:436A; CTS 12:309.

118. *Inst.* I.xvii.6, OS III.210.10–13; (1:219).

119. Comm. Psalm 147 Argumentum, CO 32:425C; CTS 12:291.

120. Comm. Psalm 135:13, CO 32:361B; CTS 12:178.

121. Comm. Psalm 114:7, CO 32:179B; CTS 11:334–335.

122. Comm. Psalm 115:17, CO 32:192A; CTS 11:358.

123. Ibid.

124. Comm. Isaiah 41:20, CO 37:48B; CTS 15:268.

125. Comm. Psalm 33:11, 12; CO 31:330A; CTS 8:548.

126. Comm. Psalm 31:19, CO 31:310A; CTS 8:515.

127. Comm. Psalm 105:37, CO 32:112C; CTS 11:200.

128. Comm. Psalm 105:12, CO 32:103B; CTS 11:181.

129. Comm. Joshua Argumentum, CO 25:423–424; CTS 7:xix.xx.

130. Comm. Daniel 11:6, CO 41:226A; CTS 25:280–281.

131. Comm. Psalm 37 Argumentum, CO 31:365B; CTS 9:15.

132. Ibid.

133. Comm. Psalm 115:17, CO 32:192A; CTS 11:358.

134. Comm. Psalm 37 Argumentum, CO 31:365B; CTS 9:15.

135. Comm. Psalm 90:16, CO 31:840–841; CTS 10:475.

136. Comm. Psalm 6:5, CO 31:76A; CTS 8:70.

137. Comm. Psalm 21:7, CO 31:215–216; CTS 8:349.

138. Comm. Psalm 60:8, CO 31:577; CTS 9:402–403.

139. Comm. Genesis 16:13, CO 23:231C; CTS 1:438.

140. Comm. Genesis 22:14, CO 23:318B; CTS 1:571.

141. Comm. Psalm 16:11, CO 31:158A; CTS 8:233.

142. Comm. Isaiah 22:11, CO 36:373A; CTS 14:122.

143. Comm. Lamentations 5:19, CO 39:642B; CTS 21:511.

144. Comm. Jeremiah 29:14, CO 38:597A; CTS 19:438.

145. Comm. Psalm 75:7, CO 31:703B; CTS 10:188.

146. Comm. Psalm 121:1, CO 32:299B; CTS 12:62–63.

147. Ibid.

148. Comm. Isaiah 63:5, CO 37:395B; CTS 16:342.

149. Comm. Genesis 18:25, CO 23:263C; CTS 1:489.

150. Comm. Psalm 94:15, CO 32:26; CTS 11:25–26.

151. *De aeterna Dei praedestinatione,* CO 8:361; *Concerning the Eternal Predestination of God,* p. 179.

152. Comm. Psalm 111:3, CO 32:168B; CTS 11:314.

153. *Inst.* I.xvii.1, OS 203.6–9; (1:211).

154. Comm. Psalm 9:8, CO 31:99C; CTS 8:117.

155. Comm. Psalm 11:4, CO 31:123–124; CTS 8:165.

156. Comm. Psalm 69:20, CO 31:645–646; CTS 10:63.

157. Comm. Psalm 92:10, CO 32:14B; CTS 10:501.

158. Comm. Isaiah 62:11, CO 37:390C; CTS 16:334.

159. Comm. Psalm 92:15, CO 32:16A; CTS 10:505.

160. Comm. Zechariah 9:8, CO 44:269A; CTS 30:250.

161. Ibid.

162. Comm. Psalm 76:10, CO 31:709A; CTS 10:200. "The expressions which he uses, calling upon God to shine forth conspicuously, and lift himself on high, amount in common language to this, that God would give some actual manifestation of his character as judge or avenger; for in that case he is seen ascending his tribunal to exact punishment due to sin, and demonstrate his power in preserving order and government in the world. The phraseology is used only in reference to ourselves,

disposed as we are to feel as if he overlooked us, unless he stretched out his hand to help us in some visible and open manner" (Comm. Psalm 94:1, CO 32:18–19; CTS 11:11).

163. Comm. Psalm 9:10, CO 31:100C; CTS 8:118–119.

164. Comm. Isaiah 5:15, CO 36:113B; CTS 13:180. "And this is what we have already said, that when crimes are allowed to pass unpunished, it is a sort of cloud held before our eyes, which hinders us from beholding the glory of the Lord; but when he takes vengeance on men's transgressions, his glory shines forth illustriously" (Comm. Isaiah 2:11, CO 36:71C; CTS 13:111).

165. Comm. Psalm 66:7, CO 31:612–613; CTS 9:471.

166. Comm. Psalm 28:5, CO 31:284A; CTS 8:470–471.

167. Comm. Lamentations 3:39, CO 39:590C; CTS 21:431.

168. Comm. Psalm 38:3, CO 31:387B; CTS 9:55.

169. Ibid.

170. Comm. Daniel 4:34, CO 40:684–685; CTS 24:295.

171. Comm. Zechariah 11:10–11, CO 44:311C; CTS 30:322–323.

172. Comm. Psalm 64:9, CO 31:602A; CTS 9:449.

173. Comm. Psalm 59:12, CO 31:570B; CTS 9:389.

174. Comm. Isaiah 5:9, CO 36:109B; CTS 13:174.

175. Comm. Isaiah 22:17, CO 36:379B; CTS 16:131.

176. Comm. Isaiah 22:17, CO 36:279B; CTS 16:132.

177. Comm. Isaiah 57:1, CO 37:306C; CTS 16:196.

178. Comm. Lamentations 1:21, CO 39:532C; CTS 21:341.

179. *De aeterna Dei praedestinatione,* CO 8:355; *Concerning the Eternal Predestination of God,* p. 172. Again, Pitkin appears to trace the appearance of this metaphor to the Psalm commentary five years later (*What Pure Eyes Could See,* pp. 126–129).

180. Comm. Psalm 73:18, CO 31:683B; CTS 10:144.

181. Comm. Psalm 87:3, CO 31:801C; CTS 10:398–399.

182. Comm. Habakkuk 2:1, CO 43:518A; CTS 29:56.

183. Comm. Habakkuk 2:1, CO 43:519–520; CTS 29:59.

184. Comm. Habakkuk 2:1, CO 43:520B; CTS 29:60.

185. Comm. Genesis 42:1, CO 23:529B; CTS 2:337.

186. Ibid.

187. Comm. Exodus 2:10, CO 24:25A; CTS 3:44–45.

188. Comm. Numbers 33:54, CO 25:337B; CTS 6:303.

189. *Inst.* I.xvii.1, OS III.202.20–26; (1:211).

190. Comm. Psalm 37:9, CO 31:370C; CTS 9:25.

191. Comm. Psalm 18:38, CO 31:187B; CTS 8:294.

192. Comm. Isaiah 25:1, CO 36:414B; CTS 14:191.

193. Comm. Psalm 77 Argumentum, CO 31:711A; CTS 10:205.

194. Comm. Psalm 77:7–8, CO 31:714A; CTS 10:211.

195. Comm. Psalm 77:9, CO 31:715A; CTS 10:213.

196. Comm. Psalm 77:12, CO 31:717A; CTS 10:217–218.

197. Comm. Psalm 89:14, CO 31:816A; CTS 10:427–428.
198. Ibid.
199. Comm. Isaiah 26:4, CO 36:429A; CTS 14:215.
200. Comm. Psalm 103:8, CO 32:78B; CTS 11:132–133.
201. Comm. Psalm 145:8, CO 32:414C; CTS 12:275.
202. Comm. Jonah 4:2, CO 43:265C; CTS 28:122.
203. Comm. Exodus 20:7, CO 24:560B; CTS 4:409.
204. Comm. Jonah 4:2, CO 43:266B; CTS 28:123.
205. Comm. Psalm 85:5, CO 31:787A; CTS 10:370.
206. Ibid.
207. Comm. Psalm 130:4, CO 32:335B; CTS 12:131.
208. Comm. Psalm 138:8, CO 32:376A; CTS 12:204–205.
209. Comm. Isaiah 33:3, CO 36:560A; CTS 15:12.
210. Comm. Psalm 111:7, CO 32:169C; CTS 11:316.
211. Comm. Isaiah 63:15, CO 37:401B; CTS 16:352.
212. Comm. Zephaniah 1:12, CO 44:22B; CTS 29:217.
213. Comm. Jeremiah 5:9, CO 37:618C; CTS 17:273.
214. Comm. Lamentations 3:32, CO 39:584B; CTS 21:421.
215. Comm. Daniel 9:9, CO 41:142B; CTS 25:159.
216. Comm. Lamentations 3:8, CO 39:566A; CTS 21:394.
217. Comm. Psalm 113:5, CO 32:178B; CTS 11:333.
218. Comm. Psalm 138:6, CO 32:375; CTS 12:203.
219. Comm. Psalm 90:16, CO 31:841–842; CTS 10:476.
220. Comm. Psalm 90:16, CO 31:840–841; CTS 10:475.

CHAPTER 4. *The Manifestation of Christ in the Law and in the Gospel*

1. CO 9:791B; *Calvin: Commentaries,* p. 58.
2. CO 9:791C; *Calvin: Commentaries,* pp. 58–59.
3. CO 9:811A; *Calvin: Commentaries,* p. 68.
4. CO 9:811–813; *Calvin: Commentaries,* p. 69.
5. CO 9:811C; *Calvin: Commentaries,* pp. 68–69.
6. See I. John Hesselink, *Calvin's Concept of the Law* (Allison Park, PA: Pickwick Publications, 1992), esp. chap. 4, "Law and Gospel," pp. 155–215. Hesselink notes in particular the earthly types of the Law and the spiritual reality of the Gospel, and the shadows of the Law and reality of Christ, but also includes the metaphors of childhood and maturity, shadow outline and living image, and dawn to midday discussed below.
7. Ibid.
8. *Institutio 1536* I.E.13, CO 1:36B; *Inst.* 1536:23.
9. *Catechismus 1538,* CO 5:329A; *Catechism,* p. 13.
10. *Institutio 1539* III.53, CO 1:403C; (1:397).

11. Comm. Colossians 2:17, OE 16.434.9–15.

12. Ibid.

13. Ibid.

14. Ibid.

15. Comm. 1 Peter 1:12, CO 55:218C; CNTC 12:241.

16. Comm. Luke 16:16, CO 45:304C; CNTC 2:8.

17. Comm. Hebrews 9:13, OE 19.141.11–22; CNTC 12:121.

18. Ibid.

19. Ibid.

20. Comm. Hebrews 10:19, OE 19.162–163; CNTC 12:140.

21. Comm. John 19:30, OE 11/2.267.2–8; CNTC 5:183.

22. Comm. Exodus 31:13, CO 24:584B; CTS 4:444.

23. Comm. 1 Peter 1:19, CO 55:225B; CNTC 12:248.

24. Comm. 1 John 5:6, CO 55:364A; CNTC 5:302.

25. Comm. John 4:20, OE 11/1.127–128; CNTC 4:96–97.

26. Ibid.

27. *Psychopannychia,* CO 5:203B; *Tracts and Treatises* III:452–453.

28. *Institutio 1539* VII.1, CO 1:801–802; (1:429).

29. *Institutio 1539* VII.9, CO 1:807B; (1:435).

30. *Institutio 1539* VII.20, CO 1:815–816; (1:447).

31. *Institutio 1539* VII.25, CO 1:818B; (1:450).

32. *Institutio 1539* VII.26, CO 1:819A; (1:451).

33. Ibid.

34. Comm. Genesis 27:27, CO 23:278B; CTS 2:91–92.

35. Comm. Jeremiah 31:12, CO 38:661B; CTS 20:83–84.

36. *Institutio 1539* VII.27, CO 1:820B; (1:452).

37. Comm. Leviticus 26:3, CO 25:13–14; CTS 5:215.

38. Ibid.

39. Comm. 1 Corinthians 10:11, CO 49:461B; CNTC 9:212.

40. Comm. Hebrews 12:18, OE 19.228–229; CNTC 12:199–200.

41. Comm. Leviticus 26:3, CO 25:14B; CTS 5:216.

42. Comm. John 4:23, OE 11/1.131–132; CNTC 4:100.

43. *Psychopannychia,* CO 5:185C; *Tracts and Treatises* III:429.

44. *Institutio 1539* VII.31, CO 5:822A; (1:455).

45. Ibid.

46. *Institutio 1539* VII.20, CO 1:815B; (1:446).

47. Comm. 1 John 1:2, CO 55:302A; CNTC 5:235.

48. Ibid.

49. Comm. 1 Peter 1:12, CO 55:218C; CNTC 12:241.

50. Comm. John 8:56, OE 11/1.295.19–27; CNTC 4:234.

51. Comm. Genesis 32:29, CO 23:445–446; CTS 2:200–201.

52. Ibid.

53. Comm. Daniel 9:25, CO 41:182–183; CTS 25:218.

54. Comm. Malachi 4:2, CO 44:490B; CTS 30:618.

55. *Inst.* II.ix.1, OS III.398.13–20.

56. *Inst.* II.ix.4, OS III.402.9–11; (1:427).

57. Comm. Exodus 6:2, CO 24:78C; CTS 3:128.

58. Comm. Hebrews 11:13, OE 19.195.19–29; CNTC 12:170.

59. *Institutio 1536* IV.9, CO 1:108C; *Inst.* 1536:93.

60. Ibid.

61. *Institutio 1539* VII.29, CO 1:820C; (1:453).

62. *Institutio 1539* VII.29, CO 1:821A; (1:453).

63. Comm. Romans 3:21, *Romans* 70.10–16; CNTC 8:72.

64. *Institutio 1543* XI.41, CO 1:828C; (1:463).

65. Comm. Galatians 3:23, OE 16.84.11–21.

66. Comm. Colossians 2:17, OE 16.435.2–7; CNTC 11:338.

67. Comm. Colossians 2:12, OE 16.427.21–27; CNTC 11:332.

68. Comm. Colossians 2:17, OE 16.434.25–34; CNTC 11:338.

69. Comm. Hebrews 10:1, OE 19.153–154; CNTC 12:132. The similarity between Calvin's interpretation of Hebrews 10:1 and the homily of Chrysostom on the same passage indicates that Calvin likely borrowed this comparison from him.

70. Ibid.

71. Ibid.

72. *Institutio 1539* IV.23, CO 1:527B; (1:510).

73. *Sophist* 235d–236a.

74. Comm. Hebrews 8:5, OE 19.125–126; CNTC 12:107.

75. *Inst.* IV.xiv.20, OS V.278.29–30; (2:1297).

76. Comm. John 5:46, OE 11/1.185.14–24; CNTC 4:143.

77. *Inst.* II.vii.1, OS III.326–327; (1:349).

78. *Inst.* II.vii.1, OS III.327.13–15; (1:349).

79. *Institutio 1536* I.4, CO 1:29–30; *Inst.* 1536:17.

80. *Institutio 1539* III.105, CO 1:436C; (1:366).

81. Ibid.

82. Ibid.

83. *Institutio 1539* VII.36, CO 1:825A; (1:458–459).

84. Comm. Galatians 3:24, OE 16.85.1–4, 12–22; CNTC 11:66.

85. Comm. Colossians 2:14, OE 16.431.4–12; CNTC 11:335.

86. Comm. Galatians 4:24, OE 16.108.21–28; CNTC 11:86.

87. Comm. Galatians 3:24, OE 16.85.12–22; CNTC 11:66.

88. Comm. Colossians 2:14, OE 16.431.14–22; CNTC 11:335.

89. Ibid.

90. Comm. Galatians 4:24, OE 16.108.27–28; CNTC 11:86.

91. *Institutio 1539* VII.38, CO 1:826B; (1:460).

92. Ibid.

93. *Institutio 1539* VII.39, CO 1:827B; (1:461).

94. *Institutio 1539* VII.39, CO 1:827A; (1:461).

95. Comm. Ephesians 2:14, OE 16.191.19–34; CNTC 11:150.
96. Ibid.
97. Comm. Ephesians 2:15, OE 16.192.9–23; CNTC 11:151.
98. Ibid.
99. Comm. 2 Corinthians 3:7, OE 15.56.19–24; CNTC 10:43–44.
100. Ibid.
101. Comm. 2 Corinthians 3:10, OE 15.58–59; CNTC 10:46.
102. Comm. 2 Corinthians 3:12, OE 15.60–61; CNTC 10:46–47.
103. Comm. Hebrews 7:12, OE 19.114.14–23; CNTC 12:96.
104. Comm. Hebrews 2:1, OE 19.30.11–23; CNTC 12:18.
105. Comm. 2 Corinthians 3:12, OE 15.60.20–22; CNTC 10:46.
106. Comm. 2 Corinthians 2:14, OE 15.62.2–5; CNTC 10:47–48.
107. Comm. Hebrews 7:19, OE 19.118.16–20; CNTC 12:100.
108. Comm. Hebrews 7:19, OE 19.118.20–23; CNTC 12:100.
109. Comm. Hebrews 7:25, OE 19.120.4–10; CNTC 12:101.
110. Comm. John 1:18, OE 11/1.37–38; CNTC 4:26.
111. Ibid.
112. Comm. Genesis 32:30, CO 23:446–447; CTS 2:202.
113. Comm. John 1:18, OE 11/1.38.14–18; CNTC 4:26.
114. Comm. Exodus 26:31, CO 24:417B; CTS 4:175–176.
115. Comm. Matthew 27:51, CO 45:782C; CNTC 3:211.
116. Comm. Acts 16:3, CO 48:371B; CNTC 7:65.
117. *Institutio 1539* VII.37, CO 1:825C; (1:459).
118. *Inst.* II.vii.16, OS III.341.1–32; (1:364).
119. *Inst.* II.xi.13, OS III.435.29–32; (1:463).
120. *Inst.* II.xi.13, OS III.435–436; (1:463).
121. Comm. John 4:20, OE 11/1.128.10–14; CNTC 4:97.
122. *Inst.* II.x.20, OS III.420.3–7; (1:446).
123. Comm. John 12:12, OE 11/2.83–84; CNTC 5:29.
124. Comm. Malachi 1:12, CO 44:422B; CTS 30:504.
125. Comm. Romans 9:1, *Romans* 192.27–29; CNTC 8:190.
126. *Inst.* II.x.23, OS III.422.31–35; (1:449).

CHAPTER 5. *Visual Confirmation of the Covenant of Adoption*

1. *Institutio 1536* VI, CO 1:207B; *Inst.* 1536:187.
2. *Institutio 1539* I.19, CO 1:292B; (1:71).
3. Ibid.
4. *Inst.* IV.viii.5, OS V.137.17–19; (2:1153).
5. Comm. Hebrews 1:1, OE 19.16.1–7; CNTC 12:5.
6. Comm. Hebrews 11:27, OE 19.205.11–16; CNTC 12:179.
7. Comm. Hebrews 11:27, OE 19.205.31–35; CNTC 12:179.

8. Comm. Hebrews 12:18, OE 19.228.19–21; CNTC 12:199.

9. Comm. Acts 2:17, CO 48:33B; CNTC 6:58.

10. Comm. Hebrews 11:27, OE 19.205.24–28; CNTC 12:179.

11. Comm. Acts 7:30, CO 48:145B; CNTC 6:190–191.

12. Comm. Acts 7:30, CO 48:145B; CNTC 6:191.

13. Ibid.

14. Ibid.

15. *Institutio 1536* IV.20, CO 1:115A; *Inst.* 1536:99.

16. *Institutio 1539* X.5, CO 1:941; (2:1280).

17. Comm. Acts 7:31, CO 48:145–146; CNTC 6:191.

18. Ibid.

19. Ibid.

20. Ibid.

21. Ibid.

22. Ibid.

23. Comm. Acts 7:31, CO 48:146A; CNTC 6:192.

24. Comm. Genesis 15:1, CO 23:207C; CTS 1:399.

25. Ibid.

26. Ibid.

27. Comm. Genesis 15:2, CO 23:209A; CTS 1:401.

28. Ibid.

29. Comm. Genesis 15:4, CO 23:210C; CTS 1:403.

30. Comm. Genesis 15:4, CO 23:210–211; CTS 1:403–404.

31. Comm. Genesis 15:4, CO 23:211A; CTS 1:404.

32. Comm. Genesis 15:10, CO 23:217A; CTS 1:413–414.

33. Comm. Genesis 15:12, CO 23:217B; CTS 1:414.

34. Ibid.

35. Comm. Genesis 15:17, CO 23:221A; CTS 1:420.

36. Ibid.

37. Comm. Genesis 15:18, CO 23:221B; CTS 1:421.

38. Comm. Genesis 28:12, CO 23:364–365; CTS 2:69.

39. Ibid.

40. Comm. Genesis 28:12, CO 23:365B; CTS 2:70.

41. Ibid.

42. Comm. Genesis 28:12, CO 23:390B; CTS 2:112.

43. Ibid.

44. Comm. Genesis 28:12, CO 23:390C; CTS 2:112.

45. Comm. Genesis 28:12, CO 23:391A; CTS 2:112.

46. Comm. Genesis 28:12, CO 23:391B; CTS 2:113.

47. Comm. Genesis 28:12, CO 23:391C; CTS 2:113–114.

48. Ibid.

49. Comm. Genesis 28:13, CO 23:392A; CTS 2:114.

50. Ibid.

51. Comm. Genesis 46:2, CO 23:559C; CTS 2:387–388.

52. Comm. Genesis 46:2, CO 23:560A; CTS 2:388.

53. Ibid.

54. Comm. Genesis 32:24, CO 23:442A; CTS 2:195.

55. Ibid.

56. Comm. Genesis 32:24, CO 23:422B; CTS 2:195–196.

57. Comm. Genesis 32:29, CO 23:445–446; CTS 2:200–201.

58. Comm. Genesis 32:30, CO 23:446C; CTS 2:202.

59. Comm. Genesis 37:6, CO 23:482C; CTS 2:261.

60. Ibid.

61. Ibid.

62. Comm. Genesis 37:8, CO 23:483B; CTS 2:262.

63. Comm. Genesis 37:9, CO 23:483C; CTS 2:262.

64. Comm. Genesis 37:10, CO 23:484A; CTS 2:263.

65. Comm. Genesis 37:10, CO 23:484B; CTS 2:263–264.

66. Comm. Genesis 37:6, CO 23:481–482; CTS 2:260.

67. Comm. Exodus 3:2, CO 24:36B; CTS 3:62.

68. Comm. Exodus 3:3, CO 24:36B; CTS 3:62.

69. Ibid.

70. Comm. Exodus 3:4, CO 24:36C; CTS 3:63.

71. Comm. Exodus 19:1, CO 24:192C; CTS 3:313.

72. Ibid.

73. Comm. Exodus 19:9, CO 24:198A; CTS 3:321.

74. Comm. Deuteronomy 5:4, CO 24:211B; CTS 3:341.

75. Comm. Exodus 19:16, CO 24:201B; CTS 3:326.

76. Comm. Deuteronomy 5:4, CO 24:211B; CTS 3:341.

77. Comm. Exodus 19:9, CO 24:198B; CTS 3:322.

78. Comm. Exodus 24:9, CO 25:76C; CTS 5:323.

79. Ibid.

80. Ibid.

81. Comm. Exodus 24:9, CO 25:77A; CTS 5:323–324.

82. Comm. Exodus 24:11, CO 25:77B; CTS 5:324.

83. Comm. Exodus 33:15, CO 25:107C; CTS 5:376.

84. Comm. Exodus 33:19, CO 25:109A; CTS 5:378.

85. Comm. Jonah 4:2, CO 43:265C; CTS 28:122.

86. Ibid.

87. Comm. Exodus 33:19, CO 25:110A; CTS 5:380.

88. Comm. Exodus 33:20, CO 25:111A; CTS 5:381–382.

89. Ibid.

90. Comm. Exodus 33:11, CO 25:105B; CTS 5:372.

91. Ibid.

92. Comm. Numbers 12:6, CO 25:182–183; CTS 6:46–47.

93. Comm. Deuteronomy 34:10, CO 25:401–402; CTS 6:409.

94. Comm. Exodus 33:11, CO 25:105B; CTS 5:372.
95. Comm. Numbers 12:6, CO 25:183A; CTS 6:47.
96. Comm. Numbers 12:6, CO 25:182B; CTS 6:45.
97. Comm. Isaiah 6:1, CO 36:126A; CTS 13:200.
98. Comm. Isaiah 6:1, CO 36:125A; CTS 13:198.
99. Comm. Isaiah 6:1, CO 36:126A; CTS 13:200.
100. Comm. Isaiah 6:1, CO 36:126B; CTS 13:200–201.
101. Ibid.
102. Comm. Isaiah 6:1, CO 36:126C; CTS 13:201.
103. Comm. Isaiah 6:2, CO 36:127C; CTS 13:203.
104. Comm. Isaiah 6:2, CO 36:126C; CTS 13:204.
105. Comm. Isaiah 6:4, CO 36:130B; CTS 13:206–207.
106. Comm. Isaiah 6:5, CO 36:130C; CTS 13:207.
107. Comm. Isaiah 6:3, CO 36:128C; CTS 13:204.
108. Comm. Isaiah 6:7, CO 36:132C; CTS 13:210.
109. Comm. Isaiah 6:7, CO 36:133B; CTS 13:211.
110. Comm. Isaiah 6:7, CO 36:134A; CTS 13:212.
111. Ibid.
112. Comm. Isaiah 6:8, CO 36:134A; CTS 13:212.
113. Comm. Isaiah 6:9, CO 36:135B; CTS 13:214.
114. Comm. Isaiah 6:10, CO 36:136C; CTS 13:216.
115. Comm. Ezekiel 1:3, CO 40:29B; CTS 22:62.
116. Comm. Ezekiel 1:1–2, CO 40:26C; CTS 22:58.
117. Comm. Ezekiel 1:1–2, CO 40:27A; CTS 22:59.
118. Comm. Ezekiel 1:4, CO 40:29C; CTS 22:63.
119. Ibid.
120. Comm. Ezekiel 1:13, CO 40:40–41; CTS 22:78–79.
121. Comm. Ezekiel 1:27, CO 40:57–58; CTS 22:103.
122. Comm. Ezekiel 1:25–26, CO 40:52–53; CTS 22:95.
123. Comm. Ezekiel 1:28, CO 40:60B; CTS 22:106.
124. Ibid.
125. Comm. Ezekiel 2:3, CO 40:62–63; CTS 22:110.
126. Ibid.
127. Comm. Daniel 2:2, CO 40:558C; CTS 24:117.
128. Ibid.
129. Comm. Daniel 2:2, CO 40:558–559; CTS 24:117–118.
130. Ibid.
131. Comm. Daniel 2:2, CO 40:559B; CTS 24:119.
132. Comm. Daniel 2:2, CO 40:559B; CTS 24:119.
133. Comm. Daniel 2:2, CO 40:560A; CTS 24:120.
134. Ibid.
135. Ibid.
136. Ibid.

137. Comm. Daniel 7:1–2, CO 41:37B; CTS 25:8–9.
138. Comm. Daniel 7:15–16, CO 41:64B; CTS 25:47.
139. *Institutio 1536* IV.8, CO 1:107B; *Inst.* 1536:92.
140. *Institutio 1536* IV.8, CO 1:108B; *Inst.* 1536:92.
141. *Inst.* IV.xiv.18, OS V.276–277; (2:1294–1295). The only change made in 1559 is to add the light in the smoking fire pot shown to Abram to the list of miraculous sacraments in Scripture.
142. *Institutio 1550* I.27, CO 1:297C; (1:83).
143. Comm. Hebrews 12:18, OE 19.228.19–21; CNTC 12:199.
144. *Institutio 1550* I.27, CO 1:297C; (1:83).
145. *Inst.* I.viii.6, OS III.75.20–24; (1:86).
146. Comm. Isaiah 7:12, CO 36:153A; CTS 13:242.
147. Ibid.
148. Comm. Isaiah 7:10, CO 36:151A; CTS 13:239.
149. Ibid.
150. Comm. Isaiah 38:7, CO 36:652A; CTS 15:161–162.
151. Comm. Isaiah 38:8, CO 36:652C; CTS 15:162–163.
152. Ibid.
153. Comm. Exodus 3:12, CO 24:43A; CTS 3:72.
154. Comm. Exodus 4:8, CO 24:53C; CTS 3:89.
155. Comm. Deuteronomy 13:1, CO 24:277B; CTS 3:443–444.
156. Ibid.
157. Comm. Daniel 3:28, CO 40:642–643; CTS 24:237.
158. Ibid.
159. Comm. Psalm 18:8, CO 31:175A; CTS 8:269.
160. Comm. Psalm 68:8, CO 31:622B; CTS 10:12.
161. Ibid.
162. Comm. Psalm 114:1, CO 32:180A; CTS 11:336–337.
163. Comm. Isaiah 4:5, CO 36:99B; CTS 13:157.
164. Comm. Psalm 136:13, CO 32:366B; CTS 12:186–187.
165. Comm. Exodus 14:13, CO 24:155C; CTS 3:253.
166. Comm. Exodus 14:21, CO 24:153C; CTS 3:249.
167. Comm. Joshua 2:10, CO 25:442B; CTS 7:50.
168. Comm. Isaiah 51:9, CO 37:232–233; CTS 16:76.
169. Comm. Numbers 14:13, CO 25:200A; CTS 6:74–75.
170. Comm. Daniel 9:15–17, CO 41:153A; CTS 25:175.
171. Comm. Isaiah 4:5, CO 36:99B; CTS 13:157.
172. Comm. Psalm 27:9, CO 31:276C; CTS 8:458–459.
173. Ibid.
174. Comm. Psalm 40:5, CO 31:407C; CTS 9:93.
175. Ibid.
176. Comm. Isaiah 5:19, CO 36:116C; CTS 13:185.
177. Ibid.

178. Comm. Psalm 119:76, CO 32:247C; CTS 11:457.
179. Comm. Jeremiah 29:10, CO 38:591C; CTS 19:429.
180. Comm. Jeremiah 33:14, CO 39:63B; CTS 20:247–248.
181. Comm. Isaiah 40:5, CO 37:9B; CTS 15:207.
182. Comm. Joshua 3:10, CO 25:449B; CTS 7:62.
183. Comm. Psalm 48:8, CO 31:476C; CTS 9:225.
184. Ibid.
185. Comm. Psalm 143:6, CO 32:402–403; CTS 12:253–254.
186. Comm. Psalm 74:12, CO 31:697A; CTS 10:173.
187. Ibid.
188. Comm. Psalm 5:12, CO 31:71–72; CTS 8:63.
189. Comm. Psalm 40:4, CO 31:406C; CTS 9:92.
190. Comm. Psalm 69:7, CO 31:640B; CTS 10:53.
191. Comm. Psalm 69:33, CO 31:652; CTS 10:78.
192. Comm. Psalm 34:3, CO 31:336–337; CTS 8:558.
193. Comm. Psalm 40:4, CO 31:407A; CTS 9:92.
194. Comm. Psalm 5:12, CO 31:71–72; CTS 8:63.

CHAPTER 6. *Symbols and Types of Christ in the Law*

1. CO 9:801A; *Calvin: Commentaries*, p. 63.
2. Ibid.
3. *Institutio 1536* IV.9, CO 1:108C; *Inst.* 1536:93.
4. Ibid.
5. *Institutio 1536* IV.8, CO 1:106–107; *Inst.* 1536:91.
6. *Institutio 1536* IV.9, CO 1:108B; *Inst.* 1536:93.
7. *Institutio 1536* IV.52, CO 1:138C; *Inst.* 1536:121.
8. *Institutio 1539* VII.5, CO 1:804C; (1:432).
9. *Institutio 1539* X.23, CO 1:954C; (2:1299).
10. Comm. Romans 4:11, *Romans* 87.41–45; CNTC 8:89.
11. *Institutio 1543* XVI.23, CO 1:954–955; (2:1299).
12. *Institutio 1543* XVI.25, CO 1:955C; (2:1301).
13. Comm. 1 Corinthians 10:3, CO 49:453–454; CNTC 9:203.
14. Ibid.
15. Ibid.
16. Comm. John 5:46, OE 11/1.185.14–24; CNTC 4:143.
17. *Inst.* II.vii.1, OS III.326–327; (1:349).
18. Comm. Acts 26:22, CO 48:545–546; CNTC 7:280.
19. Ibid.
20. *Institutio 1536* IV.9, CO 1:107C; *Inst.* 1536:92.
21. Comm. Genesis 2:9, CO 23:38–39; CTS 1:116–117.
22. Ibid.

23. Ibid.

24. Comm. Genesis 3:22, CO 23:79B; CTS 1:184.

25. Ibid.

26. Comm. Genesis 4:2, CO 23:23B; CTS 1:192.

27. Ibid.

28. Ibid.

29. Comm. Genesis 4:2, CO 23:84C; CTS 1:193–194.

30. *Institutio 1536* IV.50, CO 1:136B; *Inst.* 1536:119.

31. Comm. Genesis 8:20, CO 23:138C; CTS 1:281.

32. Ibid.

33. Comm. Genesis 8:20, CO 23:139A; CTS 1:282.

34. Ibid.

35. *Institutio 1536* IV.42, CO 1:132C; *Inst.* 1536:115.

36. Comm. Hebrews 5:6, OE 19.78–79; CNTC 12:62.

37. Comm. Hebrews 7:1, OE 19.105.22–26; CNTC 12:88.

38. Comm. Hebrews 7:3, OE 19.107.24–25; CNTC 12:90.

39. Comm. Hebrews 7:3, OE 19.107.25–28; CNTC 12:90.

40. Comm. Hebrews 7:1, OE 19.105–106; CNTC 12:88–89.

41. Comm. Hebrews 7:1, OE 19.106.11–21; CNTC 12:89.

42. Comm. Hebrews 7:3, OE 19.107.8–12; CNTC 12:89–90.

43. Comm. Hebrews 7:5, OE 19.109.16–18; CNTC 12:91.

44. Comm. Hebrews 7:7, OE 19.110.9; CNTC 12:92.

45. Comm. Hebrews 7:8, OE 19.110–111; CNTC 12:93.

46. Comm. Hebrews 7:3, OE 19.107.13–15; CNTC 12:90.

47. Comm. Hebrews 7:10, OE 19.112.11–13; CNTC 12:94.

48. Comm. Hebrews 7:10, OE 19.112.21–25; CNTC 12:94.

49. Comm. Hebrews 7:10, OE 19.112–113; CNTC 12:95.

50. Comm. Genesis 14:18, CO 23:201B; CTS 1:388.

51. Comm. Genesis 14:18, CO 23:201C; CTS 1:389.

52. Ibid.

53. Comm. Genesis 14:18, CO 23:202C; CTS 1:390.

54. Comm. Genesis 14:18, CO 23:202–203; CTS 1:390–391.

55. Comm. Genesis 14:19, CO 23:203B; CTS 1:391.

56. Comm. Genesis 14:18, CO 23:200C; CTS 1:387.

57. *Inst.* IV.xviii.2, OS V.419.10–13; (2:1431).

58. *Institutio 1536* IV.9, CO 1:108B; *Inst.* 1536:93.

59. *Institutio 1536* IV.9, CO 1:108–109; *Inst.* 1536:93.

60. *Institutio 1536* V.23, CO 1:118B; *Inst.* 1536:102.

61. *Institutio 1539* XI.22, CO 1:970; (2:1327).

62. *Institutio 1539* XI.32, CO 1:978A; (2:1337).

63. Comm. Genesis 17:9, CO 23:239B; CTS 1:451.

64. Comm. Genesis 17:9, CO 23:239–240; CTS 1:451.

65. Ibid.

66. Comm. Genesis 17:9, CO 23:240B; CTS 1:452.

67. Comm. Genesis 17:11, CO 23:241A; CTS 1:453.

68. Ibid.

69. Comm. Jeremiah 9:25–26, CO 38:56B; CTS 17:508.

70. Comm. Genesis 18:9, CO 23:253A; CTS 1:472.

71. Comm. Genesis 18:22, CO 23:261B; CTS 1:485–486.

72. Comm. Genesis 19:1, CO 23:267A; CTS 1:495.

73. Comm. 1 Corinthians 10:9, CO 49:459B; CNTC 9:209–210.

74. Comm. Exodus 3:2, CO 24:35B; CTS 3:60–61.

75. Comm. Exodus 3:2, CO 24:35C; CTS 3:61.

76. Comm. Exodus 33:14, CO 25:107B; CTS 5:375.

77. Comm. Joshua 5:14, CO 25:463–464; CTS 7:87–88.

78. *Inst.* I.xiii.10, OS III.121.22–25; (1:132–133).

79. *Inst.* I.xiii.10, OS III.122.12–17; (1:133).

80. Comm. Exodus 3:2, CO 24:36A; CTS 3:61–62.

81. *Traité des reliques*, 1543, *Calvin: Tracts and Treatises* I:339.

82. Comm. Acts 8:2, CO 48:174–175; CNTC 6:227.

83. Ibid.

84. Comm. Acts 9:37, CO 48:218B; CNTC 6:278–279.

85. Comm. Acts 9:37, CO 48:218B; CNTC 6:279.

86. Ibid.

87. Comm. Acts 9:37, CO 48:218C; CNTC 6:279.

88. Comm. John 12:7, OE 11/2.81.12–17; CNTC 5:27.

89. Comm. John 19:40, OE 11/2.275.8–13; CNTC 5:189.

90. Comm. John 19:40, OE 11/2.275.20–22; CNTC 5:190.

91. Comm. John 19:40, OE 11/2.275.22–26; CNTC 5:190.

92. Comm. Genesis 23:3, CO 23:323B; CTS 1:579.

93. Ibid.

94. Comm. Genesis 5:24, CO 23:107C; CTS 1:231.

95. Comm. Genesis 50:2, CO 23:612–613; CTS 2:477.

96. Ibid.

97. Ibid.

98. Comm. Mark 16:1, CO 45:794B; CNTC 3:223.

99. Ibid.

100. Comm. Psalm 79:1, CO 31:747C; CTS 10:283.

101. Ibid.

102. Comm. Deuteronomy 21:22–23, CO 24:629A; CTS 5:47.

103. Comm. Deuteronomy 28:26, CO 25:33C; CTS 5:248.

104. Comm. Jeremiah 34:4–5, CO 39:81–82; CTS 20:275.

105. Ibid.

106. Comm. Jeremiah 22:18–19, CO 38:390B; CTS 19:108–109.

107. Comm. Jeremiah 16:1–4, CO 38:240B; CTS 18:304.

108. Comm. Jeremiah 22:18–19, CO 38:390B; CTS 19:108–109.

109. Comm. Jeremiah 20:6, CO 38:339C; CTS 19:23–24.

110. Comm. Jeremiah 36:29–30, CO 39:137B; CTS 20:357.

111. *Inst.* III.xxv.5, OS IV.439.19–25; (2:995).

112. Comm. Genesis 27:27, CO 23:378B; CTS 2:91.

113. *Institutio 1539* VII.25, CO 1:818–819; (1:450–451).

114. *Institutio 1539* VII.26, CO 1:819B; (1:451).

115. *Institutio 1539* VII.27, CO 1:819C; (1:451).

116. Comm. Genesis 46:3, CO 23:560B; CTS 2:388–389.

117. Comm. Leviticus 25:23, CO 24:706B; CTS 5:169.

118. Comm. Deuteronomy 34:1, CO 25:398A; CTS 6:404–405.

119. Comm. Jeremiah 11:1–5, CO 38:102C; CTS 18:78.

120. Comm. Jeremiah 18:16, CO 38:307C; CTS 18:413.

121. Comm. Deuteronomy 6:1, CO 24:246B; CTS 3:395.

122. Comm. Jeremiah 25:3–5, CO 38:475A; CTS 19:247.

123. Comm. 1 Corinthians 5:8, CO 49:383B; CNTC 9:111.

124. Comm. Exodus 12:1, CO 24:285–286; CTS 3:456.

125. Comm. Exodus 12:42, CO 24:142B; CTS 3:231.

126. Comm Exodus 12:1, CO 24:286C; CTS 3:458.

127. Comm. Exodus 12:5, CO 24:289b; CTS 3:462.

128. Comm Exodus 12:1, CO 24:286B; CTS 3:458. In spite of the analogy and similitude Calvin sees between Passover and the Supper, he rarely appeals to the Passover in his discussions of the Supper. The one exception occurs when he appeals to the examination before the Passover to explain why no one can partake of the Supper without a similar examination of faith (*Institutes 1539* XI.50, CO 1:990A; [2:1353]).

129. Comm. Exodus 12:21, CO 24:136B; CTS 3:221.

130. Comm. Exodus 12:5, CO 24:288B; CTS 3:460.

131. Comm. Exodus 12:24, CO 24:291A; CTS 3:465.

132. Comm. Psalm 78:23, CO 31:730C; CTS 10:247.

133. Comm. Exodus 16:4, 14, CO 24:166C, 170A; CTS 3:270, 276.

134. Comm. Exodus 17:7, CO 24:178; CTS 3:289–290.

135. Comm. 1 Corinthians 10:1, CO 49:451–452; CNTC 9:201.

136. *Institutio 1536* I.13, CO 1:36B; *Inst.* 1536:23.

137. *Institutio 1536* I.13, CO 1:36–37; *Inst.* 1536:23.

138. *Institutio 1536* I.13, CO 1:37A; *Inst.* 1536:24.

139. *Institutio 1536* I.14, CO 1:37B; *Inst.* 1536:24.

140. *Institutio 1536* I.15, CO 1:38A; *Inst.* 1536:24.

141. *Catechismus*, CO 5:329B; *Catechism*, p. 13.

142. Ibid.

143. *Institutio 1539* III.51, CO 1:402B; (1:395).

144. *Institutio 1539* III.51, CO 1:402C; (1:396).

145. *Institutio 1539* III.53, CO 1:403C; (1:397).

146. *Institutio 1543* III.56, CO 1:405B; (1:399–400).

147. Comm. Exodus 20:8, CO 24:577A; CTS 4:434.

148. Ibid.

149. Comm. Exodus 20:10, CO 24:580B; CTS 4:439.

150. Comm. Exodus 20:8, CO 24:577A; CTS 4:434.

151. Comm. Exodus 20:8, CO 24:577C; CTS 4:435.

152. Comm. Ezekiel 20:12, CO 40:485C; CTS 23:302.

153. Comm. Ezekiel 20:12, CO 40:486A; CTS 23:303.

154. Comm. Exodus 24:5, CO 25:75A; CTS 5:320.

155. Comm. Exodus 24:5, CO 25:75C; CTS 5:321.

156. Comm. Hebrews 9:20, OE 19.146.20–23; CNTC 12:126.

157. Comm. Hebrews 8:5, OE 19.125–126; CNTC 12:107.

158. Comm. Hebrews 9:9, OE 19.137.17–21; CNTC 12:118.

159. Comm. Hebrews 9:24, OE 19.149.16–23; CNTC 12:128.

160. Comm. Acts 7:44, CO 48:158–159; CNTC 6:207–208.

161. Comm. Exodus 25:8, CO 24:404C; CTS 4:153–154.

162. Ibid.

163. Ibid.

164. Comm. Exodus 26:1, CO 24:415C; CTS 4:172.

165. Ibid.

166. Comm. Exodus 25:31, CO 24:409–410; CTS 4:163.

167. Comm. Exodus 26:31, CO 24:417B; CTS 4:175.

168. *Defensio Doctrinae de Sacramentis*, CO 9:221B; *Tracts and Treatises* II.228–229.

169. *Institutio 1536* V.64, CO 1:189–190; *Inst.* 1536:169–170.

170. Comm. Hebrews 5:1, OE 19.74.19–21; CNTC 12:58.

171. Comm. Exodus 28, CO 24:426B; CTS 4:191.

172. Ibid.

173. Ibid.

174. Comm. Exodus 28:2, CO 24:428C; CTS 4:194.

175. Comm. Exodus 28:4, CO 24:429–430; CTS 4:196–197.

176. Comm. Exodus 28:9, CO 24:431–432; CTS 4:199.

177. Comm. Exodus 28:4, CO 24:430–431; CTS 4:198.

178. Comm. Exodus 28:31, CO 24:432C; CTS 4:200–201.

179. Comm. Exodus 39:1, CO 25:71–72; CTS 5:314–315.

180. Comm. Leviticus 16:3, CO 24:501C; CTS 4:315.

181. Comm. Leviticus 21:1, CO 24:448B; CTS 4:227.

182. Comm. Numbers 6:2, CO 24:304C; CTS 3:487.

183. Comm. Numbers 3:5, CO 24:444B; CTS 4:220–221.

184. Ibid.

185. Comm. Numbers 17:8, CO 25:231B; CTS 6:127.

186. Comm. Numbers 20:25, CO 25:243B; CTS 6:146.

187. *Institutio 1536* IV.9, CO 1:109B; *Inst.* 1536:93–94.

188. *Institutio 1536* IV.51, CO 1:136–137; *Inst.* 1536:119–120.

189. *Institutio 1539* IV.23, CO 1:527B; (1:510).
190. *Institutio 1539* XII.67, CO 1:1034C; (2:1440).
191. Comm. Hebrews 9:13, OE 19.141.11–15; CNTC 12:121.
192. Comm. Hebrews 10:1, OE 19.154.22–26; CNTC 12:133.
193. Comm. Psalm 26:7, CO 31:267–268; CTS 8:445.
194. Comm. Psalm 18:2, CO 31:170C; CTS 8:260.
195. Comm. Psalm 57:11, CO 31:553C; CTS 9:358.
196. Comm. Psalm 66:15, CO 31:615B; CTS 9:475–476.
197. Comm. Hosea 4:8, CO 42:278A; CTS 26:155.
198. Comm. Amos 5:21–23, CO 43:94B; CTS 27:288.
199. Comm. Hosea 5:6, CO 42:303C; CTS 26:192–193.
200. Comm. Exodus 29, CO 24:489–490; CTS 4:295.
201. Comm. Exodus 29, CO 24:489A; CTS 4:293.
202. Comm. Exodus 29, CO 24:490A; CTS 4:295.
203. Comm. Leviticus 3:1, CO 24:513A; CTS 4:333.
204. Comm. Exodus 29, CO 24:490C; CTS 4:294.
205. Comm. Leviticus 16:2, CO 24:501A; CTS 4:314.
206. Comm. Leviticus 1:5, CO 24:508B; CTS 4:326.
207. Comm. Leviticus 6:1, CO 24:526–527; CTS 4:357–358.
208. Comm. Leviticus 4:22, CO 24:519B; CTS 4:345.
209. Comm. Leviticus 6:1, CO 24:526C; CTS 4:357.
210. Comm. Leviticus 17:10, CO 24:619–620; CTS 5:31.
211. Comm. Leviticus 4:22, CO 24:519B; CTS 4:345.
212. *Institutio 1536* IV.9, CO 1:108C; *Inst.* 1536:93.
213. *Institutio 1536* IV.9, CO 1:109B; *Inst.* 1536:93.
214. Comm. John 19:34, OE 11/2.270.10–15; CNTC 5:186.
215. Comm. Psalm 51:7, CO 31:518A; CTS 9:297–298.
216. Comm. Psalm 51:7, CO 31:515C; CTS 9:294.
217. Comm. Leviticus 12:2, CO 24:312; CTS 3:499.
218. Comm. Leviticus 15:2, CO 24:329C; CTS 4:32.
219. Comm. Numbers 21:8, CO 25:249; CTS 6:155–156.
220. Ibid.
221. Comm. John 3:14, OE 11/1.98.13–17; CNTC 4:72.
222. Comm. John 3:14, OE 11/1.98.27–29; CNTC 4:73.
223. Comm. John 3:14, OE 11/1.98.29–30; CNTC 4:73.
224. Comm. Romans 3:18, *Romans* 64.31–32; CNTC 8:67.
225. Comm. Acts 4:25, CO 48:91B; CNTC 6:124.
226. Comm. Acts 13:33, CO 48:301A; CNTC 6:378.
227. Ibid.
228. Comm. John 19:28, OE 11/2.266.1–7; CNTC 5:183.
229. Comm. Psalm 2:1–3, CO 31:42–43; CTS 8:11.
230. Comm. Psalm 2:7, CO 31:46C; CTS 8:17.
231. Comm. Psalm 2:7, CO 31:46–47; CTS 8:17–18.

232. Comm. Psalm 110:1, CO 32:160B; CTS 11:297.

233. Comm. Psalm 21:5, CO 31:215A; CTS 8:347–348.

234. Comm. Psalm 118:25, CO 32:210C; CTS 11:391–392.

235. Comm. Psalm 2:9, CO 31:48B; CTS 8:20.

236. Comm. Psalm 18:21, CO 31:181; CTS 8:282.

237. Comm. Psalm 18:1, CO 31:169A; CTS 8:256–257.

238. Comm. Psalm 18:44, CO 31:190A; CTS 8:299.

239. Comm. Psalm 2:1–3, CO 31:42–43; CTS 8:11.

240. Comm. Psalm 18:44, CO 31:190B; CTS 8:300.

241. Comm. Numbers 24:17, CO 25:293C; CTS 6:227–228.

242. Comm. Joshua Argumentum, CO 25:423–424; CTS 7:xxii.

243. Comm. Psalm 68:19, CO 31:628B; CTS 10:26.

244. Comm. Psalm 89:31, CO 31:822B; CTS 10:440.

245. Ibid.

246. Ibid.

247. Comm. Isaiah 33:17, CO 36:572A; CTS 15:32.

248. Ibid.

249. Comm. Psalm 22:1, CO 31:219B; CTS 8:356.

250. Comm. Psalm 41:10, CO 31:422C; CTS 9:122.

251. Comm. Psalm 20:9, CO 31:211–212; CTS 8:341–342.

252. Ibid.

253. Comm. Psalm 84:9, CO 31:783; CTS 10:364.

254. Comm. Jeremiah 17:25, CO 38:290A; CTS 18:385.

255. Comm. Micah 4:6–7, CO 43:355A; CTS 28:277.

256. *Inst.* II.vi.2, OS III.322.21–22; (1:343).

257. *Inst.* II.vi.3, OS III.324.7–9; (1:345).

258. *Inst.* II.vi.2, OS III.323.30–31; (1:344–345).

259. Comm. Acts 6:14, CO 48:127B; CNTC 6:169.

260. Comm. John 4:20, OE 11/1.128.13–14; CNTC 4:97.

261. Comm. John 7:14, OE 11/1.234–235; CNTC 4:184–185.

262. Comm. Psalm 78:69, CO 31:745A; CTS 10:278–279.

263. Comm. Psalm 78:69, CO 31:745B; CTS 10:279.

264. Comm. Haggai 1:7–8, CO 44:89A; CTS 29:332.

265. Comm. Haggai 2:6–9, CO 44:106C; CTS 29:361.

266. Ibid.

267. Comm. Haggai 2:6–9, CO 44:108B; CTS 29:364.

268. Comm. Jeremiah 7:8, CO 37:676B; CTS 17:369.

269. Comm. Jeremiah 7:22, CO 37:690A; CTS 17:391–392.

270. Comm. Jeremiah 17:26, CO 38:292B; CTS 18:389.

271. Comm. Ezekiel 4:1–3, CO 40:104–105; CTS 22:171.

272. Comm. Psalm 40:6, CO 31:413A; CTS 9:104.

273. Comm. Psalm 68:16, CO 31:625C; CTS 10:20–21.

274. Comm. Psalm 78:70, CO 31:745C; CTS 10:280.

275. Comm. Psalm 122:4, CO 32:305A; CTS 12:74.
276. *Inst.* II.vii.2, OS III.328.3–5; (1:350).
277. Comm. Jeremiah 17:26, CO 38:291C; CTS 18:387.
278. Comm. Jeremiah 33:17–18, CO 39:70A; CTS 20:257–258.

CHAPTER 7. *Symbols of the Presence of God to Israel*

1. Comm. Isaiah 6:1, CO 36:126B; CTS 13:200.
2. Comm. Genesis 3:8, CO 23:65C; CTS 1:161.
3. Ibid.
4. Comm. Genesis 33:8, CO 23:451B; CTS 2:210.
5. Comm. Isaiah 1:25, CO 36:53A; CTS 13:79.
6. Comm. Isaiah 10:3, CO 36:212A; CTS 13:335.
7. Comm. Isaiah 64:1, CO 37:406C; CTS 16:361–362.
8. *Institutio 1539* III.25, CO 1:385C; (1:102).
9. Comm. 1 Corinthians 10:1, CO 49:452B; CNTC 9:201.
10. Comm. Psalm 105:39, CO 32:113B; CTS 11:202.
11. Comm. Psalm 78:17, CO 31:728B; CTS 10:242.
12. Comm. Psalm 99:6, CO 32:53A; CTS 11:80–81.
13. Ibid.
14. Comm. Exodus 13:21, CO 24:145B; CTS 3:236.
15. Comm. Exodus 13:21, CO 24:145–146; CTS 3:236–237.
16. Comm. Exodus 16:9, CO 24:168C; CTS 3:274.
17. Comm. Exodus 34:5, CO 25:113B; CTS 5:385.
18. Comm. Numbers 9:18, CO 25:160A; CTS 6:8.
19. Comm. Exodus 13:21, CO 24:145–146; CTS 3:236–237.
20. *Institutio 1539* III.25, CO 1:386A; (1:102).
21. Comm. Genesis 3:23, CO 23:186C; CTS 1:186.
22. Ibid.
23. Comm. Psalm 3:4, CO 31:55B; CTS 8:32–33.
24. Ibid.
25. Ibid.
26. Comm. Psalm 9:11, CO 31:102B; CTS 8:122.
27. Comm. Psalm 26:8, CO 31:268–269; CTS 8:446–447.
28. Comm. Psalm 28:2, CO 31:281C; CTS 8:466–467.
29. Comm. Psalm 42:2, CO 31:426–427; CTS 9:130.
30. Comm. Psalm 84:2, CO 31:780C; CTS 10:355.
31. Ibid.
32. Comm. Exodus 16:32, CO 24:174–175; CTS 3:284.
33. Comm. Exodus 26:1, CO 24:415A; CTS 4:172.
34. Comm. Exodus 30:23, CO 24:445C; CTS 4:223.
35. Comm. Leviticus 26:11, CO 25:16A; CTS 5:219.

36. Comm. Exodus 40:34, CO 25:125–126; CTS 5:406.
37. Comm. Exodus 25:8, CO 24:403A; CTS 4:150.
38. Comm. Numbers 9:17, CO 25:159B; CTS 6:7.
39. Comm. Exodus 25:8, CO 403A; CTS 4:151.
40. Comm. Romans 9:4, *Romans* 196.64–69; CNTC 8:194.
41. Comm. Psalm 27:8, CO 31:276B; CTS 8:458.
42. Ibid.
43. Ibid.
44. Ibid.
45. Comm. Psalm 78:61, CO 31:741B; CTS 10:271.
46. Comm. Psalm 132:8, CO 32:346A; CTS 12:151.
47. Comm. Psalm 84:7, CO 31:783A; CTS 10:363.
48. Comm. Psalm 24:7, CO 31:248A; CTS 8:410.
49. Comm. Psalm 78:59, CO 31:740–741.
50. Comm. Psalm 105:4, CO 32:99A; CTS 11:174.
51. Comm. Psalm 132:8, CO 32:346A; CTS 12:151.
52. Comm. Psalm 78:59, CO 31:740–741; CTS 10:270–271.
53. Comm. Isaiah 46:2, CO 37:154A; CTS 15:434–435.
54. Comm. Numbers 10:36, CO 25:163C; CTS 6:14.
55. Comm. Joshua 3:4, CO 25:447B; CTS 7:59.
56. Comm. Exodus 25:8, CO 403A; CTS 4:151.
57. Comm. Exodus 19:1, CO 24:192C; CTS 3:313.
58. Comm. Exodus 32:19, CO 25:91B; CTS 5:348.
59. Comm. Exodus 25:12, CO 24:399C; CTS 4:145.
60. Comm. Acts 7:49, CO 48:160–161; CNTC 6:210.
61. Ibid.
62. Ibid.
63. Ibid.
64. Comm. John 5:3, OE 11/1.152–153; CNTC 4:117.
65. Ibid.
66. Ibid.
67. Comm. John 12:20, OE 11/2.91.3–17; CNTC 5:36.
68. Comm. Acts 17:24, CO 48:412A; CNTC 7:114.
69. Ibid.
70. Comm. Matthew 1:23, CO 45:68–69; CNTC 1:68–69.
71. Comm. Psalm 24:7, CO 31:248C; CTS 8:410.
72. Ibid.
73. Comm. Psalm 122:2, CO 32:303C; CTS 12:71.
74. Comm. Psalm 132:14, CO 32:350A; CTS 12:157.
75. Comm. Psalm 20:7, CO 31:248A; CTS 8:409.
76. Comm. Psalm 20:7, CO 31:248B; CTS 8:410.
77. Comm. Psalm 102:15, CO 32:68B; CTS 11:111–112.
78. Comm. Daniel 3:2–7, CO 40:625C; CTS 24:213.

79. Comm. Psalm 20:3, CO 31:208C; CTS 8:335.
80. Comm. Psalm 24:7, CO 31:248A; CTS 8:409.
81. Comm. Psalm 20:7, CO 31:210B; CTS 8:339.
82. Comm. Psalm 134:3, CO 32:356B; CTS 12:169.
83. Comm. Psalm 96:9, CO 32:41A; CTS 11:55.
84. Comm. Psalm 27:4, CO 31:273–274; CTS 8:454.
85. Comm. Psalm 24:7, CO 31:248B; CTS 8:410.
86. Comm. Psalm 24:8, CO 31:249B; CTS 8:412.
87. Comm. Psalm 47:6, CO 31:469B; CTS 9:211.
88. Comm. Isaiah 66:1, CO 37:437B; CTS 16:411.
89. Ibid.
90. Comm. Amos 4:2, CO 43:54–55; CTS 27:226–227.
91. Ibid.
92. Comm. Jonah 2:7, CO 43:243A; CTS 28:85.
93. Comm. Deuteronomy 12:7, CO 24:393A; CTS 4:132–133.
94. Comm. Deuteronomy 12:5, CO 24:392B; CTS 4:131–132.
95. Comm. Jeremiah 14:21, CO 38:201B; CTS 18:241.
96. Comm. Jeremiah 28:1–2, CO 38:563–564; CTS 19:385–386.
97. Comm. Psalm 99:5, CO 32:51B; CTS 11:77–78.
98. Ibid.
99. Comm. Psalm 132:7, CO 32:345B; CTS 12:149–150.
100. Ibid.
101. Comm. Psalm 132:7, CO 32:345C; CTS 12:150.
102. Comm. Jeremiah 14:21, CO 38:201B; CTS 18:241.
103. Comm. Psalm 132:14, CO 32:350B; CTS 12:157–158.
104. Comm. Jeremiah 7:1–4, CO 37:673B; CTS 17:365.
105. Comm. Ezekiel 10:4, CO 40:211–212; CTS 22:325–326.
106. Comm. Ezekiel 10:18–19, CO 40:222B; CTS 22:341.
107. Comm. Ezekiel 10:19, CO 40:222–223; CTS 22:342.
108. Ibid.
109. Comm. Psalm 132:14, CO 32:350A; CTS 12:157.
110. Comm. Psalm 48:1, CO 31:472–473; CTS 8:217–218.
111. Ibid.
112. Comm. Psalm 135:15, CO 32:363A; CTS 12:181.
113. Comm. Psalm 48:11, CO 31:479C; CTS 9:230–231.
114. Ibid.
115. Comm. Psalm 48:14, CO 31:480B; CTS 9:232.
116. Comm. Psalm 125:1, CO 32:313C; CTS 12:89–90.
117. Comm. Psalm 125:1, CO 32:314B; CTS 12:91.
118. Comm. Ezekiel 5:5–6, CO 40:121–122; CTS 22:195–196.
119. Comm. Psalm 48:14, CO 31:480B; CTS 9:232.
120. Comm. Psalm 48:4, CO 31:475C; CTS 9:223.
121. Comm. Psalm 76:2, CO 31:706A; CTS 10:194.

122. Comm. Jeremiah 22:8, CO 38:379B; CTS 19:88.
123. Comm. Lamentations 3:45, CO 39:595C; CTS 21:439.
124. Comm. Ezekiel 9:8, CO 40:203C; CTS 22:314.
125. Comm. Daniel 6:10, CO 41:10–11; CTS 24:361.
126. Comm. John 5:3, OE 11/1.152.18–19; CNTC 4:117.
127. Comm. Deuteronomy 18:17, CO 24:274A; CTS 3:438.
128. Comm. Jeremiah 23:33, CO 38:449B; CTS 19:206.
129. Ibid.
130. Comm. Ezekiel 3:25–26, CO 40:102B; CTS 22:167.
131. Comm. Ezekiel 13:19, CO 40:291B; CTS 23:32.
132. Comm. Isaiah 37:16, CO 36:627B; CTS 15:121–122.
133. Comm. John 5:37, OE 11/1.179.11–20; CNTC 4:138.
134. *Institutio 1536* I.10, CO 1:33B; *Inst.* 1536:20.
135. *Institutio 1536* I.10, CO 1:33–34; *Inst* 1536:20–21.
136. *Institutio 1539* III.29, CO 1:389A; (1:108).
137. *Institutio 1550* III.29, CO 1:389C; (1:109).
138. Comm. Acts 3:12, CO 48:67B; CNTC 6:96.
139. Comm. Acts 7:40, CO 48:153B; CNTC 6:201.
140. Ibid.
141. Comm. Acts 7:40, CO 48:153–154; CNTC 6:201.
142. Ibid.
143. Comm. Acts 7:40, CO 48:154A; CNTC 6:201.
144. Ibid.
145. Comm. Acts 7:49, CO 48:161A; CNTC 6:210.
146. Comm. Acts 17:24, CO 48:411A; CNTC 7:113.
147. Ibid.
148. Comm. Acts 17:24, CO 48:411B; CNTC 7:113.
149. Ibid.
150. Comm. Acts 17:24, CO 48:411C; CNTC 7:114.
151. Comm. Acts 17:24, CO 48:412A; CNTC 7:114.
152. Ibid.
153. Comm. Genesis 33:21, CO 23:454B; CTS 2:215.
154. Comm. Psalm 115:4, CO 32:186C; CTS 11:348–349.
155. Comm. Psalm 115:8, CO 32:187C; CTS 11:350–351.
156. *Inst.* I.xiii.1, OS III.108–109; (1:121).
157. Comm. Hosea 13:2, CO 42:477B; CTS 26:453.
158. Comm. Exodus 34:17, CO 24:382B; CTS 4:116.
159. Comm. Deuteronomy 12:7, CO 24:393A; CTS 4:132–133.
160. Comm. Deuteronomy 12:5, CO 24:392B; CTS 4:131–132.
161. *Inst.* IV.i.5, OS V.10.32–40; (2:1020).
162. Comm. Exodus 32:1, CO 25:80–81; CTS 5:330.
163. Ibid.
164. Ibid.

165. Ibid.
166. Comm. Psalm 42:2, CO 31:427A; CTS 9:130.
167. Comm. Isaiah 40:20, CO 37:20A; CTS 15:224.
168. Comm. Matthew 17:5, CO 45:487–488; CNTC 2:200–201.
169. Ibid.
170. Comm. Daniel 3:6–7, CO 40:620B; CTS 24:205–206.
171. Comm. Deuteronomy 4:12, CO 24:384–385; CTS 4:119–120.
172. Ibid.
173. Comm. Deuteronomy 4:12, CO 24:385A; CTS 4:120.
174. Ibid.
175. Ibid.
176. Ibid.
177. Ibid.
178. Comm. Amos 4:2, CO 43:54–55; CTS 27:226–227.

CHAPTER 8. *The Manifestation of Judgment and Restoration in the Prophets*

1. *Institutio 1536* VI.15, CO 1:206A; *Inst.* 1536:186.
2. Ibid.
3. Ibid.
4. Ibid.
5. *Inst.* IV.viii.3, OS V.135.30–32; (2:1152).
6. *Inst.* IV.viii.6, OS V.138.1–8; (2:1153).
7. *Inst.* IV.viii.6, OS V.138.8–11; (2:1153–1154).
8. *Institutio 1550* I.29, CO 1:298B; (1:88).
9. Ibid.
10. Comm. Isaiah 36:1, CO 36:600A; CTS 15:77.
11. Ibid.
12. Ibid.
13. Comm. Jeremiah 39:1, CO 39:180–181; CTS 20:421.
14. Comm. Jeremiah 51:39, CO 39:476–477; CTS 21:255.
15. Ibid.
16. Comm. Isaiah 6:1, CO 36:126A; CTS 13:200.
17. Comm. Jeremiah 24:1–2, CO 38:457–458; CTS 19:221.
18. Comm. Ezekiel 1:1–2, CO 40:27A; CTS 22:59.
19. Comm. Daniel Argumentum, CO 40:529C; CTS 24:78.
20. Comm. Daniel 1:17, CO 40:554C; CTS 24:113.
21. Comm. Ezekiel 3:14, CO 40:86B; CTS 22:144.
22. Comm. Deuteronomy 31:3, CO 25:343A; CTS 6:213–313.
23. Comm. Isaiah 50:7, CO 37:221A; CTS 16:57.
24. Comm. Jeremiah 20:3, CO 38:336C; CTS 19:18.

25. Comm. Jeremiah 15:16, CO 38:226–227; CTS 18:283.

26. *Inst.* IV.i.5, OS V.8.29–32; (2:1017).

27. *Inst.* IV.i.5, OS V.9.32–33; (2:1018).

28. *Inst.* IV.i.5, OS V.9.33–37; (2:1018–1019).

29. Comm. Haggai 1:12, CO 44:95B; CTS 29:343.

30. Comm. Jeremiah 36:7, CO 39:121B; CTS 20:333–334.

31. Comm. Exodus 14:31, CO 24:156B; CTS 3:254.

32. See Roland M. Frye, "Calvin's Theological Use of Figurative Language," in *John Calvin and the Church,* ed. Timothy George (Louisville, KY: Westminster John Knox Press, 1990), 172–194; David F. Wright, "Calvin's Accommodation Revisited," in *Calvin as Exegete,* ed. Peter de Klerk (Grand Rapids, MI: Calvin Studies Society, 1995); and "Calvin's Accommodating God," in *Calvinus Sincerioris Religionis Vindex,* ed. Wilhelm H. Neuser and Brian G. Armstrong (Kirksville, MO: Sixteenth Century Essays and Studies), 3–19.

33. *Institutio 1539* VIII.53, CO 1:900–901; (1:227).

34. *Institutio 1539* VIII.53, CO 1:901A; (1:227).

35. Comm. Genesis 6:6, CO 23:118A; CTS 1:249.

36. Comm. Jonah 3:10, CO 43:261C; CTS 28:116.

37. *Institutio 1543* XI.40, CO 1:828A; (1:463).

38. Calvin also appeals to God's accommodation to human capacities when speaking of the creation of angels. He realizes that Moses says nothing about their creation, though they appear soon after in his narrative in Genesis, but Calvin explains this as being due to the fact that Moses narrates nothing but what can be seen by the human eye. "To be sure, Moses, accommodating himself (*se accommodet*) to the rudeness of the common folk, mentions in the history of the creation no other works of God than those which show themselves to our own eyes. Yet afterward when he introduces angels as ministers of God, one may easily infer that he to whom they devote their efforts and functions, is their Creator" (*Institutes 1543* VI.29, CO 1:497A; [1:162]).

39. Comm. 1 Corinthians 3:2, CO 49:347B; CNTC 9:66.

40. Comm. Genesis 35:7, CO 23:469B; CTS 2:238.

41. Comm. Hosea 12:10, CO 42:469A; CTS 26:440–441.

42. Ibid.

43. Comm. Isaiah 40:18, CO 37:19C; CTS 15:223.

44. Comm. Zechariah 1:7–11, CO 44:139C; CTS 30:37.

45. Comm. Genesis 6:6, CO 23:118A; CTS 1:249.

46. Comm. Psalm 10:1, CO 31:108–109; CTS 8:134–135.

47. Comm. Exodus 2:23, CO 24:34A; CTS 3:59.

48. Comm. Psalm 14:4, CO 31:139A; CTS 8:195–196.

49. Comm. Isaiah 1:30, CO 36:57C; CTS 13:87.

50. Comm. Hosea 13:8, CO 42:484A; CTS 26:464.

51. Comm. Psalm 23:1, CO 31:238C; CTS 8:391–392.

52. Comm. Zephaniah 3:16–17, CO 44:72–73; CTS 29:305.

53. Ibid.

54. Comm. Psalm 81:14, CO 31:765C; CTS 10:323.

55. Comm. Psalm 135:13, CO 32:362B; CTS 12:179. "God assumes, as we shall see, the character of a father who is grievously offended, and who, while he is offended at his son, still more pities him, and is naturally inclined to exercise compassion, because the warmth of his love rises above his anger" (Comm. Isaiah 27:4, CO 36:450B; CTS 14:250).

56. Comm. Isaiah 63:9, CO 37:398B; CTS 16:346.

57. Comm. Isaiah 42:14, CO 37:69C; CTS 15:302.

58. Ibid.

59. Comm. Isaiah 46:3, CO 37:154–155; CTS 15:436.

60. Ibid.

61. Comm. Isaiah 49:15, CO 37:204C; CTS 16:30–31.

62. Ibid.

63. Ibid.

64. Comm. Isaiah 49:15, CO 37:204–205; CTS 16:31.

65. Comm. Isaiah 49:15, CO 37:205A; CTS 16:31.

66. Comm. Isaiah 63:9, CO 37:398B; CTS 16:346.

67. Comm. Psalm 35:2, CO 31:346C; CTS 8:575–576.

68. Ibid.

69. Comm. Psalm 91:3, CO 32:3A; CTS 10:480.

70. Ibid.

71. Comm. Psalm 35:2, CO 31:346C; CTS 8:575–576.

72. *Institutio 1539* VII.20, CO 1:815–816; (1:447).

73. Ibid.

74. *Institutio 1539* VII.26, CO 1:819A; (1:451).

75. Comm. Isaiah 30:25, CO 36:524–525; CTS 14:375.

76. Ibid.

77. Comm. Jeremiah 31:12, CO 38:660B; CTS 20:82.

78. Comm. Jeremiah 31:12, CO 38:660C; CTS 20:82–83.

79. Comm. Jeremiah 33:15, CO 39:67A; CTS 20:253.

80. Comm. Jeremiah 31:12, CO 38:660C; CTS 20:82–83.

81. Comm. Daniel 7:27, CO 41:82B; CTS 25:73.

82. Ibid.

83. Ibid.

84. Comm. Jeremiah 23:5–6, CO 38:410A; CTS 19:141.

85. Comm. Jeremiah 23:5–6, CO 38:410B; CTS 19:142.

86. Ibid.

87. Comm. Jeremiah 23:5–6, CO 38:410C; CTS 19:142.

88. Comm. Hosea 1:2, CO 42:204C; CTS 26:45.

89. Comm. *De Clementia* I.vi, pp. 121–123.

90. *Ad Herennium* IV.lv.68.

91. Ibid.

92. Seneca, *Epistulae Morales* LIX.6.

93. CO 5:177A; *Tracts and Treatises* III.419.

94. CO 6:229–230; *The Bondage and Liberation of the Will*, p. 3.

95. Comm. 2 Timothy 1:13, CO 52:356C; CNTC 10:301.

96. Comm. Isaiah 5:1, CO 36:102B; CTS 13:162.

97. Comm. Isaiah 28:8, CO 36:467A; CTS 14:277–278.

98. Comm. Hosea 1:2, CO 42:204C; CTS 26:45.

99. Comm. Jeremiah 5:13, CO 37:623A; CTS 17:281.

100. Comm. Isaiah 2:10, CO 36:71A; CTS 13:110.

101. Comm. Isaiah 5:14, CO 36:112C; CTS 13:179.

102. Comm. Isaiah 8:1, CO 36:165–166; CTS 13:261–262.

103. Comm. Isaiah 13:10, CO 36:263A; CTS 13:418.

104. Ibid.

105. Comm. Isaiah 34:4, CO 36:581B; CTS 15:47.

106. Comm. Jeremiah 13:1–9, CO 38:155B; CTS 18:163.

107. Comm. Jeremiah 46:14, CO 39:292B; CTS 20:586–587.

108. Comm. Isaiah 7:21, CO 36:162A; CTS 13:255.

109. Comm. Isaiah 19:6, CO 36:332C; CTS 14:54–55.

110. Comm. Zephaniah 1:10, CO 44:18C; CTS 29:211.

111. Comm. Jeremiah 4:15, CO 37:588A; CTS 17:222–223.

112. Comm. Micah 1:8–9, CO 43:292C; CTS 28:170.

113. Comm. Jeremiah 9:17–18, CO 38:43C; CTS 17:487.

114. Comm. Jeremiah 14:17, CO 38:195–196; CTS 18:230–231.

115. Comm. Jeremiah 31:15–16, CO 38:664–665; CTS 20:89.

116. Comm. Isaiah 9:2, CO 36:189C; CTS 13:298.

117. Comm. Isaiah 13:4, CO 36:259C; CTS 13:412.

118. Comm. Isaiah 43:6, CO 37:84A; CTS 15:324.

119. Comm. Isaiah 61:10, CO 37:379C; CTS 16:315–316.

120. Comm. Habakkuk 3:3, CO 43:569B; CTS 29:141–142.

121. Comm. Isaiah 34:6, CO 36:582C; CTS 15:49.

122. Comm. Joel 3:9–11, CO 42:590B; CTS 27:127.

123. Comm. Zechariah 14:4, CO 44:364B; CTS 30:411.

124. Ibid.

125. Comm. Jeremiah 49:3, CO 39:349C; CTS 21:59.

126. Comm. Isaiah 15:3, CO 36:296C; CTS 13:472–473.

127. Comm. Isaiah 15:5, CO 36:297A; CTS 13:473.

128. Comm. Acts 21:10–11, CO 48:478C; CNTC 7:196.

129. Comm. Acts 21:10–11, CO 48:478–479; CNTC 7:196.

130. Ibid.

131. Ibid.

132. Ibid.

133. Comm. Isaiah 20:2, CO 36:351B; CTS 14:86.

134. Ibid.

135. Comm. Isaiah 20:2, CO 36:352C; CTS 14:88.
136. Comm. Isaiah 20:2, CO 36:351B; CTS 14:86.
137. Ibid.
138. Comm. Jeremiah 13:1–9, CO 38:154B; CTS 18:161–162.
139. Ibid.
140. Ibid.
141. Comm. Jeremiah 16:2, CO 38:238C; CTS 18:302.
142. Comm. Jeremiah 18:1–6, CO 38:295C; CTS 18:394.
143. Comm. Jeremiah 19:10, CO 38:329C; CTS 18:447.
144. Comm. Jeremiah 19:11, CO 38:330A; CTS 18:448.
145. Comm. Jeremiah 27:1–5, CO 38:541–542; CTS 19:352.
146. Comm. Jeremiah 27:1–5, CO 38:542B; CTS 19:253.
147. Ibid.
148. Comm. Jeremiah 43:8–10, CO 39:242A; CTS 20:512.
149. Comm. Jeremiah 43:8–10, CO 39:242B; CTS 20:513.
150. Comm. Jeremiah 51:60–64, CO 39:501B; CTS 21:292.
151. Comm. Jeremiah 33:43–44, CO 39:48A; CTS 20:224.
152. Comm. Ezekiel 4:1–3, CO 40:104B; CTS 22:170.
153. Comm. Jeremiah 28:10–11, CO 38:573–574; CTS 19:401.
154. Ibid.
155. Comm. Jeremiah 28:10–11, CO 38:574B; CTS 19:402.
156. Comm. Jeremiah 28:14, CO 38:576–577; CTS 19:405.
157. Comm. Isaiah 1:1, CO 36:27B; CTS 13:36.
158. Comm. Isaiah 30:10, CO 36:514B; CTS 14:358.
159. Comm. Daniel 8:2–3, CO 41:89B; CTS 25:83.
160. Comm. Isaiah 2:2, CO 36:61A; CTS 13:93.
161. Ibid.
162. Comm. Isaiah 40:9, CO 37:14A; CTS 15:214.
163. Comm. Isaiah 49:13, CO 37:203C; CTS 16:29.
164. Comm. Haggai 2:6–9, CO 44:104A; CTS 29:357.
165. Ibid.
166. Comm. Daniel 11:31–32, CO 41:254A; CTS 25:321.
167. Comm. Isaiah 21:3, CO 36:356–357; CTS 14:95.
168. Comm. Isaiah 60:4, CO 37:356B; CTS 16:278.
169. Comm. Lamentations 1:14, CO 39:525–526; CTS 21:330.
170. Comm. Jeremiah 31:26, CO 38:683C; CTS 20:119.
171. Comm. Habakkuk 2:6, CO 43:540B; CTS 29:92.
172. Comm. Isaiah 60:5, CO 37:357B; CTS 16:279.
173. Comm. Psalm 137:8, CO 32:371B; CTS 12:196–197.
174. Comm. Zechariah 9:9, CO 44:269C; CTS 30:251.
175. Comm. Isaiah 42:1, CO 37:58–59; CTS 15:285.
176. Comm. Psalm 126:1, CO 32:317B; CTS 12:96.
177. Comm. Isaiah 52:8, CO 37:248C; CTS 16:101.

178. Comm. Zechariah 2:10, CO 44:163C; CTS 30:75.
179. Comm. Isaiah 52:10, CO 37:249–250; CTS 16:103.
180. Comm. Jeremiah 33:17–18, CO 39:71B; CTS 20:260.
181. Comm. Zechariah 2:10, CO 44:162–163; CTS 30:74.
182. Comm. Haggai 2:6–9, CO 44:108B; CTS 29:364.

CHAPTER 9. *The Living Image of God in Jesus Christ*

1. Comm. 1 Peter 1:19, CO 55:225B; CNTC 12:248. "A corollary of this is the truth that Christ cannot be rightly understood apart from the Old Testament. Even after his advent, Moses and the prophets are not made superfluous. They continue to witness to him. Apart from them we cannot understand who the Messiah of Israel is" (Hesselink, *Calvin's Concept of the Law*, p. 163).

2. Stephen Edmondson acknowledges that Calvin describes Christ as the image of the invisible God, due to the way the fountain of every good thing appears in him after it has been lost in creation. However, he claims that for Calvin Christ is the image of God as a result of Christ's saving work as Mediator, which Edmondson takes to be the heart of Christ's work. Edmondson acknowledges that this is primarily a matter of emphasis, as his interest is in emphasizing the threefold office of Christ. I highlight Christ as the image of the invisible God because of its relationship to the self-revelation of God as the author and fountain of every good thing in creation, to which Edmondson does not attend. But he is certainly correct to note that Christ would not be the living image of God were he not also the Mediator. See Stephen Edmondson, *Calvin's Christology* (Cambridge: Cambridge University Press, 2004), pp. 3, 176.

3. CO 9:819A; *Calvin: Commentaries*, p. 72.
4. *Institutio 1536* III.1, CO 1:81–82; *Inst. 1536*:68.
5. *Catechismus*, CO 5:337C; *Catechism*, p. 21.
6. *Institutio 1539* IV.1, CO 1:477B–C; (1:544).
7. Ibid.
8. *Institutio 1543* II.39, CO 1:329A; (1:279).
9. Comm. John 6:46, 47; OE 11/1.212; CNTC 4:165–166.
10. Comm. Matthew 11:27, CO 45:320C; CNTC 2:24.
11. Comm. 2 Corinthians 4:4, OE 15.73.10–23; CNTC 10:55–56.
12. Ibid.
13. Ibid.
14. Comm. Hebrews 1:3, OE 19.18–19; CNTC 12:8.
15. Ibid.
16. Comm. 1 John 2:22, CO 55:325B; CNTC 5:260–261.
17. Comm. Hebrews 1:3, OE 19.19.4–20; CNTC 12:8.
18. Comm. 2 Corinthians 4:4, OE 15.75–76; CNTC 10:57–58.
19. Ibid.

20. Comm. 1 John 2:22, CO 55:325B; CNTC 5:260–261.
21. Comm. Hebrews 1:3, OE 19.18–19; CNTC 12:8.
22. Comm. 1 John 2:22, CO 55:325B; CNTC 5:260–261.
23. Comm. Colossians 2:9, OE 16.425.15–25; CNTC 11:331.
24. Ibid.
25. Comm. Colossians 2:3, OE 16.419.22–32; CNTC 11:326.
26. Comm. Colossians 2:9, OE 16.425.15–25; CNTC 11:331.
27. Comm. Colossians 1:15, OE 16.398.8–22; CNTC 11:308.
28. Ibid.
29. Comm. John 14:10, OE 11/2.143.15–25; CNTC 5:78.
30. Comm. Philippians 2:6, OE 16. 321.23–31.
31. *Institutio 1539* IV.14, CO 1:486C; (1:137).
32. Comm. Genesis 28:12, CO 23:391A; CNTC 2:112–113.
33. Comm. 1 Peter 1:20, CO 55:226; CNTC 12:250.
34. Comm. Acts 20:21, CO 48:463–464; CNTC 7:177.
35. Comm. John 5:22, OE 11/1.165.6–17; CNTC 4:127.
36. *Inst.* II.vi.4, OS III.325–326; (1:347).
37. Comm. John 8:19, OE 11/1.269.7–25; CNTC 4:213.
38. Comm. Acts 20:21, CO 48:463–464; CNTC 7:177.
39. Comm. 1 Peter 1:20, CO 55:226; CNTC 12:250.
40. Ibid.
41. Comm. 1 Timothy 3:16, CO 52:290A; CNTC 10:233.
42. Comm. John 17:22, OE 11/2.224.14–17; CNTC 5:149.
43. Comm. Acts 20:21, CO 48:463–464; CNTC 7:177.
44. Comm. Colossians 2:3, OE 16.419.22–32; CNTC 11:326.
45. Comm. 2 Corinthians 4:4, OE 15.75–76; CNTC 10:57–58.
46. CO 9:805C; *Calvin: Commentaries,* p. 65.
47. CO 9:805–806; *Calvin: Commentaries,* p. 66.
48. *Institutio 1539* IV.14, CO 1:486A; (1:136).
49. *Institutio 1539* IV.14, CO 1:486B; (1:136–137).
50. Comm. Philippians 2:7, OE 16.322; CNTC 11:248–249.
51. Ibid.
52. Comm. John 1:14, OE 11/1.32.8–16; CNTC 4:21.
53. Comm. Acts 2:22, CO 48:37B; CNTC 6:63.
54. Ibid.
55. Comm. John 1:32, OE 11/1.50.4–22; CNTC 4:34–35.
56. Ibid. See also Comm. Isaiah 42:3, CO 37:61A; CTS 15:288.
57. Comm. John 3:2, OE 11/1.84.12–24; CNTC 4:62.
58. Ibid.
59. Comm. John 3:2, OE 11/1.84–85; CNTC 4:62.
60. Ibid.
61. Comm. Mark 3:20, CO 45:334B; CNTC 2:39.
62. Comm. Matthew 12:23, CO 45:334C; CNTC 2:39.

63. Comm. Luke 11:16, CO 45:351–352; CNTC 2:57.
64. Comm. Luke 23:8, CO 45:753A; CNTC 3:181.
65. Comm. John 1:14, OE 11.1.32.8–16; CNTC 4:21.
66. Comm. John 2:11, OE 11/1.70.3–11; CNTC 4:50.
67. Comm. John 5:19, OE 11/1.163.3–9; CNTC 4:125.
68. Comm. John 5:36, OE 11/1.178.17–19; CNTC 4:137.
69. Comm. John 11:1, OE 11/2.50.19–27; CNTC 5:1.
70. Comm. John 11:45, OE 11/2.70.7–14; CNTC 5:17.
71. Comm. Matthew 8:17, CO 45:156A; CNTC 1:163.
72. Comm. Mark 7:32, CO 45:461–462; CNTC 2:173.
73. Comm. Matthew 12:16, CO 45:330B; CNTC 2:35.
74. Comm. Matthew 12:17, CO 45:330–331; CNTC 2:35.
75. *Institutio 1539* IV.12, CO 1:519–520; (1:476).
76. *Institutio 1543* VII.12, CO 1:520A; (1:476).
77. Comm Philippians 2:7, OE 16.322.16–19; CNTC 11:248.
78. Comm Philippians 2:7, OE 16.322.19–24; CNTC 11:248.
79. Comm. Hebrews 4:15, OE 19.71.3–8; CNTC 12:55.
80. Comm. Hebrews 5:7, OE 19.80.24–27; CNTC 12:64.
81. Comm. Hebrews 5:7, OE 19.79.21–26; CNTC 12:63.
82. Comm. Hebrews 10:20, OE 19.163–164; CNTC 12:141.
83. Comm. Romans 8:3, *Romans* 159.23–29; CNTC 8:159.
84. Comm. John 6:41, OE 11/1.209.7–13; CNTC 4:163.
85. Comm. John 11:41, OE 11/2.68.3–13; CNTC 5:16.
86. Comm. John 17:3, OE 11/2.210.9–15; CNTC 5:137.
87. Comm. John 12:23, OE 11/2.92.15–17; CNTC 5:36–37.
88. Comm. John 12:12, OE 11/2.83.21–26; CNTC 5:29.
89. Comm. John 12:23, OE 11/2.92.2–7; CNTC 5:36–37.
90. Comm. John 12:27, OE 11/2.96.19–22; CNTC 5:39.
91. Comm. John 13:31, OE 11/2.130.3–10; CNTC 5:68.
92. Comm. John 14:1, OE 11/2.135–136; CNTC 5:73.
93. Comm. John 14:1, OE 11/2.137.8–29; CNTC 5:74.
94. *Institutio 1536* II.14, CO 1:69B; *Inst.* 1536:55.
95. Comm. John 18:32, OE 11/2.244.1–10; CNTC 5:164–165.
96. Comm. John 19:17, OE 11/2.259.3–15; CNTC 5:178.
97. Comm. Luke 2:16, CO 45:78–79; CNTC 1:79.
98. Ibid.
99. Comm. Luke 2:40, CO 45:104B; CNTC 1:107.
100. Ibid.
101. Comm. Matthew 14:23, CO 45:440–441; CNTC 2:151.
102. Comm. Matthew 17:9, CO 45:490B; CNTC 2:203.
103. *Inst.* II.xiii.2, OS III.451.2–6; (1:476).
104. Comm. Matthew 21:1–9, CO 45:571–572; CNTC 2:291.
105. Ibid.

106. Comm. Matthew 26:18, CO 45:699B; CNTC 3:127.

107. Ibid.

108. Comm. Matthew 26:29, CO 45:709A; CNTC 3:137.

109. Comm. Matthew 26:37, CO 45:719C; CNTC 3:147–148.

110. Comm. Matthew 26:57–61, CO 45:735–736; CNTC 3:163–164.

111. Ibid.

112. Comm. Matthew 27:11, CO 45:750–751; CNTC 3:179.

113. Comm. Matthew 27:24, CO 45:759B; CNTC 3:187.

114. Ibid.

115. Comm. Matthew 27:39, CO 45:769C; CNTC 3:198.

116. Comm. Matthew 27:46, CO 45:779A; CNTC 3:207.

117. *Institutio 1536* II.15, CO 1:69C; *Inst.* 1536:55.

118. Comm. Matthew 27:46, CO 45:779B; CNTC 3:208.

119. Comm. Matthew 27:46, CO 45:780A; CNTC 3:208.

120. Comm. Matthew 27:40, CO 45:770B; CNTC 3:199.

121. Comm. Philippians 2:8, OE 16.323.23–24; CNTC 11:249.

122. Comm. Matthew 27:45, CO 45:777–778; CNTC 3:206.

123. Comm. Matthew 27:54, CO 45:784C; CNTC 3:213.

124. Comm. Matthew 27:57–61, CO 45:787A; CNTC 3:215–216.

125. Ibid.

126. *Institutio 1536* II.16, CO 1:70B; *Inst.* 1536:56.

127. *Institutio 1539* IV.30, CO 1:531B; (1:520).

128. Comm. Romans 1:4, *Romans* 14.25–30; CNTC 8:16.

129. Comm. Romans 1:4, *Romans* 15.43–45; CNTC 8:17.

130. Comm. 2 Corinthians 13:4, OE 15.210–211; CNTC 10:171.

131. Comm. Acts 1:3, CO 48:4A; CNTC 6:24.

132. Ibid.

133. Comm. Acts 13:33, CO 48:301A; CNTC 6:378.

134. Comm. Acts 13:33, CO 48:301C; CNTC 6:378–379.

135. Comm. John 6:61, OE 11/1.222.21–33; CNTC 4:174. Not surprisingly, in his commentary on the Psalms of 1557, Calvin says that Psalm 2:7 "has a principal allusion to the day of his resurrection" (Comm. Psalm 2:7, CO 31:46–47; CTS 8:17–18).

136. *Inst.* II.xvi.13, OS III.500.16–19; (1:521).

137. Comm. John 12:23, OE 11/2.92.15–19; CNTC 5:37.

138. Comm. Isaiah 53:3, CO 37:256C; CTS 16:114.

139. Comm. John 12:45, OE 11/2.110.18–21; CNTC 5:51.

140. Comm. John 20:28, OE 11/2.301.1–7; CNTC 5:211.

141. Comm. 1 John 1:1, CO 55:299C; CNTC 5:234.

142. *Institutio 1536* II.17, CO 1:70C; *Inst.* 1536:56.

143. Ibid.

144. *Institutio 1536* II.17, CO 1:71A; *Inst.* 1536:56.

145. *Catechismus*, CO 5:340:B; *Catechism*, p. 24.

146. *Institutio 1539* IV.31, CO 1:532B; (1:522).

147. Comm. Hebrews 8:1, OE 19.123.7–13; CNTC 12:104.
148. *Institutio 1539* IV.31, CO 1:532C; (1:523).
149. *Institutio 1543* VII.31, CO 1:533A; (1:523).
150. Comm. John 7:38, OE 11/1.253.9–22; CNTC 4:199.
151. Comm. Ephesians 4:10, OE 16.227.8–12; CNTC 11:177.
152. Comm. Ephesians 4:10, OE 16.227.12–15; CNTC 11:177.
153. Comm. Acts 1:9, CO 48:11–12; CNTC 6:33.
154. Ibid.
155. Comm. Acts 3:21, CO 48:72C; CNTC 6:102.
156. Comm. John 20:17, OE 11/2.287.5–11; CNTC 5:199.
157. *Institutio 1539* XII.17, CO 1:1001C; (2:1369).
158. Comm. John 5:26, 27, OE 11/1.172.1–5; CNTC 4:132.
159. Ibid.
160. Comm. 1 Corinthians 15:27, CO 49:549B; CNTC 9:327.
161. Comm. Philippians 2:9, OE 16.324–325; CNTC 11:250.
162. Ibid.
163. Comm. Psalm 22:7, CO 31:224C; CTS 8:366.
164. Comm. John 3:16, OE 11/1.100.4–7; CNTC 4:74.
165. Comm. John 13:31, OE 11/2.130.16–22; CNTC 5:68.
166. Comm. John 13:32, OE 11/2.130–131; CNTC 5:69.
167. Comm. Colossians 2:15, OE 16.432.21–29; CNTC 11:336.
168. Comm. Isaiah 53:12, CO 37:267A; CTS 16:131.
169. Comm. Romans 1:4, *Romans* 14.27–28; CNTC 8:16.
170. Comm. Isaiah 53:2, CO 37:256C; CTS 16:114.
171. Comm. John 14:9, OE 11/2.143.7–14; CNTC 5:78.
172. Comm. John 17:1, OE 11/2.208.12–13; CNTC 5:135.
173. *De Scandalis*, OS II.173.10–17; *Concerning Scandals*, p. 19.
174. Comm. Isaiah 53:10, CO 37:263B; CTS 16:125.
175. Comm. 1 Peter 2:3, CO 55:233B; CNTC 12:258.
176. Comm. 1 John 1:1, CO 55:299B; CNTC 5:233.
177. Comm. Isaiah 53:8, CO 37:261C; CTS 16:121.
178. Comm. 1 John 4:9, CO 55:352–353; CNTC 5:290.
179. Ibid.
180. CO 9:803B; *Calvin: Commentaries*, p. 64.
181. Comm. John 5:37, OE 11/1.178–179; CNTC 4:137–138.
182. Ibid.
183. Comm. John 5:37, OE 11/1.179.11–20; CNTC 4:138.
184. Comm. John 5:39, OE 11/1.180.11–21; CNTC 4:139.
185. Comm. Isaiah 53:2, CO 37:256A; CTS 16:113.
186. CO 9:815B; *Calvin: Commentaries*, p. 70.
187. Comm. John 12:14, OE 11/2.87–88; CNTC 5:32–33.
188. Ibid.
189. Comm. Zechariah 9:10, CO 44:272–273; CTS 30:256–257.

190. Comm. John 19:28, OE 11/2.266.1–7; CNTC 5:183.
191. Comm. Micah 4:6–7, CO 43:355A; CTS 28:277.
192. Comm. Isaiah 52:14, CO 37:252C; CTS 16:108.
193. Comm. Psalm 118:25, CO 32:210C; CTS 11:391–392.
194. Comm. Numbers 6:22, CO 24:460A; CTS 4:246.
195. Comm. Matthew 26:3, CO 45:692–693; CNTC 3:121.
196. Comm. John 4:20, OE 11/1.128.3–14; CNTC 4:97.
197. Comm. John 19:30, OE 11/2.267.3–8; CNTC 5:183.
198. Comm. John 19:34, OE 11/2.270–271; CNTC 5:186.
199. Comm. Matthew 6:29, CO 45:434–435; CNTC 2:144.
200. Comm. John 12:7, OE 11/2.81.12–29; CNTC 5:27.
201. Comm. John 19:40, OE 11/2.275.8–28; CNTC 5:189–190.
202. Comm. Matthew 26:12, CO 45:696A; CNTC 3:123.
203. Comm. Matthew 16:1, CO 45:794B; CNTC 3:223.
204. Comm. John 19:40, OE 11/2.275.8–28; CNTC 5:189–190.
205. Comm. John 12:7, OE 11/2.81.12–29; CNTC 5:27.
206. Comm. John 5:3, OE 11/1.152–153; CNTC 4:117.
207. Comm. John 5:3, OE 11/1.153.24–34; CNTC 4:118.
208. Comm. John 7:14, OE 11/1.234–235; CNTC 4:184–185.
209. Comm. John 12:20, OE 11/2.91.3–17; CNTC 5:35–36.
210. Comm. Matthew 1:23, CO 45:68–69; CNTC 1:68–69.
211. Comm. Luke 2:25, CO 45:89A; CNTC 1:90–91.
212. Comm. Luke 2:36, CO 45:95A; CNTC 1:97.
213. Comm. Luke 2:48, CO 45:106B; CNTC 1:109.
214. Comm. Matthew 21:12, CO 45:580–581; CNTC 3:4.99.
215. Ibid.
216. Ibid.
217. Comm. Matthew 23:38, CO 45:644B; CNTC 3:70.
218. Comm. Matthew 23:38, CO 45:644C; CNTC 3:70.
219. Ibid.
220. Comm. Matthew 24:1, CO 45:648B; CNTC 3:74.
221. Ibid.
222. Comm. Matthew 24:2, CO 45:648C; CNTC 3:74.
223. Ibid.
224. Comm. Matthew 23:38, CO 45:644B; CNTC 3:70.
225. Comm. Matthew 24:1, CO 45:648B; CNTC 3:74.
226. Comm. Matthew 24:21, CO 45:660–661; CNTC 3:87.
227. Ibid.
228. Ibid.
229. Comm. Matthew 24:15, CO 45:659–660; CNTC 3:86.
230. Ibid.
231. Comm. Matthew 27:51, CO 45:782B; CNTC 3:211.
232. Comm. Daniel 9:27, CO 41:188B; CTS 25:226.

233. Comm. Daniel 12:11–12, CO 41:302B; CTS 25:391.

234. Comm. Daniel 9:27, CO 41:190A; CTS 25:229.

235. Comm. Daniel 9:26, CO 41:186A; CTS 25:222–223.

236. Comm. Daniel 9:26, CO 41:186B; CNT 25:223.

237. Comm. Matthew 24:21, CO 45:660–661; CNTC 3:87.

CHAPTER 10. *The Gospel as the Living Portrait of Jesus Christ*

1. CO 9:803B; *Calvin: Commentaries,* p. 64.

2. Ibid.

3. Ibid.

4. *Psychopannychia,* CO 5:185C; *Tracts and Treatises* III:429.

5. *Institutio 1536* II.3, OS 1:57B; *Inst.* 1536:43.

6. *Catechismus,* CO 5:332C; *Catechism,* p. 16.

7. *Catechismus,* CO 5:334C; *Catechism,* p. 19.

8. *Institutio 1539* IV.2, CO 1:478A.

9. *Responsio ad Sadoleti Epistolam,* OS I.482; *A Reformation Debate,* ed. John C. Olin (Grand Rapids, MI: Baker Books, 1976), p. 84.

10. *Institutio 1539* IV.12, CO 1:459C; (1:565).

11. Comm. Romans 1:17, *Romans* 26.38–42; CNTC 8:28.

12. *Institutio 1539* IV.13, CO 1:460A; (1:565–566).

13. *Institutio 1539* V.8, CO 1:690C; (1:601).

14. *Institutio 1539* XII.66, CO 1:1034A; (2:1439).

15. *Institutio 1543* III.28, CO 1:388A; (1:107).

16. Comm. Romans 1:3, *Romans* 13.89–95; CNTC 8:15.

17. Comm. 2 Corinthians 1:19, OE 15.28–29; CNTC 10:21.

18. Ibid.

19. Comm. Galatians 3:1, OE 16.59–60; CNTC 11:46–47.

20. Ibid.

21. Ibid.

22. Ibid.

23. Comm. Galatians 3:1, OE 16.60–61; CNTC 11:47.

24. Ibid.

25. Ibid.

26. Comm. Colossians 1:12, OE 16.395–396; CNTC 11:306.

27. Ibid.

28. Comm. Hebrews 9:20, OE 19.146–147; CNTC 12:126.

29. Comm. John 3:14, OE 11/1.97–98; CNTC 4:72.

30. Comm. John 16:12, OE 11/2.191.19–29; CNTC 5:120.

31. Comm. John 20:29, OE 11/2.302.10–28; CNTC 5:212.

32. Comm. Acts 1:1, CO 48:2A; CNTC 6:22.

33. Ibid.

34. Comm. John Argumentum, OE 11/1.8–9; CNTC 4:6.
35. Comm. Harmony of the Gospels Argumentum, CO 45:2–3; CNTC 1:xii.
36. Ibid.
37. Comm. Matthew 4:5, CO 45:133C; CNTC 1:139.
38. Comm. 2 Corinthians 3:18, OE 15.66.9–16; CNTC 10:50.
39. Comm. 2 Corinthians 4:4, OE 15.72–73; CNTC 10:55.
40. Ibid.
41. Comm. 2 Corinthians 3:18, OE 15.66.9–16; CNTC 10:50.
42. Comm. Titus 3:4, CO 52:428–429; CNTC 10:380.
43. Comm. James 1:23–25, CO 55:395B; CNTC 3:273.
44. Ibid.
45. Ibid.
46. Comm. 1 John 2:3, CO 55:311A; CNTC 5:245.
47. Ibid.
48. Comm. Acts 4:4, CO 48:81B; CNTC 6:113.
49. Comm. John 14:12, OE 11/2.145.11–18; CNTC 5:80.
50. Comm. Luke 2:30, CO 45:90B; CNTC 1:92.
51. Comm. Matthew 13:16, CO 45:362B; CNTC 2:68–69.
52. Ibid.
53. Comm. Matthew 26:75, CO 45:744–745; CNTC 3:172–173.
54. Ibid.
55. Ibid.
56. Ibid.
57. Comm. 2 Corinthians 3:18, OE 15.66.9–16; CNTC 10:50.
58. Comm. 2 Corinthians 4:6, OE 15.75.13–20; CNTC 10:57.
59. Comm. Acts 9:18, CO 48:209A; CNTC 6:267–268.
60. Comm. John 14:19, OE 11/2.149.15–26; CNTC 5:84.
61. Comm. Luke 2:29, CO 45:89–90; CNTC 1:91–92.
62. Comm. Matthew 16:17, CO 45:473C; CNTC 2:185.
63. Ibid.
64. Ibid.
65. Ibid.
66. Comm. Luke 23:42, CO 45:774B; CNTC 3:202–203.
67. *Institutio 1536, Epistola Nuncupatoria*, CO 1:15B; *Inst.* 1536:5.
68. Ibid.
69. *Institutio 1536, Epistola Nuncupatoria*, CO 1:16B; *Inst.* 1536:6.
70. *Institutio 1536, Epistola Nuncupatoria*, CO 1:15C; *Inst.* 1536:5.
71. Comm. 1 Corinthians 1:23, CO 49:328A; CNTC 9:42.
72. Comm. Hebrews 2:4, OE 19.32.6–21; CNTC 12:20.
73. Ibid.
74. Ibid.
75. Comm. Acts 2:22, CO 48:38B; CNTC 6:63–64.
76. Ibid.

77. Comm. Acts 3:9, CO 48:65–66; CNTC 6:93.
78. Ibid.
79. Comm. Acts 14:3, CO 48:319A; CNTC 7:3.
80. Ibid.
81. Comm. Acts 14:3, CO 48:319B; CNTC 7:3.
82. Comm. Acts 19:11–12, CO 48:445B; CNTC 7:154–155.
83. Ibid.
84. Comm. Mark 16:17, CO 45:825B; CNTC 3:254.
85. Ibid.
86. Ibid.
87. Ibid.
88. Comm. Acts 2:2, CO 48:25–26; CNTC 6:50.
89. Comm. Acts 2:2, CO 48:26–27; CNTC 50–51.
90. Ibid.
91. Comm. Acts 4:31, CO 48:94B; CNTC 6:128.
92. Ibid.
93. Comm. Acts 1:5, CO 48:6–7; CNTC 6:27.
94. Comm. Acts 8:16, CO 48:182–183; CNTC 6:236.
95. Comm. Acts 10:44, CO 48:250–251; CNTC 6:317.
96. Ibid.
97. Comm. John 1:51, OE 11/1.61–62; CNTC 4:43.
98. Comm. Acts 21:9, CO 48:477–478; CNTC 7:194–195.
99. Comm. Matthew 27:52, CO 45:783–784; CNTC 3:213.
100. Comm. Acts 9:10, CO 48:205C; CNTC 6:264.
101. Ibid.
102. Ibid.
103. Comm. Acts 10:12, CO 48:231A; CNTC 6:294.
104. Comm. Acts 10:12, CO 48:231C; CNTC 6:294.
105. Comm. Acts 10:17, CO 48:234A; CNTC 6:297.
106. Comm. Acts 10:30, CO 48:239C; CNTC 6:304.
107. Comm. Acts 16:9, CO 48:374C; CNTC 7:69.
108. Comm. Acts 16:10, CO 48:375B; CNTC 7:70.
109. Ibid.
110. Comm. Daniel 11:3, CO 41:221A; CTS 25:273. See also Comm. Zechariah 9:16, in which Calvin says that this account is no doubt true: CO 44:283B; CTS 30:275.
111. Comm. Luke 24:37, CO 45:812B; CNTC 3:241.
112. Comm. Acts 18:9, CO 48:428B; CNTC 7:133–134.
113. Ibid.
114. Comm. Acts 7:55, CO 48:167A; CNTC 6:217.
115. Ibid.
116. Comm. Acts 7:55, CO 48:167B; CNTC 6:218.
117. Ibid.

118. Comm. Acts 7:56, CO 48:167–168; CNTC 6:218.
119. Comm. Acts 9:3, CO 48:200A; CNTC 6:257.
120. Comm. Acts 26:13, CO 48:541C; CNTC 7:275.
121. Comm. 1 Timothy 1:15, CO 52:259C; CNTC 10:198.
122. Ibid.
123. Comm. 1 Timothy 1:16, CO 52:261A; CNTC 10:199.
124. Comm. John 4:10, *John* I.120.8–24; CNTC 4:90.
125. Ibid.
126. Comm. Matthew 9:9, CO 45:248B; CNTC 1:262.
127. Ibid.
128. *Institutio 1536* IV.1, CO 1:102A; *Inst.* 1536:87.
129. Ibid.
130. *Institutio 1536* IV.1, CO 1:102B; *Inst.* 1536:87.
131. *Institutio 1536* IV.1, CO 1:102–103; *Inst.* 1536:87–88.
132. *Institutio 1536* IV.2, CO 1:103A; *Inst.* 1536:88.
133. Ibid.
134. *Institutio 1536* IV.2, CO 1:103B; *Inst.* 1536:88.
135. *Institutio 1536* IV.8, CO 1:108A; *Inst.* 1536:93.
136. *Institutio 1536* IV.9, CO 1:108B; *Inst.* 1536:92.
137. *Institutio 1536* IV.4, CO 1:104C; *Inst.* 1536:89.
138. *Institutio 1536* IV.4, CO 1:105B; *Inst.* 1536:90.
139. Ibid.
140. *Institutio 1536* IV.7, CO 1:107A; *Inst.* 1536:91.
141. *Institutio 1536* IV.9, CO 1:108C; *Inst.* 1536:93.
142. *Institutio 1536* IV.10, CO 1:109C; *Inst.* 1536:94.
143. *Catechismus,* CO 5:349C; *Catechism,* p. 34.
144. *Catechismus,* CO 5:349B; *Catechism,* p. 33.
145. *Catechismus,* CO 5:349C; *Catechism,* p. 33.
146. Ibid.
147. *Institutio 1539* X.5, CO 1:941A; (2:1280).
148. Ibid.
149. *Institutio 1539* X.9, CO 1:944A; (2:1284).
150. *Institutio 1539* X.5, CO 1:941B; (2:1280).
151. *Institutio 1539* X.9, CO 1:944B; (2:1284).
152. *Institutio 1539* X.5, CO 1:945B; (2:1286).
153. *Institutio 1539* X.14, CO 1:945A; (2:1289).
154. Ibid.
155. *Institutio 1539* X.17, CO 1:950–951; (2:1293).
156. *Institutio 1543* XVI.1, CO 1:939A; (1:1277).
157. *Institutio 1543* XVI.2, CO 1:939B; (1:1277–1278).
158. *Institutio 1543* XVI.3, CO 1:940A; (1:1278).
159. *Institutio 1543* XVI.4, CO 1:940A; (1:1279).
160. Ibid.

161. *Institutio 1543* XVI.4, CO 1:940C; (1:1279).

162. Ibid.

163. *Institutio 1543* XVI.15, CO 1:948C; (1:1290).

164. *Institutio 1543* XVI.15, CO 1:949B; (1:1291).

165. *Institutio 1543* XVI.16, CO 1:949B; (1:1291).

166. *Institutio 1543* XVI.16, CO 1:950A; (1:1292).

167. *Catechismus Ecclesiae Genevensis*, OS II.130.17–20; *Calvin: Theological Treatises*, p. 131.

168. *Catechismus Ecclesiae Genevensis*, OS II.131.3–6; *Calvin: Theological Treatises*, p. 131.

169. *Catechismus Ecclesiae Genevensis*, OS II.131.15–18; *Calvin: Theological Treatises*, p. 131.

170. *Catechismus Ecclesiae Genevensis*, OS II.132.13–18; *Calvin: Theological Treatises*, p. 132.

171. *Catechismus Ecclesiae Genevensis*, OS II.132.19–26; *Calvin: Theological Treatises*, p. 132.

172. *Vera Ecclesiae Reformandae Ratio*, CO 7:621A; *Calvin: Tracts and Treatises* III.277.

173. Ibid.

174. *Vera Ecclesiae Reformandae Ratio*, CO 7:622–623; *Calvin: Tracts and Treatises* III.279–280.

175. *Vera Ecclesiae Reformandae Ratio*, CO 7:623A; *Calvin: Tracts and Treatises* III.280.

176. Ibid.

177. *Defensio Sanae et Orthodoxae Doctrinae de Sacramentis*, CO 9:22B; *Tracts and Treatises* II:229.

178. Ibid.

179. *Defensio Sanae et Orthodoxae Doctrinae de Sacramentis*, CO 9:25C; *Tracts and Treatises* II:232.

180. *Secundo Defensio Piae et Orthodoxae de sacramentis Fidei contra Ioachimi Westphali Calumnias*, CO 9:84A; *Tracts and Treatises* II:296.

181. *Ultima Admonitio Ioannis Calvini ad Ioachimum Westphalum*, CO 9:202C; *Tracts and Treatises* II.428.

182. Comm. Jonah 2:4, CO 43:240A; CTS 28:81.

183. *Institutio 1536* V.64, CO 1:189C; *Inst.* 1536:169.

184. *Institutio 1536* V.64, CO 1:189B; *Inst.* 1536:169.

185. *Institutio 1536* V.64, CO 1:1190C; *Inst.* 1536:170.

186. *Institutio 1536* V.65, CO 1:1190C; *Inst.* 1536:170.

187. Ibid.

188. *Institutio 1536* V.65, CO 1:1191A; *Inst.* 1536:171.

189. Ibid.

190. Ibid.

191. *Institutio 1536* V.65, CO 1:1191B; *Inst.* 1536:171.

192. *Institutio 1536* V.67; CO 1:192C; *Inst.* 1536:172.

193. *Institutio 1536* V.64, CO 1:191C; *Inst.* 1536:170.

194. *Institutio 1539* XVI.33–35, CO 1:1095–1097.

195. *Projet d'Ordonnances Ecclesiastiques*, CO 10:18A; *Calvin: Theological Treatises*, p. 59.

196. *Projet d'Ordonnances Ecclesiastiques*, CO 10:18C; *Calvin: Theological Treatises*, pp. 59–60.

197. *Institutio 1543* VIII.50, CO 1:571B; (2:1066–1067).

198. *Institutio 1543* VIII.50, CO 1:571C; (2:1067).

199. Ibid.

200. *Supplex exhortatio ad Caesarem*; *Calvin: Theological Treatises*, p. 210.

201. *Institutio 1543* VIII.50, CO 1:572A; (2:1068).

202. *Institutio 1543* XVI.20, CO 1:952–953; (2:1296).

203. *Institutio 1543* XIX.30, CO 1:1086C; (2:1476).

204. Ibid.

205. *Institutio 1543* XIX.33, CO 1:1094C; (2:1479).

206. Comm. 1 Timothy 4:14, CO 52:302–303; CNTC 10:247.

207. Comm. 2 Timothy 1:6, CO 52:349–350; CNTC 10:293.

208. Ibid.

209. Ibid.

210. *Vera Ecclesiae Reformandae Ratio*, CO 7:632A; *Tracts and Treatises* III:291.

211. Ibid.

212. Comm. Acts 6:6, CO 48:122C; CNTC 6:163.

213. *Institutio 1536* V.3, CO 1:142C; *Inst.* 1536:125–126.

214. *Institutio 1536* V.5, CO 1:144C; *Inst.* 1536:127.

215. Ibid.

216. *Institutio 1536* V.9, CO 1:146–147; *Inst.* 1536:129.

217. *Institutio 1536* V.10, CO 1:147A; *Inst.* 1536:130.

218. *Institutio 1543* XIX.4, CO 1:1068C; (2:1452).

219. Ibid.

220. *Institutio 1543* XIX.4, CO 1:1069A; (2:1452).

221. Ibid.

222. Comm. Hebrews 6:1–2, OE 19.89–90; CNTC 12:73.

223. Ibid.

224. Comm. Acts 19:7, CO 48:443A; CNTC 7:152.

225. Ibid.

226. *Institutio 1539* V.3, CO 1:142C; *Inst.* 1536:125.

227. *Institutio 1539* V.3, CO 1:143A; *Inst.* 1536:126.

228. *Institutio 1539* V.3, CO 1:142C; *Inst.* 1536:126.

229. *Inst.* IV.xix.6, OS V.440–441; (2:1453–1454).

230. Comm. Acts 8:16, CO 48:182–183; CNTC 6:236.

231. Comm. Acts 8:17, CO 48:183–184; CNTC 6:237.

232. Comm. Acts 19:5, CO 48:442–443; CNTC 7:152.

233. Ibid.

234. *Institutio 1536* V.45, CO 1:178A; *Inst.* 1536:159.

235. Ibid.

236. *Institutio 1536* V.46, CO 1:178B; *Inst.* 1536:159.

237. Ibid.

238. *Institutio 1536* V.45, CO 1:177C; *Inst.* 1536:158.

239. *Institutio 1536* V.47, CO 1:178–179; *Inst.* 1536:160.

240. *Institutio 1536* V.47, CO 1:179A; *Inst.* 1536:160.

241. *Vera Ecclesiae Reformandae Ratio*, CO 7:630C; *Tracts and Treatises* III.289–290.

242. *Vera Ecclesiae Reformandae Ratio*, CO 7:631A; *Tracts and Treatises* III:290.

243. Ibid.

244. Ibid.

245. Comm. James 5:14, CO 55:431B; CNTC 3:314.

246. Ibid.

247. Ibid.

248. Ibid.

249. Comm. Mark 6:12–14, CO 45:298A; CNTC 2:1.

250. *Inst.* IV.xix.19, OS V.454.6–8; (2:1467).

251. *Inst.* IV.xix.19, OS V.454.3–4; (2:1467).

252. *Institutio 1536* V.44, CO 1:175C; *Inst.* 1536:157.

253. *Institutio 1536* V.44, CO 1:176A; *Inst.* 1536:157.

254. *Institutio 1536* V.44, CO 1:1776B; *Inst.* 1536:157.

255. *Institutio 1536* V.44, CO 1:176–177; *Inst.* 1536:158.

256. *Institutio 1536* V.44, CO 1:177A; *Inst.* 1536:158.

257. *Institutio 1539* V, CO 1:685–736.

258. *Institutio 1539* XVI.17, CO 1:1078B; (2:1465).

259. *Institutio 1543* XIX.14, CO 1:1075C; (2:1462).

260. *Institutio 1543* XIX.14, CO 1:1076B; (2:1462).

261. Ibid.

262. *Institutio 1543* XIX.14, CO 1:1076B; (2:1462–1463).

263. *Institutio 1536* V.68, CO 1:1097C; *Inst.* 1536:172–173.

264. *Institutio 1536* V.68, CO 1:1099A; *Inst.* 1536:174.

265. Comm. Ephesians 5:32, OE 16.274.15–19; CNTC 11:210.

266. *Institutio 1536* IV.12, CO 1:110A; *Inst.* 1536:94.

267. *Institutio 1536* IV.14, CO 1:110–111; *Inst.* 1536:95.

268. *Institutio 1536* IV.15, CO 1:111B; *Inst.* 1536:95.

269. *Institutio 1536* IV.15, CO 1:111C; *Inst.* 1536:95.

270. *Institutio 1536* IV.12, CO 1:112B; *Inst.* 1536:96–97.

271. *Institutio 1536* IV.19, CO 1:114A; *Inst.* 1536:98.

272. *Institutio 1536* IV.21, CO 1:114C; *Inst.* 1536:99.

273. *Institutio 1536* IV.21, CO 1:115A; *Inst.* 1536:99.

274. Ibid.

275. *Catechismus*, CO 5:350A; *Catechism*, p. 34.
276. Ibid.
277. *Institutio 1539* XI.19, CO 1:968B; (2:1324).
278. *Institutio 1539* XI.20, CO 1:968–969; (1325).
279. *Institutio 1539* XI.22, CO 1:970C; (2:1327).
280. *Institutio 1539* XI.23, CO 1:971A; (2:1328).
281. *Institutio 1539* XI.24, CO 1:972A; (2:1329).
282. *Institutio 1539* XI.27, CO 1:974A; (2:1332).
283. *Institutio 1539* XI.27, CO 1:974B; (2:1332).
284. *Institutio 1539* XI.51, CO 1:990A; (2:1359).
285. *Institutio 1539* XI.27, CO 1:974C; (2:1332).
286. *Institutio 1539* XI.46, CO 1:986–987; (2:1349).
287. *Institutio 1539* XI.2, CO 1:958–959; (2:1305).
288. Comm. Romans 2:25, *Romans* 52.16–18; CNTC 8:54.
289. Comm. Romans 2:25, *Romans* 52–53; CNTC 8:55.
290. Comm. Romans 6:4, *Romans* 122.85–90; CNTC 8:123.
291. *Institutio 1543* XVII.1, CO 1:957C; (2:1303).
292. *Supplex exhortatio ad Caesarem*; *Calvin: Theological Treatises*, p. 203.
293. Ibid.
294. *Catechismus Ecclesiae Genevensis*, OS II.133.12–16; *Calvin: Theological Treatises*, p. 133.
295. *Catechismus Ecclesiae Genevensis*, OS II.134.9–15; *Calvin: Theological Treatises*, p. 133.
296. *Catechismus Ecclesiae Genevensis*, OS II.134.16–20; *Calvin: Theological Treatises*, p. 133.
297. *Catechismus Ecclesiae Genevensis*, OS II.135.7–10; *Calvin: Theological Treatises*, p. 134.
298. Comm. 1 Corinthians 12:13, CO 49:501C; CNTC 9:264.
299. Comm. 1 Corinthians 12:13, CO 49:501C; CNTC 9:265.
300. Ibid.
301. Ibid.
302. *Acta Synodi Tridentinae cum Antidoto*, CO 7:499A; *Tracts and Treatises* III:180.
303. Comm. Galatians 3:27, OE 16.86–87; CNTC 11:68.
304. Ibid.
305. Comm. Galatians 3:27, OE 16.87.7–11; CNTC 11:68.
306. Comm. Galatians 3:27, OE 16.87.15–17; CNTC 11:68.
307. Comm Galatians 3:27, OE 16.87.22–24; CNTC 11:69.
308. Comm. Ephesians 5:26, OE 16.267.16–17; CNTC 11:206.
309. Comm. Ephesians 5:26, OE 16.267.18–21; CNTC 11:206.
310. Comm. Ephesians 5:26, OE 16.268.1–5; CO 11:206.
311. Comm. Ephesians 5:26, OE 16.268.9–11; CO 11:206.
312. Comm. Ephesians 5:26, OE 16.269.13–20; CO 11:207.

313. Comm. Titus 3:5, CO 52:430C; CNTC 10:382.
314. Comm. Titus 3:5, CO 52:431A; CNTC 10:382.
315. Ibid.
316. Comm. Titus 3:5, CO 52:431B; CNTC 10:383.
317. Comm. 1 Peter 3:21, CO 55:268B; CNTC 12:296.
318. Comm. 1 Peter 3:21, CO 55:268C; CNTC 12:296.
319. Comm. 1 Peter 3:21, CO 55:269A; CNTC 12:296–297.
320. Comm. Colossians 2:12, OE 15.31–33; CNTC 11:333.
321. Comm. Acts 8:38, CO 48:197–198; CNTC 6:254.
322. *Institutio 1536* IV.21, CO 1:115A; *Inst.* 1536:99.
323. *Institutio 1539* XI.14, CO 1:965B; (2:1314).
324. *Inst.* IV.xv.14, OS V.295.26–28; (2:1314).
325. *Inst.* IV.xv.15, OS V.296.7–9; (2:1315).
326. Comm. 1 Peter 3:21, CO 55:268C; CNTC 12:296.
327. Comm. Ephesians 5:26, OE 16.268.9–11; CO 11:206.
328. Comm. Galatians 3:27, OE 16.87.15–19; CNTC 11:68.
329. *Institutio 1536* IV.24, CO 1:118–119; *Inst.* 1536:102.
330. *Institutio 1536* IV.25, CO 1:119A; *Inst.* 1536:102–103.
331. *Institutio 1536* IV.25, CO 1:119B; *Inst.* 1536:103.
332. *Institutio 1536* IV.26, CO 1:119C; *Inst.* 1536:103.
333. *Institutio 1536* IV.26, CO 1:120A; *Inst.* 1536:103.
334. *Institutio 1536* IV.28, CO 1:121B; *Inst.* 1536:104–105.
335. *Institutio 1536* IV.29, CO 1:123B; *Inst.* 1536:106.
336. *Institutio 1536* IV.29, CO 1:123C; *Inst.* 1536:107.
337. *Institutio 1536* IV.30, CO 1:123–124; *Inst.* 1536:107.
338. *Institutio 1536* IV.33, CO 1:125C; *Inst.* 1536:109.
339. *Institutio 1536* IV.33, CO 1:126A; *Inst.* 1536:109.
340. *Institutio 1536* IV.42, CO 1:132B; *Inst.* 1536:115.
341. *Institutio 1536* IV.40, CO 1:129C; *Inst.* 1536:112.
342. *Institutio 1536* IV.47, CO 1:134C; *Inst.* 1536:117.
343. *Institutio 1536* IV.26, CO 1:120B; *Inst.* 1536:104.
344. *Deux Discours de Calvin au Colloque de Lausanne*, CO 9:884A; *Calvin: Theological Treatises*, p. 44.
345. *Confessio Fidei de Eucharistia*, CO 9:711–712; *Calvin: Theological Treatises*, p. 168.
346. Ibid.
347. *Catechismus*, CO 5:350C; *Catechism*, p. 35.
348. Ibid.
349. Ibid.
350. *Catechismus*, CO 5:351A; *Catechism*, p. 35.
351. Ibid.
352. *Institutio 1539* XII.1001B; (2:1368).
353. *Institutio 1539* XII.17, CO 1:1002A; (2:1369).

354. *Institutio 1539* XII.18, CO 1:1002B; (2:1370).

355. *Institutio 1539* XII.18, CO 1:1002C; (2:1371).

356. Ibid.

357. *Institutio 1539* XII.18, CO 1:1002–1003; (2:1371).

358. *Institutio 1539* XII.10, CO 1:997C; (2:1385).

359. Ibid.

360. *Institutio 1539* XII.10, CO 1:997C; (2:1385–1386).

361. *Institutio 1539* XII.29, CO 1:1009; (2:1381).

362. Ibid.

363. *Institutio 1539* XII.15, CO 1:1000C; (2:1367).

364. *Libellus de Coena Domini*, OS I.505; *Calvin: Theological Treatises*, p. 144.

365. *Libellus de Coena Domini*, OS I.506; *Calvin: Theological Treatises*, p. 145.

366. Ibid.

367. *Libellus de Coena Domini*, OS I.507; *Calvin: Theological Treatises*, p. 146.

368. *Libellus de Coena Domini*, OS I.508; *Calvin: Theological Treatises*, p. 147.

369. Ibid.

370. Ibid.

371. *Libellus de Coena Domini*, OS I.509; *Calvin: Theological Treatises*, p. 148.

372. Ibid.

373. *Libellus de Coena Domini*, OS I.510; *Calvin: Theological Treatises*, p. 149.

374. *Libellus de Coena Domini*, OS I.530; *Calvin: Theological Treatises*, p. 166.

375. *Libellus de Coena Domini*, OS I.520–521; *Calvin: Theological Treatises*, p. 159.

376. *La Forme des Prieres et Chantz Ecclesiastiques*, OS II.48.7–12; *Tracts and Treatises* II:121.

377. Ibid.

378. *La Forme des Prieres et Chantz Ecclesiastiques*, OS II.48.24–29; *Tracts and Treatises* II:121–122.

379. *La Forme des Prieres et Chantz Ecclesiastiques*, OS II.48.29–35; *Tracts and Treatises* II:122.

380. *La Forme des Prieres et Chantz Ecclesiastiques*, OS II.48.5–7; *Tracts and Treatises* II:121.

381. *Institutio 1543* XVII.1, CO 1:991B; (2:1361).

382. *Institutio 1543* XVII.3, CO 1:993C; (2:1363).

383. *Institutio 1543* XVII.5, CO 1:994C; (2:1364).

384. *Institutio 1543* XVII.5, CO 1:994C; (2:1364).

385. *Institutio 1543* XVII.19, CO 1:1003A; (2:1371).

386. *Institutio 1543* XVII.22, CO 1:1004C; (2:1381).

387. *Institutio 1543* XVII.22, CO 1:1005A; (2:1382).

388. *Institutio 1543* XVII.30, CO 1:1010A; (2:1403).

389. *Institutio 1543* XVII.32, CO 1:1012A; (2:1412).

390. Ibid.

391. *Institutio 1543* XVII.36, CO 1:1015A; (2:1416).

392. *Catechismus Ecclesiae Genevensis,* OS II.139.4–8; *Calvin: Theological Treatises,* p. 136.

393. *Catechismus Ecclesiae Genevensis,* OS II.140.9–13; *Calvin: Theological Treatises,* p. 137.

394. *Catechismus Ecclesiae Genevensis,* OS II.140.17–20; *Calvin: Theological Treatises,* p. 137.

395. *Catechismus Ecclesiae Genevensis,* OS II.140–141; *Calvin: Theological Treatises,* p. 137.

396. Comm. 1 Corinthians 11:24, CO 49:486C; CNTC 9:245.

397. *Institutio 1539* XII.10, CO 1:997C; (2:1385).

398. Comm. 1 Corinthians 11:24, CO 49:486C; CNTC 9:245.

399. Ibid.

400. Comm. 1 Corinthians 11:24, CO 49:488B; CNTC 9:247.

401. Ibid.

402. Ibid.

403. *Supplex exhortatio ad Caesarem; Calvin: Theological Treatises,* p. 205.

404. *Institutio 1543* XVII.32, CO 1:1012A; (2:1412).

405. *Vera Ecclesiae Reformandae Ratio,* CO 7:622C; *Tracts and Treatises* III:279.

406. *Vera Ecclesiae Reformandae Ratio,* CO 7:623A; *Tracts and Treatises* III:279–280.

407. *Vera Ecclesiae Reformandae Ratio,* CO 7:623A; *Tracts and Treatises* III:280.

408. *Vera Ecclesiae Reformandae Ratio,* CO 7:623C; *Tracts and Treatises* III:280–281.

409. Comm. Acts 7:40, CO 48:153B; CNTC 6:201.

410. Comm. Acts 7:40, CO 48:153C; CNTC 6:201.

411. Comm. Acts 7:49, CO 49:161A; CNTC 6:210.

412. Ibid.

413. Comm. Acts 7:49, CO 49:161B; CNTC 6:210.

414. Comm. Genesis 3:23, CO 23:80; CTS 1:186.

415. *Defensio sanae et orthodoxae doctrinae de sacramentis,* CO 9:22B; *Tracts and Treatises* II:229.

416. Ibid.

417. *Defensio sanae et orthodoxae doctrinae de sacramentis,* CO 9:25C; *Tracts and Treatises* II:232.

418. *Secunda defensio contra Ioachimi Westphali calumnias,* CO 9:48–49; *Tracts and Treatises* II:250.

419. Both Brian A. Gerrish and Thomas Davis note the way Calvin combines the language of descent with the language of ascent. However, Gerrish makes the notion of the Supper as an instrument central to Calvin's teaching on the Supper, whereas Davis makes the idea of exhibiting the reality that is being represented central. Both ideas emphasize the downward direction of the Supper, which reaches its culmination in the 1543 *Institutes,* and miss the emphasis on the Supper as a ladder, vehicle, or hand reaching out from heaven that increasingly emerges in Calvin's

writings from 1543 onward. B. A. Gerrish, *Grace and Gratitude: Calvin's Eucharistic Theology* (Minneapolis, MN: Fortress Press, 1993), p. 168; Thomas Davis, *The Clearest Promises of God: The Development of Calvin's Eucharistic Teaching* (New York: AMS Press, 1995), pp. 41–42.

420. *Dilucida Explicatio Sanae Doctrinae de Vera Participatione Carnis et Sanguinis Christi in Sacra Coena,* CO 9:470–471; *Calvin: Theological Treatises,* p. 268.

421. *Secunda defensio contra Ioachimi Westphali calumnias,* CO 9:48–49; *Tracts and Treatises* II.250.

422. *Dilucida Explicatio Sanae Doctrinae de Vera Participatione Carnis et Sanguinis Christi in Sacra Coena,* CO 9:486B; *Calvin: Theological Treatises,* p. 287.

423. *Inst.* IV.xvii.24, OS V.375–376; (2:1390).

424. *Inst.* IV.xvii.15, OS V.360.23–26; (2:1377).

425. *Inst.* IV.xvii.16, OS V.362.33–34; (2:1379).

426. Comm. Acts 17:24, CO 48:412A; CNTC 7:114.

CHAPTER 11. *The Manifestation of Piety in the Church*

1. *Institutio 1536* III.9, CO 1:87B; *Inst.* 1536:73.

2. Ibid.

3. *Institutio 1536* VI.34, CO 1:227A; *Inst.* 1536:206.

4. *Institutio 1539* IX.24, CO 1:919C; (2:893).

5. *Institutio 1539* IX.24, CO 1:919–920; (2:893).

6. *Institutio 1539* IX.24, CO 1:920B; (2:893).

7. Comm. 1 Corinthians 11:22, CO 49:483B; CNTC 9:241. Calvin gives a more succinct description of worship earlier in the chapter. "For there we listen to God's teaching; we offer prayers; and celebrate the mysteries" (Comm. 1 Corinthians 11:17, CO 49:480A; CNTC 9:236).

8. Comm. 1 Corinthians 13:12, CO 49:514B; CNTC 9:281.

9. Ibid.

10. Ibid.

11. Comm. Ephesians 3:10, OE 16.209.8–17; CNTC 11:163.

12. Comm. Acts 7:40, CO 48:153B; CNTC 6:201.

13. Comm. Genesis 28:17, CO 23:394C; CTS 2:118.

14. Comm. Luke 2:12, CO 45:76A; CNTC 1:76.

15. Comm. Acts 17:25, CO 48:412B; CNTC 7:114–115.

16. Comm. Psalm 24:8, CO 31:249C; CTS 8:412–413.

17. Comm. Psalm 26:8, CO 31:268B; CTS 8:415–416.

18. Comm. Psalm 27:4, CO 31:274A; CTS 8:454–455.

19. Comm. Acts 24:11, CO 48:521A; CNTC 7:249.

20. Comm. Psalm 42:2, CO 31:426A; CTS 9:128–129.

21. Comm. Psalm 42:2, CO 31:426B; CTS 9:129–130.

22. Comm. Psalm 81:1, CO 31:760B; CTS 10:311.

23. *Inst.* IV.i.1, OS V.1.8–14; (2:1011).

24. Comm. Psalm 63:3, CO 31:594C; CTS 9:435.

25. Comm. Psalm 63:3, CO 31:594–595; CTS 9:435.

26. Comm. Daniel 9:20–21, CO 41:164C; CTS 25:191–192.

27. Comm. Psalm 52:10, CO 31:529C; CTS 9:318.

28. *Inst.* IV.i.3, OS V.10.16–17; (2:1019).

29. Comm. Hosea 9:5, CO 42:388–389; CTS 26:318–319.

30. *Institutio 1536* I.9, CO 1:32A; *Inst.* 1536:19.

31. *Institutio 1536* III.10, CO 1:88A; *Inst.* 1536:74.

32. *Institutio 1536* III.11, CO 1:88B; *Inst.* 1536:74.

33. *Institutio 1536* III.12, CO 1:89A; *Inst.* 1536:75.

34. *Catechismus,* CO 5:344A; *Catechism,* p. 28.

35. *Articles concernant l'Organisation de l'Eglise et du Culte a Geneve,* CO 10:12A; *Calvin: Theological Treatises,* p. 53.

36. *Institutio 1539* IX.27, CO 1:922B; (2:896–897).

37. *Projet d'Ordonnances Ecclesiastiques,* CO 10:26B; *Calvin: Theological Treatises,* p. 67.

38. *Institutio 1543* XV.26, CO 1:921A; (2:895).

39. Ibid.

40. *Institutio 1543* XV.26, CO 1:921B; (2:895).

41. Comm. 1 Corinthians 14:15, CO 49:522C; CNTC 9:293.

42. Comm. 1 Corinthians 14:7, CO 49:520A; CNTC 9:289.

43. Comm. 1 Corinthians 2:11, CO 49:341C; CNTC 9:58.

44. Comm. 1 Corinthians 14:11, CO 49:520B; CNTC 9:389.

45. *Theaetetus* 206d.

46. *Republic* 588b.

47. *De Interpretatione* 16a 2–8.

48. Comm. John 1:1, OE 11/1.11.25–29; CNTC 4:7.

49. Comm. 1 Corinthians 2:11, CO 49:341C; CNTC 9:58.

50. Comm. John 15:15, OE 11/2.169.13–24; CNTC 5:100.

51. Ibid.

52. Comm. Jeremiah 23:20, CO 38:429C; CTS 19:175.

53. Comm. Genesis 32:9, CO 23:439B; CTS 2:190–191.

54. Comm. Matthew 12:34, CO 45:344A; CNTC 2:49.

55. Ibid.

56. Comm. Psalm 34:13, CO 31:341–342; CTS 8:567.

57. Comm. Psalm 15:2, CO 31:144B; CTS 8:206.

58. Comm. Psalm 91:1, CO 32:2B; CTS 10:479.

59. Comm. Psalm 116:10, CO 32:196A; CTS 11:366.

60. Ibid.

61. Comm. Isaiah 44:5, CO 37:108C; CTS 15:364.

62. Comm. Jeremiah 10:11, CO 28:74C; CTS 17:33.

63. *Catechismus Ecclesiae Genevensis,* OS II.115–116; *Calvin: Theological Treatises,* p. 121.

64. Comm. Psalm 102:1, CO 32:61–62; CTS 11:97–98.

65. Ibid.

66. Comm. Daniel 9:18, CO 41:157C; CTS 25:181–182.

67. Ibid.

68. Comm. Psalm 5:2–3, CO 31:66A; CTS 8:52.

69. Comm. Psalm 139:4, CO 32:378B; CTS 12:209.

70. *Institutio 1536* IV.33, CO 1:125C; *Inst.* 1536:109.

71. Comm. Hebrews 2:12, OE 19.40.29–32; CNTC 12:27.

72. Comm. Psalm 22:23, CO 31:231B; CTS 8:378–379.

73. Comm. Psalm 22:24, CO 31:232A; CTS 8:380.

74. Ibid.

75. Comm. Psalm 31:19, CO 31:309C; CTS 8:513–514.

76. Comm. Psalm 145:1, CO 32:413B; CTS 12:272–273.

77. Comm. Psalm 111:1, CO 32:167A; CTS 11:311–312.

78. Comm. Psalm 109:30, CO 32:158C; CTS 11:294.

79. Comm. Psalm 66:13, CO 31:614C; CTS 9:474.

80. Comm. Jeremiah 33:11, CO 39:61A; CTS 20:244.

81. *Institutio 1543* IV.4, CO 1:439C; (2:1258).

82. *Institutio 1543* IV.4, CO 1:440A; (1258–1259).

83. Comm. Jonah 1:16, CO 43:232–233; CTS 28:68–69.

84. Comm. Jonah 1:16, CO 43:233A; CTS 28:69.

85. Comm. Genesis 40:19, CO 23:514–515; CTS 2:312.

86. Comm. Jeremiah 20:14–16, CO 38:353; CTS 19:45.

87. Comm. Genesis 40:19, CO 23:514–515; CTS 2:312.

88. Comm. Psalm 34:4, CO 31:337A; CTS 8:558–559.

89. Comm. Psalm 42:12, CO 37:68B; CTS 15:300.

90. Comm. Psalm 76:12, CO 31:710A; CTS 10:203.

91. Comm. Psalm 145:10, CO 32:415–416; CTS 12:276–277.

92. Comm. Psalm 145:4, CO 32:413C; CTS 12:273.

93. Comm. Ezekiel 11:18, CO 40:241–242; CTS 22:370.

94. *Institutio 1536* I.9, CO 1:32B; *Inst.* 1536:19.

95. *Institutio 1536* IV.20, CO 1:114C; *Inst.* 1536:98.

96. *Institutio 1536* VI.26, CO 1:219C; *Inst.* 1536:198.

97. *Institutio 1536* VI.34, CO 1:227–228; *Inst.* 1536:206.

98. *Institutio 1536* IV.52, CO 1:139B; *Inst.* 1536:122.

99. *Institutio 1536* VI.34, CO 1:228A; *Inst.* 1536:206.

100. *De Fugendis Impiorum Illicitis Sacris,* CO 5:272A; *Tracts and Treatises* III:404.

101. *De Fugendis Impiorum Illicitis Sacris,* CO 5:254A; *Tracts and Treatises* III:379.

102. *De Fugendis Impiorum Illicitis Sacris*, CO 5:259A; *Tracts and Treatises* III:386.
103. *De Fugendis Impiorum Illicitis Sacris*, CO 5:262C; *Tracts and Treatises* III:391.
104. *De Fugendis Impiorum Illicitis Sacris*, CO 5:267B; *Tracts and Treatises* III:397.
105. *De Fugendis Impiorum Illicitis Sacris*, CO 5:252B; *Tracts and Treatises* III:377.
106. *De Fugendis Impiorum Illicitis Sacris*, CO 5:241B; *Tracts and Treatises* III:362.
107. *Institutio 1539* IX.27, CO 1:922C; (2:897).
108. *Institutio 1543* XIII.14, OS 1:848C; (2:1192–1193).
109. *Institutio 1543* XIII.12, OS 1:846C; (2:1190).
110. *Institutio 1543* XIII.14, OS 1:848C; (2:1192).
111. *Institutio 1543* XIII.28, OS 1:858B; (2:1206).
112. *Institutio 1543* XIII.29, OS 1:858C; (2:1207).
113. *Institutio 1543* XIII.29, OS 1:858B; (2:1206).
114. Comm. Galatians 4:1, OE 16.91.20–36; CNTC 11:72.
115. Comm. Acts 7:47, CO 48:160B; CNTC 6:209.
116. Comm. Isaiah 1:30, CO 36:57A; CTS 13:86.
117. Comm. Isaiah 29:13, CO 36:493C; CTS 14:324.
118. Comm. Joel 2:1, CO 42:535A; CTS 27:45.
119. Comm. Jeremiah 5:3, CO 37:608C; CTS 17:256–257.
120. Comm. 1 Corinthians 7:1, OE 15.119.23–32; CNTC 10:93.
121. Comm. Isaiah 18:7, CO 36:326B; CTS 14:44–45.
122. Comm. Daniel 3:2–7, CO 40:624B; CTS 24:211.
123. Comm. Exodus 4:31, CO 24:68A; CTS 3:111.
124. *De Fugendis Impiorum Illicitis Sacris*, CO 5:246C; *Tracts and Treatises* III:369.
125. *De Fugendis Impiorum Illicitis Sacris*, CO 5:264A; *Tracts and Treatises* III:393.
126. *Institutio 1539* IX.27, CO 1:922C; (2:897).
127. *Institutio 1543* XIII.31, CO 1:859B; (2:1208).
128. Comm. Philippians 2:10, OE 16.326.15–21; CNTC 11:251.
129. Comm. Acts 10:25, CO 48:237B; CNTC 6:301–302.
130. Ibid.
131. Comm. Acts 10:25, CO 48:237–238; CNTC 6:302.
132. *Traite des reliques*, 1543, *Tracts and Treatises* I:329.
133. Comm. Acts 10:25, CO 48:236–237; CNTC 6:301.
134. Comm. Genesis 23:7, CO 23:324–325; CTS 1:581–582.
135. Comm. Matthew 8:2, CO 45:231A; CNTC 1:243.
136. Comm. John 9:38, OE 11/2.21–22; CNTC 4:254.
137. Comm. Psalm 95:6, CO 32:31A; CTS 11:34–35.

138. Comm. Ephesians 3:14, OE 16.212.23–26; CNTC 11:166.

139. Comm. Acts 9:40, CO 48:220C; CNTC 6:281.

140. Ibid.

141. Comm. Acts 20:36, CO 48:474–475; CNTC 7:190.

142. Comm. Daniel 6:10, CO 41:11C; CTS 24:362.

143. Comm. John 9:38, OE 11/2.21–22; CNTC 4:254.

144. Comm. Psalm 95:6, CO 32:31A; CTS 11:34–35.

145. Comm. Matthew 26:38, CO 45:721B; CNTC 3:149.

146. Comm. Ezekiel 9:8, CO 40:202–203; CTS 22:313.

147. *Institutio 1536* V.65, CO 1:191A; *Inst.* 1536:171.

148. Comm. 1 Timothy 2:8, CO 52:274A–B; CNTC 10:214–215.

149. Ibid.

150. Ibid.

151. Comm. Psalm 28:2, CO 31:281B; CTS 8:466.

152. Comm. Isaiah 1:15, CO 36:41C; CTS 13:60.

153. Comm. Lamentations 2:19, CO 39:558–559; CTS 21:382–383.

154. Ibid.

155. Comm. Lamentations 3:41, CO 39:592C; CTS 21:435.

156. Related to me by Max Engemarre at the Sixteenth Century Studies Conference in November 2003.

157. Comm. Acts 20:36, CO 48:474–475; CNTC 7:190.

158. Comm. John 11:41, OE 11/2:67.11–30; CNTC 5:15.

159. Ibid.

160. Ibid.

161. Ibid.

162. Comm. John 17:1, OE 11/2.207–208; CNTC 5:134–135.

163. Comm. Matthew 14:19, CO 45:439A; CNTC 2:149.

164. Comm. Psalm 25:15, CO 31:260A; CTS 8:431. "The keenest (*accerimum*) of all our senses is the sense of sight" (Cicero, *De Oratore* II.87.357).

165. Comm. John 17:1, OE 11/2.207–208; CNTC 5:134–135.

166. Ibid.

167. Ibid.

168. Comm. Luke 18:13, CO 45:420C; CNTC 2:129.

169. *Institutio 1543* VIII.197, CO 1:666C; (2:1241).

170. *Institutio 1543* VIII.199, CO 1:667C; (2:1242).

171. *Institutio 1543* VIII.198, CO 1:667B; (2:1242).

172. Comm. 1 Corinthians 7:5, CO 49:404B; CNTC 9:138–139.

173. Ibid.

174. Comm. Psalm 35:12, CO 31:352A; CTS 8:585.

175. Comm. Daniel 9:1–3, CO 41:127C; CTS 25:138.

176. Comm. Psalm 35:12, CO 31:352A; CTS 8:585.

177. Comm. Jeremiah 14:11–12, CO 38:188C; CTS 18:219.

178. Comm. Daniel 10:2–3, CO 41:195B; CTS 25:237.

179. *La Forme des Prieres et Chantz Ecclesiastiques*, 1542, OS II.26–30; *Tracts and Treatises* II:106–112.
180. Comm. James 5:14, CO 55:431C; CNTC 3:315.
181. Comm. Acts 20:10, CO 48:458B; CNTC 7:170.
182. Ibid.
183. *Institutio 1536* III.10, CO 1:88A; *Inst.* 1536:74.
184. Comm. Matthew 6:5, CO 45:192C; CNTC 1:202–203.
185. Comm. Matthew 6:5, CO 45:193A; CNTC 1:203.
186. Ibid.
187. Comm. Matthew 26:39, CO 45:721B; CNTC 3:149.
188. Comm. Isaiah 38:2, CO 36:647B; CTS 15:154.
189. Ibid.
190. Comm. Jeremiah 20:12, CO 38:305C; CTS 19:41.
191. Comm. Acts 9:13, CO 48:206C; CNTC 6:265.
192. Comm. Acts 16:15, CO 48:378C; CNTC 7:74.
193. Comm. Luke 1:21, CO 45:21C; CNTC 1:28.
194. Comm. Matthew 14:14, CO 45:437B; CNTC 2:147.
195. Comm. Luke 19:1–10, CO 45:563A; CNTC 2:281.
196. Ibid.
197. Comm. Mark 12:34, CO 45:615C; CNTC 3:40.
198. Comm. Acts 11:18, CO 48:258A; CNTC 6:326.
199. Comm. Psalm 88:14, CO 31:809C; CTS 10:415.
200. Comm. Joshua 2:11, CO 25:443A; CTS 7:51–52.
201. Comm. Joshua 2:12, CO 25:443; CTS 7:52.
202. Comm. Daniel 2:46, CO 40:610–611; CTS 24:191–192.
203. Ibid.
204. Comm. Daniel 6:16, CO 41:18A; CTS 24:371.
205. Comm. Psalm 101:5, CO 32:58C; CTS 11:91.
206. Comm. Isaiah 2:11, CO 36:72A; CTS 13:111–112.
207. Comm. Ezekiel 2:4–5, CO 40:68A; CTS 22:117.
208. Comm. Haggai 2:10–14, CO 44:109B; CTS 29:366.
209. Comm. Jeremiah 26:10, CO 38:522C; CTS 19:322.
210. Comm. Exodus 7:11, CO 24:90B; CTS 3:147.
211. Comm. Matthew 10:14, CO 45:279A; CNTC 1:295.
212. Comm. Acts 13:51, CO 48:316B; CNTC 6:396.
213. Comm. Acts 14:14, CO 48:323–324; CNTC 7:8–9.
214. *Institutio 1539* V.11, CO 1:692–693; (1:611).
215. *Institutio 1539* V.11, CO 1:693A; (1:611).
216. *Institutio 1543* VIII.200, CO 1:668A; (2:1243).
217. *Institutio 1543* VIII.200, CO 1:668B; (2:1243–1244).
218. *Institutio 1543* VIII.200, CO 1:668C; (2:1244).
219. *La Forme des Prieres et Chantz Ecclesiastiques*, 1542, OS II.26–30; *Tracts and Treatises* II:106–112.

220. Comm. Joel 2:1, CO 42:534B; CTS 26:45.
221. Ibid.
222. Comm. Isaiah 58:5, CO 37:328B; CTS 16:231.
223. Ibid.
224. Ibid.
225. Comm. 2 Corinthians 7:11, OE 15.129.1–4; CNTC 10:102.
226. Comm. 2 Corinthians 7:11, OE 15.129.15–18; CNTC 10:102.
227. Comm. Matthew 11:21, CO 45:312–313; CNTC 2:16.
228. Comm. Matthew 26:75, CO 45:745B; CNTC 3:173.
229. Ibid.
230. Comm. Matthew 18:21, CO 45:520A; CNTC 2:235.
231. Comm. Isaiah 22:12, CO 36:374A; CTS 14:123.
232. Comm. Isaiah 22:12, CO 36:374C; CTS 14:124.
233. Comm. Isaiah 22:13, CO 36:375B; CTS 14:125.
234. Comm. Daniel 2:47, CO 40:613A; CTS 24:195.
235. Comm. Jeremiah 36:16, CO 39:125–126; CTS 20:340.
236. Comm. Daniel 4:27, CO 40:673–674; CTS 24:279.
237. *De Fugendis Impiorum Illicitis Sacris*, CO 5:254A; *Tracts and Treatises* III: 379–380.
238. *De Fugendis Impiorum Illicitis Sacris*, CO 5:264B; *Tracts and Treatises* III:393.
239. *De Fugendis Impiorum Illicitis Sacris*, CO 5:265B; *Tracts and Treatises* III:394.
240. *Institutio 1539* II.35–36, CO 1:326–327; (1:273–275).
241. *Institutio 1543* III.34, CO 1:391C; (1:112).
242. Ibid.
243. *Institutio 1543* III.34, CO 1:392–393; (1:112).
244. Ibid.
245. *Institutio 1543* II.35–36, CO 1:326–327; (1:273–275).
246. *Institutio 1543* II.36, CO 1:326–327; (1:275).
247. *Institutio 1543* III.35, CO 1:392A; (1:112).
248. *Institutio 1543* III.36, CO 1:392–393; (1:113–114).
249. Comm. 1 Corinthians 10:14, CO 49:463B; CNTC 9:215.
250. Ibid.
251. Ibid.
252. Comm. Acts 7:43, CO 48:157A; CNTC 6:205.
253. Ibid.
254. Comm. Psalm 115:4, CO 32:186C; CTS 11:348.
255. Ibid.
256. Comm. Isaiah 42:17, CO 37:71–72; CTS 15:305–306.
257. Ibid.
258. Comm. Jeremiah 10:14, CO 38:79B; CTS 18:39–40.
259. *Inst.* I.xii.3, OS III.108.9–11; (1:120).

260. Comm. Daniel 3:2–7, CO 40:622B; CTS 24:208–209.
261. Ibid.
262. Comm. Ezekiel 8:7–11, CO 40:184B; CTS 22:286–287.
263. Ibid.
264. Ibid.
265. Comm. Acts 3:12, CO 48:67B; CNTC 6:96.
266. Comm. Ezekiel 8:7–11, CO 40:184B; CTS 22:287.
267. Ibid.
268. Comm. 1 Corinthians 11:24, CO 49:486C; CNTC 9:245.
269. *Institutio 1543* III.36, CO 1:392–393; (1:113–114).

CHAPTER 12. *The Revelation of the Thoughts of the Heart*

1. Comm. 1 Corinthians 2:11, CO 49:341C; CNTC 9:58.
2. Ibid.
3. Ibid.
4. *Institutio 1539* XII.15, CO 1:1000C; (2:1367).
5. Comm. 1 Corinthians 14:11, CO 49:520B; CNTC 9:389.
6. Ibid.
7. Comm. 2 Corinthians 6:11, OE 15.113.9–26; CNTC 10:88.
8. Comm. Genesis 11:1, CO 23:164A; CTS 1:325–326.
9. Ibid.
10. Ibid.
11. Comm. Genesis 11:7, CO 23:167B; CTS 1:331.
12. Ibid.
13. Comm. 1 Corinthians 14:5, CO 49:518B; CNTC 9:287.
14. Comm. Psalm 81:5, CO 31:761B; CTS 10:314.
15. Comm. Isaiah 33:19, CO 36:574A; CTS 15:35.
16. Comm. Jeremiah 5:15, CO 37:626C; CTS 17:286.
17. Ibid.
18. Comm. Zechariah 8:23, CO 44:258A; CTS 30:230–231.
19. Comm. Isaiah 33:19, CO 36:574A; CTS 15:35.
20. Comm. Jeremiah 9:5, CO 38:30C; CTS 17:466.
21. Comm. Psalm 34:13, CO 31:341–342; CTS 8:567.
22. Comm. Romans 9:3, *Romans* 193.70–78; CNTC 8:192.
23. Comm. 2 Corinthians 12:15, OE 15.205.7–15; CNTC 10:165.
24. Comm. Acts 10:2, CO 48:224A; CNTC 6:285.
25. Comm. Psalm 35:12, CO 31:351B; CTS 8:584.
26. Comm. 1 Corinthians 11:21, CO 49:482C; CNTC 9:240.
27. *Institutio 1536* IV.34, CO 1:126A; *Inst.* 1536:109.
28. Ibid.
29. *Institutio 1536* IV.34, CO 1:126C; *Inst.* 1536:110.

30. *Institutio 1536* IV.40, CO 1:129C; *Inst.* 1536:112.

31. Comm. Romans 16:16, *Romans* 325.30–40; CNTC 8:323.

32. Comm. 1 Corinthians 16:20, CO 49:572A; CNTC 9:356.

33. Comm. Romans 16:16, *Romans* 325.30–40; CNTC 8:323.

34. Comm. 1 Corinthians 16:20, CO 49:572A; CNTC 9:356.

35. Ibid.

36. Ibid.

37. Comm. Romans 16:16, *Romans* 325.30–40; CNTC 8:323.

38. Ibid.

39. Comm. Genesis 29:4, CO 23:400C; CTS 2:127–128.

40. Comm. John 13:13, OE 11/2.120.11–12; CNTC 5:60.

41. Comm. John 13:14, OE 11/2.120–121; CNTC 5:60.

42. Ibid.

43. Ibid.

44. Comm. 2 Corinthians 7:3, OE 15.121.28–32; CNTC 10:95.

45. Comm. John 8:6, OE 11/1.261–262; CNTC 4:207.

46. Ibid.

47. Comm. Lamentations 2:16, CO 39:553C; CTS 21:375.

48. Comm. Isaiah 36:22, CO 36:614–615; CTS 15:101–102.

49. Comm. Psalm 10:8, CO 31:114C; CTS 8:146–147.

50. Comm. Isaiah 10:12, CO 36:219B; CTS 13:346–347.

51. Comm. Psalm 123:3, CO 309A; CTS 12:82.

52. Comm. Isaiah 3:16, CO 36:91A; CTS 13:144.

53. Comm. 2 Corinthians 2:4, OE 15.37.5–16; CNTC 10:28.

54. Ibid.

55. Comm. Philippians 3:18, OE 16.364.7–13; CNTC 11:281.

56. Ibid.

57. Comm. John 11:33, OE 11/2.62.26–34; CNTC 5:11.

58. Comm. Psalms Preface, CO 31:15C; CTS 8:xxxvii.

59. Comm. Isaiah 50:7, CO 37:221B; CTS 16:57.

60. Comm. Psalm 88:10, CO 31:808C; CTS 10:413.

61. Comm. Isaiah 16:11, CO 309B; CTS 13:494.

62. Comm. Lamentations 1:17, CO 39:527–528; CTS 21:333.

63. Comm. Lamentations 2:18, CO 39:556B; CTS 21:378–379.

64. Comm. Isaiah 59:11, CO 37:343C; CTS 16:256–257.

65. Comm. Jeremiah 48:6, CO 39:317C; CTS 21:10.

66. Ibid.

67. Comm. Lamentations 3:51, CO 39:598B; CTS 21:443.

68. Comm. Genesis 35:22, CO 23:474A; CTS 2:246.

69. Comm. Jeremiah 48:3, CO 39:310C; CTS 20:612.

70. Comm. 1 Thessalonians 4:13, CO 52:164C; CNTC 8:363.

71. Ibid.

72. Ibid.

73. Comm. Isaiah 15:2, CO 36:296B; CTS 13:472.

74. Comm. Isaiah 15:3, CO 36:296C; CTS 13:472.

75. Comm. Jeremiah 34:5, CO 39:84A; CTS 20:278.

76. Ibid.

77. Comm. Isaiah 32:11, CO 36:550A; CTS 14:417.

78. Comm. Ezekiel 7:18, CO 40:166–167; CTS 22:261.

79. Comm. Jeremiah 48:37, CO 39:338–339; CTS 21:42–43.

80. Comm. Jeremiah 48:37, CO 39:338C; CTS 21:42.

81. Ibid.

82. Comm. Ezekiel 7:18, CO 40:166–167; CTS 22:261.

83. Comm. Jeremiah 16:6–7, CO 38:243C; CTS 18:310–311.

84. Comm. Jeremiah 2:37, CO 37:543–544; CTS 17:149–150.

85. Comm. Numbers 20:29, CO 25:243–244; CTS 6:146–147.

86. Comm. Jeremiah 16:6–7, CO 38:243C; CTS 18:310–311.

87. Comm. Jeremiah 15:5, CO 38:212C; CTS 18:259.

88. Comm. Numbers 20:29, CO 25:243–244; CTS 6:146–147.

89. Ibid.

90. Ibid.

91. Comm. Psalm 36:2, CO 31:359C; CTS 9:3–4.

92. Comm. Ezekiel 18:5–9, CO 40:427B; CTS 23:221–222.

93. Comm. Ezekiel 12:4–6, CO 40:257A; CTS 22:393.

94. Comm. Ezekiel 18:5–9, CO 40:427B; CTS 23:221–222.

95. Comm. Genesis 3:6, CO 23:59C; CTS 1:151.

96. Comm. Genesis 39:6, CO 23:504C; CTS 2:295.

97. Comm. Ezekiel 6:9, CO 40:146B; CTS 22:231.

98. Comm. Numbers 32:1, CO 25:323–324; CTS 6:279–280.

99. Comm. Genesis 39:6, CO 23:504C; CTS 2:295.

100. Comm. Exodus 2:2, CO 24:23B; CTS 3:42.

101. Comm. Obadiah 12–14, CO 43:192A; CTS 27:443.

102. Comm. Lamentations 3:43, CO 39:594B; CTS 21:437.

103. Comm. Jeremiah 34:4–5, CO 39:80B; CTS 20:273.

104. Comm. Psalm 13:4, CO 31:133C; CTS 8:184–185.

105. Comm. Numbers 23:13, CO 25:282A; CTS 6:209.

106. Comm. Psalm 36:2, CO 31:359C; CTS 9:3–4.

107. Comm. Psalm 73:20, CO 31:684B; CTS 10:147.

108. Comm. Genesis 13:13, CO 23:192C; CTS 1:373.

109. Comm. Matthew 13:44, CO 45:375A; CNTC 2:82.

110. Comm. 2 Corinthians 5:12, OE 15.95.27–31; CNTC 10:73.

111. Comm. Isaiah 3:17, CO 36:92A; CTS 13:146.

112. Comm. Genesis 24:22, CO 23:335C; CTS 2:20–21.

113. Comm. John 2:6, OE 11/1.67.18–28; CNTC 4:48.

114. Comm. Acts 10:46, CO 48:251C; CNTC 6:318.

115. Comm. Isaiah 66:2, CO 37:438B; CTS 16:413.

116. Comm. Ezekiel 13:19, CO 40:293B; CTS 23:35.
117. Comm. Ezekiel 13:17–18, CO 40:289B; CTS 23:29.
118. Comm. Numbers 22:15, CO 25:270C; CTS 6:190–191.
119. Comm. Jeremiah 7:22, CO 37:691B; CTS 17:394.
120. Ibid.
121. Comm. Hosea 2:13, CO 42:240B; CTS 26:99.
122. Comm. Isaiah 36:10, CO 36:606A; CTS 15:87.
123. Comm. 2 Corinthians 5:12, OE 15.95.27–31; CNTC 10:73.
124. Comm. *De Clementia*, pp. 50–53.
125. *De officiis* 2.12.43; Comm. *De Clementia*, pp. 52–53.
126. Ibid.
127. Comm. 2 Timothy 3:2, CO 52:376–377; CNTC 10:323.
128. Ibid.
129. Comm. John 11:48, OE 11/2.71–72; CNTC 5:19.
130. Ibid.
131. Comm. Philippians 2:12, OE 16.329.10–14; CNTC 11:253.
132. Comm. Numbers 22:31, CO 25:274B; CTS 6:196.
133. Comm. Isaiah 3:9, CO 36:85–86; CTS 13:135.
134. Comm. Matthew 6:2, CO 45:191B; CNTC 1:201.
135. Ibid.
136. Comm. Acts 7:49, CO 48:161A; CNTC 6:210.
137. Comm. Matthew 21:13, CO 45:582B; CNTC 3:5.
138. Comm. Ezekiel 11:3, CO 40:227A; CTS 22:348.
139. Comm. Psalm 50:16, CO 31:504A; CTS 9:274–275.
140. Comm. Psalm 50:16, CO 31:504C; CTS 9:275.
141. Comm. Hosea 5:6, CO 42:304C; CTS 26:194.
142. Comm. Hosea 8:7, CO 42:371B; CTS 26:293.
143. Comm. Micah 3:11–12, CO 43:334C; CTS 28:242–243.
144. Comm. Acts 13:50, CO 48:315–316; CNTC 6:395.
145. Comm. Lamentations 4:7–8, CO 39:612–613; CTS 21:465–466.
146. Comm. Genesis 4:5, CO 23:86–87; CTS 1:197.
147. Comm. Jeremiah 6:20, CO 37:662B; CTS 17:346.
148. Ibid.
149. Comm. Ezekiel 16:1–3, CO 40:334–335; CTS 23:93–94.
150. Comm. Psalm 90:7, CO 31:837A; CTS 10:468.
151. Comm. Hebrews 4:12, OE 19.68.19–23; CNTC 12:53.
152. Comm. Jeremiah 36:29–30, CO 39:135A; CTS 20:354.
153. Ibid.
154. Comm. 1 Corinthians 2:11, CO 49:341C; CNTC 9:58.
155. *Institutio 1536* I.9, CO 1:32B; *Inst.* 1536:19.
156. *Institutio 1536* I.2, CO 1:28C; *Inst.* 1536:16.
157. *Institutio 1536* I.9, CO 1:32B; *Inst.* 1536:19.
158. Comm. Romans 2:2, *Romans* 38.33–36; CNTC 8:41.

159. Comm. Romans 2:2, *Romans* 38.38–42; CNTC 8:41.
160. Comm. Romans 2:29, *Romans* 54.102–107; CNTC 8:57.
161. Comm. John 2:24, OE 11/1.80–81; CNTC 4:58–59.
162. Comm. Luke 16:15, CO 45:406C; CNTC 2:115.
163. Comm. Ephesians 6:9, OE 16.280–281; CNTC 11:216.
164. Comm. 1 Peter 1:17, CO 55:223B; CNTC 12:246.
165. Ibid.
166. Comm. Acts 15:8, CO 48:344–345; CNTC 7:33.
167. Comm. Jeremiah 5:3, CO 17:609C; CTS 17:258.
168. Comm. Genesis 4:4, CO 23:85B; CTS 1:194.
169. Comm. Psalm 33:15, CO 31:331B; CTS 8:549–550.
170. Comm. Psalm 44:22, CO 31:446B; CTS 9:168.
171. Comm. Jeremiah 20:12, CO 38:349–350; CTS 19:40.
172. Comm. Hebrews 11:4, OE 19.185.1–6; CNTC 12:161.
173. Comm. 1 John 5:12, CO 55:368B; CNTC 5:306–307.
174. Comm. Ezekiel 18:1–4, CO 40:425A; CTS 23:218.
175. Comm. Luke 1:18, CO 45:18–19; CNTC 1:15.
176. Comm. Isaiah 32:5, CO 36:545B; CTS 14:409.
177. Comm. Luke 2:35, CO 45:94C; CNTC 1:97.
178. Comm. 1 Corinthians 11:19, CO 49:481B; CNTC 9:238.
179. Comm. Exodus 5:22, CO 24:76B; CTS 3:124.
180. Comm. Hebrews 11:17, OE 19.197.24–29; CNTC 12:172.
181. Comm. Psalm 94:7, CO 32:21A; CTS 11:15.
182. Comm. Ephesians 5:15, OE 16.262–263; CNTC 11:202.
183. Comm. Genesis 17:1, CO 23:235A; CTS 1:444.
184. Comm. Matthew 6:4, CO 45:192A; CNTC 1:202.
185. Comm. Psalm 18:23, CO 31:182B; CTS 8:284.
186. Comm. Psalm 119:168, CO 32:291B; CTS 12:44.
187. Comm. Psalm 66:19, CO 31:616C; CTS 9:478.

CHAPTER 13. *The Distinguishing Marks of the Children of God*

1. *Institutio 1536* II.26, CO 1:75B; *Inst.* 1536:61.
2. *Institutio 1536* Epistle Dedicatory to Francis I, CO 1:20C; *Inst.* 1536:9.
3. *Institutio 1536* Epistle Dedicatory to Francis I, CO 1:20–21; *Inst.* 1536:9.
4. *Institutio 1536* Epistle Dedicatory to Francis I, CO 1:21A; *Inst.* 1536:9.
5. *Institutio 1536* Epistle Dedicatory to Francis I, CO 1:22A; *Inst.* 1536:10.
6. Ibid.
7. Comm. Acts 2:42, CO 48:57C; CNTC 6:85.
8. Comm. Matthew 16:19, CO 45:477C; CNTC 2:190.
9. Comm. Matthew 26:57, CO 45:736C; CNTC 3:164.
10. Comm. Genesis 4:26, CO 23:103C; CTS 1:224.

11. Ibid.

12. Comm. Genesis 11:30, CO 23:171A; CTS 1:338.

13. Comm. Matthew 24:1, CO 45:648B; CNTC 3:74.

14. Comm. Ezekiel 11:14–16, CO 40:237B; CTS 22:363–364.

15. Comm. Ezekiel 11:14–16, CO 40:237C; CTS 22:364.

16. *De scandalis,* OS I.179; *Concerning Scandals,* p. 29.

17. Ibid.

18. Comm. Isaiah 49:18, CO 37:207A; CTS 16:34.

19. Comm. Isaiah 4:2, CO 36:46C; CTS 13:153.

20. Comm. Psalm 87 Argumentum, CO 31:800A; CTS 10:395.

21. Comm. Isaiah 49:18, CO 37:207A; CTS 16:34.

22. Comm. Psalm 87 Argumentum, CO 31:800A; CTS 10:395.

23. Comm. Psalm 45:14, CO 31:458B; CTS 9:192.

24. Alexandre Ganoczy makes this point in his biography of Calvin. Ganoczy rightly claims that Calvin "does not break with the Church. Quite the contrary, in being converted one contributes to the purification of the Church in which one was baptized" (Alexandre Ganoczy, *The Young Calvin,* trans. David Foxgrover and Wade Provo [Philadelphia: Westminster Press, 1987], p. 266). Calvin thought that the evangelical Church represented the emergence of the Catholic Church from the midst of the Roman Church. "He never stopped claiming his unshakable attachment to the unity of the Catholic Church which he did not want to replace, but to restore" (p. 307).

25. Comm. Ezekiel 16:20, CO 40:354B; CTS 23:120–121.

26. Ibid.

27. Comm. Ezekiel 16:53, CO 40:387B; CTS 23:165.

28. Comm. Hosea 1:10, CO 42:217–218; CTS 26:65–66.

29. *Institutio 1539* IV.12, CO 1:544C; (2:1025).

30. *Institutio 1539* IV.13, CO 1:545A; (2:1025).

31. Comm. 1 Corinthians 9:1, CO 49:437B; CNTC 9:182.

32. Comm. 2 Corinthians 6:3, OE 15.108–109; CNTC 10:85.

33. Comm. Titus 2:7, CO 52:420–421; CNTC 10:371.

34. Comm. 1 Corinthians 11:1, CO 49:472B; CNTC 9:226–227.

35. Comm. Galatians 6:17, OE 16.150.1–15; CNTC 11:119.

36. Comm. Ephesians 3:13, OE 16.211.13–17; CNTC 11:165.

37. Comm. John 10:12, OE 11/2.34.1–6; CNTC 4:265.

38. Comm. 2 Corinthians 12:21, OE 15.207.25–32; CNTC 10:167.

39. Comm. Zechariah 11:15–16, CO 44:318A; CTS 30:334.

40. Comm. Colossians 1:29, OE 16.416.10–19; CNTC 11:323.

41. Ibid.

42. Comm. Galatians 2:8, OE 16.40.21–25; CNTC 11:32.

43. Comm. Zechariah 11:15–16, CO 44:318A; CTS 30:334.

44. Ibid.

45. Comm. Jeremiah 27:16, CO 38:557–558; CTS 19:376.

46. Comm. Zechariah 11:17, CO 44:320C; CTS 30:338.

47. Comm. Matthew 16:19, CO 45:477C; CNTC 2:190.

48. *Institutio 1539* IV.9, CO 1:543A; (2:1022–1023).

49. Comm. Galatians 4:6, OE 16.94.11–17; CNTC 11:75.

50. For a full discussion of the issue of the assurance of adoption, see Randall C. Zachman, *The Assurance of Faith: Conscience in the Theology of Martin Luther and John Calvin* (Louisville, KY: Westminster John Knox Press, 2005).

51. Comm. Philippians 1:6, OE 16.298.6–15; CNTC 11:229.

52. Ibid.

53. Comm. Philippians 4:3, OE 16.371.18–29; CNTC 11:287.

54. Comm. 1 Thessalonians 1:3, CO 52:140B; CNTC 8:334.

55. Comm. 1 Peter 1:1, CO 55:207B; CNTC 12:229.

56. Comm. Philippians 4:3, OE 16.371.18–29; CNTC 11:287.

57. Comm. Philippians 1:7, OE 16.229.9–11; CNTC 11:230.

58. Comm. 1 Peter 1:1, CO 55:207B; CNTC 12:229.

59. Ibid.

60. Comm. 2 Peter 1:10, CO 55:450B; CNTC 12:334.

61. Comm. 1 John 3:10, CO 55:337C; CNTC 5:274.

62. Comm. 1 Thessalonians 2:12, CO 52:150C; CNTC 8:346.

63. Comm. 2 Peter 1:10, CO 55:450B; CNTC 12:334.

64. Comm. Philippians 4:3, OE 16.371.18–29; CNTC 11:287.

65. Comm. Galatians 5:14, OE 16.127.1–16; CNTC 11:100.

66. Ibid.

67. Comm. Matthew 12:7, CO 45:325B; CNTC 2:29–30.

68. Comm. 1 Timothy 1:5, CO 52:254A; CNTC 10:192.

69. Comm. Romans 8:9, *Romans* 164–165.

70. *Institutio 1539* V.8, CO 1:690C; (1:601).

71. Comm. 2 Corinthians 3:18, OE 15.66; CNTC 10:50.

72. *Institutio 1539* III.80, CO 1:421A; (1:415).

73. Comm. Colossians 3:10, OE 16.448–449; CNTC 11:349–350.

74. Comm. 1 Peter 2:9, CO 55:241A; CNTC 12:266.

75. Comm. 1 John 4:17, CO 55:357C; CNTC 5:295.

76. Comm. Romans 2:11, *Romans* 42–43; CNTC 8:46.

77. *Institutio 1539* VI.65, CO 1:782C; (1:807).

78. Comm. Leviticus 19:1, CO 24:264C; CTS 3:422.

79. *Institutio 1539* XVII.3, CO 1:1125B; (1:686).

80. *Institutio 1539* XVII.3, CO 1:1125B; (1:687).

81. Comm. John 17:22, OE 11/2.224.10–21; CNTC 5:149.

82. Comm. Romans 6:7–8, *Romans* 124–125; CNTC 8:125–126.

83. Comm. Romans 8:29, *Romans* 182.56–62; CNTC 8:180.

84. Comm. 2 Corinthians 1:5, OE 15.11–12; CNTC 10:8–9.

85. Comm. Philippians 1:12, OE 16.304.3–9; CNTC 11:234.

86. Comm. 1 Peter 4:12, CO 55:278B; CNTC 12:307.

87. Comm. Philippians 3:10, OE 16.357.21–34; CNTC 11:376.

88. Comm. Hebrews 2:10, OE 19.38.11–16; CNTC 12:25.

89. Comm. 2 Thessalonians 1:12, CO 52:193–194; CNTC 8:394.

90. *Institutio 1539* XVII.15, CO 1:1136A; (1:702).

91. Comm. Acts 16:22, CO 48:384C; CNTC 7:81.

92. Comm. Ephesians 3:1, OE 16.200.20–26; CNTC 11:157.

93. Comm. Philippians 1:28, OE 16.314.18–30; CNTC 11:242.

94. Comm. Philippians 1:28, OE 16.315.1–19; CNTC 11:243.

95. Comm. Seneca *De Clementia,* p. 51.

96. Comm. Philippians 1:14, OE 16.305.7–15; CNTC 11:234–235.

97. Comm. James 5:10, CO 55:427–428; CNTC 3:311.

98. Comm. Genesis Argumentum, CO 23:11–12; CTS 1:65.

99. Comm. Psalms Preface, CO 31:19C, 21A; CTS 8:xl. See Barbara Pitkin, "Imitation of David: David as a Paradigm for Faith in Calvin's Exegesis of the Psalms," *Sixteenth Century Journal* 24/4 (Winter 1993): 843–863.

100. Comm. Jeremiah 37:15, CO 39:150A; CTS 20:376.

101. Comm. Jeremiah 38:6, CO 39:161C; CTS 20:393.

102. Comm. Romans 1:16, *Romans* 25.87–92; CNTC 8:27.

103. Comm. 2 Corinthians 4:3, OE 15.69.27–35; CNTC 10:53.

104. Comm. John 8:47, OE 11/1.298.11–17; CNTC 4:230.

105. Comm. Amos 8:11, CO 43:151C; CTS 27:376.

106. Comm. 1 Timothy 1:13, CO 52:258B; CNTC 10:196.

107. Comm. Matthew 12:31, CO 45:341C; CNTC 2:47.

108. Comm. Acts 5:3, CO 48:98C; CNTC 6:133–134.

109. Comm. Romans 1:24, *Romans* 33.54–62; CNTC 8:34.

110. Comm. Ephesians 4:19, OE 16.241.21–34; CNTC 11:188.

111. Comm. Hosea 9:10, CO 42:399C; CTS 26:336.

112. Comm. Ephesians 4:19, OE 16.242.1–3; CNTC 11:188.

113. Comm. Jeremiah 36:24, CO 39:130B; CTS 20:347.

114. Comm. Jeremiah 44:1–7, CO 39:248–249; CTS 20:522–523.

115. Comm. 1 John 5:16, CO 55:373A; CNTC 5:311.

116. Comm. Acts 8:22, CO 48:186C; CNTC 6:240.

117. Comm. 1 John 5:16, CO 55:373A; CNTC 5:311.

118. Comm. Romans 10:19, *Romans* 237.44–48; CNTC 8:235.

119. Comm. 1 Thessalonians 2:15, CO 52:152C; CNTC 8:348.

120. Comm. Genesis 49:10, CO 23:602B; CTS 2:459.

121. Comm. Romans 11:21, *Romans* 252.60–63; CNTC 8:251.

122. Comm. Daniel 2:44–45, CO 40:605C; CTS 24:185.

123. Comm. Daniel 4:10–16, CO 40:685C; CTS 24:258.

124. Comm. Genesis 2:3, CO 23:34A; CTS 1:107.

125. Comm. 1 Thessalonians 2:16, CO 52:153B; CNTC 8:349.

126. Comm. Seneca *De Clementia,* pp. 304–305.

127. Comm. 1 Corinthians 10:11, CO 49:460A; CNTC 9:210–211.
128. Comm. 1 Corinthians 10:11, CO 49:460B; CNTC 9:211.
129. Comm. Ephesians 5:6, OE 16.257.14–18; CNTC 11:199.
130. Comm. Colossians 3:6, OE 16.446.17–27; CNTC 11:348.
131. Comm. Zephaniah 3:6–7, CO 44:55–56; CTS 29:276.
132. Comm. Amos 6:2, CO 43:103B; CTS 27:303.
133. Comm. Genesis 4:12, CO 23:94C; CTS 1:210.
134. Comm. Genesis 11:7, CO 23:167B; CTS 1:331.
135. Comm. 2 Peter 2:5–6, CO 55:463A; CNTC 12:349.
136. Ibid.
137. Comm. Psalm 21:9, CO 31:217C; CTS 8:353.
138. Comm. Jeremiah 49:18, CO 39:367–368; CTS 21:87.
139. Comm. Ezekiel 16:56–57, CO 40:389B; CTS 23:168–169.
140. Comm. Genesis 18:18, CO 23:257C; CTS 1:479–480.
141. Comm. Psalms 37:34, CO 31:384B; CTS 9:50.
142. Comm. Zechariah 11:10–11; CO 44:311B; CTS 30:322–323.
143. Comm. Jeremiah 25:32, CO 38:505–506; CTS 19:295.
144. Comm. Isaiah 14:25, CO 36:286C; CTS 13:456.
145. Comm. Isaiah 34:6, CO 36:582C; CTS 15:49.
146. Comm. Jeremiah 41:15, CO 39:216A; CTS 20:473.
147. Comm. Jeremiah 41:15, CO 39:216A; CTS 20:473.
148. Comm. Nahum 1:15, CO 43:455–456; CTS 28:448.
149. Comm. Isaiah 1:28, CO 36:55B; CTS 13:83.
150. Comm. Isaiah 34:6, CO 36:582–583; CTS 15:49.
151. Comm. Isaiah 63:1, CO 37:393A; CTS 16:338.
152. Comm. Isaiah 63:3, CO 37:394C; CTS 16:340.
153. Comm. John 11:4, OE 11/2.52.17–23; CNTC 5:2.
154. Comm. Micah 7:18, CO 43:428–429; CTS 28:400–401.

CHAPTER 14. *The Revelation of the Children of God*

1. Comm. 1 Corinthians 4:9, CO 49:369A; CNTC 9:93.
2. Comm. 1 John 3:1, CO 55:330A; CNTC 5:266.
3. Comm. Hebrews 12:6, OE 19.218.9–17; CNTC 12:190.
4. Ibid.
5. Comm. Romans 8:31, *Romans* 184–185; CNTC 8:183.
6. Comm. Hebrews 12:6, OE 19.218.24–26; CNTC 12:190–191.
7. Comm. Romans 8:31, *Romans* 184–185; CNTC 8:183.
8. Comm. Genesis 37:18, CO 23:485–486; CTS 2:266.
9. Comm. Psalm 32:4, CO 31:319A; CTS 8:529.
10. Comm. Psalm 38:19, CO 31:394; CTS 9:68.

11. Comm. Psalm 41:2, CO 31:418B; CTS 9:112–113.
12. Ibid.
13. Comm. Daniel 11:36, CO 41:268C; CTS 25:342.
14. Comm. Lamentations 1:5, CO 39:513B; CTS 21:311.
15. Comm. Jeremiah 10:24, CO 38:93B; CTS 18:62–63.
16. Comm. Deuteronomy 28:27, CO 25:34B; CTS 5:249.
17. Comm. Acts 28:4, CO 48:560A; CNTC 7:299.
18. Comm. Jeremiah 27:8, CO 38:546C; CTS 19:359.
19. Comm. Jeremiah 20:6, CO 38:339–340; CTS 19:24.
20. Comm. Acts 28:4, CO 48:560C; CNTC 7:299–300.
21. Comm. Deuteronomy 32:24, CO 25:369–370; CTS 6:357.
22. Comm. 39:6, CO 23:504A; CTS 2:294.
23. Ibid.
24. Comm. Psalm 6:2, CO 31:74B; CTS 8:67.
25. Comm. Psalm 89:47, CO 31:829C; CTS 10:454–455.
26. Comm. Isaiah 40:1, CO 37:4C; CTS 15:199–200.
27. Comm. Psalm 30:6, CO 31:295A; CTS 8:489.
28. Comm. Jeremiah 50:17, CO 39:409B; CTS 21:150.
29. Comm. Habakkuk 3:18, CO 43:588C; CTS 29:175.
30. Comm. Romans 4:20, *Romans* 97.80–87; CNTC 8:99.
31. Comm. Psalm 22:2, CO 31:220C; CTS 8:358–359.
32. Comm. 2 Corinthians 1:9, OE 15.17.23–28; CNTC 10:13.
33. Comm. Mark 9:20, CO 45:494C; CNTC 2:208.
34. Comm. Psalm 33:19, CO 31:333B; CTS 8:552–553.
35. Comm. Deuteronomy 8:16, CO 24:249B; CTS 3:400.
36. Comm. Deuteronomy 32:10, CO 25:363A; CTS 6:345–346.
37. Comm. Psalm 11:3, CO 31:122B; CTS 8:162.
38. Comm. Psalm 6:9–11, CO 31:78B; CTS 8:74.
39. Comm. Psalm 34:19, CO 31:344A; CTS 8:571.
40. Comm. Psalm 94:18, CO 32:27A; CTS 11:27.
41. Comm. Psalm 71:20, CO 31:662B; CTS 10:97.
42. Comm. Hosea 6:2, CO 42:321C; CTS 26:219.
43. Comm. Psalm 27:13, CO 31:279B; CTS 8:463.
44. Comm. Psalm 4:7, CO 31:63–64; CTS 8:48.
45. Comm. Psalm 13:1, CO 31:132A; CTS 8:181–182.
46. Comm. Psalm 22:2, CO 31:220B; CTS 8:357–358.
47. Comm. Psalm 138:7, CO 32:375C; CTS 12:204.
48. Comm. Isaiah 14:1, CO 36:272–273; CTS 13:434.
49. Comm. Hosea 6:3, CO 42:322–323; CTS 26:221.
50. Comm. Micah 7:8, CO 43:413A; CTS 28:375.
51. Comm. Psalm 22:2, CO 31:220C; CTS 8:358.
52. Comm. Lamentations 2:9, CO 39:545B; CTS 21:361.

53. *Institutio 1536* II.3, CO 1:57B; *Inst.* 1536:43.

54. Ibid.

55. Ibid.

56. Comm. 2 Corinthians 4:18, OE 15.85.16–26; CNTC 10:64–65.

57. Comm. 2 Corinthians 5:7, OE 15.91.3–17; CNTC 10:69–70.

58. Ibid.

59. Ibid.

60. Ibid.

61. Comm. Hebrews 11:1, OE 19.181.14–28; CNTC 12:157–158.

62. Ibid.

63. Ibid.

64. Comm. 1 Peter 1:8, CO 55:214A; CNTC 12:236.

65. Ibid.

66. Comm. John 20:29, OE 11/2.301–302; CNTC 5:211–212.

67. Ibid.

68. Comm. Romans 8:24, *Romans* 177.100–107; CNTC 8:176.

69. Comm. Romans 8:25, *Romans* 178.24–26; CNTC 8:176.

70. Comm. 1 Thessalonians 1:9, CO 52:145B; CNTC 8:339–340.

71. Comm. Psalm 10:5, CO 31:112C; CTS 8:142.

72. Comm. Hebrews 11:7, OE 19.189.23–32; CNTC 12:165.

73. Comm. Jeremiah 25:29, CO 38:500A; CTS 19:286.

74. Comm. 1 Corinthians 13:12, CO 49:514B; CNTC 9:281.

75. Comm. John 16:16, OE 11/2.195.18–28; CNTC 5:123.

76. Comm. Psalms 17:15, CO 31:168C; CTS 8:256. "Hence they who fear the name of God, desire not to draw him down from heaven, nor seek manifest signs of his presence, but suffer their faith to be tried, so that they adore and worship God, though they see him not face to face, but only in a mirror and that darkly, and also through the displays of his power, justice, and other powers, which are evident before their eyes" (Comm. Malachi 4:2, CO 44:491–492; CTS 30:621).

77. Ibid.

78. Comm. 1 Timothy 6:16, CO 52:332B; CNTC 10:280.

79. Comm. 2 Peter 1:19, CO 55:465B; CNTC 12:341.

80. Comm. 1 John 3:2, CO 55:331–332; CNTC 5:267–268.

81. Comm. 1 Corinthians 13:12, CO 49:515A; CNTC 9:282.

82. Comm. 1 Corinthians 13:7, CO 49:512B; CNTC 9:279.

83. *Psychopannychia*, CO 5:190–191; *Tracts and Treatises* III:436.

84. Comm. 1 John 3:2, CO 55:331–332; CNTC 5:267–268.

85. Comm. 1 Timothy 6:16, CO 52:332–333; CNTC 10:281.

86. Comm. Hebrews 12:12, OE 19.224.5–7; CNTC 12:195.

87. Comm. 1 John 3:2, CO 55:331B; CNTC 5:267.

88. Ibid.

89. Comm. 2 Corinthians 3:18, OE 15.66.20–24; CNTC 10:50.

90. Comm. Hebrews 4:10, OE 19.63.17–24; CNTC 12:48.

91. *Institutio 1539* I.10, CO 1:286A; (1:46–47).

92. Comm. 2 Peter 1:4, CO 55:446–447; CNTC 12:330–331.

93. Ibid.

94. Comm. Matthew 22:30, CO 45:606C; CNTC 3:31.

95. Comm. 1 John 3:2, CO 55:330B; CNTC 5:266.

96. Comm. Colossians 3:3, OE 16.444.22–37; CNTC 11:346.

97. Comm. Ephesians 1:20, OE 16.173.24–26; CNTC 11:136.

98. Comm. Colossians 3:4, OE 16.445.1–5; CNTC 11:347.

99. Comm. Matthew 13:43, CO 45:371A; CNTC 2:78.

100. *Institutio 1539* IV.34, CO 1:534C; (1:525).

101. Comm. Acts 3:21, CO 48:72–73; CNTC 6:103.

102. Comm. Matthew 25:31–46, CO 45:686A; CNTC 3:113.

103. Comm. 1 Peter 1:12, CO 55:219C; CNTC 12:242.

104. Comm. Romans 8:21, *Romans* 175.28–31; CNTC 8:174.

105. Comm. Romans 8:21, *Romans* 175.36–38; CNTC 8:174.

106. Comm. Matthew 13:43, CO 45:371A; CNTC 2:78.

107. Comm. 2 Thessalonians 2:4, CO 52:198A; CNTC 8:400.

108. Comm. 1 John 2:18, CO 55:320–321; CNTC 5:255–256.

109. Comm. 2 Thessalonians 2:8, CO 52:201C; CNTC 8:405.

110. Comm. 2 Thessalonians 1:5, CO 52:189C; CNTC 8:389–390.

111. Comm. Romans 2:16, *Romans* 46.35–37; CNTC 8:49.

112. Comm. 2 Corinthians 5:10, OE 15.93.20–29; CNTC 10:71.

113. *Institutio 1539* IV.34, CO 1:534C; (1:525).

114. Comm. 1 Corinthians 15:24, CO 49:547A; CNTC 9:324.

115. Comm. 1 Corinthians 15:26, CO 49:547C; CNTC 9:325.

116. Comm. 1 Corinthians 15:27, CO 49:549C; CNTC 9:327.

117. Comm. John 14:28, OE 11/2.156–157; CNTC 5:89–90.

118. *Inst.* III.xxv.10, OS IV.453.19–22; (2:1005).

Conclusion

1. *Psychopannychia*, CO 5:191; *Tracts and Treatises* 3:436.

2. Comm. Psalm 17:15, CO 8:256; CTS 31:168C.

3. Comm. 1 Timothy 6:16, CO 52:332–222; CNTC 10:281.

4. "For the religious experience of the Christian, transformed through the proclaimed word, transforms but never destroys its roots, its grounds and its envelopment in the reality of the manifestation of the sacred" (David Tracy, *The Analogical Imagination* [New York: Crossroads, 1986], p. 217).

5. Hans Urs von Balthasar, *The Glory of the Lord: A Theological Aesthetics*, trans. Erasmo Leiva-Merikakis (New York: Crossroads, 1983).

6. "However, I acknowledge that the sign of the cross is very old in the church, and that the wooden cross falls somewhere between the sign and images. For this reason, the earliest usage of the cross was sound, but as time elapsed it has become worse. Nothing but the sign of the cross was practiced until the time of Constantine, who lived between the third and fourth centuries, and at the time it received no adoration" (John Calvin, *Calvin's Ecclesiastical Advice,* trans. Mary Beaty and Benjamin W. Farley [Louisville, KY: Westminster John Knox Press, 1991], p. 74).

7. *Institutio 1539* XI.32, CO 1:978A; (2:1337).

8. Comm. Psalm 17:15, CO 8:256; CTS 31:168C.

General Index

Aaron, 17, 148, 183, 190, 192, 229, 388
    Aaronic priesthood, 190–92, 314
Abednego, 157
Abel and Cain, 169–70
Abimelech, 71
Abraham, 10, 17, 71, 114, 404
    appearance of God as three angels to, 175
    burial of Sarah, 176–77, 178, 360
    and Christ, 117
    and circumcision, 173–75
    and covenant of adoption, 133–34, 140–41, 146, 157, 159, 163, 173–75, 181–82, 183, 214
    God's promises to, 114, 139–41, 146, 159, 181–82, 183, 368
    and Melchizedek, 170, 172, 173
    and Sodom and Gomorrah, 94
    suffering of, 412
    visions and dreams of, 138–41, 146, 150
accommodation to human capacities
    by Christ, 266–67, 273, 305
    by God, 40, 41, 49, 113, 114, 115, 129–30, 131, 139, 143–44, 147, 148, 149–50, 152, 168, 176, 182, 218, 221, 229, 236–37, 261,

272, 280, 283, 306, 308, 309, 311, 312, 328, 334–35, 336, 337, 339, 340, 346, 347, 481n38
    in prophetic speech, 232, 236–43, 252
    sacraments as, 306, 308, 309, 311, 312, 321–22, 334–35, 336, 337, 339, 340
Adam, 17, 133, 164
    sin of, 17, 61, 62, 63, 64, 65, 107, 169, 258, 290, 380, 398, 409, 438, 453n102
affliction. See suffering
Agabus, 249–50
agriculture, 59
Agrippa, King, 167, 305
Ahaz, King, 155
Alexander the Great, 97, 304
Ambrose, St., 32
Anabaptists, 56–57, 112–13, 138, 165, 181–82, 242
anagogic relationships, 8, 12, 13–14, 15–16, 113, 114, 159, 204, 236, 241, 243, 265, 268, 270, 439–40
    circumcision and baptism, 174, 325
    sacraments as ladder to Christ in heaven, 311–12, 313, 340–42, 501n419

representation of God, 1
reprobates
  distinguishing marks of, 10–11, 401, 402,
    413–15, 422–23
  divine punishment of, 402, 415–18,
    422–23, 460n164
  and God's power, 2
  Jews as, 414–15
  prosperity of, 76–77, 94, 99, 100–101,
    390, 402, 417–18, 420, 422
  See also ungodly, the
Reuben and Gad, 389
Richard, Lucien, 4, 7
righteousness of God, 2, 27, 28, 29, 41, 49,
    64, 260, 410, 435
  and Christ, 296, 434
  and providence, 75, 76–77, 80, 83, 89,
    90, 94–98
rites of burial, 176–81
rites of purification, 164, 195–96
Ritschl, Albrecht, 21
Roman Church, 21–22, 98, 175, 438
  bishops in, 407
  consecrated spaces of worship in,
    344
  doctrine of transubstantiation, 225,
    339, 340, 358
  evangelical Church as emerging from,
    402, 404, 405, 514n24
  extreme unction, 319–21
  fasting in, 365
  foot washing in, 384
  holy days of obligation in, 344
  hypocrisy in, 394
  images in, 3, 22, 238, 356, 360, 373, 375,
    376
  laying on of hands in, 313–17, 321, 438
  Mass, 1, 3, 112, 170–71, 172, 173, 190,
    316–17, 332, 339, 356–57, 359
  and miracles, 298, 299–300, 301
  ordination, 313–17, 321
  papacy, 18, 112, 128, 137, 358, 402, 403,
    404, 405, 433
  penance in, 321–23
  power and glory of, 404–5
  priesthood in, 170–71, 190, 313–17, 321,
    322

relics in, 177, 300, 360
rites and ceremonies in, 108, 110, 112,
    128, 170–71, 172, 173, 206, 252, 283,
    355–59, 366, 376, 383, 392, 394
sacraments in, 1, 133, 143, 150, 170–71,
    172, 173, 250, 309–10, 311–12, 313–23,
    326, 329, 337, 356–57, 359
saints in, 224, 299, 376–77, 430
sign of the cross in, 438, 521n6
symbols in, 17, 206
unwritten apostolic tradition in, 356
vows in, 354
rulers
  earthly power of, 83–84, 88, 97
  as images of God, 10, 68, 198–99, 243
  as sons of God, 198–99, 273

Sabbath, 32, 35, 42, 109–10, 185–87
sacraments, 4, 5, 6–7, 9, 20, 289, 345, 356
  as accommodation to human
    capacities, 306, 308, 309, 311, 312,
    321–22, 334–35, 336, 337, 339, 340
  anointing the sick with oil, 319–21
  Augustine on, 13–14, 15, 37, 165, 306,
    308, 309, 310, 321–22
  confirmation, 313, 317–18
  as confirmation of Gospel, 306–13
  defined, 306, 308, 309, 310–11, 314, 323
  and grace of God, 140, 306–7, 309, 324,
    328, 329–30, 335
  and Holy Spirit, 155, 156, 302, 307,
    308–9, 310, 310–11, 327, 328, 329, 330,
    332–33, 334, 338, 339, 341
  as ladders to Christ in heaven, 311–12,
    313, 340–42, 501n419
  of the Law, 133, 164–65, 185, 223, 257,
    280, 307
  lawful administration as mark of true
    Church, 402–3, 405, 407, 408, 413
  laying on of hands, 18–19, 313–19,
    322–23, 438
  marriage, 323
  as mirrors, 307, 345
  natural vs. miraculous, 155–56, 168
  penance, 321–23
  and promises of God, 6–7, 13, 154,
    155, 184, 306–7, 308, 310–11, 312, 314,

Scripture Index